THE VITAL FEW

THE VITAL FEW

The Entrepreneur and
American Economic Progress

EXPANDED EDITION

Jonathan Hughes

New York   Oxford
OXFORD UNIVERSITY PRESS
1986

Oxford University Press

Oxford   New York   Toronto
Delhi   Bombay   Calcutta   Madras   Karachi
Petaling Jaya   Singapore   Hong Kong   Tokyo
Nairobi   Dar es Salaam   Cape Town
Melbourne   Auckland

and associated companies in
Beirut   Berlin   Ibadan   Nicosia

First edition published in 1966 by Houghton Mifflin and issued in
paperback in 1973 by Oxford University Press, Inc., under the title
The Vital Few: American Economic Progress and Its Protagonists
Expanded edition first published in paperback in 1986 by Oxford
University Press, Inc., 200 Madison Avenue, New York, New York 10016

Library of Congress Cataloging-in-Publication Data
Hughes, Jonathan R. T.
The vital few.
Bibliography: p.
Includes index.
1. United States—Biography.
2. Entrepreneur—Biography.
3. United States—Economic conditions.
I. Title.
HC102.5.A2H8   1986   330.973′0092′2 [B]   85-28504
ISBN 0-19-504038-4 (pbk.)
2 4 6 8 10 9 7 5 3 1

Printed in the United States of America

The author wishes to thank the authors and publishers of the following books for permission to quote passages from them:

My Life and Work by Henry Ford, in collaboration with Samuel Crowther, Doubleday, Page & Company, 1923. Copyright 1922 by Doubleday, Page & Company. Reprinted by permission of Mary Owens Crowther.

My Forty Years With Ford by Charles E. Sorensen, with Samuel T. Williamson, W. W. Norton & Company, Inc., 1956. Copyright © 1956 by Charles E. Sorensen. Reprinted by permission of A. Watkins, Inc.

J. Pierpont Morgan: An Intimate Portrait by Henry L. Satterlee, The Macmillan Company, 1939. Copyright 1939 by Herbert L. Satterlee. Reprinted by permission of the publisher.

The Great Pierpont Morgan by Frederick Lewis Allen, Harper & Brothers Publishers, 1949. Copyright 1948, 1949 by Frederick Lewis Allen. Reprinted by permission of the publisher.

The Early Writings of Frederick Jackson Turner, edited by Everett E. Edwards, The University of Wisconsin Press, 1938. Copyright 1938 by the University of Wisconsin. Reprinted with permission of the copyright owners, the Regents of the University of Wisconsin.

The World of Eli Whitney by Jeannette Mirsky and Allan Nevins, The Macmillan Company, 1952. Copyright 1952 by Jeannette Mirsky and Allan Nevins. Reprinted by permission of the publisher.

A Theory of the Labor Movement by Selig Perlman, Augustus M. Kelley, 1949. Copyright 1928 by Selig Perlman. Reprinted by permission of the publisher, A. M. Kelley, Bookseller.

E. H. Harriman by George Kennan, Houghton Mifflin Company, 1922. Copyright 1922 by George Kennan. Reprinted by permission of the publisher.

The Autobiography of Andrew Carnegie, Houghton Mifflin Company, 1920. Copyright 1920 by Louise Whitfield Carnegie. Copyright renewed 1948 by Margaret Carnegie Miller. Reprinted by permission of the publisher.

The Life of Andrew Carnegie by Burton J. Hendrick, 2 vols., Doubleday, Doran & Company, Inc., 1932. Copyright 1932 by Burton J. Hendrick. Reprinted by permission of Dr. Ives Hendrick.

Beyond Bureaucracy: Mary Elizabeth Switzer and Rehabilitation, by Martha Lentz Walker, University Press of America, 1985. Copyright 1985. Reprinted by permission of the publisher.

Economic Balance and a Balanced Budget: Public Papers of Marriner S. Eccles, edited by Rudolph L. Weissman, Harper & Brothers, 1940. Copyright 1940.

Beckoning Frontiers: Public and Personal Recollections, edited by Sidney Hyman, Alfred Knopf, 1951. Copyright 1950, 1951.

Marriner S. Eccles: Private Entrepreneur and Public Servant, by Sydney Hyman. Reprinted with the permission of Stanford University Graduate School of Business, © 1976 by the Board of Trustees of the Leland Stanford Junior University.

Quotations from the writings and papers of Marriner Eccles are printed by permission of Mrs. Sara M. Eccles.

Preface to the Expanded Edition

W hen Oxford University Press suggested a second edition of *The Vital Few* I was excited by the prospect. This has given me the opportunity actually to finish the work. The original scheme was dual sets of biographies to illustrate the role of entrepreneurship in five ongoing stages of economic life, all occurring simultaneously. Since in the late 1950's and early 1960's, when I did the original work, I was mainly concerned only with economic growth and development and not with the problems of stagnation and decline, I did not write Part V. I merely set it out in the original Preface and then briefly treated the conceptual role and problems of bureaucracy in the final chapter, "The American Legacy." After *The Vital Few* was originally published in 1966 we received from the hands of the fates the Great Society, the subsequent explosive growth of government, and then the puzzling and as yet unresolved problems of "stagflation"—inflationary growth with continuing high levels of unemployment. Our "welfare state," now grown unimaginably in cost, administers an economic puzzle. Many of our greatest corporations have stagnated and faced the prospects of actual failure. They are the organizational residues of once dynamic business firms created long ago by some of the individuals treated in this book. To aid in comprehension of bureaucracy in general and the development of our modern problems with economic policy and the welfare state I now have added two new biographies for Part V. There is also a short essay on the nature and inevitability of bureaucracy in the private economy as well as in government.

Since the American government now contains one of history's major bureaucracies I chose both subjects from the federal government's modern history. My subjects are Mary Switzer and Marriner Eccles. They were contemporaries in life and in government service, but were utterly different from each other in style and effectiveness. When I was an undergraduate I attended a lecture by Eccles and never forgot the experience. Many years later at Northwestern University I served on the Ph.D. dissertation committee of Edward Berkowitz and was introduced by his work to the extraordinary career of Mary Switzer. So, when Oxford suggested that I might now (two decades after *The Vital Few*'s first appearance) complete the original scheme of my book, I already knew who my two bureaucratic entrepreneurs would be.

In Mary Switzer's long (48 years) government service we trace the development of the modern welfare state. Switzer was a Radcliffe woman, a professional civil servant, and a fascinating person who "aided and abetted" for most of her career, acting as a catalyst and then as a major force in motivating programs, legislation, and permanent government institutions. Changes in the economy and in medical science determined the ultimate course of her career. Like those of any private entrepreneur her innovations came from astute perceptions of new opportunities. In 1950 she became Director of the Office of Vocational Rehabilitation and achieved a pervasive influence on the rehabilitation movement and its philosophy as it moved out of narrowly based medical, educational, and therapeutic applications into wider areas of general social policy. The welfare state moved apace, and in 1967 she was made Administrator of the new Social and Rehabilitation Services, with responsibility for virtually all of HEW's "do-good" functions.

Within a year the Great Society exploded with burning cities and the marching poor. From then until now the welfare state has expanded in size, but not in conception, and Switzer's career enables us to understand that. She managed a truly entrepreneurial career within the confines of the professional civil service, and millions are better off today because of her work. Whatever is the future of the American welfare state, it will remain in part the consequence of Switzer's great contribution. It is a better, more humane spender of the nation's resources than it would have been without her. Her style was persuasion, the creation of workable compromises between opposing interests and factions, always, or nearly always, managing to move the inchoate mass of contending special interests toward the creation of a more humane society.

Marriner Eccles was a different kind of person and bureaucrat. He stayed in Washington for 17 years, a period of his long life sandwiched between two careers as a major American entrepreneur in the private sector. He was 44 years old and already a millionaire banker and business tycoon when he joined Henry Morgenthau's Treasury Department in 1934. Eccles was a brilliant man, a graduate of no institution of higher learning except the school of experience. His contribution was partly frustrated by the constantly powerful opposition he faced, for he was the ultimate logician of economic policy. Washington politicians like to talk about logical economic policies, but their motivation is politics and not economic reason, and the two are usually in conflict. In the career of Marriner Eccles we follow from the New Deal to the Korean War the evolution of "compensatory" fiscal and monetary policies, never really existing in practice, but always in the mind and efforts of Eccles, and then, after Keynes's *General Theory of Employment Interest and Money* (1936), increasingly in the minds of professional economists inside and outside government. Price stability and full employment were the goals, never achieved for any substantial length of time.

Eccles entered government with a high-level appointment. He was a brusque man, sometimes tactless, and awesome in argument. He was responsible for major historical changes in the laws and economic institutions of this country: In 1951, in his sixty-second year of life, he finally gave up on Washington, walking out of a government whose policies he believed would be hopelessly inflationary and economically destructive. No doubt he would have been thrown out of the government by Harry Truman at the time, but Eccles had "tenure"—he was a member of the Federal Reserve System's Board of Governors, and still had some years of his 14-year appointment left to serve.

After 1951, acting on his belief in the inevitably inflationary consequences of modern fiscal practices (deficits nearly every year, in both dearth and plenty), Eccles returned to his old ways and made another private fortune riding the crest of Washington's never-ending inflation.

In the two careers of Switzer and Eccles, we see from the inside the growth of the modern welfare state and the supposedly discretionary management by the federal government of the nation's economy, the two functions of modern government to which all else must adapt. The welfare state consumes three-quarters of the federal government's resources automatically, and discretionary economic policy determines what is to be done to acquire and spend the rest. The bureaucratic entrepreneur's role is to change the flow over time of these vast resources, for good or ill, within the framework of a popular democracy and its elected representative institutions.

Our special subject—entrepreneurship—has recently enjoyed one of its periodic rejuvenations in the world of public opinion with the appearance in Washington of Ronald Reagan and his neoconservative following. There have been some best-sellers about entrepreneurship. There has also been a modest flicker of interest amongst the economics profession per se, nothing dramatic to compare with Professor Schumpeter's original treatment of entrepreneurship. But there have been several attempts to find a place for the subject within the body of logic, theory, governing the thought of economists. The problem of entrepreneurship for economists is that the best-developed and best-understood part of economic theory—neoclassical microeconomics—is really mathematics. Business firms in that system are merely formulas, "production functions." There are no people, no institutions; it is a timeless paradigm of resources shifting back and forth according to changes in relative prices and costs. This has meant that entrepreneurship, the most forceful, dramatic, and obvious phenomenon in all of economic life, has perforce been ignored by theoretical economists in their story of how economic events happen. I. M. Kirzner's little book, *Competition and Entrepreneurship* (University of Chicago Press, 1973), has probably been the most estimable single contribution in the realm of microeconomic theory.

There have been, of course, many nontheoretical or quasi-theoretical contributions to the literature in the past two decades. But to academic economists such works really do not matter; *only pure theory matters*. So in the classroom, except possibly for Kirzner's arbitraging entrepreneur acting to equalize prices in competitive markets, there still are production functions instead of firms, and there are no people or institutions. It has long been so, and presumably will remain so. Toyota is one production function, American Motors another; labor, capital, and raw materials go in, and a homogeneous product (motor cars) comes out. The differences between the two firms are mainly the scales and shapes of their production functions and the subsidiary production and cost functions derived therefrom. If you think that business firms are different from each other in richer and more meaningful ways, that is because you haven't taken a really rigorous economics course.

The word *entrepreneur* actually occurred in President Reagan's first inaugural address, and that, probably more than anything else, brought the subject into the foreground of popular knowledge again. In addition, the appalling failure of several great American business firms in the face of foreign competition made people remember that *once* it was American business firms that could beat the competitive world. That was when there were people like Andrew Carnegie and Henry Ford making steel and autos. The idea of new businesses creating jobs and new products became fashionable in the scholarly world in the early 1980's, and hence entrepreneurship became one of the buzzwords in high-level "thinking circles." Money has flowed again into the study of the subject in universities and private think tanks.

The Vital Few by now has a venerable history of its own in the study of entrepreneurship. Its outline and method have even been adapted to an exceedingly successful educational motion picture. The book has been read in many parts of the world, and I am gratified that it has helped foreign readers to understand the American economy's development and prime motive force. In recent years it has been thrilling to receive letters from younger scholars who have just read *The Vital Few* for the first time. This new edition will make the book more readily available and even more useful than before. The two new biographies have been added. The rest, having earned its place in the world by honorable service, I have left unchanged.

J.R.T.H.

Evanston, Illinois
1985

Preface

In this book I attempt to expound some of the main lessons of American economic development, as I see them, to that remarkable individual "the intelligent reader." This is a serious, but not a "technical," work. I have not written it for my colleagues, although they may learn something new in these pages. There is no "scholarly apparatus"; whenever my debt to any single author has been unusually heavy I have so noted it in the text, and I have appended a short bibliographical essay for any who might wish to pursue more intensively the subjects treated. This book is history, economics and, in some respects, an exercise in entrepreneurial history, a fledgling discipline which, thus far, has not produced a harvest in proportion to the sowing and cultivation.

Bearing in mind that "straight" history bores many readers, and that unembellished economic analysis tends to mystify most, I have resorted to a kind of "economic biography" to make my points. It has always seemed to me to be regrettable that the solid materials relating to the growth and development of the American economy have been so extensively locked up in university lecture halls and in technical treatises, while the general reader has been fed a diet of lighter stuff. I hope this work redresses the balance a bit. In a sense the method I have employed here is a study in human ecology, the study of men under the full influence of their environments. Since it is economics that mainly concerns me, the ecological circumstances are composed primarily of ideas, technology and economic change. My hope is that I have brought to bear upon my subjects the precision of the historian, the logic of economic analysis and the art of the biographer. If I have succeeded with such a large order, the reader should emerge from these pages with a new and enriched understanding and appreciation of the kinds of forces and men that combined to build the American economy.

I have utilized a system of conceptual "stages" (categories) purely as the historian's intellectual scaffolding, a framework upon which to hang the substance of the work. The system used is a device of convenience, one of any number of perfectly valid stage schemes which might have been used, depending upon the ends the historian had in view. Since my viewpoint is primarily focused upon the roles of ideology, invention and "entrepreneurship" in the development and use of the nation's resources, the stages are largely technological and the subjects are primarily capitalists rather than workers. A similar study could be written regarding labor and economic change.

Finally, as biographical subjects I deliberately have chosen well known historical figures because I am attempting to use their lives to illustrate my views concerning the economic development of the United States, and the introduction of more obscure figures would further complicate my task. Therefore, while I have not relied extensively upon primary sources, I hope, nevertheless, that these men will be seen in a new perspective because their stories have been written in a way which gives maximum exposure to the interplay between their actions and the circumstances in which their lives were lived. For the most part this technique does in fact make each biography "new" because a great deal of information is used which has not previously been considered to be biographically relevant.

Our history speaks to us only if we ask it to. "Facts" do not speak for themselves; we select the facts we want from a universe of them. My own notions about American economic growth and change determined the facts I have selected. It is my hope that the reader will find the exercise both diverting and meaningful. To those who find this interpretation excessively disturbing, let me add that I think this is "how it was," and not "how it should have been." There are many ways to write history.

Of my debts to individuals, one in particular, to Mr. Richard E. Roberts, an old New York friend, must be acknowledged. I also have some institutional debts. The final part of this book was completed while I was on sabbatical leave from Purdue University. The John Simon Guggenheim Memorial Foundation inadvertently contributed a small part of a general grant given to me for other research, and I am grateful to the Warden and Fellows of Nuffield College, Oxford, for their hospitality during the final stages of this work.

J. R. T. H.
Montmorenci, Ind.
1961–64

Contents

To
R. E. W. H. B.
To the memory of
A. T. W.
and
For
Mary Gray
who talked about all this with me

"Every perceptive European visitor to America perceives that, in a society lacking Europe's aristocratic and medieval distinctions, the captain of industry is a hero-type for adult men and women."

Graham Hutton
(*We Too Can Prosper*)

THE VITAL FEW

CHAPTER 1

Introduction: Men, Events and Economic Change

This is a book about a group of men. They are well known figures in American history and, in fact, that is why they are in this book. These men are going to be used as surrogates, or substitutes, for scores of others like them who did the same sorts of things in life—and still do—but whose biographies are inaccessible, or perhaps not so interesting as those in this book. We want to examine why the American economy developed the way it did. To do this, among other things, we must attempt to form some coherent view of the way individual contributions to the flow of economic life affected the direction and speed of that flow. We need to come to grips with the dog-eared problem of "the role of the individual in history" for an extremely simple reason: by far the larger part of the American economy, as it exists today, is a social artifact, the remains of the past actions, successes and failures, of individuals engaged in economic enterprise of all sorts.

The organization of the American economy, since its beginning, has been centered around the contribution of the individual following his own interests and motives. Except for certain well known forms of explicitly collective endeavor, such as road-building, canals, railroads, harbors, tariffs, territorial acquisitions, surveys, establishment of the legal framework and so forth, the allocation of scarce productive resources between an infinity of possible uses has been left largely to the forces of the market place. Buyers and sellers, users and producers of goods and services, good men and bad, have reacted to each others' tastes and desires for profit and satisfaction, by spending their money in the ways that suited each of them best. Or at least what they thought was best in the circumstances. But given the role of government, as tastes and technology changed over time and the population grew, all those individual actions, decade after decade of allocating the supply of resources, *produced the pattern of American economic growth.*

That is what happened in our economic history, and it

makes no difference whether the reader or the historian approves of such a haphazard method of changing the national income and its structure over time. We need not applaud something to understand it, in history any more than in everyday life. It is useful to understand history sometimes, even if one finds it distasteful. If we are fully to comprehend our economic history, our national "experience" in the world of production and trade, then we cannot ignore the terrible problem (from the historian's point of view) of the millions of individual contributions.

To ignore the impact of individuals in our historical development would be like studying physiology without considering the actions of the organs and cells of the body and their effects upon each other. We cannot assume, as many have done, that somehow or other the individuals have cancelled each other out and change has come automatically from the "masses" and the "forces of history." There are no "masses." There are only individuals. There are no "forces of history," only human action, and the human beings involved are individuals as well as parts of society. Men make economic change. The American economy, even including government, is the sum product of the acts of individuals. It was so in the past, and it is so now.

This view is uncongenial to all sorts of people, especially to those who rely upon the simplified notions of causality in history which can be derived from formal theorizing about human action. We have, in fact, long been embarrassed by the problem of individual contributions in our economic development. That is paradoxical. Whereas we unflinchingly accept that a Ulysses Grant or a George Patton, or a Jackson, or a Roosevelt, may have imposed his will and personality upon "history" to some extent, we find it awkward to admit as much of an Astor, a Vanderbilt, a Gould, an Insull or men of little renown who have initiated economic change.

The acknowledged importance of personality in war and politics somehow cannot make the passage in our minds to the less romantic fields of commerce and industry. This is due partly to the fact that many leaders in economic life have had unfortunate, if interesting, personalities; partly to the Puritan heritage which applauds only the work and not the earthly rewards of it; partly to the egalitarian ideals of our democracy which admit of no special roles in everyday life, partly to the political ideologies of the past and present incompatible with an objective view of the work of "big shots" in a capitalist economy, and, partly, to everyone's familiarity with money making, occasional contempt of it, frequent boredom with it. This leads to a fundamental misunderstanding of American history: in too many accounts the economy lies silently in the background growing miraculously to support and nourish the actions of the gods and heroes the professional historians so love to study in war and politics. But just as men must be mobilized and led in war, voters organized and persuaded in politics, so economic resources must be mobilized and directed intelligently for economic growth to occur. As the great economist, the late Ragnar Nurkse, used to emphasize, the question of economic growth *is* the question of the mobilization of resources. In capitalist America, this mobilization has mainly been done through the market mechanism by individuals acting upon their own motives—and that is what this book is about. We are going to study individual action by studying our eight surrogates.

Whom do we choose to study and why? The answer to this question depends upon what interests us. Since it is the whole economic development of the United States that interests us here, the basis for choosing surrogates must be perfectly general regarding both time and function, limited only by the decision to concentrate upon leaders in the mobilization of resources, and this means "entrepreneurs," men who have, as Joseph Schumpeter put it, put together "new combinations" of economic factors to change the flow of economic life. Such men, numbered in the tens of thousands in our history, are really a handful, a vital few, as a proportion of the total population at any time. The efforts of men in economic life may be classified according to the general character of their major achievements in their historical and economic environments. We begin then, with a problem of taxonomy, of classification.

Since our problem is set on a most ambitious scale, the basis of selection, the system of categories, must be extremely simple to be useful. I asked initially, "What happens in economic life in the most general sense?" From the infinity of possible answers, I have chosen an inclusive five-part "stage system" in which the stages are functional, and not chronological as is the current fashion among economic historians. Events flow through our system of stages, but the stages are analytical and choose the nature of our cast of characters and the relevant facts for us. Time is passive, to be used as we please. This functional stage system (like the conventional chronological stage systems) is wholly arbitrary, of course, and is defensible only according to how well it performs its task—in this case, creating a framework in which the role of the individual in the economic history of the United States may be illuminated by the study of the contributions of a few men.

The fact that the system of categories, or stages, is functional and is not chronological means that we will argue that the nation lives simultaneously in all these stages. The nation does not move from stage I to II to III and so forth. Just as the population includes people in all stages of life, in the whole range of age distribution, so the nation lives in all of its stages—from I to V as we define them. More than that, if the nation experiences all of our stages all of the time, then history obviously can flow through the stages mirrored in the lives of our cast of characters, if that cast is chosen carefully.

Now let us briefly examine the system of choices and the men whose lives we have actually chosen to study. The five simultaneous "stages of history" or, if you prefer, "conceptual categories," are (I) idealism, (II) invention, (III) innovation, (IV) organization and (V) stagnation and decline. Consider these categories for a moment.

I. It is clear that every identifiable economic product or sustained activity represents some vested interest, weak or powerful, that will likely oppose change, since change implies that some other products or activities will be produced. Competition will thus exist to confront virtually any new idea— even ideas of a wholly abstruse nature. To overcome resistance to change is thus virtually necessarily to fly in the face of some "convention." To press ideas against existing reality in the face of argument, and perhaps threat, is to be idealistic or fanatical (I'm not sure there is really any difference). A vast and largely unplumbed region of American economic life and history is the role of systematic idealism about such noneconomic matters as religion and social organization in provoking change. The wholly recondite can be, and has been, a burning reality to men who built empires, but whose metaphysics could not be comprehended by mere reason.

II. Invention must supply the wares of economic change. Viable growth in a nation usually depends upon some self-generating inventive activity, even if there is a great deal of borrowing from others. Inventors are mainly creatures of the "state of the arts." But invention also advances the arts, and economic change crucially depends at any time upon the flow of invention that changes the technology and produces a new range of choice to the seller or user of economic products.

III. As Joseph Schumpeter correctly observed and emphasized, the man who changes the stream of the allocation of resources over time by introducing new departures into the flow of economic life is not necessarily an inventor of anything. He is an innovator, and plays a vital role in the economy. Andrew Carnegie, for example, invented nothing in the technology of the steel industry, and is credited with the remark, "Pioneering don't pay." Yet he was a mighty pioneer in the steel industry and his pioneering paid off in astronomical figures. What he meant by "pioneering" was activity in which the probability of failure seemed to him to be high. He was an innovator *par excellence,* and American history has many like him.

IV. A significant feature, in many ways a singular feature in American economic life, is the great size of enterprises at crucial junctures in manufacturing, communications and transportation. In many cases, opportunity to achieve the extra profits latent in vast capital investments meant that the nation's pool of wealth and the flow of current savings had to be tapped through capital markets. To organize and tap capital and money markets, some men had to develop the means of reconciling the demand for resources and available supplies of those resources on a massive scale. In any nation there is a pool of wealth and a flow of savings. But it may take great organizational genius to effect even the simplest markets for securities and to transfer buying power from savers to users of resources, especially where the individual sources of wealth and savings are widely dispersed.

V. Finally, as economists Simon Kuznets and A. F. Burns demonstrated more than three decades ago, the history of separate firms and industries shows a tendency for growth to slow down, and, moreover, for there to be stagnation and decline once the retardation has advanced. Because of the power of ideas and technology in individual cases, these stagnating tendencies do not necessarily find expression in aggregative measures of growth. Youth replaces age in economic life even though bureaucracy presides over retardation and decline. Bureaucracy performs useful and necessary functions. After all, someone needs to replace the burned-out light bulbs at the River Rouge. But the job hardly requires a Henry Ford. In fact, one wonders how an entrepreneurial historian would approach the problem of the role of bureaucracy. I haven't tried in this book since it is economic growth that primarily concerns us, but someone should. I'm certain that many tired economic activities have had their Robert McNamaras. The post-

1945 history of the Ford Motor Co. shows clearly enough that the arts of management contain certain powers of corporate rejuvenation.

If these categories form an operational taxonomy of the main species, who are the fishes that reflect the wealth of individuals in our historical ocean? Remember that, instead of selecting a large number of historical figures suggested by this framework, I have kept the number to a minimum, deliberately choosing men in those categories whose functional contributions cover the main part of the historical canvas, the economic growth of the United States. To gain the advantages of contrast and comparison, I have chosen my men in pairs. As I said earlier, the "stage" of stagnation and decline was not treated in this way since it is growth that presently concerns me. The final section of the book deals with the problem of stagnation generally.

The way our individuals operated within their environments illustrates the importance of personality in the shaping of actions. The framework within which the men operated explains, given the personalities, why each contribution came in the form it did. It is important to recall that the men acted upon each other, and the whole environment at any time contained men acting in all categories. One of our men, Pierpont Morgan, acted partly as a lover of order (mathematics) using the rules of an ancient art (finance) to change a world of vigorous activity created by men of elemental and sometimes undisciplined force. His achievements reflected largely the power of technique systematically applied to a hostile world. Another of our surrogates, Andrew Carnegie, had Morgan in his environment. After he went into steel, Carnegie gave up his activities as a seller of securities, and even became highly and socially contemptuous of bankers and "finance." Morgan I count as an organizer, and Carnegie as innovator. They lived in the same waters and made common cause just as the whale and the shark both contribute to ecological balance in the ocean. To lump the two together simply as "entrepreneurs" is to miss the crucial parts of the mosaic; all "big business" is not the same, and entrepreneurial activity is not a set with a single member.

My choice of men in our problem is:

I. Idealists, William Penn and Brigham Young.
II. Inventors, Eli Whitney and Thomas Edison.
III. Innovators, Andrew Carnegie and Henry Ford.
IV. Organizers, Edward Harriman and Pierpont Morgan.

I. In the first category the choice of men was easy enough. Given the supply of manpower, America required two things initially, a viable and developable institutional system and the land itself. Our institutions are largely descendants of the upheavals of 17th-century England and, in fact, largely the outgrowth of the Charter of Liberties and Frame of Government of Penn's colony. The selection of basically democratic institutions from the chaos of 17th-century English autarchy was the gift of history, and was due in large part to Penn's single-minded, perhaps even simple-minded, devotion to a set of religious beliefs which brought death, maiming, imprisonment and banishment to thousands. Much of the Leveler doctrine had permeated the Quakers', and Penn's, thinking. It was Penn's largely egalitarian democracy (allowed to operate within a private fief), and not the bigotry of the New England theocracy, that found expression in the basic American documents, and finds a home today in typical American organizational structures, economic as well as political. Penn's decisions were a product of a fanatical adherence to a system of theology. This country scarcely knows a more profound entrepreneurial contribution to its development. As a business venture, Pennsylvania was a disaster to Penn, but it was a legacy of incalculable value to future generations.

From the time of the first settlement, the taking of the Continent engaged all sorts of people. But from Plymouth onward, systematic idealistic thought, national, religious, racial, economic and political, and mixtures of all played critical roles. At the end of the trail, in the mountain deserts of the West, stood Brigham Young and the Mormons. They were not only acting out the closing of the American geographical frontier, but were themselves a kind of distillation of several main strains of American utopianism. They included the New England village, the Puritan millennialism, the social experimentation of Oneida, Brook Farm, New Harmony and a hundred other frontier settlements, and the movement of the physical frontier across the Midwest into the acquisitions of the Mexican War. Young's radical pragmatism, mixed with self-effacing devotion to his singular religious principles, were a reflection of a mainstream of American life of the ante-bellum period, which was permanently deflected after the 1840's.

Young's successes, as well as his failures, were partly the results of his personality, partly the outcome of the movement he represented and partly compromises with an alien environment. He represented, in his own way, a multitude of individuals whose lives were fulfilled on the American frontier. In the cases of both Penn and Young, the contribution of the individual to the historical outcome was striking, yet their environment was established by the actions of others. Adherents to systematic idealism today make the same sorts of impacts on the flow of events, even though, in our time, the idealism is not so likely to be a religious one.

II. Through the life of Eli Whitney (and others like him in his time) ran two fundamental threads of American development: the rise of the ante-bellum South with its slave economy, and the nascent industrial and commercial power of the North. Whitney contributed to both developments, as did scores of other men who converted the "state of the arts" to American needs. Whitney's early career, from the cotton gin, financed by expropriated British crown property, through weary negotiations and battles over his government musket contracts, was deeply concerned with the growth of governmental power and methods in the new nation. The proliferation of invention from his hands, and from those of his colleagues in the armament field, into a broader spectrum of industrial uses comprised a remarkable chapter of American industrial history.

Edison's career, on the other hand, was not importantly connected to government, but straddled a more complex technological world developed primarily in the private sector after the Civil War. The vast new world of electricity and chemistry went from crude beginnings to a powerful adolescence in the lifetime of Edison, and he participated in the new technology at its beginnings. Edison dealt with most of the great inventors of this crucial time in American history on terms that ranged from open patent infringements (the telephone) to the more subtle jostling of rivals in the old motion-picture cartel.

Both Edison and Whitney made their contributions in a certain way because of characteristics of their own personalities and private circumstances, and subtly influenced the course of economic history in the process. But they also were reacting to a changing world created, not only by men like themselves, but by men in our other "stages" of development, entrepreneurs like Westinghouse and Morgan, men whose visions were parts of circumstances which only touched the inventor tangentially.

III. Schumpeterian innovators have, of course, held the center of the stage from the very beginning of entrepreneurial studies. These were men who invented nothing but adapted and forced new technology and products into economic life. Carnegie and Ford were two such men. Their careers not only determined important departures in the course of economic change, their personalities powerfully determined their contributions—and, I hasten to add, the nature of the reaction, especially the violence and single-mindedness of labor-union action in America from Homestead to the River Rouge and after.

Carnegie's great contribution, from the establishment of the Edgar Thomson Works at Braddock Field in 1873 until Pierpont Morgan loosened the aged Spencerian's grip in 1900, was to make the American steel industry one of the wonders of industrial history. His methods were those of ruthless and unremitting competition. Carnegie Steel was the cutting edge of progress in the basic industry during the great industrial transformation of 1873–1900, an epoch in which the United States outstripped all other nations in industrial development.

Carnegie himself was a product of two deeper and older economic phenomena. His father, Thomas, was actually a hand-loom weaver, a master weaver of linen in Dunfermline, displaced by the power loom. The classic Industrial Revolution was thus one progenitor of Carnegie Steel. The other was the Atlantic migration of the 19th century, to which was added, in 1848, the little Scottish family of Thomas Carnegie. Andrew Carnegie's contributions to his new country were many-sided, ranging from steel to philanthropy, and remain with us. But the entire story is most clearly framed by the single fact that, in the growth of the American economy in the late 19th century, the poor lad from Dunfermline became the Schumpeterian entrepreneur *par excellence*. Carnegie's own development was a microcosm of much of American experience in economic affairs in the last half of the 19th century.

Possibly the greatest change in American economic history thus far in the 20th century has been due to the transformation of a European "invention" into an American innovation —the automobile. And the automobile industry was almost spelled Ford in its vital formative years, when a rich man's plaything changed into the basic mode of American transport. The automobile set off a vast change in the demographic and social structure of the country that still shows few signs of stabilizing. To understand this phenomenon and its main instrument, the Model T, one must begin by looking closely into the character of the tyrant of Dearborn, the Napoleon of the River Rouge, and oppressor of the worker, who was also a

corn-fed Bolivar to the 20th century, bringing physical freedom to millions. His greatest contribution to American life
was to free the common man from his geography. After Ford,
no man needed to stay in any locale if he had the few dollars
it cost to buy some sort of an automobile. And here I do not
mean to include only interregional mobility in the national
economy, but also, and perhaps mainly, the local freedom of
movement which has diminished the farm town and made the
new shopping-center world of suburbia a threat to the conventional city itself.

The Model T was Ford's religion, and the mass-produced
world of the automobile his monument. His own life and work
take American history from the horse-drawn plough to the
mechanical farm, from the wagon road to the superhighway.
Oddly enough, both Carnegie and Ford are now associated in
the public mind with vast philanthropies. It was not always
so. The details of their careers in industrial revolution comprise a key which unlocks a rich understanding of this country's past and its present.

IV. I chose Harriman and Morgan as my men of organization to illustrate a singular and continuous thread in economic
history, the essentially conservative power of the financial
art. Finance imposes a logic of its own upon both bor-
rower and lender. Even financial frauds and chicaneries follow
identifiable, almost predictable patterns. There is great con-
tinuity in the techniques of arts and crafts over time, and the
mind follows the action of the hand. Pierpont Morgan was
like the Medicis in more ways than his personal tastes—over
the gulf of centuries, they were essentially in the same trade.
If the users of savings, the tycoons of a new technology,
wanted contact with accumulated wealth and with current
flows of savings, that contact had to come from an intermediary whose rules were fixed by customs far older than the Newtonian science from which that new technology had developed.
Financiers set terms for repayment of debt. To meet those
terms, borrowers had to regulate their activities according to
schedules of repayment and even, commonly, to accept bankers into direct management to guarantee the necessary safe-
guards. The decisions of industry were thus powerfully influenced by the needs of the manipulators of engraved paper.
Hence, men like Carnegie and Ford, who did not use the
capital markets, had a freedom of action quite different from
that of men like Gary and Durant, who did need to come to
terms with the world of high finance.

In the late 19th century, as certain American transportation and industrial ventures generated ambitions which outstripped their own current earning capacities, the builders of these systems sought contractual partnerships with those who wanted earning assets in place of cash hoards. These unions were arranged for and sanctified by the financial organizers. The resulting era has been called such names as the "age of finance capitalism" and the "age of trusts." These phrases described a reality, and a vital one, in American economic history. Without the union of finance and industry the massive size of many of our great companies might well not have developed. There is no evidence that most of these enterprises are not based upon efficiency. The charge of "monopoly power" sounded good, but it has not held up as the origin of economic strength among the industrial giants. Internal economies made access to the capital markets desirable. In industry after industry in the late 19th century, the union of technology and the capital market provided an opening for growth, where reliance upon current earnings for expansion seemed to constrain management.

I chose Harriman as one of my financial organizers to illustrate the contribution of the specialist. It would be difficult to find a more thoroughgoing paragon of railroad finance. From his reorganization of the Ontario & Southern through the Northern Pacific Trust (in which Morgan had a hand) and on to the posthumous liquidation of the Southern Pacific empire under the Sherman Act, Harriman's activities showed a consistent pattern or rationalization and conservative reorganization and expansion. Men like Henry Villard built the railroads, but they didn't run them. Time after time it seemed that the empire builders had to "hand over" to the financial organizers.

Harriman, like Carnegie, was both thoughtful and ruthless. He also represented Thomas Mun's ideal, the man whose private ambitions embraced the public interest, or at least advanced it. Harriman was apparently not an attractive person in business, and historians have gleefully accepted the unsubstantiated and bitter charges of Harriman's defeated enemies. Yet a careful study of his career as an organizer provides a vivid lesson in the mechanics of transportation finance. Harriman was no hero to the historians, but he was a whale of a financial organizer, and his volcanic and controversial career shines a bright light on the American past when that career is viewed as an example of a particular kind of contribution.

Viewed merely as a robber baron, as the popular phrase has it
—and that is how he has traditionally been treated—Harriman has almost been lost to the history books.

My final entrepreneur is John Pierpont Morgan himself.
Sometimes it seems that all roads led to the Morgan library
until 1913 when its owner died. He was personally a great
enigma, but as a financial organizer he knew no peer, nor have
we seen his like since, nor, in my opinion, are we likely to.
Almost every facet of his life was a side of American economic history. One part of Morgan's personality, the hard-
eyed Yankee moralist studying the imperfections of his fellow
tycoons, is an essay in Americana. One imagines the astonished forefather of our race, in his threadbare suit and mud-
covered boots, looking upon his affluent progeny with both
dismay and disapproval—yet recognizing his own. On the
other hand, Morgan's tastes in matters of personal consumption, and his esthetic senses, were extravagant in his time, and
perhaps foreshadowed a future when affluence came within
the reach of millions.

Morgan had a passion to impose discipline and order upon
everything he touched. When men came to him for help, they
took away orders. And in fact, mostly, as in the panic of 1907,
when Wall Street's elite came voluntarily to the old man for
help that Sunday more than half a century ago, they knew that
orders would come which would be both painful and effective.
The portly old gentleman with the blazing eyes was a one-man
segment of American financial history. His banking house
grew out of the older tradition of merchant banking, and he
presided over the growth of American investment banking
practice virtually from its beginning. His actions in national
emergencies from 1877 to 1907 were examples for those who
yearned for the restoration of central banking to the United
States. His promotion of the arts was a great beginning of the
infusion of high quality into everyday American life—the
Metropolitan Museum of Art is as much his monument as is
United States Steel, but few remember that today.

In this scheme of organization of American economic development, the Morgans are as essential as the Penns, and if
neither kind is identifiable today on such heroic scales, it is the
scale of the national framework that has changed, not the
basic economic functions of idealism, invention, innovation
and organization. We sometimes overlook the extent to which
our society automatically systematizes useful art. Entrepreneurship of the Morgan or Harriman variety was most rare in

their time. The *talent* is still rare enough, but business schools now teach the skills those men had.

That completes the cast of characters for four of our stages, and we will treat the stage of stagnation and decline of separate industrial activities in the final part of the book, without recourse to biographical materials.

Before we move on, it should be emphasized that I claim no merits for these particular analytical categories beyond the job I have set for them here. But I do believe this way of thinking about history could be fruitful in the study of problems which are smaller in scope. But the relevant analysis would be much more complicated than is our simple system, since it is through disaggregation that the most formidable complications arise in economic analysis. The broad picture is always the most simple one—once one decides how to paint the picture.

One entirely commonplace observation has a curiously forceful impact when American economic development is studied this way, and that is the critical importance in our past of the open society. That society was the national well-spring of talent and it produced effective leadership from all segments and classes of society from the immigrant poor, Carnegie, to the Yankee aristocracy, Morgan. Any growth of formal limitation tends to restrain the nation from access to its pool of talent, the entire population. For example, educational qualifications for leadership can actually become a critical handicap to economic growth if the opportunity to achieve those qualifications is not a concomitant of the qualifications themselves. Accompanying this, one sees clearly that fear of change could easily be stultifying. Bureaucracy and stability in economic life have their places, but a growing economy needs ideas, invention, innovation and organizational virtuosity. The United States has been singularly fortunate. Lacking a comprehensive system of collective regulation of the growth path (beyond tariffs, subsidies to favored industries and the like) we relied, with enormous rewards, upon the native genius of the population to determine its own future as best it could through the market mechanism—aided at times by astute representatives of the organized political power (Senator George Norris and Gifford Pinchot automatically come to mind in connection with conservation of natural resources). The old open society was far from a perfect one, of course, but it probably provided freer access to the national pool of talent than did the social organization of any other major nation.

The alternatives for the future are obvious enough: we could substitute comprehensive planning and control for the market economy, if such were the will of the people (as it might have been in 1933). There would then be a different set of problems to contend with to gain efficiency in economic growth. In the past, our own economic progress, reflecting market forces, came from the efforts of all sorts of people in a changing world. Flexibility and mobility were crucial lubricants of growth in a changing technology impelled by the operation of the market economy. Opposition to change there always was, as there is today, but acceptance of change was usually the more powerful, and as a result the "continuous revolution" was more nearly achieved by American society than by any that emerged from the imagination of Leon Trotsky, who popularized the phrase. This continuous change made possible the particular contributions of individuals. A dynamic society incorporated those contributions and produced further opportunity for change. As a result we came to think of some of those contributing individuals as "great" men, or scoundrels, depending upon one's point of view. The eight individuals whose lives we will now consider were men like that, like those described by Lenin's teacher, G. V. Plekhanov, in a famous essay:

> The more or less slow changes in "economic conditions" periodically confront society with the necessity of more or less rapidly changing its institutions. This change never takes place "by itself"; it always needs the intervention of *men,* who are thus confronted with great social problems. And it is those men who do more than others to facilitate the solution of these problems who are called great men.

He might have been thinking of what Lenin later became, but he was also describing J. P. Morgan.

PART I

THE SEARCH FOR A HAVEN, IDEALISM
AND ECONOMIC DEVELOPMENT

One man's idealist is another man's fanatic. While it may be clear that every fanatic is an idealist, it is arguable whether every idealist is a fanatic. In what follows I am aware that the line dividing idealism and fanaticism is unclear, yet the two words are meaningful in context. Semantics need not delay the general reader, but may pain the specialist. Was Gandhi an idealist or a fanatic, both or neither? Let us consider fanatics and idealism in American economic development.

Fanatics are curious people and do strange things. The hallmark of a fanatic is blind adherence to a "position" on some subject, perhaps religion or politics. But men become fanatical about more than just religion and politics. Money, for instance, has long had a fatal charm for the absolutist. On what other mundane subject has Ezra Pound written so much? Sir Robert Peel once said that the question of the British currency had "made more lunatics than love." Economics, educational schemes, health foods, efficiency, art, nudism, there is no end of subjects which can inspire absolutely rabid devotion. Men may even give up their lives for a complete abstraction which is unreasonable in itself and unwanted by any except a small coterie of lunatic devotees. But the abstraction might be of great importance and sway millions in the end. Freedom, Communism, the Supremacy of Rome, the Inner Light, Polygamy, all these and a thousand more have their martyrs. I am not equating these and other ideals on a scale of values. I simply observe that the fanatic needs only a cause, not consistency.

Most nations, including our own, have relied again and again upon the driving force of fanaticism to provide intellectual strength in the face of powerful challenges, human or natural. Idealism has been a tremendous force in human affairs. It doubtless will continue so to be; it is a kind of fuel which human institutions need to renew their strength. Moreover, we need not fear that there will soon be any shortage of ideals and fanatics. Our only problem is to continue to recognize and encourage constructive idealism. There will always be an abundance of idealism simply because the fountain of abstract thought flows endlessly. As Lord Keynes once said, the world is ruled by little else except abstract ideas.

Abstract ideas lie at the root of most of our institutions. Even savings banks were originally a scheme to "uplift" the poor mechanic. An inquiry into our notions about the "right" to profit and property leads directly back to "natural law" or else to the Book of Genesis. It is not a great distance from a meeting of a local schoolboard to the upheavals of the 18th century and the establishment of direct representation in government as a human "right." But we are used to our rights and have largely forgotten their controversial origins.

Ours is an age of sophistication and cynicism. When relativism rules so many sectors of American life, modern idealists appear to us usually as misguided innocents or complete fools. The jaded political boss views the reformer with derision as well as with alarm. The "fundamentalist" in religion, economics, art or politics is likely to be an object of scorn. So our sophisticated age generally rejects as "too crude" the absolutes of thought which in earlier times led men into mortal conflict, razed towns, massacred populations and built nations. Nor do we generally feel anything but relief when modern fanatics fail to achieve their ends. We do not really miss the fanatics who shook half a world over the forms of religious faith. Why should we? Is it worth a massacre whether a man believes in transubstantiation or not?

Yet modern Americans know, and many fear, the power of abstract belief in the confrontation with modern Communism. There is a deep apprehension about Communist idealism. Our own stated beliefs seem to attract too few new converts while the Marxists seem to have gone from triumph to triumph since the Second World War—selling tyranny! It is a sad dilemma. A recent committee on "national goals" appointed by an American President was a pathetic attempt to find our bearings in the storm. Yet in the basic American documents, the Declaration of Independence and the Constitution, there exist history's most profound set of political ideals, never realized completely, and yet evidently no longer sufficiently recognized as an adequate set of goals for Americans to achieve. One hopes that this is just a passing phase.

We are a nation that thrives on idealism and always did.

The great drama of the occupation and economic development of this continent was written in large measure by the interplay of fanatical beliefs which needed a transformation of wilderness into civilization so that those beliefs could take root. Idealism made great achievements possible in the face of opposition which had all the forces of reason, law, and power behind it, but which was wrong in the circumstances.

Immigrants, alienated from the older European societies, brought their ideals as well as their fortunes to the New World. Here the elements and the people were engaged against each other and produced a nation with unique characteristics, a people who were no longer merely displaced Europeans. Just the initial acquisition of the land called for special qualities in the people. There were the initial (and sometimes longer lasting) hardships of life in the wilderness which were the *best* the new settlers could expect. At worst there was death in all its forms, possibly pestilential, possibly violent. Did such an environment constitute a force which would fundamentally change men, or were there men who actively sought such an environment, who found it congenial in important respects? Or were both processes active in the settlement of the land?

Looking back over the long history of development the noted American historian, Frederick Jackson Turner, in 1893 argued that the act of taking and subduing the frontier altered European man and imposed upon him certain fundamentally "American" characteristics:

> The wilderness masters the colonist, it finds him a European in dress, industries, tools, modes of travel and thought. It takes him from the railroad car and puts him in the birch canoe. It strips off the garments of civilization and arrays him in the hunting shirt and the moccasin. It puts him in the log cabin . . . Before long he has gone to planting Indian corn and plowing with a sharp stick; he shouts the war cry and takes the scalp. . . . In short, at the frontier the environment is at first too strong for the man. He must accept the conditions which it furnishes, or perish. . . . Little by little he transforms the wilderness, but the outcome is not the old Europe . . . here is a new product that is American.

Certainly the life of the raw frontier was bound to have profound effects upon men; their habits had to be changed, their techniques of making economic progress had to be altered. But was there not, in important cases, a critical selection of men made before the frontier was ever reached? Consider the process from the prospective colonist's point of view for a moment. Even if he knew that life in the American wilds would miraculously "Americanize" him, why should he want thus to be transformed? Is it not clear that prospective emigrants (at least the voluntary ones) had to have some very special motives to undertake a life so perilous? The fact is that many of our ancestors had powerful reasons to seek the new land; they were clearly ready for some change, even "Americanization," when they reached the edge of settlement. This was true, not only for those originating in Europe, but for those native-born Americans who, after all, made up the vast majority of our frontiersmen and women.

To a large extent they were a strange lot indeed, those Puritans, the free-thinkers, the mountain men, the primitive communists, the religious maniacs of all varieties, the desperados and ne'er-do-wells, the homeless ones who were the advance guard of civilization as America moved westward from the Atlantic. Some were patriotic; some were just greedy; some were ambitious; some were humble. But many were haughty in special ways. The Pilgrim Fathers make a good case in point. Lip service is paid on Thanksgiving Day to the role of idealism in the life of our country. On that day we are celebrating the harvest, the success of a brave band of men and women who fought for a place to worship in their own way. But we are also saluting a people who would not find a welcome in any but the most intellectually arid parts of modern America. They would hang a man for his religious beliefs; they conducted torture in their jails, and public humiliation of their malefactors. They could kill their Indian neighbors and *rejoice* that the pagans had gone to their reward. They transported slaves; they pressed men to death for the crime of witchcraft. The Pilgrims were narrow-minded fanatics. But who else would have come to the inhospitable Massachusetts shore in those days? Hard beginnings called for a hard people. If the frontier transformed people in the style suggested by Professor Turner, it transformed a raw material that already had strong proclivities toward adaptation to the necessary rigors for survival.

Violence against man was only a part of the story. It should not be overdone. It was one kind of a reaction to challenge. With equal zeal men might oppose all violence or authority. A man of militant peace might also tame a wilderness. The militant man of action or of peace might be a good farmer or artisan, a sturdy adherent to a given religious movement, or partisan of some perhaps esoteric social scheme. What was required was a willingness to expose oneself to conditions which might call forth either the extremes of violence or pacifism, and a positive willingness at that, for one had to travel long distances to reach the spot where the stimulus lay. Was this a special kind of devotion? It certainly was. We are all given some degree of contemplative turn of mind. We are usually adherents of some cause, religious or political. But we are not all prepared to cross an ocean in a sailboat or to walk from Illinois to Utah (as the Mormons did) to defend a religious belief. We are not all candidates for extreme idealistic beliefs of the most abstract kind. Yet the abstract ideal of some sort again and again brought men to the edge of the American wilderness.

Nor should it be surprising that this should be so. America offered an opportunity, to be sure, for the flourishing of dissident groups, but America was also a haven from persecution. There was a "pull" effect as well as a "push." Idealists, if their positions are held resolutely and if there is active opposition to those positions, can be difficult to live with indeed.

A society produces conventions which seem to satisfy the requirements essential to orderliness (the required degree of it—some societies require more orderliness than do others). Primitive tribes have their conventional systems of conduct, and advanced industrial societies have theirs. Such conventional systems are based upon adherence to abstract principles, freedom, justice, right reason and what have you. Such abstractions can always have many interpretations. For every ideal there can be an opposing one. Should a faction arise which vigorously opposes existing conventions, the rest of the society may feel threatened. Just as the military–religious order of Europe in the 16th and 17th centuries was threatened (and at length overthrown) by opposing ideals of freedom in thought and action, so modern political societies are threatened by present-day revolutionaries. In a few happy cases compromise so amended the framework of convention and control that the continuous life of society was not disrupted. In other cases the classic reaction of society to the threat of faction was either suppression or expulsion or a combination of both.

To those idealists facing suppression the American wilderness came to be a traditional haven where a new order might be established free from the power of other conventional systems. For those of a religious caste the wilderness had the promise of "the good land" of the Book of Deuteronomy. The idealists may have gone singly to the frontier or in groups. But even as groups they were nothing but aggregations of individuals ruled by some sort of governing body and led by individuals possessing both the requisite qualities of leadership and the necessary adherence to the doctrinal beliefs of the group. Of course, some fanatics made their own hardships and dangers worse than they might have been, given a more liberal frame of thought. Who can say at this distance in time? In most cases, the mere fact of survival in the face of suppression in the land of origin attested to the strength of the belief.

Whether or not it was necessary where it existed, idealism in the abstract, driven by hard and fanatical belief, proved in fact to be a powerful weapon against the American wilderness.

Later on, the strength of original beliefs seemed to make little difference. Initially the strength of belief in ideals and the qualities of leadership were critical factors determining the degree of success or failure in the struggle to build a firm economic foundation in the wilderness, a foundation which was necessary if the new utopias of the spirit were to have any chance of survival. Some utopias succeeded better than others. Prof. Frederick Jackson Turner, the historian, was generally correct, however. Means and ends became inextricably confused, as they do. Economic progress grew where spiritual utopias were supposed to exist, and liberal constitutional government flourished even on ground cleared and planted by totalitarians. American civilization grew to some extent upon the intellectual ruins of the idealistic systems of the fanatics, just as fields and flowers grew over the graves of the idealists, the leaders and the led—and their victims, their persecutors, their enemies. The wilderness shrank; the physical frontier of America disappeared. An imprint, of course, remained: puritanism, toleration, political freedom, a tradition of thrift and industry, but also racial and religious discrimination—all pieces, good and bad, of the great structure of the American civilization as it developed, and continues to develop. In such isolated pockets as the Amish settlements, the ideal remained in force, or nearly so. But for the most part, the reality of America, the growth and transformation of the great American economic and political system engulfed all, absorbed all.

We see the colonial and frontier idealists today as quaint figures with curious clothes and even more curious beliefs and customs. As it grew, the American "conventional system" of conduct in all spheres of life developed on too broad a basis, and with too great a power, and burst asunder the narrow strictures of our forefathers. The physical handiwork of their exertions remains as our heritage. Paradoxically enough, so far as the idealists were concerned, American economic development was left to their progeny largely as a residual. Do we appreciate the idealists less if we look again critically at some of them and their leaders? I doubt it. In times of trouble, and certainly for us the 20th century has been a time of great trouble, we might learn again the lesson of hardship and sacrifice which was part of our tradition of idealism and diversity. That we now frown upon such extremism should not blind us, as students of history, to what was once a powerful reality.

CHAPTER 2

William Penn and the Holy Experiment

I owe my conscience to no mortal man.
William Penn, 1668

America began in England. American institutions have mainly English ancestors. The man who first transplanted liberal, humane democracy to America in a systematic way, on a large scale, was William Penn. One can think of him as a gifted social gardener. The English garden contained liberal institutions, or the first shoots of them, but in the 17th century was overgrown with a proliferation of plants, and the totalitarian ones were thriving mightily. Penn was a selective gardener, and he chose plants of vast potential to move from the chaos of the old English garden to a new start in the American wilderness. It is in 17th-century England that one discovers America, and, oddly enough, in the Quaker courtier, William Penn, that one finds amidst the squalor of old London a recognizable American—even before there was much America to recognize.

William Penn founded Pennsylvania in 1681, and died in 1718 in his seventy-fourth year. Queen Anne had reigned in an England that knew comparative peace at home and power and ascendency abroad. But those happy conditions were achieved only after the English nation had been torn by internal revolution and bled and scourged for the best part of a century. During that time Great Britain passed through profound changes in her internal life, in politics, in religion and in economics. At the same time, she established an overseas empire; the colonies that raised the standard of independence in 1776 were the products of 17th-century England—a time and place of upheaval and tyranny.

Penn's life had been mostly lived in the aftermath of the Puritan movement in England, that "tremendous storm" as R. H. Tawney called it. The world of Penn's youth was the Civil War, the world of his adulthood was the Restoration and the accession of William and Mary. Penn was a product of his times. It is paradoxical, for although Penn was a pacifist and a man of liberal sentiments, his great colonizing venture was in every respect deeply embedded in the violence of 17th-century England. The paradox is more apparent than real though, for that England was a tumultuous kaleidoscope of ideas. William Penn chose carefully. To understand the founding of Pennsylvania we must comprehend the character of Penn's times. It was from that fantastic world that Penn made his choice of ideas, his beliefs which became an historical fabric of human relations and institutions so identifiably "American."

The seeds of American nationalism were planted from the start in the differences between England and her colonies. But the profundity of the differences was not immediately clear. Events magnified and clarified the differences. The great events of the 17th century shook the very foundations of the English constitution, were felt in all parts of the English-speaking world, even across the broad oceans; and the American colonies were English land.

That a separatist national feeling eventually grew up on the American side was viewed in England as an aberration to be deplored, just as it was a reality in American life to be insisted upon. Hence the extreme bitterness on both sides of the great conflict when it came in 1776. It was an English civil war as well as a war for American independence. Even in William Penn's lifetime the inevitable conflict began to appear in the strained relations between Penn and his colonists; between a man who, operating within the older legal framework, had given his colonists unprecedented freedom, and the colonists themselves, who sensed the chance to found a completely new order and chafed at the existence of *any* of the old symbols and restrictions. It was essentially in this form that the conflict, limited in magnitude but ubiquitous in extent, would finally come to an eruption in 1776, extinguishing not only the feudal institutions of Pennsylvania, but England's hold altogether.

Why did Englishmen leave their homeland to settle in the American wilderness? How did it happen that these Englishmen and their descendants developed a separate nationality? Here we will concern ourselves primarily with the first question. But the answer to the first contains elements of an answer to the second, because in the methods of colonization there was the germ of separatism. English ideals, unrealized at home, became the foundations of settlement—abstract ideas in England became, at the same time, American institutions. As those institutions proliferated and developed, the people, beneficiaries of English idealism, became, paradoxically, no longer English.

The American historian, Edward Channing, in an address to the American Historical Society in 1906 argued that, more than any other single person, William Penn should be considered "the founder" of the United States. To some that opinion might seem exaggerated. Yet there is no doubt that the spirit of liberty and the egalitarian democracy which we have as our legacy from Penn comprise the main wares America has to sell in the 20th-century market place of ideas. Anyone can make automobiles.

I

For most American readers 17th-century history is either that of the early colonies or it is as remote as the pyramids. It was the age of the Pilgrims, of Miles Standish and Governor Stuyvesant. As such it seems a quaint-enough age if we know it vaguely and view it from a distance. What was going on in England is an unrelated blur. But if we move up close, we see that 17th-century England was a maelstrom and the colonies reflected it.

From 1603 to 1688 we are concerned with six main political divisions in English history: the governments of James I, Charles I, the Interregnum, Charles II, James II and William III (with the Declaration of Rights following in 1689). Within these units can be traced in the political sphere the movement from divine-right monarchy to Parliamentary domination in the English Constitution. In the realm of the intellect we move from a narrow religious totalitarianism to the appearance in England of a shaky acceptance of religious diversity (the Toleration Act of 1689). In the realm of economics, England built an empire across the seas as a byproduct of her interminable conflicts with Continental political forces. The expansion of commercial activities in Britain was based upon rising capitalist organization in English life, together with a more general movement toward the regulation of trade by market forces rather than by Crown monopolies. The original American colonies were consequences of these primary forces in the 17th century, and they were molded by these forces just as the structure of English life itself was changed forever by them.

Basic political and economic differences often appear as arid doctrinal disputes. Thus it was in the 17th century. Religion was the great arena for learned and not-so-learned dispute. To the modern mind, the 17th-century concept of religion is almost impossible to comprehend, although the totalitarian political disputes of our own time resemble the doctrinal battles of the 17th century by analogy. The first operating political parties, the Whigs and the Tories, were only just forming at the end of the Stuart epoch. Before that, only the Levelers resembled a political party. The state was ruled by the Crown and its agents, which included the state church, contested widely by representatives of the ruling aristocracy in the Parliament. Until the Act of Toleration a man's religious practices were potentially an index of his agreement with his rulers.

There was of course no question of separation of church and state. After Henry VIII's Act of Supremacy in 1534 the King of England was the head of England's church. In an age of theological upheaval this was doubly unfortunate. The state's actions were given theological interpretations, and the state was automatically involved in doctrinal disputes and discords which occurred among the feuding divines. Under such circumstances there could clearly be no peace. Whether or not a man approved of the wearing of surplices by the clerics or believed in the Holy Trinity were 17th-century equivalents of the modern demands for belief in the "historically necessary" role of the Soviet dictatorship or in the ultimate victory of Socialism in the modern totalitarianism of the left. Religion was, in the 17th century, a mortally serious business. To the 17th-century Englishman, or at least to important ones throughout most of the century, there was room for only a single religious faith within society and free religious thought was, both to Anglican and Puritan, "tantamount to anarchy or rebellion."

The Puritan movement was essentially fundamentalism. Puritan divines wanted deep reform; they wanted all popish practices expunged from the church services, and they wanted the Bible to be the absolute authority upon which the reforms were to be based. They wanted simplified church organization ("no bishops") and a more fundamental and simplified dogma —notably recognition by the church of the doctrine of predestination. Such demands were bound to be resisted by the Anglicans, not only to protect hierarchical vested interests, but because the Church of England was not, after all, a descendant of European Protestantism. Henry VIII considered himself a Catholic, and the Six Articles of 1539 imposed penalties for Protestant heresies. But once loosed by Henry's break with Rome, the wind of religious, and hence political, reformism stopped at no English barriers, and in the end claimed the head of a king.

When Henry VIII died (1547), the reform movement began to gather momentum. John Knox came back to Britain in 1549 and other exiled reformers like John Hooper and Miles Cloverdale reappeared on English soil. The reaction under Queen Mary (Bloody Mary died in 1558) blessed the Puritan cause with martyrs—an estimated 250 to 300 heretics were burnt alive. Elizabeth also suppressed the Puritans but not so bloodily—her interests lay elsewhere than in interminable religious debates. At her death (1603) Puritan hopes ran high, the new king James I (and James VI of Scotland) had ruled a Protestant land. But James had already had enough of royal compromise with Protestant clergy, and the Puritans received from him a rude shock at the Hampton Court Conference (1604): "If this be all they [the Puritans] have to say, I shall make them conform themselves, or I will harry them out of the land, or else do worse." James would have in England ". . . one doctrine and one discipline, one religion in substance and in ceremony."

James' repressions drove separatist Puritans into exile, first to Leyden in the Netherlands (1609) and then in 1620 to Plymouth. The Massachusetts Colony of Puritans which followed (chartered in 1629; Boston founded in 1630) was a "nonseparatist" group; that is, they considered themselves to be the "true church" of England. But they accommodated themselves easily enough with the survivors of the separatist Plymouth group, and then, true to the style of their times, established a repressive theocracy of their own in which religious conformity continued to be imposed by totalitarian methods. There was no paradox here. The zealots of Massachusetts believed in their vision; they had finally established the conditions for building God's kingdom. Freedom and toleration were not their wares, either in their dealings with white men of differing beliefs or with the unfortunate red men who lived near their settlements.

Meanwhile, the mainstream of Puritanism in England was becoming a political force of major proportions. Among the tradesmen and merchants of the towns and in the countryside nonconformism in matters of religion was a growing attraction to those whose interests did not reside in conformity with the king's political or economic practices. It was inevitable that the economic and political oppressions of the early Stuarts have their religious counterpart. King James I was a vocal and ardent theorist of government, never missing an opportunity to write or orate on the theory of the divine right of kings. The established church, whose offices and powers were filled and armed by royal prerogative, echoed the monarch's totalitarian views. There was of course stout opposition, and Parliamentarians from Sir Edward Coke down to the outbreak of the Civil War in 1642 attempted to bend the Stuarts to compromise with the Parliament and the common law, but to no avail. The Protestation of 1621 was an outburst against rule by divine right, and in the great Petition of Right of 1628 (the work of Sir Edward Coke) both houses of Parliament passed a basic statement of English freedoms. Yet in that year Charles I argued that his actions were answerable "to God alone." Moreover, on the scaffold in 1649 he reiterated his view that the people had no right to a voice in their government.

High-handed in politics, totalitarian in religion, and autocratic in economic matters, as we shall see, the early Stuarts drove their opponents toward nonconformism, separatism and, crucially, into increasingly united opposition in Parliament. As Charles I faced off his opponents the Civil War drew closer. His Archbishop of Canterbury, Laud, pressed conformity in religious matters; the King dissolved Parliaments and thus destroyed the only voice the English people had in their government at the national level, and his grants of monopoly and privilege to raise revenues widened the schism between his government and the rising commercial community. Thus the lines of politics, religion and economics were hardened.

In 1638 the Scots raised the standard of revolt. There followed three years of fighting, treaties, negotiations. The Scots occupied Northumberland and Durham. To buy them off Charles called Parliament back in November, 1640 (the Long Parliament). Following his attempt (January, 1642) to arrest "the five members" and Parliament's new demands upon him, Charles raised his standard at Nottingham and the English Civil War began. King and bishop, lord and gentlemen, all came to know the force of the aroused English Puritans and their allies, and the fabric of monarchical supremacy in English government was irretrievably torn by the Commonwealth and Cromwell's reign as Lord Protector. Tawney's great descriptive passage of the character of the victorious forces tells how.

> On a world heaving with expanding energies, and on a Church uncertain of itself, rose, after two generations of premonitory mutterings, the tremendous storm of the Puritan movement. The forest bent; the oaks snapped; the dry leaves were driven before a gale . . . amid the blare of trumpets, and the clash of arms, and the rending of the carved work of the Temple, humble to God and haughty to man, the soldier-saints swept over battlefield and scaffold their garments rolled in blood.

With the Roundhead victories and the Lord Protector's dictatorship, Puritanism was spent as a force in English political history. It remained for Bunyan and Milton to make the "good old cause" immortal. But the Anglicans had not learned their lesson, and conformity by force in politics and religion stayed on a while longer. With the Restoration and the Cavalier Parliament (1661–78) the force of politics, once more allied with Anglican divines, resulted in religious oppression; and in the Clarendon Code, the Test Act and other legislation pressed down conformity once again upon the English people. Once more the thoughts of men were to be regulated, or at least it was imagined that such was possible. Charles II and James II both fell afoul of Parliament on matters of religion. But unlike the situation in 1603–40, after 1660 it was Parliament which would forcibly impose the Anglican rite upon all.

Just as James I's persecutions peopled Massachusetts, so the Anglican persecutions of the Restoration peopled Pennsylvania and other American colonies. James II's efforts to restore rights to his Catholic co-religionists and to dissenters contributed to his downfall in 1688, and in 1689 the English, in the Act of Toleration, began their long evolution toward religious freedom. Only in the 19th century were political restrictions removed from Catholics and others. Church and state were never separated but the church became more or less dormant in politics.

The mixture of religion and politics in 17th-century England was a sanguinary one, not unlike the mixture of economic determinism and politics in the U. S. S. R. of our own time. Indeed, in the political sphere, at least, elder statesmen in the 17th century seemed to be almost as rare as in Stalinist Russia. Among outstanding political figures executed were Sir Walter Raleigh and Sir Edward Digby (treason, the latter in the Gunpowder Plot); Charles I's Archbishop, Laud, and his minister, the Earl of Strafford; Commonwealth statesmen Sir Henry Vane and John Lambert (revenge during the Restoration); Arthur Capel (Earl of Essex), Lord Russell, Algernon Sidney (the Rye House Plot); the Duke of Monmouth and Earl of Argyle (Monmouth's Rebellion). In addition, of course, Charles I was beheaded, and Sir Arthur Hesilrige, one of the "five members," died in the Tower in 1661.

Political heads fell on other occasions as well. The most famous are well known. In the Popish Plot (1678) thirty-five were executed (*all* were innocent) including Viscount Stafford and Oliver Plunket, Primate of Ireland. Following Monmouth's invasion there was a regular judicial slaughter and an estimated three hundred and twenty were executed. Political vengeance even went into the crypt after its victims. In modern Russia the offending corpse of Stalin was merely removed from the holy place; in 1660 the corpses of Cromwell, Ireton and Bradshaw were taken out of their graves in the Abbey, hanged in their shrouds and dumped into a common pit (along with the corpses of Pym and Admiral Blake). The estates of Cromwell, Ireton and Bradshaw were forfeited. At the Restoration thirteen "regicides," including six judges of Charles I, were hanged, drawn and quartered. Pepys went to see Sir Henry Vane beheaded but complained that he couldn't actually see the blood flow because of the crowd.

There was also murder not sanctioned by the legal authority. In the reign of James I, Sir Thomas Overbury, one of the courtiers, was poisoned by the mistress of the royal favorite, the Earl of Somerset, who languished long in prison for the crime and died there. Charles I's favorite, George Villiers, the Duke of Buckingham, was assassinated. Among those who died in exile under attainder or threat of death were Edmund Ludlow, a prominent Parliamentarian who was impeached in 1660; the Earl of Shaftesbury (a member of Charles II's Cabal) and even Edward Hyde, the great Earl of Clarendon.

Of impeachments by their enemies space does not allow mention except perhaps Sir Francis Bacon, whose indictment was pushed (possibly out of revenge) by Sir Edward Coke, who had been earlier a victim of Bacon's political machinations. Coke was himself the prosecutor of Sir Walter Raleigh: "I will prove you to be the most notorious traitor that ever came to the bar," a triumph which badly mars an otherwise brilliant escutcheon. Among the great ministers of the 17th century who died of natural causes at home were Robert

Cecil, James I's Earl of Salisbury, and Thomas Osborne, Charles II's Earl of Danby. Danby survived impeachment, the Tower and powerful enemies and died of natural causes in 1712 aged 80.

This list is not complete, but the grim recital is offered to underscore the violence and the totalitarian characteristics of the political life in 17th-century England. It was an incredibly dismal political performance and represented the kind of lag Albert Schweitzer complained of in his Nobel address, the dangerous tendency of human relations to stagnate behind advances in other aspects of learning. The lag represented part of the continuous crumbling of the old social system of the Middle Ages. There was a violent confrontation of the dying medieval and the rising modern practices. The death of one king and exile of another were measures of the rise of political democracy—paradoxical as that may seem.

The modern mind existed in the 17th century but it did not yet prevail. Kepler died the year Boston, Massachusetts, was founded. Galileo died two years before Charles I was beheaded. The century saw in its first twenty-six years the publication of most of Sir Francis Bacon's work which contributed mightily to the intellectual revolution of the last part of the century. The year 1660 saw not only the Restoration of the Stuart monarchy, but the founding of the Royal Society and, in 1673, when the notorious Test Act was passed obliging all officeholders to take both an oath of allegiance and the sacraments of the Church of England, Mr. Isaac Newton, the Cambridge mathematician, had already belonged to the Royal Society for two years. The rule of official ignorance and superstition was fast ending with the death of divine-right monarchy.

But the century of Harvey, Boyle and Locke was also the century of Laud, Praisegod Barebones and Titus Oates. In the co-existence of great ignorance and great science, great evil and great good, the 17th century was like our own. The lag in human affairs is an old and a sad story. In the 17th century a new world was rising amid tumult and disorder in religion, politics and science, but nowhere were signs of the future more portentous than in the realm of economic change.

II

In economic life there was during the 17th century an undercurrent of change which matched, and some scholars think contributed to, the fundamental transformation of English political and intellectual life. An age-old population structure was undergoing pervasive change. England's population in 1600 was about 4.5 million; in 1700 it was about 5.7 million, a mean annual rate of increase of just under 0.3 percent. But this growth was not evenly distributed on a geographical basis. The phenomenon of the link between manufacturing and urbanization was present in the 17th century: mixed textiles and metals manufacturing in Worcester; textiles in Norfolk, Gloucester, Wiltshire and Devon. There was extensive manufacturing in and around London, and the ancient city on the Thames already was achieving great size. In 1605, London counted just over 224,000 souls; by 1682 its population was 669,000. The great city's mean annual rate of growth was over 2.5 percent, or nearly ten times the rate of growth of the English population generally. Probably London grew more rapidly than did most cities, but the urban growth, representing the proliferation of manufacturing and commerce, had seriously drained population from the countryside and the villages and contributed to serious social dislocations there. At the same time the new towns were centers of dissent and nonconformism, and in their wealth and power were a constant affront to the landed aristocracy of the dying feudal order.

In all this England stood alone. The fact that the England of James I was one in which the last vestiges of agricultural feudalism were fast disappearing was in marked contrast with Europe. Indeed, as late as the early 19th century the social organization of feudalism was still present in Western Europe; for example, Germany was still largely a land of serfs and guilds. As Alexis de Tocqueville noted in his great study of *L'ancien régime,* there was in France, as late as 1789, pervasive, if debilitated and weakening, feudalism in the organization of the countryside, with traces of villenage (for example, obligatory labor without pay for the landlords) in French agriculture, and many of the other feudal arrangements, including landlord monopolies at the well and dye vat, still existed. In Britain there were few such vestiges even in 1600. The decline of feudalism was a significant contributor to England's economic potential in an age when, in terms of population alone, she was still vastly inferior to her Continental rivals.

The comparatively early demise of feudalism in England is traced to several partly fortuitous circumstances. First, the English developed a national government earlier than did most

European countries. A solid basis for the growth of a central governmental power was established by the Conquest, but the Angevin governments were still feudal in their organization. The Wars of the Roses (1455–85) largely eliminated what remained of independent political power exercised by the feudal lords, so that Henry VII (1485–1509) had a national government in which the Crown exercised central political power virtually unchallenged by the remnants of the feudal aristocracy. Under Henry VIII the independent ecclesiastical power was abolished and, with the sequestration and sale of monastic lands, the economic power of religion was broken. Hence Elizabeth I ruled an England in which the governmental power was undiluted except by the as yet unresolved conflict between the monarch and the main representative body, the Parliament. The division of political power between the Crown and the Parliament was finally resolved in 1688 when Parliamentary independence was assured. The long existence of a united country gave England a broad internal market compared to the petty feudal principalities of Europe; even in France, Colbert's mercantilism (1661–72) had failed to unify the French market. Indeed, by 1707, with the union of England and Scotland, Britain was actually Europe's largest free-trade area.

Second, the localized force of feudal tradition in the holding and working of the land began to crumble as a consequence of the Black Death (1348–49). It is estimated that from 30 to 50 percent of England's rural population perished in that great disaster. To occupy the land after that the English system of landholding by leasehold, copyhold, freehold and other forms of nonhereditary agricultural tenancies was developed. The old feudalism could not be re-established. The Peasants Revolt of 1381 bears evidence of that. Even though the small holders had no clear titles to their land, the new system was a long step forward from villenage. Out of this grew a race of farmers and laborers relatively free from the constricting usages of feudalism. There was, among large-scale landowners, capitalism on the land at a very early date.

The rise of outright ownership or control of land, the antithesis of feudalism, was speeded up by the growth of Britain's woolen manufactures and trades, and the consequent introduction of sheep raising. To pasture the flocks, landlords began early in the Tudor era the process of consolidating and enclosing agricultural landholdings. They also exerted their feudal rights to common land in an attempt to bring it under their own cultivation. The results of various waves of enclosing were the famous empty villages of Britain (Goldsmith's "Sweet Auburn"). The fear of rural depopulation as a result of enclosures was widespread and governments throughout the Tudor era fought as best they could against what was felt to be a great danger of rural stagnation. Even as late as the 18th century sentiment against the enclosures was strong.

> Ill fares the land, to hastening ills a prey,
> Where wealth accumulates, and men decay.

Yet the landholding of England had to be reorganized on a capitalistic basis, if new agricultural methods were to be introduced; enclosures, brutal or not, were among the main methods used. The enclosures persisted until as late as the early 19th century, until English agriculture was completely one of capitalism. However, as early as the 17th century, villenage was gone in England, and agricultural reform made possible by the end of the century the first great English agricultural techniques. The open fields, common herds, common use of wastelands, strip farming, customary tithes and dues, inherited tenures—all the inefficient methods of feudal agriculture were under assault. But if the results in the 16th and 17th centuries were better farming, they also were social upheaval and depopulation in enclosed agricultural districts. Mobs of dispossessed farmers and laborers leveled hedges and ditches on enclosed lands and justly earned the name of "Levelers" from their sentiments as well as their activities. They presented to the victorious Puritan armies the spectacle of radical egalitarian democracy in the Agreement of the People of 1647.

Dissent in religious life was a natural consequence of upheaval on the land, and the dissent produced nonconformists including Quakers. Nonconformism came naturally with the rise of agricultural capitalism. The same was true of the rise of capitalism in urban areas. The threat of rural discontent was only one effect of the rise of capitalistic techniques with its requirements of private ownership and control of productive resources, wage labor and the sanctity of contracts.

The medieval organization of industry, like that of the land, was threatened. There was no place for guilds in openly competitive markets. In the old medieval towns the trades and crafts were in the straitjacket of the guilds, but in newly established centers of manufacturing the guilds' power was broken. Contract manufacturing in the rural districts (the "putting out system") of course was not at all under guild control. Even the Crown's revenues were threatened here. Foreign trade had customarily been conducted partly by royal grants of monopolies and partly by licenses. The Crown received revenues from the guilds, bought produce at special reduced prices at the fairs and received revenues from the trading monopolies. The rise of commerce based upon the spread of manufacturing techniques throughout the kingdom, and the flow of "free" labor from the countryside changed the distribution of trade among the towns, threatening the older ones, their guilds and, through smuggling and unlicensed internal dealings, the revenues of the Crown.

These problems were met by the establishment of a brutal and ramshackle system of controls. In Queen Mary's reign the Weavers Act (1555) attempted to limit the cloth trade to the older towns. Elizabeth's Statute of Apprentices (1563) was a comprehensive control of the population. By that ·time the older guild system clearly was weakened and had experienced a fundamental transformation toward capitalistic techniques. The "larger portion" of the nation's workers had no material interest in their product, but instead worked for wages.

The statute has been correctly viewed as an early attempt at a planned economy. Output was not regulated, but many of its main determinants were. Wages and prices were regulated. Except for persons of property, those of "gentle birth" and scholars, the whole population was to choose occupations either at sea, in the crafts or in agriculture. Anyone who failed to make a suitable choice could be forced into agriculture. Certain trades—those of the goldsmiths, ironmongers, drapers and mercers—had property qualifications for entry into them. The geographical distribution of the population was to be severely limited; no employed person might leave his town or parish without a written testimonial from the proper authorities.

The effects of the statute were comprehensive enough, and had they been successfully enforced (which they were not) they would have destroyed the independent basis for the growth of manufacturing.

The law was opposed by the rising towns, and inflation made application of stated wages and prices difficult. Enforcement was characteristically brutal: whippings, ears lopped off, impressment into the silver mines, hanging for desertions from jobs and so forth. But opposition to such clumsy efforts to control labor, commerce and industry was continuous and the resulting conflicts added to the crescendo of social violence which came finally in the Civil War. Even the Crown's use of monopolies for revenues had been under periodic attack, and in 1601 Elizabeth had acceded to a court ruling that the royal charter did not make the grant of monopoly irremediable.

Thus at the beginning of the Stuart era there was great ferment in England. Society was in the throes of a deep-seated transformation in agriculture, manufacturing, commerce and, as we have already seen, in government and religion. Economic change was a political phenomenon since everywhere it contended with the creaking apparatus of economic controls. Economic change also had religious consequences because the nonconforming Puritans found ready adherents in those sectors of the economy, especially in the rising manufacturing towns and districts, where economic self-interest was not in accord with Crown laws and the Crown's devoted supporter, the Anglican Church.

The results of these conflicts were far-reaching for the American settlements made in the 17th century. As Trevelyan emphasized, the medieval serf of France or Spain could never have built a dynamic empire capable of self-government. But the early English settlers in America were a different breed: ". . . the English colonial movement was the migration of a modern society, self-governing, half industrial, awake to economic and intellectual change." The Pilgrim fathers, for example, came primarily from English villages long freed from feudal backwardness. Penn's Quakers, tradesmen and craftsmen, men of commerce and industry as well as independent farmers, needed only a free soil in which to flourish. England had already prepared them for self-government; even the convicts sent in irons.

In England the conflicts of a changing nation brought internal war and "the tears of three generations." Essentially the Stuart troubles began with, and consisted of, a reactionary failure of the rulers to change their policies as their country changed. Hence we find James I increasing the Crown monopolies, and Charles I continuing that policy in spite of the clear conflict between a system of licenses and monopoly constraints and the rising system of free commerce and innovation. Parliament in 1624 legislated against royal grants of monopolies but the Crown's revenue needs continued to find succor there. A commercial community could not abide such a system, and the feeling was expressed for all time: monopolies ". . . like the frogs of Egypt have gotten possession of our dwellings and we have scarcely a room free from them; they sip in our cup; they dip in our dish; they sit by our fire; we find them in the dye vat, the washing bowl and the powdering tub; they share with the butler in his bar; they have marked and sealed us from head to foot. . . ."

By the first few years of Charles I's reign the failure of the English to resolve their political problem meant that the government was in impossible financial straits. Not only was it out of touch with the new forces sweeping the economy, its Parliaments refused to provide beyond the narrowest short-term financial compromises. Charles resorted to personal rule and the raising of monies by methods which were particularly obnoxious to the commercial community.

King Charles' failure to get satisfactory revenue legislation from his Parliaments (when they existed) turned the Crown to actions which were viewed as predatory by the Parliamentarians. Thus, when he raised funds by imposing ship-money levies on the coastal towns, by collecting his tonnage and poundage taxes on overseas trade, by continuous grants of licenses and patents of monopoly on salt, on soap making, on mines, on the privilege to open manufacturing establishments, the operation of inns and so forth, he alienated the townsmen. When, as a matter of social policy, his government opposed the progress of the enclosures, the land-owning gentry was offended. A similar result with smaller landholders followed efforts to force those who were qualified to take up knighthoods.

As prices rose and the wages of Elizabeth's statute became increasingly obsolete, laborers and workmen found their interests increasingly in conflict with the law. Thus the Crown's efforts to maintain a balanced economy through a status quo on the land, through detailed interference in the life of commerce and manufacturing through patents and licenses, in addition to the raising of funds through taxes not sanctioned by law, inevitably hardened the attitudes of the new men of the commercial towns and the country gentry who controlled Parliament. In the end they swept away the whole paraphernalia of royal government—briefly as it turned out—from England. The armies raised from the common people and commanded by such "commoners" as Fairfax, Cromwell and Ireton became an inexorable force. Behind the ". . . smaller part of the gentry in most counties, and the greatest part of the tradesmen and freeholders and the middle sort of men, especially in those corporations and counties which de-

pend on clothing and such manufactures . . ." who made up
the Parliamentary armies stood the wealth of the towns and
of the City. In 1641 and 1642 even the old royal monopoly
of Merchant Adventurers lent money to Parliament.

As is usually the case in political revolutions, the destruction of the old system of government looses a flood which
must be stopped by some power, or political revolution becomes social revolution. The English revolutionary conflict
was no exception. With the fall of Crown, church and squire,
came also demands for a radical change in what was left of
the old social order. Such agitation became widespread, especially in the army, where it threatened to overwhelm the
gentry and "middle sort of men" who were the officers, and
went the full way to agrarian communism in the case of the
Diggers. The extreme social radicalism was clearly a threat
to established power among the merchant and manufacturing
classes, "a design against the twelve famous companies" of
London. It was a revolution "to raise the servant against the
master, the tenant against the landlord . . . the poor against
the rich . . . every beggar should be set on horseback."

From such agitation and thought arose a political party,
the Levelers (thought to be the first in modern Europe),
whose creed later passed to the Quakers and partly thence into
American history. In October, 1647, the Levelers drew up an
"Agreement of the People" which they wanted to submit to
a popular referendum. These soldiers wanted a democratic
and republican form of government with a written constitution
which was based upon "abstract principles new to English
politics." The Levelers' principal demands were a radical
affront to the well ordered Parliamentary mind of 1647. But
any American reading them today will see old friends.

The Levelers demanded that all power should go to the
House of Commons, that there should be complete and free
manhood suffrage without property qualifications for annual
or biannual Parliaments, that the government be decentralized,
that there should be equality before the law, that monopolies
should be abolished, that the enclosures should be broken up,
that small landholders should be given security in their tenures
and that there should be complete religious freedom throughout the land. The Leveler troops mutinied. They pressed their
commanders with their views; Colonel Rainsborough, a Leveler
officer, argued that "every man born in England . . . the
poor man, the meanest man in the kingdom . . ." should be
free to choose his own lawmakers. Such was "every English-

man's birth right." The Levelers' demands were suppressed. Cromwell had some of the leaders executed. The time for such radical democracy had not yet come in England. At the Putney Debates, General Ireton (Cromwell's son-in-law) argued with the soldiers against such radical alterations in the traditional British mode of government. "If you admitt any man that hath a breath and being . . . thus we destroy propertie. . . . Noe person that hath nott a locall and permanent interest in the Kingdome should have an equal dependence in Elections." A surviving Leveler leader, John Lilburne, became a Quaker, and the Quakers, adding to other practices which aroused the wrath of their persecutors, adopted the Leveler social doctrines to a large extent—Penn gave the vote to every freeholder, as we will see shortly. The Leveler doctrine found an early home in America, but it was long coming to England.

The economic revolution in England continued during the Commonwealth and Restoration, but with two crucial and related changes: England became an imperial power of major proportions, and the attendant rise of her naval and merchant fleet, together with the promulgation of trade and navigation controls over the new colonies, turned British eyes to external trade. By the mid-17th century, England's interests in foreign trade, evidenced to some extent by the rise of great new chartered foreign-trade monopolies, had become a more prominent factor in government policy. In 1663, the prohibition against the export of precious metals was lifted. The nation's treasure was not to be assured by simply making the use of it illegal, but rather, using precious metals as well as commodities, the nation's treasure was to be augmented through the balance of trade. This was a mortal blow at the bullionists and a victory for the mercantilist school of thought, which was never more simply characterized than by Thomas Mun in 1664:

> The ordinary means . . . to increase our wealth and treasure is by *Forraign Trade*, wherein wee must ever observe this rule; to sell more to strangers yearly then wee consume of theirs in value.

Trade was to be developed, with emphasis upon maintaining the domestic market and cultivating it for domestic industry. In all, the new empire was to be as nearly as possible self-sufficient. Legislation in regard to wool is a good example of such Restoration policies. There was a prohibition against its export. It could not be made into cloth in the colonies. The dead had to be buried in wool. Everyone except "ladies and gentlemen" had to wear wool hats on Sundays and holidays. "Fish Days" were decreed when no meat was to be eaten ". . . so that the sea-coasts shall be strong with men and habitations, and the fleet flourish more than ever." Even trade in agricultural products came into the scheme. After 1670 corn laws protected home agriculture from foreign grain when domestic prices were low and encouraged imports (a sop to the non-agricultural classes) when domestic prices were high.

Such doctrine and practices were clearly incompatible with a flourishing international market. But they were compatible with focusing policy upon empire building, and that was what mercantilism was all about. By 1776 the American colonies had had enough of the system, and so had economists. In that year Adam Smith dealt a death blow to mercantilism with *The Wealth of Nations,* the fountainhead of modern economic thought. But fallacious or not, for more than a hundred years the mercantilist doctrine was the intellectual basis of the British Empire's growth, with its odious mixture of political repression and economic intervention. Somehow, in England it was more attractive than in Massachusetts.

A doctrine of trade and empire was ineffectual without ships. Elizabethan sea power had seen a precarious beginning, and until Charles I the navy rotted. James I had not wanted much business with Elizabeth's "men of war." While it may be true that the voyages of discovery had transferred the potential for commercial greatness from the Mediterranean to the North Atlantic, the opportunity had to be grasped. Under Charles I the beginnings of a new navy appeared in spite of his financial woes and the incompetence of his military favorites. During the Civil War, Admiral Blake had kept the navy largely neutral and intact on the sound doctrine that the war on land was not the navy's business, that whoever won would still be an English government and it was the navy's duty to protect the government, whatever it might be, from foreign enemies.

Under Cromwell, Britain reaped a rich harvest from Blake's conservatism. The early Stuarts had passively accumulated an empire in North America—Virginia, New England and Maryland. Under Cromwell, Britain went out aggressively after empire—a policy which was continued with vigor by the Restoration government and which stopped in America only in 1776. As Sir Charles Firth put it, Cromwell was ". . . the first English ruler who systematically employed the power of the government to increase and extend the colonial possessions of England." Cromwell had a separate policy of colonial aggrandizement which was not a necessary part of his internal policies, or so it seemed. Yet it was the overseas empire which guaranteed English manufacturers and tradesmen in later years a market for their goods in excess of the absorptive power of the domestic market and which, by virtue of the Navigation Laws of 1651, could be depended upon when "foreign" markets became inaccessible because of wars, trade fluctuations or barriers raised by Britain's trading partners— countries which were equally devoted to mercantilist principles. The Navigation Act, which limited British overseas trade and colonial trade to shipping under British control, was not only a sop to the merchant shipping interests, but was also a form of guarantee (if it could be enforced) to domestic manufacturers.

Overseas expansion was thus a matter of high policy. Royalist supporters in Virginia and the Barbados faced an English fleet in 1651 which was sent to strengthen the ties with the home government (the colonists switched allegiances). Curious as it may seem today, the Caribbean was long the main focus of English attention. Those islands formed the basis of the new trade in sugar, cotton, tobacco and other exotic tropical products. Cromwell moved first against Spain. In 1655, Jamaica was taken by Admiral Penn (William Penn's father) and General Venables after an attempt against Hispaniola failed. More Spanish islands were taken in 1655 and 1656. In 1657, part of Venezuela was taken. In 1654, an untimely peace with the Dutch frustrated an attempt to do what was completed in 1664, the final removal of the Dutch government from North America and the occupation and government of their lands by the English. There was more than just conquest. Cromwell supported and engineered the transport of population to the new colonies in the Caribbean.

Cromwell's colonial policy, congenial to domestic manufacturing and trading interests, was carried on vigorously by the later Stuarts. Victory over the Dutch in 1664 added all of New Netherland to the North American empire. The Civil War added an emigré population to the Southern and Caribbean colonies. New Netherland, governed by the Duke of York, was broken up partly into royal proprietaries (New Jersey and West New Jersey were sold in 1664 to Lord John Berkeley and Sir George Carteret), and partly governed outright as a royal colony. The grant to William Penn in 1681 completed the organization of the former Dutch territories. Other additions were made: New Hampshire was set apart from New England in 1679; the Carolinas (with a reactionary feudal constitution written by John Locke) in 1670. Thus, except for Georgia, all of the original thirteen colonies were established under the British flag in the 17th century, and a large portion of the territory was added after the Restoration following Cromwell's precedent. The pace of colonization quickened in the last part of the century.

Increased interest in colonization after the Civil War was due to several causes. The spreading use of joint-stock company procedures aided the mobilization of funds for such enterprises. There was increasingly a market for lands as income rose in England with the rise of commerce and trade—the proprietors speculated with their lands in an expanding market. The supply of emigrants rose again with agricultural change, religious persecutions, increased mobility of labor as manufacturing left the older towns, the policy of transporting prisoners (the thriving slave traffic must be added). Money, people, organization. The Navigation Acts pre-empted the colonial trade (or at least the legal part of it), and the mercantilist bias of the royal governments after the Restoration kept the hand of royal protection and encouragement over the colonies—even, in the case of tobacco, to the ruin of domestic growers.

Britain in the 16th century had wrested freedom of the seas from the Spanish; in the 17th century she established her position of dominance in the North Atlantic after breaking the Dutch power. All that were left were the French. They were broken by 1763. Thus the late 17th century was a time when "conditions," the complicated combination of religious, political, economic and technological forces, were favorable for the growth of Britain beyond her shores. Indeed, Britain seems at a distance of three centuries and more to have been a kind of human maelstrom crushing men and institutions down at home, and flinging the survivors and their beliefs into the islands of the Caribbean and the wilds of North America.

III

Such was the world in which William Penn's life was lived. It was turbulent, dangerous, vital and complex. It was a world of dramatic actions and great achievements. Economic change contributed to the rise of nonconformism and hence was one of many forces involved in the rise of Penn's Quakers. An empire was being built, and Penn, by accident of birth and by his own actions, was destined to play a crucial role in that empire's growth.

Penn was of a military and cavalier family. His father, Admiral Sir William Penn, was a naval hero under both the Commonwealth (the capture of Jamaica, for which he was momentarily placed in the Tower by Cromwell—his expedition was supposed to have taken Hispaniola) and under Charles II (Penn was the victor over the Dutch at Dogger Bank). In addition to the manorhouse at Wanstead in Essex, Admiral Penn was given the confiscated property of Macroon, a large estate in Ireland, in recognition of his services to the Commonwealth. The admiral's association with the Stuart brothers, Charles and James, was an extremely close one. It was based upon a service to them which is not entirely clear in histories of the period. It is suggested that he once offered to deliver a large part of the fleet to Charles when he was in exile. Admiral Penn declared for the Stuarts in 1659 when it was clear that Richard Cromwell's government would not succeed after the death of the Lord Protector. The Admiral was elected member of the Convention Parliament for Weymouth, and was aboard the battleship *Naseby* when the fleet went to Holland in May, 1660, to get their king.

One of Charles II's first acts on board the *Naseby* was to knight Admiral Penn. Whatever had been his services to the Stuarts, they were important. Twenty years later Charles named Pennsylvania for the admiral (long since dead) over the objections of the new proprietor of that province, William Penn, the Quaker. (In accord with current tradition and usage he tried to bribe the King's secretary into changing the name, not wanting it to appear that his province had been named after himself.) After the Restoration government was organized, Admiral Penn served as Naval Commissioner with the Duke of York—in the office which employed an ambitious, observant and malignant clerk, Samuel Pepys.

Young Penn, then, was born and spent his boyhood in a home where public affairs loomed large. His was a wealthy, favored and powerful family connection. Information regarding his mother is scarce. She is variously described as Dutch and Irish. She was probably neither, but English. It is sometimes implied that she was shrewish, and Pepys described Lady Penn as "mighty homely." The father's character seems to have been much that which might have been expected in a naval hero, straightforward, blunt in speech and manner, direct in action. A good man, evidently honest enough (an attempt to impeach him failed) and, at least as far as the Stuarts were concerned, loyal.

Young Penn, born Oct. 14, 1644 in London, had a boyhood not dissimilar to that of any other young man of his rank and station, given the vicissitudes of the period. Penn is thought to have had some formal schooling in the rigid classical curriculum of a school at Chigwell, near his home in Essex. But mainly he must have been tutored, because Admiral Penn moved his family to Macroon in 1656 or 1657 when Penn was still a youth. He entered Oxford, in Christ Church College, Michaelmas term, 1660. He was in London in the spring of 1661 to see the coronation of Charles II. Back in Oxford in 1661, young Penn came into conflict with his college authorities for refusing to conform to Anglican rites. First he was fined and then in March, 1662, when not yet 18, he was "sent down" (expelled) from Christ Church for nonconformity. The admiral, as Pepys noted, was unhappy about young Penn's turn of mind, ". . . I now perceive . . . one thing that hath put Sir William so long off the hookes." Sir William in fact momentarily turned the boy out, thought better of it and later in the same summer sent him to France. Penn remained in France until perhaps August, 1664, and upon his return was enough dandified and affected by the French to put Pepys off, "Comes to visit me Mr. W. Pen. [sic] I perceive something of learning he hath got, but a great deal, if not too much of the vanity of the French garb, and affected manner of speech and gait. I fear all real profit he hath made of his travel will signify little." Pepys had no great love for the admiral, nor for his son. When, four years later, young Penn was in the Tower for writing a pamphlet, "The Sandy Foundation Shaken," Pepys thought it was too good to have been written by William Penn, ". . . a serious sort of book, and not fit for every body to read."

The only portrait of William Penn from life shows him some time after his return from France as a handsome cavalier youth, in shining armor, with flowing curls (a wig evidently, his own hair had been badly damaged by smallpox when he was an infant). He was evidently tall and of athletic build. With his fine clothes and manners, fluent French and keen mind, young William Penn must have been his father's joy at this time. In February, 1665, the young man was entered at

Lincoln's Inn to study law, a fitting course of study for the son and heir of the admiral.

However, war broke out again with Holland and the admiral almost immediately took William out of school and went to sea with him. There is some evidence here on the intimacy between the Penns and their rulers. In April, the admiral sent William to London with a message. The King, aroused from bed at dawn, received the messenger with "Oh, is't you? How is Sir William?" On June 8, news of the great victory came and Pepys went ". . . to my Lady Pen's, where they are all joyed and not a little puffed up at the good successe of their father; and good service indeed is said to have been done by him. Had a great bonfire at the gate; and I with my Lady Pen's people and others to Mrs. Turners. . . ."

But the day before Pepys recorded two or three houses in Drury Lane ". . . marked with a red cross upon the doors, and 'Lord have mercy upon us' writ there; which was a sad sight to me, being the first of the kind that, to my remembrance, I ever saw. . . ." The plague was in London. It was followed by the great fire in September of the next year. The two events, while doubtless cutting short the Penns' enjoyment of the admiral's successes, also permanently ended William's law career. Lincoln's Inn was closed throughout the plague. The family stayed in London through the double catastrophe of fire and plague. Some have speculated that the horrors of 1665 and 1666 gave William Penn's mind a decisive religious jolt. They must have impressed anyone who lived through them.

The Irish estate of the Penns, Macroon, was returned to the loyalists from whom it had been confiscated, and in exchange, Admiral Penn was given other Irish lands which young Penn was sent to administer. The admiral's son associated with the governing classes in Ireland and, in the spring of 1666, William Penn took part voluntarily (he was, after all, not in service) in a military action against mutinous troops. His fighting qualities greatly impressed his superiors and the young man even considered accepting a captaincy of foot which the Duke of Ormonde, Lord Lieutenant of Ireland, urged Admiral Penn to allow him to bestow. At this point young Penn appeared to be a chip off the old block.

Just over a year later, Sept. 3, 1667, William Penn was arrested in violation of the "Quaker Act" (an act forbidding the sect to hold meetings) at a meeting of the Friends in Cork.

Admiral Penn's heir belonged to the despised sect of Quakers. What had happened?

Biographies of William Penn indicate that from childhood there had been a distinct religious side to his personality. Penn himself indicates that he had a "religious experience" in school at Chigwell. When the family lived in Ireland, a Quaker preacher, Thomas Loe, was invited, or allowed, to preach to the household. This was most probably in 1657 when young Penn was 13 years old. Penn recalled a great emotional impact, declaring that the admiral was "moved to tears" by Loe's preaching. Penn might have heard Loe again in Oxford in 1660 (Loe was in Oxford prison in 1661) but there is no proof of this.

We know that by 1661 the "young gentleman" would not conform to Anglican rites and was clearly ready to take the consequences for his beliefs. In France, Penn disarmed his opponent in a duel over a breach of decorum (he had not returned a hat salute) and refused to kill him, noting that such a dispute was not "worth the life of a man." Late in 1662 or in early 1663 Penn spent some months studying with the great French Protestant theologian Moïse Amyraut (1596–1664), a strong advocate of personal liberty as a fundamental attribute of true Christianity. In Ireland in 1667, while looking after his father's lands, and a year or so after his brief military experience, Penn sought out a Quaker tradeswoman, and through her learned that Thomas Loe, the Quaker preacher of his childhood, was in Cork. By September, Penn was a convinced Quaker—and in jail for it.

To have made that decision in 1667 cannot have been an easy choice. By then Quakers by the thousands filled the jails of Britain. The Quaker Act of 1662 was still in force— penalty for the third violation, transportation to the American or Caribbean colonies. In addition, the Cavalier Parliament (1661–67) had passed in 1661–65 the series of vicious and tyrannical laws against dissenters called collectively "the Clarendon Code." These measures, the Corporation Act, the Act of Uniformity, the Conventicle Act and the Five-Mile Act were totalitarian devices for the suppression of free thought and discussion of matters of religion. The Anglican majority was willing to stoop to barbaric persecutions to enforce conformity to their notions of "correct" forms of religious worship. In addition, England was then still full of old Roundhead soldiers and sympathizers who were especially numerous among the nonconformists, and the Stuart monarchy viewed all sorts of nonconformity with some degree of apprehension.

Nonetheless, the England that had produced Milton and Bunyan, as well as John Saltmarsh and George Fox, was one in which heady religious feeling and controversy were nearly ubiquitous. Young Penn, in spite of an impeccably upper-class background, could scarcely have avoided contact with the myriad theological upheavals about him. Somewhere in that upheaval the young man had found the raw materials of a religious fundamentalism to which he became so devoted that he was prepared to throw away the external emblems and habits of his class and education. Much later, he was prepared to launch a major colonization project organized on the basis of his beliefs. He had become a seeker, one of the "plain people." He refused to tip his hat (even to the King, according to one account), wore plain clothes, used the familiar "thee" and "thou" in conversation, laid aside his sword, and relied for his own protection upon whatever defenses a pacifist might find in 17th-century England (an act of bravado indeed in those days for a well known and wealthy man who traveled a lot).

Penn became both a follower and the friend of the singular George Fox, founder of the Society of Friends. Penn agreed to the proposition that God speaks to every man's inner conscience, that there was no need even for churches, not to mention prayer books, priests and the paraphernalia of organized religion. But more, the leveling religious doctrine had profound political content since it was an attack upon the strongest claims of intellectual authority of the time—Pope, priest, bishop, Scripture alike. As we saw earlier, the Leveler doctrine led straight to egalitarian democracy. The great American historian George Bancroft referred to the rise of the Quakers as "one of the memorable events in the history of man. It marks the moment when intellectual freedom was claimed unconditionally by the people as an inalienable birthright."

In an age when religious authority was not infrequently imposed upon the population by military violence, the creed of the Society of Friends was an outrage and a threat to the established church and state. The earliest Quakers included many wild-eyed ones among their number; for example, Thomas Venner, who in January, 1661, attempted with a band of fifty men to establish the monarchy of King Jesus in London (he was hanged for his trouble). But the creed of the

Quakers was unique for its gentleness and its peacefulness, and despite this they were ruthlessly persecuted by the established forces of bigotry. If the Quakers themselves seemed out of joint with their times, so did their new convert William Penn seem in odd company with the common farmers, laborers, tradesmen, the followers of George Fox. Penn himself seemed as much at home among them, at least so it would seem, as he was at home at the Stuart courts. He was evidently a natural democrat, at ease with all men, king, commoner or, as it later developed, American Indian. Penn continued to be loyal to the Stuarts, but after 1667 he was additionally a Quaker leader.

By December, 1668, Penn was, at age 24, in the Tower for attacking the extant notions of the Holy Trinity, original sin and salvation without atonement—all that in a single pamphlet. While imprisoned he wrote the first of two statements of belief under the title *No Cross, No Crown* (he later wrote another of the same title thought by some to be his finest theological writing). After that, succeeding years saw a veritable flood of pamphlets and tracts from his facile pen. His first period of long confinement in the Tower seemed to give Penn time for reflection and, as it did for so many before him, strengthened his convictions. King Charles sent no less a person than the Bishop of Worcester to entreat with him. Penn was reported to have informed that eminent divine that the Tower was the worst argument in the world.

In the roughly twelve years from his first imprisonment in the Tower until he applied for his grant of land (June 1, 1680), Penn's life was a full and rigorous one. Admiral Sir William Penn died in September, 1670. Although he had turned young William out and threatened to disinherit him for taking the Quaker faith, there was a reconciliation and a revival of mutual trust and respect between the two. Before he died, Admiral Penn wrote to Charles II and asked that the Stuart favor be continued to his heir. The Stuarts were true to their word and William Penn reciprocated to the very end of James II's inglorious reign. On his father's death, Penn succeeded to the name and estate. He was 26 years old and, by the standards of the time, a man of considerable means and responsibilities.

In addition to those responsibilities connected to his substantial landholdings in England and in Ireland, Penn soon married. He married twice in his lifetime. The destiny of Pennsylvania was bound up, until 1776, with the descendants of his second marriage. His first marriage, in April, 1672, was to Gulielma Springett, a Quaker, after a four-year courtship. This was clearly a happy marriage for him, in spite of the baleful consequences of infant mortality rates in those days. Of six children by that marriage, three (including twins) died in infancy, and Springett Penn, the eldest son and heir, a gifted and virtuous boy, died in 1695 aged 21. Only a girl, Letitia, and a son, William, survived into adulthood. Young William (Billy Penn, noted by Benjamin Franklin to have been a gentleman, even in his cups) was a throwback to the cavalier, and Penn left him out of Pennsylvania's affairs after the boy had a lively visit to the colony.

Penn was widowed early in 1694. In March, 1696, he married a second time at the age of 52. Seven children were born to this marriage, the last one when Penn was 64, and two of them did not survive. Penn thus buried six of his thirteen children.

It is difficult to believe that anyone could become hardened to such losses, even though they were not extraordinary for the times. The extent to which the presence of death in his life influenced his religious feelings we will never know. Certainly he was ever reminded by the most intimate knowledge of mortality that men's works needed solid foundations from the beginning, that the chance for revision was not to be counted a certainty. If Penn's own devotion to Quaker principles needed strengthening by any awareness of the mutability of this life, the long succession of dead children must have served as a steady reminder.

In the years between his religious conversion (1667) and the granting of his charter (1681), Penn devoted his efforts mainly to espousing and defending the Quaker cause. His means gave him the resources for such activity on a full-time basis; his fervor and eloquence made his services greatly in demand and, finally, his highly placed connections both in Parliament and at the Stuart court were great advantages to the sorely persecuted sect.

He made two evangelical missions, one to the Low Countries and the other to Germany. In both cases, he was seeking converts as well as serving as a liaison between Quaker meetings in England and in Europe. The first such preaching mission was in 1671. Very little is known of it except that Penn attempted to convert the unfrocked Jesuit, Jean de Labadie, and his followers, and that he did succeed in establishing at least one Quaker meeting (at Emden). The second mission to the Continent came in 1677 and was undertaken in company with George Fox. Again Penn concentrated upon the Low Countries and Germany. The fruits of this trip later were found in the immigration into Pennsylvania of many families of Dutch and German Friends and other Protestants. Some settled at Germantown, and from a Germantown meeting of Mennonites came the first known formal protest against Negro slavery in American history (1688).

In addition to his Continental missions, the years 1667–81 were filled with the affairs of the persecuted Friends in England. The persecution increased after 1678 with the wild accusations of Titus Oates against Catholics and their sympathizers. In those years the Quakers were automatically suspect because of their refusal to accept the Communion of the Anglican Church as prescribed under the Test Act (1673). Penn was himself doubly compromised as both a Quaker and a known friend of the Duke of York who, then, as later when he was King James II, openly professed the Roman faith. In those years Penn traveled the length and breadth of the Stuart court itself in his attempt to gain the release of George Fox, who was imprisoned shortly after Fox's return from America.

The Quakers did not compromise their principles and suffered the worst consequences. This was, of course, an early experience with a kind of trouble the Quakers have always faced when confronted with the loyalty demands of the modern state. In this regard Quaker history began when, after a long session with George Fox (who was then under arrest for preaching), Cromwell threw up his hands and exclaimed ". . . there is a people risen, and come up, that I cannot win either with gifts, honors, offices or places; but all other sects and people I can." In Restoration England the religious "line" had changed from the days of the Lord Protector, but the Quakers were still in opposition to totalitarian theological laws, and hence were under the shadow of official persecution. By 1680, with Charles in open conflict with his Parliament over the Act of Exclusion of 1679 (he dissolved Parliament over this attempt to keep his brother from the throne), there were all the familiar signs of a new political and religious upheaval in the air. The Quakers, being notorious nonconformists, mainly townspeople, tradesmen, yeomen and others associated with the rising Whig movement, were obvious targets for a new reign of terror. But by then a trans-Atlantic sanctuary appeared to be possible.

IV

The Quakers had had long contact—a great deal of it most unpleasant—with the rising new English colonies on the North American mainland. In fact, George Fox himself visited America in 1671–73, and was present in 1672 at the first meeting of the Baltimore Friends. But the Quakers generally had little hope for toleration in the existing colonies. Roger Williams, to be sure, protected the Quakers in Rhode Island, but he objected to their doctrine.

As for the other colonies, the future of the Friends was all too obvious. Among the New England bigots persecution was savage. When the first preaching Quakers, two women, landed in Boston in 1655, their books were burned; they were imprisoned, stripped naked and examined for signs of witchcraft. Quakers were commonly tied to carts' tails in Massachusetts, stripped to the waist and "whipped out" of the colony. In 1658, an act was passed in Boston against the "pernicious sect" which permitted the arrest without warrant of Quakers, and their being jailed without bail and banished from the colony on pain of death. Corded whips, starvation, holes in tongues, ears cut off, such constituted the Massachusetts treatment of Friends. In Boston, three, including one woman, were hanged for the crime of their religious convictions. At one point it took an order from Charles II to New England's government to get the Quakers out of the jails. Virginia officially persecuted Quakers. They were nearly driven out of Maryland; Penn interceded personally with Lord Baltimore on their behalf.

What was needed was a Quaker colony. The older colonies held no hope. In 1664, New Netherland had fallen to the English and had been given by Charles to his brother. The seacoast was mainly inhabited. But West New Jersey had earlier been occupied and William Penn had been instrumental in drawing up the initial laws governing that settlement. In 1677 some 230 colonists had gone there and their establishment was successful. The town of Burlington, planned and run on Quaker principles, thrived. Moreover, a Quaker leader, Josiah Coale, had corresponded with Fox about the possibility of settling the Susquehanna Valley.

By 1680 it was likely that Penn could press his advantages at court to get a grant of land for several reasons. First and foremost, the Stuarts had been active in the continuation of Cromwell's empire building and the Restoration colonization had been largely done through the establishment of proprietorships. The proprietaries established after 1660 had not been entirely successful, but there was no need for Penn to repeat the errors of others, and his family had long been able to count on royal patronage.

On June 1, 1680, Penn applied to King Charles for a grant of land. In just nine months, on March 4, 1681, the deed for Pennsylvania was signed. Penn was a well known Whig and warmly supported Algernon Sidney (who, convicted of treason by a kangaroo court, was beheaded in 1683) in his two bids for Parliament in 1679 after the fall of the Cavalier Parliament. Charles obviously could not have made Penn the grant as a public favor. But the Penns' great service to the Stuarts warranted such a thing and a way was found. The Stuarts owed debts to their thousands of supporters, which largely were never paid. James, the Duke of York, had indeed earlier paid some of his main debts with grants of land after the fall of New Netherland. The royal obligations were for loans, wages never paid, gifts promised and so forth. The Stuart debt to Admiral Sir William Penn was reckoned as "at least" £11,000 (some have placed it as high as £16,000). Beyond such information, the reasons why Charles and James did Penn this great favor are not known. This is tantamount, unfortunately, to not knowing at all why the grant was made. With the rising Tory and Anglican reaction in sight it has been suggested that the King simply wanted to save Penn's head. Considering the fate of Algernon Sidney, this hypothesis may not be too far-fetched. Penn himself thought that those around the King considered the Pennsylvania land grant a bargain: ". . . the government at home was glad to be rid of us at so cheap a rate as a little parchment to be practiced in a desert 3,000 miles off. . . ."

By July, 1681, the Concessions were signed by Penn which stated the ground rules for settling the new land. Penn's "Holy Experiment" had begun.

There was no doubt from the beginning that Penn intended to grant his people liberty and assure it to their descendants. He was now a great feudal proprietor, like Lord Berkeley and Baltimore and others before him. While he hoped for profit, his immediate object was to let his ideals find expression in a new land and government. In April, 1681, he had written to Friends in Ireland: "For the matters of liberty and privilege, I purpose that which is extraordinary, and to leave to myself and my successors no power of doing mischief, that the will

of one man may not hinder the good of an whole country."
In every major document relating to the colony's government
which Penn signed, he repeated that pledge.

Within two years, in his great Frame of Government and
Charter of Liberties, Penn had given the savage political world
of the 17th century the spectacle of representative government
with religious freedom. For Europe, Pennsylvania was a rude
awakening. For America the effects were equally profound.
Penn dealt honestly and compassionately with the Indians.
As Trevelyan noted succinctly, in the new colony ". . . was
founded the most strange settlement of all: Charles II's government, at the moment of the strongest Tory reaction in
England, permitted William Penn, the Quaker courtier and
organizer, to found Pennsylvania . . . as a refuge for persecuted Friends in the wilderness, where they practised the un-
wonted principles of just dealing with the redskins."

Penn made two great formal contributions to American
political tradition and practice. The first concerned Quaker
settlers in New Jersey. The West New Jersey Concessions and
Agreements, the charter under which that region was settled
by English, was drawn up by trustees of an estate who included Penn. It foreshadowed the great Frame of Government and Charter of Liberties of Pennsylvania. The West
New Jersey concessions included representative government;
freedom from arrest except under proper warrant and from
conviction save by "twelve men of the neighborhood"; no
detainment in prison for debt (debt to be worked out by the
debtor, the man not to "lie in prison") and, of course, complete religious freedom.

The second fundamental contribution made by Penn was
the body of laws he gave to his colony of Pennsylvania. Some
rules were established in 1681 for the first settlers under his
charter, and then in the spring of 1682 he completed and
signed the original versions of the Frame of Government and
the Charter of Liberties.* These two sets of laws established
the great tradition of American constitution making. On
March 4, 1681, King Charles signed the deed granting the
proprietary colony of Pennsylvania to William Penn. The

---

* The Frame of Government was revised in 1696 when, after a period as a
crown colony, the settlers attempted to force upon Governor Markham a
restoration of the liberties they had lost under crown rule. Then, in 1701,
during Penn's last visit to the colony, the Charter of Liberties was amended.
Basically the Charter was unchanged as regards the liberties originally granted.
Penn was party to all changes in the Charter. The extent to which the changes
were his own and those of his colonists cannot now be known. They were all
discussed and mutually agreed upon.

great and "Holy Experiment" in self-government and individual liberty was foreshadowed in April, 1681, when Penn wrote to those already established in his lands (mainly Swedes, Finns and Dutch): "You shall be governed by laws of your own making, and live a free, and if you will, a sober and industrious people. . . ." Penn held to this promise. In fact, compared to the condition of government in Penn's England, the Pennsylvania settlers found a democratic utopia beyond the Delaware.

To appreciate fully what Penn did for his colonists, and eventually for the new nation, it must be emphasized that the grant of land called "Pensilvania" was considered by Penn to be entirely his own. Only the surviving incumbrances of feudal landholding rights, or the power of the King, stood between him and the treatment of his fief as he saw fit. Penn's charter had never been submitted to Parliament and he considered that he might end it at his own pleasure if he so desired. His proprietary rights were held directly from King Charles with the remaining trappings of feudal landholding arrangements. The onerous and hated "quit rents" imposed by Penn upon Pennsylvania in his Concessions of 1681 were the proprietor's just and legal feudal dues as lord of the province. In addition to his own enterprises, the quit rents were to be a primary source of income to repay him (in perpetuity) for his investment. As in England, the titles of smallholders were not entirely clear.

This was reasonable enough in the 17th century. Quit rents were an outcome of centuries of feudal development and allowed the purchaser of land to be "quit and free," for a single annual cash payment, of such feudal services as "boon" and "week" work. In keeping with feudal usage, Penn himself owed fealty to the King and had to pay quit rents of his own. They were nominal:

> . . . William Penn, his heires and assignes fore ever to bee holden to Us, Our heires and Successors, Kings of England, as of Our Castle of Windsor in Our County of Berks . . . by fealty only for all Services . . . Yielding and paying therefore to Us, Our heires and Successors, Two Beaver Skins, to bee delivered at Our said Castle of Windsor on the First Day of January in every Year. . . ."

Charles also reserved 20 percent of the gold and silver for himself, should any be found.

The rents Penn imposed were not high—about one shilling

per 100 acres. But as lord of Pennsylvania, his *seigneurie*, the rents were his right. That the American colonists didn't pay them carefully and dealt abruptly with the whole feudal apparatus after 1776—the quit rents, entails, primogeniture and the rest—is eloquent evidence of what ordinary people thought of the last remains of feudalism, however generously imposed.

Nor were the quit rents all. A further hangover from the Middle Ages is found in the Concessions of 1681—a system of quality control in the markets. "There shall be no buying and selling, be it with an Indian, or one another, of any goods to be exported, but what shall be performed in public market . . . where they shall pass the public stamp or mark." While it is true that the Quakers were traditionally in favor of morality in business dealings, this requirement was a hangover from the Middle Ages when markets were subject to such controls. The business community of the late 17th century doubtless had little enthusiasm for such "government interference."

Yet in spite of his arbitrary powers, Penn made good his promise. The people were given a remarkable (if imperfect) government, and made their own laws. They had privileges and liberties Englishmen did not have in England. Penn must certainly be ranked as history's most enlightened feudal lord.

Even in 1681 Penn made provisions for unfree men to become free: he granted land which indentured servants might take over after their term of service had been worked off. He foresaw that the society of freemen must be enlarged from below if it would prosper, doubtless a result of his experience with the Quakers, who were largely men of the humbler classes.

Almost a year after the Concessions, in April and May of 1682, in the Charter of Liberties and in the Frame of Government of Pennsylvania, a more complete set of laws together with a statement of Penn's philosophy of government were signed. The province was to be governed by a Governor, a Council and a General Assembly. Penn's democracy worked downward (among its chief defects were the difficulty of amendment and the lack of provision for initiative). The Governor and Council were to prepare laws to submit to the General Assembly, which had the right to approve or reject them. The General Assembly, composed of all freemen at first, and thereafter of their representatives, was to choose the Council members.

Of the seventy-two-member Provincial Council, the proprietary (in the person of the Governor) was to have a triple vote—three against seventy-two votes—otherwise Penn was satisfied to allow his egalitarian democracy to work. Tenure of office in the original Council was staggered, with members rotating off. Once the Council was established, one-third would be elected each year. Experience would remain among the incumbent members. Once off, a councilman was ineligible to serve in the following year ". . . so all may be fitted for the Government and have Experience of the Care and burthen of it." The Assembly had the power of impeachment but, like Parliament, could itself be dismissed by the Governor and Council.

The original laws of Pennsylvania contained some remarkable provisions for those, or any, times. The economic provisions were in accord with King Charles' general policies of attempting to encourage trade and the arts. The Governor and Council were charged to provide schools and to "Reward the Authors of usefull Science and, Laudable Inventions." In actual practice, all schools were run either by the churches or by private individuals. Trades were seen as a method of forestalling sloth and crime. All children of 12 were to be taught a trade or skill ". . . to the end none may be idle, but the poor may work to live and the rich, if they become poor, may not want." Taxes could be raised only by due legal processes. In the Concessions provision was made, along with the well known schemes to lay out the city and to entice whole families and their servants (extra grants of land were made to encourage the wealthy to bring their servants), to have one acre of every five not cleared but left uncut to preserve oak and mulberries for ships and silk.

With an eye to the notorious penal abuses in England, Pennsylvania's laws and prisons were laudably liberal. There were to be no Fleets, Newgates or Towers. All prisons were to be workhouses. And all prisons were to be free to the inmates. There were only two capital offenses, treason and murder (compared to scores in England—more than 200 as late as the 18th century). Except for those two offenses, all prisoners were bailable. Courts were to be open, justice ". . . neither sold, denied or delayed." Juries were to consist of twelve peers, and in case of a capital offense there was to be both a grand jury of twelve to make the indictment and a different jury of twelve to try the case. The state would not confiscate property. For capital offenders one-third of the estate went to *next of kin of the victim* and two-thirds to next of kin of the criminal.

It was to be a religious society, no doubt of that. Sunday ". . . according to the good example of the primitive Christians . . ." was to be set aside and no common daily labor performed. There was to be religious liberty for all. Roger Williams had provided a refuge for English dissenters from Puritanism and Lord Baltimore's fief had provided toleration for a time. But in Penn's Charter the breakthrough to religious freedom for Christians was intended to be complete and unequivocal (as in Rhode Island, religious liberties were not always recognized in practice). He *invited* settlers of all Christian sects: Article XXXV of the Charter of Liberties, laws agreed to in England by Penn and certain of his settlers, set a tremendous mark in an age of nearly universal religious totalitarianism.

> That all persons living in this province, who confess and acknowledge the one Almighty and eternal God, to be the Creator, Upholder and Ruler of the world; and that hold themselves obliged in conscience to live peaceably and justly in civil society, shall in no ways, be molested or prejudiced, for their religious persuasion, or practice, in matters of faith and worship, nor shall they be compelled at any time, to frequent or maintain any religious worship, place or ministry whatever.

These laws were written by an Englishman, ascribed to by Englishmen, at a time when the English King was ruling without Parliament, when England was still trembling from the terrors of the Popish Plot, when religious persecution was raging, the prisons filled and when, in the fight between the Tories and the Whigs, religious nonconformism was again to be linked by association with treason. On the Continent, Protestants were soon to be harried again when Louis XIV revoked the Edict of Nantes in 1685. It was not a time in England, or in Europe, of toleration in religious matters or of liberalism in politics. Yet in this storm of the products of the totalitarian mind Penn wrote his great liberal constitution. As we have seen, it would have been possible in England to believe these things by 1681—if one had a very great power to be eclectic and knew just what one wanted to believe. It would be difficult to find a more striking example of the power of idealism to choose its own and to be untouched by the rest of the world around it. In Penn's Frame of Government his serene vision was made explicit. The origin of government was seen to be divine with two main functions:

> . . . first, to terrify evil doers; secondly, to cherish those who do well; which gives government a life beyond corruption, and makes it as durable in the world, as good men shall be. So that government seems to me a part of religion itself, a thing sacred in its institution and end. For, if it does not directly remove the cause, it crushes the effects of evil, and is as such . . . an emanation of the same Divine Power, that is both author and object of pure religion . . . I know what is said by the several admirers of *monarchy, aristocracy* and *democracy,* which are the rule of one, a few, and many, and are the three common ideas of government, when men discourse on the subject. But I chuse to solve the controversy with this small distinction, and it belongs to all three: *Any government is free to the people under it . . . where the laws rule, and the people are a party to those laws,* and more than this is tyranny, oligarchy, or confusion. . . . Governments, like clocks, go from the motion men give them; and as governments are made and moved by men, so by them they are ruined too. Wherefore governments rather depend upon men, than men upon governments. Let men be good, and the government cannot be bad; if it be ill, they will cure it. But if men be bad, let the government be never so good, they will endeavor to warp and spoil it to their turn. . . . we have . . . to the best of our skill, contrived and composed the *frame* and *laws* of this government, to the great end of all government,: *To support power in reverence with the people, and to secure the people from the abuse of power;* that they may be free by their just obedience, and the magistrates honourable, for their just administration; for liberty without obedience is confusion, and obedience without liberty is slavery. . . .

In spite of such philosophical predecessors as Penn had, such a document written in the year 1682 was an astonishing performance—especially for a feudal lord. The spirit of it permeated American political tradition. Channing, the historian, studying the various manuscript drafts of Penn's Frame, ruled that it was entirely Penn's own doing. He could find no support for the theory that other minds (John Locke and Sir William Petty have been candidates for the honor) were involved. Channing's examination of the Frame ". . . failed to reveal any steps of progress in the formulation of that remarkable document: nor did it give any reason for supposing that Penn received any important suggestions from outside sources."

Penn early saw the prospects of union in the North American colonies, and in 1697 was author of the first known Plan of Union. It was also a scheme for representative government. The colonies were to send picked representatives at least once every two years ". . . to debate and resolve of such measures as are most advisable for their better understanding and the public tranquility and safety." The presiding officer was to be a commissioner of the Crown. This deliberating body was to be a "congress" and was to devote itself to intracolonial affairs. In time of war the commissioner was the commander of the colonial forces.

Carlyle, in a famous essay, once noted that "the Time" often cried out for the appearance of a "Great Man," but ". . . the Time, calling its loudest, had to go down to confusion and wreck because . . . the Great Man . . . would not come when called." In Penn's case we have the opposite. No one seemed in 1681 to be calling for a colonizer who was also a great democratic lawgiver. Indeed, the wonder is that he appeared at all. Colonization and economic innovations one might expect in the later years of Charles II's reign. These were certainly "in the air" in the times. But a *political* vision like Penn's was an unlooked-for piece of good fortune. Or so it would seem. In Penn's life one finds some explanation of this, of the unique forces which, in combination with his historical environment, made Penn's great contribution to America possible. He was a singular individual in almost every respect.

After years of indifferent success in their colonization schemes, the Stuarts had granted a charter which would not only soon attract thousands from Britain and Europe, but would absorb settlers from other colonies as well. Virginia and New York during the late 1680's were losing young men of military age to Pennsylvania; army garrisons were threatened by desertions to the Quaker settlements, and Maryland's border had to be patrolled to intercept deserters from the British fleet. Moreover, Pennsylvania attracted men of wealth as well as those of poverty. Her institutions were free, her land rich and the new colony was soon a success in the New World.

Pennsylvania's freedom reflected the great liberal mind of her proprietor. Penn represented the best of the 17th century. It was, to be sure, the century of the Stuarts, the Puritans, the Popish Plot, of witch hunts, massacres, Judge Jeffreys, judicial murders, of political executions and all the horrors of a dark age. But it was also the age of Coke and Selden; of

Eliot, Pym and Hampden; of Locke, Mandeville and Petty; of Bunyan and Milton. In law, government, philosophy and letters the Age of Enlightenment was beginning to stir even in the darkness of religious and political totalitarianism. As we noted earlier, the founding of the Royal Society in 1660 witnessed the rise of science. Penn was elected a member in 1682 just before his departure for America.

Penn and his colony were the vanguard of a new age. By 1689, an act of religious toleration was passed by Parliament, and that Parliament's power in the British constitution was forever established in 1688 when William and Mary came over from Holland. William Penn, born in 1644, who was imprisoned for his religious beliefs, who once saw a woman burned alive for hers, lived into the age of Swift and Pope. The times were violent, but fast-changing. Penn had greatly contributed to the change. The Cavalier Quaker, a man of his times, grasped an opportunity. The "times" favored his effort. The growing commercial progress of England, the rising spirit of independence among England's common people, the triumph of British naval and mercantile sea power, the growth of a new American empire, all these were in his favor. But that was not all. Others failed to build great colonies in the same time and circumstances. Penn's colony succeeded primarily because of its institutions, and those reflected the intellectual man, the interior world of William Penn, not the models in the world around him.

V

Such a story ought to have a glorious ending. Unfortunately, history is not always so accommodating. Penn's tumultuous career contained several disastrous episodes after the successful establishment of his colony in America. First let us consider the colony itself.

Penn's lands contained about a thousand white inhabitants when he received the charter from Charles II. The people there were mostly Swedes and Dutch, with a sprinkling of English, Finns, Germans, Welsh and others. Penn gave them full rights as citizens in the new colony. The boundary with Maryland was an almost immediate source of contention between Penn and Lord Baltimore. This was due largely to initial ignorance in England about the true survey lines (originally Penn was to have from 40 degrees latitude north, which would have excluded much of the present site of Philadelphia). Penn met in America with Lord Baltimore in an attempt to settle favorably, but the dispute was finally thrown back into litigation in Britain, a slow and costly process. For years the boundary dispute dragged on and, at one period, Maryland actually armed a fort in Pennsylvania to protect its own borders.

Penn was in his colony twice, first from October, 1682, until October, 1684. His second visit was from December, 1699, until November, 1701. There is no doubt that he was completely taken with his colony. He had provided for it well. His city was laid out in squares and with spacious dimensions, possibly as a reaction to his having witnessed plague and fire sweep London, alerting him to the ill effects of urban congestion. Probably in December, 1682, his famous treaty with the Indians was negotiated (Penn, a considerable linguist, prided himself with having learned their language, which he thought to be similar to Hebrew). The treaty was not broken during Penn's lifetime and, when it finally was, it was not broken first by the Indians.

The site of Philadelphia contained perhaps ten buildings when Penn arrived. Land sales went well and, in the first three years, fifty ships brought in settlers under the terms of the Concessions of 1681. About two-thirds of the settlers up to 1700 were English, and another 20 percent Welsh and Irish. There was also immigration from the Low Countries and Germany. Partly this was the fruit of Penn's missionary work for the Quakers, and partly the result of the Revocation of the Edict of Nantes in 1685.

During his first trip Penn built his estate, Pennsbury, to which he was devoted. He went back to England in the fall of 1684 to defend his boundaries against Lord Baltimore and did not return for fifteen years. On his second visit in 1699–1701 he revised the Frame according to the wishes of his colonists. On this trip he was accompanied by his second wife, Hannah Callowhill Penn, and several of his children, of whom one, John, "the American," was born during that trip. It was on this visit that Penn drew up a proposal for union of the North American colonies. By 1699 Philadelphia had 5,000 citizens and was second only to Boston in the New World. The colony thrived on exports of grains and fruits, timber, hides, etc. Penn went back to England again in 1701 to fight to keep his charter; a new war with France was brewing, and there was agitation to turn Pennsylvania into a Crown colony. Penn never saw his colony again.

Penn loved his colony, would have liked to live there himself and urged his family to do so. But Pennsylvania made him a poor man. His own estimate of his loss in the venture was £30,000. His Irish estates were seized by the Crown when Penn was an outlaw, and at the time his health failed he was negotiating with Queen Anne's government to sell his proprietary grant back to the Crown, since the settlers would not pay their quit rents and Penn's debts were mounting. He tried to borrow £10,000 from settlers in Philadelphia (interest free) and was refused.

Moreover, he was systematically swindled over the years by his steward, a man named Ford, to whom he was in danger of losing all his property in America. When Ford's widow sued Penn in chancery, and won the case, Penn could not pay and went to debtor's prison, in 1708. A settlement was finally made with a payment of £7,600 to the Ford family. The sum was raised by the Friends against a new mortgage upon Penn's American estate.

When Penn died on July 30, 1718, he was not penniless, although he came close enough. His heirs, Tories in 1776, were awarded £500,000 by the Crown for their loss after the American Revolution, though the Penn properties taken by the Americans were valued at about £1,000,000, an enormous sum in those days.

The long-run effects of Penn's life have been profound—beyond measure perhaps—and, one hopes, may yet have their greatest days ahead. Penn was an advocate of justice, law and individual liberty. The world as yet has no surfeit of these. Penn's achievements all represent decisions made in his life on the basis of his "abstract" beliefs, uncompromised by advantages or convenience. For some modern Americans it is useful to note that in no case did Penn make his great decisions on the basis of "practical" or "common sense" or "expedient" considerations. A famous court case illustrates the point.

In August, 1670, Penn was arrested for causing a riot, as he was preaching in the street in London outside the Friends meetinghouse, the doors having been barred by soldiers. The trial, called "Bushell's Case" after one of the jurors, began in September. Penn urged the jury not to have their verdict dictated by the bench. He argued heatedly and persuasively from the prisoner's box, challenging the court on every point; and then, locked in the bale dock at the back of the courtroom, he shouted out his defense to the jury. Penn having reminded them of their rights as Englishmen, they were convinced and would not bring in a verdict satisfactory to the bench even after being locked up for two nights. When the verdict of "Not guilty" was finally brought in, the jurors were placed in Newgate Prison and fined. Four of the "phenatique jurymen" refused to pay, appealed their case eventually and won it in Common Pleas under Chief Justice Vaughan's ruling that no jury could be punished for its verdict. "It is absurd, a jury should be fined by the judge for going against their evidence. . . ." Penn's father paid his fine to get him out of Newgate. The principle of a free jury remains to this day.

Penn's beliefs were not easy to hold. He suffered a great deal for them. Not only did Pennsylvania, his "Holy Experiment," ruin him financially, but he was jailed at least four times for his religious beliefs, and his loyalty to his sovereigns caused him to be outlawed. Penn's criminal record is a useful reminder of the reality which lies behind the words in history. The phrase "suffered for his religious beliefs" is not just a way to "pad" books. In 17th-century England it meant filthy prisons, public humiliation and exorbitant fines and bails, threats of a life in prison and worse.

In September, 1667, Penn was jailed in Cork, Ireland, under the Conventicle Act. In December, 1668, he was arrested (age 24) and placed in the Tower of London for publishing a religious pamphlet, "The Sandy Foundation Shaken," without license from the Bishop of London (under the same law which earlier had induced Milton to write *Areopagitica*). Penn lay in the Tower under threat of life imprisonment until the following spring. In August, 1670, he was again arrested under the Conventicle Act and from this arrest came the ruling against punishment of juries for their verdicts. In February, 1671, Penn was in Newgate Prison for preaching in London. Just before leaving for America in 1682 he was again threatened with arrest for the same offense.

In addition to these problems involving his beliefs, William Penn, friend of the Stuarts, was sought under a warrant of "suspicion of High Treason" in 1689 which was issued by William and Mary. He was not apprehended, but as a fugitive from the King's justice, he now lost the income from his Irish lands, estimated at as high as £12,000 or £13,000, and was reduced to poverty. In July, 1690, he was arrested on a similar charge and placed in the Tower. In February, 1691, another warrant for treason was out for Penn, and he "disappeared" for three years (a perjuring informer was involved in this case, and Penn wisely did not risk arrest). He was finally pardoned in December, 1693.

Broken by his expenses and lack of financial return from his colony, and swindled by his own employees, Penn went to debtors prison for some months beginning in January, 1708. He thus shared to the full the experience of his co-religionists *and* the political losers of the era. He was no stranger to prisons.

Some have argued that Penn's important achievements as statesman and lawgiver ought rightly to be separated from his career as a Quaker leader. This is difficult to understand. It is true that Penn was a shrewd and sophisticated politician and courtier, and a man of action in a debauched age. But his use of these facets of his personality were surely the means, the ends being consistently, so far as we know, peace, justice, mercy, toleration and the rule of law. Penn, heir to a fortune and friend of the Stuarts, used his personal wealth, his estates and his influence to organize his great experiment in Pennsylvania. The profit motive was there to be sure, but the organization of that particular profit-making venture could have been much different than it was, and that is the only important point. Penn's legacy to Americans was the work of a statesman and politician all right, but it was also the work of a tolerant and democratic pacifist.

Those who argue that Penn's career as statesman and lawgiver are best understood in isolation from his career as an early leader of the Quakers are presuming that in Penn's own mind the two were separate. That was clearly not the case. In the turbulent 17th century whose statesmen were Straffords, Lauds, Cromwells and Clarendons, totalitarian doctrines and actions ruled. The democratic peace-loving beliefs and policies of Penn obviously grew out of his own extraordinary motives and choices among the infinity of alternatives open to him. As Trevelyan noted, in 1689 when the British first tried religious toleration as national policy, they were experimenting on new and novel ground. By that time Penn had already occupied the greater part of his life in pursuit of that end. His was an idealism which had been acquired by choice, not inherited.

The Penn family's loyalties to the Stuarts proved their fortune, but almost cost William Penn his own fortune if not indeed his life. Charles II's reign closed ingloriously with a battle between the Crown and Parliament over religion and the line of succession. Charles, cavalier to the end, after medical science failed to save him (". . . they opportunely blooded and cupped him, and plied his head with red-hot frying pans"), apologized for lingering so long, and finally expired in the arms of Rome on Feb. 5, 1685. Charles having no legitimate son, the succession went to his brother James, the Duke of York.

Penn's close association with James II was much to his advantage until the King fled in 1688. If Penn was indeed a close adviser, it could only be said that even the best advice could not save James from his ill-fated course. Penn went on a personal mission for the King to Holland in a vain attempt to gain the approval of William and Mary for James' policies of religious toleration. James' efforts to free his Catholic co-religionists from persecution in England were supported by Penn, it is suggested, because the Quakers, also a proscribed sect, gained from any move toward religious toleration. Through James, Penn got George Fox once more out of prison, and saved at least one Friend from the gallows. Penn is supposed by some to have influenced James to grant the indulgences which released thousands of dissenters from prison.

Penn stuck with the Stuarts to the end, was accused of being secretly a Jesuit and, in 1688, when William and Mary came to England, he was high on the list of Stuart favorites destined to suffer.

By 1693, when three members of the peerage, Lords Rochester, Ranelagh, and Sidney procured Penn's pardon from King William, Pennsylvania had been temporarily taken over by the Crown. Penn got his charter back only on the promise that his colony would contribute to King William's war with the French. The colony continued for years to cause Penn great difficulties and there seems little doubt that he would have sold it to Queen Anne's government if his health and mental powers had not failed him. Penn's widow was a good manager of the colony but his sons by that marriage, John and George, were thoroughly disliked in the colony. When the end came for the proprietary government in 1776, Penn's grandson Richard was Governor under the revision of the government which had been negotiated and signed by Penn.

VI

Penn's contribution to American development was one of many achievements in his long, complicated and eventful career. His affairs were vast for a man of any age. He was involved in his country's life at all levels, from the royal entourage to the lowest levels of governmental proceedings, the magistrates' courts where he and his co-religionists were hailed for their nonconformism. As a loyal supporter of the Stuarts he lived through the political upheavals of his time. As a pioneer practitioner of the Quaker faith his affairs were inextricably entangled in the great and bloody religious revolution which gripped England from the Act of Supremacy to the Toleration Act. As an absentee landlord he participated in the economic subjugation of Ireland by the English. As Proprietor of Pennsylvania he was a great figure in the extension of the British Empire which had consciously been started by Cromwell.

Penn was thus a complex and forceful representative of a revolutionary age. Yet his greatest achievement, the founding of Pennsylvania, displayed a kind of ultimate simplicity in Penn's character. Perhaps as a counterpart to his ineptness in business affairs, he was naive to the point of childishness in his straightforward belief in man's goodness, and in his abilities to know and understand the good, the true and beautiful. Penn's "Holy Experiment" was a portent of the *ideal* in America's future tradition—men of all classes, races and religions striving to live in harmony, governed by laws of their own making, with equality for all before the bar of justice.

Penn the man of action was also a man of peace. Following his ideals undid him in his own time, but they created a great force for the future. There is no paradox here. A cynical age might view Penn and his "peaceable people" with a smile, yet in affairs of war, we have the examples of Washington and the American cause at Valley Forge and of Churchill in the summer of 1940 to teach us that simple faith can achieve great things. Such was true in the case of Penn. In American liberty and freedom Penn lives on. Some historians, for example, S. E. Morison and H. S. Commager, consider that the ability of the United States to resist the totalitarianisms of a modern dark age is due more to Penn's resistance to an earlier totalitarianism than to the efforts of any other man. The experience of individual liberty has been nearly universal with our people and human freedom is a cherished ideal among Americans. Imperfectly realized, unequally distributed, liberty is still "natural" to Americans and autocracy is still "foreign." It is a great legacy.

Part, a large part, of American economic prowess as it later developed, came from the assumption of the legitimacy of complete freedom in economic as well as political life. Since the rights of the state already existed, there was, as the country developed, a difficult, fruitful and continuous conflict between government and the individual in economic life; a conflict which has never been perfectly resolved, either in legislation or in the minds of Americans. The conflict itself, an apparently endless dialogue, came to be part of our legacy of economic and political freedom.

CHAPTER 3

Brigham Young and the Great Basin Kingdom

> Before the troops reach here, this city will be in ashes, every tree and shrub will be cut to the ground, and every blade of grass that will burn shall be burned. Our wives and children will go into the canyons and take shelter in the mountains . . . as God lives, we will hunt you by night and day till our army or yours is wasted away. No mob, armed or otherwise, can live in the homes we have built in these mountains.
>
> Brigham Young, Salt Lake City, 1858

In July of 1857 an expeditionary force of the United States Army left Fort Leavenworth, Kansas, on a long march across the plains and mountains. The total force (counting the supporting personnel) numbered about 5,000. Their destination was Salt Lake City, in Utah Territory. Their objective? That is not easy to determine now. The minimum they proposed to do was to install Alfred Cumming to replace Brigham Young, the territory's first Governor. The troops were to be stationed in Utah indefinitely to enforce the laws of the United States which, President Buchanan charged, were not receiving due respect under the aegis of Governor Young.

The Utah War, or "Contractors War" (so named because, it was said, the army suppliers were the ones who chiefly understood what the war was all about), is not one of the more illustrious pages in American history. In fact, textbook writers usually give it short shrift. As it turned out, the Mormons did not burn their city, and the United States Army did not occupy it. The new Governor was properly installed and some $15,000,000 was expended. The Contractors War is not an important part of our military history. Few men died in that conflict and no new heroes were added to the American military pantheon. The commander, Albert Sidney Johnston, U. S. A., was spared for bloodier work, later, when it was C. S. A.

There is something significant about the Utah War though: it was the last act of a bloody and murky sequence of events in our history; it was the last time that force and violence, without the sanction of court procedure, were used to attempt to suppress the Church of Jesus Christ of Latter-day Saints—the Mormons. By 1857 the Mormons had clearly won their piece of American real estate, and had clear title to their place in America's present and in its future. Their role in the last great American continental expansion, from the Missouri to the Pacific in 1846–48, constituted an act of human sacrifice and achievement of such magnitude that the colonization of the Great Basin remains one of the chief glories of American pioneering history. Like them or not, by 1857 the Mormons had a claim on the United States which could not be repudiated. The Mormon leader, Brigham Young, had proved to be a very great American leader indeed—however esoteric. The "peculiar" Mormon customs and their even stranger theology might be changed to harmonize with the national laws, but the Mormons were not to be, as Governor Lillburn Boggs of Missouri had hoped in 1838, exterminated. Their destiny was not to be traced on the Mississippi, but in the mountains of Zion, in the Far West, beyond the Rockies on the last American frontier.

I

The American frontier has long cast a spell over our historians. Frederick Jackson Turner considered the frontier to have been both a "safety valve" for the discontented of the earlier settlements, and a kind of forge which burned out foreign matter, leaving a refined and unique American character. The frontier was even more than that for Americans. It was a great emptiness to be filled, giving scope for originality in men and institutions—the Mormons were one group of many such "new" American phenomena of the frontier. Their history followed the frontier from the 1820's onward. The frontier was also a vast field of investment—first investment in land for speculation, then investment in domestic and agricultural arts, and later in the exploitation and development of mineral and other natural resources. The application of prevailing techniques to the settlement and development of the new land produced social variations according to the character of the human "inputs" and the character of the land and its products. Human institutions were part of the "technique" and the frontier required new forms of institutions as it moved across the land. The social systems and values which sufficed to settle the Western parts of the original colonies underwent change in the pioneer experiences of the prairies, more change in the deserts and mountains of the West and on the Pacific Coast. In the end, the America of the West differed markedly, as it still does, from the original domiciles of American institutions on the Atlantic seaboard.

The early history of the Mormons, and hence the life of Brigham Young, was in large part determined by the character of the moving frontier. First the Mormons shared the experience of the great movement of people into the fertile lowlands extending to and bordering upon the Mississippi and the lower portions of its main northern tributaries. The Mormons were swept along with the tide (driven along with it) of Americans moving from New England into the Middle States, through Ohio and Indiana into Missouri, Illinois and eastern Iowa. In this wave of migration and settlement which lasted until 1846, the Mormon religion was born and grew to both economic and political power. That power ended in tragedy, with the assassination of the Mormon Prophet and leader, Joseph Smith, Jr., in Carthage, Illinois, in 1844.

In 1846 the last major acquisition of American land was under way. Again the Mormons were among the migrants. Persecuted and reviled, their great trek across the plains and mountains to the Salt Lake valley in 1846–47 was an epochal achievement of American frontier history. It was one Mormon contribution which even their mortal enemies did not belittle. At that juncture in history the Mormons ceased playing a minor role in the frontier movement and, in the settlement of the Great Basin under Brigham Young, they became the cutting edge of American civilization. The frontier was no longer one of deciduous forests and oceans of prairie grass. Between the Rockies and the Sierra, the frontier was stark desert set among towering mountains. Annual rainfall in Illinois had been 34 to 43 inches; in the Salt Lake valley it was 5 to 15 inches. The elevation in Illinois had been about 600 feet above sea level; at the edge of the Great Salt Lake it was some 4,300 feet, rising to the base of the Wasatch Mountains which range from 9,000 to 12,000 feet. Pioneering now required a very special kind of organization and planning, the kind, as it turned out, supplied by Brigham Young's Mormons.

Until the decade following the Civil War, Brigham Young's America continued to be deeply influenced by the great westward movement. It was a world of land and people when settlement and farming were of primary concern, and industry was of secondary importance for most of the people. Americans were preoccupied with the physical possession of their continent. All else in our economic development seemed to be constrained until the physical possession of the land was completed. It was an enormous task. How enormous it was, and how slow the development of industry in ante-bellum America was, may be illustrated by a few economic statistics.

After the second war with England ended with the Treaty of Ghent (December, 1814) the United States was free to exploit her interior, the old Northwest and the southern lands up to the Mississippi. There was also the area acquired by the Louisiana Purchase of 1803 and the Spanish treaties of 1819. In 1790 the territory of the United States totaled 888,811 square miles. The Louisiana and Spanish territories added another 827,192 square miles. By 1820 a population of 9,638,000 souls faced the enormous territory of more than 1,788,000 square miles of land to develop—five and a half people (the number is now more than fifty) per square mile.

Until the Mexican War (1846) this was the main theater of American expansion. The fertile plains could hold millions, and millions came. Ohio, with 581,000 in 1820, had 1,519,000 twenty years later. The westward tide continued. Illinois, with 55,000 in 1820, had 476,000 in 1840, and 851,000 ten years later. The East North Central states grew from 792,000 in 1820 to 4,523,000 by 1850. At that date those states (Ohio, Indiana, Illinois, Michigan and Wisconsin) had surpassed New England and had almost overtaken the old Southern tidewater states. There had been growth of almost equal power in the East South Central states and out of this parallel growth, of course, came the great political contests of the era over slavery which rent the territories with bitter political conflict and guerilla warfare right up to 1860.

The Midwestern frontier had drawn its population in waves of settlement. Certain uniformities in these waves are of interest to us. An extensive expansion movement which started just after the Treaty of Ghent ended in a general economic crisis in 1819. After a period of relative quiescence, a new expansion began in the 1830's. In both cases the nation's infant financial system had been deeply involved in land speculation, and banks multiplied as land sales boomed and prices rose. Then, as depression followed the financial crisis, retrenchment everywhere included a sharp reduction in the number of banks. Thus from 1830 to 1836 public land sales rose from 1.9 million acres to 20.1 million acres; wholesale prices rose from 91 (1910–14 = 100) to 114 and the number of state-chartered banks from 330 to 713.

In the panic of 1837 land sales slumped, down to 5.6 million acres in 1837 and to only 1.2 million in 1842, the trough of the depression. The number of banks also was reduced by the early 1840's (692 in 1842), and prices, on the 1910–14 base, had fallen to 82. This episode, linked with Jackson's veto of the charter of the Second Bank of the United States and the issuance in 1836 of the Specie Circular (all public land sales were to be made on a metallic-money basis), provided a backdrop of financial upheaval to the process of occupying and settling the frontier. The "wildcat" banks engaged heavily in land speculation, and a constraint upon them was a constraint upon land speculation. Once the land boom had ceased, the more unstable banks failed. With the bank failures came the inevitable bankruptcies and foreclosures.

The "new land" bubble was momentarily pricked. Consider a specific case: Among the casualties of the 1837 crisis had been the Kirtland (Ohio) Safety Society Anti-Banking Co. It was called an "anti" bank because the state refused to give it a license to do banking business, which it had done anyway. Its banking business was, typically, a considerable operation in real estate "development." The anti-bank's president was Sidney Rigdon; its cashier, the Mormon Prophet, Joseph Smith, Jr. Smith and Rigdon decamped for the West (in this case, Missouri) shortly after their bank failed to meet its obligations. The Prophet's people followed later. There was nothing unique in their action, however dramatic the circumstances. The great depression which spread across America after the 1837 crisis lasted long into the 1840's and dislodged thousands who would be willing to strike out again for new lands if the opportunity came.

Unstable or not, the Midwestern frontier had been one of momentous achievement for Americans. There had been roads built, and canals, with the Erie, completed in 1825, linking the Great Lakes with the Hudson. By 1846 there were nearly 5,000 miles of completed railway lines in the Eastern and Southern parts of the country linking together the river systems. It had been an age of expansion of the cotton economy to match (and more than match) the expansion of textile-producing capacity in Britain and in New England. Corn and wheat were being grown for export too, and the new lands of the Midwest promised a great abundance in the future.

There had not been an equally impressive growth of American industry; by 1850 it was still "infant" indeed. Only textile manufacturing in New England had achieved anything like impressive proportions. Even so, we were still a major textile importer; we were still importing most of our railway iron, and English engines too. Our imports from Europe still showed an overwhelming proportion of finished manufactured goods, both for consumer and for industrial uses. What kind of industry the nation of 1845 might have developed is one of the tantalizing if's of history. Adam Smith's dictum that the division of labor is limited by the extent of the market refers to technology and productivity, not necessarily to geography.

Intensive American industrialization doubtless could have been achieved with the national domain of 1845. The population was growing at a rate in excess of 3 percent per annum compound, doubling every twenty years or so. The land was filling up rapidly enough to supply labor and to see a market developed if investment turned to productivity-raising industrial pursuits. But it was not to be—yet. There was to be more frontier. Texas was annexed in 1845; war was declared upon Mexico in 1846, and a settlement was reached with Britain over Oregon in 1846. As a result, by 1848 an additional 1,204,741 square miles of territory were added to the United States: the Western and Southwestern plains, the mountains, the Pacific Coast.

The rush of emigration began again. The entire West was the new target for settlers, miners, speculators, tradesmen and professional men, making the trip either by wagon overland or by ship around the Horn. This great new Western frontier was the mother of legends: the Oregon Trail, the Donner party, the Mormon trek, the California emigration and the rest. By 1850 the area of the present Mountain and Pacific states had 179,000 people; ten years later it contained 618,000. From 1850 to 1860 another 2,500,000 settlers came to the East North Central states, and the Northern Plains states (Minnesota, the Dakotas, Iowa, Missouri, Nebraska and Kansas) increased in population by a million and a half.

This new land, added to the old, completed the great storehouse of nature's abundance which awaited the wand of industrialization to transform the nation. Industrialization came to the West, however, when it came on a giant scale elsewhere in the United States, a decade after the Civil War. There is a tempting hypothesis in this brief history: that in American history investment turned to industry only after the more fruitful areas of land speculation had been tapped of their highest profits. It need not have been the case, of course. But the fact is that the United States became decisively an industrial nation only after the Civil War and only after the frontier was closed.

Before the Civil War there had, of course, been some industrial growth and the great land area was being tied together with transportation routes. Yet we were surprisingly underdeveloped in industry. Consider some comparative data for the United States and the United Kingdom. Our population in 1860 was larger than the British, 31.4 million to 28.8 million. Yet British pig-iron output was 3.8 million tons to our mere 920,000 tons. The figures for coal were: U. K., 84 million tons; U. S. A., 20 million tons. British exports totaled $661 million; ours only $316 million.

At that time our exports were of great importance, since we were so heavily dependent upon them to buy needed manufactures. Most of our people were farmers: 28.7 million were rural while only 6.2 million lived in places of more than 2,500 population. We had no city of a million people. Yet at that time London's population was 2.8 million, and England contained twenty-nine cities with populations in excess of 50,000, and twelve larger than 100,000. Urbanization figures are just another way of saying the same thing: we were not yet an industrial country because urbanization and industrialization in the 19th century were two sides of the same coin. What we were in 1860 was a large agricultural nation with the beginnings of industry, but still backward compared to Britain.

This was probably a natural consequence of America's first great compulsion, the conquest and physical possession of the continent. A decade after the Civil War the "extent" of the market became altogether technological, and America finally turned to industrialization and a new set of problems which still plagues us. The transformation of America to an "industry state" became a dominant force in the lives of Americans during the final years of Brigham Young's life and will not detain us here. He was a man of the earlier age, of settlements and beginnings. He was a staunch believer in "self-sufficiency" in manufactures out in the deserts, and he abhorred the great market economy of the United States. But Utah was to be drawn inexorably into the vortex of the national market, and the little Mormon communities in the mountains were to specialize, too, for sale in that market. Young's resistance to the market economy was a consequence of his experiences in frontier America. The frontier was his environment in both a spiritual and a physical sense. His career as the great American colonizer began where so many ended—in the 1840's, in violence.

II

Joseph Smith, Jr., was born Dec. 23, 1805, in Sharon, Vermont, and was shot and killed by a mob, when he was 38 years old, on June 27, 1844, in a little jail at Carthage, Illinois. Brigham Young was born in Whitingham, Vermont, on June 1, 1801, and died peacefully at his home in Salt Lake City, Utah, on Aug. 29, 1877, at the age of 76. These two lives, one short and one long, encompassed enough time to see the Church of Jesus Christ of Latter-day Saints grow from a most insubstantial origin to great and enduring affluence. Joseph Smith founded the church and was the fountain of all its unique theology and practices; all the evidence testifies that Brigham Young believed every word of it implicitly. It was a faith for which many gave up their lives and many more were willing to die. "God's smuggest people," as Bernard De Voto called the Mormons, were fanatically dedicated to their principles, and that devotion was why, in large measure, the Great Basin was settled. Like Penn and his Quakers, Young and his Mormons were prepared to follow their ideals to a new Canaan where ideals might become a way of life. Unlike the Quakers, the Mormons were not pacifists, a fact of no small consequence.

Just as the Quaker origins were rooted in the institutional changes of 17th-century England, so the Mormon origins were deeply embedded in the institutional experiments of 19th-century America. As the frontier moved across the Appalachians, it became the scene of a powerful religious upheaval. The reforming religious zeal of colonial America still had momentum, which in the frontier revivalism of the 1820's and 1830's seemed to run riot. God was to be found in nature, so the sophisticated transcendentalists believed. So did others, and where better to continue the reform and purification of religion than in the fevers of the evangelical frontier? In day and night camp meetings the frontier families and their preachers gathered for marathon preaching, shouting and hymn singing. Personal "religious experiences" were encouraged. As the pine knots blazed and lanterns lit up the forest, men and women were struck dumb, groveled and rolled about on the ground or, alternately, were granted "the gift of tongues" and babbled incoherently to the wonderment of their rustic companions. All this was encouraged by the exhortations of a barely literate clergy. There were deeply felt cries of "Hosannah," "Amen," "Hallelujah" and "Glory," as men barked like dogs, hopped about like frogs, were convulsed with the "jerks" (one minister is reported to have boasted that his entire congregation jerked simultaneously). God was a personal experience.

In that atmosphere the sects splintered, and splintered again, as each group found some unique view of the gospels and the true church. Between 1814 and 1830, four Methodist groups appeared; there were also Shakers, Free-Will Baptists, Hard-Shell Baptists, Seventh Day Baptists, Footwashers and a score of others. As religious orthodoxy reeled before this onslaught, so did other related institutions and, inevitably, there was "free love" at Oneida, primitive communistic experiments at a dozen outposts in addition to Brook Farm. Amid great publicity, Owenism came to New Harmony, Indiana. Jemima Wilkinson believed herself to be Christ and on that basis organized a community near Palmyra, New York. In 1817 Isaac Bullard, clad in his beard and a bearskin, had organized his Pilgrims in Vermont. In Ohio, Joseph Dylks claimed divine origins and attracted a following. William Miller proclaimed that the millennium would begin in 1843. He founded a religion on that basis.

The sects multiplied, vanished, reappeared in new guise; latter-day prophets abounded in a whirlwind of Christian heresy and deviation. And in that heated religious atmosphere there appeared a new faith of stupendous novelty. On April 6, 1830, the Church of Jesus Christ of Latter-day Saints was founded in Fayette, New York. Its founder and prophet, Joseph Smith, had talked with God and other celestial personages intermittently over a period of years. Through these heavenly agencies he had restored the true church of Christ to the earth, together with its lost priesthoods. The millennium was near, of course, so these were the Latter Days. The Bible was accepted as holy writ, but there was also the Book of Mormon, first published in 1830—scripture translated by Joseph Smith from "reformed Egyptian" written on ancient golden plates. This was the history of certain peoples on the American continent. The American Indians were descendants of one group, the Lamanites. The plates were found, under angelic guidance, in the Hill Cumorah near Palmyra, New York. Other scriptures and collections of divine revelations received by the Prophet in succeeding years were later published by the church. To the skeptical modern mind, the story hardly bears close scrutiny but, then, to the skeptical mind what religion does?

The new religion grew rapidly. We will concern ourselves with the doctrinal details of the new religion only as they bear upon our story. It is sufficient for our purposes at this point that thousands of people believed in the new faith. The Prophet moved his church to Kirtland, Ohio, in 1831, where certain economic experiments, including the anti-bank, were promulgated. The "Law of Consecration and Stewardship," a kind of community economic organization, didn't work in Kirtland. It would appear again in Utah. The church established a branch also in Independence, Missouri, near the original site of the Garden of Eden, destined to be the ultimate gathering place of the Saints in the "last days."

After the crisis of 1837 and the collapse of the anti-bank, the Prophet fled (January, 1838) to the settlement in Missouri. Some 600 of his people sold their holdings and followed him. But conflict had also come to Eden. In 1834 the Prophet and his lieutenant, Brigham Young, had led a small army from Kirtland to Independence to assist their brethren against the surrounding Gentiles (non-Mormons). The Gentiles won that conflict and the Saints were driven out of Jackson County. They established settlements in Clay County and then in Caldwell County, where there was the town of Far West. The Mormons were then, as they still are, a hard-working and an enterprising people and Far West soon was a thriving town.

In 1838 the intermittent guerilla warfare blazed up again and more blood flowed. This time the Prophet and most of the church leaders, excluding Brigham Young, were captured. Governor Boggs ordered them shot. Brig. A. W. Doniphan (later of Mexican War fame) refused to execute the order. The church leaders were incarcerated. State militia and irregulars had beaten the Mormons and burned their settlements amid massacre and general plunder. Brigham Young, temporarily the leader, took 12,000 to 15,000 Mormons across the Mississippi into Illinois early in 1839. In this flight Young's organizational genius was already evident.

The Prophet and his colleagues, allowed to escape after six months of imprisonment, rejoined their flock in Illinois, and the city of Nauvoo was founded. Once again—industry, enterprise, hard work and organization. By 1844 Nauvoo had some 11,000 people. And yet again violent conflict came, and in

June of 1844 the Prophet and his brother were dead. Brigham Young, senior member of the Twelve Apostles, succeeded to the leadership over his rivals. But still there was no peace and, on Feb. 16, 1846, Young led the van of some 16,000 Mormons back across the Mississippi into Iowa, to prepare for the great exodus to Utah.

It does not seem possible to separate clear fact from fiction about the Mormons' troubles with their neighbors. It is clear that, whatever the origins, the results were violent and unremitting. The flamboyant Joseph Smith had created a radically different religion. The interested reader should consult "Mormon" in any good library. Since we are interested primarily in the fate of Mormonism under Brigham Young, our treatment of Mormon history up to 1844 is desperately brief.

It is useful to consider some of the charges made against the Mormons in order to understand something of the opposition to them, and why they migrated. The Mormon charges against their enemies are myriad, and, as in any war, tragedy was ubiquitous. It is important for our purposes to see Mormonism in its original setting, as a product of frontier America: western New York, Missouri, Illinois and then Utah —the moving frontier. (Like other faiths on the frontier, Mormonism also had its schisms and apostates. Some, including "King Strang," on Beaver Island, Michigan, were very odd indeed. There is also a Reorganized Church of Jesus Christ of Latter-day Saints in Missouri, led by descendants of Joseph Smith by his first wife Emma and their adherents who chose not to follow Brigham Young.)

There were, of course, many potential sources for the violent and bloody conflicts between the Mormons and their neighbors. Polygamy was one. It was introduced by divine revelation to the Prophet and thence to his closest advisers in July, 1843, at Nauvoo. The "Frontier Mohammed," as Smith was called by his enemies, was notorious. (The Reorganized Mormons deny forty-eight of the catalogue of forty-nine wives.) Polygamy has been the most weighty cross the Mormons have had to bear out of Joseph Smith's theology. The religion itself, with its secret temple rites, was so strange, even to the most rickety backwoods heretics, that deep animosity was almost a natural concomitant of Mormonism on the violent frontier.

Then there was politics. In Missouri the Mormons, Easterners, were thought to favor abolition. There was plenty of violence to season it too. The Mormons were not only a

tightly knit economic and social community, thus arousing
the enmity of their neighbors, but they fought back, giving
blow for blow. In the Nauvoo Legion (a militia group) the
Prophet, glorying in the rank of lieutenant general, had a
private army of some 3,000—well drilled, disciplined, uni-
formed and equipped. In Illinois the Mormons voted as a bloc
and became a vital divisive political force. Smith was a
dramatic, garrulous, flamboyant person who attracted enemies
as easily as converts. His Old-Testament-style denunciations
were printed in his newspaper for all to see. At the end, in the
election of 1844, the Prophet announced his candidacy for the
Presidency of the United States. His Illinois enemies were
outraged.

The religion, with its own scriptures, was viewed as a profound blasphemy even by the footwashing frontier schismatics.
There was economic and financial disaster in Ohio, talk of
Danites—destroying angels of the Lord, a sort of frontier
secret police—and "whittling deacons" who shadowed Gentiles
about the Mormon settlements. After the escape from Missouri there was continued conflict over the Missouri episode,
threats and exchanges of violence. An attempt was made in
May, 1842, on the life of Gov. Lillburn Boggs after Smith
had prophesied his violent death. Boggs lived, and a renowned
Mormon roughneck, Porter Rockwell (who later boasted
of the crime and who lived out a full and fabled life in Utah),
was charged with the crime but was not convicted.

Smith was Mayor of Nauvoo, and his courts made it virtually impossible for the Missourians to get his enemies to arrest
him on their warrants. The Prophet fell into his enemies'
hands on a minor slipup. He ruled his kingdom in a free-
handed and totalitarian manner and had wrecked the presses
of an opposition newspaper; he was finally apprehended (gave
himself up) on that charge after a short flight to Iowa (where
there was also a price on his head).

The Prophet's life was a short one and tumultuous almost
to saturation. The annals of American history contain few
biographies as dynamic and strife-ridden. After his death there
was still no peace. Hatred of the Mormons had produced a
smashing victory for their enemies in the Prophet's assassination, and the taste of blood stimulated the urge for more violence. The Illini continued their attacks. Harassment mounted.
Smith had once planned a move to the Rocky Mountains to
escape his tormentors, and his successor determined to carry
out the plan. There was, in 1846, precious little evidence that

Joseph Smith's church could continue to function among the Gentiles in the Midwest.

The faithful once again prepared to abandon their homes, farms, orchards, meetinghouses, their great stone Temple and "Nauvoo the beautiful" to follow Brigham Young into the wilderness to seek their Canaan. Time was running out for the Saints in Illinois. Mobs burned and sacked outlying settlements, and Governor Ford, advising the Mormons to leave Illinois, stated that he could not guarantee their safety in his state. Brigham promised that the spring of 1846 would be the date of the exodus. Nauvoo was transformed into a workshop for preparing wagons and gathering provisions and stock for the journey. There was insufficient time to make adequate preparation for the coming ordeal. Farms, homes and the great Temple were put up for sale. Enormous losses were taken by those fortunate enough to sell at all. A large part of the Mormon property was simply abandoned. The great Temple had been rushed to completion as an act of religious devotion. It was later sold to the French Communist Étienne Cabet, and his Icarians and was burned by an arsonist.

Evidence that the Mormons were leaving emboldened their enemies, and acts of violence became everyday experience. First the mobs struck outlying settlements like Lima, Illinois, where 175 homes were burned. The result of this, which had tragic consequences, was Young's decision to start the emigration in the dead of winter in the hope of saving the majority of the Saints from persecution by taking himself and his main counselors out of Illinois. It was, it turned out, a vain hope. Feb. 16, 1846, was the fateful day when Young and his party crossed the Mississippi from Nauvoo. Some Mormons had already made the crossing.

The Iowa shore on that day presented a picture of chaos and tragedy which was painfully etched on the memories of the survivors. It was snowing. Wagons were stuck, some without teams, pointing in every direction; baggage was piled about, and children and animals running loose amid the shouts of wagoners and the cries of women searching for families. There seemed to be no direction. Young stayed on the top of the bluff until the last wagon was safely up. The disorganized vanguard then slowly pulled through the snow and mud to Sugar Creek, nine miles from Nauvoo. Sleet continued to fall through the night on this, the first of the Mormon migration encampments. Snow had to be shoveled out to make beds; trees cut and wood gathered for fires. That night nine babies were born in the "camp of Israel."

A significant change began to appear at Sugar Creek. The Saints began to receive systematic instruction on the techniques of migratory living, down to the smallest detail, even how to make "salt-risen" bread. At first the problems of the migration seemed overwhelming. Slowly they were solved, and for the next thirty years the Mormons were not without close "counsel" from their leader. His personality increasingly determined their affairs. The character of Brigham Young flowered in adversity, and the great colonizer was coming into his own in the snow and chaos at Sugar Creek.

III

Brigham Young was then not quite 45 years old. He was about five feet ten inches in height, solidly built (although not stout as he was in later life), vigorous and healthy. His head was massive; a strong and forceful jaw was set off by thin, tightly stretched lips. His hair was light brown (in later years it was curled with curling irons at the edges). His face held the appearance of all the power and intelligence which characterized his life. Brigham's eyes have especially been the subject of remark by those who saw him. Some thought they were hard and cruel—icy blue. Mark Twain, in *Roughing It,* wrote that Brigham had ". . . a gentle craft in his eye that probably belonged there." In a charming memoir a daughter, Clarissa Young Spencer, recalled her father as "good to look at." She thought that his blue eyes radiated "love and tenderness." Young's features and personality powerfully impressed his contemporaries. Even today the physical presence of Young in Utah is not forgotten, and he is one American historical figure who can hardly be painted larger than life. He was a man of towering wrath, great decisions, ruthless and hard-driving leadership, but also he delighted in the simplest pleasures and many times himself led the dancing after a hard day's trek, when the Saints "formed sets under the stars." Like so many of his brethren, he lived and enjoyed his life to the full. He inspired deep love and hatred, and was as vivid a character as the 19th century produced.

His own childhood contained little that was unusual. Young was born in a family of old Massachusetts Puritan stock. His father was a soldier in Washington's command in the Revolution. The family moved out of Massachusetts into lower

Vermont and lived there when Brigham, the ninth of eleven children, was born. The fact that all the children lived to adulthood is, considering the time and the humble circumstances of the Youngs, perhaps evidence of an especially strong physical heritage. Brigham's father was a deeply religious man, in whose home the Sabbath was kept with great rigor. The children had an equally rigorous upbringing. Brigham recalled his father: "It was a word and a blow with my father, but the blow came first." The children worked on the farm, but, being in poor circumstances, the boys were apprenticed to learn trades when they were old enough. Brigham's mother taught him to read although he later recalled that he had only eleven days of formal schooling. Brigham was apprenticed at 14, on the death of his mother, and became an accomplished carpenter, painter and glazier. He was successful at his trade, and to the end of his life was proud to the point of vanity about his prowess at his craft. Doubtless no small part of present-day Mormon utilitarianism comes directly from the long rule of Brigham Young, the master carpenter, painter and glazier.

Brigham's first wife, Miriam Works, was married to him on Oct. 8, 1824. She died about eight years later. The family settled in Mendon, New York, where Brigham followed his trade. But his family was swept along in the revivalism of the period. At one point he was a Methodist, but a copy of the Prophet's Golden Bible came into his hands, and he joined the Mormons on April 15, 1832, being baptized in his own millstream. He journeyed to Kirtland, Ohio, a few months later to meet the Prophet and, from that time on until Young's death in 1877, the history of the Mormon Church and of Brigham Young were inseparable.

Brigham was evidently an obedient and unquestioning subordinate of Joseph Smith throughout the Prophet's life. Smith exploited Brigham's abilities in every way and trusted him implicitly. He was sent on long proselytizing missions all over the Eastern states, to Canada and to England with his longtime friend Heber C. Kimball in September, 1839, just after the establishment of Nauvoo. The families of the two missionaries were ill, and Brigham had to be carried to the riverboat. Yet he answered his "call" unquestioningly. In 1834 Brigham had assisted the Prophet in his ill-fated military expedition from Ohio to Missouri, and, as noted earlier, in 1839 it was Brigham who organized and led the exodus from Missouri when the Prophet was jailed following the guerilla warfare there. Young served in all the highest councils of the church before the Prophet died, and he was one of those in a select group who were first enlightened in the mysteries of celestial marriage according to the "divine revelation" received by the Prophet before the revelation was made more generally known. Young obediently took his first plural wife immediately. Many more followed.

At this point we must digress to some extent and treat Brigham's polygamy. It is the sad fact that he is to this day probably better known among his countrymen for his plural marriages than for his vast accomplishments as a frontier leader. Brigham married twenty-seven women in all, but they were not all alive at the same time. He was survived by seventeen wives. He fathered a total of fifty-six children (thirty-one girls, twenty-five boys) by sixteen of his wives. The largest number born to any single wife was to his "beloved Emmeline," who bore him ten children.

This was an impressive family to be sure. But Brigham's polygamy was not a record, even by early-day Mormon standards. The Prophet Joseph is credited with a total of forty-nine wives; Heber C. Kimball was the husband of forty-five and fathered sixty-five children. The same number is estimated as the progeny of John Doyle Lee, the Danite fighter, by his nineteen known celestial brides. The point here is not to belittle Brigham Young's polygamy but to emphasize that he was not unique in that regard, perhaps not even in the front rank. To worry his married life is like deploring Joe Louis' golf game. The really impressive thing about Joe Louis was not his golf game, and the really impressive thing about Brigham Young was not his family life. But it does help to understand Young and the Mormons if one bears in mind that, according to their religious beliefs, polygamy was virtuous.

Polygamy was inseparable from Mormonism, and so Brigham Young, "the Lion of the Lord," did his part to maintain the system. He was, incidentally, a splendid father according to his children. Life in his house was great fun for the children, with as many as fifty people commonly sitting for meals. His houses were efficiently organized to deal with his "peculiar" marital problem (an accurate and charming account can be found in Clarissa Young Spencer's *One Who Was Valiant*). The wives, "aunts" to the other children, contributed to the common household according to their special talents. There was a family bakery. Young built his own school for his children and one of the wives was school mistress. His children were a credit to him. Only one of the twenty-seven wives, the last one, was unfaithful to him—and since he was 66 when he married her, one might assume that his judgment regarding the fair sex was beginning to slip. She sued him for divorce and extortionate alimony (the courts finally ruled that her marriage to Young was not legal) and wrote a book about her life with Young which still titillates the reading public.

Polygamy was an affront to 19th-century Americans. It doubtless would still be so today. Yet a nation which extensively practices sequential polygamy as we do (one divorce for every five marriages—350,000 to 400,000 a year, and all that implies in terms of sexual license) is not so impeccably ensconced in its marriage institutions that it can with impunity castigate the long-suffering Mormon patriarchs of the last century with their frontier "harems." Mark Twain, investigating the matter for himself, expressed an opinion which was noted for its justice as well as for its humor. After observing the pioneer Mormon ladies he argued that:

> . . . the man that marries one of them has done an act of Christian charity which entitles him to the kindly applause of mankind, not their harsh censure—and the man that marries sixty of them has done a deed of open-handed generosity so sublime that the nations should stand uncovered in his presence and worship in silence.

The picture of Mormon polygamy as a kind of perfumed Turkish empire on the Western frontier is wildly off the mark. Nearer to it for most frontier polygamists was the picture of old Danite fighter John Doyle Lee (whose diary was in the third person) struggling in the winter of '49 to keep fires in his plural hearths:

> J. D. Lee from necessity removed Sat., 10th, Rachell his 6th wife and her child to his farm till the weather would get more mild; his team being so much reduced that he was unable to haul wood for 2 fires in the city and 2 on his farm.

Each fire representing at least one family to provide for in near-famine conditions, one can appreciate his problems. Frontier polygamy was no sensual romp. Under the sharp eyes of Brigham Young and his Holy Priesthoods every man was responsible for his family obligations, however extensive. The pure sensualist must have been, then as now, strongly constrained by the financial obligations involved in establishing more than one household.

Polygamy was an integral part of the social, economic and theological apparatus taken over by Young at Joseph Smith's death. Plural marriages were built into the theology of Mormonism, in what Kimball Young (a descendant of Brigham and a noted American sociologist) aptly called "the Quantum Theory of Salvation." They believed that an extensive family enhanced the degree of celestial glory a man might achieve in the next world. The object of polygamy was to provide as many "tabernacles" on this earth for spirits as a man could. Only legal action against individual Mormons under special Federal legislation sufficed in 1890 to break the *official* church position on the *practice* of polygamy. For Brigham Young polygamous marriage was of divine origin, as it was to his coreligionists (and is today among the Mormon "fundamentalists"). Polygamy, unhappily enough, must be counted by the objective historian as part of the idealistic drive which motivated the Latter-day Saints in their great migration.

But the subject can be overdone. Not all Mormons were polygamists. About one married man in ten had more than one wife. There is much more than plural wifery to Mormonism. It is a shame that for all these years Young should have been obscured by his wives' petticoats. Perhaps it is a perverse working of historical justice, the payment in full to a man who "should have known better." Yet one of the singular characteristics of religious beliefs is the absence of doubt, the tendency for believers to believe it all—gods, saints, spirits, hell and damnation, the whole lot. In that regard, Young was not unusual. In the volumes of his *Discourses* one is struck again and again by the way in which the whole body of Joseph Smith's theological creation was believed and acted upon by Brigham Young. Modern Americans should probably be grateful that Young and his people believed so fervently, polygamy and all, if that was necessary to carry American civilization into the Western desert. And most students of the subject agree that, without the Mormons' passionate—even fanatical —religious beliefs, the Great Basin would not have been settled as it was.

IV

On modern highways the distance from Nauvoo, Illinois, to Salt Lake City is about 1,300 miles. By immigration trails, fording rivers and skirting the canyons and Indian country, it was, in 1846, a great deal farther. It was, any way you care to measure it, a long way to walk.

The great Mormon trek was carried out in two primary stages: first, from Nauvoo, on the eastern bank of the Mississippi, into Iowa with the vanguard at a mud-hut settlement called Winter Quarters (now Florence, Nebraska) on the western bank of the Missouri; second, from Winter Quarters to the Salt Lake valley. The expulsion from Nauvoo began in early February, 1846; as early as the spring of 1849, an estimated 6,000 Mormons had completed the migration, and, by 1852, 20,000 of them were in the Great Basin. After that a nearly continuous immigration into Utah was maintained by the church, now established in its new home. The primary migration began in the greatest confusion, suffering and tragedy, but was completed as the classic of American pioneering organization. By the fall of 1847 when the 1,681 Mormon settlers of Utah were preparing for their first Wasatch winter, the organizational gifts of Young and his deputies, together with the ingenuity and discipline of his people, lay on the threshold of legend.

Young had three great fundamental problems of a social and economic nature to solve on the trek: (1) the scarcity of Mormon resources to stage such an expedition, (2) the requirements that the Mormon communal life be maintained during the migratory period and (3) the organization for the journey itself. The three problems were, of course, related to each other and were all solved by the use of the communal discipline latent in the church organization. On top of these problems there were still those of geography and the elements to overcome. Let us consider each of the primary problems separately.

Mormon resources were meager. As we noted, the wealth of the community at Nauvoo was largely sacrificed because of the pressing necessity to leave Illinois and avoid further fighting and bloodshed. Investment in land, buildings, roads and other improvements, the labor of seven years, was realized at only a tiny fraction of its cost. Buyers did not exist in sufficient number to create a reasonable market so quickly. Much of the property had to be abandoned outright and yielded nothing but regret and heartache to the owners. The migrants had little time, even if they had had proper funds, to prepare for such a journey. They needed to make much of their equipment, and this meant that many (and the poorest were poor indeed) had virtually what they could carry on their backs or in a wagon or two as their total supplies to sustain them over a period of two to six years in the wastes of the Western prairies, deserts and mountains.

The lack of sufficient preparation was terribly wasteful of life and equipment when the migration had to begin in winter and to labor through the mud and snow of an Iowa winter and spring. It was a terrible ordeal, the memories of which are sacred to the Mormons, but the circumstances of which constitute one of the black marks in American history. Hundreds died, 600 at a single camp in Iowa. When summer finally came, the initial energy and resources of the exodus were spent. Preparations for a wintering had to be made with the thousands scattered in a long string of encampments across Iowa. In September, 1846, mobs drove the pitiful remnant of Mormons, too poor, old or ill to have left for the West, from Nauvoo after a pitched battle. These destitute ones had to be absorbed and cared for at the Iowa camps, thus completing the disaster. It was necessary to try to rebuild and replenish the equipment and livestock before going farther.

The Mormons earned what they could from the sparse (Gentile) settlements along the route (the two brass bands in the migration played concerts wherever they could and "passed the hat"). Missionaries raised funds from converts in the East, South and in England. Brigham negotiated the enlistment of 500 of his men (the famous Mormon Battalion) in the service of the United States Government to march to California in the war against Mexico. This provided an initial cash payment of $21,000 ($42 per man for clothing allowance) and "free transportation" (they walked) for the men to the West. The church authorities promised to care for the families of the men and to transport them to Zion. The men could rejoin their families at the end of the war. Negotiations with the Indians were successfully conducted to allow the Saints to plant crops and graze their animals and hunt on Indian lands to replenish food supplies. The men foraged for lumber and shot game, the hides to be made into clothing and robes, and to be used to tie up equipment. At various camps on the route semipermanent settlements were established, fields broken and crops put in which were to be harvested by succeeding companies of migrants.

All possible efforts were thus made to mobilize resources to sustain the trek. It was barely enough. The total resources were, in fact, pitifully inadequate for comfort. Cash was spent to buy what could not be made, salvaged, earned or begged. One of Brigham's own wives walked most of the way from

Winter Quarters in Indian moccasins, and he estimated that not one of four of his own family had shoes. Had there been anything for sale at the terminus of their journey the Mormons could scarcely have bought it for cash; the historian H. H. Bancroft reported that the $50 brought into the valley by Brigham in 1847 was, initially, the whole cash supply, and that a year later he brought in an additional $84 in cash—and that when the population of the valley had reached 4,200.

The fields of grain planted and tended at the main camps across Iowa underscore the singular characteristics of the second problem—the necessity to maintain community life among the Mormons. Only as a group could they survive the rigors of the trek; collective action made continued Mormon life and discipline possible. Their migration was no romantic journey across the empty wastes; it was a *moving settlement*. Thousands of families had to be sustained off the land as much as possible while slowly shifting the mass of the community toward Winter Quarters, preparatory to the long march up the North Platte into the mountains and down into the valley. By the time the slowest (and largest) segment of the vast line of humanity was across Iowa and ready to mount the last stretch of the journey, the earliest portion would have made a start at providing the agricultural basis of life in the Great Basin. Thus, two hours after his arrival in the Salt Lake valley in July, 1847, Wilford Woodruff planted his half bushel of potatoes. Seed grain went into the ground that day also, and Brigham and his companions were at work surveying their city-to-be. No time could be lost. On July 24, 1847, when Brigham first entered the Salt Lake valley, the Mormons were farming land across a long migration route from the Mississippi to Great Salt Lake. The new root had to be planted immediately because the old root was being inexorably removed from the nourishing but hostile soil of the Midwest. Mormon survival depended upon the success of the whole enterprise, from Iowa to Utah, and as we shall see, these exhausting efforts scarcely sufficed.

None of these actions could have succeeded had the camps lost their discipline, their willingness to suffer heat, cold and exposure, to ration their food severely, to bury their dead without despair, and—above all—to wait. The church organization provided part of the means. Wherever possible the camps were organized as wards (Mormon parishes), with a Bishop presiding over the affairs of each and the two priesthoods, from High Priest down to deacon, performing as the apparatus, the chain of command, through which the "counsel" and orders of the superior officers could be transmitted, and the wishes of the brethren made known to their leaders. In the camps strict order and discipline were maintained, with daily work allocated as efficiently as possible so that, in addition to caring for and maintaining the livestock and rolling equipment, work details might be easily raised to create the chain of bridges and ferries built along the route, which was to be the permanent road of the migration. The wagons in camp were arranged in rows, like houses along a street.

On the march the wagons encamped in a circle. After the first winter stop in 1846–47, the order of march was made efficient by the division of the migration on more military lines into wagon trains of one hundreds, fifties and tens with captains over each company and subdivision, a chain of command and obedience which gave a tighter order to the trek. Each company was then ordered to be roughly independent as to departure for the mountains, within a general timetable established by Young. (The timetable was not followed to the letter, with the result that more trains made the trip to the valley the first year than Young had wanted.) Crops were to be put in and houses built for those who stayed behind the first migrants. Each company was to care for its poor, widows, fatherless, and the families of those in the Mormon Battalion. The organization of this system was promulgated as a "divine revelation" to Brigham Young. He was not yet elected President of the church.

After 1847 Young's own signature was usually sufficient to govern his church, and he had no further need for divine revelations to impress his people with the weight of his authority. In the trek, as in the early settlements, the "ideological" system was a mixture of private enterprise tempered by cooperation wherever private means did not provide the ends sought by the church leaders. This view of economic organization never left the Mormons. It now pervades economic thinking throughout the United States, of course. In modern times the leaders of the Mormon Church have constituted a curious ideological paradox. Conservatives, they preside over a most extensive cooperative welfare enterprise. But the paradox has its own tradition—the church was both "free enterprise" and "collectivist." Young wasn't interested in political ideologies, just results. The Great Basin Kingdom, as we shall see, owed its success to Young's undogmatic mixed economy.

Thus the Mormon trek to Utah was a singular masterpiece of organization, a living mechanism, nourishing itself as it slowly moved some 20,000 souls across the long trail to Utah. Without such organization the Mormon pioneers doubtless could not have succeeded as they did in their efforts to build their Zion in the wilderness. They were too ill-equipped to have made the trek on an individual basis and to have withstood the initial rigors of life in the high deserts. Until the organization was completed, they suffered terribly. No reader can come away from the surviving accounts of the Mormon trek without a profound realization of the magnitude of the achievement. There was incredible suffering and dying in the snow and mud and swamps of the prairie. A great many accounts dwell upon the suffering of the ordinary people. It is difficult to exaggerate their trials; they were terrible enough. Whole families perished. Col. Thomas L. Kane, a long-time friend of the Mormons, described a summer encampment where there were not enough men in condition even to dig graves as people died—mothers sat vigil over the dead bodies of their children, brushing off flies, waiting for sufficient graves to be dug.

Births, deaths, suffering, hardship. But it was taken in stride. The Mormons today believe that their success in that arduous journey was miraculous. I would argue that it was better than miraculous; it was organized and accomplished with a will. Young's apparatus of command was a plan to solve the terrible logistics of the march, and the Mormons themselves assured its success. Driven by their enemies, spurred on by their leaders, and sustained by sublime faith in their religion, the Mormons rose above their afflictions. Our history reveals no hardier people. Partly their faith was suited for such a trial. Mormonism gave them a fatalism which enabled them to accept hardship as their lot. The sentiment was probably best expressed in their great hymn, "Come, Come Ye Saints," written on the trek by William Clayton. The fourth stanza reads:

> And should we die before our journey's through,
> Happy Day! all is well!
> We are then free from toil and sorrow too;
> With the just we shall dwell.
> But if our lives are spared again
> To see the Saints their rest obtain
> O how we'll make this chorus swell
> All is well, all is well!

No self-pity. These were a people who would succeed.

Heber C. Kimball took six wagons out of Winter Quarters on April 5, 1847. Brigham waited two days to get a report from the returned missionaries, John Taylor and Parley Pratt. They had just come into camp from England with gold and with the scientific instruments which Young had sent for. Brigham, with the instruments for mapmaking and surveying in hand, followed Kimball on April 7. The two parties composed Young's specially picked company for exploration and settlement which was to push down the first roots in Zion. There were 148 people in all, 143 men, 3 women and 2 children. Also 72 wagons, 93 horses, 52 mules, 66 oxen, 19 cows, some chickens, and 17 dogs.

Not much drama accompanied this last stage of the initial movement to the valley. This time, for once, Young could conduct his affairs with a minimum of external interference. The result was another of what was to be a long succession of pioneering masterpieces. The Mormon leaders had carefully studied all available information about the Salt Lake valley. They knew a great deal about it. They knew that they might have to irrigate and they knew, once the final route was taken, which creek (City Creek, as it was afterward called) to camp upon and to plant beside. En route, Brigham talked with Jim Bridger, "Old Gabe," the famous mountain man who knew the Great Basin country better than anyone. Later Mormon mythmakers to the contrary, Brigham knew about as much as was possible concerning their destination before the party arrived in the valley. The Mormons followed the north side of the North Platte to avoid the main emigrant trains, for by 1847 there were many migrating parties on the plains heading for California and Oregon. The company crossed the Platte near Fort Laramie, then went through the South Pass, Fort Bridger and, after exploring alternative routes, followed the old Donner Trail through the canyons out of the mountains and down into the valley.

Young's party was attacked by "mountain fever" once they were well up into the Rockies. Young himself was unable to be in the first group which descended the western slope of the Wasatch and came into the valley on July 22, 1847. That party went directly, as Young had earlier ordered, north of the canyon entrance to the City Creek and camped. On July 24, Brigham, still bedridden with fever and lying in Heber Kimball's wagon, first looked out over the desolate but spectacular landscape of the great valley. There seems to have been no doubt in his mind that the correct piece of desert was now being put to the plough by his brethren. He is reported to have immediately stated, "This is the place."

"The place" cannot have inspired much confidence on first sight. And, indeed, surviving records indicate that there was initially abundant doubt among the party about Brigham's wisdom or Joseph Smith's or the Lord's or whoever was responsible for choosing the place. Few landscapes on earth present a more inhospitable look than the western base of the Wasatch Mountains in late summer. In its natural state it is devoid of trees of any consequence. The June grass has already gone yellow by late July. The escarpment of the Wasatch is largely reddish-brown in color, but that contrasts all the more with the sullen gray of the sagebrush and white-streaked alkali dirt of the valley. But beauty is in the eye of the beholder. Brigham Young wanted a difficult land, one which would both keep his Saints hard at their labors and which would not seem an inviting place for Gentile settlers. He chose the right place all right, and even after Utah's enormous mineral wealth was exploited in later years the Mormons were long a preponderant majority. Brigham was not a man much given to introspection (at least his writings so indicate), but he was a man of feeling, so that Bernard De Voto's lines in *The Year of Decision* may be a fair suggestion of Young's feelings when his feet first touched the dusty ground of the Salt Lake valley.

> . . . Brigham Young must have permitted himself a moment or two to taste and savor such triumph as few have known in all our history. *The thing was done!* Fayette, Kirtland, Jackson County, Clay County, Nauvoo, the frozen Mississippi, Sugar Creek, Pisgah, Winter Quarters—and now Zion. Seventeen years, the angel and the golden plates, the prophet murdered, hundreds of Mormons dying in the passion of battle or the salt frenzy of flight or shaken by ague or starving at slackened breasts or just going down into the dark after too much strain at Misery Bottoms. The faithful and the recreant, the persecuted and the damned, the mobbers and the politicians . . . Israel's fear had ended.

After that "Israel" had plenty of trials, but they were on Israel's own ground and Brigham Young, the great leader of the trek, became the great colonizer, political figure, entrepreneur and legend of the Western desert. Young went back to Winter Quarters in September to prepare the migration of 1848. Behind him in the valley more immigrants had arrived;

a city was laid out; a fort built; fields were fenced in and a foundation for the new life of the Mormons was laid.

In case the Saints did not understand all his wishes, Brigham wrote them from the trail back to the Missouri giving detailed instructions for their winter life. It was a typical epistle from Young, matter-of-fact, practical and plainly written. Reminiscent of his only published "divine revelation," this time Young's pen showed that the man who could relate God's will about emigrating companies of hundreds, fifties and tens could, on his own account, tell settlers the best time to secure salt supplies, advise them on irrigation, locate places of recreation, deal with the Indians, build and staff schools, care for the stock, trim the seedling trees, reward the virtuous, chastise the wicked, and glue it all together with holy benedictions. The style would become a familiar force in the coming years of trial and triumph.

V

Brigham came back into the valley in the summer of 1848, leading the immigration of that year, and for the next three decades confined his activities primarily to building up the "Kingdom of God" in the Great Basin. This part of his career was once the subject of enormous controversy because of political conflicts, national agitation against polygamy, and charges made against his attempts to exclude the Gentiles from economic life in Utah. Following his death attention more and more turned to the trek and only in recent years has interest revived in the way in which the "Kingdom of the Saints" in the Great Basin was built. But now, with the passions of 19th-century politics long forgotten, it is possible to gain a clear appreciation of the accomplishments of Brigham Young and his colleagues, as well as their follies, in the development of the Mormon Commonwealth.

First, it is of primary importance to recall once again that Mormonism had been a product of the Ohio and Mississippi valley frontiers of the 1830's and 1840's. In those days the role of the Federal Constitution as the "law of the land" was not settled, to say the least. Not only in Congress itself did the states-rights debate rage from session to session, but among the states government varied considerably in its structure and performance. Many of the settlements made on the frontier were economic experiments. This had been the period of pre-Marxian socialism in Europe and in America. The utopian socialists were full of ideas for improving upon primitive capitalism's sometimes baleful performance with its child labor, dangerous working conditions, complete absence of job security, periodic mass unemployment, and all the rest.

In Europe, as in America, it took a long time to patch up the tatters of early capitalism. With men like Godwin, Engels and Owen in England; Fourier and Saint-Simon in France; Marx in Germany and France (until 1848); the transcendentalists at Brook Farm, and Alfred Noyes' communism and "free love" at Oneida—and a host of other American experiments in primitive communism—it had not been so certain in the minds of thinking Europeans and Americans that capitalism had much of a long-term future (indeed *that* capitalism did not).

The Mormons had been at the far edge of these experiments with a theocratic democracy, experimentation in family life and an attempt at communal organization of property rights in the Law of Consecration at Kirtland and in later communal and cooperative efforts in Missouri and Illinois. When the Northern victory in 1865 and subsequent amendments to the Federal Constitution settled many of the ante-bellum problems of the forms and practices of government in America, the country was approaching its intensive industrial development with capitalistic enterprise (private ownership and control of productive resources) leading the march toward the new age. Brook Farm was forgotten, a dead issue.

All this had largely bypassed the Mormons and their leader, Brigham Young; they continued to try solutions to economic problems which had been long abandoned in the Eastern United States and, in fact, forgotten. In his monumental economic study of the Mormons, *Great Basin Kingdom*, Prof. Leonard Arrington traces the origins of Mormon collectivist economic enterprises, "Jacksonian communitarianism," back to their true American roots, showing that the economics of Mormonism in Utah was no aberration in the national experience, but was, in fact, virtually the last stronghold of the utopian and idealistic social and economic schemes so well known in an earlier America.

To understand this is to understand a great deal about the "peculiar people" of the intermountain West. Utah was not developed as a system of roaring mining camps and vast cattle "spreads" like its neighboring states. In Utah, an Eastern and largely European people came with all their customs and institutions intact, and simply planted them in new ground. The settled agricultural villages of Utah provided a permanence to life there which even today forms a striking contrast to much of the mountain West. Utah had the first university west of the Mississippi. The church poured funds into music and fine arts of an "uplifting" kind, and Brigham built a splendid theater and brought in the best actors. Such activity gave Utah and the Mormons a cultural lead over their neighbors which remains in glaring evidence.

This Mormon area is an interesting place today. In many respects it is as De Voto believed—what all the Brook Farms, New Harmonies and Oneidas might have been. The great achievements and triumphs, conflicts and calamities of Brigham's last three decades must be read in the context both of Mormonism and the "new" America which grew up around Utah's peaceful valleys and, in the end, penetrated them. Brigham and his brethren were trying to build their utopian dream in the bosom of a rising capitalist economy such as the world had never seen. In the end, the Mormons had to compromise to survive. But the Mormons built well enough that the difference remained.

VI

The difference between Mormon colonizing and all others was there at the beginning, deeply rooted in their religion. They were (and are), it is true, an energetically materialist people. Their economic achievements make one suspect that somehow an excessive dosage of the Protestant ethic was imbibed along with the rest of their theology. However, there was a special ingredient in the Mormon colonization: it was the unique mixture of theocratic and egalitarian democracy, with both individual and communitarian ownership and responsibility in economic affairs. Individuals were generally encouraged to "lay up" and improve their earthly treasures, but not at the expense of projects and principles deemed important by Brigham for the welfare and development of the community as a whole.

To be a Mormon involved a commitment to make economic sacrifices freely if called upon by the church leadership. The Mormon concept of "just" distribution of income and wealth seemingly straddled all ideological positions. It was taught that economic equality was in the interest of unity of the church; yet the Parable of the Talents was important too—

some should have more than others, according to both ability and need. However, all property was held as a "stewardship" from God and was not to be abused by the "owner" at his own will (many times individuals were called upon to "consecrate" their property to the church, and the property was then returned as a stewardship). In the Book of Mormon (Alma 1, 26–28) the old utopian principle—"from each according to his ability and to each according to his need"—was put forward, together with the hint of progressive taxation, as an ideal form of organization of economic life. Among the Nephites each man labored:

> . . . according to his strength. And they did impart of their substance, every man according to that which he had, to the poor, and the needy, and the sick, and the afflicted; and they did not wear costly apparel, yet they were neat and comely.

The Mormon economic philosophy was one of hard work, but also of direct responsibility. Those who were blessed according to their abilities were responsible according to their means for their less-fortunate brethren. None should suffer, but virtue was to be rewarded. Logically the Mormon position on income, wealth, property and responsibility was and is paradoxical and full of contradictions. Yet it makes enormous ethical sense. Over-all, the church leadership exercised divine authority in the general direction of economic affairs. As Brigham phrased it in 1864:

> We cannot talk about spiritual things without connecting with them temporal things . . . They are inseparably connected . . . we will not be satisfied with anything short of being governed and controlled by the word of the Lord in all our acts, both spiritual and temporal.

In addition to general "counsel" to the members concerning economic affairs, the church had various more direct methods of mobilizing and controlling economic resources. First, of course, was a general tithe of 10 percent of the net product (income) of the membership. Here was a source of investment funds to build roads and canals, to finance settlements and immigration, to purchase supplies and to pay for the host of other "social overhead" expenditures made by the church over the signature of President B. Young, the "Trustee-in-Trust."

In addition, individual members were called to "fill" "eco-

nomic missions" just as they were (and are) called to go forth
among the Gentiles on evangelical missions. Just as Brigham
Young and Heber Kimball, in most difficult circumstances,
had unhesitatingly obeyed Joseph Smith's orders to go to England as missionaries, so thousands of Saints pulled up stakes
in Salt Lake City and settled outlying valleys; built canals,
dams, roads, sawmills, a telegraph system; labored on railways, and hewed granite, to build up tithing credit or to fill
missions for the benefit of Zion in the Great Basin.

The result was a powerful engine of colonization and settlement. It did not always succeed. But it succeeded well
enough to settle the Mormon part of the West with a thor-
oughness and cohesiveness that was not seen elsewhere on the
Western frontier. At its peak, the Mormon system had planted
settlements over a vast area from southern California far up
into Oregon Territory, eastward into Colorado (with immigration stations all the way to Iowa), southwestward into northern Arizona with Salt Lake City at the center. With the final
settlement of state boundaries, Utah alone is today considered
to be proper Mormon territory. The line of Mormon settlements is actually much more extensive, spilling over into all
the neighboring states. In 1849 the Mormon claims on the
Far West were practically ubiquitous. In that year Young's
government, the "Council of Fifty," petitioned Congress for
statehood for the State of Deseret (land of the honey bee); it
included virtually all of the present Far West including California.

At first Brigham's colonization system seemed to be uniquely suited for the West. But the Mormons were soon outnum-
bered in the more fertile areas on the coast and in the rich
mineral-producing areas of the mountains when the national
expansion overtook the persecuted exiles from Illinois. In their
own domain, the arid Great Basin, the Mormons faced no
such competition for decades. Americans quickly occupied
the best parts of their last frontier after the Civil War. But
the Mormons had plenty of time to plant their roots in the
alkali desert before having to contend with the Gentiles again
in great numbers. The wisdom of Brigham's choice of Zion
was soon apparent. Zion was located in a most intractable
region. The Mormons had to learn to master their harsh environment. Once this was done they were no longer an easy,
or perhaps even possible, prey for their enemies. Survival at
least was assured.

VII

Survival itself was in doubt at first. The pioneers of 1847 had no opportunity to put in extensive crops. A fort had been made; a city laid out; some fields plowed and planted; logs were cut for cabins; a sawmill was put in operation and other essential preparations were made to sustain the nearly 1,700 Mormons who spent the first winter in the valley. According to Professor Arrington, the colonists had 450 log cabins built by winter. Mormon Battalion members coming in from California brought $5,000. This was used to send to California for cattle and provisions to be brought in the following spring, and the settlement was without cash funds when Brigham Young returned with his $84. Winter wheat was planted on 872 acres.

Thus the Saints utilized their meager resources to the limit. This they had had long experience in doing. Even so, the winter of 1847–48 was one of great hardship in the valley. The colonists grubbed for roots, shot what game could be found (including wolves), and measured out their scarce rations. A nephew of Brigham Young later recalled:

> For several months we had no bread. Beef, milk, pigweeds, segoes and thistles formed our diet. . . . At last the hunger was so sharp that father took down an old bird-pecked ox hide . . . and converted it into delicious soup which was enjoyed by the family as a rich treat.

Hunger was a constant companion that first winter. Conditions scarcely improved in the spring. A late frost damaged the vegetables, and the famous infestation of "Mormon crickets" in May and June threatened and greatly reduced the grain crops. By September, 1848, when Brigham arrived back in the valley with the second immigration, there were more than 4,000 to feed and very little to be used to accomplish this. The second winter was worse than the first, so far as the food supply was concerned. Again the problem was survival, and again the communitarian organization of the Mormons carried them through. Once again the buffalo robes and raw hides went into the cooking pots, and the Saints dug sego lily roots and thistles and watched a long, hard winter grind slowly on.

Inevitably those with sufficient private food stocks began to succumb to the temptations of this world—price gouging. There was demand among the Saints for price controls. Characteristically, Brigham met the problem in his own way. There was no need for price control. Let the markets find their own level. There was, instead, to be a system of voluntary rationing. Those with surpluses were asked to turn them over to the Ward Bishops and to deal fairly with their brethren. In case some brethren missed the point of this "counsel," Brigham was more explicit. Lee's diary described the views President Young held:

> Pres. B. Young said that we are safe . . . for he believed all the while that corn was not so scarce as Many had expected . . . if those that have do not sell to those that have not, we will Just take it [and] distribute amoung the Poors [and] those that have [and] will not divide willingly May be thankful that their Heads are not found wallowing in the Snow.

Moral suasion. The Lord moves in mysterious ways.

In the spring of 1849 the Mormons planted their fields again and held on in their mountain valley hoping for the best. By then the California gold discoveries were known in the valley and some of the weaker Saints left for the diggings and more were thinking about it. Young held steadfast to his desert, promising that the Saints who stayed in the valley would prosper. His advice was to avoid the "God of this world." Zion had to have an agricultural foundation. Man could not eat gold; ". . . we will cultivate the soil . . . plow your land and sow wheat, plant your potatoes."

Throughout the hardship period, 1847–49, Young continued to expand his plans for the settlement of the desert. The city was laid out in what came to be the classic Mormon scheme: small lots, houses set back among fruit trees and gardens, farm lands and pastures outside the settlement, wide streets with clear mountain water running down the gutters. No "unearned increment" was encouraged; land speculation, so prominent a feature at Kirtland and Nauvoo, was not allowed.

Most important among the initial organizational achievements in the valley was the control and conservation of water and timber. It was apparent from the beginning that these resources were extraordinarily scarce and had to be husbanded accordingly. There could be no reckless waste of natural resources or the colony would fail. Brigham stated his desires in his usual style:

> There shall be no private ownership of the streams that come out of the canyons, nor the timber that grows on the hills. These belong to the people: all the people.

Canals, dams and ditches for irrigating the fields were built by the labor of the individuals applying for water, according to each individual's needs. A ward "water master" distributed the flow according to the labor contributed. Here, again, the communitarian system made possible an agricultural plan which no individual could have provided by himself. This system of irrigation gave the settlement the necessary agricultural base which assured its eventual survival. Timber rights were similarly exploited and controlled by the church organization. The pioneer Mormons were far ahead of the rest of the nation in the conservation of natural resources—they had to be.

In the midst of this struggle came manna. The California gold discoveries, starting in 1848, produced profound repercussions throughout the commercial world. Linked with the Australian gold discoveries of the early 1850's, the California mines initiated a long period of rising prices and economic expansion (generally until 1873). In less than a decade the world's supply of monetary gold was increased by a third. In the United States the immediate effect was a great overland migration; perhaps 50,000 made the journey in 1849 and as many more in 1850. The nation, which had acquired California in a comic-opera military operation during the Mexican War, now reached out seriously to embrace the Golden State. The Saints, struggling in the isolation of their mountain Canaan, were suddenly on the main highway. Complete isolation was at an end.

To many the gold mines in balmy California seemed a threat to the austere future Brigham planned for his people—"hard work, good food and sound doctrine." By exhortation, threat and promises, he minimized his losses of people, and the Mormons turned the gold rush to their own account. The gold rush and the subsequent rapid rise in California's population caused the first of two relatively sudden shocks given to the Mormon economy of Utah by the expansion of the national economy. The second was the completion of the transcontinental railway in 1869. Brigham used the first to turn poverty and hunger into a small inland empire. It was his greatest triumph. As we shall see, his reaction to the second shock was different. It was defensive and was partly an attempted withdrawal into economic isolation and utopianism. This response was due to a third and increasingly ubiquitous force, which the Mormons had sought to escape—conflict with the non-Mormons. Even in the Great Basin, once the Gentiles came into close contact with the "peculiar people," open conflict became an everyday affair. Brigham's triumphant life in his desert, and the lives of his people, were destined long to suffer under the shadow of a mainly hostile national government. The laws of that government and the actions of its officials looked to the Saints much like the persecuting mobs of Missouri and Illinois. Mormon ideals and institutions were just as abhorrent to the Gentiles in the West as they had been on the Mississippi. From 1849 onward, the Mormons again had to compromise with the Gentiles; after 1869 the compromise was increasingly on the Gentiles' terms.

In spite of many troubles, the two decades from 1849 to 1869 saw Brigham's second great achievement—more striking even than the trek—the establishment of a viable Mormon economy in the Great Basin. News of the gold discoveries had reached the valley quickly. Mormon laborers at Sutter's mill (members of the Battalion were still in California because the church leaders feared that the valley could not yet feed them) had made the discovery. By late 1848 gold dust was coming into the valley, and the church even printed "banknotes" against the gold to provide a more convenient circulating medium. In spite of Young's efforts, the temptation to leave the valley for the mines was great when the snows melted in the spring of '49. (Young sent a gold "mission" which made about $60,000.) In the heat of the persuasion, Heber Kimball had been so rash in the fall of 1848 as to "prophesy" that commodities would soon be "cheaper and more plentiful" in Salt Lake City than in St. Louis or New York. It would be folly to leave. *Mirabile dictu*, he was right! It is almost anticlimactic that, in the midst of their great strivings and hardships, the Saints suddenly found their foundering Utopia virtually afloat in a small sea of provisions.

Salt Lake City seemed close to California for thousands of Forty-Niners who, having made the long journey from the plains to the Great Basin, were glad to trade food, provisions and equipment for a fast horse or a fresh team to get over the Sierra before winter. The Saints had suffered their second terrible winter in Utah and were waiting apprehensively for their second harvest when the real "Harvest of '49" roared out of the mountains. The gold rush was a godsend to the Mormons. Indeed, one can fairly ask if, but for it, Brigham Young would not have proved to have led his long-suffering followers to their final disaster. The gold rush banished the specter of failure in the mountains. As Professor Arrington puts it:

> The effect of the Gold Rush upon the Mormon economy of 1849 and succeeding years is clear and unmistakable. Faced with hunger, inadequate clothing, poor housing, and a gross insufficiency of tools and equipment, the Mormon colonists would most likely have had to give up. . . .

Our diarist, John Doyle Lee, recorded the windfall:

> About the 1st of July 1849 the Emigration for California or Gold Regions commenced rushing into the Valley, bringing in with them groceries, clothing, [and] provisions in great Abundance, Much of which were sold [and] exchanged to the Saints for Butter, cheese, Milk, garden vegitables . . . at a very low rate. Waggons that was rating from 50 to 125 dols. before the Emigration commenced rolling in, were sold [and] traded during the summer [and] fall of 1849 from 15 to 25 dollars; Harness from 2 to 15 dollars . . . which a short time Previous would have brought 30 to 50 dollars . . . Oxen, Cows, Horse, Mules . . . were sold [and] exchanged upon the most reasonable terms. Fresh Horses [and] Mules were soon raised to $200 each, so great was the demand for them. Most of the Emigrants abandoned their waggons when they reached the Vally. . . ."

On the road from the valley, Lee described a scene reminiscent of a military route:

> . . . the Road was lined with waggons from the Vally to this Point that one would scarcely ever out of Sight of Some Train. Dust verry disagreeable but not to compare with the Stench from Dead cacases which lye along the Road . . . Destruction of Property along the Road was beyond discription . . . waggons, Harness, Tools of Every discription, Provisions, clothings, stoves, cooking vessels, Pouder, Lead . . . the Traveler would not be at a loss to find Roads [and] yet be puzzled to keep the main one.

Anything for faster transportation. The Saints were given incredible trades. Lee, and doubtless many others, made small fortunes just "picking up" along the trail over which the gold-crazed Forty-Niners littered the equipage of a substantial army. Trade flourished. The Mormons had their rough flour, horses and oxen, and the Forty-Niners had everything else. The Saints displayed then, as they do today, a considerable pecuniary virtuosity. Their flour went at $10 to $15 a hundred pounds. Just as Brigham had let the market, properly exhorted, find its own level in the previous winter, so his policy continued, properly embellished *ex cathedra*. Arrington quoted him:

> What! sell bread to the man who is going to earn his one hundred and fifty dollars a day, at the same price as you do to the poor laborer, who works hard here for one dollar a day? I say, you men who are going to get gold to make golden images . . . pay for your flour.

The Mormons had mechanics, wheelwrights, blacksmiths and other craftsmen to help the Forty-Niners along; there were Mormon ferries, established on the rivers along the route, which earned impressively for the Saints. California was a golden spur to American economic growth, to the Mormons no less than to others.

VIII

After so many calamities Young's organization now had resources to carry out their great plan—to "gather in" the Saints from the plains, the Eastern states and from Europe, and to settle them in the Utah valleys within the economic, social and theological framework of the church. The work went forward with great energy. The cooperative, quasi-collective methods, mixed with individual enterprise, now flourished. The Mormons are great respecters of physical labor. An old and rousing Mormon hymn expresses the sentiment:

> The world has need of willing men,
> Who wear the worker's seal;
> Come, help the good work move along;
> Put your shoulder to the wheel.

Each colonizing mission sent out from Salt Lake City was thoroughly organized with respect to skills and resources, and placed under trusted leaders selected by Young. Every Mormon life and soul was precious; neither should be wasted by want or unemployment. As the Saints came into the valley, a system of public works kept them employed until they could be settled. The public works were part of the cooperative system of the Mormons. (When such works were adopted by the Federal Government in the 1930's, they were already an old story in Utah.) Young had interesting views on charity— he didn't like it. He believed that the best charity you could give a man was employment. He preferred that work be made available even at a loss. The old carpenter–glazier respected the dignity of labor.

> Some have wished me to explain why we built an adobe wall around this city. Are there any Saints who stumble at such things? . . . I build walls, dig ditches, make bridges, and do a great amount and variety of labor that is of little consequence only to provide ways and means for sustaining and preserving the destitute. I annually expend hundreds and thousands of dollars almost solely to furnish employment to those in want of labor. Why? I have potatoes, flour, beef, and other articles of food, which I wish my brethren to have; and it is better for them to labor for those articles, so far as they are able and have opportunity, than to have them given to them. They work, and I deal out provisions . . .

In case there were any further questions:

> . . . Should it enter my mind to dig down the Twin Peaks, and I set men to work to do so, it is none of your business, neither is it the business of all earth and hell, provided I pay the laborers their wages.

A lot of work on the buildings of the church, as well as upon public works, was done by Mormons who were temporarily "in inventory" in Salt Lake City waiting to move to a permanent home. Public works were in fact long a mainstay of employment stability for Young—churches, temples, roads, paid for from tithing resources whenever the developing economy faced maladjustments which might produce prolonged unemployment among the swelling population of Zion. Public employment gave the private economy time to work out its kinks. Young hated idleness.

Renewed contact with the Gentile world—the gold rush— now enabled Young to see his economic theories in action. The initial economic bottleneck had been broken, and in spite of many setbacks, the Kingdom was not in danger of economic failure again. All that was needed was land, tools, people, faith and hard work.

In 1849 the Perpetual Emigrating Fund was established. The people in the Salt Lake valley pooled some of their resources to equip and transport the poor from the Missouri River camps. The immigrants were then to contribute their labor and resources to pay back the P. E. F. when they could, thus renewing the fund and financing further immigration. In 1850 the P. E. F. brought in some 2,500. A year later an equal number were transported. Ezra Taft Benson (grandfather of President Eisenhower's Secretary of Agriculture) and Jedediah Grant, two of Young's most trusted lieutenants, were given the job of clearing out the remnants of the Nauvoo exiles, and with a tremendous effort 10,000 were brought home to Zion in 1852. In addition, thousands of English and European converts were brought into the valley by the P. E. F. They came in all states of preparedness and equipage. Some even walked, pulling their possessions in handcarts (one such company came to a tragic end in 1856 when it started for the mountains too late in the season). By such means, a decade after the fateful July of 1847 there were more than 60,000 Mormons in the Great Basin. Young had his human raw materials.

The settlers went out in companies to their colonies. Young was entirely systematic about the colonizing and here, even more than on the trek, his unique organizing genius was apparent. The valleys of Zion were surveyed and sites for Mormon villages were selected. The members of each colony were then selected, balanced as well as possible according to skills and needs. The wagon trains were organized like the trek, with the priesthoods having ultimate authority. (Some of these companies were very large. In October of 1861, in a single mission to grow cotton in southern Utah, 309 families were "called" and went; in a few months 400 wagons rolled into the place now occupied by the town of St. George.) Upon arrival at the chosen site the group organized the land into town lots and smallish farming plots. A cooperative "church farm" was sometimes laid out to provide a central store of provisions. The public works such as dams, canals and roads were built, as always, cooperatively.

As additional immigrants arrived at the mouth of Emigration Canyon they were given temporary work, quartered over the winter among the Salt Lake wards and then dispatched where they were needed. According to Arrington, some 500 such settlements were planted in the 19th century, 96 of them in the decade after 1847.

The rules of the original settlement were adhered to, no man got more land than he needed; water, timber, grasslands and minerals were "public" property. Mormon unity was maintained in spite of the disbursement of the population. The church hierarchy entered every home where an adult male was a member of the priesthood (the Mormons are their own clergy, every man; there are no paid clergymen). The semiannual church "conference" brought the leaders back to Salt Lake City from all over Zion. The business of the church was done at the same time that the faith was renewed at the great meetings—first in a temporary "bowery" and then in the fantastic wood-pegged and rawhide-thonged Tabernacle. The organization thus did not weaken as it grew and expanded its area of operations. Success was simply a function of effort—or so Brigham Young viewed it.

Young's economic thinking was as curiously paradoxical as was the official Mormon view on income distribution we noted earlier. He was a capitalist, a collectivist, a free enterpriser and a mercantilist. Is it possible? These are labels with fairly definite meanings in economics, and they all apply to him at one point or other in his career. What he was really was a practical utopian. He wanted the ideals of his faith, but he also wanted policies which worked. He cared nothing about labels; he was purely pragmatic. But what he wanted most was self-sufficiency and exclusiveness—freedom from the Gentiles.

With the immigration, the public works, the agricultural and colonization system pouring people and resources into development, the way seemed to be open for the growth of a self-sufficient Kingdom. Brigham passionately wanted to limit contacts with the outsiders. He believed that the Mormons had all the means at their disposal to create their own manufactures to supplement their agriculture. Economic missions were sent to grow cotton, flax, tobacco; to erect and operate textile mills; to dig and smelt iron. He especially recruited workers from Britain's industrial districts—textile workers from Lancashire, miners and iron workers from Wales and the Midlands. In the 1850's dozens of his pet manufacturing projects were set going throughout the length and breadth of Zion.

As always, the Mormon system of organization, together with the priesthoods as the organic chain of command and communication, permeated all enterprises. The scale of Brigham's ambitions was magnificent. The record of success in manufacturing was, however, not impressive. But failures were taken in stride and new starts made. This was a wasteful procedure. But colonization is by its very nature partly wasteful.

By pushing against every natural and technological limit, the Mormons slowly found the economic boundaries of their realm. No one could have told them where those boundaries were. Everything had to be tried. Most of it would have been tried anyhow since self-sufficiency through individual and co-operative effort, a "balanced" economic system, were articles of Young's mercantilist faith. His economic beliefs were not all that unusual. There had been Alexander Hamilton's *Report on Manufactures*, mercantilism on a national scale. Even by the mid-19th century there was scarcely a tradition of specialization and free trade in the United States, and it was no different in Utah except that those Americans had a more provincial view. Their "economy" was Zion. Resources were thus "misallocated" in the interests of self-sufficiency. Brigham expounded his views on it everywhere.

> I have no hesitation in saying that our true interest is, and will be most wisely consulted in domestic manufacturing, to the exclusion of almost every article of imported goods.

This doctrine, the *reductio ad absurdum* of the classic protectionist fallacies, would have reduced the people of the Great Basin to a Lilliputian model of the world economy, and it stayed with Brigham to the end of his days. It was the product of the utopianism of the experimental American frontier colonies of the 1820's and 1830's and which had been part of the original Mormon creed. Utah finally sloughed it off, grew its food, mined its metals, sheared its sheep, all for export, and imported textiles from New England and autos from Detroit. But not in Brigham's time. In the 1850's, the church programmed its development for self-sufficiency. The world outside Utah intervened again.

IX

In 1857–58 there was the "Utah War." Utah was organized as a Federal Territory in 1850 with Brigham Young as its first Governor (and Indian Agent). Federal judges, apparently of not excessively savory character, soon ran afoul of the religious organization, and strife intensified until the judges left the territory, charging that the laws were not enforced and that the Mormons had burned court records. The affairs of Federal Judge W. W. Drummond, it appears, were especially gamy. He brought his mistress to Salt Lake City and she sat alongside him on the bench while, he charged, the Saints on the juries exonerated their brethren. Heber Kimball denounced him in a typically straightforward sermon. The disease

> . . . that is in him shall sap and dry up the fountain of life and eat him up. Some of you may think he has not the disease

I allude to; he is full of pox from the crown of his head to
the point of its beginning.

The Federal officials charged that Mormon polygamy mo-
nopolized all the women ". . . which made it very inconvenient
for the Federal officers to reside there." Brigham and the
Mormons were charged with all sorts of crimes, including
various murders. The Mormons did not make it easier for
themselves. In 1856 they conducted a "reformation" (if not
a purge, at least a most vigorous "revival") among themselves
which raised a lot of strong language and charges of worse.
Once again, Danites, ritual murder and so forth filled the
Eastern papers. The Mormons were news again. Anti-polyg-
amy feeling was strong in the States—so strong it had even
figured in a Presidential election. At last President Buchanan
was persuaded to launch an expedition to install a new Governor and to "enforce the Federal Constitution." The Mormons harassed the Federal supply trains (the Mormon guerilla leader, Lot Smith, burned seventy-five wagons of Federal supplies) and forced the army to spend a cold and hungry
winter near the ruins of Fort Bridger, burned by the Mormons.

Young knew that he could not really defeat the Federals if
it came to all-out war. But the Mormons were determined not
to let the fruits of their enterprise fall once again into the
hands of their enemies free of charge. It would all be burned.
The Saints prepared their own scorched-earth "Sebastopol
plan," packed their goods in northern Utah, filled their homes
with straw, and then some 30,000 abandoned their hard-won
dwellings, moving slowly south out of Salt Lake valley.
Young, in negotiations with the new Governor, had extracted
a promise that the army would not be quartered in Salt Lake
City if the troops were allowed to come into the valley. That
promise was as good as he could get in the circumstances. He
took no chances. If the army broke the terms, the city would
be fired. The soldiers marched straight through the deserted
city, watched only by a few Gentiles and Young's militiamen
who stood ready to burn the city if the soldiers fell out of line.
The army eventually established Camp Floyd, far out from
the city in the desert. The Governor begged the Mormons to
stop the evacuation. Finally Young determined that his terms
had been met and, on June 30, 1858, told his people that he
was going home and they could do as they pleased. The Saints
came back into their valley.

The army at Camp Floyd introduced a lot of dissension into Utah, but the quartermaster paid good prices for provisions until the troops were called back to the states in 1861 to choose up sides. The Mormons, who had flourished provisioning Camp Floyd, tasted the final victory by purchasing the Federal stocks at "war surplus" prices. On a single day, it is recorded, $4,000,000 worth of stores were sold for $100,000. In that encounter with the Gentiles, as in 1849, the Mormons profited materially. But not without paying, and exacting, a terrible price. The war spirit instilled in them by their leaders had gotten out of hand and innocent blood was shed.

In September of 1857 some Mormons in southern Utah, in the company of local Indians, butchered most of a California-bound emigrant train at Mountain Meadows in one of the most squalid atrocities in the history of the West. Our diarist, John Doyle Lee (adopted son of Brigham), was executed in 1877, almost twenty years later, for his part in the massacre. Historians have now cleared Brigham of direct complicity. The Mormons were facing their mortal enemies again in 1857; they were contemplating the abandonment of their homes, and worse. It could have been Far West and Nauvoo all over again. The ill-fated wagon train included people from Missouri and Arkansas (where Apostle Parley Pratt had recently been murdered). It was "war" and feelings ran high. Like John Brown's massacre of the innocents at Pottawatomie, Kansas, in 1856, the Mountain Meadows massacre was an atrocity committed in an era of open frontier violence Americans have now forgotten. But the specter of Mountain Meadows hangs over the Mormons and haunted Brigham to his grave. One of Young's daughters recalled in later years that her father "wept bitterly" when the news of Mountain Meadows reached him.

During the Civil War, Brigham's loyalty was again in doubt. His attitude of "a plague on both their houses" was widely known. Indians threatened the Overland Mail and the telegraph line which had been completed in 1861 (with an important contribution by Mormon labor). Young offered to protect the lines with a militia, but in 1862 a new Federal armed force, commanded by one Patrick Connor, arrived in the valley to maintain Federal interests. Connor established a camp (later well known as Fort Douglas and now part of the University of Utah campus) on an elbow of the Wasatch overlooking Salt Lake City from the east. It is said that he trained a cannon on Brigham Young's house. Connor caused lots of trouble. His force and hangers-on brought both business and vice into the valley. Camp Douglas was a center of opposition among dissident Saints. Connor published an anti-Mormon newspaper and attempted to encourage a mining boom. This was a portent of things to come. In 1862 and 1863 rich deposits of gold, silver, copper, lead and other minerals were found in the areas surrounding Zion, and after the war, when the great Western mining boom was combined with the transcontinental railroad, the developing national economy once again reached out to embrace more of its new Western provinces. First the economies of the present states of Colorado, Idaho and Nevada were developed as raw-materials producers for the industrial East. Utah was next.

Until then, Brigham Young hammered away at his colonization and self-sufficiency schemes. He organized a large-scale wagon train which went each year from 1861 to 1867 to the Missouri, carrying Utah products. Commodity imports and immigrants were brought back by the returning wagons. More than 20,000 were brought in during the '60's by this method. A famous theater was built in Salt Lake City (Brigham liked the theater, but not tragedies; he once stopped one during the performance: "There is enough tragedy in everyday life . . . we ought to have amusement when we come here.") In 1863–67 the Tabernacle was constructed; work was pushed forward on the Salt Lake Temple (it took forty years, and was not completed until 1893). In the Deseret Agricultural and Manufacturing Society efforts were made at self-improvement in agronomy and in manufactures. In 1866, the Women's Relief Society was organized under one of Brigham's wives, Eliza R. Snow (a poet and Mormon feminist, and also formerly a wife of Joseph Smith), to mobilize Zion's women in the interests of community activity. A silk industry was attempted and renewed efforts with church participation were made to manufacture import-competing commodities. Brigham the mercantilist was still at work. A great triumph was the Deseret Telegraph, a system built largely with tithing labor, ward by ward along its entire route of 500 miles, to connect up the outlying Mormon settlements. It was in operation in 1867. Operators were trained at a special school, their training counting as a "mission."

In 1869, Brigham reached his 68th birthday. Less than a decade of life was left to him. He was by then a renowned figure, grudgingly respected even by his enemies. Visitors to Utah pressed to see him. The population of Utah alone was

now more than 85,000; the Mormon institutions were intact
and thriving. The old man might have settled into a triumphant retirement. Kirtland, Far West, Nauvoo, Winter
Quarters and the trek must have all seemed far away indeed.
His life was a triumph. Brigham was a very wealthy man for
the times, with sufficient houses, lands and flocks to support
his abundant family handsomely. Like his people, he had had
his failures, but like his people, he had tasted success.

> You know my life; there is not a person in this church and
> kingdom but what must acknowledge that gold and silver,
> houses and lands . . . do multiply in my hands. There is not
> an individual but what must acknowledge that I am as good
> a financier as they ever knew, in all things that I put my
> hands to.

Like John D. Rockefeller at a later time, Brigham was convinced that God had rewarded him. Young's winters were
spent at St. George, in Utah's "Dixie" and the movement of
his entourage between Salt Lake City and St. George was a
regular Roman triumph. Most of his people were inordinately
attached to him. In spite of Federal Governors and courts, his
enemies charged that Brigham ruled Utah as an absolute
monarch. When, on his travels, his party approached a settlement, they were met by mounted cavalry, and bands played;
it was a parade. Yet in 1869 Brigham still faced many crises.
He met them head on.

X

With the completion of the transcontinental railway, a
combination of latent conflicts came into the open. When the
railway came into the valley at Ogden, Utah's physical isolation, shattered in 1849, was eliminated. Over the years a
Gentile trading and mining population had grown up in the
valley. There was a newspaper operated by excommunicants.
Many of Young's best Saints had taken to commerce and to
close association with the Gentiles. In the past Brigham had
dealt roughly with this opposition. If they were Saints, he had
them excommunicated. Now there was need of new rigor in
the faith. He organized the "School of the Prophets" among
the elite of the priesthoods, a special cadre to debate church
policies and enforce a new rigor in the everyday practices of
the church. His whole organization was put to work to move
Zion toward an exclusive Mormon life. But the enemy had to
be met on its own terms, in commerce.

An attempt was made to squeeze out Gentile and "apostate" merchants by amalgamating Mormon retail establishments into a single giant enterprise, Zion's Cooperative Mercantile Institution (1868), and then by "counseling" the Saints to trade only with their own people. In 1870 an attempt to meet the competition with "outside" mineral interests was made with the Union Iron Works and similar enterprises. Further efforts tried to establish cooperative textile mills at likely sites. The Mormons had previously refrained from banking, but in 1869 Brigham entered into a cooperative banking enterprise which was chartered in 1870 as the Bank of Deseret (for such actions Young, the Mormon Prophet, became known as "the Profit" among his enemies).

When the railways approached, Brigham, always an alert combatant, joined an enemy he could not beat. He took a contract for more than $2,000,000 to do the final 150 miles of grading and tunneling for the Union Pacific. The church also took a contract for about $4,000,000 to do the final 200 miles of grading for Central Pacific. The church leaders reasoned that if Mormons did the labor in Utah for the railways Zion might at least be spared a direct invasion by the railway construction gangs and their mobile "Hell-on-wheels" communities. The work might also prove to be profitable. When the railways proved unable to meet their contractual obligations to the Mormons with money, payment made in machinery, ties and iron was turned to good account. The Saints built their own railways linking the various parts of Zion north and south. Even railway construction was amenable to the church organization and, along the routes of the lines, loyal Mormons turned out with teams and equipment to answer the call of their religious leaders.

In 1873 the burgeoning new industrial capitalist economy was temporarily derailed by a profound financial crisis and depression. Mass unemployment spread in the great market economy of the United States, and wherever the Mormons had joined forces with the "outside" there was now unemployment and distress. Brigham saw this as just and inevitable payment for the folly of mixing with Babylon. His own position of leadership had recently faced a new and powerful kind of challenge, an intellectual one, the so-called Godbeite Heresy. William Godbe, a friend of Young's, joined with other prominent Mormons of Utah's growing new "business" world in an attempt to reverse the Mormon policies of agrarian life and home manufactures. In the "New Movement," a powerful

dose of Ricardian logic was introduced into Brigham's mil-
lennial empire, pointing out the economic facts of life about
Utah's great mineral reserves (a product, long range, of
Connor's earlier work at Camp Douglas). Utah, like other
civilized commonwealths, should specialize and trade with the
rest of the world. Exploitation of minerals was the road to
greater prosperity and "progress." To Brigham it was the road
to Babylon, and the New Movement theorists were excommunicated.

Now, with the new industrial America of the first post-
Civil War decade opening markets for Utah's minerals, Brigham, an old man, faced a hopeless battle. The Gentiles were
coming upon Zion by railroad; they were weaning away his
trusted lieutenants; they were moving people into mining and
away from agriculture, the classic Mormon villages and the
self-sufficient Kingdom. By then America had changed, and
so had the Mormons. Sophistication was encroaching upon
the millennialists. Brigham Young reacted to the depression
and to the entanglements his people faced by returning to the
fundamentals of Joseph Smith's visions, The Law of Consecration and Stewardship, now reintroduced as the United
Order of Enoch—equality, virtue, generosity—utopian ideals.

In 1874 Young got his followers in St. George to subscribe
to a charter establishing a United Order. Several kinds of
United Orders were eventually established, running the gamut
of various modes of cooperation to the most extreme, at
Orderville, Utah—a self-sufficient commune. Young pushed
the United Order vigorously. He described his visions at the
church conference in October, 1872:

> . . . when it comes evening, instead of going to a theater,
> walking the streets, riding, or reading novels—the falsehoods
> got up expressly to excite the minds of youth—repair to our
> room, and have our historians, and our different teachers to
> teach classes of old and young, to read the Scriptures to them;
> to teach them history, arithmetic, reading, writing, and paint-
> ing; and have the best teachers that can be got to teach our
> day schools. Half the labor necessary to make a people
> moderately comfortable now, would make them independently
> rich under such a system . . .

And again Brigham Young, 19th-century cooperating capitalistic mercantilist:

> A society like this would never have to buy anything; they
> would make and raise all they would eat, drink and wear, and

always have something to sell and bring money, to help increase their comfort and independence.

Back to Brook Farm! or rather, back to Kirtland and the
Prophet Joseph. In 1874, Young was an old man, worn out
by one of America's incredible lives, and the visions of his
youth seemed all the sweeter to him.

How did the frontier utopianism of the 1830's look in the
Utah of 1874?

. . . the most preposterous and crackbrained fantasy that ever
deluded the judgement of a spiritual or temporal leader.

Such was the judgment of the *Salt Lake Daily Tribune,* the
opposition paper and the voice of progress and the New
Movement. The loyal Saints tried the United Order in spite of
progress, and all their attempts failed. Well, times had
changed. The Lion of the Lord was now a quaint figure, with
his odd religion, his "peculiar people" and all the wives and
children. There is a time for everything. A "preposterous and
crackbrained fantasy." But then, perhaps Brigham Young was
thinking of Far West, or Sugar Creek, or Winter Quarters, or
1847! A people once cried out for his fantasies and were
saved.

XI

President U. S. Grant came to Salt Lake in 1875. Brigham
went to see him in his private railway car. Both men took
off their hats. The old Prophet was a favorite for touring
dignitaries. He continued to have troubles. His last wife tried
to divorce him and get an enormous financial settlement amid
great splashes of publicity. He had been charged with murder
when Bill Hickman, an old frontier cutthroat, published his
"memoirs" claiming to have murdered men at Brigham
Young's suggestion. There was no rest. A polygamist, Young
was arrested at 70 for "lascivious cohabitation." Such a charge
for another man might have been considered a triumph. For
Brigham Young it was further persecution of the true church
by the Gentiles.

In his old age, the Lion of the Lord had softened considerably. Sir Richard Burton thought Young resembled nothing so
much as a New England gentleman farmer. Young's enemy,
T. B. H. Stenhouse, in his *Rocky Mountain Saints,* describes
the septuagenarian as "very regular in his habits," rising be-

tween seven and eight in the morning, going first to his office to survey the day's business, and then to breakfast (codfish gravy was a favorite at breakfast according to a daughter). He might "saunter out and look at his premises." He was ready for business at nine, was barbered and shaved in his office at ten "no matter who may be present," and so on through the day. Stenhouse further noted "no lady or gentleman is denied admittance to his office on simply sending in a card . . . Brigham is very human, and he can button himself up to an unwelcome visitor in a style that the stranger is not likely to forget; but when he is in excellent humor, he is a perfect Chesterfield."

At 70, Brigham still kept a keen interest in the affairs of the youths of Zion; sometimes, it was charged, even censoring and purging invitation lists to dances. He sat in his box at the theater in a rocking chair with his stovepipe hat on. His biographer, M. R. Werner, notes that he managed to control his faculties until the very end. He had the kind of gift of decision and command so common among "natural" leaders, and Stenhouse noted that Brigham had "schooled himself into the habit of never thinking twice upon any subject; and, when once it has received his attention, and he has pronounced his decision, he never wants to hear of it again." The old Prophet was no original thinker. His was the gift of organization and action. Ideally suited to combine the raw elements of people and the land, his rough methods had become "old-fashioned" by the end of his life.

Brigham Young died on the afternoon of Aug. 29, 1877, at his house in Salt Lake City in his seventy-seventh year. Years before when his great lieutenant, Jedediah Grant, died, Brigham delivered the funeral oration. For himself, when his time came, he wanted no elaborate funeral ". . . nor make any parade, but give me a good place where my bones can rest, that have been weary for many years, and have delighted to labor until nearly worn out; and then go home about your business, and think no more about me, except you think of me in the spirit world, as I do about Jedediah." In 1873 Young wrote specific instructions for his own funeral. The master carpenter wanted a coffin of "plain one-and-a-quarter redwood boards, not scrimped in length." There was a place prepared for the coffin on his property. There was to be no mourning or crepe. If any of his friends wanted to say a few words, "they are desired to do so . . . I have done my work faithfully. . . ."

XII

Utah's valleys were integrated into the national economy. The "peculiar people" became outwardly about like everyone else. After much litigation the church gave up most of its remaining cooperative enterprises. Polygamy was officially abandoned in 1890. Utah's minerals were exploited as the Godbeites wanted them to be. The Saints slowly adjusted to their role in modern American society. The agricultural base established by Brigham and his frontier utopians thrived and provided a firm foundation for the growth of modern industrial Utah. The best scholars agree that without the religious idealism of the early Mormons the colonization could not have been done. Moreover, by pushing for every means of self-sufficiency, Brigham's Mormons, with all their failures, did find the full capacity of varied economic enterprise their domain could support. This gave Utah a better balance in her economy than the other mountain states achieved. Utah could not only support her own population but supply the mineral settlements in the surrounding states as well.

There are many powerful contrasts between our two sets of idealists—Penn and his Quakers, and Young and his Mormons. Penn's Quakers were passive, law-abiding English subjects, asking only peace and the chance to live according to the dictates of the Inner Light. Young's Mormons were largely of the same national stock, but the stock had been tempered by nearly 200 years in the New World. The Mormons wanted peace, too, and if their religion was a delusion, they wanted the opportunity to live thus deluded. They were also 19th-century Americans on the frontier and were ready to take their rights by force if necessary. In both cases, the driving power was religious idealism.

When hard times came to America again in the 1930's, the Mormons went back a bit to Brigham's "fantasies" and developed a church welfare system—cooperative farms, canneries and so forth—which continues now to provide their people with a buffer against those vagaries of industrial fluctuations in free-market capitalism that Young had hoped to avoid. The church went back into various businesses and, paradoxically, the agrarian Mormons became, as a group, phenomenal in their mastery of the ways of modern finance, industry and government. But the difference always remained. The Saints remained to some extent tied to the soil. Brigham would still recognize them. Not long ago, I spoke to a sophisticated Mormon elder who labored mightily in Babylon's financial headquarters—New York City. The Elder talked of the evenings each week he spent on his knees with his hands in the dirt working on the cooperative "church farm" over in New Jersey. Self-sufficiency. Brigham Young would have liked that.

PART II

THE INVENTORS

The Mormons built a great temple of granite in Salt Lake City. Like the European cathedrals of the Middle Ages, the massive structure was an act of faith, of sacrifice. The men were tithed for their labor and for materials, the women for food and drink during the long years while the temple was being completed. The granite was hewn from a Utah canyon and transported many difficult miles to the building site by teams of oxen. The physical environment of the Mormon empire was wild and imposing, and building a settlement there had changed many of the Mormons' preconceived notions about life on many levels. The physical environment was totally different from that of the Middle West, the East or of Europe. The strange nation of Deseret on the shores of the Great Salt Lake seemed to be without any similarity to anything else in America or elsewhere. Why then, asked Aldous Huxley, does the Mormon Cathedral look like a Victorian church?

Invention is made possible by environment to some extent; environment may provide opportunity or inspiration. But the methods employed to make a given invention at any time are largely determined by extant technology, by what economists call "the state of the arts." Few inventors discover all of the mechanical or artistic principles utilized in their creations.

The combination of environment and the state of the arts gave American inventive genius an enormous opportunity. The work of conquest and settlement which comprised the great economic legacy of the idealists and others who forced back the American wilderness provided the material basis for Jefferson's vision of Arcadia. But America's destiny was not to be a nation of independent yeomen working their largely self-sufficient family farms. The great challenge of America to Americans was the full development and exploitation by all physical means of the continent's massive natural endowment —the land, the forests, the minerals, the waters and even the open skies of a continent. Almost anything can be improved upon by human genius. The application of known principles of physical science could transform the nation's primitive agricultural economy if men of invention had scope for such application.

Throughout all of American history such employment of science has been "in the air." We have grown up as a nation in the harsh and stimulating light of technological change. We are not a nation formed by the constricting usages of the Middle Ages, but one which was from the beginning in revolt against those usages. We had no aristocracy of land and blood and church. We explicitly forbade the development of that European curiosity on American soil. Ours was to be a society of work and industry governed by ordinary people. It was to be an open society so far as laws and men could create it. An open political and social structure was also an open economic one, and the chance for change stemming from invention was always present. As we have come to learn over the long period of our history, technological change in an open economy is cumulative, never final. Change is the stimulus for further change.

There was a "practical" side to the American need for invention which was given by the physical environment of the new land. The kinds of agricultural commodities grown were not the same as in Europe, and indeed varied remarkably throughout the United States. The planting, tending, harvesting, transport and storage of the basic crops would stimulate the inventors endlessly. The same sorts of challenges lay waiting in the minerals, forests and waters. The physical challenge of America to man's inventive ingenuity was, and is, tremendous.

Given the physical environment and the state of the arts, invention might flourish. But "time is money" and both the planning of invention and the creation of machines and processes involves the command of funds to finance the movement of resources. In an open and changing society with its economic counterpart, the free market, the opportunity of personal profit for inventors made invention all the more congenial.

In the historiography of capitalism the profit motive has achieved a very nasty reputation indeed. It is crude; it is sinister; it is vulgar. The love of money debases the "higher" values and so forth. There is, of course, a long history of this line of thought going back to biblical times. A learned literature traces the emergence and transcendence of the profit motive in the modern Western world from the collapse of the medieval church in the face of the Protestant storm of the 16th century. Historians of American industry have pilloried the robber barons and the masters of capital for their heartless plundering of a nation and a people to satisfy the baser motives of private greed—and worse. It sometimes seems to the reader of that literature that profit is, *ipso facto,* a crime.

In a colder light, profit is a measure of something else. Profit is defined by economists as *total revenue minus total cost.* If efficiency in economic life has any meaning it must have a measure of some sort. The customary measure of efficiency (in the short run), under competitive conditions, is the net return to the factors of production employed—profit. Such a measure has no moral value. It is not good or bad. An enemy of capitalism such as Stalin found it useful; in his *Problems of Socialism in the U. S. S. R.* Stalin urged his industrial managers to pay close attention to their net returns over their outlays for factors of production, and to the employment of cost-accounting methods in the pursuit of efficiency thus measured. Recently, in the U. S. S. R., the measure of profitability has received even more emphasis.

The economist customarily assumes that men enter upon economic undertakings for economic reasons. It is useful to assume that they desire to "maximize" their profits. That is another way of saying that man, in the pursuit of economic betterment in a given situation, seeks to reduce waste of labor, capital, and materials by employing them to a minimum. The manufacturer knows what the buyer wants and at what price. Can he meet the price with any margin above cost? How large should the margin be? As large as possible without raising the price and losing the buyer, is the most efficient principle of production. If quality is lowered to increase profits, the customer goes elsewhere. Efficient production comes within the constraints of consumer demand and the prices of the factors of production. In such a market there are other conditions to be met. There should be perfect knowledge of the market by all participants; there should be perfect freedom of entry and exit of sellers and buyers—no single seller or buyer should be able to influence the "equilibrium" prices of goods and services. When such conditions are not met, elements of imperfect competition or "monopoly" exist and the rate of profit is no longer an overall measure of efficiency but of monopoly power and the absence of competition.

Clearly such perfectly competitive markets rarely can exist.

There are only close and not so close approximations. But it is an imperfect world. No one can say what is a "fair" profit and what is an excessive one—where "profit" becomes "profiteering." In the Middle Ages attempts were made to say what a "just" price was. We have given that up except in the curious conditions of public utilities.

If an inventor was greedy, prospective profits spurred him on; if he had other motives as well, profit gave him the wherewithal to achieve his ends. Through "profit" American economic growth was guided by the dollar and cents choices of the people. It is not paradoxical, it is the natural economic corollary of an open society. Such a system may not build roads and schools and hospitals. But it builds better mouse-traps. For invention, the demand for better mousetraps is critical.

The "state of the arts" could provide method for creativity as it did for the Mormon church builders. But the creative efforts of others also could be a lesson and an inspiration to the aspiring inventor. The state of the arts was a fund of knowledge available to all who had a scientific or mechanical aptitude, and who had the opportunity, willingness and ability to tap it. If the physical environment was a source of inspiration to men with an inventive turn of mind, the technical environment was even more of a stimulus, for it was ever changing, ever presenting new problems, the solutions of which simply generated more problems. Thus has our complex technical society grown.

In the long history of the economic development of the United States certain conditions favoring the emergence of specific sorts of inventions coalesced and inspired and made possible the contributions of invention. Combinations of the physical challenge, the state of the arts, profit and other motives, enabled men of invention to make their permanent contributions to the nation's progress. The work of the idealist made improvement possible; the inventors were many times the instruments of that improvement.

CHAPTER 4

Eli Whitney and American Technology

> I have not only the *Arms* but a large
> portion of the *Armourers* to make.
> Eli Whitney, 1798

The years of Eli Whitney's life were from 1765 to 1825, from just after the French and Indian Wars to the opening of the Erie Canal. In that period the nation won its independence and passed from a delicate and stormy infancy to a sturdy economic youth. Whitney was an inventor of machines. He was one of a small group of men who planted on the American shore the skills necessary to produce a self-sustaining flow of technological ingenuity. It was a rare gift which enabled the new nation to grow industrially, raising productivity per man as new techniques were introduced, providing every American with an increasing supply of resources to be used in building the national economy. Without men such as Eli Whitney our economic development would have been immeasurably slower, depending altogether upon borrowed ideas. The interplay of markets, investment and invention would not have produced that burgeoning economic virtuosity which became so quickly the virtual birthright of every American. Without the generations of stubborn and independent "Yankee mechanics" at the beginning, our history would have been a far different tale.

It is easy now to use facile phrases like "processes of invention" to describe our technological beginnings. But to do that is to miss the whole point. It was not a matter of blind "processes" at all; it was a matter of men, one at a time, individuals who saw possibilities for improvement and found the opportunity to make changes. There was nothing automatic about it; the world is filled today with nations, with millions upon millions of population, that never had their Whitneys; nations whose histories comprise dismal catalogues of economic frustration and backwardness. Their development even today is blocked by lack of inventiveness, even where natural resources exist. Such problems seem as ridiculously simple to us as they seem insurmountable to those who do not have an efficient technology and have only the faintest hopes of acquiring it.

Whitney's story begins when America was not so favored in technology, when it was a "backward" country in that respect. In fact, at the end of the American Revolution technological backwardness seemed, in the eyes of discerning Europeans, to doom the new republic to a humble role indeed in the affairs of nations. It was the contribution of Whitney, and others like him, to liberate us from technological backwardness. We begged, borrowed and stole ideas. But we had men of original invention too. That was our good fortune.

Whitney's story also contains the seeds of the great national disaster, the Civil War. It was Whitney's fate to contribute fundamentally to the economic success of Negro slavery in the South, as well as to the rise of an industrial technology in the North. Someone else might have invented the cotton gin—many claimed the honor—but it was Whitney whose contrivance launched King Cotton on its turbulent career. That is always the danger with a Prometheus, even a primitive one. A machine is neither good nor evil; the men who use the machine determine what its moral impact will be. Some things, at least, do repeat themselves in history.

I

At the end of the 18th century, Great Britain was the main country which had achieved substantial economic development so far as the factory system was concerned. But, unlike the situation in our own times, Great Britain in the late 18th century was in no mood to provide technicians, teachers, information or anything else to aspiring backward countries such as the United States. The same was true among the Continental powers wherever mechanical skills existed. Great Britain contained, and was attempting to keep, most of the newly developed techniques which, since about 1750, had been transforming the British land in the classic Industrial Revolution. But even then the British were hoarding relatively little, since technical knowledge was still crude. Moreover, the hoarding was not very successful either in keeping ideas or skilled men in Britain. Newton's *Principia* was available, and publications of mechanical principles were becoming daily more commonplace. The whole family of machinery and machines to make machines was tiny, in its infancy. The range of application of tools and mechanical energy to production was growing but still primitive. In those times, even if a nation started from "scratch" it might not be too far behind the leader for very long. An inventor of tools and machines might reasonably hope that his own creations were as good as a similar object anywhere. They might also be the *only* ones of their kind.

In such circumstances the United States very quickly joined in the mainstream of industrial development—if at the edges at first. As a serious competitor to Britain, as well as a powerful supplier of raw materials and as a growing market, our quick appearance after the American Revolution was a remarkable achievement. It is doubtless true that inventive genius is distributed randomly throughout the human race. It is nevertheless clear that only a handful of nations have been fortunate enough to realize the potential of native inventive genius. America realized the potential of many great inventors. The early ones like Oliver Evans, Eli Whitney, Simeon North and Robert Fulton had a hard enough time of it, but did not fail altogether. Consider what we were, economically, at the end of the 18th century.

It is important to bear in mind that Eli Whitney's America was a very small-scale affair in many respects. The United States in 1790, two years after the adoption of the Constitution, contained 3,929,000 people, roughly as many as modern Philadelphia. At that time Great Britain had about 14,000,000; Spain had 10,000,000, and France 27,000,000. Compared to the main European powers the United States was unimportant so far as population alone counted. Little Portugal with 3,400,000 was close to the new American republic in population. More than one out of every seven persons in the United States was a Negro slave, with the vast majority of those, 657,000 out of 697,000, living in the South. The median-sized household contained more than five persons (compared to three today) and the median age was about fifteen (compared to thirty today). The nation was overwhelmingly a farming society, with only 5½ percent, or 202,000, of the total living in urban areas. Only Philadelphia and Boston contained more than 25,000 people; the cities of any consequence were the seaports. The population, except for Kentucky and Tennessee, was situated in the coastal states. Virginia, with nearly 750,000, was the largest, followed by Pennsylvania with 434,000 and North Carolina with about 429,000. (Virginia then included the present state of West

Virginia, and North Carolina included the present state of Tennessee.) It was a young, rural society based upon the large family, self-sufficient farming and a small commerce. It was hardly prepossessing. It was Jefferson's "Arcadia."

The armed forces of the country were composed of 718 men on active duty, of whom 46 were officers. The Federal debt, mainly a legacy of the Revolution, was $75.5 million; the whole Federal expenditure in 1789–91 was $4,269,000, of which $2,349,000 was interest on the debt alone. Since there were few taxes of any sort, customs duties provided virtually the sole source of income for the Federal Government. The total employment of government officials was a few thousand. The First Congress was in session in 1790 at the nation's capital—Philadelphia, and that Congress, with just 106 members, passed 118 of the 144 measures introduced. It all seems Lilliputian compared to the sorts of "national numbers" Americans have since regarded as typical. In our foreign trade of 1790, $23 million worth of imports (with England by far the largest supplier) just overbalanced the $20 million of exports (with England taking more than a third). There was a net capital inflow of about a million dollars, and the balance of services made up the rest. Our exports were mostly primary products—tobacco, rice, some wheat and naval stores. We mainly imported manufactured goods. We had little of consequence in the way of manufacturing.

The new nation's financial arrangements were even more quaint. In 1790 the struggling commercial activity of the new republic was financed, to the extent that American finance was involved at all, by four commercial banks, one of which, the Bank of Maryland, was chartered in that year. There was a Bank of Pennsylvania (chartered in 1781), a Bank of New York (chartered in 1784) and the Massachusetts Bank (chartered in 1784). The Federal Government was to enter the banking field in 1791 with the nation's first attempt to conduct central banking, the First Bank of the United States.

The money system was simple chaos, with foreign currencies holding precedent; not until 1792 was a national monetary standard established by Congress. The inflated Continental currency was still in circulation; during the years of the Confederation (until the new Constitution was ratified in 1788) many of the states had issued their own paper currencies. All such paper fared poorly in exchange against foreign coins, although efforts were under way to reform the currency. Bills of exchange, domestic or foreign, representing the movement of commodities were better "money" than domestic currencies. In many places the need for a circulating medium reached ludicrous proportions. In 1789 the provisional state of Franklin (soon to be Tennessee) proposed to pay His Excellency the Governor 1,000 deerskins; the Chief Justice was to receive 500 deerskins; the Attorney General 500 deerskins. A county clerk was worth 300 beaver skins a year, the Members of the General Assembly were to get a *per diem* allowance of three raccoon skins, and a justice of the peace could charge one muskrat skin for signing a warrant. In the more sophisticated areas, trade was invoiced in British currency, but the price of that currency varied widely even against coins, depending upon the state of the market. As Ross Robertson put it in his *History of the American Economy*, the price of anything "could be arrived at only after an agreement had been reached as to the medium of payment." First you decided what you were going to use for money, then you worried about price.

Roads were scarce, rivers and the sea providing the only dependable routes for transportation. Except for production of clothing and tools at home, there was no important manufacturing. The new republic faced outward, to England and Europe. Its future hardly excited the ordinary statesman, and indeed it was widely believed in Europe that the United States would soon subside into a permanent stagnation now that the nourishing ties with the mother country had been cut.

This belief was buttressed by the realization that a great change in the affairs of British manufacturing had taken hold, a development simply beyond even the imagination of the agrarian Americans—the Industrial Revolution was churning up old England in a way that it had rarely experienced. Fundamental improvements in British manufacturing were already beginning to sweep that nation far beyond all others as an economic power; not yet so powerfully as later, but enough so that the English recognized the change in the balance of economic power and were taking measures to protect their advantage.

Important improvements in metallurgy were already productive; by 1788 there were fifty-nine coke-using furnaces in blast in the British iron industry, and coke-refined iron was nearly equal to that refined by charcoal in the output of iron bars. The great innovations of Dud Dudley, the Darbys of Coalbrookdale, John Smeaton, Henry Cort, Thomas Newcomen, James Watt, the Cranage brothers and iron-master John Wilkinson were already history, or rapidly becoming so. As a result, iron was being smelted in Britain with coal, in blast furnaces with a constant blast pressure powered by steam engines, and rolled mechanically. In textiles, John Kay's flying shuttle, James Hargreaves' spinning Jenny and Samuel Crompton's mule had speeded enormously the processes of manufacturing. Richard Arkwright, the "Barber of Bolton," had successfully established large-scale factories making yarns. In 1785 Edmund Cartwright's power loom was patented, and the age-old weaving of cotton cloth on hand looms was about to become an oddity (although the power loom was decades making its effect universally felt in textiles). Skilled mechanics and engineers found occupations in the new British industry, and their skills and innovations reinforced each other in an explosion of technological progress. Britain was on the edge of that economic, and therefore political, pre-eminence which would soon make her the world's first power and its legendary workshop. British exports in 1790 were over £18 million, perhaps five times the value of American exports.

The British also exported men, but the skilled ones were "encouraged" to remain at home. The United States was always fortunate about immigrants. In Samuel Slater the British exported the wrong man. In 1790 he set up shop in Rhode Island for the manufacture of cotton textiles. Slater had been a workman at the firm of Arkwright & Strutt in Milford, England. He had memorized the main features of Arkwright's machinery and would soon (1793) set up Almy, Brown & Slater, the first extensive textile factory in America. This was a beginning, and reinforcements were on the way. Eli Whitney was in his second year at Yale in 1790, and was the oldest member of his class. He would soon, in 1793, produce the cotton gin, the first of his inventions which would put the United States on the road to vast economic development. Whitney would live to be the much-disputed father of "the American System of Manufacturing"—the origins of mass production.

II

Joseph W. Roe, in his *English and American Tool Builders*, noted that as an inventor Eli Whitney was greatly favored by his Yankee origins: "He came from that best school of mechanics, the Yankee hill farm." Whitney was born in Westborough, Massachusetts, on Dec. 8, 1765, and died Jan. 8, 1825 in his sixtieth year. His lifetime thus spanned the period of the Revolutionary War, the Louisiana Purchase, the War of 1812 and the beginnings of the great movement of Americans across the Appalachian barrier. Whitney witnessed the beginnings of the American nation as a political and economic entity; the years in which the initial patterns of economic and political growth were established. In many respects, modern America still bears identifiable characteristics acquired in those years: for example, the love of machines and gadgetry.

Whitney came of typical Yankee stock. The family was originally English and settled near Boston. The grandfather, Nathaniel Whitney, had moved from Boston to Westborough some 20 years before a son, Eli (the father of our Eli Whitney, who might also have been called Eli Whitney, Jr.) was born. There were ten children in that family.

Eli Whitney the inventor was the eldest of four children. His siblings were named Elizabeth, Benjamin and Josiah. Their mother never recovered from the birth of the youngest and died when Eli was only 7 years old. There was later a stepmother, a widow, who, according to Elizabeth Whitney, had two "silly" daughters who lived in the home with the Whitney children. The stepmother was not remembered kindly by the four Whitney children. The father was more or less the town intellectual. He could write better than most, had a farm and was also an office holder and justice of the peace. Most important, he kept a small workshop which contained a forge, tools and a lathe.

Information about the young Eli Whitney is scarce. But modern scholarship has produced some interesting fragments. Jeanette Mirsky and Allan Nevins, in preparing their book, *The World of Eli Whitney,* were able to examine some of the family papers and get some information about Whitney's childhood. Also some of it is known because of a sketch of Whitney written by Dennison Olmstead, a friend and contemporary, a few years after Whitney died. From such evidence it appears that certain of Whitney's adult traits were apparent in childhood: he was awkward, laconic, yet firm and decisive. But most of all, he had a highly independent mind and a perfect willingness to follow his own curiosity. Young Whitney, according to his sister, was slow to read and disliked farm work (which included at 11 years of age, watering sixty head of cattle before going to school each morning). But

Whitney was gifted at mathematics and applied himself regularly in his father's workshop. That is obviously where the story of Eli Whitney begins. Invention, so an old saying goes, is the besetting sin of the mechanic.

The Whitneys, like other enterprising Yankees, found prosperity in 1776–83. The American Revolution was a seedbed for early American manufacturing. With supplies cut off, or nearly so, for eight years, many country workshops took advantage of inflated prices to enter into relatively high-cost production of goods which ordinarily would have been imported. These new home manufactures mainly did not long survive the end of the war and the return of foreign competition but, while the war lasted, the country workshop did a good trade. During that time the Whitneys made nails.

After the Revolution, Eli Whitney turned briefly to the manufacture of hat pins, making equipment to draw the pins. Ambition led him beyond the country forge, however, and he determined to get a formal education. Yale was to be the college. First he had to learn enough to pass Yale's entrance exams. This he did by the simple expedient of enrolling at Leicester Academy and at the same time hiring out as a school teacher. Whitney used his education at Leicester Academy instantly, selling it as he acquired it. His father was committed to help pay his expenses at Yale—about $1,000 was needed to take him through. His teaching earnings were $7 a month plus board, and he clearly would not have earned enough to pay his own way. From his earnings, he had to pay his expenses at Leicester, where resources were so sparse that the principal and associate preceptor shared a bed. But by the spring of 1789 his father made some funds available and in April young Eli was matriculated at Yale at the age of 24, in a freshman class of forty-three students. Before matriculation he had been privately tutored in mathematics by Elizur Goodrich, professor of both mathematics and divinity. In the late 18th century, a man at Yale might still wear both those hats in comfort.

Yale and New Haven were eye-opening experiences. New Haven was then a town of a few thousand. It was a time when flocks of passenger pigeons flew over the town and blocked out the sun for hours. Although Whitney announced that he would study for the law, he took advantage of Yale's scientific instruments and books—Yale then had "some reputation" in "Pneumatics, Mechanics and Electricity." Whitney was a mediocre student and had a hard time of it financially, but he was able to do the work, borrowing enough money from his father to pay his debts, and graduated in September, 1792.

A Yale alumnus, Whitney was now certified an educated man. He also shared the great first experience of millions of American "college men"—he had no job. His father, who was by then hard-pressed financially, informed Whitney that he could not help to establish him as a lawyer. In desperation, the young man turned to his old profession, teaching, and by October, after suffering a shipwreck and a slight case of small-pox as preliminaries, was on his way to Georgia as a private tutor to the family of a Major Dupont, for a stated salary of 80 to 100 guineas a year. He had been hired for the post by Phineas Miller, a Connecticut gentleman who had gone South earlier as tutor to the family of Gen. Nathanael Greene, and who, watching his chances, had formed a "tender relationship" with the general's widow which in 1796 evolved into marriage.

Phineas Miller was destined to be Whitney's partner, and the Widow Greene's money was to provide their resources. It appears from the surviving evidence that Catherine Greene was slightly "fabulous." She had wintered with her husband at Valley Forge and now occupied Mulberry Grove, the estate of the last Royal Governor of South Carolina, which had been confiscated and given to Greene by his grateful compatriots. Widow Greene apparently knew just about everyone worth knowing in post-revolutionary America. She summered in Rhode Island, and her soirees there were great favorites with the neighboring lights. At Mulberry Grove she seems to have dispensed a lavish hospitality, and the local gentry was much in evidence in her parlor. She took an immediate liking to Whitney and, when it appeared that Major Dupont's job was less than a solid offer, and probably paid less than half the money Whitney had been told about in New York, Whitney took the easy, and the more intelligent, way out. He lingered a year or so with Catherine Greene and her gay companions —by invitation.

A young man of intelligence, education and ambition sud-denly cast upon loose ends in the South Carolina of late 1792 and the growing season and harvest of 1793 might be expected to study his own and the surrounding country's prospects pretty closely. Whitney was astonished at the amount of labor involved in growing rice. He also discovered a way to break one of the great economic bottlenecks in American history. In a letter dated Sept. 11, 1793, Whitney wrote:

> There were a number of very respectable Gentlemen at Mrs.
> Greene's who all agree that if a machine could be invented
> which would clean the Cotton with expedition, it would be a
> great thing both to the country and to the inventor.

The kind of cotton grown on the mainland, with its small green seed and short staple, was not suited to the techniques used in separating the long-fiber, black-seeded "sea island" cotton then enriching the Caribbean planters. The short-staple cotton thrived on the mainland but was expensive to prepare for market. The South having no real staple crops except tobacco and rice, the lack of economic alternatives made for a dismal future prospect. The system of Negro slavery, already fastened firmly onto the South, was a steady threat to free labor. The slave system also held the prospect of ruin for the slave owners and of social chaos, it was believed, if agriculture did not continue to absorb labor in large numbers, thus using the mass of Negro slaves.

In 1793 Whitney gave the nation a unique gift and a nemesis. The cotton gin which he invented gave the South its great staple, provided the nation with a bounteous export commodity, assured industrialism in England, in New England and its introduction elsewhere. The cotton culture induced the vast expansion across the Gulf states into Texas of a one-crop plantation system. The cotton gin also made Negro slavery immensely profitable and cursed the nation that used slaves with degradation, a deep political rancor, war, a degenerate social and political system which enervated half the nation, and a racial discrimination which still pollutes the rest. There is, by the way, no evidence that Whitney cared a fig about slavery one way or another.

By late September of 1793 Whitney had a model of his cotton gin completed. He was immediately offered 100 guineas for it. Like many great ideas the cotton gin was extremely simple. Wire hooks on a roller reached between wooden dividers, edging a bin full of cotton and tearing the cotton off the seeds. The seeds, being too large to pass through the space between the wooden dividers, dropped into a hopper. A large brush cleared the cotton from the wire hooks. The cotton could be taken easily and quickly from the brush by hand and pressed into bales. All moving parts could be run by turning a single crank, belts and pulleys making the necessary connections. The gin also could be run by animal or water power.

The numbing simplicity of the gin, "teeth wires working

through slats and a brush," bespoke a mind of great ingenuity in its inventor. The numbing simplicity of the gin also meant that anyone who saw the model (and Catherine Greene evidently showed it to virtually all of her *aficionados*) could copy it. The potential profit of the gin meant that it would be copied, copied at once and used. After all, by Whitney's own conservative estimate, one man working a gin could do the work of ten men a day. A man and a horse could do the work of fifty men using the old methods, and that ". . . without throwing any class of people out of business," as Whitney put it.

The great importance of Whitney's first invention meant that its author was automatically in trouble. Miller and Mrs. Greene formed a partnership with Whitney, "Miller & Whitney," in which they agreed to divide the profits in half. Miller was to establish gin sites and handle the Southern end of the business; Whitney was to go North and build works to manufacture and improve the gins. Also, Whitney was to get the patent under the terms of the new patent legislation, a scheme for the encouragement of native inventive genius. Whitney and Miller evidently planned to gin *all* the cotton in the South. They would return one pound of clean cotton to the planter for every five pounds of raw cotton delivered, seeds, dirt and all. About two-thirds of a pound of the clean product were to go to Miller and Whitney as their fee, and the rest was waste. Such were the initial plans. Whitney went North to get his patent application processed and his works going, and the cotton planters who saw the little machine at the gay Widow Greene's establishment went home to copy it, to "improve" it, but above all to use it; and without paying a third of their pure cotton to the partners for ginning their crops. Miller and Whitney were already against the wall.

From that point on, the story of Eli Whitney and his cotton gin is one of continuous, sometimes comical, sometimes tragic, complications. Whitney applied to Secretary of State Thomas Jefferson personally for his patent, and it was finally signed by President George Washington on March 14, 1794. The patent's processing was held up by difficulties in making a working model in New Haven (where Whitney was setting up his works). Whitney's affairs were further complicated by an outbreak of yellow fever in Philadelphia which killed 4,000 and cleared the Federal Government out of the city along with the 17,000 inhabitants who fled.

Initially there seemed to be grounds for optimism. Once the

New Haven works were organized, some cotton cleaned by a newly built gin sold in New York at the highest price. Building the works was slow. Whitney had to make his own tools, even his own lathe; machinery was invented on the spot for drawing and cutting and bending his wires. But gins were built, packed in standard crates (indicating that they were all copies of a single model) and shipped.

The South's response to the gin was so tremendous that the partners were immediately aware that they could not conceivably produce a sufficient quantity (this might have led them to adopt immediately, as they eventually did, the idea of licensing the process; but they also might have realized that their initial schedule of charges, which would have given them ownership of a third of the nation's cotton output each year, was ridiculous). Miller wrote Whitney to speed his efforts: "Do not let a deficiency of money, do not let anything hinder the speedy construction of the gins. The people of the country are almost running mad for them . . ." More than that, "the people of the country" were making their own. Why wait for Miller and Whitney who could not provide gins even if the Georgia and South Carolina planters waited for them to arrive? Anyhow, who knew if a patent monopoly could ever be enforced?

In the fall and winter of 1794 New Haven was gripped in panic as scourges of scarlet fever, yellow fever and another pestilence, unknown to medicine then and hence never named (sore throat was one of its properties), swept the city. Then in 1795 Whitney's New Haven works burned to the ground, tools, gins, materials and all. He had to begin again. The planters did not wait. By 1797 there were an estimated 300 illegal copies and "improved" cotton gins (with round saws substituted for the wire teeth) at work. Miller & Whitney went to the courts in desperation. They failed to get redress. The patent law was so worded that they could not sue. The law would need to be reworded before they could realize any of their rights under the patent. The fact that Phineas Miller had been involved extensively in the Yazoo land frauds did nothing to ease the problems of Miller & Whitney among the Southern planters or in the Southern courts.

Meanwhile a revolution in Southern agriculture was under way. In 1784, when eight bales of American cotton had been landed in Liverpool, they were seized for having been falsely documented; cotton clearly could not be grown on the American mainland. But it was, and the crop was spreading; only the cleaning held back exports. American cotton exports in 1791 had been 189,000 pounds; a year later the figure was down to 138,000. Then, in 1793, 487,000 pounds were exported; in 1794, 1,601,000 pounds; in 1795, 6,276,000 pounds and, by 1800, nearly 18,000,000 pounds. That was roughly a hundredfold increase in a decade.

In 1800 Congress finally changed the wording of the patent law so that Miller and Whitney could sue those who had used their process without leave. Vindication was still years away, and Miller, who died in 1802, never lived to see it. The South Carolina Legislature voted to pay Miller and Whitney $50,000 for the patent rights but soon rescinded the law. Whitney induced North Carolina and Tennessee to pay him for his rights (users of the gin paid a tax to the state, and the state paid the patentees a lump sum). When he went to South Carolina in 1804 for a hearing on the reinstatement of his claim, Whitney was actually arrested and jailed by his opponents. South Carolina finally declared him "the true original inventor" of the cotton gin and paid the firm of Miller & Whitney for the rights. Those who had used the gin without leave had been able to claim that they had "different" models; that Whitney hadn't invented it anyhow; that it had been seen in England, and so forth. In one courtroom the noise of the gins working next door drowned out proceedings in which the defendants denied that Whitney's gin was being used.

The firm of Miller & Whitney hired lawyers and kept up suits against all unlicensed users and finally got a judgment in their favor in Georgia for damages of $2,000. Judge Johnson's decision of Dec. 19, 1806, became justly celebrated.

> The whole interior of the southern states was languishing and its inhabitants emigrating for want of some object to engage their attention and employ their industry, when the invention of this machine at once opened views to them which set the whole country in active motion.

In that year 167,000 bales of cotton were produced in the United States against a mere 6,000 bales the year before Whitney invented the gin.

Doubtless someone else would have invented the gin if Whitney had not. But in fact it was Eli Whitney who invented it and gave the South its future. In Roe's opinion: "There is not another instance in the history of invention of the letting loose of such tremendous industrial forces so quickly." In 1812 Congress, expressing the profound esteem of a grateful nation, refused to renew Whitney's patent. Whitney said in later years that he lost more actual cash than he gained in cash income from his cotton gin. In point of fact, in 1797 he faced the bleak prospect of a New England bankruptcy because of the gin.

III

The nemesis grew without any further help from Eli Whitney. The country's cultivation of cotton continued to mount and, with it, the scourge of Negro slavery. The gin made possible the expanded output of large-scale plantations. The new Southern lands, as the politics of 1803–60 emphasize with deadly clarity, were opened largely by planters using slaves. The cotton culture was the slave culture. The United States was becoming inextricably sunk in a barbarism almost too rank to be discussed in polite company. Hence the South's "peculiar institution," the breeding, sale and commercial depletion of human life, was clothed in a gossamer of sophistry. But few believed it. Jefferson wrote the fears of many in prophetic words:

> I tremble for my country, when I reflect that God is just; that his justice cannot sleep forever.

The time of "his terrible, swift sword" would come; in combining cotton and slaves America had made a fatal blunder.

On the surface one might have supposed that the slave system was safe, in spite of the moral scruples of abolitionists and others. It was, after all, the basis of the world's largest industry, cotton textiles. Great Britain's textile industry grew rapidly on the basis of American raw materials; so did the American and Continental industries. Samuel Slater's legatees were given a powerful boost by Whitney. The United States came to supply three-fourths of Great Britain's raw cotton imports, and by 1860 Great Britain consumed about half of the whole world's cotton supply (the American share was just under 20 percent). By 1860 Britain contained nearly 3,000 factories employing just under 400,000 power looms, with nearly half a million people employed *directly* in cotton, and as many as three times that number in dealing with the commodity outside the factories. The estimated value of British cotton output was £60 million by 1857, more than the value of output of the British coal and iron industries combined.

In the North, United States investment in cotton textile output was without a peer in *any other industry* up to 1860. From 1790 to 1860 the consumption of cotton in America rose eight times as rapidly as did the population. Cotton manufacturing in the Northeast was done by individual corporations, several of which had capital of more than a million dollars each. It is small wonder that cotton was "King" to the South. In 1860, of total American exports worth $316 million, $192 million, or more than 61 percent, was raw cotton. Of total British exports of £140 million in 1850, £52 million, or more than 37 percent, was cotton textiles. The South had good reason to expect the North to heed her wishes and good reason to hope for powerful British support.

The South also had good reason to fear her future. Slavery was turning the region into a nightmare of force and cruelty. The slave trade was as old as the South itself: the first slaves were landed at Jamestown in 1619—that famous year, famous for the House of Burgesses in Virginia. After 1811 the African slave trade was abolished in the British dominions (the climax of decades of legislation). From 1808 on, the United States had prohibited imports of slaves. With the Ashburton Treaty of 1842 the English, French and American governments agreed to search the seas for slavers. The peculiar institution had become the source of bitter politics in the United States, pushed by abolitionists in the North. The great compromises held off any fundamental split until the election of 1860, but the South by then was hopelessly enmeshed in slavery. The South's population was 11 million and nearly 4 million, just over one in three of the population, were human property. If it was dangerous and debasing, slavery was also profitable.

The Negroes had not increased as rapidly as had either the white population or the demand for hands in the exploding cotton culture (U. S. output just about doubled in the last decade before 1861). The breeding of Negroes was big business. By the end of the 1850's a number-one field hand 15 to 21 years old fetched more than $2,000 in Texas, $1,900 in Georgia and $1,300 to $1,400 in South Carolina and Virginia, the prime breeding areas. In 1800 a prime field hand had been bought for as little as $500. By the end of the 1850's children cost that much. "Wenches" brought from about $1,000 up, and a pregnant girl, age 18, cost the purchaser $1,500—but he got the "colt." "Best grown girls" cost $1,275 to $1,375. A lot of 39 separate sales, "mostly children," averaged $566 each. Even a "small girl" cost as much as $880 although small girls were selling in the late 1850's for as little as $350 if they were very small. A skilled slave cost a lot more; in 1860 a good carpenter might bring as much as $4,000. In 1859 the "entire Pimlico stock" was sold at an average price of $750, old folks, infants and all, 235 of them.

The young republic had become a disgrace to Western civilization and well might the cultured European sneer at "Brother Jonathan" (as "Uncle Sam" was then known in the European press) with his "whips" and "niggers," some of them nearly as white as Brother Jonathan himself, and for obvious reasons. There was clearly no end to it. As the consumption of cotton soared, demand rose—at one point in 1856 Great Britain was down to a mere three weeks' supply for her mills; the Manchester Cotton Supply Association of 1857 was the consequence. The British desperately wanted a new source of cotton. American slaves, in spite of great efforts to raise output, could not provide a steady dependable supply. In trying though, the American planters reaped the profits of slavery, both from breeding slaves and working them. Then the American planters reaped the whirlwind.

Some American historians have tried to believe that the Civil War was all a tragic mistake. It wasn't necessary. Surely there was something "wrong" economically with slavery so that by 1860 it was being crushed by various weights. Something as morally outrageous *must* be inefficient. Alas, that was not so. Lincoln's soldiers killed a thriving, growing system. Alfred Conrad and John Meyer, in a celebrated paper published in 1958, "The Economics of Slavery in the Ante Bellum South," destroyed the comfortable notion that Southern slavery was not profitable, a position which they called "a romantic hypothesis which will not stand against the facts." Conrad and Meyer argued that slavery was "profitable to the whole South" (an argument that has been disputed), that the slave economy contained no "self-destructive" economic problems, that the slave economy could have been expanded farther (west and south into Mexico and South America), also that the reopening of the slave trade, a political cry of the 1850's, was always possible. Finally, that the South might even have developed her own industrial structure on the basis of cotton and slaves and the use of slaves in factories. In such conditions, said Conrad and Meyer in a general way, ". . . the elimination of slavery may depend upon the adoption of harsh political measures. Certainly that was the American experience."

The American Civil War was a harsh solution indeed.

Whitney's gin need not have necessarily spread slavery; cotton is grown without slaves and has been for a long time. But the American tragedy was that Whitney's invention did in fact give slavery a new lease on life. Doubtless the shade of Eli Whitney is comfortable enough about it. Whitney lost money on the cotton gin; the profits were for others. After 1812 Whitney cut his losses and showed no further interest in cotton. By then he was well along with the large-scale production of muskets, and the South was mostly a bad memory to him. Miller was dead, and Catherine Greene would soon be.

IV

The question of the origins of mass production has always been volatile enough to raise steam among historians. While it is generally agreed that Eli Whitney deserves the major share of the credit in America, his fellow Yankee, Simeon North, has had many supporters for the laurels. Some historians, moreover, would deny to Whitney any major claims. Of course there are also English claimants, notably the famous engineer, James Nasmyth. Jefferson interviewed a French artisan who was making musket locks with interchangeable parts some years before Whitney's famous demonstration in 1801. There were others. Also Whitney gets credit for many machine-tool inventions, notably the milling machine, which have been disputed, and still are, for that matter. All this, while useful in the interests of strict historical accuracy, is partly futile since nearly any machine has an antecedent, and partly these deliberations obfuscate the main issue, that mass production, wherever invented (Russia perhaps?), is known to history as a peculiarly American contribution, and it was Eli Whitney who pioneered mass production for all to see. But remember that, for us, Whitney is a surrogate, representing all of his colleagues.

There is no doubt that Whitney invented his own methods without copying others, and that he invented machine tools that he had never heard of from outside sources. The same may probably be said of Simeon North, and doubtless a number of other Yankee mechanics now lost to history. It was the American genius that put the system of standardized output and interchangeable parts to work for the good of mankind. The colonial seaports, the mines, forges and blacksmith shops of a hundred Yankee towns, the workshops of young America —these were the cradles of American invention. Eli Whitney is the best known of the early American inventors, and deserves his honors, but the environment in many ways helped a man like Whitney.

H. J. Habakkuk, in his *American and British Technology in the Nineteenth Century,* noted that within a decade of Whitney's death the Yankees had already seized the new system of manufacturing. Americans were desperate to reduce the amount of skilled labor involved in manufacturing. Their easy access to farm land, and hence to a poor but proud economic independence, meant that wages had to be high to hold men in workshops and mills. If productivity were not as high as that of foreign firms, enterprises would be priced out of the market by importations. Labor had to be economized, and it was as early as 1835 that Richard Cobden saw labor-saving machinery that was superior to contemporary English methods at work in a machine shop and woolen mill at Lowell, Massachusetts. English technicians visiting America in the 1850's:

> . . . reported that the Americans produced by more highly mechanised and more standardised methods a wide range of products including doors, furniture and other woodwork; boots and shoes; ploughs and mowing-machines, wood screws, files and nails; biscuits; locks, clocks, small arms, nuts and bolts.

Habakkuk noted that in the 1850's the English were still far ahead of Americans generally in manufacturing, but that the "greater stress on standardisation" in America was sufficiently striking to seem to call for some sort of an explanation. In the 1850's the famous British small arms factory at Enfield was forced to equip itself with machine tools made at Windsor "in the backwoods of Vermont."

In general, Professor Habakkuk argues that access to a huge market in the United States enabled American manufacturers to concentrate upon quantity production. It was quantity production that justified the extensive capital equipment needed to engage in mass production. That is doubtless a good argument, and it applies both to Eli Whitney and to Simeon North. But not in the way Habakkuk imagines. The *private* American market was small, far smaller than the English one. Whitney and North had a large-scale market independent of the small private sector: they started their separate establishments to make arms for the Federal Government. Difficult as it may be to swallow for those who like to credit *the whole* of American enterprise to individual efforts in a free market, the narrow truth of the matter is that "the American system of manufacture" got its main initial nourishment from that age-old friend of the manufacturer, the government contract.

In 1797, at 32, Whitney was near bankruptcy. The firm of Miller & Whitney was getting nowhere with its cotton-gin business; the fire had made it necessary to expend more resources for rebuilding, and the workmen had little work to keep them going. Miller had married Mrs. Greene in 1796 and had become extensively involved in other interests. Whitney was near the end of his financial rope and faced the prospect of closing down his New Haven shops. He needed to manufacture something for somebody. Only the Federal Government seemed to be a possible market. First Whitney tried to get the government to finance him in the construction of a screw press. Then he offered to make 15,000 "stands of arms," muskets, bayonets, ramrods and other equipment. A benevolent and interested government saved him. He got a contract for 10,000 stands in June, 1798, with a $5,000 payment on closing the contract and arrangements for advancing funds as they were used up. The total contract was worth $134,000. That would keep his works going for years. Whitney, a Federalist who disapproved of the "democrats," was perfectly blunt about his good fortune. He wrote: "By this contract I obtained some thousands of dollars in advance which has saved me from ruin."

The making of muskets was strictly a custom job before Whitney. America had few arms makers. Armories had been established at Springfield and Harpers Ferry, but they could not arm the country. During the Revolution, the French had supplied us; the Battle of Saratoga was won with the aid of French muskets imported just in time. They had been made in 1763, and in 1798 Whitney was given two of them to use as models for new production. In Europe the musket maker, whose trade was passed down from father to son, was the descendant of the medieval armorer. Each musket was a work of art in itself. Repairs were serious bottlenecks to any army's operations, and hence the horse and sword were still worthy opponents of an infantry whose weapons, likely as not, would not fire after protracted use and could not be repaired in the field to any great extent. In 1812, for example, Whitney reported that the British had a backlog of 200,000 stands of arms awaiting repairs.

There were two problems that Whitney determined to avoid, both of which stemmed partly from the single fact that the

United States had few skilled gunmakers. First, if all the guns were made alike, then any parts from any musket could be used to replace the same parts on any other musket; all the parts coming from the same mold, no skill would be necessary to make replacements. Second, since there would be no skilled workmen involved, Whitney must devise tools which could be operated by the unskilled and yet do the job. As he wrote to Oliver Wolcott, the far-seeing Treasury Secretary who awarded Whitney the contract on faith:

> One of my primary objects is to form the tools so the tools themselves shall fashion the work and give to every part its just proportion—which when once accomplished, will give expedition, uniformity and exactness to the whole.

There were already models in life from which he could take his inspiration:

> . . . the tools which I contemplate are similar to an engraving on copper plate from which may be taken a great number of impressions perceptibly alike.

Whitney had used standardized methods with the cotton gins. In fact, as a schoolteacher he had built an enormous model of a quill pen, put it in front of the classroom, and had the students cut their own quills accordingly. The idea of interchangeable parts and mass production must have been with him a long time, possibly since the days of the nails and hatpins at Westborough. Mill Rock, or "Whitneyville," Connecticut, near New Haven, was purchased in November 1798, and by January 1799, the first of Whitney's buildings was up. He went to Massachusetts to get his workmen. He believed that their lack of experience would be of advantage to him. He proposed to make muskets like none other, and it would be better if his men did not have to unlearn old habits. Ignorance in workmen employed in manufacturing was made a valuable asset—over a century later Henry Ford would be advancing Whitney's arguments when mass production meant, not only interchangeable parts, but the assembly line as well.

When Whitney received the contract for his muskets in 1798, the United States faced the threat of war (with France at that moment) and could not arm herself. Whitney's proposals sounded fantastic, but Wolcott was willing to gamble on him and, a year later, on Simeon North. The country was desperate for the means of its own defense. When Whitney needed more money than his contract called for, and needed it quickly, Wolcott wrote to him: "I should consider a real improvement in machinery for manufacturing arms as a great acquisition to the United States." Whitney got an additional $10,000 (the leading citizens of New Haven signed a bond for him). It took a good deal of courage for Wolcott to advance more money on such a scheme. Whitney was engaged in making machinery to produce the various parts of the musket. He was not making muskets at all, but tools to make parts. Who knew if anything would come of it? Joseph Wickham Roe, in his *English and American Tool Builders,* noted that the experts were scarcely friendly and foreign experts, as some of the denser ones would do for a hundred years, laughed off the whole idea of improvements in manufacturing coming from a mere Yankee: ". . . Whitney's determination to introduce this system of manufacturing was ridiculed and laughed at by the French and English ordnance officers to whom he explained it."

Wolcott resigned in November 1800, and Whitney, worried about the future of his contract (his delivery rate was then zero), went to Washington in January 1801, and gave his personal demonstration in Jefferson's presence. He took some prototypes of his musket locks, disassembled them, piled the parts in a heap, and the gentlemen present were invited to reassemble the locks. The government officials got the point quickly. After that Whitney was called by such titles as "the Artist of his Country." The contract seemed to be safe enough. Jefferson said that he had seen such musket-making by a French workman, and had tried to get him to come to the United States. The workman, a man named Leblanc, was hired by the French Government, according to Mirsky and Nevins. Leblanc clearly had the idea of interchangeable parts, but nothing came of it in France, while the idea was destined to spread quickly in American industry. It is known that by 1808 North was using the same methods. The system was adopted at the government armories, spread from there throughout the New England arms trade and, as we already noted, by the 1830's was found extensively in other industries.

The secret of Whitney's system was, of course, the machinery and the tools. He had to devise and invent his own tools as he went along; since he was the first man to try such methods, there was nowhere to turn for help. Being both a theorist and a practitioner, with talents ranging all the way from those of a mathematician to those of a blacksmith,

Whitney was able to do the work himself. It took longer than he or anyone else had contemplated. After all, 26 contractors had offered to supply the government with 30,000 muskets; most of the contracts were for fewer than a thousand, some for one thousand. These would all be made by tried-and-true methods. Whitney was obligated to make 10,000 muskets by no known methods. His whole scheme was widely viewed as being simply fantastic.

It was 1809 before Whitney completed his contract for the first 10,000 muskets. The long days and years wore on with the lonely bachelor working at his private industrial revolution. The picture of Whitney in his mature years is that of the familiar American mechanic, much overburdened with work, a mind which sought after details with relish, and a scolding, dry, matter-of-fact personality which, by being involved in *all* stages of business, was close to being overwhelmed. Whitney was a tall man, not much gifted with speech, but who wielded his pen with a nice flourish. He had an oval face, a long, hooked nose; his eyes were deepset, with eyebrows arched above them in an inquiring way. His small mouth turned up slightly at the corners and touched off a look of penetrating intelligence and humor. He lived in an old farmhouse at Mill Rock with his apprentices and a succession of housekeepers. His nephew wrote of these arrangements: "Uncle has a widow and an old maid to keep house for him; has got nine apprentices . . ." Sometimes there were more apprentices.

Whitney was always worried about his long bachelorhood, but with his tangled affairs, his shops and workmen to oversee, machinery to make, and his load of debts, he counted himself a poor marriage prospect and many times despaired altogether of finding a wife. Mirsky and Nevins published a letter written by Whitney in 1800 to a friend describing the inventor–manufacturer's life. It deserves an extensive quotation.

> I meet with many delays which I did not expect but cannot avoid. I am many times impatient and unhappy that I progress so slowly—at other times I look around & see that I have done a great Deal and feel more satisfied with the progress which I have made. But my principal solace arrises from the consideration that my machinery and modes of doing the work will certainly answer a better purpose than any heretofore devised. I shall be able, by and by, to work well & to execute with Dispatch. My works will be much superior to any in America & I have the vanity to suppose they are equal to any in the world. But I have a great task before me and when I shall

get thro' God knows. I live constantly out at my place & tho
I have at least forty People around me every day—I am yet
a solitary *Old Bachelor*. I am incessantly occupied in my
Business and after laboring hard thro' the day I am obliged
to leave ten times so much undone (which ought to have been
done) as I have in the course of the day accomplished, and
lie down under a load of cares ready almost unsupportable &
still accumulating. I flatter myself. . . . I am so totally en-
grossed at home that I am almost entirely ignorant of what
is passing in the world. I think of my friends sometimes—sigh
for their society—hope, wish, and believe that they are happy
—curse the stars that have imposed Ixion's task—& return
again to the Wheel.

A few months later he described himself as a ". . . forlorn Old
Bachelor—making guns yet—always in a Dam'd hurry without
bringing anything to pass." There was the outlook of the
Yankee inventor. The world was bleak and inhospitable, but
life in it was a test to be overcome. "The Giant, Despair, Lived
in Doubting Castle, but Christian was not Long delayed there."
Failure, ever present, was something one understood and
worked to avoid. The result was economic progress, but that
was not the driving force. We sometimes speak of the "Puritan ethic" when we try to understand the old Yankees who
built the first stages of American industry. There was among
the "proper" Yankees a simple compulsion to work.

Whitney's loneliness and troubles were augmented by the
fact that he was often in poor health. At this distance, given
the surviving evidence, one sees Whitney as a brilliant, slightly
crotchety and fussy general factotum of his works, living in
his farmhouse, served by his cook and housekeeper, working
in his shops, chasing after runaway apprentices, making occasional trips to New Haven and Washington; a man of affairs,
but a man living in a world mainly of his own making. Whitney was generally esteemed by the great men of his day. He
was the "Artist of his Country" for good reason. In a country
that small there were not many Whitneys. He knew personally
every President down to John Quincy Adams. If one could
sympathize with Whitney, it would be because he simply had
too much to do and could get no dependable help. He took
in his nephews to solve that problem (they later managed the
business). Whitney had a capable pen and his Chesterfield-like
letters of advice to a nephew at Yale, on the importance of
good manners, are charming. That nephew, Eli Whitney Blake,
wrote of an uncle who was simply rushed in all directions for
time.

In those early days, when technical expertise was so rare an item, Whitney's advice and experience were regularly sought by others in the same and allied businesses. These activities took up some of his "spare" time, and he was also a regular advisor to the government armories. But, however much time he may have spent on activities in an advisory capacity at Mill Rock or elsewhere, it is clear that the middle two decades of his life were simply absorbed in his inventions and in overseeing his works. Whitney knew the theory of classical mechanics and had the rare ability to reduce it to practice in his inventions. However, his affairs could not run themselves and he had to manage closely.

The fact that he had no assembly line, but simply a series of shops, meant that a great deal of time was wasted. The continuous assembly line, the moving creation, was still a thing of the far future. What Whitney had at Mill Rock was a very efficient division of labor and specialization making interchangeable parts. The separate shops did the work, essentially, of stations on the modern assembly line, but not continuously. Since muskets were inordinately unsusceptible to mass production (few linear or rectangular shapes), and Whitney made no attempt to deviate from his French musket design (he invented machines, not firearms), his presence was constantly required to keep production bottlenecks open. In addition to all these matters was the main problem of invention and adaptation of machinery to replace skill. It is small wonder that Whitney had little time for social life or even for marriage, if wooing the bride was going to require time away from Mill Rock.

Most early American industry got some sort of special treatment from the government; for example, tariff protection (a form of subsidy) for textiles. Was it necessary for government to give American industrial capitalism such boosts at the beginning? Probably so, and for fairly simple reasons. Even if a market had existed for the finished product (and that is not at all certain in Whitney's case), there was the overwhelming problem of getting capital. It is useful to recollect that even the cotton-gin factory had been built by "government" resources and "British" at that. General Greene's estate, out of which Whitney got his first capital funds, had been provided free to the general by the government of Georgia from the confiscated properties of the last British Governor. Since those properties were largely provided by British taxpayers and consumers, by a tortuous, but relatively uninterrupted chain of events, British Government resources and Georgia government resources went into the cotton-gin factory, just as American Government funds built the musket factory.

Whitney had found in the cotton-gin experience that industrial capital, long-term credit, was desperately short in early America. Indeed, to a large extent Americans relied upon Europeans to provide long-term funds for economic development until late in the 19th century. Credit available for industry in Whitney's time was mainly relegated to commercial, short-term credit. Had there been a money market like London, such credit might have been used, as it was commonly used in England, for long-term investment by renewing short-term paper and getting finance bills. But in America there were no such opportunities. In the early days at Mill Rock, Whitney pointed out that he could get sixty-day credit readily,

> . . . but that is not a credit which, in the present state of the business can be of much service to me. . . . In mercantile transactions, where quick turns are made and the property for which the credit was obtained can at all times be turned into cash, commodities may be purchased with safety on this short credit. But manufacturing is very Different. More time is required to work up raw materials . . .

To have capitalism you needed "capital," so Whitney built his works on advances from the Federal Government. There had to be someone willing to wait, as the Federal Government ultimately was willing to wait, a long time, before the payoff. One also needed capitalistic thinking, a calculation of risk and waiting in the process of investment, so Whitney the inventor had to explain to government officials that capital was "time and trouble." Investment had to be made in failure as well as in success. The work needed time and thought and equipment before manufacturing could actually be done. For example, of the manufacture of sabres, Whitney argued that he would need funds for experimentation.

> A substitute for European skill must be sought in such an application of Mechanism as to give all that regularity, accuracy . . . which is there affected (sic) by a skill . . .

There is no complete record of the number and kinds of machines, tools and combinations created by Whitney. His nephew, Philos Blake, wrote to his sister that all of the machinery was run by water power; that there was a drilling machine, a boring machine, a machine to make screws, a shop to make gun stocks, a blacksmith shop and a trip-hammer shop. Whitney evidently was fairly informal about his inventions. In fact, after the fiasco with the cotton gin, he actually withheld his creations from his countrymen. We do not know how extensive the withholding was. He viewed his situation with some humor—anger and outrage had passed over into a measured cynicism. In 1815 when the Springfield Armory needed a machine to turn musket barrels Whitney wrote:

> If yours should not answer the purpose I have one which I invented more than ten years ago . . . I would put it into operation if I could see any prospect of a fair remuneration for the invention & expence, & risque of the Experiment. But the probability is that some person would contract to make all the barrels & not only take advantage of my invention but intice away the workmen. . . .

Whitney is ordinarily credited with inventing a milling machine some time before 1818 (although some scholars dispute that he made the *first* one). The materials presented in the Mirsky and Nevins biography show overwhelmingly that Whitney's factory was his own creation, whether or not anyone had done anything like it earlier. Once, in defense of his work on a government contract, Whitney bared his breast on the extent to which his own manufacturing establishment was the creature of Eli Whitney, and *only* of Eli Whitney:

> I am indebted to no man for planning or executing any part of my machinery. I have always directed in person the intire detail of the business both as to the form and modes of working. The more difficult branches I have executed myself.

Doubtless Simeon North, his son Selah and the handful of other early machine-tool builders could have said much the same thing about their own works. It was the case that the independent American technique and tradition of mass production came from the inventor–manufacturer–mechanics. That it spread powerfully in the United States may have been a function of the market, as has been suggested, but one cannot avoid the conclusion that, at the beginning, the character of the Yankee experimenting mechanic, with his craving for efficiency, together with the high price of skilled labor, led Americans to mass-production techniques.

Whitney never had an easy time of it. He did finally marry. Constance Green, one of his biographers, noted that he had tried to arrange a marriage for himself by mail in 1800, possibly with a daughter of Catherine Greene. After that he gave up for seventeen years. As a result he passed his adult years virtually alone, and, indeed, it is asserted with "no personal life" at all beyond his shops and his multifarious affairs. Finally, in 1817, at 51 years of age, he took a bride: Henrietta Edwards, spinster daughter of his friend Pierpont Edwards, and granddaughter of New England luminary Jonathan Edwards. A son, Eli Whitney, Jr., was born in 1821 when his father was 55. There were two older girls, born in 1817 and 1819, while another daughter died in infancy.

The arms business never seems to have given Whitney much joy. Unless he was a natural comic, his letters seem to indicate that he always was crushed by the scope of his involvements. In 1818, urging his nephew Eli Whitney Blake (whose education at Yale had been financed by Whitney) to come and help at Mill Rock, Whitney wrote:

> . . . my affairs . . . have been so numerous, embarrassing and oppressive that I am almost driven to delerium. I find it almost impossible for me to accomplish one half of that for which there is the most pressing necessity.

After completing his first contract in 1809, Whitney had been faced again with the prospect of closing down his works, but was tided over when he managed to get contracts for arms for some state militias, including New York and Connecticut. In 1812 he got a contract from the Federal Government for another 15,000 muskets. This job was not completed until 1822, and brought Whitney more irritations. During most of the War of 1812 he feuded with Callender Irvine, Commissary General, an upstart politician with large hopes. For a long time Whitney could not even get the government to take delivery of the finished muskets, suffering impertinent rebukes by petty functionaries for his troubles. Several times he had to go to President Madison for his money. The trouble stopped after the British burned Washington (on Aug. 24–25, 1814, to the unfeigned delight of many in New England who wanted the capital moved back to Philadelphia, its "natural" location). Then the works were guarded and the muskets wanted.

Whitney finally thrived on the arms business and became a New Haven capitalist, with investments in everything from banks to ships. He knew the important people of Yale and New Haven, and many seemed to have formed attachments for the solitary, querulous arms maker. Ill luck did not entirely desert him, however; he began suffering from an enlarged prostate gland in 1822. He evidently made his own flexible catheter, which gave him some relief from the pain. The trouble got worse in 1823 and Eli Whitney died Jan. 8, 1825, after nearly three years of painful suffering.

Whitney's company lasted as an independent entity until 1888 when it was absorbed by Winchester. The nephews and the son ran the works in their turns. Whitney's great contributions were almost lost. After the cotton gin, he lost his appetite for patents. His machines therefore are not known to us except that modern research has indicated that in almost every line of early machine-tool building Whitney is mentioned among the first pioneers. He shared his knowledge with his friends and associates, possibly most of his ideas too. But he never made machine tools for profit. Whitney's wife seemed to sense that her husband was in fact an historic figure and therefore took the trouble to preserve his papers (taking care to destroy all references to herself; three of Whitney's biographers think Henrietta Whitney was no belle). That gave the historians their chance in later years, although friends of Whitney like Dennison Olmstead, who published a memoir of the inventor in 1834, tried to keep his memory alive.

The great Yankee inventor seems somehow to be a man of our own times. In his passion for systematic production processes he would have felt at ease in any automobile or appliance or electric motor factory—or at an aircraft factory or shipyard in World War II, or at a guided missile plant in our own unhappy era. Wherever interchangeable manufacturing is done, there is the spirit of Whitney. Mass production, it is charged by some, has reduced American life to a dull sameness, has taken the "quality" out of workmanship. But *only* that system of manufacture has ever been capable anywhere in the world of raising the workers' productivity, and the living standards of most people to levels appreciably above subsistence. Everything has its price.

Perhaps the greatest irony in Whitney's life was the role his works played on both sides in the Civil War. He gave the Southern economy and its slave system a reason to expand and a way to thrive. He then contributed to the North's industrial growth and hence to its ultimate ability to crush the slave system. Whitney was not only the archetype of the American genius, but his works reflected the driving and largely incompatible modes of life which developed in America up to 1861. The tragedy of 1861 had its seeds planted at the very beginning of the country's development.

CHAPTER 5

The Wizard of Menlo Park

Results? Why, man, I've gotten a lot of results.
I know several thousand things that won't work.
                          Thomas Edison, 1900

Edison spent nearly a decade in the search for a dependable storage battery which could make electric automobiles competitive with those driven by internal-combustion engines. As he said, he found several thousand things that wouldn't work. He never did find one that would, but he did develop a superior storage battery for other uses. It was not untypical of the man, or of his career, that his battery project ended up far afield of the original goal. Very little that he did came directly from long-term plans, and many of his major inventions led to consequences other than those for which he had labored. Moreover, some of his major inventions were, so far as he was concerned, purely fortuitous and not even well understood by Edison himself, or anyone else at the time of the discovery.

Edison was an adventurer in strange seas. He traveled in the company of many kindred spirits, and they fought among themselves for the prior claims and rights of discovery. Many of them gained very little from their discoveries, but mankind gained the whole host of new industries which arose from the harnessing of electrical energy and from induced chemical change, industries which made so powerful a contribution to the transformation of everyday life from the epoch of the steam engine and animal motive power.

In the age of Eli Whitney we saw industrial invention in its infancy in the United States. In Edison's lifetime we see the growing stream become a torrent. The number and virtuosity of the inventors of the late 19th century became a legend— too much of a legend in fact, because, although the pace of invention never slackened, the very number and complexity of them overwhelmed the minds of the publicists and historians. As a result, the old-time inventors became congenial specters of a rustic past, and the notion arose that, whereas there was now an age in which the individual inventor had been displaced by research laboratories, there was in the 19th century an "heroic age" of invention. It is a myth, both parts.

In that myth of the "heroic age" of invention Edison holds a special place because he was supposed to be the "last" of the great individual inventors. And because of his lack of formal education and his Barnumesque personality, he gained a special place in the hearts of his countrymen. He is mainly known as just a common man who used his head about things. Eli Whitney had been a Yale man, and Edison's great rival, Alexander Graham Bell, was not only a university man but a college professor as well. Intellectuals. Edison gloried in his role as the practical man among the eggheads. Actually it is odd that Edison saw himself that way, since he was a complex man of singular genius. It is even odder that so many were taken in by his "common man" image. Very few men in history could have surmounted his background and risen to a great role in the world. What is nearer the mark about Edison is a remark made by an American writer that "Edison was the last great hayseed." He was a great hayseed, but what an uncommon hayseed he was!

I

Thomas Alva Edison was born Feb. 11, 1847, in Milan, Ohio, and died Oct. 18, 1931, at West Orange, New Jersey, in his eighty-fifth year. When he died, well over a thousand patents had been entered in his name. They include the phonograph, the incandescent electric lamp and a whole system of electrical generation and distribution, a workable motion-picture camera, patents to improve telegraphy and the telephone, patents to separate iron from ore by electromagnetic devices, patents to make prefabricated concrete houses. He tried to make a helicopter; he had discovered principles of primary importance in the development of modern electronics; he invented the direct forerunner of the mimeograph. He made an improved typewriter, a workable electric locomotive and a multitude of other inventions from the simplest household gadgets to giant electric dynamos. He also took a flyer in patent medicines. At the height of his powers, between his first patent in 1869 to his 1,328th in 1910, the average number of patents applied for by Edison came to one every eleven days. He had assistants working for him, and they gave him credit for involvement in every invention.

Edison's mind was bursting with originality and invention, and even at the end he was trying to develop rubber from goldenrod for his cronies Henry Ford and Harvey Firestone (he had bred out, by Mendelian methods, a goldenrod plant 14 feet high that yielded 12 percent rubber).

As was the case with so many inventors, nearly everything Edison invented was disputed by someone or just stolen outright. It is said by some that Edison did his own share of such piracy. Like Whitney before him, Edison stopped patenting intermediate inventions in order to try to keep his competition honest. In his old age, he ruefully said of the patent procedure that it was simply "an invitation to a lawsuit." It cannot be denied that Edison knew a great deal about patents.

Edison came from an "old American" family (not as old, however, as rumor had it at one time, that he was of Aztec descent) and his progenitors had suffered through British colonial policy like a drunk in a revolving door. His paternal ancestors seem to have been strong-willed and unbending about their affairs, especially about politics. His great-grandfather, John Edison, came to New Jersey from the Netherlands with his widowed mother in 1730. A solid, middle-class citizen, he was on the losing side in the American Revolution and, in 1783, with some 35,000 other Tories, was expelled from his country by the victorious republic. He settled first in Nova Scotia and then, in 1804, moved with his son and grandchildren to Ontario, where Thomas Edison's grandfather, Samuel Ogden Edison, was a farmer (old John Edison lived until 1814, and died in his ninetieth year).

Edison's father, Samuel Ogden, Jr., was cut from the family's hard-woven cloth, joined in Mackenzie's Rebellion against the government of Canada in 1837, and was forced to flee on foot across the border to the United States. He settled first at Milan, Ohio, where he operated a lumber mill. The Edisons were Americans again.

The boy Thomas was the last of seven children born to Samuel and Nancy Elliot Edison. The melancholy statistics of 19th-century infant mortality were felt powerfully by the Edisons, four of whose children, two boys and two girls, died in infancy or childhood. As a baby, it is said that the unnatural size of Thomas Edison's head led to fears that he suffered from "brain fever." He was in fact a healthy and bright child who spent much of his time with his nose pressed against the window of the local steam-driven flour mill, watching the machinery, and who was publicly whipped by his father at the age of 5 for setting the barn afire "to see what would happen."

The Edison family flourished in middle-class respectability in Milan, where the family business grew with the settlement. However, in 1853, the new Lakeshore Railroad bypassed Milan. The town's prosperity had been based upon a canal link with Lake Erie. Now that advantage was gone, and Milan quickly lost four-fifths of its population, including the Edisons, who moved on to Port Huron, Michigan. Another venture was started, this time combining the lumber business with a feed and grain store. This project did not prosper, and the Edisons began to know hard times.

It was in Port Huron that young Thomas had his only bout with formal education—three months at the local school. His scholarly pursuits there ended abruptly when the schoolmaster pronounced him "addled" and sent him home (in later years the aging schoolmaster suggested to Edison, in a plea for charity, that Edison's father had not paid the school fees, and the grateful inventor replied with a check for $25). After that, Edison's mother, a former teacher herself, gave the boy his daily lessons at home, and he quickly showed the fierce aptitude for study which stayed with him throughout his life. "Inept" at mathematics, he was precocious at chemistry and mechanics, performing experiments described in adult practical-science manuals and filling the basement with wire, chemicals and discarded pieces of machinery. He remembered reading Paine's *Age of Reason* as a 12-year-old and the ". . . flash of enlightenment that shone from his pages." Edison's father said that the boy never really had any childhood, preferring his experiments and machines to children's playthings. There was a further reason for not having a childhood, since he was soon enough "on his own." He never really had much time to be a child.

As the Edison family fortunes declined, the necessity for extra earnings increased, and at 12 years of age Thomas applied for, and received, a concession to sell food and newspapers on the Grand Trunk Railroad between Port Huron and Detroit. The distance was 126 miles, and the boy left Port Huron at 7 A.M. and was back again at 9.30 P.M. During the day-long layover in Detroit, he ransacked the libraries and explored the town, visiting the various machine shops, forges and other points of interest. He had no memories of hardship with such a schedule. There is a photograph of him at about this time—a bright, "cheeky"-looking lad, with twinkling eyes, a wide-awake expression on his face, and a firm jaw.

Those who recalled him in later years told of a kind of rail-roading Huck Finn, alive to every possibility, pursuing multifarious schemes in selling food and newspapers, but also in boy-fantasy adventures directly connected to running a train (Edison recalled being allowed at the throttle by a congenial engineer). Edison had his chemicals on board (in the baggage car), acquired a small printing press and published his own newspaper on the train, *The Weekly Herald,* which reported local news and gossip (he was once pitched into a nearby river by one of his subjects), accounts of Civil War battles, prices of eggs, beans and potatoes, all done with a flourish and in somewhat random grammar and spelling. The little paper sold at eight cents a copy and had a circulation of 400. Edison showed a precocity for business as a lad that he did not possess as an adult. In later years he said of his days on the Grand Trunk:

> The happiest time of my life was when I was twelve years old. I was just old enough to have a good time in the world, but not old enough to understand any of its troubles.

He remembered the trains loaded with Norwegian immigrants heading for North Dakota and Iowa. Young Edison was, for all the world, a "real go-getter" on the Grand Trunk. It was at this time that deafness began to afflict him. It was evidently the result of a childhood fever and grew nearer to total deafness as Edison grew older. The oft-told stories that his deafness was due either to being pulled aboard a caboose by his ears or, alternatively, having his ears boxed soundly by an irate railroad conductor after his chemicals caught fire, have no basis in fact, according to his most recent biographer, Matthew Josephson. It is true, apparently, that the train conductor did throw the boy's chemicals off the train once and for all.

Edison's mercantile and journalistic career ended abruptly when he was 15, in 1862. It was then that he was given the opportunity to learn telegraphy after he rescued the 3-year-old son of J. U. Mackenzie, the Mount Clemens, Michigan, stationmaster, from the path of a moving boxcar. Mackenzie, out of gratitude, offered to take Edison as a boarder in his home long enough for him to learn the telegrapher's trade. As a portent of the future, young Edison appeared with a perfect set of telegraph instruments he had made in a Detroit gunsmith's shop. There was a pressing demand for substitute telegraphers as the Civil War raged.

Edison learned his trade well enough, and quickly enough, to be on his way as an itinerant telegrapher in his sixteenth year, early in 1863. There followed five years of wandering from town to town, largely on foot, during which the young man's mind slowly formed out of that of the precocious boy. Edison traveled throughout the Middle Northern states, starting at Stratford Junction, Ontario (where his negligence nearly caused a wreck, forcing him to flee back across the border), and going on to Adrian, Michigan, and Fort Wayne and Indianapolis, Cincinnati and other cities. He lived in cheap boarding houses, slept in Western Union offices on the floor, and is remembered generally during this period of his life as a serious, unkempt young man in shapeless shoes and no overcoat, cold and hungry in winter, who spent most of his money on electrical apparatus and chemicals, using the premises of his employers' businesses as makeshift laboratories. Not surprisingly, he was often fired, since his interests in his employers' affairs were strictly limited by his own much deeper interest in "what made things tick." Matthew Josephson phrased it tactfully in his biography of Edison: "In most cases he was fired, either because he was not amenable to office discipline, or was at times inattentive to his duties." In fact, he seemed to do pretty much as he pleased and, if it cost him a job, he moved on gladly enough. He was scarcely a budding "company man."

By the end of the war, the peripatetic telegrapher was earning top wages ($105 a month) and went into the South. He worked in Memphis and Louisville and, in 1867, was again in Cincinnati. He continued to conduct experiments on the company's time and with their telegraphic equipment. He continued to be discharged regularly for these actions. At one point, down on his luck, he got as far as New Orleans in a scheme to go to South America. A major turning point came in 1868 when, after a fruitless stay in Port Huron at his parents' home, Edison arranged through a telegrapher friend for a job in the Western Union office in Boston. He arrived there after a long, partly snow-bound, train ride. From that time on, the telegrapher "on the bum" began to emerge as a prodigy of invention.

II

Men who worked with Edison in Boston recalled a disheveled country bumpkin, uncouth of manner, an excellent telegrapher, and a "loner" who lived in the cheapest quarters, incessantly reading and experimenting with whatever materials he could gather. He was overflowing with ideas for improving the telegraph, and his colleagues apparently were treated to a running account of those ideas whether they wanted to be enlightened or not. Even then he evidently liked publicity about his ideas—later on, his penchant for newspaper releases got him into tight corners again and again. He admitted that he worked best under pressure, and his serial descriptions of his ideas constituted a method of building up steam.

Edison was steadily educating himself in the mysteries of electricity. He continued to experiment with chemicals, too, and his hands and clothes were often stained and burned by chemicals and acids. Edison said that Michael Faraday's *Experimental Researches into Electricity* first introduced him to a systematic knowledge of the subject. Faraday's pages were clear and were meant for the interested reader. His accounts of his discoveries were written lucidly: "His explanations were simple," Edison said. Faraday had turned Edison back toward the extant body of scientific information after years in which he had shunned formal treatises; Newton had alienated him. At 15, Edison had tried to make a "scientist" of himself by attempting Newton's *Principia* and received a body blow; he had seen, for the first time, "the wilderness of mathematics" which ". . . gave me a distaste for mathematics from which I have never recovered." It was different with Faraday; here was a man writing of electricity at its very beginning as a useful source of power, patiently describing each experiment and its consequences with the object of educating his readers.

Edison jumped for the bait and pored over the volumes day and night, reproducing the experiments and learning about electrical forces by repeated application of principles. There was nothing unusual in this process except that the person doing it was totally without "schooling." For a man with no formal education this method was probably the best for learning known applications of electricity. Such knowledge was by itself no bridge to the future. It was left to the divine spark in Edison's mind to carry him from the known into the unknown, into the field of invention. But given that Edison did possess a powerfully original mind, the repeated experiments doubtless contributed critically to the mixture of hypothesis, fact and intuition out of which original ideas ultimately were formed. The originality in Edison's mind enabled him to store up unrelated bits and pieces which could be put together in a new way—an "inspiration."

We know very little about the mainsprings, biological, social or intellectual, of originality in thought. But as Jewkes, Sawers and Stillerman put it in *The Sources of Invention*, the "essential feature" is that the path to original invention is not known and that the less ". . . an inventor is pre-committed in his speculations by training and tradition, the better the chance of his escaping from the grooves of accepted thought." The argument can easily be taken to the extreme that "ignorance is strength." That is emphatically not so, but scores of scientists, scholars, inventors and innovators have attested to the virtues of *some* degree of ignorance so that what cannot be done is not too well known. Edison had plenty of ignorance, some formal knowledge (from his reading), and through experimentation was learning about the possible as well as the impossible. The main factor in his favor, however, was *not* his ignorance— something he and his admirers too often forgot in the later years of triumph—but rather, it was his driving determination to overcome that ignorance which made the bridge to the future. The method of experimentation is, after all, an accepted way to gain knowledge. So is the reading of books. Edison was blazing no new trails by reading Faraday and reproducing his work, but he was giving himself an excellent education in certain fundamentals of physics. The first fruits of that education came quickly.

In 1869 Edison received his first patent. During his spare time in Boston, the young man nosed about in the various shops making telegraphic equipment. He occupied a corner in the shop of one Charles Williams—the same shop to which Alexander Graham Bell would soon come to conduct his experiments with the "speaking telegraph." Edison was soon immersed in experiments to send messages two ways on a single wire. The premature publication of "success" in these experiments in a technical journal brought a general (and limited) offer of financial support, and Edison received his first patent, for a telegraphic vote recorder. Naive in the mysteries of parliamentary processes, Edison had reasoned that it would "speed things up" if the statesmen could instantly record "yes" or "no" verdicts on bills introduced for discussion and vote. He contrived machinery to do this, two buttons on each solon's desk connected to a recorder of the results near the speaker's chair.

To his genuine dismay, Edison discovered that politicians

were appalled by his invention. After failing to sell his device to the Massachusetts Legislature, he took it to Washington, giving a demonstration to a Congressional committee. It was patiently explained to the young inventor why efficiency is not necessarily a virtue in the discussion and horse trading that is invariably a part of the legislative process; in fact, that minorities find their rights to some extent in the inefficiency itself, getting the chance to be heard *because* of the amount of time involved. Edison himself said that his experience with the vote recorder determined him to invent in the future only those devices which had a good prospect of finding a market. After that, knowledge for its own sake played only a negligible role in Edison's work. Perhaps he believed that about his experience with the vote recorder, but, considering his career as a whole, it is difficult now to conceive of him as a "pure" scientist even had he nursed such ambitions. He educated himself only about scientific problems as they arose in his work and, more often than not, the "pure" scientist gets his formal education first, in a broad spectrum of science, and then moves out to the frontiers of knowledge in the world of research into narrowly specialized subjects.

Edison always liked to refer to himself as "only" an inventor. From the invention of the vote recorder onward, he nursed the ambition to make his way entirely on the basis of the commercial exploitation of the products of his own imagination. He searched for some "practical" invention and devised a series of improvements on the existing "stock ticker" which printed market quotations on a moving paper tape. A company was formed, machines were rented out and men were employed to string wires from the central office to the offices of the customers. But Edison soon fell out with his backers, and the patent rights were sold to an existing telegraph company. This was a serious setback. Worse followed, and after a series of failures with his telegraphic experiments, Edison, heavily in debt on his personal notes and without further prospects in Boston, borrowed enough money for boat passage to New York City.

It was late May or early June of 1869 when the 22-year-old inventor reached New York. He was broke, without even the price of a meal, and spent his first night walking the streets. L. S. Laws, inventor of a machine for telegraphic relays of daily gold-market quotations, had heard of Edison and allowed him to sleep on a cot in the cellar of his place of business, the Gold & Stock Telegraph Co. Edison was able to repair the

Laws machinery during a critical breakdown, and Laws, recognizing talent when he saw it, hired Edison at the handsome salary of $300 a month. Edison had now made his first profitable step in the direction of success as an inventor. Although there was some mechanical work involved in his job, he was mainly being paid just for his inventive powers. He continued to patent improvements on the Gold & Stock machinery and, further, devised equipment to transmit stock as well as gold quotations to the company's customers.

He was working at Gold & Stock in September of 1869 when the market was thrown into disorder by Jay Gould's attempt to corner the available gold supply. By the time the Subtreasury stepped into the market as a gold seller (an action Gould thought he had forestalled through his connections with high officials in the Grant Administration) the market was a shambles, and it took hours for the equipment at Gold & Stock to catch up with the market quotations. It was Edison's first experience with "high finance," although it was not his last with "Mephistopheles" Gould.

The young inventor's mind was deeply impressed by the gold corner of 1869, and the belief remained with him to his dying day that men who merely manipulated money in the markets were somehow dangerous to society. He never did try to comprehend the function of money and capital markets in a capitalist society, and in later years fed his ideas on the subject to his friend Henry Ford, who made an issue of it.

After the gold corner, Edison's employer sold out to Western Union, then a rising giant in the new communications industry. Edison made another attempt to make a living by his inventions alone. In October, 1869, a notice appeared announcing the commencement of the firm of Pope, Edison & Co., electrical engineers. Edison made improved machinery to transmit foreign-exchange rates at fees below those of Western Union. Accordingly, an offer of $15,000 was made by Western Union for the patents. Pope, Edison & Co. had three partners, all anxious to be bought out; Edison's share was $5,000. It was his first substantial earning from his inventions, and he promptly wrote to his hard-pressed parents offering them financial assistance. Edison was glad to see the firm dissolved. He wrote of the venture:

> I got tired of doing all the work with compensation narrowed down to the point of extinguishment by the superior business abilities of my partners.

The young inventor was immediately retained by Western Union itself. Within a year after his arrival in New York he had applied for seven patents on improved telegraphic equipment. Gen. Marshall Lefferts, the new president of Western Union, who was an engineer, recognized Edison as a "genius," said so, and gave him an open-end offer for his inventions. Lefferts knew that the industry was only just starting, that machinery was crude and untrustworthy, that significant improvements were bound to come, and that with Edison's brain committed to Western Union, the company could expect to gain a rapid technological lead over its rivals. Edison's fee was not fixed and, as the technical improvements came from him fast and thick, Lefferts decided that an arrangement had better be made. He asked Edison how much money he wanted as a settlement for all of his inventions to date for Western Union. Edison didn't know; why didn't the General make an offer? So the General did. Edison recalled it as $40,000 and said that at that moment he was ". . . as near fainting as I ever got."

The actual amount involved, according to Josephson (who examined the documents relating to the transaction), was $30,000—Edison was so careless about money that he could have easily remembered the amount involved with an error of $10,000. In his lifetime he made much larger errors than that with "mere money." Edison signed a contract, "as obscure as Choctaw," and was given a check. At the bank he panicked and fled when the teller asked him for some identification. When the young man reappeared at the bank, led by the hand, his check was paid out by the amused teller in ten- and twenty-dollar bills. Edison went back to his room in New Jersey with $30,000 in small bills bulging from his pockets and sat up all night with his hoard, fearing robbery and murder. The next day a friend took him back to the bank, where he was introduced to the wonders of a bank deposit. A man of some means in 1870, he actually knew that little about the ways of the world; he was less than a decade from his concession on the Grand Trunk Railroad, and in another decade he would be one of the most famous inventors in history.

Shortly after his first financial settlement with Western Union, Edison became a manufacturer of various telegraphic apparatus, including his improved stock ticker. Like Eli Whitney, he was an inventor and an innovator, and he was both on a much grander scale than was Whitney. But there was a fundamental difference in the external circumstances with which the two men had to contend. After the fiasco of the cotton gin, Whitney, working at the very beginnings of industrialization in the United States, was forced to rely largely upon the benevolence of the Federal Government for resources to carry on his experiments. By the early 1870's, however, the industrialization of the country was gaining momentum and Edison's inventions were financed by, and related to, the burgeoning private sector of the national economy. Certain industries like railroads were near their peak rates of expansion; others, like steel, were nearing a period of rapid growth. The new telegraph industry was just entering a period of expansion, change and rationalization.

S. F. B. Morse in America, and Wheatstone and Cooke in England, had evolved a radical change in human communications with the telegraph. (In many cases of invention, not the least Edison's main contributions, there are several claimants to priority, each country generously celebrating its own contributor. The Russians did not invent the custom.) In 1844 the first message had been sent in America from Washington, D. C., to Baltimore. The system grew steadily. The Morse code had been mastered by thousands, the Civil War having facilitated the adoption of the telegraph for more general purposes of communication. Moreover, linked to the railways, the telegraph had an automatic vehicle of expansion. With the laying of the Atlantic Cable in 1866, America was tied to Europe. In addition to railroads and private communications generally, markets in commodities, stocks and foreign exchanges were now linked by telegraph. The new industry had become an integral part of the expanding national economy. Even in Utah the "Lion of the Lord" exhorted his brethren to build the Mormon telegraph to link up with the outside world.

Representative data for the Western Union Co. show the extent of growth during the late 1860's and 1870's. Western Union had 2,250 offices in 1866, nearly 4,000 by 1870, 6,500 by 1875 and nearly 10,000 by 1880. Miles of wire owned by the company grew from 76,000 in 1866 to 234,000 by 1880. Messages handled in 1867 numbered just under 6 million; the number was nearly 30 million by 1880. Net income grew from just under $2 million in 1866 to $4.7 million in 1880, a mean annual rate of growth of about 10 percent. The data exaggerate the growth to some extent because of Western Union's absorption of already-existing companies, and because of technological advances which varied the capacity of existing equipment. But it is clear that it was an industry of growth, and as such made room for a man like Edison (several like him) to supply equipment.

Prof. Jacob Schmookler recently demonstrated from the record of growth of leading American industries that ". . . the evidence strongly suggests that the output of a commodity and invention relating to it vary together. . . ." Edison's initial attachment to the telegraph industry was a case in point. Part of the growing industry's resources were made available for the improvement and invention of equipment—invention was profitable. Time and again Edison's inventions, or the practical (profitable) introduction of them into the economy, were made possible by industrial growth. He thus had a great advantage in the expanding industrial economy of his time that Whitney never had.

The appearance of Edison as both a manufacturer and an inventor in the telegraph industry in the early 1870's meant that he was inevitably involved deeply in the competitive warfare that characterized those times. He learned to "play the game" and successfully profited from the rivalries of the tycoons until Jay Gould simply swindled him. Without getting too far ahead of our story, it is worth noting that when Gould finally got control of Western Union—partly due to Edison's efforts—the inventor gave up inventing telegraphic apparatus, saying that Gould would stifle growth in favor of monopoly profits and that further invention in telegraphic equipment would be pointless.

By the winter of 1871, Western Union had given Edison 1,200 orders for his improved stock ticker. To make these, General Lefferts gave the inventor financial support to set up manufacturing premises in Newark, N. J., sending along a trusted Western Union man named Unger to watch over Western Union's interests; accordingly, the firm was called Edison & Unger. Edison set to work interviewing prospects after advertising for "mechanics" and "engineers." About fifty men were hired initially. Some remained with Edison the rest of their lives, and were doggedly loyal to him. The loyalty was reciprocated. Edison was congenial with practical mechanics in a way that he could not be with others; there was a deep community of interest in the workmanship itself. But the men may well have wondered about the prospects of their employer during the interviews. John Ott, a long-time Edison employee, described the Edison of 1871:

He was an ordinary-looking young fellow, dirty as any of the other workmen, unkempt, and not much better dressed than a tramp.

In a letter written at the time, Edison, the populist, was describing himself grandly as a "bloated Eastern manufacturer."

Edison was no more of a "company man" in Newark than he had ever been. He hired men largely for their capacities for originality; watched for, and took for himself, new things which came out of the work on the stock tickers. He now had few illusions about the world he served. He wrote in his notebook about one device: "Invented by & for myself and not for any small-brained capitalist."

In the shop it was clear to the other men that Edison's mind was extraordinary indeed. Observations made by his workmen told of his great reliance upon his singular powers of intuition, the "nicety" of his solutions of problems, the "refinement" with which he made changes in equipment. There was also something uncanny about him. One shop assistant wrote of him at this time:

> He displays cunning also in the way he neutralizes or intensifies electro-magnets, applying strong and weak currents, and commands either negative or positive directional currents to do his bidding.

The legend of "the wizard" was starting in his own shop. But Edison's astonishing energy for work was also much in evidence. In 1871 a new kind of high-speed telegraph sender, invented by George D. Little, was brought to Edison. Little had sold his patent rights to a group called the Automatic Telegraph Co. One of the company's directors, George Harrington, brought the device to Edison, offering him a $40,000 advance if he would undertake to perfect the instrument and make it commercially feasible. This was the origin of Edison's famous (and ill-starred) "automatic printing telegraph." Edward H. Johnson, for two decades an associate of Edison's, described the beginning of the inventor's attack on the problem. The scene was not untypical and should, by itself, explain something of what Edison meant by his oft-quoted phrase that "genius is ninety-nine per cent perspiration and one per cent inspiration." It also shows how far off the mark is the widely held belief that Edison was strictly a blind-luck, trial-and-error inventor.

I came in one night and there sat Edison with a pile of chemical books that were five feet high when laid one upon another. He had ordered them from New York, London and Paris. He studied them night and day. He ate at his desk and slept in a chair. In six weeks he had gone through the books, written a volume of abstracts, made two thousand experiments . . . and produced a solution, the only one that could do the thing he wanted.

Edison had the automatic printing telegraph system perfected in 1873. In that year Jay Gould acquired control of Automatic Telegraph. He also controlled the much larger Atlantic & Pacific Telegraph Co. Gould had found the telegraph industry congenial to his talents, a fact that boded little good for the industry. When he bought control of Automatic Telegraph, he took over Edison's improvements and, to a growing extent, Edison's services. The inventor was now serving two competing masters, Gould and Western Union, and, accordingly, his affairs became complicated. In 1872 the firm of Edison & Unger was "wound up," but Edison continued working for Western Union along with his work for Automatic Telegraph. In the winter and spring of 1873 he contracted to make improvements in Western Union's central equipment, sleeping on the floor of the New York office. It was a marble floor and ". . . a very hard kind of floor to sleep on," he wrote. By then Edison had been married a year and a half, had a house on which he owed $10,000 and was pressed for cash to meet his weekly payroll. He went to England in the summer of 1873 in an unsuccessful attempt to get the British Post Office to adopt his new equipment.

When he returned in the fall, the Panic of 1873 was raging, and credit was virtually unobtainable. Edison was desperate after the profitless English venture; not only did he owe current payments, but his properties, including his home, had been attached. He had been working on a method of sending four messages simultaneously on each telegraph wire, two each way. This was the quadruplex system. Western Union would not pay. To get funds he played some office politics; he agreed to make its head engineer, George B. Prescott, his "co-inventor."

Edison, a man of enormous ego, later suffered the agonies of the damned whenever his great achievement was referred to as the "Prescott–Edison" system. By the summer of 1874 the new system was shown to be assured of practical application. In a single stroke Edison had multiplied Western Union's output capacity, but the company (probably also hard-pressed) still would not pay him. To keep his affairs going, Edison had continued to draw heavily on the funds of Automatic Telegraph, to whom, in desperation, he finally promised to sell his quadruplex telegraphy system.

It is clear that Edison was playing with great potential fire. But he sailed straight in. He intended to take care of himself. In the summer of 1874, Western Union still held back its payments for Edison's work, but Jay Gould at Automatic Telegraph helped out with a check for $10,000. That check saved Edison's house from the hammer and put the inventor deeply into the wily Gould's personal debt. Gould was now using some of Edison's equipment, but Western Union claimed the patent rights and got an injunction against Gould's Atlantic & Pacific Telegraph to stop their using the critical equipment, the relay system. Gould, always up to the competition, offered Edison another $10,000 to invent a substitute for the apparatus claimed by Western Union. Edison succeeded in time for Gould's company to ignore the injunction. Edison and Gould now were in each other's debt, or at least each had reason to be grateful for the other's existence. By November of 1874 when the quadruplex system was working for Western Union, Edison's hopes for compensation were dashed; Western Union still stalled on payment. It offered an initial $5,000, but Edison now needed much more to pay his men and hang onto his properties. Again he turned to Mephistopheles, and the beady-eyed little man gratefully replied with a check for $30,000 for Edison's part of the quadruplex system. Both Western Union and Atlantic & Pacific were now using the system, Western Union by Prescott's patent rights, and Gould by Edison's.

In the court battles which followed, Edison was flamboyantly excoriated by Mr. (later Senator) Roscoe Conkling as the "professor of duplicity and quadruplicity." Jay Gould, by one of his "little tricks," cut his losses, merging his Atlantic & Pacific with Automatic Telegraph, cutting the Automatic Telegraph stockholders and creditors (including Edison) off at the pockets. Edison, fleeced, entered suit against Gould, along with the other victims who finally won a judgment in 1906, long after Gould was dead, in the sum of one dollar each.

Edison had been "conned" by one of the greatest sleight-of-hand sharks in American financial history. But he had also made some money out of it, a fact of which the meticulous

Mr. Gould later reminded Edison. The inventor actually admired Gould because he was "so able in his line." He said of the financier that "his conscience seemed to be atrophied," but he went on to suggest that perhaps Gould's competitors had no consciences at all.

Western Union, more interested in profits than in spite, forgave Edison for his temporary defection and in 1875 began channeling research funds to him again for experiments on the improvement of telegraphy equipment. Edison finally quit working on telegraphy after 1881 when Western Union and Atlantic & Pacific merged, and Gould ruled it all. Edison had played the competitors against each other for nearly a decade, and had made it pay.

In those times, before the passage of the Federal anti-trust legislation, American capitalism rode out a rugged shakedown cruise as the national social fabric was stretched and changed to accommodate a whole new range of enterprise, industrial, financial and organizational. Invention was necessarily dependent upon the developing infrastructure of the new system, and Edison, however much a hayseed in many respects, used his native wit and adaptability to stay solvent. Nor should that have been surprising; the Midwestern Adam is not noted for his inability to look after his own interests.

Edison was involved in business and friendship with a whole range of the classic American tycoonery from Gould to Henry Ford and Pierpont Morgan. It was not a world for the faint of heart. There were not even clear legal bench marks at first, and business ethics tended to be marvelously flexible whenever the pursuit of profit conflicted with conservative notions of probity. Edison was no saint. He was a man who intended to have his own way, whatever the game. The picture of Edison using for his own ends the conflicts of the growing telegraph industry is one which becomes a familiar view in his life, in the cases of the telephone, the phonograph, the electric light, the motion picture and all the rest.

Did such involvement in worldly affairs interfere with Edison's inventive efforts? As he later said, when he left the electrical industry, he needed the pressure of competition to force him to invent. In fact, some biographers have argued that he preferred victory for its own sake, the sweet taste of the triumph itself, over all the monetary rewards he ever got from his work. He was thus a compulsive achiever. There is little evidence that he cared for anything more than the fame and prestige which came from his highly publicized triumphs of invention. And Edison was his own best and most constant publicity agent. It was the case, moreover, that he did not like to share his fame with other claimants.

III

In the spring of 1876, construction was progressing on the crude wooden-frame buildings of Edison's laboratory at Menlo Park, New Jersey, a whistle-stop settlement. The laboratory was to be devoted to the invention of useful (profitable) industrial equipment. Edison had cleared his debts, and had $20,000 in cash. He wanted to get out of Newark and the manufacturing business. Perhaps his experiences in the telegraph wars had given him a momentary urge for a more "ivory tower" atmosphere. He wanted to try again for his old dream, the life of the pure inventor. He had no doubts that he could make industrial research pay. He was then under contract again with Western Union, this time to experiment with sending sound by telegraph. He had many business contacts and had some notion of what his markets might be for patented industrial improvements. Edison said confidently that he would make a minor invention every ten days and a major one every six months. He was finally to achieve, for a little while, his ambition to make his living by invention alone.

He also may have wanted to get his family away from the city. On Christmas Day, 1871, he had married a 16-year-old employee at Newark, Mary Stilwell. A child (Marion, called "Dot") had been born within a year, and during the period up to 1875 his private affairs had been convulsed in the same money troubles that had plagued his business life. In other ways his married life was less than perfect. He was, by all accounts, a careless and unthinking husband to a young woman who comprehended little of his affairs. Their home life was irregular and haphazard, starting with the wedding day, when Edison worked halfway through the night at his laboratory. Later he would go weeks at a time without coming home, sleeping on the floor or in a chair at his laboratory whenever exhaustion at last overcame him. He liked to have his crotchety old father around (his mother had died in 1871 at Port Huron), and Sam Edison was evidently a bit strong for Mary's tastes. She was a good housekeeper and seems to have made Edison a comfortable home whenever he was in it.

Menlo Park was a solution of sorts. At least the laboratory would be within eyesight of the house. There was room there for a growing family (a son, Thomas Jr., "Dash," was born in 1876 and another, William Leslie, in 1878). There were a few other houses for Edison's married associates. A Mrs. Jordan kept a boarding house for the other employees, initially about thirteen "mechanics." The land was cheap enough, selected by Sam Edison. There were few diversions to interfere with the work, and Edison's wild and wooly working habits could be imposed upon his men more easily (for example, during day-and-night sieges each man was allowed four to six hours sleep under a table at the lab and was then awakened). He said that when a long stretch of full-out work had been completed in the days at Menlo Park:

> . . . I used to engage a brick sloop at Perth Amboy and take the whole crowd down to the fishing banks on the Atlantic for two days.

Edison was a born tyrant, and life at Menlo Park suited his ideas about work and life. Josephson argues that Menlo Park, the nation's first laboratory devoted to general industrial research (the Smithsonian Institution was devoted mainly to pure science), was as great and influential as any of Edison's inventions, and was a transitional phase in the process of invention passing over from great individuals to team research. It is true that a great deal of inventive research is now done in laboratories in which there is team research, but the argument can easily be overdone. In the first place, as Jewkes, Sawers and Stillerman have demonstrated, on the basis of an investigation into the primary inventions of this century, it is emphatically not true that the individual inventor has been displaced altogether by great laboratories and team research paid for by giant industrial firms. But second, Menlo Park was not an industrial research laboratory, with a formal hierarchical structure, director of research and all the rest that we have come to know. It was instead a one-man show with a supporting cast. It was indeed almost a physical projection of Edison's character: even the architecture, judging by the photographs, was old-style "Midwest barn" in its configuration, with a little front porch tacked on to give the dreary two-story main building some "class." Inside were the rows of chemicals and equipment and piles of materials. Used-up materials were simply tossed out the door (Henry Ford later sifted the very earth at Menlo Park in search of Edison relics). Edison ruled it all; the experiments were his; he "hired and fired . . . ," and the work went on day and night, nonstop whenever Edison felt like it, and he often did. It is more likely that Menlo Park was the forerunner of the small research laboratories that thrive in the United States today under the leadership of gifted individual scientists. It was left to Alexander Graham Bell to father the modern research octopus: his laboratory, founded in 1881 in Washington, D. C., was an ancestor of "Bell Labs."

Edison's working habits set the tone at Menlo Park. He reminded those who met him there of a somewhat down-at-the-heels working man, perhaps a night printer, with the air of a mechanic. His graying hair fell over his great forehead in a tousled mop. He frequently had a distracted look about him, which could give way to a "big, careless schoolboy" air, or perhaps to one of his not infrequent bursts of temper. He "catnapped" anywhere that sleep overtook him, and awoke from deep sleep (often he had to be shaken awake by one of his men) completely refreshed. His men were expected to keep up the pace. George S. Bryan, in his biography of Edison, quoted Francis Jehl, an old Edison man, on his employer's habits.

> It often happened that when Edison had been working up to three or four o'clock in the morning, he would lie down on one of his laboratory tables, and with nothing but a couple of books for a pillow, would fall into a deep sleep . . .

In spite of his own aversion to mathematics, Edison was prevailed upon at the time of the search for an incandescent lamp to hire Francis Upton, a professional mathematician with a wide scientific background. Upton saw, perhaps more clearly than those with narrower experience, what an extraordinary person was behind the twangy voice, the dirty clothes, the knotted handkerchief "necktie" and the rough manner. He was deeply impressed by many facets of Edison's personality, but by none more than his furious energy. Upton wrote:

> . . . I have often felt that Mr. Edison could never comprehend the limitations of the strength of other men, as his own physical and mental strength have always seemed to be without limit. He could work continuously as long as he wished, and he had sleep at his command.

The kind of boss Edison was at Menlo Park seems appalling. But his men evidently gloried in it. Asked once by an applicant about the pay and working conditions Edison told the man, "We don't pay anything and we work all the time."

Edison used his men remorselessly. The work day started officially at 7 A.M. with the blowing of a whistle and then lasted as long as it needed to. Edison himself told of one man whose capacities were unequal to the task:

> I put him to work on a mercury pump, and kept him at it night and day. At the end of sixty hours I left him for half an hour, and when I returned, there he was, the pump all broken to pieces and the man fast asleep on the ruins . . .

Edison was a "team worker" all right, but at Menlo Park he worked the team like any mule skinner.

He was at Menlo Park from 1876 to 1881 and then, characteristically, he just walked off, abandoning it all, letting it fall to ruin. Those years were Edison's best, most productive and original years as an inventor. They started amid ridicule and triumph. The ridicule came from his stumbling onto (and publicizing) "etheric forces." The triumph came in another patent battle, this one over the telephone. Then came other inventions including the phonograph and the Edison incandescent lighting system.

In late 1875 Edison had observed that he could induce "peculiarly bright, scintillating sparks" from the core of a vibrator magnet. Work on electromagnetism had been going forward since that of Lord Kelvin in 1853. In 1865 James C. Maxwell had shown that, just as a varying electric field produces a magnetic field, so a varying magnetic field produces an electric field. Edison knew nothing of that. He thought the sparks he observed were nonelectric and rushed to the newspapers with an announcement that he had discovered a new "etheric force." Ridicule rained down upon him from the scientists and professors. It is argued by some, including Josephson, that the experience with electromagnetism poisoned Edison against academic scientists. If it did, the effects were short-lived because, in spite of his wisecracks, Edison had plenty of contact with such people. In any case, no one really understood what the uproar was about until much later in 1888 when Maxwell's theories were proved by the classic experiments of Heinrich Hertz and radiotelegraphy became a possibility.

Edison's happier experiences at the beginning of the years at Menlo Park came from his continuing business connection with Western Union and from the discoveries of Bell.

It was known that experiments relating to sending sound over wires had been conducted by Elisha Gray, Alexander

Graham Bell and others. In fact, such work had been done since the 1830's, by Wheatstone in England and Page in Massachusetts; Charles Burseul, a Frenchman, contributed in 1854 and, in 1861, a German, Phillip Reis, had made a fundamental contribution. Western Union was interested, and in the spring of 1876 gave Edison a retainer of $500 a month to conduct experiments.

When Bell's invention was first announced earlier in 1876, Edison discovered that he, too, could send the sound of his voice over the apparatus he had already constructed; possibly his deafness had cheated him of the necessary hunch that would have made him beat Bell to the patent office. Such parallelism in invention is not unusual because of the extent to which invention is usually a further development of the given "state of the art." Indeed, Bell beat Gray into the patent office by only a few hours. In fact, it took the courts to grant Bell the patent, since Gray charged that he had actually beaten his rival, but that a functionary at the patent office had been bribed to give Bell's application precedence. Whatever else this three-way parallelism shows, it is a considerable piece of evidence in itself against the "hero" theory of invention. How many others besides Bell, Gray and Edison had a "telephone" by February, 1876?

Western Union blundered on Bell's invention. He offered to sell his patent rights but the company's president dismissed the contraption as a "toy." After successfully demonstrating his invention at the Philadelphia Exposition in 1876, Bell got backers and proceeded to launch a new industry. (Thus Hollywood, in its initial estimate of television, was simply following a time-honored path.) Bell's telephone was primitive, the same instrument being used for both speaking and listening. Moreover, messages could be sent only short distances without excessive fading, and the voice sounds were indistinct. There was clearly room for improvement in the telephone if it could be "re-invented" in a way that would circumvent Bell's disputed patent. Western Union, after a careful second look at the "toy," came to Edison for help, and a new war was launched in the rapidly changing communications industry. Edison was confident that he could make Bell's telephone look like the work of an amateur.

Edison went to work on the telephone in the fall of 1876 and, by January of 1877, had made considerable progress getting around Bell's patent. Edison loved this sort of mental combat, possibly the more so in this case because he had to overcome the handicap of his deafness (he held a metal plate connected by wire to the telephone between his teeth to "hear"). He decided to use separate instruments for listening and speaking. In April, 1877, Edison filed for a patent on his new transmitter, which used carbon buttons (after a search involving some 2,000 experiments) between the external metal covering and the housing for the inside wiring. This eliminated the parchment diaphragm used in Bell's model. The carbon-button transmitter obtained the variable resistance necessary in the circuit to improve the quality of the voice. By adding an induction coil Edison defeated the problem of distance; the voice "spoke" to the coil and the coil sent the message. Edison now had conquered the main defects in Bell's telephone. The Edison telephone had clear articulation, greater volume (so much so that in England it was called the "shouting telephone") and distance than Bell's apparatus, and with the two-part hearing and speaking arrangement, it was convenient. In February of 1878 Edison filed for a patent on the whole apparatus, and a demonstration of his telephone in New York in March caused a sensation. Western Union, trusting Edison's titanic self-confidence, had set up a company, American Speaking Telephone, in November, 1877, and now was clearly into the new telephone business—or so it thought.

Bell was alert to the threat, and soon found a way into the courts. Emile Berliner, a German immigrant living in Washington, had independently made a workable transmitter. Moreover, he had "filed a caveat" (given warning of work in progress, an old-time patent procedure no longer in use) two weeks before Edison had filed on the first parts of his new transmitter. Learning of this, the Bell forces quickly bought out Berliner's patent rights and filed suit against Edison under the existing patent legislation. The case dragged through the courts long after anyone was interested in it, and Edison's patent rights were finally sustained in 1892. By then it was a mere formality.

Meanwhile, both sides plunged in with their equipment. Pending any court settlement, it paid both sides to establish themselves as securely as possible. The battle lines stretched across the Atlantic. Edison described the struggles in London:

> In England we had fun. Neither the Bell people nor we could work satisfactorily without injuring each other. They infringed on my transmitter and we infringed on their receiver . . . we were cutting each other's throats.

Edison had to train technicians to install the equipment in England. He took sixty men out to Menlo Park. The whole place was strung with telephones and Edison gleefully mixed them up in every conceivable manner. When any man could successfully unsort the chaos ten consecutive times, he was shipped off to England to install equipment. Twenty of the sixty men survived Edison's examinations. In London, the new sales force included a young, angular Irishman who, in his introduction to *The Irrational Knot,* described the American workmen as he saw them through his class-warfare prisms. George Bernard Shaw wrote:

> These deluded and romantic men gave me a glimpse of the skilled proletariat of the United States; and their language was frightful even to an Irishman. They worked with a ferocious energy which was out of all proportion to the result achieved. Indomitably resolved to assert their republican manhood by taking no orders from a tall-hatted Englishman . . . they insisted on being slave driven with genuine American oaths by a genuine free and equal American foreman. They utterly despised the artfully slow British workman who did as little for his wages as he possibly could. . . . They were free-souled creatures, excellent company; sensitive, cheerful and profane; liars, braggarts, and hustlers; with an air of making slow old England hum. . . .

Shaw naturally served himself the lion's share of the credit for any successes the Edison people had in Britain. But at this distance in time one wonders, one even doubts. Shaw a salesman?

The combatants eventually made peace among themselves. Western Union recognized Bell's patent, sold its lines to the Bell System for a seventeen-year royalty payment of 20 percent on telephone rentals. Edison was given $100,000 for his transmitter. Like the man who keeps his watch running fast to avoid being late for appointments, Edison asked that the money be paid to him in annual installments, being afraid that he might spend it all at once if it were paid in a lump sum. He did not escape temptation. He accepted out of hand a cabled offer of "thirty thousand" for his English rights, and to his astonishment found that it was pounds sterling and not dollars, so that from England he received over $145,000.

Edison had done well indeed from his campaign to circumvent the Bell patent. He also, incidentally, turned the telephone into a commercially successful innovation, and his improvements formed the basis of the telephone as the world came to know it. Bell "invented" the telephone, or at least the courts said his patent was filed before Gray's. Edison made the telephone that sparked the industry's beginning.

Is is agreed that Edison's most completely original invention was the phonograph. He had no precursors. Edison was a master of intuition and hunch, and in his work, no matter how dull and repetitive, he continued to store up unrelated pieces of information, putting them together in different combinations to form hypotheses, informed speculation about possible relationships which could be tested. While he was working on the automatic telegraph, in February, 1877, he applied for a patent on a device to record telegraphic impulses on a paper disc. According to Josephson, it was some time in June, 1877, that Edison's laboratory notebooks first indicate that he thought the impulses coming over the telephone might be recorded and then reproduced.

Experiments proceeded, and he finally decided to try simply shouting into a diaphragm with a stylus attached to see what might be etched onto a revolving tinfoil-covered cylinder. He sent one of his assistants, John Kruesi, off to make a device to accomplish this—Kruesi thought that the scheme was a waste of time. There was a grooved, foil-covered cylinder, 3½ inches in diameter, mounted on a foot-long shaft which was turned by a hand crank. The grooves guided the stylus. Attached were two diaphragms which were connected to the two styli, one for recording the impulses and one for reproducing whatever might have been recorded—it was not known what that might be.

When Kruesi brought in the model, Edison turned the handle and shouted the first verse of "Mary Had a Little Lamb" at the recording diaphragm. He then pulled away the cutting stylus, put the reproducing stylus at the front, and turned the crank. The Mother Goose rhyme came cackling out. Those who recalled the moment agreed that great shock was registered by the faces and actions of all present. Some remembered a dumfounded oath in German from Kruesi breaking the silence. Edison said:

> I was never so taken aback in all my life. I was always afraid of things that worked the first time.

Awe gave way to jubilation, and Edison and his men stayed all through the night playing with their new toy. Edison could scarcely contain himself and appeared the next day, Dec. 7, 1877, at the New York editorial offices of *Scientific*

American. The editor, F. C. Beach, recorded the events of that morning:

> I had not been at my desk very long that morning when Mr. Edison was announced. He came in and set his parcel, which he appeared to handle somewhat carefully, on my desk. As he was removing the cover I asked him what it was. 'Just a minute,' replied young Edison. Presently with a 'here you are,' he pushed the quaint-looking little instrument towards me. As there was a long shaft having a heavy steel wheel at one end and a small handle at the other, naturally I gave the handle a twist, and, to my astonishment, the unmistakable words emitted from a kind of telephone mouthpiece, broke out, 'Good morning! What do you think of the Phonograph?' To say that I was astonished is a poor way of expressing my first impressions.

There followed an excited mob scene which Beach finally broke up, fearing that the office floor would collapse. The patent was applied for on Dec. 15, 1877. It must have been a peculiar kind of triumph for Edison because of his deafness. He could still hear a little, but to hear nuances of sound he had to bite into the instrument to "get it good and strong."

For those who had made such sport of Edison's "etheric forces" the previous year, there was now a time of bitter crow-eating. In its 1877 supplement *Scientific American* went overboard altogether.

> We are inclined to regard him as one of the wonders of the world. While Huxley, Tyndall, Spencer and other theorists talk and speculate, he produces accomplished facts, and with his marvelous inventions is pushing the whole world ahead in its march to the highest civilization.

The effects upon Edison's fortunes were immediate. As Josephson put it:

> Fame entered the door of the Menlo Park laboratory at the end of 1877; thenceforth Edison was never to escape the attentions, flattering or irksome, which the great public pays to an accepted national hero.

At first he wallowed in his new-found eminence. The seed of thespianism in him flowered. He loved to demonstrate the machine to the throngs that now made the journey out to Menlo Park just to gawk. Putting on his most rustic airs, his most eccentric clothes, exaggerating his Midwest accent, Edison played Barnum. In April, 1878, he appeared before the

American Academy of Sciences to demonstrate his invention. The same day, he showed the phonograph to a group of Congressmen. That evening he was the guest of President Hayes, and the President went upstairs and got his wife out of bed at 12.30 A.M. to come and see the phonograph. It was 3.30 A.M. when Edison left the White House.

There followed a "phonograph craze," and a lot of money was made exhibiting the machine around the country as a side-show attraction. Edison had all sorts of ideas for using his machine in the long run. All of them eventually came to pass, but not in the sequence or order of importance he had forecast. Mainly, Edison failed to understand the future of his invention as part of the world of the arts and entertainment. He thought of it mainly as an adjunct of business in uses like the modern dictaphone. He thought it would be used to make a speaking family album, to preserve the speeches of great statesmen, to teach languages and to provide books for the blind. Perhaps the poor quality of the early reproducing apparatus together with Edison's deafness made him miss the possibilities for the reproduction of music. Moreover, he was soon absorbed in other work and his little phonograph languished. When he did come back to it, he was responding to the competition of a superior adaptation, the gramophone and the flat discs and turntables that brought professional music standards for the first time into the lives of millions. Edison would not comprehend the later developments in electronics and the modern industry evolved from his competitors, making the world of high-fidelity and stereophonic sound possible. But his invention was used as he predicted too. In fact, he could not have imagined the proliferation of uses to which the recording of sound was eventually put.

From 1877 onward, Edison became increasingly accustomed to the company of distinguished scientists. It was because of this that he initially became connected with the development of incandescent lighting. George F. Barker, Professor of Chemistry and Physics at the University of Pennsylvania, invited Edison to take part in a scientific expedition to Rawlins, Wyoming, in the summer of 1878 to observe an eclipse of the sun. Edison greatly enjoyed himself on this excursion, and was allowed to ride on the "cow catcher" from Omaha westward. At the expedition's headquarters he was fascinated by the work of the astronomers, and by their mathematical calculations, which he said ". . . looked like the timetable of a Chinese railroad."

While Edison may have felt like a fish out of water among the hard-working scientists at Rawlins, Professor Barker clearly comprehended the potency of Edison's special talents. He talked at length with the inventor about the problems and possibilities of lighting by electricity; about the work currently being done and about past failures, and urged Edison to apply himself to the problem. At length Edison agreed to look into it. Back in the East, in September, a special party including Edison, Barker, Charles F. Chandler (Professor of Chemistry at Columbia University) and Dr. Henry Draper (a pioneer in celestial photography) went to Ansonia, Connecticut, to see the firm of William Wallace and Moses Farmer, which was then experimenting with arc lighting and making equipment. As Edison toured the works he became increasingly excited by what he saw, not by what was being done, but by what was not being done. Finally he told his hosts that he would bet them that he could beat them to an electric light of general commercial usefulness. Edison said afterward: "I saw that what had been done had never been made practically useful."

The arc lights already lighting streets in Europe and America offered nothing for the home. Edison had the greatest respect for Wallace (and, in fact, always claimed that Wallace had done much for which others received credit). But he saw a potentiality that others had not seen. The great future for electricity, Edison wrote in his notebook, was to replace gas lighting and heating in the home! Not only would he need to strike out in a different direction, but he would need to create a whole system of inventions and innovations. He said of his ambitions:

> When it is known how I have accomplished my object everyone will wonder why they never thought of it. . . . I can produce a thousand—, aye, ten thousand lights from one machine.

True to that prediction, Lord Kelvin would soon be admitting in England, when asked why he had not thought of incandescent lighting: "The only answer I can think of is that no one else is Edison."

IV

In the fall of 1878 Edison began the search for a system of practical lighting for common use. It was to be his greatest adventure, and in many respects his most disappointing and disillusioning experience. He is probably better remembered for this achievement than for any other. Yet in no case were his claims more hotly disputed nor, probably, were his achievements more seminal. Also he was probably never more wrong about the ultimate development of any of his contributions than he was about the incandescent light when he opposed the introduction of alternating current. He emerged years later a richer, a wiser and a sadder man.

Initially all was hope, and Edison in September, 1878, even told a newspaperman that success would take him only six weeks. But he soon enough realized that the battle of his lifetime lay ahead. This early publicity did him little good beyond encouraging his financial backers. There was an initial decline in the prices of gas-company shares when it became known that Edison would turn his attentions to the electric light. He quickly achieved a small success by producing a short illumination of a platinum-wire filament within a partially vacated bulb in October of 1878 (the illumination lasted about eight minutes before the wire burned up). His announcement from the pulpit of a (necessarily) short but sensational public demonstration, that he would light up as many as 500,000 small lamps in downtown New York from a few steam-driven dynamos, produced a panic in sales of gaslight shares. The gas companies of course scoffed at Edison's claims, but their statements had little effect in the face of his sensational pronunciamentos.

Edison was also attacked by some, not all, men of science. His scheme to subdivide the current immediately brought many experts down around his ears. He showed ". . . the most airy ignorance of the fundamental principles both of electricity and dynamics," crowed the London periodical *Engineering*. A few months later, following a Parliamentary inquiry into the sudden decline in gaslight securities, that same journal contained a piece of that species of fatuous patronizing the British have long been fond of delivering to their "American cousins" (usually quickly forgotten when proved wrong). Edison's scheme might be ". . . good enough for our Transatlantic friends . . ." but obviously would be ". . . unworthy of the attention of practical or scientific men . . ." in England.

By then, early in 1879, Edison knew how difficult his problems were going to be, but he said that he was never discouraged, although ". . . I cannot say the same for my associates." Edison had to solve a whole series of problems, some of which had blocked experimenters for years. First there was the incandescent bulb itself: how to get anything to glow under intense heat for a long period of time without burning up. Second there was the problem of distributing electricity cheaply and safely to a mass market at a profit.

These problems were tackled along with one that often seemed to be equally formidable—money. Edison soon saw that he would need some new backing, that he would not be able to finance the work from his own resources. A prominent New York lawyer, Grosvenor Lowery, undertook to find the money. As happened so many times with enterprises of that period, but almost never at the *beginning* of any venture, the financial path led to the front door of Mr. Pierpont Morgan. It is here that objection must be raised to certain interpretations of events, including Josephson's. The facts themselves are clear enough. After raising some $30,000 from Western Union people, a Morgan syndicate, the Edison Electric Light Co., was formed. Morgan's brilliant partner, Egisto Fabbri, was the "Morgan man" in the directorate. There were 3,000 shares, with a nominal value of $300,000, in the new company, but only 500 shares (worth $50,000) were "paid up" initially. Edison held the remaining 2,500 shares himself. Josephson both applauds the "robber barons" of the Morgan syndicate for "real vision" and then, joining Edison himself, damns them for their later conservatism and monopolistic tactics.

Actually both views are somewhat overdone. As for their "real vision," the amount of money involved was mere "chicken feed" for a Morgan syndicate, and it is clear that the view of Morgan's son-in-law and biographer, Herbert Satterlee, was essentially correct: that, initially, the Morgan syndicate was something of a lark. To Morgan it might have been viewed almost as charity. Then, not unlike many capitalists, the syndicate was flummoxed when the scale of the prospects went suddenly far beyond their expectations (in a later part of this book an account is given of a man who sold out his shares of Ford Motor Co. after the first successful year to invest in a gold mine). Organized as a safe little holding company for Edison patents relating to electric lights (for a five-year period), the future changed the company from a possible small-scale success into a gigantic imponderable. Morgan himself can hardly be faulted. He never balked when difficulties came. And, still in the spirit of adventure, had his own house wired for light immediately, putting an optimistic face on it when the lights malfunctioned, and when a short circuit set part of his library on fire. Morgan did view Edison Electric at first as a monopoly holding company. There was no illegality in such an operation in 1878. Also Morgan did, evidently, suggest a merger (which Edison hotly vetoed) after two other inventors claimed to have beaten Edison to a successful electric-light system. Such a merger would have been typical of Morgan.

There is no point either in handing out unnecessary laurels or maintaining a doctrinal interpretation of events for the sake of consistency. Morgan doubtless felt a bit odd as a "pioneer," although, for him, the stakes involved at first were simply pocket money. On the other hand the great banker was never against expansion when it looked profitable. He was no Edison; he was probably wholly ignorant of the prospects for electric lighting beyond the confines of downtown New York, even after the lights were installed there. It took Edison's sublime faith in himself and his own ideas to start up a real expansion of the electrical industry. J. P. Morgan's syndicate initially financed Edison's electric-light venture. As a group they showed less than undeviating enthusiasm as the bills and failures mounted, although there is no written evidence what the impassive Morgan thought of it before success came, beyond his laconic statement that he was "perfectly willing to go on" in the spring of 1879 when more money, perhaps a lot more, was needed. Edison finally fell out with his backers, but it was not the first time he had done that. Edison made a lot of mistakes and some money (although he always belittled it) out of Edison Electric Light; so did the Morgan syndicate. Edison also made, as even his detractors admit, "an immense engineering achievement" and for that he alone gets the credit —suitably discounted to accommodate the claims of rival inventors.

When Edison began work on the incandescent electric light in the fall of 1878, he was following a beaten track, but one which previously had led to a dead end. Up to then the most successful application of electric power to lighting had been in arc street lighting. Sir Humphry Davy had produced an arc-lighting effect as early as 1801 and had demonstrated it publicly in 1808 (using a 2,000-cell battery as his power source). In 1831, Faraday's dynamo made the generation of electrical from mechanical energy a reality. By the 1860's electric arcs were being used in lighthouses. Then, in 1870,

Siemens developed an improved direct-current dynamo, and further improvements in arc lighting followed. A Russian officer, temporarily in Paris, Paul Jablochkov, in 1876 demonstrated an arc light made of two carbon rods separated by insulation, which was run by an alternating current dynamo. C. K. Brush, an American, in 1878 advanced the arc light with a superior dynamo and a system of connections which would allow the lights to operate effectively in series. There was a successful stream of work on electric arc lighting up to 1878.

Contrasted with that, attempts to make a commercially feasible incandescent light had achieved only repeated failures. In France, as early as 1820, De La Rive tried to get a successful incandescent glow in an evacuated glass container. In England, E. A. King made an imperfect incandescent lamp in 1845. Sir Joseph Swan, ultimately the English "inventor" of the incandescent lamp, had conducted experiments as early as the 1860's. But Swan, although holding the English patent for the incandescent lamp, did not have a commercially practicable one. There were also Russians who had experimented with incandescent electric lighting before 1878, and others, some American, whose names are no longer mentioned. At the end of this line of work there was still no successful incandescent lamp when Edison started his work. He knew that commercial success depended upon the subdivision of current into thousands of outlets to power incandescent lamps in individual households and businesses. He could have had no inspiration, except a negative kind, from expert opinion. Paget Higgs, an English electrical expert, in his book *The Electric Light* said in 1879 that the subdivision of electrical current was "incompatible with the well proven law of the conservation of energy." The English scientist, Prof. Sylvanus Thomson, said flatly in 1878 that ". . . any system depending on incandescence will fail," and no less a person than Sir William Preece stated in a lecture in 1879 that ". . . a subdivision of the electric light is an absolute *ignis fatuus*." It could not be said that Edison was embarking upon a promising quest so far as received doctrine was concerned. The main problems, the production of a continuous glow, its possible distribution and its effective supply of current, had never been solved. Edison solved them all.

As we noted earlier, Edison succeeded in getting a short incandescence in 1878 from a platinum filament in a partially evacuated glass container. He saw that he needed to create the entire system to make any of it a commercial success. As pieces of the puzzle were put together other parts "fell into" place. Edison's first real breakthrough came from his interpretation of Ohm's law—roughly, that current delivered is equal to the voltage (potential difference) relative to the resistance in the circuit. Edison decided—he said "in a flash of inspiration"—that a practical light would need to have a high resistance relative to voltage to use less current to produce the incandescence. This was a departure from his precursors, who had concentrated on low resistance and high voltage. It solved one of his distribution problems, too: the reduction in the weight, and hence the cost, of copper wire needed to tie the entire system together. By this time Edison was relying upon mathematics, but not his own.

Lowery had persuaded Edison to hire Francis R. Upton, the mathematician, to help in the work on the light. Edison was at first skeptical and referred, at least partly in jest, to his new associate as "Culture" Upton. But he soon came to value Upton's skills and talents. For his own part, Upton said he was simply astonished by Edison's "wonderful flow of ideas." In later years Upton recalled:

> I cannot imagine why I did not see the elementary facts in 1878 and 1879 more clearly than I did. I came to Mr. Edison a trained man with a year's experience in Helmholtz's laboratory . . . Yet my eyes were blind. . . .

They worked together; Edison would talk out his ideas, and Upton would turn them into rigorous form. Edison's hunch that he could subdivide current without losing it turned out to be correct according to Upton's calculations—the "experts" had forecast a serious loss of power from such subdivisions. Then on Edison's hunches about using a high-resistance filament to achieve incandescence, Upton found that, over a given length of line, the weight of copper could be reduced as much as 99 percent, depending upon the voltage and resistance selected. There would be no bottleneck on the cost of wiring. Even those changes in the course of experimentation put Edison on a track far different from that traveled by other experimenters. They, using high voltage and low resistance, not only experienced the melting of their incandescing materials, but the cost of the copper wire needed for the high-voltage transmission was prohibitive.

The next group of developments brought ultimate success for the lamp itself. Edison had to find a material which would glow in a vacuum under great heat for a long period of time without melting. He also had to produce a better vacuum than he had. He borrowed a newly developed English vacuum pump from Princeton and set about making it work even better. He also tried again with platinum; by January of 1879, he had a high-resistance platinum lamp which would burn for a couple of hours. By April that lamp had been improved, but was still not a real possibility for successful commercial development. He then began to ransack the world of fibers and minerals, and his search involved him in the testing, under all sorts of conditions, of some 1,600 materials. In the process he learned to eliminate occluded (trapped) gases from fibers by burning them while pumping out the containers. This improved the general performance. Still the search continued. After his earlier bursts of optimism, not only his backers were beginning to wonder. Gas-stock prices recovered. A prediction was made by W. E. Sawyer, a rival inventor, that Edison was doomed to "final, necessary and ignominious failure."

Edison noted the apprehensions of his backers and the doubts of his public. In later years he remembered the fantastic series of experiments:

> The electric light has caused me the greatest amount of study and has required the most elaborate experiments. . . .

At the time he issued an oft-quoted statement at an interview given to a newspaperman (quoted here from Josephson):

> Just consider this: we have an almost infinitesimal filament heated to a degree which is difficult to comprehend, and it is in a vacuum under conditions of which we are wholly ignorant. You cannot use your eyes to help you, and you really know nothing of what is going on in that tiny bulb. I speak without exaggeration when I say that I have constructed 3,000 theories in connection with the electric light, each of them reasonable and apparently likely to be true. Yet in two cases only did my experiments prove the truth of my theory.

The search for an incandescing material continued without success. Edison even tried a hair from the beard of J. U. Mackenzie, his old telegraphic mentor, who was then at Menlo Park as a laboratory assistant. Finally, he turned to carbonizing fibers again. He had tried carbon before because of its extremely high resistance to heat, but he had no luck. Now that he knew that the removal of occluded gases made a difference, carbon would clearly be worth another set of experiments.

He concentrated on the development of a carbon filament of 1/64 inch in diameter and which had a high resistance. The reader is referred to Josephson for a detailed blow-by-blow account of the whole search for the incandescent light. For our purposes, the technical information need not be extensive, but some of the numbers are important to consider at this point. Edison was trying to make a filament 0.0156 inch in diameter yielding 200 ohms resistance. The man who gets credit in England for inventing the incandescent light (Swan) produced a filament 0.185 inch thick. The resistance of experimental filaments before Edison was of the order of 1 or 2 ohms. It is clear that Edison was in a world of his own making, far beyond the conception of his rivals. His work was on a different plane, as the difference in the orders of magnitude of the numbers cited above indicate. Those who give Edison too little credit for the incandescent electric light bulb are reckless. There is a difference between grape juice and wine.

On Oct. 21, 1879, Edison snipped off a piece of cotton thread, put it in a mold and carbonized it in a furnace. Tests of the resulting piece of carbon for incandescing properties seemed to show promise. So they tried putting the carbonized thread in the glass container so that it could be tested for incandescence under vacuum. Things kept going wrong, and had to be done over. It was the ninth time they tried before the fragile carbon was successfully put in place under glass. By then the usual night shift had run over into the small hours of the next day. Everything was set up to test. Edison described the moment:

> The bulb was exhausted of air and sealed, the current turned on, and the sight we had so long desired to see met our eyes.

The light burned from 1.30 A.M. to 3.00 P.M. on Oct. 22 and then they put it out. The carbonized thread had burned for 13½ hours (Edison later said it was left to burn for 45 hours, but he evidently had forgotten the details), and Edison said: "If it can burn that number of hours, I know I can make it burn a hundred." He kept his own counsel and refrained from sending his usual broadside to the press. Much was still to be done to perfect the whole distribution system, together with the constant-voltage dynamo on which he had also been laboring. Some interim announcements about this had been greeted with derision, and he may Ħave decided to fell all of his detractors with a single blow. The blow fell on Nov. 1, 1879, when Edison filed for his patent. The application read in part:

> I have discovered that even a cotton thread, properly carbonized and placed in sealed glass bulbs, exhausted to one-millionth of an atmosphere, offers from one hundred to five hundred Ohms resistance to the passage of current and that it is absolutely stable at a very high temperature.

By early November, when Fabbri and another of Morgan's partners journeyed out to Menlo Park, they found the houses of Edison and Upton brilliantly lit by incandescent light. The whole system was now nearing completion. Edison had also succeeded in greatly improving the dynamo. It had previously been argued that the dynamo needed the same internal resistance as that which existed outside the dynamo, and could deliver only 50 percent of the power it generated. Edison did not believe those arguments and set to work to construct a dynamo with a small internal resistance relative to the external resistance, saying acidly that he ". . . wanted to sell the current outside the station and not waste it in the dynamo and the conductors, where it brought no profits. . . ." Upton had described their work in an unsigned article in *Scientific American* in the summer of 1879 which was greeted with the kind of ridicule to which Edison had lately become accustomed. When the dynamo was finished, Edison's guess, supported by Upton's calculations, was correct. The new dynamo was 90 percent efficient.

Work on the parallel wiring, switches, meters and fixtures had been successful enough so that Edison was in fact producing the nucleus of a new industry in itself, with, as it was nicely put in the article in the Eleventh Edition of *Encyclopaedia Britannica* (1910) by the great J. A. Fleming, "copious ingenuity." Edison hoped to sell electric current and fixtures to thousands of customers based upon central power stations connected to homes, businesses, factories and wherever else electricity could be used. According to the New York *Herald Tribune,* the news from Menlo Park "shook the scientific world to its foundations."

Perhaps some of the scientific world was shaken, but it wasn't as easy as all that. Edison's claims had always been distrusted by a significant part of the scientific fraternity, possibly because he wasn't "properly educated." In addition, his extravagant claims amounted to the crying of "wolf" too many times in the case of his light. Even the slightest difficulties were seized upon. The (British) *Annual Register* for 1880 had this to say:

> Towards the end of 1879 the American correspondents of the London daily papers telegraphed in rather sanguine language accounts of a new electric lamp invented by Mr. Edison. The extraordinary simplicity and marvellous cheapness . . . of this wonderful lamp, and the brilliancy and steadiness of the light it gave out were represented in glowing colours. . . . At the end of January, however, the reports were not quite so satisfactory.

The scientists were hardly shaken. Edison might be able to overcome his difficulties, of course, but in fact was there anything in it? They noted that Mr. J. W. Swan had, after all, pointed out that he also had developed an incandescent light just like Edison's 15 years ago, and had recently perfected it. There was nothing really new evidently. Even when electric lights were being put in London, their radical character was not widely appreciated. It is useful to recall how much work had already been done, that arc lighting already existed. In fact, in 1881, Werner Siemens turned down a chance to produce Edison systems in Germany, believing that the incandescent light would soon be displaced by arc lighting. It was not just Edison's backers who wondered what it would all come to. Once he had carried his point through, it was promptly stolen. When it was seen that Edison did, in fact, have an innovation of enormous economic potential, his patents were plundered right and left. In a sense, too many people believed in him then. He then faced the inventor's nemesis, the pirate and the law courts. Moreover, he would eventually lose control of even that part of the electrical industry which he was destined to establish. In the end he said bitterly:

> I fought for the lamp for fourteen years and when I finally won my rights there were but three years of the allocated seventeen left for my patent to live.

There was a long, hard road ahead, and it was to end for Edison in frustration and disillusionment. He would, however, live to see a grateful nation credit him for his accomplishment. But, at first, he had fun with his new toys. Menlo Park was overrun. On New Year's Eve, 1879, 3,000 people descended upon the little settlement to see the lights. Edison was prepared. Switches were set up, and through the night the pilgrims turned the little lamps on and off, on and off. For a gas-company agent there was surprise and disappointment when he succeeded in producing a short circuit at the height of the celebration and found that the parallel wiring had forestalled him—all the lights did not go out. It is reported that a few of the lamps were stolen that night, but Edison was in his glory, explaining it all and freely predicting that the little bulbs would soon be selling for 25¢ each.

V

Edison learned quickly enough that if the bulbs were going to sell for 25¢ he would have to make them. A whole new era in electricity began, and Edison battled with some of the greatest tycoons of the age. He almost gave up inventing in order to become one of the major innovators of the period. Harold C. Passer, in his fine history of *The Electrical Manufacturer*, called Edison a ". . . pioneer innovator whose contribution to economic development has been exceeded by very few persons." From our point of view, his power as an innovator was secondary to his importance as an inventor, but Edison the innovator was an impressive figure. By the end of the 1880's he would lay the foundations of Consolidated Edison, General Electric and a dozen other great new regional electrical firms. He would also, in the end, sell out his interest in that which he had so largely built.

After 1879 rivals were soon in the field, charging that Edison had pre-empted their inventions, offering copies of Edison's lamps to the market, and building, on all sides, the foundations of the new industry. Edison, now an old hand at the patent-rights game, knew that the courts would be years sorting it all, that he had to be able to avoid injunctions, pay his lawyers and fight it out with the competition. He soon changed over to a carbon-paper filament (already done by Swan) and then, after a search of thousands of fibers, began making filaments out of carbonized bamboo. Work continued on the perfection of his whole system. He wanted to use underground power lines; he wanted better equipment all around. In the initial research, $43,000 of Edison Electric's funds had been absorbed. The financiers agreed to put up another $58,000 in cash to continue the work, but by the end of 1880 he had used up $150,000 and no end was yet in sight for the development of the system. This was no longer mere pocket money and the syndicate became restive.

Meanwhile Edison had been experimenting with an electric locomotive. Henry Villard, the Northern Pacific mogul, had begun putting money into Edison Electric in 1880 and was interested in electric locomotives. He also had Edison wire a ship, the *Columbia,* belonging to his Oregon Railway & Navigation Co. The *Columbia* then sailed to California without mishap. That was good publicity, and it meant that electric lighting would be sea-going, too. Early in 1881 the backers at last saw what the completed Edison lighting system would look like as an operating business proposition, and perhaps some of them saw the truth in Edison's declamation: "After this we will make electric light so cheap that only the rich will be able to burn candles."

The Morgan combine had envisaged themselves as a general patent-holding company, income to be derived from licenses, and had little taste for actually pioneering the industry. Edison, on the other hand, spoke ambitiously of "raising millions." The inventor and his backers were at loggerheads. As Edison described the situation:

> We were confronted by a stupendous obstacle. Nowhere in the world could we obtain any of the items or devices necessary for the exploitation of the system. The directors of the Edison Electric Light Company would not go into the manufacturing business itself.

Edison decided to do it himself: "The issue is factories or death." He went to several of his Menlo Park associates, among them Edward Johnson, Charles Batchelor and Francis Upton, for support. They agreed to risk their savings and credit. He also went into a partnership with Sigmund Bergmann, a New Yorker who had done some production work for him. They pooled their funds, and Edison risked his entire fortune (by then a not inconsiderable accumulation), the gains from a decade of profitable inventing. He also sold some of his Edison stocks outright, and used the rest for collateral. He was now entering a period as a great entrepreneur, when he became a millionaire, but a millionaire who was usually starved for cash. An estimated 40 percent of the original funds to start manufacturing came from Edison himself.

As so many times happened, the early stages of industrial growth were self-financed; the capital market was of no importance until much later, when success was a fact. Early in

1881 Edison and his associates left Menlo Park behind them and crossed the river to New York. The famous laboratory soon became derelict (so to remain until the faithful Henry Ford, Edison's disciple, moved and restored it, plank by plank, red dirt and all, at Greenfield Village in Dearborn, Michigan).

The new offices were at 65 Fifth Avenue, a four-story building. Out of this the new enterprises were to be directed. "We're up in the world now!" Edison exclaimed, recalling that ten years earlier he had lacked the price of a bed for the night in the great city. In January, 1881, the directors of Edison Electric voted $80,000 to start up in business in New York. A separate company, the Edison Electric Illuminating Co. of New York, was organized to start the sale of electric power (later, allied with the Consolidated Gas Co., this became "Con Ed").

A franchise had been squeezed from the Tammany officials to put in the first Edison system on a tax-free basis (although a certain number of "inspectors" had to be added to the payroll—Edison never saw them except on payday). A site on Pearl Street, on the lower East Side, was purchased. Edison wanted to begin by lighting the financial district. There were miles of power lines to be put in, in addition to building the power station. Work started in the fall of 1881.

In downtown New York, Edison acquired the buildings of an old iron works, where the heavy manufacturing was to be done (later, moving up to Schenectady, this was the origin of General Electric's massive manufacturing divisions). There was also some subcontracting for equipment.

In addition to the beginnings of Edison's electrical enterprises in the United States, the year 1881 also saw the organization of Edison companies in Europe. Edison was covered with prizes including the Legion of Honor, for his exhibit at the Paris Exposition in 1881. His main rivals, Swan, St. G. Lane-Fox and Hiram Maxim, received lesser honors. On the Continent, Edison thus had some primacy. But in Britain, Edison had to compromise with Swan, who held British patents for his incandescent light and had his own company. The result was a merger, Edison & Swan United Electric Co. Ltd. Work was soon under way in London to set up a system; in fact, London had the Edison lighting system before New York did. (Parliament soon put the British electrical industry into a technological deep freeze with legislation empowering local authorities to absorb the lighting system—the British went ahead only in the 1920's when the national grid was formed and the nation was freed from a host of tiny light plants.)

By all accounts Edison was in his glory as New York City experienced the first of its visitations by the ancestors of the present ubiquitous Con Ed excavators. Crowds gathered at the door of the Fifth Avenue office just to see the inventor. He did not disappoint them, emerging with top hat and cigar and a disheveled costume with a crumpled swallow-tailed coat finished off by a handkerchief necktie. He had several variations of this picturesque inventor's costume (it is said that Tennyson used to stalk the English lanes in an opera cape). As the work progressed, Edison often slept nights on the concrete floors at Pearl Street, "in the rough." By July, 1882, everything was ready for the first run of the system (some millionaires, including Morgan, had isolated power plants installed in their homes). Amid considerable fanfare, Edison launched the new system. It was a fiasco.

Edison said that nothing worked by itself, you had to "make" it work. So they went to work to get the "bugs" out. Leaks in the power lines and distribution system were corrected. More efficient steam engines were designed and installed (Edison got help for that). Then, amid very little publicity indeed, on Sept. 4, 1882, the system was started up again. This time it worked. There were 85 paying customers using 400 lamps. By then more than $600,000 had been expended on the Pearl Street installation. At Drexel, Morgan & Co., wired with 106 lamps, Edison himself pulled the switch.

At first, development of the Edison system was slow. By 1884, for example, there were still only 508 customers of the Pearl Street station, and no new stations had been built in New York City. There were plans to organize Edison companies in Boston, Cincinnati, Chicago and Detroit (where Henry Ford was destined to be hired as night engineer). Small, independent electrical systems for ranches, hotels and factories were much in demand, and the Edison Isolated Lighting Co. was organized to exploit that market. Progress there was, but it was too slow for Edison's tastes.

Meanwhile Edison, now a celebrity, was grandly feted and enjoyed every minute of it. In New York City he personally placed the lights in the costumes of the dancing girls of the dramatic ballet "Excelsior" which plugged Edison Electric from the Broadway stage. The Pearl Street station created some sensations of its own, leaking underground power lines occasionally turning surprised men and horses passing over the surface into "grounds" (no fatalities came from the low voltages used in the Edison system).

In 1883, Edison created an unfamiliar kind of sensation in very select circles. He observed that he could place an electrode between the positive and negative poles of his incandescent lamp and draw out a negative current which had as part of its circuit the vacuous space in the lamp. This was odd indeed, to conduct current without wires in a near-vacuum. In November, 1883, he patented this variation of his lamp, but he scarcely knew what to do about it. He made a voltage indicator out of this strange device and exhibited it in Philadelphia. Sir William Preece came to Philadelphia and inspected the phenomenon, went back to England and reported it to the Royal Society, calling it "the Edison effect." Edison, finding no practical use for his discovery, laid it aside. "I'm not a scientist," Edison said, "I'm an inventor . . . I measure everything I do by the size of the silver dollar. If it don't come up to that standard, then I know it's no good."

The work of Hertz, Fleming, Marconi and Lee De Forest made something of the phenomenon though, and the vacuum tube and the radio were the results. In 1897, F. F. Thomson demonstrated that *electrons* were passing to the cold element inside Edison's lamp. The new science of electronics was now developing, and Edison was simply nonplused by it all. He admired Marconi and assigned him the patent rights to the "Edison effect." Edison remarked that: "In experimenting I find a good many things I never looked for. . . ."

In 1884 there were still only a dozen Edison lighting systems at work, and Edison's patience with the management of Edison Electric was exhausted. His own profitable manufacturing businesses depended for their growth upon the installation of more Edison systems. He had sold so much of his stock he no longer controlled Edison Electric. When he heard that the Morgan people wanted to merge the parent company with the manufacturing businesses, Edison began gathering support for a stockholders' fight. He succeeded in ousting the president of Edison Electric, got in a more congenial management and began proceedings against his competitors. The Morgan people eventually backed the inventor, and the way was open for expansion.

By the end of 1886, 58 city light plants were using Edison's system; there were two new plants "uptown" in New York (26th Street and 39th Street), and there were more than 500 "isolated" plants. As output expanded (800 men were employed at the downtown works in 1885), unit costs fell and lamps were used by millions of Americans. By then Thomas Edison was a millionaire, and the combined Edison businesses had assets worth $10 million. The new system was firmly established.

The growth of the Edison electrical enterprises now passed through two clearly defined stages, one of internal integration and growth, followed by one of financial reorganization and control. Edison's carelessness about his finances (personal as well as business—he used to just hold out money to clerks by the handful, disdaining to count it) got him into continuous and complex difficulties as his affairs became more extensive. He always had contempt for mere bookkeeping; he never comprehended any systematic connection between his internal management and ease of access to external finance. He was usually in financial straits.

Early in the career of Edison's manufacturing businesses a young Englishman, Samuel Insull, began to direct financial affairs for Edison. Insull was always an enthusiast for borrowing short-term money (say, payable in 90 days) to make long-term commitments (say, to build a factory with no hope of making anything for a year). Edison systems were placed in municipalities, Insull accepting the obligations of those cities as payment. The securities were then used as collateral for borrowing from banks. Insull thus used short-term money to do the work of long-term money. There were certain advantages to this system. It was possible, at least for a while, to utilize external funds for growth without going into the capital market and thus (by necessarily bringing in the influence of investment bankers) jeopardizing the managerial freedom of Edison. There would be no bondholders, or new stockholders, to worry about. Insull's methods also meant continuous (and for Edison, nerve-racking) strain as the companies were continuously pressed for cash to meet constantly maturing short-term obligations. Eventually Insull brought Edison to grief.

The managerial freedom thus attained gave Edison great flexibility. An example of both the ills and the virtues of Insull's financial methods came in the late 1880's when the main manufacturing was moved from New York to Schenectady. As an employer, Edison was always an old-time autocrat ("Hell, I'm doin' the hirin' and firin' here . . ." he told one of his sons when dismantling a personnel staff the son had assembled). Edison saw no use, especially, for unions among his workmen. He once designed and secretly produced machine tools to replace the work of some skilled men in anticipation of their next strike. When the union finally "went out," the machines were installed. That was all for the union: "It has been out ever since," Edison remarked. The men at the downtown works called a strike over wages. Edison, writhing under Insull's financing, was short of cash to meet his payroll anyhow, and decided that the strike ". . . would give us a couple of weeks to catch up. . . ." At the same time, Edison could still do anything he pleased about the management. He was tired of labor troubles in New York City and decided to accept an offer of land and tax concessions from the city fathers of Schenectady and he simply moved the machinery out of the downtown works and shipped it up to Schenectady. When the workmen tired of the strike and asked to be allowed back into the shops to resume work, their employer was nothing but cooperative.

> Finally they said they would like to go back. We said all right. . . . When they went back to the Goerck Street shops they found them empty of machinery.

Edison's "playfulness" and "streak of boyishness" have often been the subject of comment by his biographers. With a sense of humor so mortal, and with "industrial relations policies" like his, Edison was bound to find endless frustrations as a manufacturer. But his finances were even more ragged. At about the same period as the Schenectady move, he once paid $4,000 interest on a short loan of $20,000. He was clearly the victim of sheer usury because of Insull's cavalier methods. Edison was evidently not a good risk in a banking sense. The Morgan connection was of no use for that sort of thing; Morgan had an infinite distaste for seedy financing methods, and he stayed clear of the problems of Edison's manufacturing establishments. Once, when he refused to lend Edison a red cent, James Stillman, president of the National City Bank, acidly told the inventor that he needed a partner.

What Edison had instead was "financial genius" residing in the persons of Insull and Henry Villard. To concentrate his efforts, Edison sold most of his remaining shares of Edison Electric, the parent company, and in 1885 put his money into United Edison Manufacturing Co. of New York City, an attempt to integrate his sprawling empire of manufacturing, distribution and sales. Insull presided over that operation with predictable results. Then, in 1888, Villard became the dominant figure. After his Northern Pacific combination collapsed into bankruptcy in 1884, Villard had gone back to Germany. There he became closely associated with leaders in German banking, with the great inventor, Werner Siemens, a leader in the German electrical industry. Villard also established close personal relations with Emile Rathenau, head of the largest German electrical combine. To these and similar Germans, Villard described the future of Edison's manufacturing enterprises in roseate terms as investment projects. They were convinced. Now Villard needed Edison's agreement to a reorganization.

Villard proposed to unite all the Edison businesses with Edison Electric, the parent and patent-holding company. This would involve a very considerable piece of financial diplomacy; the Morgan interests would have to be compensated for accommodating the German financial group. For his own part, Edison was glad for the chance to reorganize the whole business. First, under Insull's financial guidance Edison, a man who had known too well what the word "poor" meant, spent a great deal of time in a state of near panic, wondering where the money to meet his constantly maturing obligations was coming from. Perhaps he needn't have worried so much, but he said he did. The proposed reorganization would combine his interests with the Morgan syndicate again and assure a steadier financial structure. But by then, 1888, Edison no longer had control of his companies anyway, and for some time past had had little interest in Edison Electric itself.

There was another reason, too, why Edison was probably glad to see this particular denouement. He doubtless was hoping to realize a stiff capital gain and to get out of the electrical business altogether. In addition to the costs and uncertainties of the continuing patent-right litigation, he had lost touch with the rapidly changing technology, or was fast losing touch. He had been a stanch, and then a rabid, opponent of alternating-current transmission. There was no part of Edison's career that was so unworthy of the man and, in fact, sordid.

Edison's main competition was made up of two companies: Thomson-Houston and United States Electric. Both were using lamps under patent arrangements with W. E. Sawyer and Hiram Maxim. Edison was suing those companies after 1885. In 1886 the intrepid George Westinghouse got control of United States Electric. Alternating-current engineering had been making rapid strides since 1883 when a successful a.c. transformer was patented in England by Lucien Gaulard and

J. D. Gibbs. Now high voltages could be carried long distances and then "stepped down" by transformers for ordinary household use. You could (and Westinghouse soon did) harness Niagara Falls itself and sell its power. You could run heavy industrial prime movers from high voltages. A new age was dawning in industry. Edison's short-range (each central station covered only about one square mile) and low-voltage system was suddenly obsolescent. The Gaulard–Gibbs a.c. transformer was improved by an American, W. A. Stanley, in 1885 and the rights were quickly acquired by Westinghouse. Nikola Tesla, the Serbian genius who had once worked as a laboratory assistant for Edison, made a great improvement in electrical distribution with his polyphase system. Westinghouse got Tesla's patent rights too. The competition was about to go into the lead.

For some reason Edison could not comprehend the a.c. system. He was convinced that, transformers or not, the high-voltage of the a.c. system made it extraordinarily dangerous. He said:

> Just as certain as death Westinghouse will kill a customer within six months after he puts in a system of any size.

Arguments got nowhere with Edison on this issue. The fact that he considered the main proponents of a.c. systems to be common thieves made him even more unwilling to see any virtue in their arguments. He began demonstrating the dangers of high voltages by cruel exhibitions in which stray dogs and cats were electrocuted for the enlightenment (and doubtless, entertainment) of potential customers and representatives of the press. Edison openly charged that the "patent pirates" were trying to put a lethal force into the American home indiscriminately. He refused to meet Westinghouse to talk it over. Westinghouse, smarting under such abuse, and unable to find an audience for his defense, considered suing Edison for libel. He had a point when, in discussing the possible instant execution of condemned criminals by electricity, Edison suggested that the process be called by the infinitive "to Westinghouse." (Out of that came the adoption by New York State of electrocution. The first hapless victim, a condemned murderer, William Kemmler, was electrocuted Aug. 6, 1890, but had to be "burned" twice, the first charge being of insufficient power.) Even though he refused to see reason about a.c. electrical distribution, Edison doubtless realized that technology was passing him by, if for no other reason than that the proponents of a.c. distribution included men of science whose opinions Edison respected. Once, a few years later, when an assistant came to ask him a question, Edison sent him to consult an associate, Dr. A. E. Kennelly (later Professor of Electrical Engineering at Harvard and MIT). Edison said that Kennelly knew far more about electricity than he did, and then added ruefully, ". . . in fact I've come to the conclusion that I never did know anything about it."

In January, 1889, Edison General Electric was incorporated in New Jersey with the chief promoter, Henry Villard, as president. Edison realized $1,750,000 out of the reorganization of his companies. Of the new stock issue of $12 million, Deutsche Bank took more than half for its German customers. Villard's work had paid off. Morgan interests took a major block of the stock, and Edison himself held about 10 percent of it.

Now came the last stage in the formation of General Electric, the stage of merger with competitors. In October, 1889, the United States Circuit Court in Pittsburgh upheld Edison's patents. Edison's competitors now faced the possibilities, if appeal failed, of extinction or else of an expensive settlement. In July, 1891, Federal Judge W. A. Wallace upheld Edison's patents again in New York.

There had to be a settlement. Westinghouse was nearly ruined by the court costs. Whatever the jubilant Edison thought, he no longer had control, and it is not in the nature of mature industrialists to watch vast physical resources fall into disuse, and the collapse of financial apparatus because of the courts—not without trying for an accommodation.

What to Edison was justice and a triumph, for the others was a legal threat but also an opportunity for salvage. Thomson-Houston was the main competition for Westinghouse in the a.c. business. Both firms were threatened by the court decision. The head of research at Thomson-Houston was Charles Steinmetz, no mean piece of property. Villard was anxious to merge with Thomson-Houston, but Edison remained opposed. He still thought that a.c. transmission was "unworthy of practical men." Villard hoped to form a national cartel, perhaps even linking up with the foreign companies in a vast international price and output-fixing arrangement— something which, under the Sherman Act of 1890, would soon be frowned upon. Edison wrote in 1890 that a company "could no more control the price than the tides," and prices were generally too high anyhow. Besides, Edison wanted to get out altogether. He had written to Villard in 1890: "I feel that it is time to retire from the light business and to devote myself to things more pleasant. . . ." Edison had been selling his stock and would soon own none. His opinions would soon cease to matter altogether in the practical business of Edison General Electric.

Villard pushed ahead with the merger. But now, just as the time had come for a Steinmetz to take over from an Edison, so Villard and Insull had to give way to a different kind of professionalism, Morganization. J. Pierpont Morgan had no taste for dramatic personalities. Villard was dropped from the presidency. Insull's financial genius now had to be paid for. Morgan examined the position of the two companies. Edison General Electric had excessive short-term obligations, which would have to be paid off and scaled down. It was clear that, in the merger, Thomson-Houston interests would actually get more than the Edison interests ($18.5 million of the new stock compared to $15 million for Edison General Electric) even though the Edison company was, in terms of sales, the larger of the two. Other factors had to be taken into account; for example, the street railways that had grown up since Edison's experiments for Villard at Menlo Park. Edison had played no role in these enterprises.

In April, 1892, General Electric was organized by Morgan on that basis, merging the two competitors and bringing in some smaller organizations. Edison's name was dropped altogether (it caused Edison pain and bitterness to have his name obliterated from the company and industry he had done so much to build).

Morgan liked smooth, efficient—and silent—management. The "Morgan man" who replaced Villard as president was Charles Coffin, whom Morgan trusted. Insull declined a minor post and went to Chicago, where history heard from him again because of his odd notions about finance which ended in another catastrophe. Morgan's fine touch in company reorganization usually did not create combines which could be called "monopoly" with ease, so Westinghouse was left out of the merger as the major "independent." Suitable arrangements could be made about the patent problems. When Morgan was finished, he hoped, as was the case with nearly all of his great reorganizations, that a smooth-working profit machine had been created where once chaos and fierce competition had reigned. He did not fail with General Electric.

By 1892 the industry was no longer a beginner and Morganization took over where the fruit was ripening. The average cost of each lamp had already fallen from 70 cents in 1881 to less than 31 cents in 1884, while average revenue per lamp rose from 38 cents to over 44 cents. Lamp production itself was profitable, and sales soared. By 1888 there were 185 central stations in operation supplying nearly 386,000 lamps, and there were 1,281 isolated stations supplying an additional 344,000 lamps. In 1880 the Census had listed 40 electrical manufacturing establishments employing fewer than 900 workers; in 1890 there were 189 such establishments employing nearly 46,000. The central power stations of 1890 employed an additional 2,000 workers. By 1902 some 3,620 stations would be employing more than 30,000 men, and total income in the industry, negligible in 1880, would be some $100 million. As was usually the case, Morgan knew what he was doing when he finally stepped in with his full force and organized General Electric.

In our scheme of thought the incandescent electric lighting business, and those parts of the electrical industry closely associated with it that received the benefit of Edison's inventions, had gone from the invention "stage" through innovation into financial organization and control in about thirteen years. This much was accomplished largely by the same cast of characters (Edison and Morgan had both been in it from the start) in an industry which experienced an explosive expansion after the initial difficulties. At the end of the first decade after the Pearl Street station, Morgan was left to tidy up. Edison went back to inventing things in other fields. Perhaps it would have been a happier story had Morgan taken a more active interest from the start, at least that has been said by some commentators.

As a manufacturer, in spite of his complaints, Edison in the end had not suffered from too much Morgan, but rather, from too little; there had been too much Insull, too much risky financing. It might be called "inevitable" though. Morgan was no pioneer. He only entered "in the Morgan manner" into the finances of Edison's greatest contribution when it was big enough to benefit from Morganization—and to justify the cost of Morgan's energies. That was too late to help Edison much, but he said, when he sold out his manufacturing holdings in 1890:

> I have been under a desperate strain for money for 22 years, and when I sold out, one of the greatest inducements was the

sum of cash received, so as to free my mind from financial stress and thus enable me to go ahead in the technical field. . . .

It is easy to be wise after the event. A strong argument can be made that it was virtually inevitable that the early electrical industry had to grow up as it did. There was a time for the Insulls, Edisons, Westinghouses and Villards. That time was when there were great risks to be taken. No one knew at the beginning whether electricity would grow up into the great industry we now depend upon so heavily, or whether it would just be a toy.

However admirably solid Morgan's reorganizations usually were, it was *not* solid financing that usually made pioneering possible in American industry (James J. Hill's Great Northern Railroad was a notable exception). Risk and growth were the business of the men who came before Morgan, his business was stability—or as it turned out, immense growth with very little risk. Both growth and stability were desirable, obviously, but they were rarely found working the same ground in the period from 1879 to 1892 when the American electrical industry was in its unstable days of invention, innovation and mushroom growth.

Conservatism has its place in economic growth, but so do risk and the men who are willing to take it. So one can applaud Morgan for bringing order out of chaos, but it is myopic not to applaud the men who made the chaos. Without the chaos there would have been nothing.

VI

By 1892, when General Electric was organized, Edison's private life had undergone some marked changes. He had re-established a base for continuing his work as an inventor, and had a multiplicity of new interests. So, when the electrical industry left Edison in the dust of history, he was ready to be abandoned by his ungrateful stepchild.

During the great push toward the successful establishment of his electrical businesses, Edison had virtually abandoned his wife and three children for long stretches of time. When he was at home he was abrupt, could be cruel, tended to ignore the children, usually wolfed his food and left the table immediately. His irregular overt attempts to play the "heavy father" left little beyond bitterness in the hearts of his children. His fierce temper frightened them. He continued to oppose formal education of any sort for his sons; they were, in fact, a source of deep disappointment to him (what might Thomas Edison's fatherly expectations have been?). Mary Edison, the simple working-girl wife, evidently worked out her frustrations in the kitchen and became exceedingly stout. She understood little of her husband's affairs, could not talk with him and was thought to have been "lonely."

All in all, it would seem that Edison's home life was the stuff of recent novels about preoccupied executive types; except that unlike the gray-flanneled heroes of contemporary fiction, Edison had neither time nor tastes for promiscuous sex or alcohol—or drugs—so his life would not provide material for a "best seller." In August of 1884 Mary Edison died of typhoid fever. She was not yet 30. It was too late for the inventor to make amends to her. His success had been hemlock in more ways than financial.

Faced with a widower's life and with three children, Edison, a rich man with crushing responsibilities and vaulting ambitions, made some changes in his way of living. He slowed down the interminable round of sandwiches, day-and-night work schedules, sleeping in office chairs or on floors of construction projects. He had to create an orderly private life before he could go on. A notable transformation occurred. His biographers report that he got fitted out with a decent wardrobe, and began to appear at fashionable soirées, just as affable as you please. He was wife hunting. Friends willingly provided "prospects" for him to look over. In Boston, at the home of an old friend, Ezra T. Gilliland, Edison met Mina Miller. She was the daughter of an Ohio industrialist and was in Boston at a finishing school. She was intelligent, cultured, high-spirited, independent and half his age. He was smitten. He pursued the courtship with some vigor, partly by mail from Florida where he was establishing a winter home. In the summer of 1885 he journeyed to Lake Chautauqua (the prospective father-in-law was a firm supporter of the Chautauqua Association) to intensify his suit. He taught the young lady Morse code and proposed to her in that medium. She accepted, subject to her father's approval. A photograph of a letter written to Mr. Miller in Edison's striking hand, adhering to the sternest forms of *Hill's Manual* etiquette, is reproduced by Josephson.

> I need only add in conclusion that the step I have taken in asking your daughter to intrust her happiness into my keeping has been the result of mature deliberation. . . .

Mr. Miller approved the match, and in late February, 1886, guests assembled in Akron for a gala wedding. Edison was 39 and Mina was 20. Crowds cheered the newlyweds, the girl and the famous inventor, as they drove through the streets. The couple went directly to the partly finished winter home in Fort Myers.

Edison's second marriage reflected the influence of an independent young wife with ideas of her own. The new Mrs. Edison was a real companion, and the marriage was a more equal partnership than the first one had been. Edison met his match in many ways. In later years Mina Edison complained mildly: "You have no idea what it means to be married to a great man," but she had her victories. The two sons of this marriage (Charles, born in 1890, and Theodore, born in 1898 when Edison was 51) both went to prep school and graduated from MIT. The younger son, in fact, became a mathematical physicist, much to his father's chagrin. The daughter, Madeline (born in 1888), went to Bryn Mawr and married well. There was no repetition of the wretchedness and failure of Edison's first marriage (his first two sons had disappointing lives; neither left children, and one was a suicide in 1936 and the other died in 1941 after unsuccessfully trying to break his father's will). The inventor's ideas about education were ignored.

Mina also tried to make a home for the children of the first marriage, but with indifferent success. She was always close to Marion, the eldest (who was nearly as old as Mina), but had difficulty with the two boys, who had grown up "wild" under their father's indifferent gaze. The two sons of the first marriage gave their father a great deal of misery throughout their adult lives, so long as Edison lived.

The Edisons bought a huge mansion, "Glenmount," in West Orange, New Jersey, and kept a winter home in Florida. It is said that Mina Edison succeeded in smoothing over many of the inventor's rough corners and imposing, at times, some limits on his working hours. Faced at last with a formidable schedule of private duties, the inventor was forcibly "domesticated" by his second wife. In West Orange, Edison began building new works, including a new laboratory. He said, optimistically, of the West Orange establishment:

> I will have the best equipped & largest laboratory extant. . . . Inventions that formerly took months & cost large sums can now be done in 2 or 3 days with very small expense, as I shall carry a stock of almost every conceivable material.

By 1913 he employed 3,600 men at his West Orange enterprises, developing and exploiting new ideas related to the
changing economy. Edison was no one-shot inventor, and the
man who wearily dropped out of the electrical business in
1890 was, in spite of his trials and tragedies, a man of vast
affairs and influence. It was a far cry from the days at Menlo
Park, even farther from the tramp telegrapher of 1869. By
1890 the origins at Milan and Port Huron must have seemed
remote indeed.

In 1887 Edison had returned to one of his abandoned children, the phonograph. Others had entered the field and found
a vast market. Emile Berliner invented the gramophone in
1887. Edison, ignoring the claims of others to patented improvements in the device he had invented a decade earlier,
referred to his competition collectively as "patent pirates." He
reorganized his old Speaking Phonograph Co., putting his
friend Ezra Gilliland in charge of it. Edison was now involved
in a new battle in which his education in the ways of the
world was rounded off—he was double-crossed and swindled
by his closest friends. The trouble began when, after improving
his own machine, he still resisted the obvious, that the machine's greatest potential was for music and entertainment.
His deafness may have inured him to the scratchy charms of
early phonograph music. He insisted that his machine be used
as an adjunct of business:

> I don't want the phonograph sold for amusement purposes. It
> is not a toy. I want it sold for business purposes only.

He was bucking the market. That was bad enough. But he
was also scalped by his own men. His old competitor, Bell, in
collaboration with Charles S. Tainter, developed a phonograph
which they called the "graphophone." They sold their rights to
J. W. Lippincott, a millionaire businessman. By June of 1888
Lippincott's new company was selling machines and records
in the market. The heat was on Edison to meet the competition. But Lippincott wanted to merge with Edison against the
other manufacturers. Lippincott approached Gilliland and
John Tomlinson, Edison's attorney. They convinced Edison
that he should merge with Lippincott for a cash payment of
$500,000. Both Gilliland and Tomlinson then left for Europe,
after Tomlinson touched Edison for $7,000 for expenses.

Edison had asked originally for $1,000,000 for the merger.
Lippincott, knowing his men, had offered to pay Gilliland and
Tomlinson $250,000 if they could talk Edison down to

$500,000. The flesh was weak. The offer was taken. Edison was cheated. Lippincott evidently could not face a business relationship with a man whose swindling he had subsidized. He confessed all to Edison. The inventor was crushed by the betrayal. Gilliland and Tomlinson had been two of his most intimate friends; Gilliland had even introduced Edison to his wife. It is said that Edison never again allowed intimacy to develop between himself and another man—except of course Henry Ford, a man who could not have any motive to cheat anyone for mere money.

Adding insult to injury, the new phonograph firm was soon in bankruptcy. Lippincott was trying to license their machines, as Bell had done with his telephones, to rent the phonographs for an annual charge. But to be a monopolist, one needs a monopoly. Lippincott and Edison were trying to exploit a monopoly market where none in fact existed. The business just went to their competitors. Not only were competing machines selling cheaply, but the flat-disc record was on the market bringing music and entertainment to buyers.

Although Edison's company had made some records of music, their main effort had been in the wrong direction. Edison got his patent rights back and made money on nickel-odeons. Later Edison resisted improvements in phonographs. He hated radio, considering it a mere "craze"; too long refused to incorporate vacuum tubes in his machines and, by 1930, his companies no longer made phonographs. No one wanted to listen to his old-fashioned machine any more. Again technology had passed him by. Once, after Edison had fired a gifted electronics engineer, his son Charles remarked: "My father's past experience had simply got in his way."

As the years passed, such stories increasingly were part of Edison's life. He had invented the phonograph and made a good thing of it for a time, but he resisted change in that machine as he did a.c. power systems. He exhibited a curious rigidity in his thinking, being unable in many cases to follow what he had once brilliantly invented, or developed, when others began the inexorable process of technological advance. Whether his limited vision was the result of his lack of formal training is an interesting, although perhaps academic, question. Perhaps it is simply unreasonable to expect unlimited ingenuity in a single mind, no matter how brilliant. Every field of endeavor experiences the same phenomenon; the Young Turks are quickly transformed into the Old Guard. Few indeed are the artists, scientists or scholars who remain at the frontiers of knowledge throughout their careers.

Edison almost, but not quite, missed out on the exploitation of motion pictures. It is now generally denied that Edison made any important contribution to motion-picture technology. Indeed, his biographer in the *Dictionary of American Biography* states flatly that he made "no original contribution to motion-picture invention." Recent scholarship is largely in agreement on this point, although Josephson defends his hero stoutly. But even if it be agreed that Edison was not the "father" of the motion-picture camera, for once he successfully exploited the talents of others along with his own work and, as a result, has some claims to being one of the fathers of the motion-picture *industry*.

Following the work of others, Edison began work on a motion-picture camera in the late 1880's (he had seen demonstrations of other attempts). In 1888 he filed a caveat: "The invention consists in photographing continuously a series of pictures occurring at intervals. . . ." While the work was in progress under the direction of a talented English assistant, W. K. L. Dickson, in the summer of 1889 Edison and Mina made a triumphal tour of Europe. Under Mina's pressure Edison had consented to the enrollment of his daughter Marion in a European school. Their trip was to visit her as well as for Edison to enjoy the perquisites of prestige.

Edison was lionized, made a Commander of the Legion of Honor by the French, made a Grand Officer of the Crown of Italy. He also rode in a stagecoach in Paris pursued by howling Sioux in Buffalo Bill's Wild West show, and regularly sneaked off to their encampment for a good old American "grub-stake" meal whenever the exquisite tortures of French cuisine became excessive. He met Louis Pasteur in Paris. In Berlin he met Helmholtz and Werner Siemens. In London he met S. Z. Ferranti and got a first-hand introduction to a.c. lighting systems. "Too ambitious," Edison said of Ferranti's schemes. When the Edisons got back to New York in August, he went straight over to West Orange where an image of Dickson, one of his assistants, appeared on a screen in a darkened room and said: "Good morning, Mr. Edison, glad to see you back. I hope you are satisfied with the Kinetophonograph." Edison's first version of the motion picture was a reality, "talkies" at that.

From 1890 to 1894, Edison continued work on his motion-picture camera. He got special films made in strips by George

Eastman in Rochester and developed the 35-millimeter picture that is still the standard size in commercial motion pictures. The work was extremely difficult; some of his patents were faulty, and men who worked for him left and joined competitive efforts. Perhaps influenced by the success of his phonograph as the nickelodeon, he developed little penny-arcade "peepshow" boxes, operated by coin, to exhibit his motion pictures. The boxes were called "kinetoscopes." At West Orange a studio was built and films of dancers, cockfights, cowboys, knife throwers and the like were produced for the thriving kinetoscope business. In fact, the kinetoscope parlors seemed to be making him another fortune and, at first, he rejected the suggestion that his pictures might more profitably be projected onto a central screen in an auditorium. Oddly enough (perhaps harking back to his first experiences with the phonograph when the side-show market finally died out), he believed that the market for the motion picture would be too quickly saturated if customers were allowed to see the novelty in crowds.

He was finally persuaded that the motion picture might be more than a passing fad, and that someone else would capture the market. The rush was on to get a working projector. Thomas Armat, an inventor in Washington, D. C., had perfected a projector. Edison got that. Then, seeing how it worked, he made a better one of his own. Armat withdrew his machine and charged Edison with patent infringement. Edison by then was an old campaigner in such matters. There would be a splashy lawsuit, to be sure, but meanwhile he pushed forward using a disputed process as others had done with his electrical patents in the 1880's. Adjustments could be made all around, later. In a music hall in Herald Square on April 23 (Shakespeare's birthday), 1896, Edison put his "enlarged kinetoscope" before an audience. The motion picture had come to Broadway. The little studio at West Orange kept grinding out films. The films began to incorporate simple plot lines, and then, in 1904, Edison's company produced and distributed "The Great Train Robbery." The novelty became something quite different altogether.

Edison knew the ways of the old-time tycoons, but evidently had not comprehended the meaning of the Sherman Anti-Trust Act of 1890, or of the Northern Securities decision in 1904 which had cut down Pierpont Morgan, E. H. Harriman, James J. Hill and a galaxy of other *illuminati* at a single stroke. So as the war over the motion-picture patents built up momentum, and after a Chicago court upheld his patent claims in 1907, Edison got together with his competitors and formed a quiet little patent-pooling company. When the company, the Motion Picture Patents Corp., was ordered broken up by the Supreme Court in 1917, Thomas Alva Edison may have been surprised, but doubtless few others were. Until then, Edison's share from his motion-picture monopoly had been a neat $1,000,000 each year.

During the 1890's Edison had been heavily involved in other affairs. Like so many of his contemporaries, the hidden treasures of the earth proved an overwhelming lure, and Edison lost millions in experiments near Ogdensburg, New Jersey. There he established works filled with giant machinery to separate iron from crushed low-grade iron ore by electro-magnetism. There was sunk the fortune he made out of the electrical industry (a fortune he denied ever existed). Once, upon being told what his electricity shares would have been worth had he kept them, Edison said: "Well, it's all gone, but we had a hell of a good time spending it." He meant that too. After his worrisome years in the patent wars over the incandescent lighting system, the struggles at Ogdensburg gave Edison release. Visiting the site in later years he said:

> I never felt better in my life than during the five years I worked here. Hard work, nothing to divert my thought, clear air and simple food made my life very pleasant. We learned a great deal. It will be of benefit to someone some time.

Even after Edison left the electrical industry he continued to be a central figure at annual conventions, and he enjoyed the fun. At one such convention, at a dinner in New York in 1896, he was introduced to an awkward-looking engineer, Mr. Henry Ford, from the Detroit Edison Co. (many power systems kept Edison's name, and still do, after it was dropped from the escutcheon of General Electric). Edison questioned Ford about the automobile powered by an internal-combustion engine that Ford had recently made. Edison said words of encouragement to Ford, even though at that date it was still thought that electric-powered autos held the future. It was a small enough thing to Edison, but Ford always considered that conversation to have been the great turning point in his life; he had been without much encouragement, and then the great Edison had said that Ford was on the right track. Ford became Edison's fervent disciple. By 1904 Edison had in hand orders for a superior storage battery from Henry Ford, the auto manufacturer whose firm, the Ford Motor Co., had just started. By 1909, some 50,000 experiments later, Edison had made a fine storage battery; it would not power a car, but Henry Ford, the rising auto magnate of Detroit, was too enchanted to care. Before long, Ford, the Croesus of Detroit, would finance Edison in anything his heart desired.

Edison liked Ford. The two men had a common bond in their rough-edged views of things. Ford's friendship was reciprocated and was a valuable asset as well as a source of amusement. By 1911 Edison had thirty businesses going and incorporated them all in a single company, Thomas A. Edison Inc. The man proved to be irrepressible, making and losing, and then making again fortune after fortune. He was making no more great inventive breakthroughs—he hadn't really done that since 1883, but by application of his efforts to existing technology, he continued to see commercial openings for successful inventions (which he defined in his Populist way as ". . . something that is so practical that a Polish Jew will buy it"). The works flourished at West Orange. Then came disaster. In December, 1914, his buildings were gutted by fire. As he stood watching the conflagration, he asked his son Charles to go fetch Mina: "Get her over here, and her friends too. They'll never see a fire like this again." It was a major disaster, but it was too late then for Edison to be ruined by anything this side of the grave, the Fairy Godmother in Detroit saw to that. Ford soon was at his idol's side, surveyed the losses and handed Edison $750,000 to rebuild—an interest-free loan.

Edison had reached his sixtieth birthday in 1907. He was now entering his "grand old man" stage. By now he looked like the famous pictures. He was not a tall man, standing five feet nine and one-half inches, and had a portly build, with broad square shoulders and a deep chest. His huge head was topped by unruly gray. His blue-gray eyes were set deep under huge, long, black eyebrows; the whole face dominated by a prominent nose and a powerful jaw. He was a striking figure of a man. He smoked one cigar after another, chewed tobacco and spat it on the floor where he wanted to, and swore a great deal. In spite of Mina Edison's best efforts, the great man cared nothing for his appearance and continued to appear at public events in suits with the slept-in look. He really just didn't care, although he had given up looking like a tramp by then. William Inglis described him in 1911:

Looking at the hands alone, one would classify Edison as one who lives entirely in the world of delicate but vast imaginations. It is the squareness of the jaws, the width and depth of the back head and the fulness of the torso that indicate his limitless combativeness and robust energy. . . .

By then Edison's views on most matters were "news." Often enough his off-the-cuff remarks made headline materials. In 1911 he had been voted the country's "most useful citizen" in a newspaper poll. It is apparently true that he gloried in that sobriquet far more than he did in the honors heaped upon him by governments at home and abroad. That was fitting too. The brash "hayseed" who made good had mellowed into "a simple, democratic old man." He was that in many ways. He was an admirer of Tom Paine, and Edison's views on religion got into controversies. He saw (and said) that "billions of prayers" clearly had done mankind no good; there was no scientific evidence that "the God of the theologians" exists. But Edison did say, "That there is a supreme intelligence I do not doubt." He thought that some sort of immortality was possible. It was rumored (and denied by him) that he tried to make a machine to communicate with the hereafter. That was extreme enough, but it was Henry Ford who went the limit, saying:

> The greatest thing that has occurred in the last fifty years is Mr. Edison's conclusion that there is a future life for all of us.

As Josephson points out, Edison called him Henry—no one else did—but Henry always referred to "Mr. Edison." By the outbreak of war in Europe in 1914 Edison, in spite of his grass-roots ways, was beginning to be "Mr." to an extent that he must have regretted. He was that rare phenomenon, a hero in his own country.

VII

In 1916 Edison, nearly 70, marched down Broadway in the Preparedness Day parade, and supported Woodrow Wilson for a second term. The European war was, in Edison's opinion, inevitable. The Europeans were infatuated with war. He said: "This war had to come. Those military gangs in Europe piled up armaments until something had to break." He was sympathetic to Henry Ford's pacifism, but did not believe that pacifism, even propelled by Ford's millions, would have any effect upon the belligerents. He saw Ford's "Peace Ship" off at the dock, but refused to humor his friend by joining in that ill-fated voyage. Then the septuagenarian Edison joined the Naval Consulting Board with other noted scientists. During the war Edison worked hard at his job, conducting experiments with explosives and with submarine detection devices. At the war's end he emerged with a profoundly unfavorable view of the navy's bureaucracy, saying that it had apparently been especially designed to stifle independent thought. He refused to accept the Distinguished Service Medal in 1920 for his war work, saying that he deserved no honors above those of his collaborators. He was still crusty.

Edison did not retire from his business until 1926, when he was nearly 80 years old. He said he didn't believe in retirement, that he didn't think it was good for a man. He had continued to work hard, attempting to maintain a "double" shift of 16 hours a day until he was well into his seventies and his wife successfully restrained him. His son Charles complained that although Edison thought nothing of firing younger men, he kept the old veterans at their benches long past any reasonable retirement age. As in the all-night sieges of the past, Edison made no rules to which he would not himself adhere. He stayed in the public eye, treating his admirers to his deeply heretical views about religion, politics, money and especially education. He considered conventional education to be perfectly useless. He would, he claimed, hire only graduates of institutes of technology: "They aren't filled up with Latin, philosophy and all that ninny stuff." What the country needed was technicians, engineers and business managers. His view of America was completely out of date, but he hadn't noticed it. He said: "In three or four centuries, when the country is settled and commercialism is diminished then will be time for literary men." That was his opinion in the early 1920's. Scientific writers have complained that Edison was excessively ignorant of fundamental scientific principles. He was more ignorant of other things.

The fact is that Edison was an entertaining, if absurd and crotchety old man, alive with opinions on subjects about which he had merely the slightest understanding. That made him all the more fun. I.Q. testing was becoming popular so Edison devised his own, the "ignoramometer." His questions were largely examples of the kind of learning he claimed to detest, sheer memory feats and nothing else. They measured nothing more than the volume of random facts lodged in the heads of the examinees. From a test given in 1921 the following questions are chosen to illustrate the point.

"What city in the United States is noted for its laundry-machine making?"

"Where do we get prunes from?"

"Who was Solon?"

"Who invented logarithms?"

"In what cities are hats and shoes made?"

"What voltage is used on streetcars?"

"What country makes the best optical lenses and what city?"

Not surprisingly, very few people passed Edison's examinations. He announced that his results showed that only 2 percent of the people "think." It is a shame that he never gave his examination to his disciple Henry Ford. But then neither man valued training that was not "practical." They talked about "original perception" as the fundamental basis of intellectual progress, but what they meant was that formal training harmed the original mind, cluttered it up and made it less able to perceive new things than it would in its pristine state. When Edison in turn was quizzed, some of his answers showed a mind that "thought" in a way no one was trying to test.

Q. The American people have lost confidence in their political leaders. Why?
A. I can't remember that they ever had very much.
Q. If the population of the world continues to increase at the rate of the past half century, what will be the result in two hundred years?
A. War.

As he grew older there was more of this. He reveled in this kind of repartee and of course his pithy views were always worth looking at in the newspapers. But the American people, like Edison and so noticeably unlike his biographers, had a far-reaching sense of, and appreciation for, the ridiculous.

Edison's old age was much brightened by his association with Henry Ford. The friendship had ripened during the war years. In 1914 the great naturalist, John Burroughs, took Edison and Ford for a tour of the Everglades. The world of botany fascinated Edison, and he found a new interest which made his old age and eventual retirement simply a change to new experiments. Ford was interested in botany too, and the subject was pursued in 1915 when, after receiving the salute in an open car on "Edison Day" in San Francisco, Ford and

Edison together with Harvey Firestone visited Luther Burbank's place in Santa Rosa.

From these outings came the famous camping trips, when the industrialists communed with nature. In 1916 Burroughs, Edison and Firestone camped through the Adirondacks (Ford was otherwise occupied). In the summer of 1918 Ford joined the safari and, like boys again, they camped through the Big Smoky Mountains, their rough garb and talk comprising prime news items for the reporters and photographers. Edison amused himself with his magnets and geologist's hammer, astonishing observers by his readiness to sleep anywhere in the clothes in which he was standing (he had long training, but who could remember it by then?). Henry Ford was then running for the Senate in Michigan and Edison found the prospect of "Senator Ford" worth considering around the campfire: ". . . he won't say a damn word." The nation was diverted by the fabulous campers and when, in the summer of 1919, the "boys" hit the trail again they were followed by a caravan of fifty cars and trucks. Warren Harding even came out to be rejuvenated under the stars. Then Burroughs began to decline and in 1921 he died. That was the end of the camping. Coming away from the funeral, Edison turned to Ford and said bluntly, "I'm next."

In 1926 Edison finally retired from active participation in his enterprises. But the faithful Henry Ford made it easy. Ford and Firestone organized the Edison Botanic Research Co. in 1927, put in an initial $93,000 for expenses and then fed money in silently to keep the great man busy. Edison's contribution was his labor. He was searching for a domestic source of natural rubber and actually developed, by selective breeding, a giant strain of goldenrod for that purpose (Firestone made a set of tires for Edison's special Ford car out of goldenrod latex). Ford came down to Fort Myers, where he maintained a home next door to the Edisons, and cheered the old man on. Edison worked at his usual full-out pace, hiring a linguist to translate books and papers for him so he could read what was known about rubber. In 1929 he said that he was, he estimated, about five years away from giving the country a natural rubber crop that the farmers could "sow and mow." This research kept him busy until the end.

In 1928 Congress awarded its gold medal to the old man as a sign of the nation's gratitude. Then in the fall of 1929, on the fiftieth anniversary of his incandescent light, a unique homage was paid to him. General Electric intended to celebrate the Golden Jubilee of Light. Henry Ford pre-empted the ceremonies, it is said, because he objected to the commercialization of his idol's name. So Ford just "assumed power"—with Edison's approval. Out in Dearborn, Ford had painstakingly reconstructed Menlo Park and filled a museum with Edison trophies. (Ford's industrious search extended to Edison's place in Fort Myers, and Josephson reports that Mina Edison remarked to her husband one morning after looking out her kitchen window, "Dear me, I do wish Mr. Ford would keep out of our backyard.") A ceremony was planned on a scale that only the imperious Ford would have attempted.

The guest list began with the President of the United States and his lady, and worked down to the "Edison Pioneers," the survivors of the early days at Newark and Menlo Park. The guests included Madame Curie and Orville Wright. Blue-ribbon industrialists like Charles Schwab were invited. Even the world of finance was momentarily forgiven its transgressions by Ford, and men like Otto Kahn, Thomas Lamont and J. P. Morgan, Jr., were invited. Things had changed since 1916 and the "Peace Ship"; by 1929 few indeed would have declined an invitation from Henry Ford, and Dearborn was overrun. There was a nation-wide radio hookup and special old-fashioned incandescent lamps were distributed around the country to be turned on when Edison and his old assistant, Francis Jehl, started up a replica of their 1879 lamp.

Going into the dinner that ended the exhausting ceremonies, the aged inventor suffered a momentary collapse, but revived sufficiently to make a short speech. At the end the grateful old man turned to Ford and said:

> As to Henry Ford, words are inadequate to express my feelings, I can only say to you, that in the fullest and richest meaning of the term—he is my friend.

Few men could ever have said that truthfully, yet Edison had found in Ford a man he could trust and Ford found in Edison a man he could admire. In the friendship both men found simple, yet fundamental, values that had eluded them elsewhere.

Edison was in poor health after 1929 and died in West Orange on Oct. 18, 1931, in his eighty-fifth year. In September, Ford had made a last pilgrimage to see his friend. Ford, assisted by his ghostwriter, wrote a little book, *Edison as I Knew Him*. It was an extraordinary tribute from a man who viewed his fellows sourly indeed. For most Americans, whose opinions of people were more charitable than were Ford's, the passing of Edison was a broken link with a distant past. In everyday life one turned on lights, listened to the radio, went to the movies, played the phonograph and performed a hundred and one other perfectly routine and mundane acts which made life easier and more interesting and fruitful, and which, one way or another, bore the imprint of Edison's pragmatic genius. It was astonishing, even to Edison. He said once in an interview: "Say, I *have* been mixed up in a whole lot of things, haven't I?"

VIII

Efforts have been made to calculate the value of the annual output and the capitalization of industries Edison started. These have been futile exercises. Except for the phonograph, Edison had mainly been part of a great stream of technological advance and, as the court battles showed, someone else could claim almost everything of importance that he patented. His achievements are of incalculable value to the nation as part of the stream of ingenuity that produced America's tremendous productivity. Who could say what the value of the lights at the White House have been to the nation? Edison's achievements were a tribute to the open society that gave such a man the chance to shake the world, and those achievements remain as a warning to any who would shrink from the risk of failure.

Doubtless Edison's place in the folk mythology of America as a somehow "typical" specimen is due to several connected facts: the Horatio Alger character of his life, the American's native distrust of organized learning of all sorts, the belief (however deluded) in the reality of opportunity for all, trust in the "practical" side of life, in things that work. But also there is the ingrained American belief that new ideas are worth trying, at least once. That means hardship as well as success. If ever there was a man whose contribution to American economic growth was the product of hardship, risk, failure and sweat, it was Edison. It is no wonder that his name is so honored among his countrymen.

If success be measured by wealth accumulated (and some would have it that way) then Edison was a success—in the end. But if success be measured by the realization and fulfillment of opportunity and promise, then the poor little deaf boy from Port Huron who became the Wizard of Menlo Park was a paragon. For the nation's economic growth, neither measure of Edison's achievement is very important. We have a surfeit of success stories. We needed men of invention and ingenuity, and still do. Edison's place in American history is secured by his technical contributions alone. And that doubtless would have satisfied him—even discounted for patent suits. He liked to work and try out new things. That, one has reason to hope, will continue to make Edison seem to be a "typical" American. Economic progress depends upon the search for greater efficiency and new ideas. But most of all it depends upon a people's willingness to work hard when they need to.

PART III

CREATIVE DESTRUCTION—THE INNOVATORS

The economic growth of the United States has caused one of the most fundamental shifts in the balance of economic power in modern times. A few figures might help to illustrate the reasons for the magnitude of American growth. In 1790 there were just under 4 million persons in the continental limits of the United States; by 1860 there were 31 million; by 1900, 84 million; by 1940, 131 million; by 1960, more than 185 million. This rise in population, enormous as it was, was actually outstripped by increases in output of goods and services to such an extent that rising output per head of population came to be a thing taken for granted by Americans. We virtually consider to be "automatic" that which two-thirds of the earth's population find almost impossible to achieve.

Such declines in output as were associated with downturns in the business cycle were compensated for in the expansions in economic activity which followed. From relatively meager beginnings, the United States surpassed all to become, by the 20th century, the "industry state" *par excellence*. By 1956 with just 7 percent of the world's population, the United States produced 46 percent of the world's electrical energy, made 41 percent of its steel, mined 37 percent of its coal, made a quarter of its cement and produced some 45 percent of its crude petroleum. As late as 1880 we had been behind the United Kingdom (still the industrial leader of those days) in the production of every major manufacturing mineral and metal except crude steel—and we were only just even with the British on that. These great changes in the American position in industry were intimately related to the continuous introduction of technological change into the economy.

The prodigious increase in the size of the American economy meant opportunity for the millions of citizens, native and foreign-born alike, to improve their lives. That great story is part of the American heritage and is well known. The continent increasingly was filled with people, traversed by transportation systems and adorned with cities. But there was something special about the size of the economy and the kind of economic activity it inspired. With a productive population, such a growth should have been a stimulus to economic activity of all sorts. But the massive size of the continental market, unimpaired by internal barriers to the flow of commodities and people, was a challenge to men engaged in certain kinds of economic activity to expand the size of their operations to match the rise of a national economy which was developing on such a colossal scale. The growing giant stimulated the rise of giant enterprises.

To plan and build for markets beyond a given city or locale called for skills which bore some resemblance to that of invention, but which also called for a certain combination of both conservative judgment and audacity. The inventors had many times carried their inventions successfully into the main channels of economic life and wrought fundamental changes in techniques, tastes and organization. But in the industrial history of the United States, as was also true elsewhere, it was more common for changes in technology to be introduced by men who were not themselves inventors, but who, nonetheless, had sufficient knowledge of the economic potential of critical changes to introduce those changes successfully. Andrew Carnegie made more Bessemer steel than did Sir Henry Bessemer (or Mr. Andrew Kelly, the American who also discovered what came to be known as the Bessemer process). James J. Hill built the Great Northern Railroad on a scale which would have staggered the builders of the Stockton & Darlington—history's first railway. Henry Ford's methods and volume of output of automobiles would doubtless have surpassed the wildest fantasies of Otto Daimler or the other "inventors" of the motor car.

Invention itself has no economic effect unless it can somehow be introduced into the stream of the nation's economic life. The "innovators" who built the foundations of many of the nation's industries were primarily men who bridged the gap between the technological advances of the inventors and effective economic change.

In recent years the roles of innovation and innovators in economic progress have been the subject of a great many studies by American and foreign scholars. The great economist, Joseph Schumpeter, was largely responsible for this shift of emphasis away from the study of abstract "forces" and toward this particular human element in economic progress.

Schumpeter used the French word *entrepreneur* ("beginner" or "undertaker") to designate the individuals who, by their own decisions, wrought economic change. His entrepreneurs played no passive roles. They were the effective agents of economic change, shrewdly judging the moment when existing technological advances, changes in taste, technique and so forth could find profitable expression in the open market. This function of innovation was sharply differentiated from that of invention, as we noted above.

The wisdom of Schumpeter's functional differentiation between invention and innovation is sharply illustrated in the studies of American innovators. For example, biographers of Commodore Vanderbilt were especially impressed by his unwillingness to involve himself or his funds either in steam navigation or railway enterprises until it was clear to him that these radical evidences of technical progress would "work." Then he plunged in. He was a terror as a competitor, but a pretty cautious "pioneer." He was no inventor and "pushed" no inventions on principle. Unlike inventors, innovators live in history primarily by their financial successes. Andrew Carnegie was strikingly similar to the old Commodore in that one respect: he introduced both Bessemer and open-hearth steel production techniques only after, in his judgment, the processes were relatively perfected and the market was ready for their product. The "Old Man of Steel" invented nothing; he knew a good thing when he saw it, but a thing was not always "good" the first time he saw it.

The role of innovation in American economic development is one of the most dramatic parts of the whole story. The innovators both built and ruined. Schumpeter referred to continuous innovation as a process of "creative destruction." In an open economy where consumer demand ultimately regulates the allocation of resources (what doesn't sell ultimately is not produced), a new technique or a change in taste, while opening an era of economic progress for some, can mean ruin for others. Business failures, in this view, are part of the cost of economic progress, if resources are going to follow changes in the economy produced by fundamental innovations. Canals, street cars, railway passenger service—one by one these have succumbed to new methods of transport which have gained the public's favor.

Creative destruction due to innovation in American history has introduced a great deal of instability into economic growth. First one industry or group of industries, then another, has led the growth of output. Thus growth was quite uneven or "unbalanced" so far as the distribution of output over the whole range of production was concerned. This was necessarily so because some economic activities expanded more rapidly than others and some, of course, were simply killed off by innovation.

The pattern of this kind of innovation-induced economic change was quite simple and can be generally divided into four parts. First, of course, there is the change in the flow of resources created by direct demand for a primary innovation.

Second, increased demand for a given product might stimulate demand for other products which combine (the intermediate products) to make it; for example, demand for automobiles created a demand for engine blocks, the latter being "derived" from the demand for autos since automobile engine blocks customarily have no separate economic life except as parts of autos.

Third, some products find their demand influenced by other products in a complementary way: beer and pretzels, for example. A rise in beer consumption might give rise to a "complementary" increase in demand for pretzels.

Finally, there is the case of direct competition. Successful market expansion by a product or service might breathe new life into the manufacture of a directly "competitive" product and both products experience a rise in output because of an initial innovation affecting one of them. One is reminded here of the great improvement since World War II in the quality and price of cotton textiles in the face of stiff competition from artificial fibers. In all these ways innovation can stimulate economic advance. Hence the process of innovation becomes the source of new life in any economy which provides scope for continuous and pervasive change. The growth process here described is of necessity "unbalanced" and creates problems, but also it brings rising output per capita—net economic growth.

The innovators were, and still are, the natural revolutionaries of a dynamic free-enterprise economy. They are the initiators of economic change. Since they also destroy, their activities have not been viewed as an unmixed blessing by their contemporaries and competitors. Too many times in our history, combinations of producers have coalesced, intending to stop the introduction of innovations. The present-day opposition to "automation" is a good case in point. But while we may appreciate the viewpoints of those who oppose the innovators, our own history, as well as logic, suggests that the suppression of innovation is the road to economic and social stagnation. Unless the free market is replaced by overall economic planning *and control,* innovation by individual entrepreneurs is our only method of gaining the rewards of technological progress. This is a lesson Americans can forget only at their peril.

CHAPTER 6

Carnegie and the American Steel Industry

> It would be safe to wager that a thousand Americans in a
> new land would organize themselves . . . and go ahead
> developing their country before an equal number of
> British would have discovered who among them was the
> highest in hereditary rank and had the best claims to
> leadership owing to his grandfather. There is but one rule
> among Americans—the tools to those who can use them.
>
> Andrew Carnegie, *Autobiography*

I

Andrew Carnegie's life contained so much that was great
mixed with the absurd, such giant achievements amid the
commonplace failures, that the historian's hand necessarily
falters momentarily at the prospect of it all. The poor, but
deserving, Scottish immigrant lad, laboring in the Allegheny
cotton mill lived to carry his version of the American "success
story" beyond the sublime, almost beyond belief. He rose to
be the greatest innovator in the American steel industry, and
in his own lifetime gave away over $350 million of the result-
ing personal fortune for the benefit, as he saw it, of humanity.
He left a host of institutions to influence the future of the
world, paid for by the interest on the residue of his personal
estate.

Like so many self-educated men, Carnegie believed that his
own investigations into the wisdom of the ages (embellished
by the musings of the great men of letters, learning and politics
he so assiduously cultivated) had revealed important truths;
and through his benefactions, books, articles and personal influence, he wanted to favor the world with the fruits of his
wisdom.

Carnegie also believed that the great material successes
of his own life justified his actions in the world of ideas and
institutions. He set the pace of philanthropy in his time—for
all time, for that matter—enunciating his gospel of wealth
that "he who dies rich dies disgraced." Carnegie's talents as a

competitive innovator made him enormously wealthy; his intellectual leanings made him a social reformer, and the improving gospel Carnegie spread was the Social Darwinism of Herbert Spencer. Carnegie was destined to experience total disillusionment as the price of his naïveté. In the last years before 1914, Carnegie the steelmaker had been transformed in the public eye into a kind of holy man, a great prophet of peace and progress, who was able to achieve his ends by simply buying what he wanted with his vast wealth. Then war came, and during Carnegie's last years, while his old mills at Pittsburgh waxed rich on the sinews of war, the terrible 20th century ground out the first of its major horrors.

In August of 1914 hope died in Western Europe. Progress was not inevitable any more. Carnegie's health as well as his spirits were utterly crushed by the sudden vision of reality. His idol, Herbert Spencer, was irrelevant. The tools of war had improved. Mankind's "spiritual progress" was a tragic joke.

The magnitude of the conflict in 1914 illuminated the extent of Carnegie's Victorian naïveté, as well as the abandoned folly of the world's statesmen. In 1904 Carnegie had set up the first of his Hero Funds. He wanted to reward those who helped their fellow men. There were little gold, silver and bronze medals to be given for heroic acts: "Ours is an heroic age," Carnegie said. The "heroes of civilization," he noted, are many times

> . . . injured or lose their lives in attempting to preserve or rescue their fellows. . . . The heroes of barbarism maimed or killed theirs.

Carnegie believed this. He also believed that universal education was not only a good thing but possible. He believed in the whole corpus of the doctrine of the spiritual evolution of man. He noted in his *Autobiography* that, when he was losing faith in organized religion, he found a suitable alternate philosophy.

> When I, along with three or four of my boon companions, was in this stage of doubt about theology, including the supernatural element, and indeed the whole scheme of salvation through vicarious atonement and all the fabric built upon it, I came fortunately upon Darwin's and Spencer's works 'The Data of Ethics,' 'First Principles,' 'Social Statics,' 'The Descent of Man.' Reaching the pages which explain how man has absorbed such mental foods as were favorable to him, retaining what was salutary, rejecting what was deleterious, I re-

member that light came as in a flood and all was clear. Not only had I got rid of theology and the supernatural, but I had found the truth of evolution. 'All is well since all grows better' became my motto, my true source of comfort. Man was not created with an instinct for his own degradation, but from the lower he had risen to the higher forms. Nor is there any conceivable end to his march to perfection. His face is turned to the light; he stands in the sun and looks upward.

In accord with this hopeful belief in man's inexorable progress, Carnegie built the Peace Palace at The Hague to assist the nations to settle their differences without war. The Palace was dedicated in 1913. Indeed, ceremonies to unveil a bust of Carnegie, with Lord Bryce as the principal speaker, had actually been scheduled for August, 1914.

When the old man died in August of 1919, his whole ideological world was gone; there had been more than 37 million casualties among the Western nations (except for Turkey, "Christendom" as people used to say) in 1914–18; 8,500,000 "killed and died" in the armed forces: nearly a million from Britain and her empire, 1,700,000 Russians, 1,358,000 Frenchmen, 1,800,000 Germans, 1,200,000 from Austria-Hungary. The smaller nations also made their contributions. Rumania alone lost 336,000 dead. Our 126,000 dead in 1917–18, a hard sacrifice, was not of the same order of magnitude as, say, France's losses. The end of Carnegie's dreams was described by his widow in her memorable preface to his *Autobiography*.

> . . . when the fateful news of the 4th of August reached us, we immediately left our retreat in the hills and returned to Skibo to be more in touch with the situation. These memoirs ended at that time. Henceforth he was never able to interest himself in private affairs. Many times he made the attempt to continue writing, but found it useless. Until then he had lived the life of a man in middle age—and a young one at that. . . . Optimist as he always was and tried to be, even in the face of the failure of his hopes, the world disaster was too much. His heart was broken . . . two serious attacks of pneumonia precipitated old age upon him.

The demolition of Carnegie's personal fantasy world was, in microcosm, the end of an epoch. From 1815 to 1914, the age of the *Pax Britannica* had seen such material and scientific progress that general war among the great powers had become "unthinkable" because men assumed that there had been parallel ethical progress. The Victorian faith in the goodness

ANDREW CARNEGIE / 223

of man and in his perfectibility is slightly unbelievable now, but was real enough then. In that progress and faith America grew to a robust eminence among the nations, and Carnegie with his steel mills and hopes and self-improvement had played a critical role in its development. Economic progress was thought to be virtually a guarantee of peace—an old notion. Hence Carnegie had written regarding a dinner with the Kaiser in 1907:

> . . . I believe the peace of the world has little to fear from Germany. Her interests are all favorable to peace, industrial development being her aim. . . .

The question "Industrial development for what end?" was not asked. Carnegie assumed that "progress" was the end sought by Germany. Instead, the hand of the barbarian in European history reached out for conquest and slaughter once again in 1914, dashing the hopes of Andrew Carnegie's world and, for the most part, our own. Carnegie's life was in many respects America's life; his hopes were ours, his tragedy our own. American economic power, which Carnegie so greatly helped to build, was the decisive force in the 1914–18 war. But the fruits of victory were bitter, and America came into her own in a flawed world, one of uncertainty and terror.

Carnegie's dreams had not been complicated enough. The world was much more complex than he imagined it to be. Why? Because men of good will also start wars, and with the best of intentions. Half a century later the imperfection is still not corrected. Carnegie's dreams were crushed in 1914 by the flaw in Western man, his evident inability to live in peace.

The agnostic Carnegie had acted as if he believed in miracles. He thought that the study of the causes of war by men of good will, and the general improvement in the education of the masses, would by themselves eliminate war. Men already knew the causes of war, and it was the most educated populations of mankind that indulged themselves in 1914.

II

The story of Carnegie and America begins with the Atlantic crossing and the troubles of 1848. Europe's greatest contribution to American development was the people, the millions of immigrants, most of them in poverty, who sailed for the Golden Shore. In the "theory of noncompeting groups" economists developed the thesis (recently utilized by Brinley Thomas in his pioneering *Migration and Economic Growth*) that the migrants could not have been assimilated at home once their jobs disappeared under the forces of free trade and economic change. This was so primarily because of the constricting social system of Britain and, by analogy, of Western Europe in general. Economic change in Europe was a detonator; the force of the explosion was felt in the waves of migrants for whom America was the only hope. Europe lost part of its hardiest stock as a consequence, and America was the beneficiary.

In the little Scottish family of William Carnegie, Britain gave America in 1848 one of history's greatest industrial prodigies. Britain's curse was our blessing. The New World was, in the song the child Andrew Carnegie heard sung by the silent looms of famine-ridden Dunfermline, "as broad as all England and free to us all." There used to be two kinds of "success stories" in America: log cabin to the White House for the native born, and immigrant ship to independent wealth for the foreign born. For the wide-eyed American schoolboy of fifty years ago, Abraham Lincoln exemplified the first, Andrew Carnegie the second.

Carnegie's life was overshadowed by technological change, the most thoroughgoing revolutionary force man has contrived. Carnegie was at first a victim of this force; he then became one of the virtuoso industrial innovators in history, imposing technological improvements in the wide-open American steel industry with such skill that none could stand against him. In the end, the great economic innovations he had so largely fostered warranted vast financial organization for continued progress, and Carnegie, the industrial innovator, stepped out. He hated finance. As he once put it, he "manufactured steel, not securities."

Andrew Carnegie was born Nov. 25, 1835, at Dunfermline, the ancient seat and burial ground of the Scottish kings. On the paternal side, his family had produced three generations of hand-loom weavers, and Carnegie's father, William, had risen to the position of master weaver. In Carnegie's childhood, therefore, the family had reached working-class opulence. The Carnegies were of the agnostic, independent Scottish tradition, haters of the established church and the aristocratic British social organization which was indissolubly linked with crown and religion. Carnegie's maternal grandfather, Thomas Morrison, was a shoemaker and a local political radical, and

Andrew's uncle Morrison had once, during the Chartist agitation of the early 1840's, been jailed.

On both sides was the strong Scottish tradition of learning. The paternal grandfather, Andrew Carnegie, had been a local pundit, "The Professor" (also "Daft Andrew"), and had helped form a workingmen's library and "college." Little Andrew was brought up in both Carnegie and Morrison traditions at his father's and his uncle's knees with a strong primary education in Scottish history and literature and a powerful dose of political and social radicalism. There was little formal education: a few years, only, at a Dunfermline elementary school. Scottish history, political radicalism, agnosticism, independent thinking and hard work mixed with a strong dash of Celtic emotionalism were the bricks and mortar of Carnegie's character. These and an egotism which came near to being boundless.

Carnegie's father did not long enjoy his success as a master weaver. The power loom for weaving textiles had been perfected and was being widely used; by 1835 there were already some 110,000 power looms at work in the British cotton textile industry. The loom was also adapted to other textiles quite rapidly, and its use suddenly reduced thousands to grinding poverty. The Carnegie family had the misfortune to become part of one of economic history's great *cause célèbres,* the case of the hand-loom weavers, their impoverishment and destruction by the power loom. The use of power looms spread to linens, and the hand-loom weavers of Dunfermline were doomed. Moreover, after the crest of the British railway boom of 1845–46 and the Panic of 1847, mass unemployment and industrial depression, together with the potato blight and poor harvests, brought the dread of famine to Britain for the last time. The worst year was 1848, the nearest Britain ever came in modern times to "the edge" of social revolution.

All of these forces converged upon the Scottish hand-loom linen weavers in the 1840's. Power looms had come relatively late in linen but by then they were introduced, and by 1850 there were already more than 1,000 of them at work. The end was in sight for people like William Carnegie; within a decade there were 15,000 power looms at work making British linens. Under the pressure of technological unemployment compounded by general economic stagnation, the Carnegie family, on May 17, 1848, joined the tide of 1,300,000 that emigrated from the British Isles between 1845 and 1850. There was nothing to do but leave Britain forever. William

Carnegie, a master weaver of Dunfermline, had been converted into a ruined man. Reduced to poverty, the looms sold, the household effects auctioned for a pittance, money borrowed from relatives and from a neighbor woman, William, his wife Margaret and their two sons Andrew and Thomas followed the path of millions to the new world. "Home" had now become only a place of dream and memory for the Carnegies, a phantom.

The great 19th-century trans-Atlantic migration is sometimes viewed as an "economic process." It was also a human experience, many times heartrending to all concerned. In his old age Andrew Carnegie wrote of the heartbreak of leaving the place of his birth and childhood, watching the fabled tower of Dunfermline Abbey disappear behind them. He had to be torn from his uncle's arms by a watching sailor and pressed aboard the ship. He vowed to return. The imprint of Dunfermline was on him for life. In his first published book, *An American Four-in-Hand in Britain,* Carnegie told how deeply his birthplace was rooted in his life: "What Benares is to the Hindoo, Mecca to the Mohamadan, Jerusalem to the Christian, all that Dunfermline is to me." Partly this was due to the simple fact that the only childhood Carnegie had was in that Scottish village. In America, work began for him immediately. His childhood was closed, a private, treasured world of his imagination.

The Carnegie family settled in Allegheny, Pennsylvania, in the immigrant slums. Mrs. Carnegie had two sisters there. At first the family continued to live in poverty. William was unable or unwilling to leave his only skill and try to adapt himself to new circumstances. He used his brother-in-law's hand loom to weave tablecloths, which he sold door-to-door himself. Thomas, the youngest son, could go to school; but Andrew, then in his fourteenth year, had to work to contribute to the family treasury. Failing to earn enough at the loom, William took a job at a textile mill and got young Andrew on as a bobbin boy at $1.20 a week, hours 6 A.M. to 6 P.M. William soon gave it up and went back to the hand loom and its submarginal earnings. He was lost in America. He never found himself. The loom was all he knew, his only employment. He was dead in 1855, aged 50. America for him had been the end of a catastrophe. He was, and his wife and children seemed so to consider him, a failure. Not all of the immigrants tasted success.

For young Andrew, on the other hand, the cotton mill was

a beginning. The new country held few terrors for him. He soon had a job tending a boiler for $1.65 a week, a dirty job, but an "improvement," and in less than a year he got a job as a messenger boy for the telegraph company. When Carnegie applied for the job, his father accompanied him to the telegraph office but did not go in—his son was ashamed of his father's accent—a familiar American story. Andrew Carnegie was always known for his quick wits, overwhelming self-confidence and ability to make decisions. Accordingly, by going to work before regular office hours he independently learned to send and receive messages. Thomas A. Scott, superintendent of the Pennsylvania Railroad's Pittsburgh Division, hired the boy at the princely salary of $35 a month to be his secretary and telegrapher. Scott soon learned that Carnegie could run the division unaided—and did so one morning when Scott was late to work. Scott went to Philadelphia in 1859 and Carnegie, at 23 years of age, was made superintendent of the Pittsburgh Division. He was then only eleven years from Dunfermline but already far up the road to power, controlling the affairs of thousands.

By 1859 Carnegie had also discovered capitalism. A year after his father's death, Mrs. Carnegie had mortgaged their home to stake Andrew to ten shares of telegraph company stock. Soon the first dividend came. Carnegie described the great event in his *Autobiography*.

> I opened the envelope. All it contained was a check for ten dollars. . . . I shall remember that check as long as I live. . . . It gave me the first penny of revenue on capital—something that I had not worked for with the sweat of my brow. 'Eureka!' I cried. 'Here's the goose that lays the golden eggs.' It was the custom of our [group of young people] to spend Sunday afternoon in the woods. I kept the first check and showed it as we sat under the trees in a favorite grove. . . .

There was the spirit of capitalism unadorned: invest, earn.

Carnegie met a man named Woodruff who had built a railway carriage which could be converted at night into a sleeping car. Carnegie took Woodruff to Scott and arranged for the Pennsylvania Railroad to buy two cars. The grateful Woodruff offered Carnegie one-eighth interest in his company. Carnegie took it, borrowing without collateral from a banker, his first payment. The amount involved was $217.50: ". . . here I made my first note, and actually got a banker to take it. . . . The first considerable sum I made was from this source."

In 1860, when he was 25, Carnegie's income from this investment alone was $5,000. In 1863, at 28, Carnegie had the income of a blossoming millionaire—$47,860.67—of which a paltry $2,400 was his salary from the Pennsylvania Railroad. He had $17,868.67 that year from his oil company (he and a partner, unaware of how much oil there was in the world, had gone to the first field in Pennsylvania, dug a large artificial lake into which they poured oil for storage hoping to corner the market eventually). By then he already had money invested in a company to make bridges. He had purchased a country home for his mother, started his brother Thomas in business, lent money to friends to stake their careers. Where his father had been totally unable to cope, Andrew Carnegie had triumphed with all the flippant airs of the born virtuoso. America would be Andrew Carnegie's romping ground.

About 1860 Carnegie, known as "the little boss" by his men, was an appealing picture of precocity. Small of stature, slightly built, with icy blue eyes and a shock of white hair, the future steel tycoon lived a life of Bohemian irregularity. Tramping about the Pittsburgh Division in oversized boots, inspecting, cajoling, admonishing, hurrying out to railway wrecks, sleeping in cabooses or even in box cars, Carnegie was all vitality and his division of the Pennsylvania Railroad was enormously efficient. The "little boss" did not run his railway from a padded chair. Carnegie was "vain, boastful, cocksure." As his biographer, Burton Hendricks, described him at that time: "That he could ever fail in life, that any possible ambition could not be achieved—such doubts never entered Carnegie's mind." He already exhibited his "unerring instinct in his choice of men." He had taken the trouble to make some improvement in his manners. Earlier he had the advantage of Col. James Anderson's generous loan of his private books to "working boys." Now Carnegie met Leila Addison, a neighbor in Pittsburgh. She was educated in Europe, and Carnegie ". . . realized the immeasurable gulf that separates the educated from people like myself." Evenings at the home of the Pennsylvania Railroad's general counsel further impressed Carnegie with his own ignorance. His intellectual horizons were expanding, and he developed a life-long craving for formal learning. More than his intellectual horizons were stimulated in 1861.

Early that year, Washington, D. C., had been cut off from the North by Confederate railway wreckers. Carnegie's old boss, Scott, was ordered to Washington to organize the Union's rail transport system and took Carnegie with him. Carnegie organized a railway and telegraph repair crew, used the men of Benjamin Butler's Eighth Massachusetts Regiment for labor, and in three days opened the rails to the capital. Carnegie was injured in the process but was able to enter Washington with the first Federal troops. He then organized the Telegraphers Corps, calling upon old friends from the Pittsburgh region to serve. He was in charge of dispatching trains at Burke's Station, behind Bull Run, and came out on the last train with the wounded. Later in the year the Pennsylvania Railroad ordered Carnegie back to Pittsburgh; he had suffered what was evidently sunstroke at Bull Run and was unable fully to recover. When, in May 1862, he was granted leave of absence to recuperate, Carnegie took his mother and a friend on a triumphal return to Scotland.

After Pittsburgh, the old country and Dunfermline seemed incredibly small to Carnegie. "You over here are all playing with toys," he said to a relative. But after Washington, the Pennsylvania Railroad also seemed too limited a world to Carnegie. By 1861 he had an investment in an iron forge; by 1863, although still superintendent at Pittsburgh, he had entered upon his career as a manufacturer.

III

The next decade saw Carnegie emerge as a great capitalist and then turn away from all enterprises except steel. Carnegie saw the great wartime demand for iron and determined not to miss the opportunity. With Thomas Miller he organized a company in 1864 to construct blast furnaces and a rolling mill at Pittsburgh. "There was no difficulty in obtaining partners," he noted. Nor should there have been, with iron at $135 a ton. Earlier, in 1862, he had gone into the business of making iron bridges. He had seen one built at Altoona in the Pennsylvania Railroad's shops, and formed a partnership with the men who had built it. In 1863 this firm was reorganized as the Keystone Bridge Co. It was the first such company in America, and over the years no Keystone bridge ever collapsed. Carnegie referred to his product affectionately, quoting Carlyle, as "an honest brig."

In 1865, at 30 years of age, Carnegie resigned from the Pennsylvania Railroad and was thereafter the complete master of his own affairs. Ties with his former employers were maintained, however, and were highly profitable, Carnegie's enterprises receiving a lion's share of the Pennsylvania's orders. When, in 1866, Carnegie and Miller organized the Pittsburgh locomotive works, Carnegie already had an extensive interest in the iron-founding firm of Andrew Kloman, and had lent his brother Thomas the money to buy a partnership. By 1867, Andrew was able to integrate his interests. The blast furnaces and rolling mills supplied beams for the bridge business, as well as rails. Carnegie was making iron through the basic reduction process to a finished product. This was a small beginning of the sort of "vertical integration" for which he would one day become singularly famous.

Carnegie's comment, made when he first refused to install "Bessemer's Volcano" in his works, has often been quoted: "Pioneering don't pay." What he meant was that unnecessarily risky pioneering didn't pay, or rather, that new ideas which didn't pay could be called "pioneering." He was a great innovator and took risks when he thought they would pay—that wasn't "pioneering."

Carnegie's "nonpioneering" innovations included the first steps toward scientific management in the iron business. First was the introduction of accounting in the shops. He quickly discovered that the cost of each individual process in iron-making was unknown and that only at year end did his competitors really know how their net positions had changed. As an old railway man, Carnegie saw a fabulous opening here. Accountants and strict costing in the shops were introduced. The new system took years to perfect, but from the first was a powerful source of strength to Carnegie. He introduced the Siemens gas furnace into his iron works because his accounting methods showed him that it would raise his profits by cutting his unit costs. His competitors took years to understand this. They thought that the furnaces were "too expensive" because of their high initial costs. Carnegie knew how much they cost per ton of product, a very different sort of information. Carnegie's appreciation of the accountant's art gave him immense advantages in competition with his "practical" Pittsburgh colleagues, whom he was fond of referring to derisively as "the Fathers-in-Israel" because of both their Quaker origins and their hide-bound conservatism. As Carnegie put it:

> One of the chief sources of success in manufacturing is the introduction and strict maintenance of a perfect system of

accounting so that responsibility for money or materials can be brought home to every man.

The old rule-of-thumb Pittsburgh was destined to be badly shaken by this man who was a perfectly ruthless competitor. His system of information included the details of his competitors' businesses. He could make calculations fine beyond belief in the iron business of the time. Once, when calculating whether to continue to respect his competitors' steel price agreements, his lieutenant, Charles Schwab, was able to advise Carnegie to cut his competitors down; it would be more profitable to run his vast operations full at one-tenth of a cent less per pound than, at the current prices, to use them at three-fourths of capacity—the amount allotted to him by the "pool." Accounting! As Schwab once described the Carnegie accounting system: "We made a careful . . . statement of each manufacture, with the cost as compared with each department. . . ." One of Carnegie's employees, Julian Kennedy, recalled that he was expected to show a saving in cost in each accounting period. Even when vacationing in Scotland, Carnegie could detect a 5 percent increase in coke consumption in the accounts of his company's operations which were regularly forwarded to him.

Another important innovation made by Carnegie in the Pittsburgh iron industry was the introduction of chemistry into the blast-furnace operations. To his astonishment Carnegie, upon entering into the iron manufacturing business, learned that the Pittsburgh iron masters really knew very little about the production of iron. The content of the furnace was a mystery until it was poured. "Practical men" ruled at the blast furnace. Carnegie describes the manufacture of pig iron at the beginning of the 1870's:

> The blast furnace manager of that day was usually a rude bully, generally a foreigner, who in addition to his other acquirements was able to knock down a man now and then as a lesson to the other unruly spirits under him. He was supposed to diagnose the condition of the furnace by instinct, to possess some almost supernatural power of divination, like his congener in the country districts who was reputed to be able to locate . . . water . . . by means of a hazel rod.

Where might a solution lie? Obviously a chemist might have something beyond rule-of-thumb information to contribute. However, as late as 1867 Sir Lowthian Bell, the great English iron mogul (and himself a chemist), had noted that science had little to offer the ironmaster.

> With regard to the application of science the ironmasters in other countries, as here, can only lament how little chemistry has been able to effect in the blast furnace or puddling process.

Carnegie broke ranks. In 1870 a huge new furnace, the Lucy Furnace (named for his sister-in-law), had been erected at his works and he was determined to increase its efficiency by applying science and getting rid of his "rule-of-thumb-and-intuition" furnace manager. A mere youngster, Henry Curry, a shipping clerk, was raised to manager, and a chemist was hired to find out what happens inside a blast furnace. No one has ever told the story better than Carnegie himself.

> We found the man in a learned German, Dr. Fricke, and great secrets did the doctor open to us. Iron stone from mines that had a high reputation was now found to contain ten, fifteen, and even twenty per cent less iron than it had been credited with. Mines that hitherto had a poor reputation we found to be yielding superior ore. The good was bad and the bad was good, and everything was topsy-turvy. Nine tenths of all the uncertainties of pig-iron making were dispelled under the burning sun of chemical knowledge. . . . What fools we had been! But . . . we were not as great fools as our competitors. . . . We were the first to employ a chemist at blast furnaces. . . . The Lucy Furnace became the most profitable branch of our business, because we had almost the entire monopoly of scientific management.

It was years before the "Fathers-in-Israel" understood why the hiring of a chemist was not an extravagance. By then Carnegie, with his cost accounting and chemical analyses, was the industry's most efficient producer by far and it was too late to catch him. His chemist told him where to acquire ore lands, and his partners even bought from his competitors waste materials which were converted into rails at the Carnegie mills.

Carnegie also introduced the modern technique of marketing iron and steel—he went out after business. He solicited. His main customers, railways and manufacturers, had offices in New York City. Instead of waiting in Pittsburgh for their orders to come, Carnegie went out after them. He moved his mother to New York in 1867 and opened an office there, commuting to Pittsburgh whenever his presence was required at his works. Carnegie now became a "commercial traveler on an heroic scale." He was selling iron bridges and rails. No journey was too arduous, and his Keystone bridges began spanning the rivers and gorges of America.

His methods baffled his competitors. Sometimes, as when negotiating a contract with his fellow Scotsman, John Garrett, president of the Baltimore & Ohio Railroad, the "wee drap o' Scotch bluid atween us" gave Carnegie a competitive advantage none could overcome. But Carnegie also had less subtle methods. He lent money to his buyers when necessary; he accepted mortgage bonds as payment; he was as good as any at squeezing special rates out of the railways for shipping his products. He personally marketed his customers' bonds abroad to enable them to buy his bridges. Continuous improvements at his mills allowed him to undercut the competition whenever it was necessary. He *sold* his products on a scale hitherto unknown in the iron business.

During the years 1867–72 Carnegie's affairs become increasingly widespread. He merged the sleeping-car company with that of George Pullman in 1869, and thus gained a monopoly position. Carnegie became a director of the Union Pacific in 1871 and might have gone back into railroads, since in 1871 George Gould offered to buy control of the Pennsylvania if Carnegie would oust his old superiors and take over as president. Carnegie declined. His travels to England gave him an opportunity to place American railway securities on a large scale with English investors, and by 1873 he had sold some $30,000,000 worth of them there. A banking career seemed a distinct possibility. He became friendly with, and did a great deal of business with and for, the American investment banker in London, Junius Morgan, whose son, Pierpont, was by then well established as a merchant banker in New York. Here was a connection pregnant with possibilities to a rich and powerful young tycoon.

But a career in finance was not to be, for essentially two reasons. First, Carnegie hated finance and financiers; the word "speculator" was a nasty one indeed to him and one he reserved for men he intended to be rid of. Carnegie ran his businesses on hard, old-fashioned principles, as partnerships. His stocks never sold to the public; there were no Carnegie bonds. He never understood the role of high finance in industry, and distrusted it. But second, and most important, in 1872 Sir Henry Bessemer personally demonstrated his converter to Carnegie and acquired a disciple.

Carnegie came home from England in 1872 a changed man.

He had "seen the future." From then on his world was steel. He now followed his own maxim "Put all good eggs in one basket, and then watch that basket." Carnegie the innovator now created an industrial revolution of his own, either destroying his competitors outright or dragging them "kicking and screaming" into the age of steel. Incredible as it was, the Dunfermline lad, already a millionaire, was not yet 40 and had not yet embarked upon the career which made him a legend. All that began in 1873, at the scene of General Braddock's defeat, near Pittsburgh.

IV

Up to the 1870's Britain's position as the leading producer of iron and steel seemed secure. In 1870 British pig-iron production was 5,963,000 tons compared to American output of 1,865,000 tons. Moreover, much of the American product, tariff-protected, was vastly inferior to the British, and most of America's railways had been built with British rails (made especially exempt from the tariff by a friendly Congress). The best locomotives and rolling stock in the world came from the great British engine shops. New British ore fields in the northeast of England and in Cumberland and Lancashire, along with the older deposits, seemed to assure continued British superiority. Ironmaking had long been a British prerogative; the industrial revolution had its home in Britain; the major advances in ironmaking had been British, and the British were girdling the globe with railways. Iron steamships, built in Britain, and machinery were exported to all countries from "the workshop of the world." In Wales inferior rails were called "American" because they could be sold to Americans even though they found no market in Britain. Thirty years later Americans produced more than 17,700,000 tons of pig iron to Britain's less than 5,000,000 tons.

In 1870 the British made 275,000 tons of steel ingots compared to a mere 37,500 tons turned out in America. Steelmaking was a slow and expensive process, involving puddling furnaces and forging, unless made by the Bessemer converter, and even then special ores and pig iron which cost twice as much as the ordinary kind were required. Steel was an expensive proposition. Even in England there was great trouble with Bessemer's converters, and in America that method had ruined more than a few experienced ironmasters. Although Americans had been trying to make Bessemer steel since 1864 when a converter was established at Wyandotte, Michigan, the results were unimpressive. In fact, Americans had taken to importing Bessemer-type pig iron from Europe. Carnegie had refused to touch it.

In 1901 the British made 5,000,000 tons of steel, the Americans over 13,000,000 tons and Carnegie Steel alone made 4,000,000 tons. Sir Lowthian Bell (still alive in 1901) was publicly apologizing for British failures to come "up to the American standard." Charles Schwab claimed he could roll steel rails for 40 percent less than the British, and still make a profit, and Andrew Carnegie was selling Pittsburgh steel plates in England to British shipbuilders. America made more steel, cheaper than anyone; steel rails, which cost $160 a ton in 1875, were down to $17 a ton in 1898. The 4,000 men at Carnegie's Homestead works in Pittsburgh made three times as much steel as did Krupp's 15,000 men with all their "Prussian" discipline.

Iron and steel were at the base of the great transformation of the United States into an industrial nation, and in the years 1870–1900, Andrew Carnegie led the fierce competitive battles which made the age of steel so much an American achievement, and the American steel industry the wonder of the manufacturing world.

Carnegie was hardly pioneering when he got back to Pittsburgh in 1872, but he was using an innovation perilously close to the frontier, and he had to undertake his new vocation without his old partners, his brother Thomas, Henry Phipps and Andrew Kloman. They quoted Andrew Carnegie to Andy Carnegie regarding the Bessemer process and elected to stay in the iron trade. So Carnegie organized a new company to make steel (he brought brother Thomas and Phipps in later, when they saw the light). He rounded up new partners, sold his holdings of Pullman stock and put up $250,000 of his own money. He bought land at Braddock's and, in 1873, began construction of his steel mill, later to be called the Edgar Thomson Works, after his old chief on the Pennsylvania Railroad. That dignitary noted, without losing his composure, that since the Braddock location gave Carnegie access to the Pennsylvania Railroad, the Baltimore & Ohio and the Ohio River, the Pennsylvania would be unable to bottle Carnegie up completely as it had done the Pittsburgh producers. Carnegie had learned a thing or two about railway rates and rebates. Now in 1873 he learned some further valuable lessons about the steel business.

Once he was in the steel business, Carnegie's competitive instincts were given full rein. Even by 1873, when the Edgar Thomson Works were under construction, many of Carnegie's business habits were evident. He operated his various companies, almost until the end, as partnerships. Considering that he was operating in one of the greatest periods of corporation development, this was surprising. But surprising or not, the partnership and not the corporation was Carnegie's instrument (here perhaps he was influenced by his British ironmaster friends who also stuck blindly to the partnership form of organization), and he built the partnership into a fabulous organizational machine.

Carnegie was a staunch believer in internal financing, plowing back profits into new plant and equipment at the expense of dividends. He left the capital market strictly alone, emphasizing his sizzling contempt for "speculators" and "financiers." Finally, he seemed to have an innate sense of timing as regards the business cycle and learned quickly, and applied the lesson again and again, that cash money goes a long way when the economy is idle, and that taking advantage of low construction costs in depressions meant low production costs when demand revived.

One major advantage of the partnership to Carnegie was his own control; in times of stress, partners who had become financially "embarrassed" could not bring in outside capital by selling equity in the Carnegie companies. If a partner had to raise money, he had to sell out to his other partners or to the wealthiest ones. After the 1873 crash, six of Carnegie's new partners in the Edgar Thomson Works were forced to sell to him and Carnegie ended with 59% of the ownership. He was majority owner from then on, and became quickly the wealthiest man of his time. He resented the notion that he had taken advantage of his partners and always maintained that he had done them a favor by buying them out at the pit of the depression. In later years Carnegie didn't like to recall the rapacious competitor he once was. As he described the acquisition of majority control of Edgar Thomson in later years: "So many of my friends needed money that they begged me to repay them." He did.

Carnegie watched silently as men, including his old boss Thomas Scott, were ruined by calls on stock that had been purchased on credit, and learned the fundamental truth that when the banking system contracts, all of the credit cannot be honored. In 1873 Carnegie, relatively free of current debt personally, found himself esteemed as a "rock" in the industry. His credit was as good as gold, and the "old men" of Pittsburgh ceased to refer to him as a parvenu and a plunger. Carnegie never forgot the lesson. He was convinced thereafter that absolute virtue resided with the man who had cash in depressions. It was of course advantageous on other grounds, too; you could buy extraordinary amounts of labor and materials when prices were low.

In the depression following 1873 the steel men first learned to sweat out Carnegie's virtuoso game of purchasing and rebuilding in depressions. It was Carnegie who initiated, and maintained throughout his lifetime, the policy of continuous cost and price-cutting competition in the steel industry. His competitors were considered enemies, not gentlemanly rivals. The Edgar Thomson Works were built with maximum efficiency and at minimum cost for the best. Carnegie's net marginal returns were enormous compared to those of his competitors. Hendricks quotes one of Carnegie's managers in later years: Carnegie knew

> ... that the real time to extend your operations was when no one else was doing it. Whenever there would be a boom in the steel trade most manufacturers would start in and build new steel works. They would have to pay the very highest prices for the materials that entered into these constructions on account of boom times, and about the time they were ready to operate the bloom was off the peach and the works would have to lie idle.

Or, they could sell out to Carnegie. In 1883 when the steel market began its collapse, the price of rails had been $85 a ton. Soon they were well down toward the $27 a ton which they reached in 1885. Carnegie found that his erstwhile competitors at the newly constructed mills at Homestead were "willing" to sell to him. Homestead had been built in the boom to roll steel rails and now lay helpless as Carnegie sold rails profitably below Homestead's costs. The men who built Homestead had openly boasted that they were going to undersell Carnegie. Carnegie summed up the situation bluntly, "They were in no condition to compete with us." He offered the Homestead owners either partnerships, dollar for dollar, or cash. All but one of the Homestead owners took cash. They had already seen enough of Carnegie to satisfy their curiosity (the one who stayed in saw his $50,000 share grow to $8,000,-000 in fifteen years). Again, in 1890, the new Duquesne steel

works was "swallowed up" by Carnegie after its builders were
unable to continue.

After Carnegie retired he told his business "philosophy" to
a Congressional committee. Business was war.

> I was in business to make money. I was not a philanthropist
> at all. When rails were high we got the highest prices we could
> get. When they were low we met the lowest price we had to
> meet.

He bought in depressions, rebuilt in depressions, restaffed in
depressions, then undercut his competitors when business was
good. His competitors had to stay awake to remain in the
game with him. Efficiency was the result. The whole point of
the competitive system, after all, is to reward the efficient
producer and chastise the inefficient. In many ways Carnegie
was the *laissez-faire* economist's delight; he maximized his
profits by competitive ruthlessness and the survivors in the
steel industry, by meeting his competition, reduced the price
of steel until it became a basic metal.

When Carnegie went into business at Braddock's in 1874,
steel was still virtually a luxury item. It was not even certain
in the trade that steel rails could be rolled efficiently in America. In a short time steel, American steel, was the metal of
American railways. After being battered by Carnegie, who in
the late 1890's refused to "play ball" with his competitors,
Judge Gary, head of the giant Illinois Steel Co. (and later to
be Morgan's man at United States Steel when the banker tried
to "stabilize" the industry) ruefully said goodby to further
hopes of comfortable monopoly pricing and output. It was no
longer possible, he said, "to do business on the basis of high
profits for comparatively small tonnage."

But that was after Carnegie had triumphed. Before the early
1890's Carnegie's tactics included joining in the multitudinous
cartels and pools which the industry tried to maintain to produce monopoly profits. The opportunity was there because of
the protective tariff. A tariff of $28 a ton on steel rails, for
example, kept out foreign competition and American producers could mulct their compatriots if they could only agree
among themselves. Part of the game was to act as if they
could agree (such agreements were not illegal before the Sherman Act of 1890). But one fundamental characteristic of a
cartel is its instability. The opportunity to undercut the agreed
price could hardly be resisted and Carnegie, playing the game,
double-crossed his competitors with as much regularity and

glee as they double-crossed him. Judge Gary and the "Fathers-in-Israel" took a long time to become convinced competitors. In fact Gary never did; he always hankered after "order" in the steel market.

Carnegie, on the other hand, never liked to cooperate with his enemies. When he entered his first rail pool, he was allotted only a small part of the market by the other members. Carnegie leaped up, announced that he wanted an amount equal to the largest quota, moved his finger around the table from magnate to magnate telling each one his own business and costs and threatening to undercut them all. It was a typical Carnegie display, and it worked.

Until the '90's Carnegie entered pools periodically, using the period of the price agreement to prepare for his next competitive offensive, if there was time. Most of the pools were, in fact, too short-lived. Schwab once said of pools: ". . . many of them lasted a day, some of them lasted until the gentlemen could go to the telephone from the room in which they were made. . . ." Carnegie ceased playing the game with much grace after 1893 when he told a Pittsburgh competitor that he wanted no more price agreements. "The market is mine whenever I want to take it. I see no reason why I should present you with all of my profits."

From the time of the building of the Edgar Thomson Works (it started making rails in 1874), Carnegie's spirit poisoned the would-be convivial atmosphere of the Bessemer Steel Association's meetings—the Pittsburgh rail pool. Even in the late 1870's and early 1880's, before Carnegie's aggressiveness reached its height, his methods were having astonishing effects. It wasn't all Andrew Carnegie, of course—he had help at his mills, but the growth of the competitive steel industry before 1900 was due more to Carnegie personally than is commonly realized today. Carnegie was too good a propagandist and the image of the kindly old philanthropist obscures the man who made Pittsburgh the capital of steel. He could use all the vagaries of the violently fluctuating market to his own advantage. That was remarkable enough. But Carnegie was in a class by himself when it came to choosing his management. Indeed the Carnegie management has been considered by many to be one of his most remarkable achievements. It was also his innovation. It was a singular kind of masterpiece, and the steel industry has never really seen the like of it since 1900.

V

J. P. Morgan, the great investment banker, was renowned for the talents (and, strangely enough, for the good looks) of his partners. Carnegie's comment on that was: "Mr. Morgan buys his partners, I grow my own." At first Carnegie had taken partners in when he needed them. Some, like his brother Thomas, Henry Phipps and his cousin George Lauder, had been with Carnegie from childhood. Some men were made partners for special reasons; Andrew Kloman, for example, had the original iron firm that Thomas Carnegie had gone into, staked by Andrew, along with Carnegie partners Thomas Miller and Henry Phipps; Carnegie finally absorbed Kloman and eventually parted with him (Kloman was one of those ruined in 1873). Henry Clay Frick was already the Connellsville coke baron when Carnegie merged with him in order to have the Frick coke ovens integrated with the Carnegie blast furnaces.

Other partners, like William Coleman, went in with Carnegie when he needed capital. But as the Carnegie enterprises grew and Carnegie's personal control became established, young men coming up from the inside were made partners on a merit basis. Stock was set aside for them, paid for out of earnings, and then the fortunate youngsters were full-blown Carnegie partners.

The firm had an agreement, the "Iron-Clad," from 1887 until it was broken by Frick in 1900, which obligated any partner to relinquish his stocks back to the company "at the books" (a valuation which included no "good will" and hence was radically short of what a fair market price might be) if he left the firm. In case of death, the stocks were automatically put back into the treasury and the company had a "protracted" period to pay for them. Carnegie said he was impressed by how much harder commercial fishermen who owned their own boats worked than did those who were merely wage earners. Also Carnegie was terribly sentimental, so long as they did good work, about his friends and cronies and liked to reward good young men by making them associates.

Since a Carnegie partnership was in fact open, free, to any young man, the employees were famous for their diligence. Carnegie kept an eagle eye out for talent in his mills. One of his managers said of him in later years, ". . . he exceeded any man I ever knew in his ability to pick a man from one place and put him in another with maximum effect. . . ." His furnace managers competed fiercely with each other, always aware that "the little boss" expected repairs to show an ever increasing efficiency. It might have been slave driving, but the slaves seemed willing. Why not? Any ambitious young man had universal opportunity just sitting there waiting to be taken. No barriers. Moreover, Carnegie believed in giving every bright young man his head. "Every year should be marked by the promotion of one or more of our young men. . . . We can not have too many of the right sort interested in the profits." In the single year 1898 twenty youngsters were made partners. All had come up from the bottom through the Carnegie mills.

In keeping with the policy of utilizing the best talent, Carnegie never allowed "dead wood" to accumulate. He was perfectly ruthless about partners pulling their own weight. Men who failed to come up to the mark were forced out. In Pittsburgh the "European tour" of unsuccessful Carnegie partners became a standing joke. As Carnegie put it, "If he can win the race he is our race-horse; if not he goes to the cart."

It was a system designed to gain efficiency without regard to personalities. Carnegie, it was said, never inquired about the profits, only about the costs, which he wanted constantly reduced. It was the job of his "young geniuses" to do it—or else. Given the market, Carnegie's profits were determined by his costs. He understood, and many times lectured his sales people about the fact that the price in the market was not their affair. They should just meet the price whatever it was. The technical partners would handle their affairs so that *any* market could be met.

Not only were partnerships dangled in front of bright young men, but so were lavish bonuses for good work. Those who took the bait were known to be the highest paid men in American industry. "I can't afford to pay them any other way" was Carnegie's reply to a question about his young men's high wages. In his *Autobiography* Carnegie noted shrewdly that the most expensive labor is the only kind worth hiring because its high productivity, in a free market, is the cause of its high price.

If Carnegie's incentive system seems a bit hair-raising compared to present-day industrial practices, it is worth considering a few of the astonishing results. The system worked. Perhaps the best known and most spectacular product of Carnegie's system was Charles Schwab. He was hired out of a grocery store as a youth at $1 a day to drive stakes by Capt.

William Jones, the great Carnegie superintendent. Within six months Schwab was an assistant manager. He was a superintendent in five years and at barely 30 years of age was president of Carnegie Steel. Carnegie said of Schwab, "I have never met his equal."

Jones himself was taken on as a $2-a-day mechanic. "We soon saw that he was a character," said Carnegie and gave Jones his head. Jones is remembered today as the greatest steelmaker in American history and he is usually given credit for making the Bessemer converter a success in America. Jones was a restless experimenter and inventor; he and Julian Kennedy doubled the output of the Edgar Thomson furnace without altering the basic plant, simply by devising methods to raise the heat and increase the charge. Jones developed many of the important inventions which made possible a continuous movement of steel from blast furnace through the converters, ingot casting and rolling stages without reheating. When the British steel savant, J. S. Jeans, inspecting the wonders of the Carnegie plant said he would like to rest on a cool ingot and just admire it all, the Captain told him he'd have to go back to England to find an ingot cool enough to sit on. Jones refused a partnership, saying that his men would distrust him: "Just give me a hell of a salary if you think I'm worth it." So Carnegie simply paid him the salary of the President of the United States. "Ah, Andy, that's the kind of talk," said Jones. He was killed in a plant accident in 1889; Carnegie, to the end of his days, kept Jones' picture on the wall of his bedroom in New York.

Other young men who came up through Carnegie's system were W. E. Corey and A. C. Dinkey, who were both made general superintendents of Carnegie Steel while still in their twenties. Like Schwab, Corey was later president of United States Steel. None of Carnegie's young partners was more renowned than the Connellsville coke tycoon. In 1882 Carnegie purchased half of the Frick Coke Co. to guarantee his own supply of coke regardless of market conditions. Henry Clay Frick became a Carnegie partner, and was one partner Carnegie could not control. In 1882 Frick was operating 12,000 coke ovens and was only 33 years old. He had built his company himself. In spite of the bad blood which eventually came between them, Carnegie called Frick a "positive genius" in his *Autobiography*. In 1889 Frick, in his fortieth year, was made president of Carnegie's company (then styled "Carnegie

Brothers & Co.") and was a great success. Carnegie clearly intended at that time that Frick should be his successor.

In 1891 most of Carnegie's interests were pulled together in the reorganized Carnegie Steel Co. The capital was valued at a mere $25,000,000, following Carnegie's refusal to count the good will. By then Carnegie had supplied the steel for the first American skyscraper, the Home Insurance Building in Chicago in 1883. (In 1894 Carnegie, Phipps & Co., a special organization, issued the first handbook of steel shapes to guide architects in building skyscrapers. Carnegie's pricing methods were followed there too, selling eleven-story buildings for the price of ten-story buildings.) Carnegie supplied steel for the Brooklyn Bridge, the New York elevated railway, the Washington Monument, railways, and armor plate for the newly developing Navy. Carnegie's company was a wonder of organization, producing all the way from the mines to finished products. Carnegie himself was the "super salesman": the bright young men managed at Pittsburgh.

> There are no other works in the world under one management which have reached this remarkable output or are likely soon to attain it.

So ran a contemporary report.

By 1892 it might have appeared that Carnegie had achieved an organizational miracle and that the path was open to the future in industrial America. Was there anything missing? In July, 1892, there occurred one of the most famous events in American industrial history, the Homestead strike. There was evidently a great deal missing indeed. The whole Carnegie concept suddenly seemed to go sour—to the great and open delight of Carnegie's enemies on both sides of the Atlantic. The "positive genius," Mr. Frick, had blundered into a small-scale war with Carnegie's workmen. As a result, Carnegie and Homestead became infamous in the annals of American labor.

VI

Judging from his own recollections of the Homestead strike and the other evidence (for example, see Hendricks' account in his *Life of Andrew Carnegie*) it is apparent that Andrew Carnegie never did understand, really, why his men struck against him. He was so certain that the Carnegie Steel organization was the answer to all problems of industrial organiza-

244 / THE INNOVATORS

tion that the strike seemed to him to be the "fault" of Frick.
Affairs had been bungled. The men's demands were, in Carnegie's words, "outrageously wrong" but the issue could have
been handled without a strike. Carnegie gave as evidence a
cable from the officers of his company union: "Kind master,
tell us what you wish us to do and we shall do it for you."

Carnegie was wrong, and his own evidence explains why.
The word "Homestead" is forever written large in American
labor history precisely because men working in steel had not
been unaccustomed to referring to their "kind master." In
America that would never do. There is an enormous difference
between "kind master" and "the boss." The great new American industrial structure was rising pre-eminently in steel and,
accordingly, the men who worked in the mills were trying to
find a way to equalize the wage bargain. Carnegie was not, as
he thought he was, merely the victim of a wage dispute that
had gotten out of hand. Homestead was bound to come, and
many more strikes like it. Carnegie Steel had felt one of the
first shocks of a coming force, the formation of unions in the
mass-producing industries.

The workers lost at Homestead in 1892, and they continued
to lose until in *Jones and Laughlin Steel Company v. The
National Labor Relations Board* in 1937 the Supreme Court
fixed the public interest in collective bargaining, and the free
formation of unions by workmen. A month before that decision was handed down, United States Steel, successor to
Carnegie Steel and others, quietly agreed to bargain collectively. The United Steelworkers had finally come after decades
of bloodshed and struggle. And that is why all 3,800 Homestead employees went out in support of an exclusive union of
skilled workmen, which only had 800 members, which refused
to accept nonskilled men, which even practiced racial discrimination against the other workers, which was undoubtedly
wrong in its bargaining position in 1892, and which was refusing, by a very narrow margin, a generous Carnegie offer. The
men wanted control, or some control of their own job security.
The kindness of their paternalistic master was not enough.
Considering the opportunities he was giving them, Carnegie
simply could not conceive of such a state of affairs. Like so
many self-made men he could not understand the cast of mind
which would cause men to opt for security, to organize unions
to reduce hours instead of grasping the larger chance and
working "full-out" for the chance to be partners of Andrew
Carnegie. He would not be the last American industrialist who

had no understanding whatever of the role and force of unionism among workmen.

The history of American unionism is a violent one, more
so than in most industrialized countries. However, Americans
seem to prefer their violence piecemeal rather than by cold
political organization. Hence, although the American worker
has never been a revolutionist like his European colleague,
the American worker, again unlike his European colleague,
has always been ready to give, on the spot, blow for blow in
struggles with his employers. Homestead was a prize example
of the American version of "the barricades." Interestingly
enough, it finally was the European version that killed the
Homestead strike.

The Amalgamated Association of Iron & Steel Workers was
an A. F. of L. affiliate, organized in 1876 from several old
ironworkers and puddlers unions. In 1892 there were about
24,000 men in the union in the entire steel industry. Although
there were some 800 Amalgamated members at Homestead,
other Carnegie plants, including Edgar Thomson, were not
organized. The old ironworkers unions had been based upon
skill, and in the rapidly changing technology of steel the
Amalgamated appeared as something of an anachronism. The
union realized the difficulty of its position and made a great
many concessions to the company over technological improvements, but nothing less than complete acquiescence in the
matter of technological change was satisfactory to Carnegie.
Change had to come to cut costs. It made no sense to have
one's operations sandbagged by a union of skilled men whose
skills were no longer of great importance. It was perfectly
mad to allow the pace of technological change to be dictated
by men who neither understood nor wanted it. The union was
simply an albatross. David Brody, in his *Steelworkers in
America,* quotes Frick's complaint to Carnegie: "The mills
have never been able to turn out the product they should,
owing to being held back by the Amalgamated men."

Carnegie viewed the Amalgamated with utter contempt. It
not only was an anachronism; it also was an affront to Carnegie's sense of fair play. The skilled men kept a tight control
at Homestead, largely on the basis of nationality; the Irish
ran the Bessemer plant, the Welsh ran the rolling mills. When
vacancies occurred the Amalgamated men sent back to Britain
for replacements. The mass of the Homestead workmen, unskilled Slavs, Italians and Hungarians, were locked into their
menial jobs and could not rise. Carnegie said flat out that the

Amalgamated was "feudalism" and it was not to be tolerated in the midst of an organization which promised a partnership to every deserving man. Carnegie wanted the union out of his works for good. He was especially galled by the thought that the union had lodges in other companies—by the idea that *his* men should have brotherly associations with the men of "the enemy."

The Amalgamated men were simply trying to get the best possible wage bargain in 1892. New machinery had been installed and the skilled men's piece rates needed to be adjusted accordingly. The men made a negotiable offer but Frick, who was now president of Carnegie Steel Co., Ltd., came back with an ultimatum. Carnegie had left the country for his annual summer vacation and Frick ruled in Pittsburgh. He intended to break the union. Carnegie had forced Frick to settle with his men at an earlier strike at the Frick Coke Works. In 1889 the Amalgamated had actually won a strike at Homestead. Frick thought Carnegie's methods were "soft." In the winter of 1887–88 there had been a strike at the Edgar Thomson Works. Carnegie simply closed the works down until the men were willing to work on his terms. He refused to import "scabs." Carnegie argued that he already employed the best men in steel, the only ones worth hiring. He would simply wait until the men accepted his terms. At Homestead in 1889 when the superintendent had brought in scabs, the workers drove them out of town and won the strike. This had proved to Carnegie the folly of fighting the men. You should just lock up the works and wait. The men had to eat, so eventually they would have to work. You just waited. Simple.

The "positive genius" thought otherwise. With Carnegie out of the country Frick determined to settle with the men on his own terms. He built a high wooden fence around Homestead, topped by barbed wire with portholes at regular intervals "for observation." There were also observation towers with searchlights and even before Frick's ultimatum, Pinkerton's detectives guarded Homestead's entrances.

Facing such preparations the Amalgamated men must have sensed their defeat. In 1892 there was no National Labor Relations Act; the unions were still facing legal rulings that they were "criminal conspiracies." The Amalgamated was on very weak ground indeed, or so it appeared. It was a minority union and not well liked by the mass of the workmen. But the members of the Amalgamated had more on their side than they knew, or perhaps even wanted.

However exclusive and odious their practices, the Amalgamated men were not "the company," and the unskilled men saw the Amalgamated as perhaps a poor but *only* chance to have some freedom from the company's embrace. For the unskilled men, Carnegie's system, if they had indeed ever heard of it, must have seemed a bitter joke. The men worked seven days a week and twelve hours a day. Those were the minimum hours. It was common practice for workers to trade shifts and work twenty-four hours straight to have a day at home with their families. Death rates were staggering. Even as late as 1906–10 one-fourth, some 3,273, of the immigrant workmen in Allegheny County were killed or injured seriously in the mills. The unskilled men lived mainly in squalid river-bottom slums without running water or basic sanitation. The immigrants lived in their "Hunkyvilles." Pennsylvania's laws applied indifferently and capriciously to the foreigner who was a prey to every crooked cop and deputy sheriff. The men who spoke English saw in the Amalgamated aristocracy their own nabobs. Illnesses and death among the unskilled at least brought charitable responses from the Amalgamated, a blessing in the days when general workmen's compensation would have been considered an insane notion and the company had no liability if it could be shown, as it usually was, that the accident in question was due partly to the action of any other employee, or to negligence.

For such reasons there was in fact virtual solidarity among the workmen at Homestead. Hence, on July 1, 1892, when the works were closed after Frick had announced that the men could all be hired, but only as individuals, no union, the Carnegie Co. found to its astonishment that the whole labor force was on strike. Frick might still conquer, but he clearly had failed to divide.

When the mills closed, civil government ended at Homestead. The city and the Carnegie properties were seized by the workmen. The mayor, named McLuckie, a man destined for a kind of fame, supported the men and allowed his office to be used for partisan purposes. McLuckie was a mechanic at Homestead and became chairman of the "Advisory Committee" which was now the "government." The sheriff of Allegheny County was unceremoniously escorted out of the town. Armed guards were posted at the outskirts of Homestead, on the hills and even in skiffs on the river. No one could enter or leave the town without a pass from "the committee." Carnegie's executives were kept away from Carnegie property by the strikers who now triumphantly ruled the silent mills. Frick had lost the first round. However, the strikers were now a "committee of public safety" and were in an extremely poor legal position.

The next move was Frick's. For years the Pinkerton Detective Agency had supplied spies to the owners of the steel mills to watch for signs of organizational enthusiasm among the men. Pinkerton men were also available for various tasks related to strike breaking. Now Frick decided to raise a private army of Pinkertons and seize Homestead from the strikers. What he intended to do next is not clear. Perhaps he thought that by garrisoning the mills he could entice nonstrikers, if there were any, back to work. On the night of July 5th, 300 armed Pinkertons boarded barges at Pittsburgh, sailed at 2 A.M. on the 6th, and were abreast of Homestead at about 4 A.M. The strikers had been warned of the attempt. As the barges approached, thousands of Homestead's people, men, women and children, provided a violent reception, firing off rockets, throwing stones and shooting revolvers at the barges. The barges came up to the shore and the Pinkertons tried to land. The gunfire now became general. The amphibious operation failed. The Pinkertons were quickly driven back to their barges but five strikers lay dead and three Pinkertons were mortally wounded.

The strikers attempted to finish the job by pouring oil on the river and lighting it. Before this tactic had any success the Pinkertons negotiated to surrender on condition that they be allowed to leave Homestead immediately. The scene took on a completely barbarian character as the Pinkertons, with their wounded, were marched through the frenzied townspeople. The Pinkertons were stoned and beaten as they stumbled along. They got out of town by train before all restraint disintegrated among the strikers.

Both the strikers and Frick had now failed. The strikers had unilaterally suspended the civil government, thus making of themselves lawless usurpers. Frick's attempt to cash in on the complete illegality of the strikers' position had been crushed. The State of Pennsylvania now intervened and the law, embodied in the bayonets of 8,000 Pennsylvania militiamen, was restored to Homestead. The strike had become a national sensation. The union was now grasping at straws, it was willing to settle just for recognition. "There is no disposition on the part of the employees to stand upon a question of scale, or wages, or hours, or anything else." So said the Amalgamated leaders. But Henry Frick smelled success. He could break the strike if he kept up the pressure, and he was prepared to see the game through: "Under no circumstances will we have any further dealings with the Amalgamated Association as an organization. This is final." Now Frick watched to see what his next opportunity would be.

At this point the Homestead strike was caught up in an issue much larger than the rights either of the strikers or of the Carnegie Co. Just as carrion on the desert eventually attracts scavengers, so the deadlock at Homestead now attracted a bird of sinister and portentous properties. A stranger came to Pittsburgh. He was not a worker. He was not a capitalist. He was a logician and he had traveled far on an errand of philosophy; he came to kill a man—as a matter of principle. Alexander Berkman was the stranger. He was a Russian anarchist. Pittsburgh in 1892 probably knew little of Marx, Engels, Chernyshevsky, Bakunin, Kropotkin, of the Paris Commune of 1871 or the politics of 1848. Pittsburgh got a fast lesson in political and social theory, European style. Berkman came to rid the world of one who "embodied the tyranny of capital." He entered Frick's office, shot him and then stabbed him. Frick fell wounded, but as always, was up to the competition. Icy and cool, he refused anesthetic while the doctors removed bullets and stitched him up. Frick stayed on at the office the rest of the afternoon, coldly finishing up his work, including negotiating a loan, and then was carried home on a stretcher. He was a hero, transformed by philosophy and a flair for the dramatic.

A wave of sympathy for Frick now poured forth. The strikers were covered with the opprobrium of "foreign radicalism." Hugh O'Donnell, an Amalgamated leader, said: "The bullet from Berkman's pistol went straight through the heart of the Homestead strike." Frick continued from his bed to direct Carnegie affairs, and Andrew Carnegie, who in private believed, and said, that Frick had bungled the whole operation, stood by his president. By fall the men, long without pay, with the forces of law and public opinion firmly against them, gave up and began filing back to the mills, signing up each one individually on the terms offered. The union was beaten and dead at Homestead. Writing four decades later, Carnegie's biographer, Hendricks, was able to say: "Not a union man has since entered the Carnegie works." The victory was complete for Frick. He wrote to Carnegie: "We had to teach our employees a lesson, and we have taught them one that they will never forget." They never forgot it all right.

The Homestead strike came to Carnegie as a body blow. He hadn't expected that kind of trouble in getting rid of the Amalgamated. He confessed years later that: "No pangs remain of any wound received in my business career save that of Homestead. . . . I was the controlling owner. That was sufficient to make my name a by-word for years." By then Carnegie was already well along with his second career, that of philanthropist extraordinary and general panegyrist of the American democracy. He not only was traveling in the company of great men of letters and politics, but had enemies of equal rank. Homestead delighted Carnegie's enemies, and the vitriol poured down upon the "benefactor of mankind." The strike became an issue in the Presidential campaign of 1892; Carnegie was a renowned Republican and the Republican leaders dealt Carnegie a generous personal share of the credit for the victory of Democrat Grover Cleveland.

Homestead was a landmark in the troubled history of labor—management relations in American industry. The strike showed, mainly, that "opportunity" was not destined to mean the same thing to most American workers that it did to the ambitious few whose eyes were fastened only upon the heights. No amount of spread-eagle oratory combined with private philanthropy and court injunctions could change the fact. The men who worked in the mills had their own visions of America, visions which were not those of the Carnegies and the Fords. The fact has been lamented by many, and blessed by more, but the unions were destined to come, even to the steel industry.

Just as America's industrialization had its counterpart in other countries, the organization of industrial labor was an experience Americans shared with their brothers abroad. There was a difference though. American workmen have mainly resisted the mixing of politics with their bargaining over wages, hours and working conditions. Berkman's bullets were wasted. American workmen wanted more than political slogans; they wanted property and freedom of their own, individually acquired and individually controlled. They fought violently with their employers for a larger share of the pie, but not for the expropriation of the pie and its distribution on doctrinal grounds. As the great student of the labor movement Selig Perlman described the A. F. of L.'s successes in his classic, *Theory of the Labor Movement,* the A. F. of L.:

ANDREW CARNEGIE / 251

> . . . recognized the virtually inalterable conservatism of the American community as regards private property and private initiative in economic life . . . [the A. F. of L. demanded] . . . only that the employers should concede the union's right to control the jobs through "recognition" embodied in the trade agreement; and in this attitude it remained unperturbed in the face of all the charges by socialist intellectuals of treason to labor or even corruption. . . .

American industrial unionism has been no different. The American labor movement as a political force has remained a myth and a threat, never a reality. Such an outcome might have surprised both Frick and Berkman. It might have delighted Carnegie. It wouldn't have surprised O'Donnell. The fact has long been a peculiarity of American labor. Politics has to do with politicians; contract negotiations have to do with "the company." The two things have largely remained unrelated in the minds of American workmen.

Hence Homestead was not the opening shot of "the Revolution." Homestead was one of scores of places where American workmen fought against their employers for the chance to achieve a workingman's vision of America. This vision was not Carnegie's, nor Frick's, nor Berkman's. Carnegie's industrial system was efficient; it worked wonders of innovation and competition. Like most systems it was inflexible, and the Homestead strike showed, in case there was any doubt, that labor organization in the mass-producing industries had a violent future in the development of the national economy. There is a fairly straight line from Homestead in 1892 to the Republic Steel massacre in Chicago in June, 1937. The peculiar violence of industrial organization in this country is probably best the subject for a study of the national psyche. Homestead was an example of American-style violence, good murderous fun until someone got wind of it who was *really* interested in violence—systematic violence. Then the strike ended. Americans seem to prefer spontaneous killing; systematic murders sicken us. We would make a poor "People's Democracy."

VII

In 1892 Carnegie was already planning for an early retirement from business. His idea of retirement was to escape into the world of ideas. He always hoped somehow that he could overcome his lack of formal education. Then there was a facet of Carnegie's personality that was little known in the rough and tumble of his early business days in Pittsburgh. Andrew Carnegie the philanthropist was hidden behind the image of the steel tycoon. He wanted desperately to live his "other" life. He was long torn between his competitive instincts and his benevolent feelings. Andrew Carnegie was a curious mixture. He had married late, in 1887 at 51, Louise Whitfield, who was then 30. Carnegie's long bachelorhood had been guarded by his mother, although that alone doubtless does not explain the tardiness of his marriage. In November, 1886, Margaret Carnegie died, only a few days after her son Thomas had died of pneumonia. Carnegie himself was bedridden with typhoid fever at the time and was not expected to live. His loneliness was short-lived. Within five months he was married. In 1887 his income was $1,850,000. There were no income taxes. It was enough to retire on.

For years Carnegie had treasured a memorandum written to himself in 1868. The paper came to light after his death and showed that even at the beginning of his business career Carnegie had interests far beyond the accumulation of wealth. He had noted that at 33 he already had an annual income of $50,000. He could soon quit business altogether and "spend the surplus for benevolent purposes." He could now get that which had been denied him, a formal education. He could settle in Oxford for three years (long enough for a B. A.), then buy a newspaper and take an active part in public affairs, ". . . especially those connected with the education and improvement of the poorer classes." He was, it seems, a congenital do-gooder. It doubtless would have nonplused those engaged daily (usually losing) in business warfare with Carnegie to discover that they were victims of a social reformer. For those who regarded Carnegie as "the greediest little gentleman God ever created" the ending of the 1868 memorandum would have come as an unnerving shock.

> Man must have an idol—the amassing of wealth is one of the worst species of idolatry—no idol more debasing than the worship of money. Whatever I engage in I must push inordinately; therefore should I be careful to choose that life which will be the most elevating in its character. To continue much longer overwhelmed by business cares and with most of my thoughts wholly upon the way to make more money in the shortest time, must degrade me beyond hope of permanent recovery. . . .

Carnegie knew himself well. In the following years he made considerable headway in his nonbusiness ambitions, piling up his millions at the same time. He never did spend his three years in Oxford, but by 1892 he had certainly engaged himself in public affairs. In America, Carnegie was just another tycoon in politics, and there were a lot of them by 1892, with little or no impact, but in Britain, where he spent each summer, he was widely viewed as a menace to the existing social order, as indeed he was. As a former Scottish emigrant his career was something of an affront to those who had long argued that Britain had no room for such riffraff. Unless Britain were destined only to be an old-folks home, such theories were wildly wrong. By 1892 Carnegie, after all, had shown the British how to make steel. He was also vocal about the glories of "Uncle Sam's great farm" and the need for the British to learn the lessons of equality and Republican institutions. By early 1880 he had entered into a partnership in England with Samuel Storey, M. P., and was publishing radical newspapers for the working classes, agitating for universal suffrage and a British Republic. The British "establishment" found little humor in their local boy who had made good. "Mr. Carnegie is at the head of a conspiracy . . . which seeks to destroy both the Crown and the House of Lords." So spake the *St. James Gazette* glumly and accurately. In 1885 Carnegie gave up his Hearstian adventure, finding that radical newspapers for the "lower orders," all preaching the same editorial line, lost money (it took a few decades before the British press lords learned the correct formula for such newspapers, lots of sex and sensationalism mixed with the political message).

In 1885 Carnegie was in print with his book *Triumphant Democracy,* largely a cannibalization of the 1880 U. S. Census, proclaiming the infinite glories of New World Democracy and rubbing salt liberally into wounded British pride. The book opened with a broadside: "The old nations of the earth creep at a snail's pace; the Republic thunders past with the rush of an express." British reviewers were unkind to the book. But it sold 40,000 copies in the United Kingdom alone.

Carnegie was seriously approached by the Liberals to stand for Parliament for Birmingham. Several Scottish constituencies also approached him, but the errant son of Scotland was after bigger game. In the first place, he was something of a crank on Anglo-American union, on "Race Imperialism." He wanted to see all of the British chicks—including the United States—and the old hen united again (his personal standard over his

Scottish castle was fashioned by uniting the Stars and Stripes and the Union Jack on a single field). Also he wanted to be free for a literary life, for personal influence and to direct his own immense domain. Carnegie's first book, *An American Four-in-Hand in Britain,* had been something of a success when it came out earlier. He had continued to contribute to the press and periodical literature, and by the early 1890's counted as his friends many of the chief luminaries of Victorian England, including Matthew Arnold, Herbert Spencer and William Gladstone.

Carnegie was already using his own wealth for the benefit of others; in 1873 he had given public baths to his native Dunfermline, which in 1881 also received the first of all Carnegie libraries. Then in 1889 Carnegie's ideas on wealth, now suffused with Social Darwinism, were given formal and sensational form in an article, "Wealth," published in the *North American Review*. The only justification for wealth was the betterment of mankind in general.

The leaders of Victorian thought saw in their world the triumph of man over both the elements and over "the baser instincts," as they used to say. The line from the French Enlightenment ran straight through the English and American romantics, down through Shelley, Arnold and Tennyson, down through Emerson and Walt Whitman. Men spoke, in all seriousness, of "noble souls," "high natures," of "improving and uplifting sentiments." Serious people sought "the good, the true and the beautiful" with straight faces. Just as Carnegie was the child of his age in industry, so he was in spirit a true Victorian romantic. Science and philosophy together were raising the curtain of poverty, ignorance and superstition, and mankind was at last on the threshold of universal peace and ethical and economic progress. Evidence to the contrary was ignored. "Conditions" for most people in Victorian England and America were bad enough, but there were signs and hope of improvement. The Victorians had a beautiful dream and Carnegie shared it. Rich men, he wrote:

> . . . have it in their power during their lives to busy themselves in organizing benefactions from which the masses of their fellows will derive lasting advantages, and thus dignify their own lives. . . .

It ruined one's children to leave them too much money. Charities treated only symptoms. Build with your own wit and mind sure and long-lasting methods to eliminate the causes of poverty, disease and ignorance. There was a real program for a rich man. Carnegie ended "Wealth" with a prediction.

> The day is not far distant when the man who dies leaving behind him millions of available wealth, which was free for him to administer during life, will pass away 'unwept, unhonored, and unsung,' no matter to what uses he leave the dross which he cannot take with him. Of such as these the public verdict will then be: 'The man who dies thus rich dies disgraced'. Such, in my opinion, is the true gospel concerning wealth. . . .

The optimism of the Victorians was a fantastic thing, and doubtless Carnegie was more optimistic than most. Some received his message with derision. Some doubtless considered him to be a certifiable lunatic, but Mr. Gladstone himself caused the article to be reprinted in *The Pall Mall Gazette*. The fact is that such notions did receive a serious audience. One could scarcely imagine it today.

By 1892 Carnegie's life was already virtually a continuous triumph. He had his friends with "high natures," scholars, poets, statesmen. With his young wife a new life was opening to him. In 1888 they rented Cluny Castle in Scotland for their summers and continued there until they bought a castle of their own, Skibo, in 1889. Carnegie did not take up an interest in art collections as did some of his fellow millionaires; the fact that the walls of one of his New York apartments were papered with Scottish tartans explains why, with more eloquence than mere words could ever achieve. But he did care enough for the performing arts to build Carnegie Hall in 1892. Reflecting both his Scottish and American backgrounds, Carnegie's interests in literature and practical things gave him enormous intellectual rewards. The demands of his vaulting ego were kept satisfied by the continuing parade of honors which came to him—in the end he had the "freedom" of no fewer than fifty cities in the United Kingdom. Gladstone himself accumulated only seventeen of those.

Carnegie thus had worldly success to the point of saturation when the Homestead strike came in 1892. It is easy enough to understand why he considered Homestead as a great blow, as an assault on all his beliefs and practices. It is also easy to understand why his enemies found in it a purifying and life-giving balm. If one was not a Victorian of the "noble soul" variety, Mr. Andrew Carnegie must have been an awful pain.

Especially if one was rich and intended to be greedy about it.

If Homestead was a great personal defeat for Carnegie, it also was a challenge, and the ruthless competitor came home in the fall of 1892 to give his opponents a thorough and continuous trouncing until he quit the steel business altogether. From 1892 to 1901 Carnegie proceeded to shake the steel industry as he had never done before. His last decade in business was his greatest. Retirement had to wait.

VIII

In 1893 there was another crash, followed by a deep and long-lasting depression. While his competition stared at idle plants, Carnegie used his powerful financial position to play his old game once again. The capacity of Carnegie steel was expanded as never before. Moreover, much of the old plant was destroyed or modernized, so that from 1893 to 1898 most of the mills were rebuilt. When prosperity came again, Carnegie was far under his competitors in production costs. In the 1890's he went all out for vertical integration, self-supply of all inputs from the mines to the retail trade. Carnegie, as we have seen, had been building a vertically integrated system since the days of the Keystone Bridge Co., slowly freeing himself from dependence upon independent suppliers. In the 1890's he completed the process.

It was the Mesabi Range that finally impelled Carnegie to go the distance to complete integration. Lake Superior ores had been used at Pittsburgh since the early 1850's, steadily after the Sault Ste. Marie canal was opened in 1855 and ore boats were able to go regularly to the blast-furnace centers along the lower margins of the lakes. By 1870, with the inauguration of steam-driven ore barges, the lake-ore trade boomed and so did the Great Lakes steel locations. Pittsburgh still had certain advantages and used both the Lake Superior ores and others, mainly from Iron Mountain in Missouri. By the late 1880's however, ores were getting scarcer, and Carnegie, already benefiting from owning his own coke supply, was becoming increasingly aware of the potential need to acquire ore reserves on a large scale, something which he had long avoided, preferring simply to buy his ores at market prices, or lease the mines from others and let them take the risks of exploration and development.

In 1891, Leonides and Alfred Merritt discovered the vast deposits of iron ore in the Mesabi Range in Minnesota, and the

American steel industry came to a revolutionary turning point. Ore was to become plentiful and, in addition, technological change on a giant scale came again, this time displacing the Bessemer process with the basic open-hearth furnaces. Carnegie lived to see open-hearth steel overwhelm Bessemer steel in America, and he led the movment so long as he remained in the industry. His competitors had to change over with him or perish.

Carnegie could be conservative. On the subject of Mesabi he dragged his feet as he originally had with Bessemer. Frick had acquired some ore rights with a $500,000 loan to an old Carnegie playmate, Henry Oliver, a "speculator" who had gone into Mesabi quickly. But Carnegie still held back and by 1893 was not yet committed to an extensive operation there, even though he did want to acquire dependable ore supplies of his own. He distrusted the Mesabi development. One couldn't tell when a vein would give out. He had earlier made a similar estimate of the oil business when he and a partner tried to corner the market. Years afterward Carnegie commented about Mesabi: "Fortunately, I woke up in time."

"In time" was after the Panic of 1893. The events of that year wiped out would-be ore developers by the score. According to the Carnegie formula, that was the time to move in. Carnegie, pressing for new construction during the depression, refused to pay dividends to his partners and was so fully committed that he was actually forced to borrow money on his own notes from bankers—a rare thing for him. It was in such conditions that Carnegie discovered, when he finally decided to go to Mesabi, that he would be forced to deal with the "Magnate of 92 Broadway," history's mightiest virtuoso monopolist.

"I was astonished that the steelmakers had not seen the necessity of controlling their ore supply," said John D. Rockefeller. Naturally, Rockefeller controlled his astonishment and made his move, buying Mesabi ore lands from bankrupt developers, buying railroads, buying lake steamers. Carnegie's main competitor, Illinois Steel, was established already at Mesabi through contacts with the Minnesota Iron Co. Carnegie realized that he would have to take nearly all of the ore property he wanted from Rockefeller, an interesting predicament for anyone, even for Andrew Carnegie. Merely the ore lands would not be enough because Rockefeller, following his natural instincts, also controlled the railroads in the area and the lake steamers, and "That's like owning the pipeline," said

Carnegie. He had a fine appreciation of Mr. Rockefeller's methods. But unlike so many, Carnegie did not fear Rockefeller. The scale of Carnegie's operations put him in a powerful bargaining position.

The great oil monopolist was now well placed to build his own steel works, but he would have to fight Carnegie, and even for Rockefeller, that was a sobering prospect. On the other hand, Carnegie could easily absorb all of Rockefeller's iron interests, and that might satisfy both sides. Rockefeller was interested in money, not steel. Carnegie leased the ore lands for 25 cents a ton, making provisions for the employment of Rockefeller's mines, ships and railroads. Even Carnegie, interestingly, was impressed by Rockefeller's diabolical acquisitive prowess and confessed that he had found John D. Rockefeller "a hard bargainer." Thousands would have agreed with that verdict.

Carnegie now turned to solve the Pittsburgh end of his transportation problems. As early as 1883, when he entered into an abortive construction scheme with William Vanderbilt, Carnegie had attempted to escape from the Pennsylvania Railway's coils by building his own railway. The Pennsylvania squeezed Pittsburgh shippers regularly and gave more favorable rates and rebates to Carnegie's lakeside competitors. Now that Carnegie had his ores, he did not intend to lose his advantages to railway-rate discrimination. In 1896 he bought the Pittsburgh, Shenango & Lake Erie Railroad, a small line which came to Butler, 30 miles from Edgar Thomson, and ran to the lake port of Conneaut, Ohio. Carnegie announced that he would rebuild and extend this road to connect Pittsburgh with the lakes. Moreover, he would build a railroad to carry his own coke from Connellsville, thus cutting off the thriving coke trade from the P. R. R.

The Pennsylvania men panicked and asked for a parley. Carnegie knew their business, and presented them with their own secret rebate data (which he had obtained by espionage). He agreed to allow the Pennsy to continue to transport his coke from Connellsville if they would no longer discriminate against him in favor of his competitors. He would, however, go ahead with his railroad from his mills to Lake Erie. Renamed the Pittsburgh, Bessemer & Lake Erie, the road was finished in 15 months. It carried coke from Pittsburgh to Conneaut and ore from there back to Pittsburgh. The railroad was a great success. Carnegie also built more lake steamers to handle his ore traffic.

His organization was now unrivaled. Carnegie himself owned 58 percent of his stock, and thus had easy control and, thanks to the Homestead strike, had no unions whatever to oppose any changes he might want to make in his plant layout or equipment. The other partners, Henry Phipps with 11 percent of the stock, Frick with 6 percent, Carnegie's cousin George Lauder with 4 percent, Charles Schwab with 1 percent, together with the many smaller partners, were scarcely in a position to oppose Carnegie even if they all united against him. Carnegie could carry out reorganization measures as he pleased. He intended to become independent of everyone else in the trade. "The more I study the situation the more I feel that our policy is to own every factor in the process of making steel," he wrote in 1896. The profits were there because of his efficiency; he could undersell everyone in the trade. "Take orders and run the mills full, the margin is there" was increasingly the substance of his instructions.

Carnegie's steel works had been built around his own blast furnaces and the Bessemer converters that Captain Jones had made the most efficient in the world. Now Carnegie began a massive scrapping and rebuilding program, carried out during depression at rock-bottom costs. It is said that during these years Carnegie started one January meeting of his associates with a cheerful: "Well, what shall we throw away this year?" He had seen a Siemens open-hearth furnace, with a basic lining, making steel in Europe. He came home and asked Schwab to try it. In March, 1888, the first open-hearth furnace was installed at Homestead. Now, in the pit of the depression Carnegie intended to completely equip himself with the new open-hearth technology. His partners protested for a division of the profits but Carnegie voted his 58 percent to reinvest. Rebuild, tear down, rebuild. "The perfect mill is the way to wealth," said Carnegie. The great converters were torn down wherever necessary. Carnegie was only sentimental on a selective basis, and his sentiment did not extend into technology; if a machine, or a plant, was obsolete it was fit only for a museum.

Schwab told an interesting story of this period. Carnegie, upon a plea that a new mill could save 50 cents a ton, had authorized Schwab to build it. When Carnegie came to see the mill, Schwab told him that if he could build the mill again he could save a dollar a ton. "Can't you make the needed changes?" asked Carnegie. "No," answered Schwab, "I would have to tear it down again." "Then go ahead," said Carnegie. "Which we did," said Schwab.

By the end of the Nineties, with his ore, coke, ships, railroads, new mills, superb organization, Carnegie made a quarter of America's steel output. He was impregnable wherever he operated. He could easily, as he later said, have ruined any other steel producer in open competition. He viewed the giant Federal Steel (put together by Judge Gary from Illinois Steel and others with the assistance and blessings of J. P. Morgan) with open contempt; "speculators" and "manufacturers of securities" he called them. But Carnegie was increasingly restive now about his "other life." He was in his sixties. In 1897, at 62, he had become the father of a little girl, a dividend which he wanted time to enjoy. He also wanted to savor the fabulous personal triumphs which were pouring in upon him from kings, emperors, presidents, prime ministers and others. He also wanted to indulge his philanthropic urges. He wanted to sell out. But to whom? And how much would Carnegie's fantastic steel empire be worth if it were put on the block? The answers to those questions have, of course, become part of the folklore of American industrial history.

IX

For years Carnegie fought against all attempts by his partners to raise the valuation of his capital stock. Assets were carried on the books at the most conservative possible figures, and the capital stock, representing the partners' ownership of the assets, was valued accordingly. This arrangement was convenient to Carnegie if he decided to force out a partner "at the books." It also was congenial to Carnegie in other ways, representing his distrust of "finance." The result was that with a capital stock valued at $45,000,000 the Carnegie Steel Co. was in danger of presenting to the world the spectacle of a company with annual profits equal to the capital stock, a 100 percent net return each year. With the completed integration and the new mills, Carnegie steel was increasing its profits at a fabulous rate while maintaining the lowest prices in the industry. Profits in 1896 were $6 million; in 1897, $7 million; 1898, $11 million; 1899, $21 million; 1900, $40 million. Of the last figure Andrew Carnegie's share, his personal *income* for the year from his steel works, was $25 million. How much would a man want for an investment which was nominally valued at $27 million, but which yielded $25

million or more a year? How much was $45 million of stock
at face value actually worth in a free market if, at face value,
that stock made a net income of nearly 100 percent each year,
or perhaps more, much more?

Such were the questions which faced any purchaser of
Carnegie Steel. With Carnegie's conservative valuations, his
refusal to allow his stock to be marketed, the fact was that
no one, including Carnegie himself, knew what the capital
stock of Carnegie Steel might fetch in the market. Carnegie's
notions that a gigantic steel empire could exist as a comfortable little partnership run on the principles of a fishing fleet
had produced a financial dilemma of enormous proportions.
How could Carnegie sell at all if he refused to sell on the
free market? His contempt for the world of finance was
colorful; this was doubtless a refreshing thing in a tycoon,
but now that he wanted to sell out no one knew what to
offer him and he did not know what to ask. It was as simple
as that.

Carnegie had approached some English capitalists in 1889
but they shied away from the problem. Frick was the heir
apparent, so in 1899 he and Henry Phipps made an attempt.
They settled on a valuation of Carnegie Steel of $320 million,
$250 million for the Steel Co. stock and $70 million for the
Frick Coke Co. Carnegie's personal share was to be $157
million. Carnegie asked for an "earnest money" deposit of
$2,000,000 and gave Frick and Phipps ninety days from April
24, 1899, to sell him out.

They failed. Carnegie had not known to whom they intended
to apply. He personally expected that it would be, it would
nearly have to be, a combination of Morgan, Mellon and
Rockefeller interests. In fact, Frick and Phipps tried another
group which included the Moore brothers, two flamboyant
Chicago plungers. J. P. Morgan refused to participate; the
Moores were not "Morgan men." When the attempt failed,
Carnegie pocketed $1,170,000 of the earnest money, which
included $170,000 from Phipps and Frick personally. Car-
negie was also "hopping mad." The two partners had can-
vassed bankers all over the country and had intended to pay
themselves a brokerage fee of $5,000,000. Carnegie's ego was
badly burned at seeing his name and empire peddled from
banker to banker—and unsuccessfully too. He announced
that the next time anyone wanted to talk about buying Carnegie Steel the earnest money was going to be $5,000,000.
Just to talk.

He also turned his wrath upon Frick. The two men had always had a curious, almost boyish, brotherly relationship. It was by turns hot and cold, and always emotional. Now Carnegie determined to squeeze Frick out, and under the iron-clad "at the books" figure. Between 1890 and 1900 the shares of fifteen of Carnegie's partners had been returned to the treasury under those drastic valuations. But Frick was a different kind of man. He was as strong a character as Carnegie, and was determined to fight. The fight included starting a price war with Carnegie over the cost of coke delivered to the Carnegie steel works from the Frick coke ovens. That was an odd circumstance since Frick was an officer in both companies. He now ominously acquired a choice steel-mill site near Pittsburgh that Carnegie wanted. Frick also instituted a suit against Carnegie over the "at-the-books" figure. Finally, Frick offered Carnegie a fist fight.

The nation's industrial leaders were deeply unhappy about the Carnegie–Frick feud, and worried too about possible repercussions. George Westinghouse came to Carnegie and pleaded with him to settle quietly with Frick. Carnegie finally bowed to necessity. In 1900 the partners reorganized Carnegie Steel as a New Jersey corporation. The capital was $320,-000,000—Frick's figure—$160 million in common stock, $160 million in 5 percent bonds. This was a $250 million valuation for the Carnegie company and $70 million for the Frick company. The partners did the work by themselves and paid no banker's or broker's commissions to anyone. No stock was marketed. Frick's share was $31,284,000 of the total. He was also excluded from the management. Carnegie abolished Frick's job and gave the supreme power to Charles Schwab as president of Carnegie Steel. Carnegie's share of the ownership was now valued at $174,529,000.

Carnegie's competitive energies were running full again. He now turned upon his competitors with fury. Federal Steel had been organized out of the Illinois Company and others. The new companies were mainly manufacturers of finished steel products; they had previously relied largely upon Carnegie for steel ingots, bars and rods. The Federal companies now began to rely upon their own blast furnaces and ingot mills. This affront was simply a red flag to Carnegie. If it was to be war, fine. He told Schwab to take them all on. "You have only to meet the occasion, but no half-way measures."

Carnegie would enter into the manufacture of nails, wire, tubes, hoops and all other steel products. With his integrated works, he would make short work of Judge Gary and his colleagues at Federal Steel, the "securities manufacturers." Carnegie wrote to Schwab, master to student: "It is with firms as with nations; 'scattered possessions' are not in it with a solid, compact, concentrated force." Carnegie proposed to rule it all. In the spring of 1900 when American Steel Hoop began to reduce its orders from Carnegie Steel, Carnegie wrote to Schwab: "That should be stopped or we should go into making their product promptly."

This last competitive effort of Carnegie's showed every sign of being his most successful. There was no doubt that he was in it heart and soul. He wrote to Schwab: ". . . crisis has arrived, only one policy open; start at once hoop, rod, wire, nail mills. . . ." He wanted more ore boats, his railways extended: ". . . have no fear as to the result; victory certain. Spend freely for finishing mills, railroads, boat lines." Once more he admonished his sales people to meet *any* prices. "Take orders and run the mills full." Just meet all prices: ". . . the head of the sales department is not responsible for market prices." Whatever the market might say about the price of steel, it would be Carnegie Steel that could sell most cheaply and profitably. He planned to drive to the wall quickly companies with capital of $80 million. The rest would be taken care of in due time.

Carnegie also decided to make it a clean sweep and settle the Pennsylvania Railroad once and for all. He entered into negotiations with George Gould to build a railway from Pittsburgh through Wheeling, West Virginia, to Baltimore and the sea. Carnegie Steel would at last be free altogether of the Pennsylvania Railroad.

The result of these operations was upheaval in the industrial world. Who could stop him? Carnegie had led one of the greatest industrial transformations the world had ever known, the rise of the American steel industry. The nation's industrial machine, based upon cheap steel, was without peer. The resulting rise in national output had in turn nourished the continuing revolution in steelmaking. The process had created the most rapid rise in per capita income the nation had ever known (or has known since, for that matter). It was at once ruthless and wasteful, productive and efficient. Now Carnegie was pushing again. What would be the result? History was cheated of its answer. At this point Carnegie was bought out. The man who did it was John Pierpont Morgan. There was no "earnest money" involved; there was not even a contract at first, just a slip of paper with Carnegie's terms written on it.

Morgan was at the peak of his career as an industrial organizer and financial Caesar. Carnegie's contempt for financiers stopped short of the Morgans. Junius Morgan had applauded and aided the youthful Carnegie in London, and Carnegie had discovered that the Morgans were not like other bankers at all. In fact, Carnegie held the memory of J. S. Morgan in a sort of awe. In his *Autobiography* he wrote concerning business dealings with the Morgans in which they gave him several thousand dollars more than he thought he had coming, and gave it to him as a matter of course, ". . . I determined that so far as lay in my power neither Morgan, father or son, nor their house, should suffer through me." Carnegie certainly did not hurt the House of Morgan now.

In the face of Carnegie's onslaught on his competitors, Morgan's men in steel, and at the Pennsylvania Railroad, pressed the banker for help. Morgan must have been deeply perplexed. A solution to these problems was not evident. But a solution existed, and Morgan got it in the winter of 1900 from Charles Schwab. At a dinner in New York in his honor, Schwab, the 38-year-old president and boy wonder of Carnegie Steel, discoursed at length upon the opportunities in steel for further specialization, the wastefulness of so much duplication, and the advantages, as Carnegie Steel had shown, of vertical integration. Morgan was there, and after dinner conversed alone with Schwab at some length. Carnegie dropped in for a few minutes, but there is no evidence that Schwab was acting on his orders. Morgan was interested in Schwab's ideas and a later meeting was arranged. It was a familiar Morgan conference; it lasted all night. Schwab spread his vast knowledge of the steel industry before Morgan, explaining which firms should be consolidated, which ones should be left alone as independents. A giant steel firm could be constructed around the Carnegie and Federal companies. Carnegie himself posed a problem. Sometimes he talked longingly of retirement, then the mood left him and he sailed gleefully into his plans to carry out his new campaign. At dawn Morgan rose from his chair; his mind was made up. He said to Schwab: "Well, if Andy wants to sell, I'll buy. Go and find his price."

Louise Carnegie suggested to Schwab that he play a round of golf with Carnegie before bringing up the subject of the meeting at Morgan's. This Schwab did, on the wintry links of

St. Andrew's Golf Club. At first Carnegie presented a "pathetic figure" when Morgan's offer was presented. Here was the end, quite suddenly. There could be no doubt. Morgan was no gambler, no speculator; he was the man who could end Carnegie's career in steel. But now that the moment had come Carnegie couldn't let go. He asked Schwab to come back the next day for an answer. Years before, another age it must have seemed, Junius Morgan had watched the tow-headed youngster on the road up. Now Junius Morgan's son was offering to officiate at the end of the road. If Carnegie felt sentimental about these events, he stifled his emotions and wrote down a good stiff price. The next day Carnegie handed Schwab a slip of paper asking for $400 million for the whole enterprise. Carnegie's own share of $178,784,000 in Carnegie stocks and bonds (it was growing steadily under the new accounting system) was to be exchanged for $225,639,000 of 5 percent mortgage bonds in the new corporation. A tidy one-year capital gain of about $50 million.

When Schwab handed him Carnegie's terms, Morgan simply glanced at the paper and said: "I'll take it." Andrew Carnegie was out of business, and the organization of the United States Steel Corp. was under way. Morgan never looked back except to notice some weeks later that there existed no legal document to represent the transaction and sent some men to Carnegie to get one.

In March, 1901, the formation of U. S. Steel was announced to a stupefied financial world. In March, 1901, Andrew Carnegie was in his sixty-sixth year, and his personal fortune exceeded $300 million. It was just two months short of fifty-three years since the impoverished little Scottish family of William, Margaret, Andrew and Thomas Carnegie had forsaken Dunfermline for the Golden Shore.

X

The great American statesman, Elihu Root, said of Carnegie: "He was the kindest man I ever knew." That was after Carnegie died, and it must have raised a few eyebrows around Pittsburgh. Root's verdict does not necessarily mean that his experiences had been remarkably circumscribed. The Andrew Carnegie now generally remembered was the philanthropist. Once Carnegie gave up his steel empire, he followed his own beliefs about the "true gospel concerning wealth" to their logical ends. A man who could cheerfully give away more than $350 million could easily be remembered as the kindest man ever known. After 1901 the "little boss" of Pittsburgh was slowly blotted out of men's memories and replaced by the gentle Laird of Skibo Castle. Carnegie now became a "pioneer." His actions no longer needed to "pay" in a conventional sense. He went to work to see if his enormous wealth could be productive in a nonprofit way.

In 1919 the Carnegie Endowment for International Peace published *A Manual of the Public Benefactions of Andrew Carnegie*. The total figure at that time was $350,695,653.40. There were the costs of constructing 2,811 free public library buildings, more than $60 million. The Carnegie Corporation of New York, the first of the great private foundations, received an enormous $125 million ". . . to promote the advancement and diffusion of knowledge and understanding among the people of the United States. . . ." Carnegie, who also wanted to "reform" the spelling of the English language, charged the trustees:

> My desire is that the work which I hav been carrying on, or similar beneficial work, shall continue during this and future generations. Conditions upon the erth inevitably change; hence, no wise man will bind Trustees forever to certain paths . . . I giv my Trustees full authority to change policy. . . . They shall best conform to my wishes by using their own judgement.

The wisdom of that endowment and charge needs no comment. The Carnegie Foundation for the Advancement of Teaching had, by 1919, received more than $29 million; the Carnegie Institute was endowed with nearly $27 million (which included $13.5 million for the Carnegie Institute of Technology); the Carnegie Institution of Washington had received $22.3 million; the Hero Funds were endowed with more than $10 million; the Carnegie Endowment for International Peace, the Scottish Universities Trust, and the United Kingdom Trust each were endowed with $10 million. Pensions for the steelworkers had received $4 million. The Dunfermline Trust received $3.7 million.

There were smaller public gifts. The Simplified Spelling Board received $280,000; the Koch Institute of Berlin received $120,000; the Sorbonne received $50,000 for the Madame Curie Fund. Carnegie gave away 7,689 church organs at a cost of more than $6 million. That represented his childhood objections to the rigors of the Scottish Kirk. Each benefaction has a personal story behind it.

The Carnegie Corporation of New York, a great "pioneering" adventure, came in 1911 when Carnegie feared that he might not live to disburse his wealth, so he set up the corporation with $125 million of U. S. Steel bonds. It was the first of great open-end foundations, and it is amusing to reflect that Mr. Rockefeller, who had become a friend of Carnegie's and who was having the same problems as Carnegie grappling with personal wealth so enormous as to almost defy the imagination, followed suit with the Rockefeller Foundation (Rockefeller, who lived until 1937, actually outdid Carnegie on the scale of his gifts, giving away almost $600 million).

The Carnegie Institution of Washington represented Carnegie's interest in pure science (he was personally captivated by the Mount Wilson Observatory). The Carnegie Institute of Pittsburgh was part of a continuing effort on the founder's part to assist the people who lived on the scene of his great triumphs (for years after he retired Carnegie could not bear to look at the city when traveling in the United States, pulling down the shade in his car and turning his face away as his train passed through it).

The Scottish Universities Trust brought a basic reform to higher education in Scotland. The United Kingdom Trust was set up in 1916 when Carnegie was down to his last $25 million of U. S. Steel bonds; in it he gave away $10 million for the general betterment of the people of his homeland. The motives behind the Dunfermline trust might seem obvious. The same could be said of the pension system for the steel workers. The system of retiring college professors through their contributions to the Teachers Insurance & Annuity Association is an outgrowth of the Carnegie Foundation for the Advancement of Teaching.

And so the list continues. Noted here have been only the main public gifts. The point is that Carnegie turned out to be a man of his word and simply gave away virtually all of the fruits of the great campaigns he fought and won in the building of the American steel industry. This is not the place to write in detail of the many and great achievements of Carnegie's endowments, nor to try to fathom the deeper motives underlying Carnegie's philanthropic urges. Once out of business, he was generous to a fault. He was egotistical; he was energetic; he was curious, curious about everything he encountered. Most important, he was the Dunfermline lad; Carnegie had the training of his childhood; agnostic or not, he knew the difference between "right" and "wrong" within the framework of Scottish Calvinism and its discontents. Carnegie knew what the word "ought" meant and acted upon it in the long process of dismantling and disbursing his enormous fortune. The result is that, in libraries, laboratories, churches, schools, concert halls, universities, government chancellories and private homes from Pittsburgh to Melbourne, in any direction, the name Carnegie is known today in connection with public virtues of the highest order.

Carnegie also kept a private pension list, indulging himself and providing for whomever and whatever he pleased. He offered to pension Grover Cleveland, the "mean-honest" President, when Cleveland was leaving the White House nearly broke. Carnegie pioneered there too, leaving $10,000 a year for ex-President Taft, $5,000 a year for Cleveland's widow, $5,000 for the widow of Teddy Roosevelt. From 1890 on he kept the White House supplied with the best Scotch whisky "in the wood." An indigent female descendant of the Scottish poet, Robert Burns, was pensioned. The friends and benefactors of his youth were tracked down and endowed. Letters poured in upon Carnegie by the thousands and hundreds of thousands soliciting funds. The telegraphers of the Civil War had not been given pensions—they were not considered by Congress to be soldiers, so Carnegie pensioned them, and their widows.

Except where he was personally involved, Carnegie was no easy touch. He tried to understand where every grant was going, and he kept his sixth sense in spotting talent. James Bryant Conant told a story of a young scientist being sent by a university (unnamed) to get funds from Carnegie for a new laboratory. Carnegie turned down the proposal cold, but proceeded then to provide personal funds for the young scientist himself, to free him for research. The scientist had a Nobel prize fourteen years later.

Carnegie bought Skibo Castle in Scotland in 1897 and rebuilt it into his permanent summer home, restoring the forests and streams, rebuilding the farms of his tenants. As Laird of Skibo Carnegie ruled a feudal domain of about 32,000 acres. In his retirement his days were increasingly filled with the great men of the age. There seems to have been no patronizing in this at all. Carnegie was a great man in his own right and was accepted as such by people to whom the world of industry must have been the deepest mystery. Even the King of England came to Skibo to view Carnegie's grounds. The old steel baron somehow attracted the genuine esteem of people in all social classes and occupations. No better evidence of this could be given than that he was elected Lord Rector of St. Andrews University in 1902 and was re-elected for a second term. The Lord Rector of St. Andrews is elected by the students. In his first address as Lord Rector, Carnegie anticipated the Common Market by half a century, pointing out that Europe would have to be "federalized" to be able to compete economically with the United States.

A sweet triumph came in 1903 when Carnegie acquired the dreamy vales of his childhood, Pittencreiff Glen in Dunfermline, with King Malcolm's Tower, and St. Margaret's Shrine, the ancient seat of Scotland's kings. As a child he had been barred from Pittencreiff by its owners. He gave it all to Dunfermline with an endowment ". . . to bring into the monotonous lives of the toiling masses of Dunfermline more of sweetness and light." An old debt was repaid.

The process of building the thousands of public libraries gave Carnegie special satisfaction. He built them but only if the cities receiving them would provide an annual upkeep of from 10 to 15 percent of the cost of construction. The libraries were thus a "bargain" and difficult for any politician to walk away from. Carnegie loved this arrangement, pointing out that he was forcing tight-fisted city fathers, who ordinarily would never tax themselves to buy a book, to tax themselves heavily in perpetuity for the benefit of educating the masses. He was also pleased to see this idea of his put the public library into the center of American public education.

The first decade after his retirement was a continuous triumph, but the triumph for Carnegie, as well as for the industrial nations of the world, was beginning to be clouded in the second decade of the century. It was becoming clearer that the Europeans were getting set to play their bloody game again. In 1907 Carnegie proposed that a "League of Peace" be established among the nations. This was when the Hague Conference on international peace was at work. Carnegie was in Europe during the period, June to October, of the conference and worked behind the scenes. Although a private citizen, he had the confidence of the emissaries of the major powers and was used as a go-between on an informal basis. An extraordinary role.

Carnegie became increasingly obsessed with the desperate need to maintain peace and not let war come again. He agitated for peace steadily among the rulers of the Western world, who somehow found Carnegie worth listening to. It is conceivable that, even though the generals thought that a new war would be on the scale of 1866, or at worst, 1870–71, and the professors believed that war could be fitted into the framework of the civilization of the West, the statesmen who listened to Carnegie had an inkling that the little white-bearded man was right, and that a new outbreak of Europe's old disease might well fatally weaken their civilization. Even the German "War Lord," Kaiser Wilhelm II listened to Carnegie. The two talked peace together in 1907 and, seeing Carnegie again in 1912 in the Grand Palace in Berlin on a state occasion (the twenty-fifth anniversary of his reign), the Kaiser opened his arms to him and exclaimed, "Carnegie, twenty-five years of peace, and we hope for many more."

In 1910 Carnegie transferred $10 million to the trustees of the Carnegie Peace Fund, the Endowment for International Peace. The new organization, led by the most eminent men (the president was Elihu Root), on an international basis, was an effort to focus men's eyes upon the causes of war, to search them out, to study them and thus to remove ". . . the foulest blot upon our civilization." American statesmen could easily identify their lives and missions with Carnegie. He represented, after all, the virtuous, practical and successful voice of the New World speaking to the Old. If Carnegie could hope and work for international peace, why not all men? The English could sympathize with a Victorian view of the destiny of man they understood. The dream of peace brought honors from the Europeans too. So Carnegie had every hope that he might be instrumental in stopping wars, at least in the West. In 1913 the Peace Palace at The Hague was built with Carnegie's money. It was to have been the scene of that gala celebration in August, 1914.

As it was, the Germans decided to play the "great game" again. On Aug. 1, 1914, a "state of war" existed between Germany and Russia, even though Russia had not yet had time to move against Austria and thus give Germany a treaty reason for war. On Aug. 2 German troops entered France, on Aug. 3 came a formal declaration of war against France. The next day, the Germans crossed the Belgian frontier, a line drawn by Lord Palmerston in 1839 and guaranteed by Great Britain. Now the German Chancellor, Theobald von Bethmann-Hollweg, could cry out in anguish and disbelief that Great Britain was going to make war upon Germany for a "scrap of paper," the Belgian treaty. The British declared war and in that war the centuries-old ascendency of Western Europe was ended. With its kings, and queens, and emperors and parliaments, universities and culture and science, its social stability and its economic progress, old Europe committed suicide. General war reigned in its lands for more than four years, and when it was over the destiny of Western civilization was no longer well understood.

Carnegie's old friend and ally in the peace crusade, Lord Morley (for whom Carnegie had acquired Lord Acton's private library), resigned from the British cabinet, unwilling to accept any responsibility for the war. But Carnegie managed to face up to the new situation. He was a realist, but a broken one. When the news was brought to him by the local minister, Carnegie said: "All my air castles have fallen about me like a house of cards." And then pathetically, "Can't America do something to stop it?" Carnegie supported the British government, and later the American government in the prosecution of the war, although he could never accept that the Kaiser was in any way personally responsible for the catastrophe. But the great last act of the career of Andrew Carnegie had ended; there was no way to square off his beliefs and hopes with the terrible reality. He came home to America in September, 1914, a sad figure indeed. He never saw Skibo again.

XI

Carnegie lived to see his daughter married in April 1919. He was an invalid from 1915 on. He could still do some of his work, and amused himself sitting on a bench in Central Park talking to whoever happened along. Since he never carried money on his person, he had no fear of the public. Pictures of him in the last years show a much shrunken figure, the fire gone from his eyes, with a slightly quizzical expression. In 1917 the Carnegies bought Shadowbrook, a home in the Berkshire hills of Massachusetts, for their summers. Carnegie's health slowly failed him and he died in his sleep on Aug. 11, 1919, in his eighty-fourth year. He was buried in Sleepy Hollow Cemetery, in Tarrytown, New York, a spot he had personally selected. Washington Irving is also buried there. The tenants at Skibo cut a granite block from a local quarry and out of it was fashioned a great Celtic cross which stands over Carnegie's grave.

Doubtless Carnegie died satisfied that he had done his best by his own lights. The spectacle of the great millionaire endowing mankind right and left with uplifting and improving benefactions certainly left a sweet taste in the mouths of his beneficiaries and those who wrote his obituaries. No one suggested that he was not a good man, that he was not sincere in his expressions of love and concern for his fellow man. There was a tendency to forget what he built, and how he built it, before he sold out to Mr. Pierpont Morgan. That has been unfortunate, since Carnegie was also one of the greatest competitors in American history and, as a people, we value competition in industry. Carnegie's competitive innovations in steel constituted a mighty legacy he left to his country. It was a fabulous patch of seed corn. Carnegie invented nothing. But he made the inventions of others enormously effective, and the growth of the American steel industry was largely his masterpiece.

Carnegie's own memory was not clouded by the Olympian triumphs and gigantic failures of his last two decades of life. He remembered everything and how it happened. He sought out those who had befriended him and his wealth showered down upon them. It was the memory of Homestead, his permanent wound, that caused him to provide pensions for the strikers too. Years after the strike a friend of Carnegie's found McLuckie, the Homestead mayor of 1892, in Mexico. McLuckie was broke. His wife had died. He had been forced to flee from Pennsylvania, and the blacklist had hounded him to Mexico. Carnegie was informed of this and sent word to "Give McLuckie all the money he wants, but don't mention my name." McLuckie refused the offer saying that he'd make out on his own. Some time later when McLuckie's fortunes had recovered he was informed that the money he had refused was Carnegie's. The dumfounded McLuckie said: "Well, that was damned white of Andy, wasn't it?" Carnegie wrote: "I would rather risk that verdict of McLuckie's as a passport to Paradise than all the theological dogmas invented by man."

An anonymous bard did Carnegie a favor and left McLuckie's verdict in a form that vastly amused Carnegie. Included here are the first and last verses of "Sandy on Andy":

Oh hae ye heared what Andy's spiered to hae upo' his tomb,
When a' his gowd is gie'n awa an' Death has sealed his doom!
Nae Scriptur' line wi' tribute fine that dealers aye keep handy,
But juist this irreligious screed—'That's damned white of Andy.'

Sae when he's deid, we'll gie good heed, an' write it as he askit;
We'll carve it on his headstone an' we'll stamp it on his casket:

'Wha dees rich, dees disgraced,' says he, an' sure's my name is
    Sandy
'T wull be nae rich man that he'll dee—an' 'That's damned
    white of Andy.'

The nation that still cherishes the old man's memory, and,
year by year, receives the continuing benefits of his largesse,
could hardly disagree.

CHAPTER 7

Henry Ford and the Automobile Age

America is not a land of money, but of wealth—not
a land of rich people, but successful workers.

Henry Ford, 1935

In 1938 Henry Ford and his wife Clara celebrated their
golden wedding anniversary and Henry celebrated his seventy-
fifth birthday. The people in the auto industry in Detroit and
Dearborn, and to a lesser extent the rest of the nation, joined
in the festivities. The wedding anniversary was illuminated by
a special ode from the facile pen of Edgar A. Guest, Ford's
favorite poet, and President Roosevelt invited Ford to Washington for a luncheon. Henry Ford at 75 was as uniquely
American in the public mind as Lincoln or Whitman, and
people felt an easy familiarity with the sage of Fair Lane, the
mighty industrialist of Dearborn and the River Rouge. In an
editorial, "Clara and Henry," the New York *Herald Tribune*
wrote a folksy tribute.

> Clara has seen Henry put his imprint upon his country and
> has heard him described, for better or for worse, as the man
> most responsible for the growth of the new industrial age . . .
> they remain essentially simple people. Clara never dyed her
> hair purple or had her face lifted or won the prize at the
> Beaux Arts Ball. Henry . . . has had his share of odd notions
> [but] never bet twenty grand on a dice game, never had to be
> psychoanalyzed . . . and has never been reported by the gossip
> writers as carrying the torch for either a countess or a show-
> girl. More, they still dance with each other. It may be that,
> in more matters than one, they are the richest people in the
> world.

At that time Ford was half as old as the United States. He
had been a pioneer in the auto industry. He had also tried to
stop the First World War by his own efforts; he had been sued
for publishing anti-Semitic materials in his private newspaper.
He had himself sued a great newspaper for calling him an
"ignorant idealist" and an "anarchist." He was, in 1938, fight-

ing against the organization of his workmen under the Wagner Act. ("There is nothing a union can give them that they haven't already got.") Ford had successfully withheld his signature from the automobile industry code, which the (by-then defunct) N. R. A. had attempted to impose upon him. Ford was a vociferous opponent of the New Deal. He believed that Wall Street ran both the government and the labor unions.

He believed some other curious things too. But even his great competitor William C. Durant, founder of General Motors, said that Ford, more than any other person, was responsible for carrying the industrial revolution into every American home, for re-creating the nation's physiognomy on the basis of cheap mass transportation.

Ford was an American figure all right, almost homespun—but not quite. He was comical, down-to-earth and grass-rootsy, and indeed, he tended to be almost a stereotype of the Great American Kid, if you didn't look too closely. He was also unnaturally suspicious, ruthless, hard-headed, bigoted and "tough"—very tough. He was a hard-driving task master. Ford was more than just a figure though; he was, in a very real sense, a creation of American history.

In Henry Ford several strains in the growing American tradition came to fruition and joined. He and his friend Edison represented, each in his own way, the "folk" figure in America, the natural American, able to achieve almost anything without formal training simply by virtue of birth on American soil. Their doctrine of "original perception" was not only a recognition of the power of insight combined with pragmatic objectivity, it was also a thumbed nose at "experts," "scientists," "specialists" and the like. Ford and Edison were the old wise-cracking rural American laughing at the "green-horns." Yet Ford and Edison created a world in which their own kind would find life increasingly difficult.

Ford's extension of mass production techniques, the legacy of Whitney, was the payoff of a century of American industrial development; in Ford's factories the substitution of machinery for skilled hands, the serialization and standardization of production went from the realm of technology into the meta-physical. Ford virtually made a religio-social and economic system out of mass production.

Out of his frontier home, out of McGuffey's *Readers,* out of the people he knew and the little reading he ever did be-yond his primary school, Ford managed somehow to distill the clearest essence of American Puritanism. His statement against the N. R. A. codes included the phrase "the world was built to develop character. . . ." Cotton Mather couldn't have said it more succinctly. Ford was in many respects a living monument to the economic and social extremism of the New England forefathers. Ford's ideal economic system, as put forth in *My Life and Work*, resembles nothing so much as an ant hill. Aldous Huxley, in *Brave New World*, showed a deep understanding about Henry Ford.

Like Carnegie, Henry Ford carried his virtuosity in industrial innovation to revolutionary extremes, tearing up a whole way of life on the basis of technological change and price competition. Like Carnegie, Ford believed that the act of "making" things was a positive virtue in itself, when done efficiently. The manufacturer was the salvation of the country, but the "financier" was its curse. Ford had no more use for bankers than he did for professional historians.

He liked to wear gray suits, ready-made, black shoes and a high starched collar with striped neckties. The iron-gray hair, the thin tightly drawn lips, deep-set gray-blue eyes, the lithe figure, the sensitive hands—that image remains. Until he died April 7, 1947, the odd old man continued to fascinate Americans. He was a living piece of their history. In old age he jumped fences and ran foot races, but he made fewer and fewer public pronouncements. There was a good reason for that. From the 1930's onward he evidently realized that history was somehow running against him and his kind. When history was with him, however, in the golden age of the Model T, Henry Ford thought he spoke for the nation.

I

Henry Ford was born July 30, 1863, on a farm near Dearborn, Michigan. He was the second of eight children, three of whom died, the last at birth in March of 1876. The eldest child had died as an infant and the seventh, a boy, Robert, died at the age of 4. The mother, Mary Litogot Ford, never recovered from her last delivery. Hence, Henry knew well the meaning of the terrible infant mortality statistics of 19th-century America. At 13, he was motherless, with two younger brothers and two younger sisters. He said their home was like a watch without a mainspring after his mother died. The family of William and Mary Ford had suffered 40 percent mortality in the process of family creation, the mother and three children dying and the father and five surviving. Even so, the Ford family was not unusual in that regard. The "good old days" were bad indeed when so many died so needlessly.

It was thought until recently that Ford was partly of Irish descent, but, according to recent research, Henry's grandfather, John Ford, was an Englishman and a Protestant, tenant farming in Ireland, who was evicted during the famine in 1847 and came to Dearborn, following two brothers who had immigrated in the 1830's. Henry's father, William, could remember Ireland. Little is known of the ancestry of Mary Litogot except that her parents were either Dutch or Flemish. She was orphaned early and grew up the adopted daughter of Patrick O'Hearn and his wife, a childless immigrant couple. Mary Litogot married William Ford in 1861. Thus it was that Henry Ford had an Irish "grandfather" and yet had no known Irish ancestor; Patrick O'Hearn was the only grandfather Henry Ford ever knew, his father's father having died in 1864.

Like Andrew Carnegie, Ford was indelibly marked by the example and precepts of a strong mother. Mary Ford was the ruler in her house. So powerfully did she shape her son's motives and thought that even as an old man he told an interviewer, "I have tried to live my life as my mother would have wished." Her Calvinism had been partly learned in the nearby Scotch Settlement school. Henry also started his schooling there. Ford learned his little Calvinist catechism well; he used to repeat his mother's maxims—for example, "The best fun follows a duty done." Such an outlook was a great asset in the circumstances. Mary Ford was a farm wife in frontier Michigan; her eldest living son, Henry, had to help with the work as soon as he could. It was a life of drudgery to a large extent, and success could come only from hard physical work. The mature Henry Ford, prating endlessly about the virtues of work, is more easily understood if his origins are taken into account. He was his mother's son.

Ford, according to a sister, was not always fair to the memory of his father. That is also quite unremarkable. Henry hated the inefficiency of the old-time farm, hated it with a life-long fury (as a result he was a leader in mechanization of the farm and in the application of science to agriculture). His father was a farmer and a satisfied one. He wanted Henry to be a farmer, too, naturally enough. William Ford was a good and generous father to the boy. But when is a parent good and generous enough?

Henry was precocious at mechanics and backward at other things. He said he could read McGuffey's first *Reader* before he entered school, that his mother had taught him. Perhaps he could, but reading was never his strong suit; "tinkering" was. As a boy he was fascinated by machinery, repaired clocks for neighbors, and even considered at one point the possibilities of manufacturing them (the night he met Clara, Ford was showing off a watch which told two different times simultaneously).

Inevitably the boy's interest in mechanics led him away from the horse-driven world of his father's farm. In 1879, without informing his father of his plans, the 16-year-old Henry went to Detroit and took a mechanic's job with the Michigan Car Co. He quit within a week, but not before he had seen a self-contained manufacturing plant in operation. The next step was an apprenticeship at the Flower Brothers machine shop. In nine months Ford was apprenticed at the Detroit Drydock Co., and it was there that he passed his apprenticeship as a machinist.

The last point—that Ford was himself a master mechanic— is an important one, especially in contrast to Carnegie. Although his claims to the role of an inventor are thin, Ford was able to be an industrial pioneer on his own mechanical ingenuity. Carnegie was contemptuous of pioneering. Ford was not. Carnegie had general ideas about steelmaking, which he relied upon others to put into practice. Ford used the skills of others, but he could also rely to a great extent upon his own knowledge of the detailed processes of manufacturing, and did. One result was that Ford stayed at his factory, leaving the selling to others, whereas Carnegie spent more time in New York than in Pittsburgh. Carnegie saw the role of his business and the industrial sector of the economy within the cradle of a wider world of men and events; Ford tended to view the world at large only from the point of view of the manufacturing industry or, even more narrowly, simply through the lens of the Ford Motor Co.

Carnegie became increasingly a man with broad and diverse interests based upon a wide acquaintance with men of letters and public affairs. Ford's sources of inspiration came from his factory. He viewed and organized human relations on the basis of production economics. That is what he understood. He was no believer in the perfectibility of man, or even that the ordinary man was especially an admirable character; or, indeed, that it was necessary that man have any particular aspirations beyond simple self-interest, so long as that self-interest could be acted upon. In many respects Ford was simply a master mechanic all his life, and to a large extent the world, to him, was indistinguishable from the shop. Those first years in Detroit not only extended Ford's education beyond McGuffey, they very nearly saw the completion of his education except for the inevitable accumulation of details. McGuffey, Mary Ford and the shop. What was good, and what worked.

Ford went back to the farm briefly after "Grandfather" O'Hearn died in 1882. There followed three years in which he obviously had no distinct ideas about his future. He helped with the farm; he worked for Westinghouse, putting together steam traction engines to be used for threshing, woodcutting and so forth. Also in these years (1882–85), according to evidence uncovered by Allan Nevins and F. E. Hill, Henry seems to have taken some courses from a "business college," probably some instruction in accountancy. In 1885 Henry was employed by the Eagle Iron Works in Detroit to repair an internal-combustion engine—evidently the first upon which he had worked—the "Silent Otto," a product of the German motor builder, Nikolaus August Otto.

This first contact with the internal combustion engine apparently had no powerful influence on Ford. He still thought of steam as the major source of power for self-propelled vehicles. In 1888 he married Clara Bryant, settled on an eighty-acre farm (Ford calls it forty acres; it seems to have been eighty acres with forty in timber) which his father provided for the young couple, on the understanding that Henry would give up the machinery trade and settle on the farm. Henry immediately built a proper workshop and began trying to build a steam-driven tractor. It is suggested that he took up his father's offer *in order* to have more time to conduct experiments. Henry and Clara did well on the farm with a sawmill, run by a steam engine, which Henry constructed. They built a comfortable house and lived a settled rural life. But in a few years the forty acres of timber was almost all cut and there was either the prospect of living off job saw-mill operations, farming, or leaving.

At this point Henry and Clara made the momentous decision to leave their country life, their new home and their friends and to move to Detroit where Henry had a job with the Detroit Electric Co. (the Edison Illuminating Co.). Just why Ford made that decision is not known as nicely as many historians would like. Ford encouraged a "cult of personality" atmosphere and his biographers have therefore tended either

toward a shameless species of idolatry or toward hypercriti-
cism. The idolatrous biographers insist that Ford realized
almost immediately that his steam tractor would come to
nothing, that he at once had set his mind upon building an
automobile powered by an internal-combustion engine, and
that *therefore* he decided to leave the farm. He would need
to learn about electricity; *therefore* the job with Edison Electric. The question is important only regarding how much
sheer chance was involved at this point in Ford's career. It is
most likely that his notions about an internal-combustion
engine were not yet fixed when he left the farm. He was explicit about his reasons for giving up: "The timber had all
been cut," he said. Besides, he went on, the Edison Electric
job paid $45 a month and "that was more than the farm was
bringing me and I had decided to get away from farm life
anyway."

In later years Ford continued his interest in farming (in
mechanizing it); he even idealized rural life to a large extent,
but he wanted no more of it himself. Henry and his wife
settled in a house on Bagley Avenue in Detroit in 1891, and
there the first Ford car was made. Soon after the move Ford
was at work on engines again, but this time it was an internal-
combustion engine and it was for an automobile, not a tractor.
On Christmas Eve, in 1893, Clara helped Henry operate part
of a one-cylinder engine in their kitchen. Ford had made it
in the woodshed workshop in the back of the house. He
worked there on most nights (after being promoted from night
engineer at the electric company) after work, laboriously
making a motor car. He read about other motor cars, adapted
ideas from them, but even then he wanted one on his own
terms, light in weight relative to the power delivered by the
engine.

Making the car was a matter largely of trial and error,
night after night. It is said that the neighbors soon thought
Clara Ford's husband to be very odd indeed, although no one
considered him a dangerous enough lunatic to get in touch
with the authorities. Very few people in Detroit had ever seen
a motor car in the early 1890's and many probably had never
even heard of such a contraption. Yet there was Henry Ford
making one in his woodshed.

Ford was hardly a lonely pioneer. He had seen plans for
other motor cars. He was trying to reproduce what others
had done. He used all the help he could get, got other mechanics to help him and had parts made wherever he could.

He contracted for the iron work, but the wheels, sparking mechanism, most of the motor, were made in his shop. The seats, bolts, nuts and screws along with other parts were bought from established firms. Ford couldn't remember where he got the balance wheel. The point is that his car, however original, was largely a matter of adaptation. There was no startling invention in it. Ford even got the advantage of direct observation; in March of 1896, while his own car was moving rapidly to completion, he watched a demonstration on the streets of Detroit by his friend, Charles King, of the King four-cylinder "powered wagon."

Early in the morning of June 4, 1896, between 2 and 4 A.M., an excited Henry Ford seized an axe and knocked down part of the brick wall of his woodshed. Like the proverbial do-it-yourself basement boatbuilder, he had made his machine too wide for the doors. He wanted it out of the woodshed *now*, no matter what. After all those months, the work and the expense, he wouldn't wait longer. It was still dark. Rain was falling. Clara watched, holding an umbrella. One of Ford's helpers, Jim Bishop, got on his bicycle to ride ahead and warn off any drivers of horses who might be out so early. Ford started up the little engine, climbed up onto the seat which he had placed on top of a box over the motor, grasped the tiller, put the car into gear and the first Ford automobile moved down the alley into the street. Except for a minor breakdown, the trial run was successful and uneventful. Afterward Clara served both men their breakfasts before they reported for work. The momentous day continued, just like any other.

In fact, although Ford's life began to change because of his automobile, the change came slowly. It was one thing to make an automobile in one's spare time out in the woodshed, it was quite another thing to get together enough money and men to make cars, in 1896, and then attempt to displace the horse. It was not at all certain that an automobile factory would be a good business investment. How much of a market would there be for such a contraption? Ford was not overrun with encouragement, financial or other. But in August, 1896, Thomas Edison told him that he could see a great future for the automobile driven by an internal-combustion engine. Ford always claimed that encouragement as decisive in his own mind. He had met Edison at a dinner in New York. Ford had risen to a position high enough (ultimately he was to be senior engineer at a salary of $1,900 a year) to be included in such affairs as annual company dinners in New York; he had gone there and had been introduced to Edison as "a young fellow who had made a gas car." Ford found no financial backers, but he soon sold his first car to a Detroit man for $200 (it was still running in 1899) to get funds to start building a new car. Meanwhile he continued to work for the Edison company.

More than three years after his first car was tested successfully, Ford resigned from the electrical company. It was Aug. 15, 1899, and ten days earlier Ford and some backers had filed articles with the county clerk to establish the Detroit Automobile Co. Ford parted amiably with the electric company—he was given no ultimatum about his tinkering, as some biographers have stated. His boss, Alex Dow, was an admirer of Ford and thought that he might be able to promote his car and remain with the Edison company. But Ford made a complete break with the security of a job with a going concern, the kind of break that every man must make if he is to start something new. It is easier for some than for others. Ford was then 36 years old. He had "dawdled" to some extent if you consider where he ended in his life. He was middle-aged, for his times. In 1899 the road ahead was still a long one. Ford had a family to support (Edsel, his only child, was born in November, 1893); he was a man of modest means, little education, and had only the product of his own hands for his future. Most people who attempt new enterprises fail. Ford knew that. The automobile industry was already strewn with the wreckage of failures when Ford entered it in 1899. He would contribute some wreckage of his own before he became the Henry Ford of legend.

II

The Times of London wrote of Henry Ford: "So closely is his name associated with motor cars and mass production that it is perhaps hard to realize that he did not originate either." That is important to remember. Henry Ford's company carried certain technological developments to a very high level. Those developments were not invented by Henry Ford, or his men, and the level of their ultimate perfection in Ford's hands was possible only because of the parallel and prior development of the national economy as a whole. It is important to bear these things in mind because of the extraordinary amount of calculated misinformation put out by Ford's own people, his admirers and his enemies. Indeed a large part of the available literature on the man is a really extraordinary mass of fabrications, ignorance, near and outright plagiarism. In recent years, the opening of the Ford archives to scholars has made it possible for historians to untangle fact from fiction. The life revealed is perfectly astonishing, and the historian can only approach it with utmost care. Ford said history was "bunk" and a great deal of the history about Henry Ford is bunk indeed. There is some justice, however, in the fact that Ford himself, the way he operated and lived, is partly responsible for the bunk in his own history. But more of that as we proceed.

The reader of this book saw the origins of mass production in Eli Whitney's time. Automobiles were already developed and being sold when Ford entered the business. Neither of these considerations need detract from Ford's legitimate accomplishment. The innovator need not originate anything, he need only find the way to introduce change into economic life. Ford did originate some things, and he was without a peer in his successful introduction of change into American life. He used all of the tactics others before him used, including some shrewd advertising, luck and a superior product. He also used what Carnegie used, the price mechanism. He used it in a slightly different way, but the result was the same; the successful innovator drove inefficient producers out of business, made the efficient producers even more efficient, and permanently changed the flow of resources and the pattern of economic development as a result.

The change in the pattern of development was the appearance in, and complete permeation of, the American economy by the automobile. The age of the automobile began in the United States early in the 20th century; motor-car ownership spread like wildfire. By the 1920's the motor car was ubiquitous, and it has been permeating the economies of other countries progressively as industrialism spreads and national incomes rise. The important point about the automobile is *energy*. For both transportation and communications, as well as in the performance of stationary work, the internal-combustion engine has been a massive infusion of mechanical energy into economic life. The attachment of that engine to wheels has meant a massive freeing of mechanical energy from stationary sources. The result is that men with engines can do the work of hundreds of horses wherever a motor car can be driven (or shipped, or dropped by parachute).

In America the automobile obliterated a whole culture and

way of life. In addition, it quickened the long-term rise in national income both by introducing greater efficiency in output, and perhaps more important, by inducing men to work harder and to perform better. Americans, it turned out, all wanted motor cars. Ford was right. As a result we are still trying to adjust to the monster; our highways and superhighways span the continent in all directions; cities sprawl because of the motor car; through it, the farmers have become part of the urban culture. Much has been destroyed by it, and much created. Now it is difficult even to imagine America without the automobile. A curse and a blessing, the horseless carriage largely dictates the way our nation lives. Not only was this not always so, it was, as Dr. Seuss might say, not so not so very long ago. The motor car came to America in numbers quite suddenly, and that was when Mr. Henry Ford was so important in our history.

In 1905 the three main Western European nations, Britain, France and Germany, boasted 81,000 registered passenger vehicles between them, compared to only 77,400 in the United States. By 1913 the Europeans had 426,000 registered vehicles, but the United States by then had 1,258,000. The gap widened and by 1926, when the whole of Western Europe had 3,139,000 passenger vehicles, the American figure stood at more than 22,000,000. By then there had been 15,000,000 Model T Fords made in the United States. In 1926 total U. S. motor vehicle output was 4,301,000 compared to a mere 495,000 in Europe.

Henry Ford's company had accustomed itself to more than half of the American output. Ford could have made all of Europe's automobile output in less than three months—if by "automobile" you meant Model T, and that is what Ford and millions of Americans meant. It would be decades (the late 1950's) before Europe would see the motor car as it was seen in America by 1913—a piece of mobile mechanical energy at the disposal of virtually anyone with a job. That was Ford's dream come true, and it had happened in America in the space of a mere decade.

Ford did not create his world. He made the most of a world of economic expansion and change into which he had been thrown. What many historians and biographers of Ford and the phenomenal rise of the automobile have utterly failed to understand is that Ford, a great innovator, was riding the crest of an enormous wave, the secular expansion following the Civil War which, given the vagaries of the business cycle, did not really end until the 1930's.

When the present Ford Motor Co. was organized in 1903, the economy was still showing some of the vigor of the great secular expansion of the late 19th century, although there were some rough short-term ups and downs in business activity. Measured over longer periods, by decades, national output of goods and services was still rising rapidly, although not so rapidly as had earlier been the case. From 1903 to 1926 are the years from Ford Motor Co.'s beginning to the end of the Model T, the years of Henry Ford's greatest triumph. In those years net national product rose at a mean annual rate of over 10 percent (about 7 percent compound), doubling itself roughly every decade or so. (What this means can perhaps be better appreciated by comparing the figure of more than 10 percent in 1903–26 to the roughly 3 percent per annum of 1950–61.) Net national product stood at roughly $22 billion in 1903, was nearly $37 billion by 1913 (a mean annual rate of growth of nearly 7 percent after passing through two serious recessions that followed the crises of 1903 and 1907), and then with World War I and its aftermath reached $89.9 billion in 1926. Those decades did not see *the* most rapid rates of growth of income for such periods of time in American history (those occurred earlier, in the years from 1869 to 1883), but the rates of expansion achieved in 1903–26 have not been seen again except in the Second World War.

Ford entered the automobile industry near the end of one of the greatest epochs of economic expansion in history, but he entered that epoch in time to prosper. Carnegie had seen the beginning of that economic epoch, Ford was to see its end.

Ford was making nearly 10,000 cars a day in 1925. In those days he claimed (his ghost writers and publicists claimed), and too many historians believed, that Ford himself was somehow the key figure in the great economic expansion. Curiously, when the national economy slowed down drastically in the 1930's none of Ford's claque of trained-seal biographers and historians said it was any of Ford's doing. It was not, of course, beyond their share of the downturn in the national income that Ford's own production cutbacks accounted for. But the same logic holds for the expansion up to 1929. Ford's share of that great rise in output was only a tiny fraction of the total. The *influence* of the methods in his factories upon the rest of the economy is another matter altogether. Here

Henry Ford was important (and still is) out of all proportion to the value of his own production.

To cut Ford down to size, compared to where his most hot-eyed admirers left him, is still to deal with a colossus. He was the greatest leader in the creation of the automobile culture which now embraces the national economy. For that he is an important figure in American history. But he was a *product* of our great industrial transformation, and in some respects his company was the most perfect representative of certain aspects of American industrialism before the Great Depression. Ford could make cars with his bare hands. He hired others who could, too. He had a vision, and together Ford and his men changed the world. Charles Sorensen, Ford's production boss, put it well when he pointed out that Ford would not have gone far without his key men, but, as Sorensen emphasized, those key men would not have gone anywhere at all without Ford. Ford organized men into the right economic activity at the right time, and he did it in a unique and successful way. Hundreds of others failed.

At first it looked as though Ford might fail too. His early ventures after he left the electric company in 1899 suggested nothing of what was to follow.

III

The Detroit Automobile Co., organized in 1899, had a nominal capital of $150,000 of which a mere $15,000 was paid in. Ford was a stockholder but he paid no cash; his interest was in his designs. The mayor of Detroit was among the stockholders, and Ford was superintendent of the company. They made perhaps twenty-five motor cars before giving up in late 1900. It is not clear precisely what was wrong with the car. Ford later said it was not what he wanted to produce. He needed new backing. To get it he took up racing.

The automobile, then a rich man's toy and a source of amusement (or harassment) to the public, provided a chance for quick fame at the race tracks. Ford challenged Alexander Winton, another pioneer, whose car had beaten the best Europeans. Winton held the American speed record. Ford built his entry in a rented loft so cold that he and his mechanic, "Spider" Huff, had to stop periodically and box each other with boxing gloves to get warm. The race was held at the Grosse Pointe track on Oct. 10, 1901. Ford drove his racer and Winton drove his. Ford won, and Detroit had a new hero.

He now got a new set of backers, including some from the defunct Detroit Automobile Co. who wanted to try again. The Henry Ford Motor Co. was organized on Nov. 30, 1901. Ford was now listed as "engineer." He was given a $10,000 interest; total capital was $60,000, of which about $30,500 was paid in and comprised the company's initial resources, those that were supposed to be used to develop a salable motor car. Instead, Ford spent his (and his company's) time and money on racing cars. Henry Leland was brought in over Ford's head to develop a salable commercial car out of what Ford had already done. Leland was a great precision mechanic, and Ford's backwoods trial-and-error methods inevitably led to friction with the boss. By early 1902 Ford and his second set of backers parted company. Ford's idolater biographers have put it out that Ford left both of the early companies because he wanted to build an economy car and his backers wanted a luxury model. After a fresh examination of the evidence the verdict of Nevins and Hill was:

> Ford was obsessed with the racing idea . . . he unreasonably resented Leland's expert counsel, and he seemed to be chiefly responsible for holding back production which the corporation must have to survive.

Ford got $1,800 for his carburetor and a promise that the company would not call its car "Ford." The car Leland developed was called Cadillac instead. Leland later designed and built the Lincoln automobile and was, still later, bought out of bankruptcy for a song by Henry Ford, the legendary one. The automobile was still in infancy when Ford went back to racing in 1902. There was still time for experimentation. Ford, Tom Cooper and C. H. Wills built the famous 999 in 1902 and in October of that year, with Barney Oldfield at the wheel, the 999 set a new American speed record.

Ford now got more backing. A. Y. Malcomson, a moderately wealthy Detroit coal dealer, wanted to get into the automobile business, and of Ford, Cooper and Wills, Ford was the most promising, or so Malcomson thought. The result was the present Ford Motor Co., incorporated in June of 1903. Henry Ford was then in his fortieth year, a sometime racing-car driver, mechanic and car producer with two false starts behind him since his successful car back in 1896. Extraordinarily shy, unable to explain himself to strangers, and with a general hayseed personality, Ford did not seem a good business bet to many reasonable investors. James Couzens, about whom more

288 / THE INNOVATORS
288 / THE INNOVATORS
288 / THE INNOVATORS

later, said that he was thrown out of so many offices around
Detroit in his money-raising efforts that he once just sat down
on the curb and wept. Who wanted to invest money in Henry
Ford?

The Ford Motor Co. had twelve shareholders initially. Ford
and Malcomson each had 25½ percent (255 shares) of the
nominal issued capital of $100,000 (there was another $50,-
000 in reserve as treasury stock). A banker, John S. Gray, put
up $10,500 cash and got 105 shares. Albert Strelow, a man
with a woodworking business, refurbished and rented his two-
story workshop on Mack Avenue for a manufacturing plant,
and put up $5,000 in cash for 50 shares. The Dodge Brothers,
John and Horace, had an established machine shop. They
were to make the motor, transmission and other parts. They
got 50 shares each in return for $7,000 in materials and their
note for $3,000. V. C. Fry, C. H. Bennett, Horace Rackham
and John W. Anderson put up $5,000 apiece for 50 shares
each and Charles J. Woodall had 10 shares. James Couzens
came in for 25 shares (one of which belonged to his sister,
Rosetta, who lent him $100; that one share was her fortune).
Rackham and Anderson were lawyers connected with Malcomson who did preliminary legal work. Malcomson wanted
to have a man of his own in the front office to watch the
books, so his employee, Couzens, was brought in. Fry was
Malcomson's cousin and had some money he wanted to invest;
Bennett had manufactured the Daisy air rifle and had succumbed to the sales talk.

Those were the charter members of one of the greatest private money-making ventures in the history of the world. For
a total of just $28,000 in cash they founded the Ford Motor
Co. It was a tiny shoestring for such a venture. No other
"outsiders" got a chance; so long as Henry lived, no money
was raised by stock issues. Strelow sold his stocks to Couzens
in 1905 in order, wildly enough, to invest in a "gold mine" in
British Columbia. Malcomson, trying to promote another automobile company, got into trouble, nearly went bankrupt and
was squeezed out, selling to Ford and Couzens for $175,000
in 1906. Fry, Woodall and Bennett followed Malcomson out.
Ford ended up with 58½ percent of the stock by the end of
1906 and Couzens had 10 percent.

Ford now had control and would, before long, run the company as he pleased. By 1908 there were eight stockholders left
(counting Couzens' sister Rosetta and her one share). The
eight between them had owned a nominal $33,100 in 1903, of

which only part was paid for in cash. Ford bought them out, the "parasites," for $105,000,000 in 1920; by then they had received $33,000,000 in dividends. They were all rich; all except Rosetta were multimillionaires. Couzens got more than $29 million; his sister received more than $262,000 for her $100 investment. Banker Gray's estate received $26,250,000 for his original $10,500 investment. The Dodge Brothers got $25,000,000, and Anderson and Rackham were paid off $12,-500,000 each for their troubles. For a sixteen-year capital gain the Ford Motor Co. had nearly passed all understanding. Yet in a few more years Henry Ford would laugh off an offer of a cool billion dollars for his interest.

By the time Ford bought out his shareholders the Ford Motor Co. was one of the wonders of the modern world and Ford had been transfigured; the humble mechanic, the Michigan farm boy, was now widely called the supreme "genius" of a new industrial order. The Model T Ford was the reason.

IV

The newly organized Ford company was given one more piece of publicity from Ford's racing. As a last fling, Ford took a racer out to the frozen surface of Lake St. Clair in January of 1904 and, on a measured mile of cinders laid over the ice, set a new world record. A few days later he did it again officially, making the distance at just under 100 miles per hour. Ford never drove a racing car again at top speed. He used this last venture for advertising. Leaning heavily on Ford's name as a car racer, Couzens, now Ford's office manager, tried the advertising slogan "Don't Experiment—Buy a Ford."

In 1904–05 the new company offered a Model F at $1,000 and Models B and C. Model B had four cylinders and sold for $2,000. Ford made it as a concession to his stockholders, who wanted a heavy, impressive car to "meet the competition." The Model C, however, was a light car and sold for only $950. In 1905 dividends of $288,000 were paid on the $28,000 of cash investment that launched Ford in 1903. Ford's company was a success and was not destined to join the hundreds of auto companies that would go to oblivion. In 1904–05 Ford had sold 1,745 automobiles. Ransom Olds were selling more than 6,500 in the same year, and his "runabout" sold for around $650 at the factory.

There was still a division between Ford and his management about the kind of car they should make. The experimentation continued. There was a Model K in 1907–08, a six-cylinder job, rated at 40 horsepower, which ran 50 miles an hour, weighed a ton, was expensively got up (it looked impressively like an old-time locomotive with brass fittings) and which sold for $2,500. That was for the stockholders. Ford himself was still trying for a light car, perhaps watching Olds, so there was a Model N with a 15-horsepower engine, which ran 40 miles an hour and had four cylinders. Ford's stockholders were for concentrating upon production of Model K; after all, nearly half the cars sold in the United States in 1906 were priced at between $2,275 and $4,775. Since 1903, the "trend" had been running toward big, heavy, flashy cars (as it usually seems to be in Detroit).

The company's sales declined when it went into heavier cars. In 1905–06 sales fell to only 1,599 cars from the level of 1904–05. The cheapest model then was selling at $1,000, and the company's hopes were on the Model K, a regular limousine. Ford saw the message. He began to concentrate on producing the Model N, a cheap $600 car. By then Ford had control of the company, having forced out Malcomson and the minor stockholders, and he now began to do as he pleased. As a result, the men who had sold out to Ford and Couzens soon had reason to weep. In 1906–07 a record-breaking 8,423 cars were produced and sold by Ford Motor Co., and the Model N was going like wildfire. In December, 1907, the directors suddenly saw Henry Ford in a new light, a very new and different light indeed. He got a salary increase, his pay was raised in one step from $300 to $3,000 a month. Ford was now general manager and president and owned a majority of the stock. Dollar sales of Ford cars had been $1.5 million at the end of September, 1906; a year later the figure stood at $5.8 million.

From September, 1907, through the next twelve months, the nation witnessed the Panic of 1907 and the short but sharp depression that followed. Ford sales in 1907–08 held up fairly well at 6,398, and the gross sales figure fell only a million dollars from the previous year's level; but by reducing costs, the decline in net income was held to less than $20,000. Five of the largest companies, including Malcomson's, had gone bankrupt in 1907. But Ford emerged from that crisis strong and ready to ride the recovery with his new Model T.

Charles Sorensen published a book, *Forty Years with Ford,* in 1956. His eyewitness account upset a lot of biographical applecarts. Sorensen said that although parts of the Model T were the work of several mechanics, it was all Ford's idea generally.

The Model T was started at Ford's Piquette Avenue plant in Detroit in a special room, sealed and locked, in the winter of 1906–07. Ford was unable to read blueprints, and the car had to be "thought up" from day to day by trial and error, building models and drawing pictures of parts on a blackboard. Ford was sold on the idea of using vanadium steel, a light, strong alloy with a tensile strength of 170,000 pounds, compared to the 60–70,000 pounds of the steels in use in motor cars at the time. Ford knew that he could make a car light in weight relative to the engine power by using vanadium steel in the heavy parts. (Ford said he first met vanadium steel when he picked up a valve strip stem from a wrecked French racer at Palm Beach.) He put his best designers and mechanics on his secret Model T project. He himself was personally involved in every piece of the work; he was responsible for choosing the Model T's planetary gears; he thought of making a detachable head for the block, the first one made (at the time this decision was made, no one knew how to make a head gasket strong enough, but Sorensen said they decided to work out such details later).

With their magneto ignition system (which eliminated the need for a battery), a small and light forged crankshaft, the pressed-steel transmission case and all the rest, Ford and his men made a revolutionary machine and a revolution. They made a light, strong, powerful, efficient, simple, dependable and cheap automobile.

During 1908 and early 1909, Ford continued selling two other models, R and S. He unloaded the remaining Model K limousines for a $1,000 discount. The Model T, introduced in October of 1908 swept the field, however. In the next twelve months Ford Motor Co. produced and sold 10,607 cars, the most ever sold by any firm up to that time. The gross sales figure topped $9 million.

It was in 1909 that Ford made his great decision; it was autocratic and characteristic of the man. He would make only one model car and paint it only one color. The car would sell initially for $850 and up. It was then that Ford laid down his famous edict about color: "Any customer can have a car painted any color that he wants so long as it is black." Model T became Ford's religion; announcing his decision to the

motoring public (his competitors gave him six months to fail),
Ford put his advertising in the form of a manifesto.

> I will build a motor car for the great multitude. It will be
> large enough for the family but small enough for the indi-
> vidual to run and care for. It will be constructed of the best
> materials, by the best men to be hired, after the simplest
> designs that modern engineering can devise. But it will be so
> low in price that no man making a good salary will be unable
> to own one—and enjoy with his family the blessing of hours
> of pleasure in God's great open spaces.

The age of the classic Model T began. There has never been
anything like Ford's masterpiece. It would go through snow,
mud and desert sands. It was seven feet high, top to ground.
Clearance? Boys in the West could drive out *over* the sage
brush and rocks chasing jackrabbits. In 1909 a Model T won
a transcontinental race from New York to San Francisco
(changing motors en route, which was against the rules):
4,106 miles in just over 22 days. The achievement is difficult
to comprehend now because Americans seldom see ungraded,
unsurfaced mule tracks traversed by automobile.

It was said in the early days of the automobile that the
American public was in a quandary; they owned cars but had
no place to drive them because there were so few miles of
improved roads. That was the glory of the Model T though;
you could drive it on roads but you didn't have to. In 1911
Henry Alexander drove a Model T to the top of Scotland's
Ben Nevis. In 1912 a man drove a Model T down into the
Grand Canyon and out. A Texan drove a Model T from
Dallas to San Antonio over plain open country. You could put
the Model T into reverse while going forward. Even Sorensen
never got over Ford's planetary transmission; he wrote about
it nearly 50 years later.

> This was a remarkable transmission. I'm sure many old-timers
> remember the stunts they could perform with it. It was pos-
> sible to teeter the car back and forth simply by stepping first
> on the low and then on the reverse pedals. By releasing the
> low and then reversing that motion a man could do almost
> anything he wanted to get the car out of difficulty when in
> danger of bogging down in a rough country road. No trans-
> mission in today's cars could give that type of performance.

R. L. Strout and E. B. White, in "Farewell My Lovely,"
also described the transmission.

The Fords were obviously conceived in madness: any car which was capable of going from forward into reverse without any perceptible mechanical hiatus was bound to be a mighty challenging thing to the human imagination. Boys used to veer them off the highway into a level pasture and run wild with them, as though they were cutting up with a girl.

Ford's Model T quickly became a way of life. It was an immensely practical machine. It was simple. A generation of automobile mechanics was made on the spot. Parts were cheap and readily available. With a crank and the magneto ignition, you could run the Ford in almost any weather if there was gasoline in the tank and you could turn over the engine at all (my grandfather used to "warm up" the engine on his old Ford truck by direct application of a blow-torch to the block on wintry Idaho mornings). If the motor got hot, you simply let it cool off by stopping the car. You could drive along in your "flivver" with the sides of the hood up and "tucked under." In this state a Model T coming straight on resembled a panicky hen fleeing the farm dog.

Americans loved "Tin Lizzie" in an incredible way, and the car simply crushed instantly and forever the barrier that had existed between rural America and the application of mechanical energy to the farm. From the Model T the farmer was easily converted to tractors and electric motors. A machine so cheap and so practical as the Model T appealed powerfully to that child of pragmatism, the farmer. American farmers came off the prairies, down the back roads and into the towns and bought flivvers by the millions.

You could "put on the dog" if you wanted to. If you didn't like to call your Ford a "flivver," you could call it a "Phourde" or a "IV D." There were endless possibilities and, accordingly, the cars began to take on personalities. Garet Garrett, in his impressionistic study of Ford, *The Wild Wheel*, described the raw individualism of Ford's creation.

It was a mechanical animal such as never existed before and will never be seen again. . . . It had some of the characteristics of a mule, the patience of a camel, the courage of a bull terrier, and in bad situations it could be very gallant, although there was latent in it a whimsical hostility to the human race. When you cranked it on a cold morning it might come at you.

Naturally enough the fun-loving Yankees converted Tin Lizzie's traits into jokes and a whole literature was born. The Ford jokes were the cheapest and most effective advertising

Ford could get (in fact, the Ford car became so famous that Ford quite wisely gave up paying for advertising for years): The Devil allowed anyone coming to his kingdom to make a tour of it in any car from his car pool. When a visitor remarked that all Satan's autos were Model T's, he answered: "Ah yes, that's the hell of it!"

The car's passengers were its shock absorbers. Will Rogers argued that Ford could easily be elected President if he would promise to change the front end of the Model T. Ford said that the price of the Model T was "part of the design," and his system of operations was reflected in the falling price of his car which, finally, when the Model T had been simplified to "a thing of stark utility," was a mere $260 delivered at the factory.

Woodrow Wilson had said earlier that the motor car was "the new symbol of wealth's arrogance." He was thinking of the great, ornamental, creaking machines with the long-gloved chauffeurs in uniforms and puttees. He thought that the motor car was to be (as it was for decades in Europe) a permanent physical barrier between the classes. The "lower orders" could tend the machines owned by the rich.

A Detroit newspaper as late as 1909 suggested that former coachmen made the best chauffeurs because of their ingrained habits of obsequious obedience; they would always know "exactly what is expected of them by their masters." It will be to Henry Ford's undying glory that he ended all that, that he made the automobile perhaps the most powerful instrument of classlessness, of egalitarian American democracy. Any man who owned a car was on equal terms with any other. And virtually anyone could afford to own a car. The Model T could perform as well as any. In fact, Ford's great Tin Lizzie would go where Rollses feared to tread. The owner of a Model T was "as good as" any man. Ford liberated the common man on a greater scale than any hero in history. Ford said that of Edison. But it applied to Ford himself. That much has got to be granted to Ford's memory. After the Model T, no American had to work or live or *be* in any place that did not appeal to him. As Ford said in one of his moments of raw wisdom, unadorned by his hovering ghost writers:

> Everybody wants to be someplace he ain't. As soon as he gets there he wants to go right back.

As on the morning in 1896 when his first car was finished, Ford was wild with excitement the morning the first Model T was built and running. Nevins and Hill record a workman's memories of him on that day.

> Every time he'd meet somebody, he'd give him a kick in the pants or a punch between the shoulders.

Ford knew what he had done, or at least that he had done something with great potential. How great no one could have known. "Well, I guess we've got started," he said, after whipping the Model T about the streets of Detroit that first day.

"Got started" indeed! Sales of Model T's hit 10,607 in 1908–09, so that for a while the factory was swamped and had to refuse orders. In 1913–14, 248,307 were shipped; in 1920–21, 933,720, and Ford's gross sales of $546 million brought in profits of more than $75 million. Ford left everyone else behind and, for a while at least, became an industry and a law unto himself. By then the Ford Motor Co. was an empire and the emperor, Henry Ford, was an international figure.

V

As Ford's automobile began to appear on the nation's roads by the thousands and hundreds of thousands, the personality of Henry Ford became a public property. The growth of the Ford "image" is in itself one of the prodigies of American communications history. Unfortunately for the advertising fraternity, it would not be possible to build a Henry Ford by ad slogans alone or even by planned misinformation. As the manufacturer of the Model T, Ford was bound to achieve a measure of public fame, perhaps rivaling Cyrus McCormick's or even Edison's. Ford tried to assure that much fame with Stalinesque press handouts like the one announcing that the forthcoming Model T would ". . . stand clearly defined as a monument to the genius of America's master builder of automobiles." Anyone can give himself that sort of publicity, but who would believe it? The singular thing about Ford's self-apotheosis is that a great many people believed it all, and Ford achieved a fame and esteem nearer to Lincoln's than to Edison's. In Ford's prime, in the early 1920's, he must have been more widely known than any other American.

In the first place, the car was everywhere. Ford quickly built up foreign assembly and distribution outlets as his resources grew. He also spread his assembling plants across the American continent. In addition, the little car was exported in vast numbers from the United States to the four corners of the earth. That much spread his name at home and abroad. But that, the ubiquitous knowledge of the mere word "Ford," was not the important part of the Ford public relations success. What was unusual, phenomenal, was the successful communication from Dearborn to the world of a personality, a character and a "philosophy" of life. Partly this achievement was designed, partly it was accidental, but mainly Ford was himself such an "original" that his words and deeds became front-page copy the world over. Also words which were not his, but which came from his organization, and deeds that never happened, but were said to have been done by Ford, became front-page copy. What Keith Sward aptly called *The Legend of Henry Ford* was born.

The biography of the Henry Ford of legend runs somewhat like this. There was once a successful Midwest farm boy, who worked hard and stuck to his principles and became the world's most successful industrialist. He was a simple and good soul who loved the common people, and was indeed one of them. His works were models of efficiency and humanity; he was generous to a fault with his employees, who loved him, and he lived a spotless personal life. He was a benefactor to his people, sharing his wealth with them through prodigious good works. He was gay and fun-loving, and in spite of his astonishing successes he kept that basic common-sense approach to life that so characterized his people, the solid, hardworking folk of the Midwestern farm families. Ford lived, in the years of triumph, as he always did, a simple, almost Spartan life, and died at an advanced age beloved of his people in the bosom of his devoted family. Or, as the Right Honourable Lord Perry (Percival Lea Dewhurst Perry), chairman of Ford Motor Co., Ltd., the English branch, put it, in a piece of obituarial pap that would have made Ford himself blush:

> He was a man not only admired and respected, but beloved by everyone who came into contact with him.

That was said at a company meeting in London a month after Ford died, and is surely a record of some kind in the extent of its calculated inaccuracy. Perry knew Ford well, intimately, and yet he said that anyway, in the presence of people who also knew Ford well. Thus the legend of Ford grew.

Keith Sward's comprehensive assault upon Ford, on the other hand, left almost nothing standing, and one remains, in spite of the excellence of Sward's writing and thinking, in a state of wonderment, because Sward's Ford was an ogre beyond any kind of redemption. Could Ford have been all that bad? Several biographers certainly thought so. There were thus diametrically two opposed schools of thought about the creator of the Model T.

There was also a middle ground, represented by such biographers as Roger Burlingame (*Henry Ford*) and most recently by Allan Nevins and F. E. Hill. Their volumes represent the most complete man, although, in my opinion, they lean a bit too much toward Lord Perry's encomium.

Every man who studies Ford's career is bound to form some general notions about the man. Here are mine. They begin just like the Ford of legend. There was once a successful Midwest farm boy who worked hard and became the world's most successful manufacturer. He had certain simple, but operational, principles regarding life: that hard and efficient work gave life its meaning, that one should not drink alcoholic beverages, smoke cigarettes or eat very much because such activities, like other "worldly" pleasures, were sinful. Carrying such thoughts to extremes, Ford soon became a food and diet faddist.

Beyond such notions Ford's principles were entirely mechanical, consisting of the implications or direct consequences of applying his notions of work and efficiency to every sphere of human activity. Thus, although Ford disdained all things "intellectual," he was himself possessed by the ultimate vice of the intellectual, the willingness, or even desire, blindly to press humanity into a received intellectual system without regard to the expressed wishes of the human beings themselves. Thus the German word, *Fordismus,* was coined to cover something real: Ford's blueprint of a totalitarian industrial society put forward in 1922 in his book, *My Life and Work. Fordismus* in application resulted in fantastic economic efficiency and the most appalling "industrial relations" in American history. Men were killed at the gates of the Ford Motor Co., sprayed with fire hoses in subfreezing temperatures, beaten and maimed in the streets out front, and at least one in the offices of Ford Motor Co. by Ford policemen, with Ford officials watching, like so many SS officers.

On the factory lines total job insecurity, together with physical violence passed out liberally by the thugs of the Ford

Service Department, made naked terror an "input" in Ford cars. Ford's workmen hated him and his organization; and nearly all of Ford's "great men," from Walter Flanders and William Knudsen down through Sorensen, were either purged outright by Ford or given working conditions which were intolerable and which led to resignations. Even the eulogizing Lord Perry was "fired" by Ford twice, but unsuccessfully the last time, because the English directors refused to act upon their instructions from the failing old tycoon.

Ford's vast ignorance of the world beyond the machine shop contributed to his morbidly suspicious and vindictive nature (even Nevins and Hill, striving heroically, for middle ground, concede a "mean streak") which came to rule Ford's actions when he grew old. He was bigoted and small-minded. Possibly the younger Ford would have been more responsive and responsible as his position in life changed, but Henry Ford was in middle age when success came, and was on the threshold of old age and senility, and then into it, when he was famous. To be fair to him, we should bear in mind that virtually all of the Henry Ford known to posterity was an old man. He died long after his prime and upon his death it was necessary for his grandson to reorganize the company completely.

Henry Ford finally passed from this world at the age of 83 and there were many who were glad to see him go. Yet he made a unique contribution to America's industrial development, and, even those who hated him the most conceded that much to the old man's memory.

Through all the conflicting interpretations of Ford, his work and his character, there remains an outstanding fact which must be reckoned with: the Ford of legend, the benevolent farm boy who remade the world, is the strongest memory of the man that remains with the American people. Why the Ford of legend remains, in spite of all attempts to illuminate his vices, is partly because of the success of his own publicity compared to the failure of his detractors to reach the public; but also the Ford of legend remains simply because a large part of the legendary man was truth. That it is that part of Ford's image that appeals most to Americans is easy enough to understand: they want to believe, and do believe, that a poor but honest farm lad could rise up and shake the world and remain an unspoiled child of Arcadia in the process.

The building of the legendary Ford began with seven events which transpired within two decades after the Ford Motor Co.

was formed: (1) the Selden patent case, which established Ford as a defender of competitive capitalism, (2) the Five Dollar Day, which established Ford as a friend of labor and an original economic genius; (3) the Peace Ship, which established that Ford was naive beyond belief, but more wise than the "statesmen"; (4) his Senatorial campaign, which established Ford as a political force on the side of virtue; (5) the *Chicago Tribune* suit, which established Ford as an authentic folk figure; (6) the purchase of the remaining Ford stock, which established Ford as a financial wizard as well as a new kind of industrial autocrat; (7) the *Dearborn Independent*, which established Ford as a bigoted anti-Semite—an appealing philosophical position to many Americans and to interested parties abroad.

The Selden patent case grew out of the ignorance of American patent officials and jurymen, and the gullibility of the main motor-car manufacturers. The case is important because Ford, by winning it, broke an artificial constraint upon the development of the automobile. The German, Gottlieb Daimler, is usually given credit for "inventing" the automobile, although of course no one actually invented it, because the automobile, a combination of wagon and internal-combustion engine, was a complex apparatus and represented the triumphs of a multitude of inventors in many ages. The wagon goes back to the chariot and beyond.

The first patent for a commercially successful internal-combustion engine was granted in 1860 to Jean Joseph Étienne Lenoir, a Belgian who lived in Paris. Early in his career Gottlieb Daimler saw Lenoir's shop. Nikolaus August Otto, a German, later tried to patent internal-combustion engines, but the Prussian patent office repeatedly turned him down because his engines were too much like others. Otto, in partnership with Eugen Langen, finally made an engine which was patented and won a gold medal at the Paris Exposition in 1867. A later and improved version of the Langen and Otto engine was the "Silent Otto," the first internal-combustion engine upon which Ford worked. The "Silent Otto" was primarily the product of Langen and Otto's chief engineer, the brilliant Daimler.

In 1875 another German, Siegfried Marcus, built a horseless carriage which incorporated the main features of later automobiles and resembled King's and Ford's cars remarkably. Daimler fell out with Otto in 1882 and a year later was running an automobile of his own design. This was no mere experiment like the Marcus machine. "I have created the basis of an entirely new industry," Daimler said; he patented his four-wheel, motor-driven carriage in 1886.

A year later Carl Benz had patented a three-wheel, motor-driven vehicle. By 1892 Panhard and Levassor were selling French motor cars, powered by Daimler's engines, in numbers. In September, 1893, the Americans, Charles and Frank Duryea, had a successful motor car running. A year later came Elwood Haynes; then the other pioneers: Winton, Olds, King, Ford and others, many, many others. Motor-car manufacturing, which started primarily as a German and French industry, had spread to the New World.

In the face of such a history, in 1900, George B. Selden and the Electric Vehicle Co. successfully sued two motor-car manufacturers, one of them Alexander Winton, for infringing upon Selden's patent for the motor car. This had been granted in September, 1895. Selden had first applied in 1879, but had continuously delayed completing the patent procedures. The automobile manufacturers agreed, after the Winton case, to pay the Selden interests a fixed royalty for "using" the ideas (which were, of course, continuously changing) of the automobile, and a manufacturers' trade association, the Association of Licensed Automobile Manufacturers, was formed. A manufacturer had to apply for membership, and the application might be refused, although it scarcely ever was in practice. More than 90 percent of the automobile manufacturers joined. Suit was brought against Ford in 1903 after he angrily dared the A. L. A. M. to try to interfere with his operations. Ford fought the suit, lost the first trial, but on appeal finally won in 1911. It was then ruled that the Selden patent was legal, but that it did not apply to the kinds of automobiles, including Fords, then under production in the United States.

Curiously, Ford was evidently willing to sell out his company to William Durant (then building General Motors) in 1908 and again in 1909. Durant, a considerable financier, had been unable to meet Ford's conditions ($3 million in 1908, and $9 million in 1909) because Ford, characteristically, wanted his payment in hard cash.

Although he might be willing to sell his business, he would not pay ransom on it to the A. L. A. M. or be bullied by them. As a mechanic, Ford claimed that the Selden patent was ". . . a freak among alleged inventions and is worthless as a device." When the association threatened to sue purchasers of Ford cars, Ford offered bonds (only about fifty of his thousands of buyers took the offer) against the threat. Ford said flat out that no workable automobile could be built from Selden's patented ideas. That was the master mechanic talking. He simply thought the whole of the Selden claim a hoax. It is said that Edison, who understood well the problems of patent-right litigation, encouraged Ford to fight the Selden claims. As a businessman Ford was outraged that any should try to limit competition in what was obviously a vast potential market. He said (with flamboyant and awkward ghosting):

> . . . the automobile industry must take its course with other industries, must allow the weeding out of the unfit, and must permit of the continuance of the industry by those who were left with the survival of the fittest. This is exactly as in other lines of trade.

He showed in the Selden patent case a trait that was one of his strongest. When properly aroused to an issue, he was almost demoniacal in his adherence to his own notions of what was right and just. Sometimes those notions were mercurial, but many times they were unchanging. Sometimes they were unchanging when reason cried out for change.

The A. L. A. M. took its defeat with eagerness, the manufacturers being actually grateful to Ford for breaking the power of the Selden forces and, at a dinner in New York, the silent Ford received their thanks and praises. Ford's treasurer, James Couzens, gave the response. The A. L. A. M. soon found its way into oblivion.

Doubtless no other single act by Henry Ford did so much to spread his fame, and at the same time to fix his reputation, as did the Five Dollar Day. Ford was hailed as an industrial-age Messiah by some, called a lunatic by others, and some considered him to be a threat to the established order—and they were right. The *Wall Street Journal* said that Ford was a willful troublemaker and perhaps a criminal, a man who was acting on "religious" principles (Ford said he wanted to help the common man) in "a field where they don't belong." The paper went on, ". . . he has in his social endeavor committed economic blunders if not crimes." Ford had more than doubled his minimum wages.

In 1913 Ford's total sales grew from $42 million to $89 million. Net income, which had been $13.5 million at the end of 1912, hit $27 million at the end of the following year. The Ford Motor Co.'s net assets grew from $21 million to $35 million in a single year, and the unorthodox former farm boy said his profits were "awful" and that he intended to share his gains with his employees and with the public.

There are many conflicting versions of how the Five Dollar Day came about. Couzens, for example, once gave himself credit for the idea and Keith Sward, at least, believed him. Others said that Couzens objected to it when Ford proposed it; still others said Couzens never heard of the decision until the day after it was made, and then objected to it. Nevins and Hill accept the view that the decision was taken after extensive deliberations by a large group which included Couzens and others. Fortunately, one of those present, Charles Sorensen, wrote down his eyewitness account, in the full knowledge of conflicting versions of the famous incident. It was in January, 1914. Sorensen's account is explicit, and no one can seriously suggest that he had a faulty memory.

> Myth also surrounds the participants at that Sunday morning meeting. Couzens, Wills and Hawkins were said to have been there. They were not. The only ones present were Mr. Ford, Ed. Martin, [John R.] Lee and I. The events of that day are still very clear in my mind. . . . I am the only man alive who took part in that meeting; and since none of the others ever set down their accounts, mine is the only first-hand recollection.

Sorensen had been making some projections for Ford of costs and profits in the future based upon various assumptions about price, cost and output. At the meeting Sorensen chalked up on a blackboard a computation of cost, sales and profit data in such a way that changes in the wage rate enabled a quick transfer of sums from projected profits over to cost, the profits being reduced accordingly. The men present toyed with various wage rates, raising them by steps of 25 cents from the existing range of $2 to $2.50 until the figure $5 was reached. It took four hours of discussion. According to Sorensen, Ford said: "Stop it Charlie, it's all settled. Five dollars a day minimum and at once." Couzens was told of the decision by Ford the next day. Either Sorensen's evidence must be shown to be faulty on the basis of better information or that is how the Five Dollar Day was decided.

In later years, people became used to such completely outlandish actions from Ford. But the Five Dollar Day was the first of his many sensational innovations in the sphere of wage and social policy and it attracted enormous attention. Even when Ford's beliefs and practices seemed to be in accord with orthodoxy, his reasoning was bizarre enough to be headline material for newspaper reporters, and he had a lot to say to the gentlemen of the fourth estate about the Five Dollar Day, and a lot to say about other things from that time forward.

Many, including Charles Sorensen, have thought that the great publicity of the Five Dollar Day "ruined" Henry Ford by making him such a newsworthy figure. He loved the publicity and, as Garrett pointed out, never seemed to ask himself why it was that *whatever* he said was news. It is argued that Ford was too simple a man for the position into which he was thrust by his successes. Power corrupted him; absolutely, in the opinion of people like Sward. What was worse, the instantaneous successes of his pronouncements, even the off-the-cuff ones, tended to convince Ford that, not only were his views newsworthy, but correct. He got into a lot of trouble after 1914 by not questioning his own views and actions.

The doubling of his minimum wages Ford called "profit-sharing and efficiency engineering." All sorts of explanations have been given for the dramatic action: that Ford had become frightened of the I. W. W. agitation among his workmen; that his wife put the idea into his head for ethical reasons; that Percival Perry got the idea from his English experiences and passed it on to Ford; that Ford intended to fire all of his workmen and rehire only the best, thus raising output per man enough to profit by the doubling of minimum wages.

When the new plan was flamboyantly announced—that there would be $5 minimum pay (for the "deserving," of which more later) for eight hours' work, there was a "tremendous surge" in output at Ford's plants. The Ford people said this was due to skyrocketing morale among the workmen. Ford's detractors said it was the consequence of sheer terror. Ford was going over to three eight-hour shifts and a call for workers was issued. The result was mob violence at the factory gates as thousands of unemployed descended upon the Ford works. It was said that Ford's workers were simply terrified for their jobs, which had suddenly become the most desirable laboring jobs in the world. Ford, in *My Life and Work,* viewed it all as an Olympian benefactor of mankind, with an eye on profits.

> The payment of high wages fortunately contributes to the low costs because the men become steadily more efficient on account of being relieved of outside worries. The payment of five dollars a day for an eight-hour day was one of the finest cost-cutting moves we ever made. . . . How far this will go we do not know.

It did not go on indefinitely. Soon enough, Ford's wages were not noted for their generosity. And even in 1914 the Five Dollar Day was, it has been charged, a speeded-up one, for which not all of Ford's employees qualified. It is worth noting though, that thousands of Ford workers did get the $5 straight off, and in the haste of historians and others to pontificate about the motives and consequences of the plan the effects have been largely overlooked so far as they applied to individual workmen. There, where the facts counted too, Ford had done a great thing. W. A. Simonds published some newspaper reports on the immediate consequences of the wage boost. The wife of a stockroom helper told a reporter:

> My husband made only $10 a week, and he was glad to get that since he is no mechanic. When he came home last night with his pay at the rate of $30 a week he was so excited he couldn't eat. It has been hard to keep the family together on $10 a week.

Ford had said that he would rather make 15,000 families happy than create a few millionaires (his stockholders). The devil must be given his due.

There is one additional point to make about the Five Dollar Day. Ford, a banking and currency crackpot, was also a "vulgar Keynesian." Long before J. M. Keynes published the *General Theory of Employment Interest and Money,* Ford's ruminations had led him to a vital economic truth: that the value of output is the national income, and that, if he were going to prosper as an automobile manufacturer, he would have to have customers. The higher the national wage bill, the more money consumers would be prepared to spend, and the more they would get for their money if unit costs were continuously cut. High wages meant buoyant markets and that is what any manufacturer needed. Ford said:

> I have learned through the years a good deal about wages. I believe in the first place that, all other considerations aside, our own sales depend in a measure upon the wages we pay. If we can distribute high wages, then that money is going to be spent and it will serve to make storekeepers and distributors and manufacturers and workers in other lines more prosperous and their prosperity will be reflected in our sales. Country-wide high wages spell country-wide prosperity, provided, however, the higher wages are paid for higher production.

When he inaugurated the Five Dollar Day, Ford said he was leading the nation toward a much greater internal market for American commodities by paying his workers large incomes. Did he believe it? Perhaps he did, because after the 1929 crash he raised his wages temporarily to help stop the recession in cooperation with President Hoover. Unfortunately for Hoover, Ford and the nation, the idea of getting out of a recession by earning and spending did not catch on; instead, wages were cut and then factories were closed down in the face of dwindling expenditures and dying markets. That was simple enough. After all, the United States could have a Great Depression any time by simply closing down a large part of the country's productive capacity as was done in 1929–32. It is interesting that Ford, for all his crudeness, if he believed his own statements, was in advance of his time with his Five Dollar Day.

On Dec. 4, 1915, the steamship Oscar II sailed out of the Port of New York, carrying a strange cargo on an eccentric mission. Henry Ford had decided to stop the World War. Andrew Carnegie had been shattered by the outbreak of that war, but Carnegie had intellectual pretensions and hence took seriously the words of statesmen and kings. Ford was different. His was the raw American view of that triumphant international leadership which had produced the great European abattoir. To Ford, the statesmen and kings were a pack of fools, crooks and charlatans, all of them victims of the munitions makers and international bankers who were reaping huge profits from the fighting.

Upon being informed that the European powers would welcome a neutral group to set up continuous mediation of differences with a view to ending the slaughter, Ford decided to take a hand in it himself. As the years passed Ford had reason to cherish his scheme. By 1922, when *My Life and Work* by Ford and his ghost writer, Samuel Crowther, was published, the magnitude of the 1914–18 disaster was becoming better understood than it had been during the heat of the conflict. What was worse, by then it was clear that the peace treaty was a catastrophe and, as J. M. Keynes said in his *Economic Consequences of the Peace,* the ruinous economic provisions might well contain the seeds of a new war. Keynes has never really received credit due for the dark accuracy of the forecast and the brilliance of his analysis. He was too incisive too quickly. The body was still warm when the sacrifice was shown by Keynes to have been in vain. About it all Ford said:

> I have never been able to discover any honorable reasons for the beginning of the World War. It seems to have grown out of a very complicated situation created by those who thought they could profit by war. . . . I financed the expedition to Stockholm in what has since been called the "Peace Ship." I do not regret the attempt. . . . I do not now know whether the information as conveyed to me was true or false. I do not care. But I think everyone will agree that if it had been possible to end the war in 1916 the world would be better off than it is today. For the victors wasted themselves in winning, and the vanquished in resisting. Nobody got an advantage, honorable or dishonorable, out of that war.

Ford made no secret of his disapproval of the war, right from the start. He said it was started by capitalists (Ford perversely considered himself a workman to the end), parasites, money lenders, profiteers, lazy military people and Jews who were trying to destroy Christianity. He even said he would burn his factories before he would produce military equipment. Madame Rosika Schwimmer, a feminist and pacifist of Hungarian origin, gained an interview with Ford on Nov. 16, 1915. She presented the manufacturer a plan for continuous mediation by a delegation made up of prominent neutrals. He gave her a luncheon interview the next day. He was convinced that the scheme was worth trying.

Ford went to Washington to talk to President Wilson about the idea. Wilson hedged, saying he could not come out in support of any single scheme to end the war (a most curious position; Ford saw the oddity of it and was momentarily disgusted with Wilson, "a small man" Ford called him as his party left the White House). Ford announced that he would finance the expedition himself. Moreover, he would "get the boys out of the trenches by Christmas." The press went into raptures. Here was the great multimillionaire hick from Michigan going to tell the Kaiser to call off the dogs, and Ford was going to take a whole shipload of peace cranks with him. It was a rare thing. The attitude of the press was close to unanimity. Amid headlines like "FORD TO STOP WAR", the Peace Ship sailed, as Walter Millis put it, ". . . to the undying shame of American journalism, upon one vast wave of ridicule."

Ford had been active in various peace groups and by 1915 had met and become friends with the principal pacifists and peace advocates in the country. He invited hundreds of these people to go. It is worth considering what the effect might have been had the Oscar II really contained row upon row of distinguished American leaders in science, education, the arts and political life. Unfortunately, nearly all of Ford's anxious pacifist friends found excuses to stay home; Edison and William Jennings Bryan came to the dock to see the ship off. Ford took almost anyone who wanted to go along for legitimate reasons.

As the *New York Times* described it, there was a plentiful cargo of "crack-brained dreamers," the peace delegation itself, some college students, clerks, journalists and others. Not a single one of the college presidents invited by Ford was able to tear himself away from his pressing engagements. The young Elmer Davis was aboard; so was William C. Bullitt. Ford's personal divine, the Rev. Samuel S. Marquis, also went along. He had tried, until the last moment, at the behest of Clara Ford, to dissuade Henry. The Reverend (and later Dean) Marquis was sent packing by Ford to the fountains of theosophical knowledge by Ford's simple question: "It is right, is it not, to try to stop war?" When Marquis answered with the only word a professed follower of Jesus of Nazareth could give, Ford said: "You've told me that what is right cannot fail."

But fail it did. The sendoff at the pier was a pitiful shambles. Ford stood at the rail tossing American Beauty roses to the mob below, which included a predictable rabble of lunatics wrapped in flags, draped with streamers and banners covered with slogans, hymn singers, preachers, four-square gospelers and what-have-you. There had been a marriage on board (with the nonplused Ford and Bryan as witnesses) and, according to Sward, that union was consummated on the Oscar II before it left the dock. Hilarious. As the ship pulled out, a man dived into the water and tried to swim after it, "to ward off submarines" he explained when he was fished out. Predictably, dissension tore the crusade badly during the journey. Ford was washed by a wave, caught cold, and came directly home. The Peace Mission continued on fruitlessly in Europe with Ford paying the bills until the United States entered the war and Ford withdrew his financial support.

The Peace Ship has usually been treated as a joke by historians. It certainly was a pitiful performance in some respects but, among those who failed to acquit themselves with honor, Henry Ford cannot be named. Considering the costs and outcome of the "war to end all wars," it is not so easy to mock Henry. Ford said of his project in 1940, on the twenty-fifth anniversary, ". . . we can afford to remember that there was once a peace ship. At least we who sailed in 1915 did not decrease the life or love that was in the world."

Today's generation, which has lived through the treadmill negotiations in Korea; the continuous mediations at Geneva, at the U. N., in Warsaw, concerning Israel, the Congo, Cyprus, and a dozen other outposts while fighting continues or is being prepared for, where mediation by "neutrals" has become the accepted way of stopping current shooting and of avoiding something far worse, we who lived through the Cuban Crisis, —*we* are in no position to laugh at Ford's scheme. We can leave that to an older generation that thought it knew better. The Peace Ship cost Ford $400,000, and it failed. But Ford never regretted his "unique argosy." As the *Detroit Free Press* wrote in December, 1940, when the truce of 1918 had run out and mankind was looking once more into the mouths of cannons, and the blood-drenched fields of Europe were sprouting death: "No peace ship has sailed since the Second World War began. It could find no port geographically or in the hearts of men."

In 1918, Ford ran for the Senate. He had already been mentioned in 1916 as a "favorite son" Presidential prospect, and he clearly considered himself to be Presidential timber. In fact, in 1924, he seems to have very seriously attempted to start up a Ford-for-President bandwagon. The Senatorial campaign of 1918 was different. Ford could possibly have been the Senator from Michigan; he was then one of the richest men in the state and thus was a long step on the road to political power ahead of others. He was also, of course, a famous man by then. His candidacy was partly President Wilson's idea because Ford was in favor of Wilson's League plans. Moreover, Ford had supported Wilson in 1916, the Ford Highland Park factory carrying a gigantic banner along its side reading "HE KEPT US OUT OF WAR."

Even Henry's friends were appalled by the apparition of the aspiring Senator. In the first place, the candidate's mastery of the forensic arts was ludicrous. He was panic-stricken before any kind of an audience; Garrett says that on a speaker's platform Ford was like a man caught in a public place with his trousers down. Two of Ford's public addresses, unadorned by ghosts, have been preserved for posterity. In 1915 he was maneuvered into addressing the inmates of Sing Sing. Ford said: "Boys, I'm glad to see you here. I've never made a speech in my life and never expect to." Later the same year, addressing a women's peace rally, Ford said: "I simply want you to remember the slogan 'Out of the trenches before Christmas,' and I thank you for your attention."

Thus armed, the Democratic candidate, Henry Ford, put his name before the people of Michigan. His Republican opponent was Mr. Truman Newberry, scion of a wealthy Michigan family. Ford made no campaign at all, but so developed was the fun-loving Michigan electorate's humor that a Ford victory began to look possible. So the politics got dirty.

Ford had fought, successfully, to get his son Edsel deferred from the draft to help run the Ford empire. In the argot of the "age of preparedness," Edsel was "a slacker and a coward." The press of Michigan had been merciless, pouring abuse down upon the Fords, father and son. Edsel, for example, was compared to the Kaiser's six sons, as one of the seven sure survivors of the World War. In spite of his anti-war attitudes, Ford had engaged in massive war work, promising publicly to turn all profits back to the government (a promise apparently not honored). The Ford plants made not only military vehicles and parts, but airplane engines, arms, helmets and "Eagle Boats" (submarine chasers).

One of Ford's greatest tool designers was a man of German origin, Carl Emde. Ford relied heavily on Emde's genius in the creation of machine tools to keep Ford's private industrial revolution moving. On Nov. 3, two days before the election, full-page newspaper advertisements appeared in Michigan headed "HENRY FORD AND THE HUNS" in which Ford's general patriotism was challenged. Carl Emde was liberally tarred with the brush of jingoism, and Ford's personal credentials were finally evaluated thus: "Henry Ford loves the Huns too much to be trusted with a seat in the Senate of the United States." Whatever else the Republicans' last-minute effort was, it certainly was in keeping with the times.

Ford had a victory dinner the night before the election and, next day, lost to Newberry by a tiny margin of 7,567 votes. Newberry now paid with his skin for the dirty business at the end of the campaign. Ford, a man whose vindictiveness knew few (if any, according to his enemies) bounds, turned loose a small army of detectives and lawyers on the Republicans, alleging corruption, bribery, the outright purchasing of votes. Specifically, they charged Newberry with spending excessive amounts under the law. Ford's millions paid off. The unhappy

Newberry was convicted and sentenced to two years at hard labor at Leavenworth. The appeal before the Supreme Court was conducted by Charles Evans Hughes. The Court ruled that the law under which Newberry was convicted was unconstitutional, and the unhappy man was seated in the Senate by a vote of 46–41. Disgraced, Newberry resigned his seat, and was replaced, ironically enough, by Ford's (by then) former treasurer, James Couzens.

In the decade of the 1920's American social history was marked by a Romanesque, vicarious public participation in certain kinds of events, spectacular events, humorous and tragic, frivolous and morbid. This was the triumph of mass communications. "Peaches" and "Daddy" Browning; the "Monkey Trial," the suffering and death of Floyd Collins in his cave, the Lindbergh flight, the Leopold and Loeb murder trial, all are examples of a kind of sensationalism in public affairs which became established in the 1920's and has remained part of the American way of life. Among the first such mass spectacles, and a harmless one, was Henry Ford's $1,000,000 libel suit against the *Chicago Tribune,* which had referred to Ford as an "anarchist" and an "ignorant idealist." For some odd reason Ford objected to being so categorized, although he had been, and would be, called worse things in print.

In 1916, incidents on the Mexican border resulted in a mobilization of the National Guard. Although Ford repudiated the story and his officials denied that it ever occurred, it was said that Ford policy would be that no man who went off to the Guard would get his job back at the Ford Motor Co. When the *Chicago Tribune* taxed Ford on this, he sued. The suit was tried in the summer of 1919 at Mount Clemens, Michigan, a small county seat near Detroit. The jury was made up of eleven farmers and a road inspector. The defense brought in witnesses of the border incidents. There were real-live Texas Rangers, who stalked the streets of Mount Clemens for days in their ten-gallon hats, six-shooters in place, spurs jangling off their fancy high-heeled boots. The little town was agog. Ford's counsel occupied twenty-five rooms in a hotel. The trial saw 2,000,000 words entered into the record. The nation watched, fascinated.

Henry Ford was the star of the show, as he sat, cross-legged in the witness chair, twanging away wrong answers to questions, amusing himself by whittling on the sole of his shoe with his pocket knife. The defense lawyer, E. G. Stevenson, pilloried the colossally ignorant tycoon. It seemed that Ford knew virtually nothing, possibly nothing at all, about the American Revolution—in fact, he may have thought it was the War of 1812, which he did describe as a revolution. Once prompted, he recalled 1776 and guessed he had forgotten about it. He could not state any "fundamental principles" of American government. He couldn't do much with "big words" (he had once referred to "commenced" as a "technical term"). He had never heard of Benedict Arnold, the traitor. He thought "ballyhoo" meant ". . . a blackguard or something of that nature." He was unable to say what *chile con carne* might be. Did Ford know anything beyond mechanics? Was he in fact illiterate? It was hard to tell from the court proceedings. Asked to save the court from the impression that he was unable to read, Ford backed off, saying he didn't have his glasses, had hay fever and would "make a botch of it."

A few times, like when he said, "Land, I guess," in answer to a question about what the United States was originally, Ford made Stevenson's inquisition backfire. The same thing was true when Ford defined an "idealist" as ". . . one who seeks to make profit for others." But mainly Stevenson roasted the helpless tycoon slowly and thoroughly. The defense summation contained the following gem:

> Gentlemen of the jury, they forced us to open the mind of Henry Ford and expose it to you bare, to disclose the pitiable condition which he had succeeded in keeping from the view of the public.

The rustics in the jury box appreciated the entertainment, evidently, because their verdict in Ford's favor, awarding the libeled millionaire damages of 6 cents, was one of the highlights of the whole show.

Ford was humiliated by the Mount Clemens trial, but it endeared him to rural America. Wherever bib overalls and gum boots met astride a row of corn, Henry Ford was a hero as never before. And in a lot of other places, too. When in 1916 Ford first uttered his famous dictum, "History is more or less bunk," he was talking about the exploits of the gods and heroes so sacred to the academic historian. Ford said: "Records of old wars mean nothing to me." And they meant little or nothing to millions of men and women in all walks of life, on the farm and in the city, people who had been nearly asphyxiated by the record of "one damn thing after another" from the first grade onward. They were grateful that the nation's new industrial colossus was also ignorant of his-

tory. He refused at the trial to say outright whether it was true
that he could neither read nor write. A few years later he
added: "I don't like to read books; they muss up my mind."
The people loved it. Huckleberry Finn's compatriots recognized the original article when it came along.

In the fall of 1915, Ford's views on peace were being
placed in Ford Motor Co. publications. James Couzens (later
Senator Couzens), the treasurer, became restive about it.
Couzens had been the man of "business" at Ford while Henry
stayed mainly in the shops. Couzens was a major stockholder,
second only to Ford, and around Detroit, he was thought to be
the main power at the Ford Motor Co. Even Henry made a
great show of deferring to his treasurer. One October day
Couzens was outraged about Ford's peace views and said that,
if Ford kept circulating them through Ford Motor Co. channels, he would resign. Ford accepted the offer "on the spot"
to the amazement of Couzens. That ended an era at Ford
Motor Co. Charles Sorensen, who had enough rapport with
Ford to watch dozens of top Ford men pick up their final
paychecks, was perfectly blunt about Couzens. Sorensen
frankly admired him. "He should be forever blessed by the
company for his relentless drive. . . . In the early days Henry
Ford could not have succeeded without James Couzens; now
he was no longer needed."

Couzens had joined what Sward called the "Ford Alumni
Association," a trickle which one day became a flood of top
executives who had been axed when Ford indulged his
periodic desires to purge his household. When Couzens left
the Ford Motor Co., the last vestiges of traditional business
management were abandoned. From then on Ford ran things
as he pleased. First he began the campaign which finally ended
in the elimination of "the parasites"—his stockholders.

The right of stockholders to receive income and increments
in capital values from their investments constitute two of the
fundamental bases of modern capitalism. Without them, the
use of the corporate form of organization would not flourish
as it does. Ford had no understanding of or use for such
niceties. The Ford Motor Co. was his. Except for Couzens
(whose resignation had been accepted), the other stockholders
were viewed by Ford as useless appendages. Indeed, the
Dodge brothers had a competing motor company of their own,
and Ford executives believed that the Dodges had made a
private fortune by overcharging Ford for parts. Ford had
made them millionaires twice, once as stockholders and once

as parts suppliers. Others knew little or nothing of the company or even of its product; one of the lawyers, Anderson, fatuously allowed in later years that he really knew very little about the Ford motor car, having never ridden in one. The Populist in Ford was never far under the surface. He could see no good reason why a pack of investors ought to be enriched by the Ford Motor Co. just because they had bet a few thousand dollars on the right horse back in 1903.

Accordingly, in 1916 Ford told the Dodges to their faces, that he was reducing the annual dividends of Ford Motor Co. to a fixed rate of $1,200,000, no more, no less. By then Ford was planning to embark upon the great River Rouge works of over a thousand acres, with raw materials coming in one end by lake steamer and railroad, and automobiles rolling out the other end. It was to be an almost completely vertically integrated factory, the most extensive on earth. Ford intended to do all this by ploughing back his profits, and if they weren't distributed to the parasites, the profits would suffice to finance everything he had in mind.

The Dodges were not willing to have the gold mine closed, and sued Ford for the company's profits. Ford said in court that he did not intend to buy out the minor stockholders (he had told the Dodges that since he owned the majority of the voting stock he could do as he pleased anyhow) either; they could just rot with their fixed earnings. Meanwhile the great Ford works went ahead at River Rouge, and a separate company, wholly owned by the family, was organized to make Fordson tractors. Late in 1918 Ford resigned the presidency in favor of his son Edsel. By then Ford had extensive other interests going and evidently felt that Edsel should at least have the nominal title.

Ford's management scheme was upset, however. In February of 1919 the Michigan State Supreme Court ordered him to pay his stockholders $19,000,000 and 5 percent interest on it from 1916. Moreover, the Court ordered Ford to continue to pay dividends proportional to profits. Edsel might be president, but it appeared that the Court intended to rule part of the company's affairs. The Court felt that Ford had no appreciation of the fundamentals of capitalism. Sward quotes one of the justices as saying:

> The record, and especially the testimony of Mr. Ford convinces that he has to some extent the attitude towards shareholders of one who has dispersed and distributed to them large

gains and that they should be content to take what he chooses to give them.

The Justice certainly knew his Ford.

Ford now showed a comical wiliness. He wanted to be rid of his stockholders, but he didn't want their "asking prices" to increase. He announced that henceforth he would have no direct interest in the Ford Motor Co.'s affairs, and went on an extended vacation to California to commune with nature. From Californian bird-watching sites the press was informed that Ford had some new plans: he was considering the creation of a new firm, wholly owned by the Fords, which would manufacture a revolutionary cheap car, a competitor to the Model T, which might even sell for a mere $250. The prospects of the Model T were thus suddenly dampened, and with them the future of the existing Ford Motor Co. together with the potential prices of the Ford stocks held by the "parasites." Ford's agents began making anonymous offers to the minority stockholders, who suddenly were given a chance to sell out in the face of public discussion of their imminent ruination. They all sold. Oddly enough, only Couzens saw through the ruse and, upon finding out who the buyer was, raised his selling price accordingly. As we saw earlier, Ford made millionaires of his stockholders, and bought them out cheaply at that.

Ford borrowed money, $70 million, a rare occurrence, from banks in Boston and New York, to give the minority stockholders cash. A large sum, $58 million, was due April 1, 1921, and on Jan. 1, only $20 million was in sight. Vast as Ford's assets were, the problem of raising the cash in just ninety days seemed overwhelming. Rumor went out that Ford was at last going to be forced to borrow on a funded basis. Ford's Treasurer, Frank Klingensmith (who had replaced Couzens), had been so rash as to discuss Ford's problems with some New York bankers.

A New York investment banker appeared at Dearborn and told Ford that, untidy as his finances were, a group of bankers would be willing to help him out, provided that "their' man be placed in a position of financial control of the Ford Motor Co. until the debt was paid. Feeling his oats, the banker continued to speak grandly of the extent of the magnanimity in the offer, since Ford was known to be "erratic and irresponsible," and hence a poor banker's risk. Sorensen, who was there, said: "It was the boldest, nastiest thing I ever saw done to Henry Ford." Ford, boiling mad, dismissed the banker; Sorensen handed the luckless financier his briefcase and said: "Here are your papers, you run along and peddle them. Good-bye." Klingensmith was called to Sorensen's office where (according to Sorensen) Ford was. Ford began asking Klingen-smith what he had been up to. "Before Henry Ford finished with him on that matter, he knew his days were numbered." The hapless Klingensmith went the way of much of Ford's managerial flesh shortly after the interview, when the great Ford purge of 1921 was under way.

How would Ford raise the cash without bank financing? He would squeeze it out of his own organization. One of his fa-vorite, and endlessly repeated, notions, was that any well conducted enterprise had all the resources *within* it that it should ever need in the way of capital (there would be neither money nor capital markets in Ford's ideal world). "Bankers play far too great a part in the conduct of industry," Ford said. But he was not just an irrational Populist in this belief. He said that businesses must take risks, and that bankers ". . . want to watch the money, not the efficiency of produc-tion. They think of a factory as making money, not goods." There was reason enough here in Ford's set of dogmas to keep the bankers out. There was his further rule ". . . the very worst time to borrow money is when the banking people think you need money."

Ford was not caught. He quit buying raw materials, con-verted his own stocks of raw materials into 93,000 autos, force-fed a total of 125,000 cars into his dealer system (cash on arrival; if you did not pay, you lost your franchise), and then closed down for "inventory" when there was virtually nothing left to count. The depression of 1921 was upon the country and Ford decided to wait for raw-material prices to break before he started up again. Which he did, and more successfully than ever.

On April 1, 1921, Ford had raised $87 million in cash from his own organization, or $29 million more than was needed to meeting his maturing obligations, which included not only the stock loans outstanding, but also income taxes and a bonus due his workmen. He had sold some Liberty bonds, and col-lected debts due, but mostly he just squeezed and purged. The banking system had financed the operation all right, by lend-ing money across the nation to harassed Ford dealers who were buckling under a steady onslaught of freight cars loaded with Model T's, cash on delivery. But Ford himself did not go to the bankers, and no banker control was instituted at Ford Motor Co.

At the same time, Ford launched one of his most famous purges. He lowered his car prices below cost, and then ordered his executives and workmen to "dig for it" and bring up a profit. A great grinding and winnowing began with executives, office employees and workmen fired right and left. The overhead cost per car was reduced from $146 to $93. As Ford told it, in the weird quasi-Olympian style that came from his amanuensis' pen:

> The house-cleaning swept out the waste that had both made the prices high and absorbed the profit. We sold off the useless stuff. Before, we had employed fifteen men per car per day. Afterward we employed nine per car per day. This did not mean that six out of fifteen men lost their jobs. They only ceased being unproductive. We made the rule that everything and everybody must produce or get out.

Ford went through his company with a great scythe. Men "ceased being unproductive" by the thousands. Half of the office force was lopped off; Ford says the men were offered jobs on the assembly line. The office force fell at a stroke from 1,074 to 528. All sorts of order blanks and forms were eliminated. A department of statistics was unceremoniously thrown overboard (although Sorensen denies the story found in biographies that he led a wrecking crew in and crow-barred the statisticians into the streets). Foremen were sent back to the line or fired outright. Executives were relieved of their offices and either turned out or offered jobs on the assembly line. Where four foremen had previously stood, only one remained. Ford goods in transit were so speeded up that the company realized $28 million "out of the pipelines." Resources tied up in inventories, stationary or in transit, were released.

Sixty percent of Ford's telephone extensions were removed from his premises: "Only a comparatively few men in any organization need telephones," Ford said. A whole trainload of office furniture was carted off and sold second-hand. The Ford "Sociology Department" was liquidated. Ford's personal divine, Dean Marquis, had been head of the Sociology Department. He was allowed to resign after a row with Sorensen over the dwindling Marquis fief, while Ford watched silently; ". . . I heard from Dean Marquis some words I'd never heard before." That from Sorensen is saying a lot. Ford fired a number of his publicity people or "allowed them to resign."

Good men left out of disgust too. William Knudsen "left the organization," as W. A. Symonds, one of Ford's "court biographers," delicately phrased it. Knudsen always said that he learned his trade from Henry Ford, but Knudsen was too much for Ford in more ways than one, as his later triumphs as president of General Motors and as head of the War Production Board indicated. (Ford was convinced during World War II that Knudsen and his government friends wanted to take the company's affairs out of his hands, and in senile periods, dreaming of the old days, he would say to Sorensen, "Charlie, there's one man I don't want to see any more. You must get rid of Knudsen.")

By April of 1921 all of the "fat" had been unceremoniously cut away from the Ford Motor Co. Using only two-thirds as many men as had been employed in 1920, the company ended up making twice as many cars in 1921, and the Fords, now sole owners, faced a net profit for the year of $75 million on a gross of $546 million. The year 1921 was a depression one, but for Henry Ford it had been the year of his headiest achievements, and he really never had such triumphs again. It began to appear that Ford's publicity department was not exaggerating about the "genius" at Dearborn.

Unfortunately for Ford, his triumphs encouraged him increasingly to favor mankind with his views on "things in general." As in the Peace Ship episode, Ford was soon in trouble again. This time it was anti-Semitism.

Sorensen was Ford's intimate for four decades; he said he knew Ford "better than any man alive or dead knew him." He went further: "I knew him better than did members of his family." Sorensen also said off-handedly ". . . I did not share his racial prejudices. . . ." Ford's court biographers have had immense difficulty ignoring or getting around the simple fact that Ford was a bigot. Except that bigotry is unfashionable in America, Ford's bigotry should not surprise anyone. It was in keeping with many of his other beliefs and practices. It was unfortunate, perhaps, but it should not have caused biographers to evade the whole subject. Insofar as Ford was religious, he was a fundamentalist as he was in most things, and "they" crucified the Lord, as the grand old Christian hymn has it.

Ford was not mildly anti-Semitic; he was enthusiastic about it. His dislike for bankers and financiers was wedded to his primitive anti-Semitism and his "devil" theory of history, so that his conversation was studded with references to the "Wall

Street kikes" and so forth (Sward said that Ford told Rosika Schwimmer, herself a Jew, that the Jews started the First World War). Even after Ford's anti-Semitism had landed him a very bad press indeed, he stayed on his topic, and the evidence suggests that, through his various flunkies, he returned to his anti-Semitic last again in the 1930's—although his apologists insist that there was nothing untoward in his accepting from Adolf Hitler, in the summer of 1938, the Award of the Grand Cross of the German Eagle. (He had a photo taken wearing it in a fancy uniform according to Keith Sward. It is not a well known photo of Ford if it still exists.) After all, he had been honored by several foreign governments.

Surrounded as he was by ghost writers, kept journalists, publicists and deputies such as Harry Bennett and W. J. Cameron, the extent of Ford's personal participation in the virulent anti-Semitic excesses conducted by his flunkies on Ford Motor Co. time, using the facilities, name, properties, personnel and resources of the concern, will never be known. That Ford's men, his biographers and historians have flat out denied that he was anti-Semitic and unaware of the extent to which his employees were slinging the ancient muck, is patently absurd. Employees were later presented with full blame for the anti-Semitism of Ford's communications network, but what can one say for Ford's own words "in collaboration with Samuel Crowther"?

One can get something of the flavor of Ford's personal thoughts on the subject in *My Life and Work*, a book published at the peak of its subject's successes and powers in this world. After denying that he had meant any harm to the Jews, Ford said:

> . . . we are not actuated by any kind of prejudice, except it may be a prejudice in favor of the principles which have made our civilization. There have been observed in this country certain streams of influence which were causing a marked deterioration in our literature, amusements, and social conduct. . . . It was not the robust coarseness of the white man . . . but a nasty Orientalism which has insidiously affected every channel of expression—and to such an extent that it was time to challenge it. The fact that these influences are all traceable to one racial source is a fact to be reckoned with, not by us only, but by intelligent people of the race in question.

Ford thought that the "Orientals" in question had taken steps to correct the nastiness, but that:

. . . there is still room to discard outworn ideas of racial superiority [the Goyim backlash?] maintained by economic or intellectually subversive warfare upon Christian society.

Ford hoped that the Jews would work ". . . to make Jews American instead of America, Jewish. The genius of the United States of America is Christian in the broadest sense, and its destiny is to remain Christian."

Ford then made a very fine distinction; it was not race and religion that he objected to, but the ideas which happened to emanate from members of the Jewish race and religion. Ford felt that he (that is, the Dearborn *Independent*—it was later, five years later, that Ford was supposed to know nothing about the *Independent*'s contents) had done the country the favor of exposing the Jewish conspiracy, and no more action by him was required. Ford said:

> Let the American people once understand that it is not natural degeneracy, but calculated subversion that afflicts us, and they are safe. The explanation is the cure.

Having thus acquitted himself of the charge of being anti-Semitic, Ford concluded his defense; time itself would show

> . . . that we are better friends to the Jews' best interests than are those who praise them to their faces and criticize them behind their backs.

How ungrateful it was of the Jews not to appreciate the efforts of their benefactor.

In January, 1919, the Dearborn *Independent*, a private weekly, was published under the ownership of Henry Ford. The paper was adorned by "Mr. Ford's Own Page," an editorial page devoted to what were given out as Ford's views. The paper was force-fed to the public through Ford's dealers (they were told that they were to sell both Model T's and the *Independent*), and at one point reached a circulation of 700,000. The first editor was E. G. Pipp. In the early 1920's, Pipp, who had left the Ford payroll (Pipp was a liberal and could not stomach Ford's views, although he had once been a staunch Ford supporter), carried on a considerable vendetta against Ford. Pipp was replaced by W. J. Cameron, a man whose syrupy inflections became known to millions of Americans in the 1930's when Cameron was narrator on Ford's nationally broadcast "Sunday Evening Hour." Cameron had been a small-town minister of the gospel in Michigan, and was thus well enough equipped for a career as a retailer of eternal verities.

As Sward put it, "Ford laid siege to the Jews on May 22, 1920." The first editorial, "The International Jew, the World's Problem," began: "There is a race, a part of humanity, which has never yet been received as a welcome part." From then on, for ninety-five weekly issues, the Dearborn *Independent* flailed away at the Children of Israel. These pieces were published separately as pamphlets: in 1920 came "The World's Foremost Problem"; followed in 1921 by "Jewish Activities in the United States" and "Jewish Influence in American Life"; and finally, in 1922, one that was reminiscent of an academic thesis title, "Aspects of Jewish Power in the United States."

The Dearborn *Independent* published the fraudulent *Protocols of Zion,* and thereby did the nation a disservice which is still felt at cell meetings of the right-wing political underworld, and in the occasional synagogue desecrations produced by the psychopathic flotsam of modern social and political stresses.

Aaron Sapiro was a successful organizer of agricultural marketing cooperatives. The *Independent* gave him as an example of Jewish fraudulence. At that point the game ended. Sapiro sued for a million dollars damages, and there was the sudden possibility that Mr. Henry Ford personally was going to be asked his opinions about things. It was March of 1927 when the case finally came to trial. It appeared from the defense evidence that Henry Ford knew virtually nothing about the *Independent,* or what was in it. In court, Cameron tried to take entire responsibility and then to pass it on to others; for example, the primary anti-Semitic articles were written actually by an ex-Hearstman, and Mr. Ford knew nothing of their content. An attempt was made to bring Ford into court but, after being displayed to the world as an ignoramus at the *Chicago Tribune* trial, Ford had no taste for courtrooms. On this issue he especially had no wishes to be publicly examined. After refusing to acknowledge that he had been successfully served with a subpoena, after a reported automobile accident (no witnesses) and confinement in his own hospital, Ford settled with Sapiro privately; made, or allowed to be issued, an abject apology to the Jews and to Sapiro, and agreed that the *Independent*'s vicious little masterpiece, now bound as *The International Jew,* should be withdrawn.

The possible consequences of Ford's anti-Semitism cannot

be fixed; of course they clearly could have been staggering. On Dec. 20, 1922, a *New York Times* article described the scene at Hitler's headquarters in Munich. Among other things, the *Times* reported:

> The wall beside his desk in Hitler's private office is decorated with a large picture of Henry Ford. In the antechamber there is a large table covered with books, nearly all of which are a translation of a book . . . published by Henry Ford.

Nazi leaders would not say why all this should have been so, and Mr. Ford was unavailable for comment. A German publisher brought out *The International Jew* in several languages. In the 1930's the book was again passing into the hands of fascists and would-be fascists all over the world. *Der Internationale Jude* had a wide circulation in Germany (Sward reports a statement that Hitler plundered large parts of the book in the original manuscript of *Mein Kampf*). It was said in defense of Ford that he did not himself write the contents of *The International Jew* (which goes without saying). After the United States entered the war, Ford's mouthpiece, Cameron, made a series of public statements against anti-Semitism, and against discrimination on the basis of religion of all kinds. Cameron himself had been closely associated with the Anglo-Saxon Federation and had published in their magazine. From there the record continues. Father Coughlin seems to have been privy to confidential Ford information; he was evidently a favorite of Bennett, Ford's policeman. Fritz Kuhn was a Ford employee, although it is said that the Ford Motor Co. did nothing to encourage his curious political activities.

Ford's notions about the Jews could well have had great influence in fanning the disastrous anti-Semitism of the interwar years. Anyone who reads Sward's documented account of the whole episode, even discounting Sward's biases (he was a C.I.O. man) can see how the possession of great wealth in the hands of a barely literate bigot could do untold harm. Ford was immensely wealthy; there is abundant evidence that he was barely literate (Upton Sinclair said that Ford could in fact read, "but slowly") and *My Life and Work* is the product of a bigot where it deals with the Jews. But the indictment can easily be carried too far, and it should not be.

Ford did not invent anti-Semitism in the world. The curiously demented European variety needed no stimulus from Dearborn, Michigan. Hitler himself was abundantly endowed with anti-Semitism without help from Ford, and the same applies to the rounding out of the maniacal views of people like Joseph Goebbels and Julius Streicher. Anyone who argues that the leaders and believers of anti-Semitism in the world, and specifically the Nazis, were simply products of Henry Ford's anti-Semitic ventures has got a lot to prove. It is lamentable that Ford did contribute to such a cause, and contribute he undoubtedly did, although in later years, hopefully during a lapse of memory, he denied having contributed "a cent" to anti-Semitism.

It is absurd to whitewash Ford's anti-Semitism now. He is long gone from this world, and one wants to know as much as possible about him. About the Jews, Ford couldn't open his mouth without putting his foot in it. "Damned if he does, and damned if he doesn't," under the pressure of wartime sentiments, in 1944 Ford made a complete gaffe of it when he issued this example of his new-found toleration:

> There's need for the Jew in the world, and it's bound to be recognized. Among the Jews are some of our ablest financiers and greatest merchants. They understand trade.

As the saying has it, he "should have stood in bed."

The position held by Ford's biographical partisans that he could somehow have been unaware of all that appeared in the *Independent* or of what was published under his own name for years and years, strains credulity beyond any reasonable limits. The life of Henry Ford does not suggest a man so unconcerned with the uses to which his great powers were put. Quite the contrary, Ford was an "activist" until the very end. Henry Ford was a man of vast and diverse affairs. His views on the Jews were no more ridiculous than his views on many subjects. For example, consider what he thought were the origins of the First World War.

> An impartial investigation of the last war, of what preceded it and what has come out of it, would show beyond a doubt that there is in the world a group of men with vast powers of control, that prefers to remain unknown, that does not seek office or any of the tokens of power, that belongs to no nation whatever but is international—a force that uses every government, every widespread business organization, every agency of publicity, every resource of national psychology, to throw the world into a panic for the sake of getting still more power over the world.

Devils everywhere. Ford's anti-Semitism was no more lunatic, or more odd, in the abstract (if infinitely more cruel and dangerous) than that view of history.

Nor was his anti-Semitism more odd in the abstract than his views on food, his nut and raw-vegetable diets, his "violent" (the word is Sorensen's) antipathy toward cigarettes, alcohol and their users. Or his views on pasteurization of milk (he was against it), on labor unions (creatures of Wall Street), old-time dancing, on the glories of village industry ("it was an evil day when the village flour mill disappeared"), and so forth.

As a bigoted anti-Semite he was, as he was in so many other ways, partly a child of his time, the late 19th century in the rural backwoods of fundamentalist, Protestant America. He was even a child of his time in the publication of his beliefs, as the timing was coincident with the upsurge of anti-Semitism in the interwar period. This does not excuse him, but it does show him against a recognizable background. Of course, not all of Ford's beliefs were so cranky; some were not cranky at all—some were shrewd and astute. He was a man of parts. Garet Garrett, who knew him well, said that Ford's mind held ". . . astonishing vagaries . . . whimsical and sometimes puerile contradictions." Ford's mind also held the vicious evil of anti-Semitism, and he loosed it upon the world as a byproduct of the Model T—the Dearborn *Independent* was sold by Ford dealers. Fortunately, the car was more successful in changing America than was the bigotry.

VI

Over a period of two decades after the founding of the Ford Motor Co., Henry Ford, by a series of remarkable events, had thus become a public figure of great renown. It was not just his eccentricities and his motor car that made him so important; in the Ford Motor Co. the techniques of mass production had reached a state of perfection beyond any previous experience or conception. People forgot about Eli Whitney and the old Yankee gunsmiths, about the proliferation of interchangeable manufacture that had come after; instead, Ford was virtually enthroned as the father of mass production —which he was not.

What Ford did was to conduct mass production at a tempo and on a scale never seen before. At the same time he experimented with labor and social relations to have a force of men tending his machines who were optimally skilled, educated, organized and domiciled in such a way as to produce maximum output from existing equipment and not only to facilitate the continuous introduction of mechanical change (and therefore social change) but also continuously to raise output and lower the production costs of the Model T Ford. The goal was to reduce to zero the skill required by men actually working on the car. Any man off the street could do the work. The skill was successively removed "back" from production into toolmaking and design. It was, in its way, the epitome of capitalist production, and input efficiency. Nothing like it was seen before, and nothing quite like it has been seen since.

Fordismus, the idea of men existing as mere appendages of a particular line of machines, to be swept away automatically as the machines changed, inspired a whole literature of terror. It was thought (feared) to be a vision of the future of industrial America, and many were horrified. Actually, of course, it was a future we did not embrace in its purity. We watered it down with ordinary humane arrangements, like job security and so forth. Ford's system was logical so long as one believed as he did that the purpose of work, the whole purpose of it, was output, and the more efficiently produced the better.

Ford's major statement of his views appeared in 1922, at the height of his triumphs, in *My Life and Work,* a book written by Samuel Crowther out of Ford's conversations concerning his affairs. The book has many inaccuracies in it regarding dates and events and other facts. It is in that sense, as has been charged, a mine of misinformation. There is no doubt that, as a source of reliable information concerning Ford's *views,* the book is unexampled. What follows relies heavily upon *My Life and Work.* In later years Ford relayed his further views to the public again in three more books (one of which was an appreciation of Edison).

What Ford thought he was doing, and what he thought about what he was doing, constitute a singular chapter in the industrial history of the United States—and the Western world for that matter. Not only was Ford the greatest manufacturer of all time, in his life Yankee Puritanism, which had its Old World origins, and the native American productive ethos (the better a thing is, and the cheaper it is sold, the more is the country benefited, no matter what the thing is) came together with explosive force. Ford was a real purist in American economic ethics; so far as he was concerned, efficiency was, by itself, the logical and ethical end of human affairs.

In the model year 1908–09, when Ford made and sold some 10,600 cars, that was unprecedented and the largest number ever made and sold by a single producer. By 1926, when the end of Model T finally came, 15,000,000 had been made and sold, nearly 1,700,000 in the single year 1923, and at the maximum daily rate ever reached, one Model T came out of the Ford factory every 15 seconds, although the more usual speed was one about every 45 seconds. Ford sold half of the new cars made in the country up to 1926, and had more than double the output of his nearest competitor, General Motors. The more than one-hundred-fifty-fold increase in annual output by Ford was due to the introduction and perfection of the moving assembly line; the work moved to the worker.

The great plant at the River Rouge was the paragon of mass production. The factory covered an area 1¼ miles long and 1⅛ miles wide. It was a complete piece of vertical integration. Raw ore could go in one end on Monday, pass through furnaces, mills, forges, machine shops and, joined by subcontracted components, emerge on Wednesday as a completed automobile. Ford had eliminated his inventories so that virtually nothing was tied up in goods in storage. It was all timed to be in constant movement; materials moving to the Rouge, cars moving out. In 1923 Ford was using a million board feet of lumber each day and one-quarter of the entire nation's output of plate glass.

The method, the moving assembly belt, spread quickly into other manufacturing industries, and like Whitney's system before it, soon became "standard" American manufacturing procedure—the line running like a river, tributaries of parts flowing into it, a finished product moving out into the economy. Ford set up assembly plants for his cars, with assembly belts, around the country. Parts were subcontracted, and automobile "factories" became simply assembly plants. The system's productive capability was immense, and the modern American economy is its monument to a large extent.

Charles Sorensen gives himself full credit for the idea of the assembly line. Previously, autos were made by workmen bringing parts to the point of assembly and putting them together. Here was the old system of interchangeability paying off. But the possible gains from specialization were clearly only partially achieved, as each man did several jobs. The Ford men knew this could be improved upon; they had learned a lot about speeding up output from Walter Flanders,

a production specialist who resigned from Ford when he heard
that Model N was being dropped for Model T. Flanders had
made them realize that the proper placement of machinery
could bring immense savings. Sorensen and Ed Martin took
over from Flanders. In 1908, when orders were far ahead of
output, the first moving assembly line in the automobile industry was tried. Sorensen had already made the delivery of
parts to the assembly point strictly a sequential operation. But
he was not satisfied. As he tells the story (italics in his version):

> It was then that the idea occurred to me that assembly would
> be easier, simpler and faster if we moved the chassis along,
> beginning at one end of the plant with a frame and adding
> the axles and wheels; then moving it past the stockroom, in-
> stead of moving the stockroom to the chassis.

On Sundays, Sorensen and an assistant would experiment
with rope and windlass at moving the frame along on a sled
past the piles of parts. The cars were assembled very quickly.
That was at the old Piquette Avenue plant. Ford saw it, and
encouraged the experiments (on Sunday it wasn't costing him
much), but it was five years later, in 1913, that the first real
moving assembly was set up at Ford's Highland Park plant.
After that the speed of auto assembly rose steadily. Sorensen
was not only entirely explicit about the role he played (that
of inventor) but he was also entirely explicit about Ford's
role.

> Mr. Ford had nothing to do with originating, planning, and
> carrying out the assembly line. He encouraged the work, his
> vision to try unorthodox methods was an example to us; and
> in that there is glory enough for all.

Ford was himself no inventor. He was more of a pioneer,
at the beginning, than was Carnegie, but there was nothing
reckless about him *until* he knew the way. Ford said: "I do
not believe in starting to make until I have discovered the best
possible thing." But then he was ruthless. He was a great innovator, and that is why the assembly line is linked forever
to his name. He let the experimentation go forward until it was
ripe; then the assembly lines were set up. When they worked,
Ford himself gave the date 1913 as the first experimental assembly line, and by not mentioning any names, allowed the
impression to exist that *he* had a hand in the actual invention.
Such slurring narrative and calculated falsehoods in *My Life*

and Work constitute the main reason the book is so distrusted by historians today. Ford really did think that history was "bunk," and that is certainly the kind he dictated to his amanuensis when names and dates were involved. He had little taste for the pursuit of truth for its own sake beyond the workshop.

In the Ford workshop, however, one saw unprecedented seeking after a kind of truth, the ultimate of productive efficiency which lay hidden beneath traditional and conventional modes of work. Ford was a complete, if careful, revolutionary; ". . . we will rip out anything once we discover a better way." He was similar to Carnegie in his disregard for obsolete methods. And *everything* was potentially obsolete. Ford said: "If we have a tradition it is this: Everything can always be done faster and better." And so it was. Every job done by Ford men was studied to see if it could be sub-divided, and thus done more efficiently; for the Ford Motor Co. became a massive monument to Adam Smith's pin factory (obviously not having read Smith, Ford seemed to think that the idea of division of labor was original with himself).

With the design of Model T frozen, all the brains at Ford Motor Co. could be applied to productive efficiency. That was in line with Ford's own beliefs. The manufacturer, Ford said, was merely an instrument of society,

> . . . and he can serve society only as he manages his enterprises so as to turn over to the public an increasingly better product at an ever-decreasing price, and at the same time to pay all those who have a hand in his business an ever-increasing wage.

How the purchaser of the ever more expensive modern auto, paying over three years or more for a product that is obsolete virtually the minute it hits the streets, might yearn for a bit more of the spirit of old Henry in Detroit!

The motor assembly of Model T was subdivided into more than eighty separate actions. There was to be no waste energy. Ford said that men should never take more than one step, and no man should stoop over. Nothing was to be lifted, the work should all be waist high. The men and tools should be so arranged as to minimize movement; gravity should be used wherever possible; tools and parts should be immediately at hand. Everything must be reduced to utter simplicity. If at all possible, no man should do more than one thing or use more than one movement to do it. The speed of the assembly was a "mini–max" problem: the maximum work should be done but with the minimum of error. Speedups were useless if the work was botched. But, of course there was room for, and there was, constant experimentation with methods. Ford himself recorded the classic description of assembly-line work.

> The idea is that a man must not be hurried in his work—he must have every second necessary but not a single unnecessary second. We have worked out speeds for each assembly, for the success of the chassis assembly caused us gradually to overhaul our entire method of manufacturing and to put all assembling in mechanically driven lines. The chassis assembling line, for instance, goes at a pace of six feet per minute; the front axle assembly line goes at one hundred eighty-nine inches per minute. In the chassis assembling are forty-five separate operations or stations. The first men fasten four mudguard brackets to the chassis frame; the motor arrives on the tenth operation. . . . Some men do only one or two small operations, others do more. The man who places a part does not fasten it—the part may not be fully in place until after several operations later. The man who puts in a bolt does not put on the nut; the man who puts on the nut does not tighten it. On operation number thirty-four the budding motor gets its gasoline; it has previously received lubrication; on operation number forty-four the radiator is filled with water, and on operation forty-five the car drives out. . . .

To those who screamed in horror that Ford's assembly line "dehumanized" industry, Ford was willing to concede a point. It was true that some people could never do the work. But such people, the creative ones, were rare. Ford admitted that he himself could never stand working on an assembly line. But, he argued, most people have little or nothing creative to think about anyhow, and would prefer jobs where no creativity or judgment was involved. After all, he argued, most business is just routine, sheer routine at the clerk level, and mostly routine at the president's level—if at a more genteel pace. So far as the ordinary workman was concerned, no problem existed.

> The average worker, I am sorry to say, wants a job in which he does not have to put forth much physical exertion—above all, he wants a job in which he does not have to think.

It was an error, Ford went on, to imagine, as creative people sometimes did, that all people abhorred routine—that simply was not so. But to pity the assembly-line worker for his dull job was "to extend quite unwanted sympathy. . . ."

The same argument held as regards skilled labor. There would always be a shortage of skill because "the will to be skilled is not general." The intelligent use of skill was to make machines that eliminated the need for skill on the job; this would provide more jobs because the mass of men had neither intelligence nor skill, had no hope or expectation of acquiring any, and the assembly line gave them employment that could not otherwise exist. As income rose from higher productivity, more jobs were created, and there was in turn more need for skilled men to improve the technology. In fact, it was an advantage to have men ignorant and unskilled "on the line" in manufacturing industry, because they did not have to "unlearn" anything as techniques were changed through the efforts of the intelligent and the skilled men at the design tables. Here, in the mind of Henry Ford, was a line of thought that was present at Eli Whitney's musket factory; now that line of thought had become the *rationale* of a whole industrial system. And so Aldous Huxley found *Brave New World*.

The internal organization of Ford's work was something to consider, and it sprang straight out of Ford's Yankee view of life and its meaning. At his mother's knee Henry learned the lessons of the Puritan boy. The whole notion of a life of ease was "abhorrent." Ford said: "None of us has any right to ease. There is no place in civilization for the idler." Ford always considered himself to be a "worker." Others were mere drones. "Labor is the human element which makes the fruitful seasons of the earth useful to men." Any kind of retailing, Ford said (he called it "speculation" in things already produced) was "just more or less respectable graft." The important work was in making things, making two blades of grass grow where only one previously grew. But work itself was sacred.

> There will never be a system invented which will do away with the necessity of work. Nature has seen to that. Idle hands and minds were never intended for any one of us. Work is our sanity, our self respect, our salvation. So far from being a curse, work is the greatest blessing. Exact social justice flows out of honest work. The man who contributes much should take away much.

The worst waste was the waste of time itself: "From time waste there can be no salvage. It is the easiest of all waste and the hardest to correct because it does not litter the floor." Since labor was noble by nature, there was no need for any man to have any sort of a title: ". . . when a man is really at work, he needs no title. His work honors him." Titles were simply devices for privileged men to set themselves apart, probably to avoid work. Ford preferred not to stratify his works with titles; let every man be always within reach of leadership, if he could grasp it from others. Let no title bar leadership from the worthy man.

The same logic held as regards backgrounds: ". . . whether he has been in Sing Sing or at Harvard . . . we do not even inquire from which place he has graduated." Experts were to be used, not paraded. "We have most unfortunately found it necessary to get rid of a man as soon as he thinks of himself as an expert. . . ." Every job at Ford Motor Co. was theoretically up for grabs at all times.

As Charles Sorensen described Ford's internal policies, "perpetual ferment" was his scheme for keeping people alert. No formal titles or duties, people's various authorities overlapping, and the men watching each other, each hoping for an opening (all this later went in the obvious direction—a secret police and a policeman, the Ford Service Department and Harry Bennett). The men were kept at razor's edge sharpness. Sorensen said, admiringly: "Henry Ford didn't let us grow stale." Keith Sward said that nervous breakdowns among Ford's men were a scandal in the industry.

The floor in a Ford factory came to resemble an ant hill. As Sorensen put it, the key to success was "You've got to get around." Managerial people scurried about looking busy; "Mr. Henry" didn't like to see time being wasted. Anyhow, with no titles and few offices, there were few places to loiter. On the assembly line the same rule held. You "looked busy," even if there was nothing to do. Idleness was unnatural. According to Sward, a Ford employee could not even sit down in the factory dispensary unless it was a "leg or head case." In a famous bit of therapy (Ford himself was especially proud of this one) the men in the Ford Hospital had aprons spread across their beds and were able to do assembly work during a period of their lives when they might otherwise be "wasting time."

Ford advocated making the prisons into factories, since the men in prison were obviously wasting time and were a charge on the community. He did not argue for convict labor; he said that the prisons should be in competitive business and the men should earn fair wages, enough to support their families and lay by some for their eventual release. Some thought Ford had difficulty in differentiating between the procedures suitable for prisons and factories respectively. Sorensen told a story of a vagrant given a job by Ford who quit in a panic after a few weeks' work saying, "I want to get out of this jail." The Ford Service bullies contributed their bit of on-the-floor brutality to make the factory seem more like a prison than it might otherwise have seemed. But the stories of the effectiveness of brutality in the factory of Ford Service were either overdone or the brutality was superfluous, because the terror imposed by systematic job insecurity would have been fully as effective as force could ever be. Nevertheless the record of Ford brutality persists. See Sward.

At one time Ford decided that his workmen should lead blameless lives. The Reverend Mr. Marquis was put in charge of Ford's Sociology Department, an investigating arm of Ford Motor Co. Those who qualified for the Five Dollar Day had to come up to Ford standards of temperance, family life and so forth. "A Ford man must be a builder," said Marquis, and he thought it was simply iniquitous that the men should resent his activities as interferences with their "liberty." Even Nevins and Hill found it difficult to see what all the complaint was about. After all, the men were improved by the Sociology Department and were better for it. But almost any body of men taken at random would be found wanting by Marquis' standards, and could be improved instantly if they could be brought up to minimal standards of Christian ethics. One of the virtues of a free society is that, barring infractions of the civil law, you don't need to come up to such standards if you don't care to. Even Ford finally came around to understand that he was beyond his tether with the Sociology Department and Marquis was eased out. Ford could still fire a man, and did, if he smoked in the men's toilet. But he gave up snooping into his employee's homes.

By the time of *My Life and Work*, Ford granted himself freedom of action along with his workmen. Ford said: "Paternalism has no place in industry." It was "out of date" and it also constrained management by creating a false hankering after good employee relations where the only criterion for work ought to be efficiency.

> I pity the poor fellow who is so soft and flabby that he must have an 'atmosphere of good feeling' around him before he can do his work. There are such men . . . unless they obtain enough mental and moral hardiness to lift them out of their

> soft reliance on 'feeling' they are failures. . . . There is alto-
> gether too much reliance on good feeling in our business
> organizations.

Ford thought of his business as virtually an act of nature:
it made families prosper; it allowed children to grow, the nation to prosper—there was, in fact, "something sacred" about
his business. But its own ends must be served first and foremost, before all merely human considerations.

> A great business is really too big to be human. It grows so
> large as to supplant the personality of the man . . . when one
> looks at a great productive organization that is enabling all
> these things to be done, then the continuance of that business
> becomes a holy trust. It becomes greater and more important
> than the individuals.

In this passage it is clear that Ford had gone over the edge
from efficiency engineering to industrial totalitarianism.
Change the word "business" to "state" and we are in the 20th
century all right, but in Central and Eastern Europe and in
politics. Since Ford was not in Europe or in politics, his ideas
about the character of industrial life constituted a blueprint
for labor trouble. Of course Ford said a lot of kind things and
did a lot of humane things, but he tried to run the Ford Motor
Co. along the lines set out in *My Life and Work*. His labor
relations were, as a result, reputed to be easily the worst in
the auto industry, which was saying rather a lot at that time.
Ford added insult to injury by the unprecedented job insecurity
in his plants.

His famous purges seemed to be completely arbitrary. (I
was told by an old-time Ford employee of office workers being
laid off by alternate rows—there are well documented samples
just as arbitrary.) He was egalitarian about it though; men
were fired out of hand from top to bottom. Ford always had
others do the dirty work. He was by all accounts extremely
devious. Both Sorensen and Bennett tell of the little errands
they had to do in their master's service. Above it all, like
Stalin in the days of the great purges in the Soviet Union,
floated the myth of the kindly and benevolent Mr. Ford. Possibly Ford's inordinate shyness (he evidently did not look
people directly in the eyes, and he is said to have actually
crawled out of windows to avoid seeing people) contributed
to what Sward called Ford's "circuitous" firing methods. His
enemies say he was crafty and malignant, that his were the
ways of a cowardly despot, and let it go at that.

There is no need to belabor here the effects of *Fordismus* on his employees. The reader is referred to the books by Sorensen and Bennett, to Sward's exhaustive catalogue of Ford's crimes against labor and humanity, and to any of the better biographies.

The ultimate consequences of Ford's appalling methods came home only in the great union battles of the 1930's. At this point it matters only that the reader understand what Ford said he was trying to do because, by only partly succeeding, Ford changed America forever. He was attempting to find the route to the highest attainable level of industrial efficiency. He said that the price of his product would be reduced continuously as his methods improved and that he had no idea how far the process could be carried.

Ford believed that management needed a completely free hand to impose technological change; that the free hand should be as blind as justice is supposed to be; that layoffs, furloughs without pay, firings and production cutbacks were unimportant if productivity could be raised in the process. If that were achieved, then the men who had "ceased to be unproductive" could find ample and more productive employment as the economy expanded. Ford was unconcerned that his employees should periodically be without work if that was the price of industrial progress. The cure was worth it, even if the medicine was bitter.

If productivity rose, so would wages and incomes. In *Today and Tomorrow* Ford said: "It is this thought of enlarging buying power by paying high wages and selling at low prices that is behind the prosperity of this country." Finally, those like Sward who were appalled by the apparent wastefulness of Ford's employee relations missed one of the main points of Ford's system: he believed that *he did not need good employee relations* if it all worked out, because he was simplifying the work so much that any man off the street could do any job on the assembly line.

Of course it did not work out. Men want job security. Their labor is their property, and they want property rights in that labor. Such rights they want to be protected by a contract between two competent (relatively equal) parties. Ford's world was one of perfect labor competition and mobility. Without doing too much violence to one of Karl Polanyi's main theses in *The Great Transformation*, it could be argued that the workmen's sense of the social contract doomed Ford's methods. Polanyi argued, in another context, that in a world of perfect competition in all forms of economic life human society would dissolve. There needed to be some constant relationships beyond the drive for efficiency. The point is arguable, but I think such considerations were at the bottom of Ford's appalling labor system. It was a total threat to labor in the auto industry, one which finally brought the young Walter Reuther and Richard Frankensteen to violence at the famous overpass. But they lived to triumph over Ford, at least formally. What had confounded Carnegie at Homestead, finally defeated Henry Ford. The workmen insisted upon protection of their "property rights" in their labor.

VII

The demolition of Ford's utopia came almost at the peak of his success. The automobile market changed dramatically in the mid 1920's. Before Ford's adjustment to that was completed, the Great Depression struck. Then came the New Deal and the Second World War. By then Ford was a very old man, and although his life had been extended beyond the normal term, he had no more triumphs like Model T.

In 1926 Ford was 63, and after all his years of battles and victories he faced great problems again. The Dodge brothers had jibed: "Think how many Ford buyers would like to own a real automobile by paying only a little bit more." By 1931 Walter Chrysler himself drove his little Plymouth to Dearborn and made a present of it to Ford so he could have a "real car." By then Model T was gone, the new Model A was going, and you could buy a slightly used Buick for nearly as little as a Ford. The automobile revolution had caught one of its most effective activists, and for a while it looked as though that revolution, like so many others, would devour its children, or at least one of them.

Ford's price policy had been conducted as if each time his prices were reduced his total revenues would increase (and for years they did). Unlike Carnegie, who took market prices for steel as given (except for the occasional rail pool), Ford, in a market where brand names were crucially important, believed that he could always reach a larger stratum of buyers with a lower price. The trouble was that, with a product as durable as the motor car, the used car became a competitive product. Ford's own past output became part of his competition; the past production of other manufacturers formed a part of the total competition along with the current output of

other car makers. Thus, even with a new Model T selling for
as little as $263, a slightly used one was cheaper, as were used
cars made by other manufacturers, and some used cars which
sold for as little as new Model T's were fancy autos which
could be repaired cheaply. Hence, in the cheap-car market
Ford's competition became increasingly rigorous.

Equally important was the change in consumer taste. The
Model T was a wonderful machine. But the Dodge brothers
were right; there were millions of Americans who wanted
something a bit fancier, more convenient, than the Model T
with its mechanical brakes (on two wheels), two-speed pedal-
run transmission, its crank, its temperamental headlights and
so forth. Knudsen at General Motors brought out his Chevro-
let, and in 1923 sold nearly 465,000 of them. Here was color,
comfort, styling, safety, modernity and dash. Against all that
the flivver suddenly became obsolete and sales started falling
off. At first Ford refused to believe that the American public
would abandon the glorious utility of the stark Tin Lizzie for
the useless gadgetry, color and yearly model changes of his
competition. Then, in desperation, the Model T was painted
attractive colors, the fenders were rounded, the body was
lengthened and lowered, the windshield slanted. In a much-
quoted passage Sward described the Model T's last months.

> Like a renovated, ancient dowager on her last fling, the Model
> T appeared in fawn gray, gun-metal blue, phoenix brown and
> highland green.

Sales of the Model T continued to slip. Finally, in May,
1927, Ford output stopped altogether. A new car was needed.
The new car took months to create, largely as before, by trial
and error. Ford was shut down for nearly a year. For months
he did not know what he wanted. Thousands upon thousands
of workers were laid off (60,000 in Detroit alone). The relief
rolls swelled with Ford workmen. The salesmen were lost to
competitors. The workmen were a matter of indifference to
Ford. The salesmen he didn't need. Sorensen quotes Ford as
saying, "I know some people think that salesmen make a car.
We believe that a car, if it is good enough, will make salesmen." The new car, the Model A, took shape slowly. Once it
was set, there was a vast problem of designing and creating
thousands of machine tools, new dies and fixtures, planning
the output of parts and so forth. The total changeover is estimated to have cost Ford as much as $100 million.

During the interregnum Ford's competitors had been presented with the quite fantastic gift of the entire Ford market to do with as they pleased. Ford said he didn't care, and possibly he didn't. Finally, in January, 1928, the Model A was shown to the public amid mob scenes at the showrooms. So powerful was Ford's "good will" that 500,000 down payments had been made on new Fords by purchasers who knew neither what the car would look like nor how much it cost.

The Model A was, of course, a real winner. It was a tough, classy little car, and it is still seen on the roads of America nearly four decades later. It had many of the virtues of the Model T and it had styling, a standard transmission, and all other modern automotive conveniences as well. More than 600,000 were produced in 1928, more than 1,500,000 in 1929 and more than 1,000,000 in 1930. Then, in 1931, only 542,000 were produced. The one-year reduction in output of 50 percent measured the impact of the Great Depression.

At that point Ford made his last personal mechanical triumph. With his competitors pressing and the depression near its pit, in 1932, Ford put the V8 engine into his cars. The technological breakthrough that made this possible was the perfection at Ford Motors of a method of casting the V8 block in a single piece (predictably, it has been said by Ford's Ode-to-Stalin biographers that Ford made this breakthrough with his own bare hands). Before that V8 engines were cast in more than one piece. This involved comparatively large-scale use of skilled labor, and foundry and machine-shop losses, so that only the most expensive cars had V-type engines.

The Ford V8 engine, cast in one piece, went basically unchanged for 21 years. It even beat the Model T for longevity, and it produced a new coterie of Ford owners, people who got used to both the surging performance of the V8 engine and to the overall economy and good sense of the Ford product. Ford spent millions going over to the V8 but it pulled his company through the Great Depression. Ford told Sorensen, ". . . I know this new car will bring in more money than ever . . ." and authorized Sorensen to spend another $50 million on retooling. By 1933 Ford sold fewer cars than either General Motors or Chrysler, but the bottom had been reached and there was no danger of extinction. In a mere six years, from Model T to V8, Ford had caught up and surpassed, technically, his competitors in many respects, He had gone from the beginnings to the present. His competition was years making a successful introduction of V8 engines in standard models.

The great days of Ford the automobile innovator were over by then, and the man himself was slipping into an old age that was prolonged and increasingly acrimonious. Ford had at least kept abreast of his vigorous and inventive competitors. He was still a man to be reckoned with in the motor-car world. But other parts of Ford's world changed beyond his recognition and powers. The world of his prime was gone; his idol, Edison, was dead. And so were most of his contemporary automotive pioneers. The society itself had changed radically; the old values seemed to be disappearing; prohibition was over. Herbert Hoover, Ford's favorite President, was a man of the past and maligned. In no time at all, the world of the 1920's seemed like ancient history. The reign of "business" was at an inglorious end and That Man was in the White House in 1933. In New Deal America, Ford and his ideological brethren were completely at sea.

The Great Depression was an awesome thing. The American economy was like a barrage balloon with the gas let out. American capitalism suddenly faltered, and a fear and doubt crept in which has never left us. For the first time, with the possible exception of the years from 1837 to the early 1840's, the American economy seemed to flounder helplessly, year after year. Economists have been at loggerheads about the "causes" of the economic debacle of the 1930's. About the facts there is no dispute: the depression that began in late 1929—or at least which was signaled by the stock-market crash of that year—was a catastrophe. Consider some of the main economic indicators.

Manufacturing production, which had stood at 110 (average of 1935–39 = 100) in 1929 declined precipitately to 57 in 1932. The Gross National Product in current prices fell from $104.4 billion in 1929 to a mere $56 billion in 1933; in terms of 1929 prices the decline in the same period was less, down to $74.2 billion, but even that much of a decline in output in four years was a disaster of the first magnitude.

Commodity prices (1929 = 100) fell to 76. Prices of raw materials fell nearly 50 percent, more than did prices of manufactured goods. The farmers, carrying debts incurred in the plush World War I years and their immediate aftermath, and who already had seen hard times in the 1920's (from 1914 to 1923 interest owed by farmers more than doubled on a per-acre basis) began to sink beneath their burdens. Mortgage debt alone had more than doubled between 1914 and 1924. Now, in the early 1930's, the payments for debts contracted at high prices were overdue when farm prices were low and farm cash income, which had stood at $11.3 billion in 1929, had diminished to a mere $4.8 billion in 1932.

One of the most significant declining sectors of the economy was building construction. There was a tendency for building construction to follow a roughly 20-year cycle. Building construction is one of the most important sectors of the economy, not only because of the sheer volume of resources employed in it, but because the materials and labor used are more largely of local origin and hence changes in building activity are felt widely and quickly.

Building also seems to be a reliable indicator of expectations as regards family formation, incomes, savings and the like. Building construction reached a peak in the mid 1920's and then declined steadily, slowly at first. Total outlays on building construction were more than $15 billion in 1926, 1927 and 1928. By 1933 total outlays were only $5.4 billion, and that included government. In the private sector alone the reduction was from $9.9 billion in 1926 to $1.2 billion in 1933, a fall of about 88 percent. There were 849,000 private dwelling units started in 1926, 509,000 in 1929, and a mere 93,000 in 1933. Here was a vital industry nearly extinguished, so drastic was the impact of the depression. For those who think that the Great Depression started instantaneously with the Wall Street crash of 1929, the decline in building construction from 1926 onward ought to give a moment's pause.

The reduction in output in heavy industry was worse even than in manufacturing industry in general; steel output, for example, fell from more than 56 million tons in 1929 to a mere 13.7 million tons in 1932. The output of locomotives in 1929–33 fell from 1,161 to 63, and output of railway passenger cars fell from 2,202 to a catastrophic 7 (seven) or was nearly extinguished. In 1929 some 4.5 million passenger automobiles were produced, but by 1932 output had fallen more than 75 percent, to 1.1 million cars.

Wage earnings of those fully employed fell by a third in 1929–32. Personal income in the nation at large was reduced by over 40 percent. The cruelest product of this gigantic deflation was, of course, the waste of men and resources through unemployment. Unemployed manpower in a nation is a waste that is lost forever. The United States in the 1930's surrendered billions in potential homes, factories, public improvements and consumer goods through unemployment (not to mention the loss of *people* as marriage and birth rates dropped sharply). In the 20th century the largest average number of known unemployed in any single year had been the 5 million of 1921, which amounted to 11.9 percent of the labor force. But a year later, in 1922, the number was down to 3.2 million and by 1923 was down to 1.4 million. Other periods of high unemployment in the past had also been mercifully brief, and the expanding economy had soon reabsorbed its displaced workmen. Thus the United States had avoided any fundamental social disruptions as the economy adjusted to cyclical disorders. The same had been true in the 19th century.

But the Great Depression was different—ominously so. In 1929 known unemployment was about 1.6 million, or 3.2 percent of the labor force. In 1930 the figure stood at 4.3 million; a year later it was far worse, more than 8 million; in 1932 more than 12 million were known to be out of work, and, by 1933, 12,830,000, a catastrophic 24.9 percent of the labor force, was unemployed. The number of partially employed added greatly to the waste of manpower, and as work weeks shortened and wages fell, a large part of the work force was simply holding on for dear life—the loss of voluntary mobility indicating an additional, and not insignificant, reduction of potential output as men feared to try to better themselves (in 1929, 3.4 percent of the labor force in manufacturing had voluntarily changed jobs; by 1933 only seven-tenths of 1 percent voluntarily changed jobs). The unemployment disaster was without precedent.

The nation was, not surprisingly, experiencing great social unrest by 1932. The Bonus Marchers were the most spectacular single reflection of the revolutionary potential of such mass unemployment in a nation that had known better times. The political and social upheaval of the Great Depression forms a separate literature. The reader is referred to general treatments of the depression; for example, Broadus Mitchell's *Depression Decade* or the relevant parts of the first three volumes of Arthur Schlesinger's *Age of Roosevelt*. Franklin Roosevelt was the electorate's answer to the disaster, and the New Deal, or the several "new deals" comprised Roosevelt's not-too-successful prescriptions. The Great Depression burned itself into the nation's experience for more than ten long years and the nation was changed forever by the experience, as the Employment Act of 1946 bore witness.

Of course, one of the sensational symptoms of the nation's economic disorder was the nearly complete rout of the financial leaders and the collapse of their system. It was so sensational that journalists and others, seeking a convenient single-cause explanation of the depression, fixed on the calumnies of the "speculators" (lovely word, in this context it means simply businessmen whose ventures failed) and careless and sometimes fraudulent characters in the banking fraternity.

The financial crisis was of course sensational; common stock prices which averaged more than 260 (1941–43 = 100) in 1929 averaged a mere 69 by 1932 (the interested reader is referred to F. L. Allen's *Only Yesterday,* and also to J. K. Galbraith's *The Great Crash* for details). The market crash in 1929 was the worst in our history. Bank suspensions, which had been high throughout the 1920's, went from 659 in 1929 to 4,004 in 1933; and in that year all commercial banks closed their doors temporarily during the "bank holiday" which immediately followed Roosevelt's inauguration. The dollar was "devalued" (the Treasury's buying price for gold increased) in a series of steps throughout 1933. Such episodes seemed to point to an obvious set of culprits.

But no recognized economist today argues that the business cycle is a moral problem. There had been great crashes and depressions in the United States before: specifically, in 1819–20, intermittently in 1836–42, in 1857–58, in 1873–74, 1882–84, 1893–96, 1903–04, 1907–08, 1920–21. In England the record went back through the 18th century and beyond—far beyond. The American economy had always staged a recovery, ever more powerful, after these depressions (and the economy had weathered some hair-raising financial storms since). Something different had happened after 1929, when the depression and its consequent unemployment of men and resources persisted year after year. In 1940 more than 8.1 million, a whopping 14.6 percent of the labor force, were still unemployed. The New Deal had not solved the problem (in a celebrated paper, Prof. Cary Brown argued a few years back that the real income effects of the whole New Deal program were in fact negligible). Only World War II brought back prosperity and full employment.

Attempts to explain the Great Depression do not constitute a bright chapter in the literature of economics. Some economists applied the profession's accumulated knowledge of the theory of business cycles to the problem (a famous explanation, in that jargon, has a coalescence of "Kitchin," "Juglar," "Kondratieff" and building cycles simultaneously in their contraction phases in 1929–32 producing an abnormally deep depression), but the net effect was unconvincing to the *cog-*

noscenti (see Simon Kuznets' demolition of Joseph Schumpeter's massive *Business Cycles*). The Dutch economist Jan Tinbergen made an empirical study of the U. S. economy in the relevant period and showed that no cycle theories were relevant to an explanation of the sequence and character of the facts.

It was thought by Alvin Hansen and others that long-term growth forces in the American economy had run their course and long-term, or "secular" stagnation was the consequence. Other economists, looking back, have seen the causes of the depression of the 1930's in the sudden, and largely unexplained, collapse of business "confidence." The British economist, Thomas Wilson, found pregnant sources of U. S. stagnation in the "maturity" of certain leading industries whose expansions had sparked the economy's growth. Of course, some argued that we imported the depression from Europe (where it is said that *they* imported it from us); others argued for "underconsumption" and some for "overinvestment."

The list goes on; it is powerfully unconvincing, and of course lapses into total crackpottery at its end. One is tempted to include among the obvious cranks those eminent economists who developed theories of business cycles without reference to any facts whatever and then rested, assuming that the Great Depression, its causes and consequences, formed simply a trivial problem of "testing" theories which were, in fact, untestable. The great British economist, J. M. Keynes, knew the way out, he thought; he published his ideas in an open letter in the *New York Times*, and talked to Roosevelt about it (he admired Roosevelt's hands). But even Keynes had little to offer, beyond the obvious, about the depression's causes. And Roosevelt and the New Deal didn't follow Keynes' advice anyway.

There was tragedy in the confusion, because President Hoover was offered useless advice by "experts" who thought involuntary unemployment was logically absurd (and therefore could not exist), and F. D. R. was treated to a great deal of similar, and even more useless, expertise. There were economists (naturally enough, if you understand the relevant part of the theoretical apparatus which underlies the analysis of prices) who refused to see that there was a depression; the whole trouble was simply that wages were somehow too high.

The fact that Henry Ford was confused thus does not mean that he was any more ill-equipped to think about the catastrophe around him than were the rest of the nation's leaders.

In the 1930's Ford was extensively involved in affairs beyond the auto industry, in experimental farming (soybeans) and with the pursuit of physical history (below). Ford refused, to Gen. Hugh Johnson's face, to participate in the National Recovery Act's industrial organization. Ford said he didn't believe that the cartelization of the nation's industry would help matters, and anyway, he said, the law was "not legal"— on the latter, the Supreme Court agreed in 1935. One of Johnson's weapons against Ford was a threat to withdraw all government contracts from Ford Motor Co. There was public outcry at this. Will Rogers found himself amused by this public defense of the Dearborn tycoon.

> You can take the rouge from female lips, the cigarettes from the raised hands, the hot dogs from the tourist's greasy paw, but when you start jerking the Fords out from under the travelling public you are monkeying with the very fundamentals of American life.

Ford's defense of his independence from the Federal bureaucracy put him on the side of the angels in the long run (the country's economy would have been pretty odd had it developed under the N. R. A. for any length of time). But Ford's attitude toward the organization of labor and the brutality of Ford methods in resisting the unions blackened his name forever.

In 1931 the Norris–LaGuardia Act was passed, which drastically limited the use of injunctions in labor disputes. In 1933, Section 7a of the National Industrial Recovery Act (passed again in 1935 as the National Labor Relations Act) made membership in labor unions a right. In 1937, in *Jones and Laughlin Steel v. The National Labor Relations Board,* the Act of 1935 was upheld by the Supreme Court. American labor was near the end of a long road. From the Philadelphia cordwainers case in 1806, down through the years of struggle, persecution and violence, over the dead bodies of labor's heroes at Homestead, Haymarket, Ludlow, Everett, and a dozen places of blood, legal status had at last been achieved under the aegis of a friendly government.

But the old alliance of craft unions, the A. F. of L., was unable to grasp its sudden opportunities, and the young men of the movement, at first led by the redoubtable John L. Lewis, organized the Congress of Industrial Organizations and moved to seize the great chance, the vertical organization of labor in the mass-production industries. In coal, steel, autos and other mass-production industries, hundreds of thousands of willing, unskilled workmen awaited their chance to organize. In a series of strikes and all-out organizing efforts, one by one the great citadels of industrial America fell before the C. I. O. onslaught. Union membership, fluctuating in the neighborhood of 3 to 7.5 million since 1923, was 4 million in 1936, more than 7 million in 1937, and more than 8 million a year later. By 1941 organized labor counted more than 10 million members. For the most part that growth was accounted for by the burgeoning C. I. O. In autos the fight was uphill. First recognition was won by the United Auto Workers from General Motors where negotiations were started in 1936, then barricades went up at Chrysler and in March of 1937 Walter Chrysler himself came forward to negotiate. Hudson followed. That much was easy compared to what was coming; if the U. A. W. was to have industry-wide recognition it had to organize the Ford Motor Co.

Ford was a long and implacable foe of organized labor. In that regard he truly represented a long line of American capitalists who viewed (and still view) organized labor as a snare and a delusion at best (Ford's view most of the time), and at worst as a plot against the golden goose, Bolshevik subversion or just general un-Americanism. The cherished tradition of rugged individualism could not be mentally squared with collective bargaining even after the courts had solved the legal problem, completing in 1937 at 180-degree swing from 1806, when the cordwainers had been found to be a criminal conspiracy. Henry Ford, the individualist *par excellence*, intended to fight against organized labor in every way, and the U. A. W. cannot be accused of underestimating their job. By 1937 there was sufficient reason for union organizers to view with apprehension the problems of reaching the workers at the Ford Motor Co.

Ford put forward all sorts of reasons for viewing unions with distaste. But mainly he thought they were hoaxes. He considered their objectives to be strictly the aims of paid union officials who were mainly devoted to the constriction of output in the interests of labor monopoly under their own control. The only people interested in unions, Ford said, were the officials, ". . . their union salaries liberating them from the necessity of work so that they can devote their energies to subversive propaganda." Ford considered union leaders to be in a class with the "blind" capitalist boss. Ford said: "Both are misfits, both are out of place in well-organized society."

Both, in Ford's mind, were instruments of financiers and other parasites. All such people were interested only in monopoly, monopoly and constriction of output by the misuse of capital, monopoly of labor through strikes and slowdowns, all of it paid for by "the people."

Ford had long put his view into everyday operation. He must be credited with indiscriminately treating both sides harshly. The bankers were never done any favors by Ford and were verbally flayed by him regularly. But organized labor never had a more intransigent enemy. Ford became obsessed with the view that all interest in labor affairs by professional politicians constituted the road to Bolshevism in industry. His policy toward the increase in welfare legislation was to oppose it all. Ford made a great point of the number of disabled men he employed (he said that the disabled in a factory should be in the same proportion as in the population at large), yet men disabled in Ford's plants had to sue him for compensation, and Ford Motor Co. had the distinction of fighting more compensation cases than all the other automobile companies combined. Ford's views on welfare legislation were perfectly uniform. Of Federal benefits for the unemployed, the official mouthpiece of Dearborn, Cameron, said that they were "a new form of permanent pauperization."

The Five Dollar Day had established Ford's reputation as a friend of labor, but as the years passed, the purges, speedups, firings and systematic job insecurity at Ford Motor Co. gave it a special place in the hagiography of labor's enemies. Ford could not understand the depression. As a result he pressed his advantages over his workers, men whose bargaining positions were gone, the depression having left them helpless pawns— they had no alternative but to accept Ford's terms or face the terrors of joining the miserable army of enforced idleness.

Ford also had little understanding of the change that had come over the automobile industry since the great days of *My Life and Work*. The automobile industry hit its peak output in the 1920's, and the 4.6 million cars produced in 1929 was not equaled again until after World War II. The industry, suffering from excess productive capacity on a gigantic scale, limped along, depending upon annual model changes to spur sales. Ford's magic touch was no more. Gone were the days when he could count upon continued increases in demand, or rising sales every time he lowered his prices, and his workers, as in the rest of the industry, found themselves facing virtual seasonal employment. Ford could not find a way to operate full out, the only way he could understand.

The workers' reaction took the form of slowdowns when possible—"spread the work"—and in attempting to protect their jobs by organization. Job insecurity and force were Ford's methods in dealing with whatever the workers did. The workers were kept at their machines (and marched up the aisles, lock-step, by Ford Service men, according to Sward, when there was reason to be in the aisles), and they were not even allowed to step back and rest when the lines stopped due to temporary disruptions. Union organizers were instantly dismissed and likely to be roughed up in the process. Ford was called in the *New York Times* "an industrial fascist" and "the Mussolini of Detroit."

By the early 1930's the aging Ford increasingly relied upon Harry Bennett to handle his labor problems. Even Sorensen, hardly a bleeding heart, found Bennett repugnant. But neither Sorensen nor Bennett relieved Ford of direct, personal responsibility for what went on at the River Rouge and at other Ford plants. That was left to white-washing biographers. Sorensen wrote: "I hold no brief for Bennett. But he had an unenviable job of being Henry Ford's man Friday." Bennett, a former sailor and prizefighter, had organized, in the Ford Service Department, a singular collection of ex-pugs, football players, former convicts and wrestlers. Their job was to keep the work force in line. Ford Service was a private Gestapo, and was famous as such. In *We Never Called Him Henry,* Bennett explained his actions. The plants were filled with Bennett's spies, and the Ford Service rough-housing treatment of recalcitrant workmen became a permanent fixture of Ford's plants. That was how Mr. Ford wanted it. According to Sorensen, Bennett always carried a gun, had a target range in his office, and ". . . his cops-and-robbers activities fascinated the older Ford."

But as Sorensen said: "Bennett never had any real power other than that delegated to him by Henry Ford. He was a yes-man who did what he was told, and promptly." Ford's morbidly suspicious nature took increasing possession of him as the years passed and Bennett and Ford Service came to reflect simply an autocrat's whims. Bennett flourished in his role, cherishing intimate connections with the underworld, and mixing liberally into state politics, placing his men in vital spots; for example, the police chief of Dearborn was a former Ford Service man. That was a happy convenience. Ford found

Bennett indispensable. Garrett said of their relationship: "Fewer and fewer people could he trust, and the fewer these were the more he trusted Bennett, whose loyalty was exclusive and personal." Sorensen described in his book how Ford even turned Bennett loose on Edsel Ford, the crown prince (and by most lights, a decent, sensible man), harassing him right and left when Edsel's enlightened views pushed him farther away from his father's notions.

Thus it was that Ford Motor Co., by its founder's design a very unpleasant efficiency mill, became as totalitarian a personal empire as was conceivable within the limits of the American Constitution. Ford, who basked in the aura of the Five Dollar Day, and who lashed out at the parasite capitalists and blind bosses, became the incarnation of both to his workmen.

The tradition of violence had been at Ford at least from the freezing morning of the Five Dollar Day when thousands of unemployed men were driven away from the company's gates with firehoses. The style was embellished through the years. The brutality increased with the rise of Bennett. Then in 1932 came the killings.

In March of 1932 an estimated 30 to 50 percent of Detroit's workers were unemployed. Some had already been unemployed for years. Suffering was acute. The depression seemed to have no end. A column of unemployed men formed near the city limits of Dearborn. Ford Motor Co. was the target for several reasons. Ford's unemployed lived mainly in Detroit, and Ford, at Dearborn, contributed little to their relief. Then there was humiliation. Ford had arranged garden plots for his men, offering them the chance to scratch out their own food from the earth, suitably supervised by Ford Service. That was virtual feudalism. Those who did not take advantage of this largesse (a throwback to Ford's earlier schemes for uniting industry and agriculture in complementary seasonal work) were discharged. Ford had laid off tens of thousands and his working conditions were notorious. But probably the fact of Henry Ford himself made Dearborn the target of the Ford Hunger March.

The march was led by a handful of Communists. The depression was the great day for the American Communists, and no one can deny that they made the most of their opportunities. While their "scientific socialism" provided convenient abstractions, "monopoly capital," "exploiting bosses," "bourgeois reptiles," "class enemies" and the like, a man was a better target than an abstraction. You could hate a man in a way you could never hate an abstraction. Ford was *the* capitalist of Detroit—in spite of his cranky views of himself as a workman and an enemy of monopolies, financiers, capitalists and governments. Besides, Ford was asking for it. He had treated the suffering unemployed to a diet of flippant jibes. He said that the unemployed were too lazy to work. They preferred to loaf. In 1930 he had said, before embarking for a European vacation, that he was glad it was a long depression, "Otherwise the people wouldn't profit by the illness." In 1931 he thought that the depression was "a wholesome thing in general." He continued to favor the nation with such nuggets of wisdom as the depression got worse. Even after the tragic hunger march, in October of 1932, Ford was still out of contact with reality: "If we could only realize it," he said, "these are the best times we ever had." By 1933 he denied that a depression existed at all.

The hunger marchers numbered several hundred. They carried banners demanding jobs, justice and improved working conditions at Ford Motors (an odd demand for men unemployed). Their march was obviously meant to be a gesture to arouse public sympathy. No one who knew Henry Ford could expect anything less than firehoses as a reception. At the Dearborn city limits the police ordered the marchers to halt. They pushed on. Scuffling began and the inevitable tear-gas shells fell on the marchers, followed by equally inevitable bricks and stones thrown at the Dearborn police. The demonstration quickly disintegrated into a riot. The waiting fire trucks were driven away from the hydrants and the violence mounted.

The critical point was the theatrical arrival of Harry Bennett. According to Sorensen, Bennett was simple enough to believe that the workers loved him, and he had come to the thick of the fighting to entreat the rioters to go home. As Bennett stepped from his car, his scalp was split open by a brick. There was immediate gunfire, some of it coming from the Dearborn police, and, according to eyewitnesses, the rest from Ford's own company police firing blindly at the crowd. Four of the marchers were killed and twenty wounded. The whole tragedy was watched by an interested party of Soviet experts then visiting Ford (one wonders what weirdly mixed feelings they must have had about it). At the burial services the "Internationale" was sung. The Ford hunger march had made its several contributions to the long list of labor's martyrs.

After that Ford hardened even more in his attitude toward organized labor, and labor people began to find a burning hatred for Ford. Surrounded by his bodyguards wherever he went, Ford was now ridiculed as a prize worth "a billion dollars on the hoof."

Even greater efforts were made by Ford to keep labor organizers out. He believed that unions would destroy his organization. He wanted no union voice in the management of his company. In early 1937, as the other major producers made terms with the U. A. W., Ford prepared for a long battle. All dealings with the union were placed in Bennett's hands. No one but Bennett was to deal with them in any capacity. The other executives, including Edsel Ford, the nominal president of Ford Motor Co., were to remain aloof. Ford said: "If things get too warm for any of us, we should take a trip and get away from the plant. I've picked someone to talk to the unions." In case the workmen failed to grasp the dangers of the union, Ford published and circulated a little card called "Fordisms." Samples:

> A monopoly of jobs in this country is just as bad as a monopoly of bread.
>
> This group is asking us to sit still while it sells our men the jobs that have always been free.
>
> A little group of those who control both capital and labor will sit down in New York and settle prices, dividends,—and wages.

The purpose of organizing strikes was to induce the men to put their necks into a collar, Ford said, and "I am only trying to show who owns the collar." The U. A. W. later charged before the National Labor Relations Board hearings that "Fordisms" was calculated to hold unions up to "scorn and contempt." Ford would hardly have disagreed.

On May 26, 1937, the U. A. W. announced its intention to distribute leaflets in Dearborn. A permit for this purpose was issued by the Dearborn city officials. The approaches to the Ford plant were filled with interesting-looking characters in various costumes, and striking time-consuming attitudes. Bennett had said that "loyal employees might" resist the intrusion of union pamphleteers. The scene, judging from eye-witness accounts, was a macabre takeoff on the usual operatic street scenes just before the main action begins. In groups of four to seven the loyal employees loitered, or cruised nearby streets. The union men and women arrived on schedule. Before the afternoon shift changed, Walter Reuther and Richard Frankensteen mounted the overpass over Miller Road, and the Ford Service rough-housing began. Reuther and Frankensteen were subjected to special cruelty, being kicked and beaten to the ground again and again—but scientifically, with due attention being paid to vital areas of the body.

The Ford Service men then attacked the remaining union people, men and women. One union man had his back broken. The newspaper men present were also beaten up, their cameras and equipment smashed and seized. The loyal employees who mobbed Reuther and Frankensteen, it was learned, included a boxer, a wrestler, a wrestling referee, two hoods (one with a record of twenty-one arrests and four convictions) and the president of the Knights of Dearborn, one of Bennett's para-fascist organizations devoted to "fighting communism and subversion."

The union brought charges against Ford Motor Co. under the National Labor Relations Act; the hearings, appeals and deliberations went on for years. Bennett organized several comic-opera company unions to represent his workmen. These unions were transparent hoaxes, their names indicating the declining levels of the inspiration at Dearborn as Bennett's power waxed. The names were: The Liberty Legion of America, the Workers Council for Social Justice, the Independent Automobile Workers Association, and the Ford Brotherhood of America. Bennett's thugs outdid themselves at enforcing discipline in the plants, and Ford himself accompanied Bennett to the American Legion's national convention at Chicago to gain support against the union subversives. Bennett bought off a U. A. W. president. The city of Dearborn passed an ordinance against union pamphleteering. Thousands of men were fired for union sympathies—each firing being, incidentally, a violation of the National Labor Relations Act.

Finally in April, 1941, the U. A. W., long torn with internal disorganization, had steeled itself for its task and struck Ford Motors. Ford ordered his executives to stay away from the plants. There was further violence. Ford had to settle, and after settling the strike the company left no stone unturned to delay a union election under the N. L. R. A., and Bennett even fired the entire U. A. W. Ford organizing committee. At last the N. L. R. B. ordered an election held at the Detroit plants of Ford Motor Co. The voters could choose the C. I. O.–

U. A. W., an A. F. of L.–U. A. W. (the product of Bennett's deal with a former C. I. O.–U. A. W. president), or to have no union at all. To the polls went some 80,000 Ford workers. The C. I. O.–U. A. W. won hands down, getting 70 percent of the votes cast.

By then the sheer volume of charges against Ford Motor Co. before the N. L. R. B. was without precedent in American labor history. The extent of Ford's illegal activity in defiance of the Supreme Court and the National Labor Relations Act for 5½ years can be gauged by a single order in which the N. L. R. B. told Ford to reinstate no fewer than 4,000 men who had been fired for union activities—those were 4,000 individual violations of the N. L. R. A. The reader is referred to Sward for a description of the entire catalogue of Ford violations.

Only 2.6 percent of Ford's workers voted to remain independent. Incredibly, Ford had actually believed that "the men" felt as he did about the unions. Sorensen wrote:

> This was crushing news to Henry Ford, perhaps the greatest disappointment in all his business experience. He had been certain that Ford workers would stand by him. This was the last straw. He never was the same after that.

Like Carnegie and hundreds before him, and like hundreds who have followed the paths of industrial leadership since, Henry Ford, in spite of his own origins as a farm boy and workman, understood nothing about the aspirations of workmen, about their passion to have some control of their labor, to have some job security beyond the mercurial good wishes of a boss, to have some leverage beyond unemployment in their contract negotiations with the impersonal industrial giants in which they labored.

Although Ford's capitulation seemed to be complete (the first union dues checkoff in the auto industry came as part of the Ford–U. A. W. settlement), Ford's labor relations remained among the worst in the industry until in 1945 when, in his eighty-second year, the old man handed over Ford Motor Co. to his grandson. Just as organized labor found its great victory in the 1930's, so did the old-time capitalists find their greatest defeat. But neither the victory nor the defeat was decisive and the great problem involved—industrial democracy—has never been solved to the satisfaction of the unions, management, stockholders or the public at large. Perhaps there is no perfect solution in a world of ever changing technology.

VIII

Death came to Henry Ford by lamplight on the night of April 7, 1947. A violent storm had cut off the power in Dearborn, and only a coal-oil lamp lighted the last minutes of Edison's crony. By then Ford was a pathetic figure. His son Edsel had died in May of 1943 and the stricken old man (thrice stricken, according to Sorensen, for having bullied and harassed Edsel through Bennett) had personally picked up the reins of Ford Motors, installing himself as president for the first time since 1918. His health failed badly after 1945 and he appeared no more in public. He died a billionaire; the family holdings in Ford Motor Co. alone were in excess of $700 million. His body lay in state at Greenfield Village and more than 100,000 people filed past to look.

Even in his last years Ford continued to make history. At Willow Run, Sorensen's great bomber plant, the arts of *Fordismus* were applied to airplanes and, in spite of many initial difficulties of all sorts, including more labor troubles, more than 8,000 Liberator bombers were produced. Ford's plants, as in World War I, also made the whole range of war equipment. But according to Sorensen, Ford took little interest in his war plants—the old pacifism remained and he blamed the war on F. D. R. Ford did unbend enough to show the Roosevelts through Willow Run in 1942 but, Sorensen said, Ford was simply in misery on that day.

> Henry Ford was gloomy, even in the final few minutes. . . . It was one of the worst days, up to that time, that I had ever spent with Henry Ford. Even during the hard days of the battles with his stockholders he had not been so gloomy or mean. He had spent a few hours with the man who was running the country and a war. Ford hated him, and he was furious because Edsel and I were giving all we had to a cause that was not his own. From then on he became even more difficult to work with.

As the years passed Ford's interests had become vast. He got back into the tractor business (with Harry Ferguson, an association that inevitably ended in the courts) and was extensively involved in experimental farming. He had a rubber plantation in Brazil, and lumber mills in the North Woods. He organized a hospital which he tried to run as efficiently as a factory. (Ford had no use for doctors either, he said: "Many physicians seem to regard the sustaining of their own diagnoses as of as great moment as the recovery of the patient.") He bought a bankrupt railroad and made it a vital and profitable part of his distribution system.

In 1936 the Ford Foundation was organized. There were trade schools and rural industries. He made an all-metal airplane in the 1920's and his researchers patented the first radio beam used in commercial air navigation. Everything that interested Ford became objects of his careful attention. Hence, in the end, his industrial interests extended far beyond the automotive industry and after his death there was a lot of untangling to do.

The Edison Institute and Greenfield Village were, to some extent, like his revival of old-time dancing, efforts to surround himself once again with the familiar sights and sounds of his far-distant boyhood. Ford was intensely sentimental about *things* connected with his past. He restored his childhood home, had the backyard dug up and sifted to find bits of crockery that his mother had thrown away three-quarters of a century earlier, and new objects were made based upon those authentic models. He even filled the closets with facsimiles of his mother's clothing. He kept a key to the house (it was not part of any exhibit) and would go out there alone, or sometimes with a guest, and cook himself supper. Once, according to Garrett, showing people through the Edison museum, the aging Ford stopped in the reconstruction of his Bagley Avenue workshop and began handling the tools. He said he felt like he could just sit down there and go right to work, and then he began to weep. The emptiness of his childhood that came with his mother's death was never filled.

The past was poignancy to Ford—the "real" past, not the records of wars and heros that bemused the historians. At the Greenfield Village and Edison Institute, Ford's vast collections of tools, furniture, machinery, motors, buildings and utensils were his answers to "history." He said he would preserve the American past (a considerable part of which he had lived) in a detail that no mere historian could even imagine. Like Carnegie before him, Ford was partly the prisoner of a disrupted childhood.

Yet Ford had little sentiment regarding people. His coldness toward his own blood relations awed even Sorensen, to whom Ford had given instructions to do no favors for his brothers and sisters. Edsel Ruddiman, whose name was given Ford's only child, was the only important childhood friend, yet Sorensen said he saw no evidence from either Ruddiman or Ford that the two men were anything more to each other than employee and employer. Ford never bothered with his childhood acquaintances. He idolized Edison.

Ford's aloofness from people doubtless came from hard experience. Ford, the *nouveau riche* to end them all, disliked being approached for money by people who knew him. His open contempt for Detroit's high society, and his refusal to mix socially with them was, according to Sorensen, due to a nagging fear that these wealthy idlers would try to "touch" him for a loan. Ford knew that most of these people could never earn their way if anything happened to their inherited wealth and he dreaded, as the richest man in Michigan, to become a one-man relief agency for a bankrupt aristocracy. It was only with the greatest efforts that Clara Ford could get Henry into the company of the "better" people beyond old-time dancing. As a maker of light conversation Ford must have been an odd companion between the minuets.

Ford's restoration of the Wayside Inn in Massachusetts was a notable gesture. It was as if he wanted to restore what the auto had destroyed. The old inn was reconstructed throughout, the fields around it were purchased, tilled with horses and old-fashioned equipment, and a busy state highway was moved out of the way to re-create the kind of silence rural America knew before Ford. Like his lament for the village mill, Ford's anguish was well placed. It was the auto that, initially, made every other rural hamlet in America useless and made rural flour mills uneconomic. By vastly cheapening the cost of transportation and communication the motor vehicle industry sealed the doom of Ford's boyhood world, the little schools with the McGuffey *Readers,* the village flour mills, the wayside inns, the spreading chestnuts—it was all smashed, abandoned or cut down.

One by one, as the years passed, the men, sights and sounds of Ford's great years disappeared. But Ford lived on, increasingly a stranger to the world around him. Sometime during World War II senility came in a serious way, clouding his brain, causing memory lapses and making him even more unreasonable when his "dander" was up. He now fired his best men out of fear that they would get too prominent and shoulder him aside. Edsel felt that pressure continuously.

After Edsel died, Sorensen himself decided to call it quits

rather than go on with Ford. By then Ford's vindictiveness was the more dangerous because of the senility—it was something uncontrollable because of the old man's absolute power within his domain. Ford was convinced that Roosevelt and Knudsen were in league to take Ford Motors away from him (he wasn't far wrong several times during the war, according to Sorensen, when his obstreperousness threatened the war effort). Sorensen wrote: "He was obsessed with the idea that he would be attacked by a government agent. I was astonished to find an automatic pistol in a holster under the cowl of his car. His chauffeur also packed a pistol." Ford assured the inquiring Sorensen that the arms were merely for target practice out at the farm.

Sorensen had an agreement with Ford that he could quit when he was 60 and become an adviser. By early 1944, when he was in his sixty-third year, Sorensen sought peace. The firings, the threats, the suspicions, the double dealing had finally overcome even him. He used a football metaphor:

> . . . the team was breaking up. The captain was a sick man, unable to call the plays. The line coaches were gone. Anyone who made a brilliant play was called out.

Sorensen told Ford he was quitting and spent several days giving the old man parting advice: "To this day I don't know whether Mr. Ford fully understood what we were talking about." Sorensen described his last sight of the great tycoon.

> On my way out I ran into Mr. Ford. I told him I was leaving in the morning and not coming back. He made no response except to say, 'I guess there's something in life besides work'. He followed me to my car. We shook hands. . . . I never saw him again.

But Ford did not acknowledge Sorensen's change of status. Sorensen could not get anything coherent on that subject from Ford's Georgia retreat. Finally Ford demanded Sorensen's resignation, accusing him of wanting to become president of Ford Motors. So in the end, after forty years with the Company, even the "Great Dane" was fired—after a fashion. Later, back at Dearborn, Ford would come out of his office, get into his car and order the chauffeur (sometimes Bennett) to take him to Willow Run to "see Charlie." Upon being told that Charlie wasn't there any more, the president, founder and owner of Ford Motor Co. would say, "Not there any more? Where is he?"

Henry Ford II came home from the Navy and was quickly groomed to take the company from the failing grip of his grandfather. In the fall of 1945 the young man was made president, and began to dig the company out from the decades of the founder's decline. There followed a giant purge: more than a thousand managerial people were turned out. One of the first to go was Bennett (who by then was a vice president and a member of the board). Not yet 30, young Henry showed some of his grandfather's toughness, and the accretions of years of Bennett and Ford Service, the beneficiaries of decades of suspicion and internal feuding, the yes-men were thrown out. The "Whiz Kids" were brought into Ford's management and Ford Motors began the long road back to the eminence it had surrendered to General Motors and Chrysler.

Nothing more was heard from the Fair Lane mansion, with its old-fashioned furniture, long porches for the summer evenings, the swimming pool and billiard room, all built for the young Edsel, but hardly used by him before he married and left the old couple there alone. Then in April, 1947, Ford was gone, and a memory became part of the long-dead past. It was all history.

PART IV

THE ARTS OF FINANCE AND CHANGING
INDUSTRIAL STRUCTURE—THE ORGANIZERS

Certain men of pure finance played crucial roles in American economic growth, just as today, they continue to do. E. H. Harriman and J. P. Morgan were two of the most important "men of money" in the past.

Unless an exchange of commodities is barter, say a pair of shoes is traded for an overcoat, the exchange involves the use of a token of value which can itself be used later in a further exchange. "Money" in its various forms is such an intermediary device and hence is called a "medium of exchange." As we know it today, money is in the form of coins, banknotes and orders to pay (bank checks). These are customary forms of exchange media. It is obvious of course that other sorts of objects—wampum, railway bonds, cigarettes, fancy rocks or what have you—can also serve the functions of money so long as they have the quality of being freely exchangeable for commodities and services. But usually we think only of notes and coins and direct orders to pay on demand as "money." The required qualities for a successful intermediary of exchange are variously described. These qualities may be conveniently divided into three parts: A good medium of exchange should represent true value; be easy to use in computing, and be readily usable as a medium of exchange. These attributes are clearly not independent of each other. A unit of money might be fine for arithmetic purposes and still not represent true value (francs and centimes are clearly easier to compute than the pound sterling and its exotic subdivisions, but not always superior in history as representatives of value). Clearly a currency which does not represent true value may not be a good medium of exchange. "Money," then, is obviously no simple thing.

But if money itself can be complex, how magnificently more complex can be the instruments of exchange which are "near" money, or money substitutes. Here are usually classified IOU's of all sorts, bonds and other dated promises and orders to pay together with such equities as common stocks. These instruments of exchange are not used as money because they are not payable on sight and thus are unsatisfactory for ordinary transactions. But as there is usually a very fast market for them (they can quickly be exchanged for money), they are clearly closer to money than is an ordinary commodity, say a bushel of wheat.

The uses of money and near money are infinite, money obviously can take many forms, and the "moneyness" of money changes constantly according to changes in the relative prices of things. Money's command over resources thus varies from day to day and the ordinary substitutes for money also fluctuate constantly in value according to the supply of them relative to the market demand for them. Just to make it all the more complex, "money breeds money"; it produces interest, and has done so since time immemorial. Thus for a dollar borrowed today you must repay more than a dollar if it is borrowed at interest—you borrow a dollar and pay back at a stated time that dollar plus interest. Similarly, if you sell a bond with a definite maturity date on it, the present value (price at time of sale) will ordinarily be less than the face value according to (1) the bond's rate of yield, (2) the current market rate of interest, and (3) the maturity (years to pay off) of the bond. Finally, the values of all securities vary from time to time according to risk, risk of default, of reduced current earning and so forth.

Thus the instruments of money and money substitutes constitute a complex and ever changing system of exchange and account. But the instruments themselves are only the work-a-day tools of the financial institutions. The Western countries have developed the art of banking as part of economic growth. Some parts of society acquired money claims which were in excess of current consumption needs. Other parts of society generated demand for money claims in excess of their own holdings of such claims. The function of the financial system was to balance out the surplus claims and the demand for them. The surplus generated at any time, not being required to pay for current consumption, could be employed in the production and movement of new goods and services. The purpose of the financial system was to mobilize the surplus claims, borrow them if necessary (deposits) and invest them or lend them to enable goods and services to be available to those whose needs were beyond the limits of their own saving.

The banks served as rationing devices, "markets," for the investable surpluses generated by economic growth.

The earliest banks in the modern Western tradition grew up in the thriving commercial states of Western Europe in the Renaissance. The Italian banks of the Bardi and Peruzzi, the Medicis of Florence, the Fuggers of Augsburg, financiers of Charles V, these were among the earliest bankers. By the 17th century, scriveners (pawnbrokers) and goldsmiths of London had developed the art of lending; the goldsmiths took in deposits, made loans and had discovered that they needed only a fraction of their money in reserve against the demands of their depositors. Fractional reserve banking was born: the banking system as a whole could lend more than it received in deposits.

In 1694 the Bank of England was formed on the basis of a loan to King William, and from that flowed the main stream of central-banking tradition in the West. By the late 18th century, Britain contained a private banking system outside of London, a group of merchant bankers (primarily engaged in international trade) and a bank of last resort—the Bank of England. Early in the 19th century specialization became more intensive; banks could become corporations (at first with unlimited liability) when the Westminster was formed in 1834 under an act of 1828. After that the houses in London which had specialized in moving the financial paper arising from trade—bills of exchange—flourished and the London market for such commercial paper became the financial center of the Western world. One of those houses, George Peabody & Co., had as a partner a solemn Yankee, Junius Morgan. His son, J. Pierpont Morgan, who knew well the London discount market, figures importantly in our story.

But let us not get too far ahead of ourselves. It is clear from this brief account of the history of banking that the United States, at the time of its start as an independent nation, could count as part of its European heritage the art or science of banking and finance. We were not backward in grasping the opportunity. During the Revolution, the Bank of Pennsylvania had been found to help finance the war. By 1810, we had 88 commercial banks. In 1860, there were some 1,500 commercial banks and, by 1910, more than 20,000 were chartered by the states or by the Federal government or by both.

By that time we had ourselves added several powerful and colorful chapters to the long history of finance in the Western world. There had been two central banks, the First (1791–1811) and Second (1816–36) Banks of the United States. The Second had, in its demise, provided the first, but not the last, spectacle in the United States of open conflict between the principles of "sound" finance as conducted by a central bank, and the expansionist desires of political authority—Nicholas Biddle of Philadelphia versus Andrew Jackson of Tennessee. Our commercial banking history had given us a tradition of unit banking (as opposed to the branch systems used in other Western countries). We had devised many systems for the control of commercial banking by the banks themselves.

Money markets developed in several cities but by the mid-19th century had come to be concentrated in New York City, where, in the stock and curb exchanges, a thriving capital market had also grown up. Specialists in the placement of commercial paper—evidences of debt arising from trade—before the Civil War had begun placing with buyers and lenders the instruments of indebtedness of the slowly rising new industrial corporations. By the 1870's there existed a giant American financial system; virtually a national market for money. Since the values of money and money claims changed constantly according to the relative demands for them and supplies of them, this was a great field of opportunity for men of talent and skill. It would, in any case, have attracted the men of ambition and nerve.

But there was something else. Recall that financial transactions have counterparts in "real" transactions in a money economy. By the 1870's some of the real transactions in industry in the American economy had taken on a character which was fundamentally different from what had gone before. Manufacturing units on a very large scale were appearing which needed financing that was far beyond the means of individual, or even small groups of, industrialists.

Within the intricate mass of financial instruments and institutions lay the means to solve virtually any conceivable money problem which might arise in connection with the vast expansion of the scale of operations of American industry. There could be "high finance," but finance imposed a logic of its own upon industrial organization. To wed the country's growing industrial structure on a permanent and viable basis to the source of finance—a nation's savings—the ancient arts of finance and banking were needed, and industry had to take on a sophistication which matched that of finance.

Reorganization of growing industry on this basis was a job for the financier. The great organizers of American industry understood the structure of financial markets, together with the instruments and institutions of capital. They could mobilize the *evidences* of command over resources. Some of them knew little or nothing of the industries they organized; in the steel industry, for example, J. P. Morgan neither invented nor innovated. But the great banker and art collector pushed the organization of the American steel industry beyond the horizons of the "old man of steel." Some enterprises like railroads very quickly were allied with financiers because of the relatively enormous amounts of money involved. Thus the career of Edward Harriman.

The intrusion of high finance into the industrialization of the United States has always been treated as a *cause célèbre* by historians. Sensational may have been the word for many of the actions of our "robber barons," but there was nothing difficult to understand about their part in American economic development. The great capital and money markets of America were not going to be linked up to the booming new industries by conventional business people. The great financiers played roles which were warranted by market conditions. The eccentricities of individuals of genius in organization were critical factors in the final form of the new industrial structures, but the headlong rush of American growth required the intrusion of financial genius, eccentric or not. As it turned out, few of the great organizers had "sympathetic" personalities. But they were not being called upon to project a desirable image to the public. The results of their activities made Americans aware that the efficiency of large size was not an unmitigated blessing. We got our anti-trust tradition as well as much of our gigantic industrial structure out of the initial union of banking and industry on a massive scale—the union of the age-old art of finance and the consequences of applied Newtonian science.

CHAPTER 8

E. H. Harriman, the Financier and the Railroads

> The people always find out what's
> what, in the end, and I can wait.
> E. H. Harriman, 1905

Edward Henry Harriman was the perfect object for all forms of derision and abuse aimed at the "masters of capital," the "robber barons," the "malefactors of great wealth" and the like. He was usually a winner, and hence was resented. He was the image of the bantam corporal. Like so many short men, he compensated with physical and intellectual vigor. With a small stature, a feverishly aggressive personality and "too clever by half," Harriman was brusque, taciturn and efficient. He was a relentless man of business; his business was making railroads pay. He was a financier, but a very special kind. Once into the railroads, Harriman devoted himself mainly to them. His great skill in finance gave him crucial advantages over most of his rivals. The railroads at the end of the 19th century were in a period of turmoil, and in the constant warring between contending interests Harriman's financial astuteness together with his general cleverness brought victories which gave him the most formidable combination of enemies any American tycoon ever had to contend with.

Harriman's methods and mannerisms made men hate him with a burning hatred. His visage, the hawk eyes peering out from behind rimless glasses over a walrus mustache, made him an easy mark for caricatures, and the yellow press "savaged" him unmercifully. He was certainly one of the most disliked public figures of his time. Theodore Roosevelt, whose spleen was vented on many a lesser victim, saved his most special, publishable epithets for E. H. Harriman; and from the White House, Roosevelt caused to be published his views that Harriman was an example of a "wealthy corruptionist" whose appeals to "the basest passions of the human soul" made him an "enemy of the Republic"; Harriman was "an undesirable citizen." That was a powerful load of official invective for one man to carry. How much kinder even was the view of a contemporary that Edward Harriman "would be a wonderful character if only he had a heart." The man seemed to inspire little enthusiasm.

Yet the role of E. H. Harriman in the country's economic history is interesting indeed, for, in point of fact, in spite of all, he never was put in prison; he was never found to have violated the criminal laws; he died surrounded by loyal friends who never doubted him, honored publicly and remembered, to some extent, as an important, if controversial, figure in the country's history. The role he played as financial organizer to much of the nation's transportation system was bound to be played by someone. Harriman played it with consummate skill.

I

America had long been the country in which the railways meant massive investment in long miles of track. Those railways were also political creatures, and bred interesting situations. The early railroads were built in a variety of ways, almost all of which involved a partnership between private railway builders and governments at some level, Federal, state or local. Carter Goodrich, in his *Government Promotion of American Canals and Railroads,* found that state and local governments provided cash and credits for internal improvements (roads, canals and railroads mainly) equal to an astonishing $425,000,000 even before the Civil War. The Federal government's cash expenditures were much less then, but it made available its Army engineers, assisted the states financially during the building of canals and railroads and, after 1850, gave the states Federal lands which were used to help railway promoters, a process which distributed 225,000,000 acres of the public domain. After the Civil War the balance shifted; the states were fast losing their appetites for further railroad ventures, but the Federal government stepped up its contributions. Goodrich dates the origin of massive Federal support from the assistance given to the Illinois Central in 1850.

The first transcontinental railroad was built by companies which had been lent $65,000,000 by the Federal government. From 1861 to 1870, 100,000,000 acres of the public domain were given to finance the roads. In Texas and the South, state governments were able to continue such encouragement to railroad builders (Texas gave them 27,000,000 acres); in New York, Missouri and Illinois, local governments contributed another $70,000,000 before the 1880's. Toward the end of the century, the *proportion* of the public's expenditures to private expenditures fell drastically. (However, the direct financial assistance of governments to railways alone totaled $350,-000,000 from 1861 to 1890, which, together with other forms of assistance, made a far larger absolute amount than the ante-bellum figure.) Perhaps 30 percent of the railroad mileage built before 1860 had been financed out of the public purse. The larger public figure after the Civil War slowly declined as a proportion of the total investment, as the American financial system increasingly achieved the ability to carry out railway finance.

Not only did government and private resources contribute to the building of the American railroads, foreign investors also played a powerful role. American transportation systems were the opiate of the English and European investor. It seemed that bankruptcies, defalcations, missing dividends, violent fluctuations in capital values, business and political chicanery and outright debt repudiation on a massive scale could not dampen the European appetite for American railway securities. In the early Forties, when some American states repudiated their own securities, British investors alone were left contemplating an estimated $100,000,000 in defaulted American promises to pay on long term. As early as 1857 an estimated $390,000,000 of American railway securities were held by the British (which made that nation, incidentally, about as significant a source of capital for railway building as were all levels of government in the United States). By the end of the 19th century, foreigners, mainly Europeans, held $2.5 billion of U. S. long-term securities, largely issued by the railway companies.

The American railroad system was a prodigy. With nearly 53,000 miles of rails in 1870, the nation saw more than 40,000 miles added by 1880, an enormous 70,000 miles added in the next decade, nearly 30,000 more by 1890, making the total more than 193,000 miles. And 47,000 miles more were built by 1910, the year after Harriman's death. By then the United States—with a fantastic total of 240,414 miles of railways connecting its towns and cities, cutting through its farms and deserts, burrowing through its mountain ranges—had about one-third of world railway mileage. After 1910 growth slowed down; there were 253,000 miles by 1930 and the figure has been falling ever since.

The roads were built by men well known to the literate American public: the Huntingtons, Hills, Stanfords, Goulds and others. They were bold, imaginative men who mobilized resources by all possible means to serve the ends of railroad construction. Much of the mileage was initially unproductive, and for decades after, even if built frugally, could not have supported the underlying bonded debt, not to mention dividends on the stock. To the extent that rascals issued railway securities and stole the money paid for them (the extent is not clear), it was just that much more difficult to make the railroads into efficient productive units. There was a great deal of parallel construction, with accompanying rate wars, and the competition to build into virgin territory produced bankruptcies by the score. Built without any overall plan, the railroads now faced a period of amalgamation and financial reorganization. Even the enormous growth of the industrial and agricultural economy could not support the system as it was originally constructed. As the great railway builders grew old and died off and empires fell into receivership, the time had come for the Harrimans and the Morgans. The railroads were a great national asset—even if some were temporarily bankrupt.

II

E. H. Harriman was born on Feb. 20, 1848, in Hempstead, New York. His paternal ancestry was dominated by men of commerce. The Harriman family line in the United States began with the arrival in New York of William Harriman from England, in 1795. He had been a stationer in London and was a man of some means. He settled first in New Haven and then in New York, where he engaged in the lucrative West India trade, chartering ships and transporting cargoes. Several of his sons were lost at sea, but one, Orlando, lived to continue the Harriman name. All of Orlando's sons but one kept up the family's commercial interests. Orlando Harriman's oldest son, also named Orlando, turned out to be the "renegade"; he went to Columbia College, did brilliantly in his studies and took the cloth. He was ordained a deacon of the Episcopal Church in 1841 and thus guaranteed that his own children would grow up in respectable if modest surroundings.

In 1841 the Rev. Orlando Harriman married Miss Cornelia Neilson, who came from an old New Jersey family. The clergyman had a difficult time of it, being usually close to poverty, or in it. He started out as rector at Hempstead but could not manage on the income. He was not a successful minister anyhow, largely because of his cold and austere personality, but instead of giving up the profession he took a job in the gold fields of California in 1850 and moved his little family the long journey by sea, going overland at Panama. There was no job waiting for him in the Golden State (the vestry had hired another man).

After a year of peripatetic preaching in the mining camps (which, if we can believe Brett Harte or Mark Twain, must have been a trial for any preacher), the family made the long trip home to a "semi-attached" curateship in Jersey City, New Jersey. In early 1860, when he got a rectorship again, it was in West Hoboken and he walked the distance from Jersey City each Sunday. He even had to give that up in 1866 when his salary was one year in arrears.

There were six children to feed by then, and the mother's small independent income was a crucial factor in keeping the wolf at bay. Nevertheless an attempt was made to preserve middle-class respectability and young Edward was placed in a good private school, Trinity, in New York. When Edward was 14 years of age, the old Harriman blood seemed to rise up in rebellion against its unnatural captivity under the roof of an impecunious minister of the gospel and, over his father's strongest objections, Harriman quit school forever. Following his instincts the boy found his natural habitat—Wall Street— and once back in friendly soil the Harriman genius flowered.

Harriman's rise in Wall Street was quick and decisive. He began at 14 as a "pad shover" at a salary of $5 a week. There were no electronic communications between offices in those days and boys were employed to go about the streets and offices gathering information on current stock prices, offers, purchases and so forth. It was the perfect training for the fledgling tycoon. By 1870, at 22 years of age, young "Ed" Harriman had a seat of his own on the New York Stock Exchange, and an office at the corner of Broad Street and Exchange Place. His uncle Oliver, a wealthy merchant in the family tradition, lent the young man $3,000 to buy the seat, and was repaid with interest in the first year.

News travels fast when the news is money, and Harriman's reputation was made almost immediately. His shrewdness quickly attracted a blue-ribbon clientele, and the young broker could list Jay Gould, old Commodore Vanderbilt himself and

August Belmont among his steady customers. They were men who appreciated a young man like Harriman who understood what the words *really* meant that were on the engraved pieces of paper that made up the stock in trade of the financial district.

Harriman's first big independent coup came in 1874. "Deacon" White, a renowned speculator, was cornering some specialized railway stocks and Harriman "sold him short." White was ruined by his failure to complete the corner and Harriman cleared $150,000. The triumphant youngster next conducted a bear raid on the stocks of the Delaware & Hudson Railway Co. The Astor interest was buying, and Harriman was badly cut up, losing all his profits from Deacon White's downfall. There were others in Wall Street, Harriman learned, who also understood the game. But those who spent Harriman's winnings were enjoying a rare delicacy. In the next thirty-five years there were few men who dined at Harriman's expense without invitation.

In spite of the great crash of 1873 the nation's growth continued, if irregularly, in the 1870's, and, Harriman's successful brokerage business became the foundation stone of what was ultimately an empire. In 1877–78 he entered the transportation field by purchasing a Hudson River steamer. Then, in 1879, he married Mary Williamson Averell, of Ogdensburg, New York, the daughter of a wealthy Ogdensburg banker and president of the Ogdensburg & Lake Champlain Railroad (he was thoughtful enough to send the young couple away in a special train with "E. H. Harriman" painted on the engine). *"Gelt geht zu Gelt,"* as an old cosmopolitan saying has it. Accordingly, in 1880, Harriman was made a director of his father-in-law's railroad. That was evidently his first railroad connection. He learned quickly, and soon made another.

There was a little railroad, the Ontario & Southern, in upstate New York, which had connections with both the New York Central and the Pennsylvania. Harriman took over the small road in the fall of 1881 in partnership with J. S. Macy and others. The road was reorganized as the Sodus Bay & Southern Railroad, and a grain elevator was built to attract traffic. But the railway still lost money and in October, 1883, Harriman offered to sell out to his partners or buy them out. He would rule or cut his losses. His partners sold to him and Harriman was now a railroad president. He poured funds into improvements, then opened negotiations with *both* the Penn-

sylvania and the New York Central. Playing the giants off
against each other, Harriman, the future "Little Giant" of
railroads, unloaded the Sodus Bay & Southern upon the Pennsylvania Railroad at a comfortable profit. Harriman said later:

> This property had great strategic value which nobody seemed
> to recognize. . . . My experience with this railroad taught me
> a lesson with respect to the importance of proper physical
> condition in a transportation property which I have never
> forgotten.

Sharp? It was clever. Was it a useful transaction, or was
Harriman just a shrewd speculator who had bilked a larger
but less cleverly run company? In a market transaction the
measure of "value" is the price paid. No one forced the Pennsylvania to buy, except their own best interests as they saw
them. Apparently Harriman's price was thought to be fair
enough.

What about the partners? Was it not immoral for Harriman
to buy them out when he must have known that he could improve the road and make a great profit? Certainly that is what
many have thought. Harriman was a free agent. He could
do as he pleased. He pleased not to have partners. They had
the chance to buy him out. They did not. Finance is not
philanthropy. Business transactions in a competitive situation
are supposed to be efficient. Equity is not business.

Harriman was not a philanthropist like Carnegie—and
neither was Carnegie when it came to business. What Harriman did in the case of the Sodus Bay & Southern Railroad was
to create value (price) where it had not previously existed,
and the market rewarded him accordingly. Such are the in-
scrutable ways of capitalism.

Morally justifiable or not, it was that sort of transaction
that made men hate Harriman and, since he made many
transactions just as shrewd and just as hard-nosed, his enemies
became legion. He asked no quarter. But he rarely gave any,
and that was evidently thought to be unethical in a winner.
His personality was no asset either when it came to the creation and maintenance of good will, and he usually created ill
will when he meant to provoke no reaction. He made few
attempts to defend his operations when called to task by the
press or by politicians. His friends urged him sometimes to
defend himself against charges made by people like the so-
called Harriman Extermination League in 1907. Apparently
he couldn't have cared less. It would have been out of char-

acter to do so. Harriman was a competitor, not a conciliator.

Harriman was a vigorous athlete. He was a hunter, a fisherman, a hiker. He was an expert amateur boxer (lightweight). He was a crack shot with a rifle. A lover of the out of doors, he had much in common with Theodore Roosevelt, who later excoriated Harriman so mercilessly from his privileged position.

There was also a lot of the "gallows" humorist in Harriman. His biographer, George Kennan, relates two stories from a favorite camp in the Adirondacks. A talkative Englishman, teller of big-game-hunting tales, began to bore. Harriman sent to New York for a stuffed bear's paw, went out at night and covered the ground with tracks and enjoyed himself immensely as the "Great White Hunter" spent his energies day and night prowling about, rifle cocked.

On another occasion Harriman imported Billy Edwards, the lightweight champion, into the camp and apparently relished the spectacle of Edwards, who had been introduced as a fellow financier, bashing the camp guides about. The guides, large, powerful young men, had boasted of their prowess at the manly art.

Kennan, who spent a significant part of his two-volume biography trying to rehabilitate Harriman from his calamitous reputation, told these stories as examples of his hero's "mischievous," "boyish," "lighthearted" side. The trouble is that Harriman was not then a boy, nor very near to it. Boys do that sort of thing, but not many grown men. Putting the better light on it (no one has ever said that the mature Harriman had anything childish about him), the stories show a grim realism mixed with the slight, cynical humor that characterized Harriman: the Englishman was simply a loud-mouthed fool who could, and should, be made to act accordingly; the camp yokels were oversized braggarts who could be easily cut down, and should be, by any young man in training who knew how to box. Harriman laughed. It was amusing; there was precious little "mischievous" about his practical jokes. Sadistic perhaps.

Harriman, like any man, had his humane side (Stalin, after all, is supposed to have been a reasonably loving father to his daughter Svetlana). Harriman, accordingly, did many admirable, and even quixotic, things. But it would be misleading not to try to see him as he was, a fairly humorless and forbidding financier, at least in his business dealings. But a very fine financier in a time when fine financiers were in short supply and the nation's transportation system was crying out for them. There was not much point in being a "nice guy," not with the row that Harriman had to hoe.

III

Harriman entered the "big time" in railway finance in 1883 when he was elected a director of the Illinois Central Railroad. From there he moved rapidly. In 1887 he clashed with Pierpont Morgan and won. Harriman was not the kind of financial colossus that Morgan was, but he knew some things that Morgan did not and, in the pantheon of the American tycoonery, Harriman stands just below Morgan in the financial wing. In 1895 Harriman clashed with Morgan again, and lost —but had a "moral victory." In 1897 he battled his way into the executive committee of the Union Pacific Railroad, and the nation had a new empire builder.

As a financier Harriman was cautious enough, but he came to understand railroads thoroughly and became a financier of railway expansion. In that he differed, for the most part, from Morgan. It was usually stabilization that Morgan sought in his railway financing. But with Morgan, railroads were only a specialty business in a larger game, a far larger game. For Harriman railroad finance became a calling.

The Illinois Central Railroad by 1883 had come a long way from its early land-development days (see Paul Gates' masterpiece, *The Illinois Central Railroad and Its Colonization Work*). The Illinois Central was no longer strictly an intrastate road, but had connections with the Gulf. Wherever the transcontinental lines crossed the Illinois Central, there was a possible competition point with Chicago for freight. There were great possibilities in the Illinois Central. Stuyvesant Fish was then a friend of Harriman's and a member of the Illinois Central board. Harriman had done some financial work for the railway and, with his own holdings of Illinois Central stock, with Fish's support and with the proxies of Dutch shareholders, he was elected to the board. Two years later, in 1885, he retired from his investment business, Harriman & Co., leaving it in the hands of his younger brother William, who was also cut from the traditional cloth of the family. From then until he died in 1909, Harriman was primarily, although not exclusively, a railroad financier.

As chairman of the Illinois Central's financial committee, Harriman initially pushed a policy of expansion, amalgamation and alliances with connecting roads. His financial wizardry was such that the Illinois Central continued to prosper, and its bonds commanded premium prices even as its obligations piled up because of its chairman's expansionist policies. In 1887, while attempting to absorb the Dubuque & Sioux City Railroad, Harriman first ran afoul of "Jupiter." Morgan's firm, Drexel, Morgan & Co., held the proxies of the D. & S. C. R.'s management, who wanted the Illinois Central to buy them out at par. Harriman controlled a large block of the stock, and, since he controlled a majority of those present at the stockholders' meeting, the Harriman forces organized it. Pointing out that proxy voting was then not legal in Iowa, the Harriman forces rejected the Morgan proxies; where Morgan controlled votes as trustee, his votes were rejected for being signed personally instead of signed as trustee. Thus the Morgan nominees were rejected. Harriman had control of the D. & S. C. R.

Morgan was outraged. He took the Illinois Central forces to court but was forced to settle for Harriman's cut-down, take-it-or-leave-it offer for the D. & S. C. R. stock. Morgan considered Harriman's resort to the minutiae of the law to be unethical, ungentlemanly, and could not completely forgive him until Harriman was on his deathbed (*if* he did then is not certain; Morgan visited the ailing Harriman, but who knows?). However, even if Harriman might never be invited to dinner at Morgan's, he still had earned the great man's outraged respect.

Harriman's control of the Illinois Central's finances made the road a legend. In 1890 he inexplicably vetoed any further expansion and urged, in a complete policy reversal, that a large cash surplus be accumulated. This was done by managers who could not fathom his motives until 1893 when another financial imbroglio left 156 railroads bankrupt and in receivership, including the Erie, the Baltimore & Ohio, the Southern, the Reading, the Union Pacific, the Northern Pacific, and the Atchison, Topeka & Santa Fe. *But not the Illinois Central.* There stood Harriman, his vaults filled with ready cash, and a veritable supermarket display of bankrupt railroad properties to be acquired at cut rates. Harriman was a phenomenon. The financier, Otto Kahn, said of Harriman's reign over the finances of the Illinois Central: "Somehow or other, it never had bonds for sale except when bonds were in great demand; it never borrowed money except when money was cheap and abundant."

One of Harriman's private investments had been Erie bonds. He commuted on the Erie to New York City from his home, Arden, and was increasingly interested in that railroad's affairs. Morgan was reorganizing the Erie in 1895 at the expense of the bondholders (Morgan liked to protect equity investment). Harriman sent a long communication to the Morgan committee on the Erie's affairs which Morgan duly ignored. Harriman took the Erie reorganizers to the New York Supreme Court, but lost his suit. The moral victory, however, was his. Morgan, casting about for a new scheme, used Harriman's ideas; the great banker recognized and valued talent, no matter how obnoxious its owner.

But the Erie was merely a diversion. In 1895 and 1896 Harriman was after bigger things. He unleashed a secret campaign to straddle half a continent. Jakob Schiff, of the firm of Kuhn, Loeb & Co., a distinguished gentleman and financier, was attempting to reorganize the Union Pacific. By 1895 the U. P. was in what seemed to be a quite hopeless receivership. Built by the notorious *Crédit Mobilier* of Reconstruction days, the railroad had been in precarious financial shape from the beginning. It is estimated that as much as half of the original construction costs had been "stolen"—spent on crooked politicians, lawyers and wildly inflated construction contracts. By 1875 the U. P.'s management had been able to arrange some dividends but was quickly forced to protect itself by doubling its mileage with bankrupt tracks.

Jay "Mephistopheles" Gould had taken over two parallel lines, the Kansas Pacific and the Denver Pacific, and by rate warfare and threats to build parallel lines wherever the U. P. had tracks, he forced it to merge with his own lines, exchanging on equal terms U. P. stocks valued in the market at $68.50 for Kansas Pacific stocks that had a market price of only $13. Gould went on to other things while the U. P. was left with more thin air to pay interest on. The price, however, was clearly "right" since Gould could have, in fact, driven the U. P. to the wall. Charles Francis Adams' reign over the U. P. from 1884 to 1890 added another 3,000 miles of branch and connecting lines running through the high—and empty— Western deserts. The Union Pacific was due in 1895 to begin paying off its government debt—which, with interest, amounted to $53,000,000—when the Panic of 1893 sent 500 banks and 156 railroads with capitals of $2.5 billion into bankruptcy. In October of 1893 the Union Pacific failed.

Once receivership was upon the U. P.'s stockholders, they

went to J. P. Morgan to see if he could save their property. Morgan, with his brilliant partners (on a committee headed by a United States Senator), tried and finally gave up, finding the U. P.'s affairs hopelessly embroiled in politics. As far as Morgan was concerned, the U. P. could rot where it lay. In the phrase of the time, all that was left of the Union Pacific Railroad was "a rusted streak of iron."

The stockholders asked Schiff if he could save them. With Morgan's blessings, Schiff put his own forces together with Vanderbilt interests and began the work of reorganization. At first things went well, but by early 1896 Schiff realized that he was being systematically blocked at every turn. Schiff could not fathom the trouble; it was financial, it was political, it was hidden. Where was the source of the obstruction? It had to be powerful to block a combination of Kuhn, Loeb and Vanderbilt money and men. Schiff went first to the most obvious possibility, Mr. Morgan, thinking that he might have changed his mind and decided to try his own hand with Union Pacific after all. Morgan assured Schiff that he still had no interest whatever in the Union Pacific, and was grateful about it. But he offered to find out what force was blocking Schiff's progress. In a few weeks Morgan called Schiff back and gave him the bad news: "It's that little fellow, Harriman, and you want to look out for him."

Schiff had never met Harriman before, but went to see him immediately and asked him straight out who was blocking the reorganization committee. The conversation is quoted by Kennan. Harriman said: "I am the man." When Schiff asked why he was doing it, Harriman answered: "Because I intend to reorganize the Union Pacific myself." Growing expansive, Harriman pointed out that, using the Illinois Central's powerful financial position, he could finance the U. P.'s reorganization at prices no one else could touch; for example, he could issue $100,000,000 of Illinois Central bonds at a mere 3 percent coupon and the market would be grateful to absorb them at par. The funds could be used to finance the Union Pacific. "I am determined to get possession of the road," Harriman said finally. Schiff, doubtless startled and sobered too by the apparition across the desk, questioned Harriman about a possible collaboration. Harriman, never backward with his opinions, gave him the stiffest possible price: "If you'll make me chairman of the executive committee of the reorganized road, I'll consider joining forces with you." Schiff thought the price too high, and Harriman dismissed him curtly.

Schiff's committee failed to complete the reorganization so he went back to Harriman, offering to make him a director and a *member* of the executive committee, pointing out flatly that if Harriman were, in fact, as good a man as he seemed to think he was, then he would soon become the chairman. He could have his price if he could earn it. Harriman knew his man, and agreed to the terms. He put in $900,000 of his own money as a starter. He was now on the approaches of empire.

IV

Unlike so many American tycoons, Harriman did not live to an old age, but died in his sixty-second year. The reorganized Union Pacific was incorporated in January, 1897, when Harriman had only about twelve years of life left to him. Perhaps the most astonishing single thing in his life was what he did in just those twelve years.

When the new Union Pacific management took over, Harriman made his usual initial impact; even Kennan had to admit that the other directors regarded Harriman "with distrust." As Otto Kahn put it: "His ways and manners jarred upon several of his colleagues, and he was considered as not quite belonging to their class. . . ." His colleagues needn't have concerned themselves. Harriman would make them rich men, or richer men. He now plunged his personal fortune into Union Pacific stock, betting on his own abilities. Observing that, a well known financier said to Kahn: "You see the man is essentially a speculator. He is putting everything he has, and more, into Union Pacific stocks. . . . He will come to grief yet."

No such luck. In 1906 when the Union Pacific, by then *the* prime railway property in the country, declared a 10 percent dividend and did not announce it for two days, there was a great outburst against Harriman—the charge being that the U. P. management had delayed the announcement in order to purchase stock in anticipation of the rise in prices assured by such a dividend. When the Interstate Commerce Commission investigated Harriman's railroads in 1907, the examiner asked Harriman flatly if he had ever bought Union Pacific stock in anticipation of the 10 percent dividend. "Yes," said Harriman. The surprised examiner then said that such an admission was admirably frank and helpful to the committee. Would Mr. Harriman mind relating the details? Harriman gave the examiner details.

I bought most of that stock, many thousand shares of it, in anticipation of the ten per cent dividend declared August, 1906, some eight years before, mainly in 1898, and I paid all the way from 20 to 30 for it. And I bought more of it in subsequent years, whenever prices were low, many thousand shares more; and all the time I was accumulating it I anticipated the declaration of that dividend.

The "malefactor of great wealth," as the President of the United States called Harriman (and some others), began his reign over the Union Pacific in a way that was characteristic of the man. Schiff's agreement stuck, and in May of 1898 Harriman was made chairman of the executive committee. He had a special train put together at Omaha with the observation car at the front, the platform facing front, and with the engine at the rear of the train, pushing. Harriman then rode on the observation platform over the thousands of miles of Union Pacific tracks (which then included lines all the way to the Pacific, lines which the U. P. had lost during its bankruptcy but which were now being reacquired) out to Portland, Oregon, and back to Omaha. The train traveled slowly so that Harriman could see everything, stopping frequently so he could ask questions and examine things. When he came back, Harriman knew, as no other mortal knew, what the Union Pacific was. (Even traveling slowly, incidentally, a man riding on the front of a train through the plains, deserts, mountains, mountain-deserts, and mountains again from Omaha, Nebraska, to Portland, Oregon, and back, in the late spring and early summer must have risked one of history's most profound combination wind-and-sun burns.)

Upon his return, Harriman asked the executive committee for an immediate commitment of $25,000,000 for a massive reconstruction effort. Other board members, it is said, thought they could see receivership coming down the tracks again; but Harriman got his money, and more. By 1902 the Union Pacific had spent nearly $45,000,000 on reconstruction. Between Omaha and Ogden, Utah, 150 miles of the old line was abandoned outright; a million new ties were laid down; 42,000 tons of new heavy-steel rails were laid down over 397 miles of roadbed; 200 obsolete locomotives were scrapped. The road's car capacity was doubled with 4,760 new cars (more than doubled if measured by workload since the new cars could be moved more rapidly over the new lines by the new engines). Tunnels were blasted out; miles of cut-and-fill straightened out the old line. All that was done in the first sixteen months of Harriman's control.

Harriman, an inveterate lover of horse flesh, the harness-racing kind, even stopped the train-robbery problem (oddly enough, still a problem that late) by stabling blooded distance-running horses along the route in the dangerous areas (mainly Wyoming) so that posses could start off immediately after the bad men. W. Z. Ripley, in his *Railroads: Finance and Organization*, had to admit that Harriman had a great success in the Union Pacific by 1901, and Ripley had little good to say about E. H. Harriman: "By 1901, therefore, the [Union Pacific] was in prime financial condition, with strong credit and unsurpassed banking conditions."

The "unsurpassed banking conditions" were, of course, mainly spelled Harriman, just as had been the case with the Illinois Central. Harriman, who had pulled in his horns as the Panic of 1893 approached, was correct again in his financial prognostications and, as the Union Pacific prepared itself to carry a great increase in traffic, the national economy recovered from the depression of the 'Nineties and provided that traffic. Each helped the other. Figures speak more eloquently than words: in 1898 the Union Pacific carried 43,000 passengers per mile of road; in 1902 it carried 751,000 passengers per mile of road. John W. Gates, the steel baron, general speculator and financial "swell," traveled over the whole route of the Union Pacific in 1901. (He liked to do that sort of thing; a more famous ride of his was between Chicago and New York on the "Twentieth Century Limited" when it was inaugurated.) About the Union Pacific, Gates declared simply: ". . . it is the most magnificent railroad property in the world."

The expansion and improvement of the Union Pacific continued so long as Harriman lived. He was always an enthusiast for the "Great West" and the country he loved enriched him. From 1898 to 1909 the Union Pacific put a total of $175 million into improvements. The average U. P. locomotive weighed 37 tons in 1898, 68 tons in 1909. In 1898 the average U. P. freight train hauled 277 tons; in 1909, with a decrease in the variable cost per ton-mile (freight rates were also reduced over the period by more than 15 percent) the average U. P. freight train hauled 548 tons. In 1898 there were 476,000 tons of freight carried for every mile of U. P. track. In 1909 for every mile of Union Pacific track more than 1,000,000 tons of freight were carried. The population of the trans-Missouri West was growing in those years at a mean annual rate of 4 percent. Harriman's Union Pacific was carrying a large part of that growth. The estimated value of farm lands along the U. P. route nearly tripled in those years.

Dividends began with a cautious 1½ percent and edged up (jumped up in 1906 from 6 percent) to the celebrated 10 percent of 1906. U. P. stock rose from $20 a share in 1898 to $195 in 1906. John Moody estimated that a man with a $1,600 investment in U. P. stock in 1898 had received, by 1906, $21,900 in dividends and capital gains and was, in addition, receiving 63 percent per annum on his original investment.

E. H. Harriman had, in his words, "many thousands" of Union Pacific stocks. He had made a vast fortune on them alone. The "rusted streak of iron" of 1897 made a pre-dividend net profit of $42,000,000 twelve years later. Harriman's Union Pacific, bankrupt in 1896, had in just over a decade become as profitable as was Carnegie Steel when Carnegie quit. That was how one of the "malefactors" got his great wealth, or a large part of it.

The U. P. also absorbed the old Central Pacific (Ogden to San Francisco) and the Southern Pacific in 1901. By then people saw Harriman as a "threat" to the established order. Harriman soon realized that he needed the Central Pacific to control his access to the Pacific. His new equipment and time tables were crippled by the dilapidated condition of the Central, over whose tracks the Union Pacific had to route freight to San Francisco.

The Central Pacific was owned by the Southern Pacific, and all of Harriman's efforts to purchase the Central Pacific had failed. In 1900, Collis P. Huntington died. Of the more than 2,000,000 outstanding Southern Pacific shares, Huntington held 400,000. Just out of receivership, the Southern Pacific had not yet paid a dividend, but the shares were worth an estimated $100,000,000. Harriman decided to go for it. On Feb. 5, 1901, the executive committee of the Union Pacific authorized a bond issue of $100 million for the purpose of acquiring railroad stocks. The bonds, priced to yield no more than 4 percent, were convertible in 5 years to Union Pacific stock. Harriman, who by 1901 did pretty much as he pleased with the Union Pacific's finances, was authorized by the committee to use the $100 million in any way ". . . as in his judgement may be practicable and desirable." *Carte blanche.*

As usual, Harriman already had the capital markets calculated and the issue was a complete success (the buyers in 5 years realized a 56 percent profit when they converted their bonds to Union Pacific stocks). By March the Union Pacific had spent $42 million on Southern Pacific stock and had 38 percent of it. The buying continued and the Union Pacific soon had over a million shares, enough for control. As Harriman put it: "We have bought not only a railroad but an empire."

Once again the work of reconstruction and rehabilitation started. The Central Pacific needed—immediately—some $18,000,000 spent on it. Julius Kruttschnitt, general manager of the Southern Pacific, asked Harriman how fast he ought to use the money. "Spend it all in a week if you can," was Harriman's reply. Work on the Central Pacific required an enormous amount of grading and straightening: more than 13,000 degrees of curvature had to be taken out over a stretch of 373 miles where the road made more than 36 complete circles. The new Central Pacific line involved filling and building the Lucin cutoff, the famous pair of straight lines that went across the Great Salt Lake's surface to a vanishing point on the horizon. Special dumping cars, "battle cruisers," had to be built to carry the fill. Huntington had started the cutoff (by 1917 it was estimated that the cutoff had saved enough energy for the Central Pacific to lift 1,000,000 loaded railroad cars a mile in the air).

Initial expenditures on the Southern Pacific came to $41 million; again, like the Union Pacific, carrying capacity of the cars was doubled and the heavier and faster trains were pulled by new and heavier engines, 540 of them. Before Harriman's death some $242 million had been spent on the entire Southern Pacific system and more than $400 million had been spent under Harriman's fescue on the Southern and Union Pacific systems in just over a decade.

In 1909, 40 percent of all new railroad construction in the United States was being done on the Union and Southern Pacific lines. Even the Interstate Commerce Commission (whose harassment of Harriman might have been Theodore Roosevelt's doing, although Roosevelt denied it, as he did so many things) had to admit in its *Report* in 1907 that Harriman's roads were the best. His financial abilities carried over into everything he did. Precision was what he wanted. He once asked Kruttschnitt why the tie bolts used had part of an inch of iron too much in them. The unfortunate Kruttschnitt, according to his own testimony, said he didn't know; he guessed the size was standard. He got the following lecture:

> . . . we have about eighteen thousand miles of track and there must be some fifty million track bolts in our system. If you can cut an ounce off from every bolt, you will save fifty million ounces of iron and that is something. . . . Change your bolt standard.

Harriman's efficiency spread rapidly throughout the new system and, except for engines, from 1904 onward the two systems, Union and Southern Pacific, began standardizing and pooling their equipment, gaining economies of specialization and scale.

Naturally the Southern Pacific acquisition caused a great uproar. It wasn't helped by Harriman's negotiations in Mexico (he had 800 miles under construction there by 1909 under a concession granted to him in 1902 by the dictator, Diaz) which raised the specter of an international railroad empire under the "Little Giant's" control. Harriman's enemies had reason to howl. By 1901 he had run roughshod over scores of the most important people in Wall Street. The battle with James J. Hill and J. P. Morgan over the Burlington & Quincy in 1901—the notorious Northern Pacific Panic—had heightened the feeling against Harriman in those who had reason to fear him, and that feeling was not dampened until Harriman had experienced a brutal Presidential rebuke and an official investigation.

V

In 1901, while rebuilding the Union Pacific and acquiring the Southern Pacific, Harriman also attempted to outmaneuver James J. Hill and the redoubtable Pierpont Morgan in one of financial history's most complex and entertaining Wall Street skirmishes. James J. Hill was the builder and proprietor of the Great Northern Railroad. His empire stretched from St. Paul to Puget Sound. In 1896 Hill had taken over the unfortunate Henry Villard's bankrupt Northern Pacific and thus achieved a virtual monopoly on the traffic of the far northern section of the United States from the Great Lakes westward. Hill had a certain contempt for mere financiers (like Villard), excepting, of course, his mentor and ally, Pierpont Morgan.

The Northern Pacific affair began with the Chicago, Burlington & Quincy Railroad, which ran from Denver to Chicago, with many branch and feeding lines. It was a prime piece of railroad property with capital stock valued at $110,500,000 and outstanding bonds worth $145,000,000. From Denver to the Missouri River, the C. B. & Q. R. ran parallel to the Union Pacific and that made Harriman deeply interested in the road's affairs. If the U. P. had the Burlington, it would also have a profitable Chicago terminus. James J. Hill was also interested in the Burlington to complete his system in the North.

Harriman had discussed a purchase with the Burlington people earlier but the two sides could not find a common ground for negotiation and the matter was dropped. Now, in the spring of 1900, hearing that Hill and Morgan were interested in the Burlington, Harriman decided to try to beat them to it. The Burlington stock was widely owned, held by some 15,000 individuals. This meant that an open-market purchase would be necessary, but that it must be done secretly without inflating the prices unduly and letting the Hill–Morgan forces become aware of the buying. It was also not certain at all that control of the Burlington could be purchased from so many stockholders. In the circumstances, however, with Hill casting his reptilian eye over the road, its purchase must be attempted.

Harriman formed a syndicate, which included Schiff, James Stillman for the National City Bank (and hence the Rockefellers) and George J. Gould, son of Jay Gould and potential heir (Jay Gould died in 1901) to the massive Gould fortune. The syndicate thought that control, with the stock so widely held, might be achieved with 200,000 shares. Kuhn, Loeb did the buying. By late July, Kuhn, Loeb had accumulated more than 80,000 shares, but at a cost of $10,000,000 and the goal was nowhere in sight. The buying ceased.

In the fall, Hill got moving on the Burlington. The buying was beautifully done by Morgan's men; there were only small supplies of Burlington stock available and Burlington prices rose some, but the Morgan buyers kept their hands steady so that no attention was attracted to the operation. As prices rose, the Harriman group decided to take some profits and quietly unloaded 60,300 shares, most of which Morgan's buyers quietly absorbed. The buying continued; share by share the Morgan buyers had to pick up the Burlington stock from the thousands of holders. So skillfully was the buying done that it was evidently March of 1901 before Harriman and Schiff realized that Morgan and Hill were after the railroad. Harriman immediately arranged for a conference with Hill through

the good offices of a mutual friend and financier, George
Baker. Harriman asked the beaming Hill if the Union Pacific
might have a cut, a one-third cut, of the Burlington. Hill said,
"No." Harriman then told the portly empire builder: "Very
well, it is a hostile act and you must take the consequences."

One supposes that such a manifesto delivered by Harriman
to Hill's face might have shaken Hill. It evidently did not.
Why should it? After all, Hill knew better than anyone by then
how difficult it was to buy control of the Burlington and he
was allied with Morgan. What could Harriman and his fancy
friends do about it?

> I did not think, at the time, that it was at all likely that any-
> one would undertake to buy in the market the control of 155
> millions of stock.

That is what the battle-scarred and shaken James J. Hill said,
later, after he discovered what Harriman had done about it.

Harriman knew the treacherous terrain of railroad finance
as well as any man. Knowing that, he knew that there was
more than one way to control the Burlington if one had the
resources, and Harriman had vast resources at his disposal.
One could, for example, wrest control of the Northern Pacific
itself from Hill. The Northern Pacific's shares were largely
available. Harriman proposed to buy out Hill's own property.

The audacity of the scheme was only equaled by its obvious
feasibility. Harriman and Schiff now proceeded to give Hill
and Morgan a return bout in the gentle art of Wall Street
tactics and strategy. Hill's biographer, J. G. Pyle, described
the Harriman–Schiff operation in Northern Pacific stock as
"swift and unsparing in execution." By March, 1901, Hill and
Morgan nearly had their Burlington campaign wrapped up.
Morgan's combination had done the buying, and in March
the Great Northern's directors officially gave Hill the authority
to use Great Northern and Northern Pacific funds to absorb
the accumulated Burlington stock. They ended up with about
97 percent of the Burlington's stock and they came perilously
close to buying that railroad for Mr. E. H. Harriman's use.

In late spring, their Burlington triumph completed, Morgan
took off for his annual tour of the European spas and art galleries, and Hill abandoned the coming Turkish bath of New
York City for the blessed climate of the Great Northwest.
Harriman and Schiff moved in.

Schiff maneuvered the Kuhn, Loeb buyers into position, and
Northern Pacific stock began to accumulate in their hands.

They were soon able to deliver to Harriman 150,000 shares of Northern Pacific common and 100,000 shares of preferred. With that platform Harriman took command and his structure of Northern Pacific holdings began to rise; it would be of colossal magnitude. The skill of the buying camouflaged the origins of the orders so completely that Hill's friends did some profit-taking themselves. There was nothing to be suspicious about in the gentle rise of the Northern Pacific stock. After all, with the Burlington acquisition it was natural enough that the prospects for the Northern Pacific should have brightened in the investing public's eye. Not only did the Northern Pacific's directors themselves sell 13,000 shares in the exhilarated market, but even J. P. Morgan's own firm presented 10,000 shares to the anonymous Harriman. The buying continued.

It was the end of April before Hill, out in Seattle, took alarm at the rise in Northern Pacific shares. His instincts were right. He knew there was something fishy, and he sensed the origins of the smell. The tracks were cleared to St. Paul, and Hill's special roared eastward. On May 3, he walked into the offices of Kuhn, Loeb & Co., and confronted his good friend Jakob Schiff with the evidence (Schiff clearly didn't mix friendship with business). Jakob Schiff was a gentleman of the highest integrity. He simply informed Hill that Kuhn, Loeb's buying was Harriman buying and that Harriman was out to control the Northern Pacific. Hill was astonished, but he said he didn't think it possible; that the Northern Pacific directors, together with Morgan, held too much stock. They, however, had been selling, taking profits, and Harriman had been buying. The stock exchange in those days was open half of Saturday. By the end of the Saturday session May 4, Hill knew how things stood and cabled Morgan (in Italy) for authority to buy immediately 150,000 shares of Northern Pacific common stock.

At that point Harriman might have controlled the Northern Pacific. The day before, his accumulations had reached a majority of the preferred shares, but was 40,000 shares short of a majority of the common. Since *both* the preferred and common had voting rights, Harriman had a technical majority. He controlled Northern Pacific on paper. However, under certain circumstances, the Northern Pacific's charter provided for the retirement of the preferred stock by the holders of the majority of the common stock. Harriman's control was thus vulnerable. He gave Kuhn, Loeb, on the morning of Saturday, May 4, orders to buy 40,000 more shares of Northern Pacific common. "I made up my mind that we should have a majority of the common shares . . . ," Harriman later recalled.

Here fate intervened in a variety of ways. Harriman was ill and unable to go downtown to attend to his affairs. It was Saturday and, accordingly, the devout Schiff was at his synagogue. He was Kuhn, Loeb's senior partner; Harriman's order was given for him personally, and the man at the office found it all simply too hot to handle. He went to Schiff's synagogue and sent in a note. Schiff studied it, sent a reply not to execute the order—he didn't think it necessary, and returned to his devotions.

The irate Morgan cabled back immediately for his lieutenants to buy the 150,000 shares of Northern Pacific common —that was all, just buy the shares. On Monday morning, Morgan's men carried out his orders quickly. A short panic developed as the Northern Pacific stocks spurted upward. But it was all over quickly, and the Morgan orders were completed. When the ailing Harriman found out that Kuhn, Loeb had not executed his buying orders it was too late to do anything.

As matters stood, anything could develop from a potential stalemate at the next Northern Pacific meeting, including a very splashy series of engagements between Harriman and Schiff with their total majority and Hill and Morgan with their majority of the common stocks. How it might have been resolved was never known because the Northern Pacific Panic now broke out.

The mechanics of the stock exchange include a "short interest"—those who bet on decreases or increases in stock prices by selling against future delivery or buying forward for future delivery. The whole Harriman campaign had been so skillfully conducted that the short interests had confidently sold right and left, believing that the final sharp increase in Northern Pacific shares could not last more than a few days. Harriman had purchased over an extended period of time and at only gently rising prices. But in the final week the Northern Pacific stocks had gone from 112 to 149¾, the strong finish provided by Morgan's purchases. That buying was, however, completed on Monday the 6th. It is clear that, between Harriman and Morgan, virtually all of the available Northern Pacific shares were controlled. Now the short sellers had to deliver.

But there was virtually no stock to deliver. In two days Northern Pacific went from 149¾ to over 1,000. The Wall

Street brokerage houses who had sold short, more than half of the total, were caught. It was as wild a panic and as weird a panic as Wall Street ever saw. The brokers dumped everything they had to try to get enough cash to deliver their Northern Pacific commitments and avoid bankruptcy (under the New York law, failure to deliver on time made a broker bankrupt). As a result, while Northern Pacific's prices soared, all other stocks plunged; some, like United States Steel common, lost as much as 50 percent of their value in two days. By 12 noon, on May 9, half of Wall Street's brokerage houses were technically bankrupt. It was as near as the Street ever came to extinction with no outside help. Since none of the Northern Pacific combatants wanted to see their colleagues swallow each other up on such a scale, arrangements were quickly made to let go of enough stock to allow the shorts to settle at $150 a share. More Northern Pacific stock had been sold than existed.

The story does not end there, but becomes confused. The Supreme Court finally straightened out the confusion in a history-making decision. There are two versions of the aftermath of the Northern Pacific affair, the humorless one and James J. Hill's version. According to the humorless version, Morgan and Harriman settled the control of the Northern Pacific by setting up the Northern Securities Trust, incorporated under the friendly laws of New Jersey in November, 1901. It was a holding company which controlled the Great Northern, the Northern Pacific and all their proliferations. The board of directors was a carefully balanced compromise of interests. Kuhn, Loeb published a statement saying that the Northern Securities organization ". . . will be left in the hands of J. P. Morgan personally"; that was enough to dampen the spirits of any prospective speculators and to assure that the compromise would be both delicate and precise. There were fifteen directors—six from the Northern Pacific, four from the Great Northern, three from the Union Pacific, and two independents. By "unanimous vote" the directors (who included Harriman) elected James J. Hill as president. Harriman surrendered all his Northern Pacific stocks in exchange for $82,500,000 worth of the shares of the new company. Morgan considered the whole arrangement something of a triumph.

According to Hill's version, he and his friends were growing old. Alarmed at the experience they had just passed through, they desired a large, solid holding company to be created to which their properties could be entrusted without fear of any further danger from outside raids. Since the Northern Securities' initial capital was $400,000,000, it seemed to Mr. Hill to be large enough for safety from the ambitions of any outside interests.

The State of Minnesota, in the persons of its highest legal authorities, declined either to view the Northern Securities Trust as a triumph of financial sagacity or as a club for aging railroad tycoons. Instead, the State of Minnesota viewed the Northern Securities Trust as "an illegal combination in restraint of trade" and so charged it in court under the terms of the Sherman Anti-Trust Act of 1890.

On Jan. 7, 1902, the State of Minnesota started action against the trust. On March 10, the U. S. government joined in with a separate suit. Two lower courts split in their opinions on the two cases, but on March 14, 1904, after two years of litigation, the United States Supreme Court, by a 5-to-4 vote, ruled that the Northern Securities Trust was illegal under the Sherman Act and had to be broken up. It was a momentous decision. It established that the lessening of competition was an illegal restraint of trade. It established the Northern Securities· Trust among scholars as the last great merger "for monopoly," which no doubt would have surprised Morgan, Harriman, Hill and Schiff.

In the dissolution of the Northern Securities Trust, Hill and Morgan got a plan through the courts for stock valuations which broke Harriman's control of the Northern Pacific. Their triumph over him must have seemed hollow though, because Harriman, with his uncanny "sense" of the market, sold out *all* of his holdings of Northern Pacific in 1905–06 at the peak of the market. The $58,000,000 he made in capital gain was the largest amount of profit ever made in a single stock transaction.

George Kennan, in his biography of Harriman, defended the Northern Securities Trust skillfully from a legal point of view (there *was* a defense after all, or else why the 5-to-4 verdict; did the justices not understand the law?), and held that a combination of politics and ignorance brought the trust to its end.

> Owing partly to popular ignorance or prejudice and partly to political demagogism, the public mind . . . was obsessed with the idea that combinations and agreements among railroad companies were made for the sole purpose of advancing or maintaining rates.

That was true; that was evidently just how the public was beginning to feel about it at the turn of the century, judging from the political capital to be made by "trust busting."

VI

In *The Robber Barons* Matthew Josephson said: ". . . by disposition Edward Harriman was a bear." It is difficult to agree altogether with that verdict (it is impossible to agree with most of the rest of Josephson's verdicts on Harriman). Cautious he was, shrewd he was, but no "bear" ever pushed the expansion-minded reorganizations that Harriman pushed. The "bearish" part of Harriman was that he knew what "enough" was, and pulled in his horns to avoid being caught in business-cycle downturns or in any other systematic fluctuations in values. Josephson also considered Harriman to be a taciturn pessimist, and many writers have thought him another Jay Gould. Such judgments just cannot be squared off with Harriman's life. In the first place, Harriman was an open-handed person in his dealings with men, whenever open-handedness was required. He was even public-spirited. He was a generous man too, and he was evidently that rarest of men, one without physical fear. Harriman also trusted people. None of these were characteristics of Jay Gould. Several incidents in Harriman's life may be cited to illustrate these points.

Harriman and his family (five children) lived a full and happy life in the community in which Arden, his country estate of thirty square miles was located, near Tarrytown, Orange County, New York. Monuments were erected there in his memory for the work he did in building up the local dairy industry, re-establishing the breeding of trotting horses, heading committees for the improvement of the county roads, dredging the river, and so forth. When he died his family gave, at his request, $1,000,000 and 10,000 acres of the estate to the State of New York as part of the Bear Mountain Park. Such a bequest does not make a Carnegie of Harriman, nor do his community interests make him a Jane Addams. But surely he cannot be classified altogether as a wrecker and malefactor on even that much evidence. In fact, Harriman even went in for eleemosynary institutions and founded a huge boys' club in New York, donated a building, actively participated in its operations and management, and made up deficits regularly from his own pocket.

In 1899 he appeared in Washington without warning to see

some scientists. He was planning a vacation cruise up the Inside Passage to Alaska and decided, entirely at his own expense, to take along a party of scientific people; he took two photographers, two artists and twenty-five scientists from leading universities, museums and government departments. Few of them had ever heard of Harriman before. Swain Gifford, John Burroughs, John Muir and G. B. Grinnell were in the party. Along the route to the coast, Harriman stopped the train periodically to show the scientists the various natural wonders. There was a stop at Shoshone, Idaho, for example, and the party went by saddle horse and wagon down into the long valley through the sage brush and over the purple-black lava rock to the edge of the Snake River Canyon to view the great Shoshone Falls in the pit of that enormous gorge.

Once under way to Alaska, Harriman allowed the scientists to plan the route as they pleased. While his family romped on the deck, Harriman went ashore with the exploring parties, carrying his full share of the pack weight. He several times risked his own life—for long hours and repeatedly—piloting the ship's launch to search for and pick up wandering exploration parties. He piloted the ship himself into fjords the scientists wanted to see when the captain and pilot refused the responsibility. The excursion went to Kodiak Island for a specimen of the Kodiak bear (Harriman shot two; they were the first ever taken for museum exhibition), and to the Pribilof Islands in the Bering Sea so the naturalists could observe the mating of the fur seals.

The ship also went across to Siberia to an Eskimo encampment. Both Hart Merriam and John Muir wrote books about the expedition, and there was an official publication of the expedition's findings in thirteen volumes. The scientific party was simply ecstatic about Harriman's good sportsmanship, personal bravery, kind and considerate character and the rest. They named a fjord and a glacier after him. The two-month voyage covered 9,000 miles and produced, in addition to the books, twenty-two scientific papers.

In April, 1906, San Francisco was nearly leveled by earthquake and a fire which lasted three days and nights. Harriman immediately ordered his railroads to put "all" their resources into the battle to save the city. He rushed to San Francisco. As he usually did, he assumed command of all who would follow his orders. His roads poured tons of supplies into the city and carried 225,000 refugees out—*all free*. Congress appropriated $2.5 million for supplies and the public at large donated another $10 million. The estimated value of tickets not sold and freight not charged by Harriman's railroads in the emergency was about a million dollars. Harriman issued a personal statement for the world's press saying that all was well enough and sound in the city, its railroads and docks intact, its prospects excellent. And that, from him, was doubtless worth much more than a million dollars in interest rates not charged when embattled San Franciscans were borrowing to restore the estimated $325 million worth of property that had been destroyed.

What Harriman's bill for his personal services might have been is unknown. In those days his services must have been worth a great deal indeed. He stayed in the city, organized work gangs and personally supervised the transportation and communications. After Harriman's death the *Railway World* wrote:

> When San Francisco was laid in ashes, it was Mr. Harriman who took personal charge of the situation. . . . It was primarily due to his organizing genius and energy, that San Francisco so quickly rallied from its great disaster.

One supposes that was something of an exaggeration. But the only question is, how great an exaggeration? He was there; he ran the railroads and river steamers; he must have contributed a great deal.

Harriman saved most of the Imperial Valley from being turned into a lake in 1906 on his own, without help from the U. S. government. The operation, carried out astraddle an international border, cost the Southern Pacific more than $3,000,000 in direct expenditures and took the resources of the Union Pacific and the Southern Pacific together, nearly stopping regular traffic for weeks.

The Colorado River had been partly diverted for irrigation and it flooded into the Imperial Valley (as it did periodically toward the Salton Sink), tearing a vast gap in its old bank, leaving its old channel altogether and emptying into the Imperial Valley. It would have made an inland sea of the valley. In a perfectly fantastic engineering operation, using thousands of workers (mainly Indians and Mexicans in special camps supervised by the Mexican *Rurales*), employing the great fill-carrying railroad cars that had been used on the Lucin cutoff, driving thousands of piles down into the roaring river, the Colorado was put back into its old bed and the weakened banks rebuilt with timbers, steel cables, stone and fill. The Southern Pacific's tracks had already been moved far above the areas threatened by inundation (the threat having been there long enough for the Southern Pacific people to take precautions) and the railroad was in no way responsible for the actions of the land-development company's earlier operations which had diverted part of the river and weakened its banks.

Moreover, Harriman pushed the work against expert advice (with the aid of insinuations from Roosevelt that Harriman himself was responsible for the flood). It is worth noting the exact words used by C. K. Clarke in his report on the saving of the Imperial Valley to the American Society of Civil Engineers.

> The writer desires to put on record the fact that the accomplishment of the work was due primarily and exclusively to the independent judgment and courage of Mr. Harriman, who persisted in his belief that the breaks could be closed, and his determination to close them, in the face of opposition, and regardless of the positive assertions of a host of eminent engineers that the closure was a physical impossibility.

Such a list of Harriman's positive contributions could go on at great length. But perhaps the point is made, as much as it could be; although Harriman was as ruthlessly efficient a financial protagonist as anyone, he in fact did not have exclusively the qualities of an "undesirable citizen" so generously attributed to him by the Rough Rider.

It was in the West that people first awakened to the fact that the grim little man might have been badly misjudged. After an official investigation had failed to find any crime in his railroads, and Harriman had saved the unhappy Erie Railroad out of his pocket, the clouds began to disperse to some extent. John Muir, whose perceptions can scarcely be questioned, said that he *saw* this in 1907, on a trip to Portland, Oregon, he made with Harriman.

> At the stations along the road he was hailed by enthusiastic crowds, assembled to pay their respects . . . and on the return trip a large body of Shriners, on their way to Eugene, stopped his train by taking possession of the track, climbing over the railing of his car, and literally took him by force and carried him away through the crowd on their shoulders, with cheers and hurrahs as straight from the heart as any I ever heard.

The careful cynic might point out that in all of these incidents Harriman was simply feathering his own nest. It obviously paid to build up the community around one's own home to keep out the riffraff. Juvenile delinquents cost more money in jails than in boys' clubs. Harriman might want to speculate in Alaska's future, or even build a railroad there, so scientific exploration was a necessary first step, and he had got the scientists cheaply enough (board and room). San Francisco was the Western terminus of his railroads; it would clearly be disastrous to allow that city to decline, so it was natural for Harriman to go out there to oversee his properties and haul in the free supplies provided by the government and the people. If the Imperial Valley were lost, the Southern Pacific would lose the freight that would otherwise accrue from the shipment of vegetables, and so forth.

Fair enough. In the year 1664, John Mun of Bearsted, County of Kent, England, had printed in London a volume of essays written by his father, Thomas Mun, a great merchant of London. The book is called *England's Treasure by Forraign Trade*. In the first chapter, "The Qualities which are Required by a Perfect Merchant of Forraign Trade," Thomas Mun says that the merchant is the "Steward of the Kingdom's Stock," that foreign commerce is a trust and should be always "performed with great skill and conscience, so that the private gain may ever accompany the publique good." In a famous passage in *The Wealth of Nations*, Adam Smith wrote in 1776:

> By pursuing his own interest (the individual) frequently promotes that of the society more effectually than when he really intends to promote it. I have never known much good done by those who affected to trade for the public good. It is an affectation, indeed, not very common among merchants, and very few words need be employed in dissuading them from it.

Accepting the cynical interpretation of his work, Harriman comes up to the highest canons of classical economic thought. If the cynic's interpretation is rejected, and it is admitted that Harriman had even less than the average quantity of human decency in him, then E. H. Harriman was an admirable character from the point of view of conventional American morality, then or now—heart or no heart.

VII

Harriman's influence in American railroads began to proliferate so extensively in the last years of his life that he was commonly pictured as a great railroad monopolist strangling the nation's arteries of commerce. This picture is one that seems to have irritated Harriman a great deal and he went so far as to write an essay about it, which he never released but which his biographer, George Kennan, did him the favor of publishing. Harriman was being charged with inflating his capital structures and then raising rates (he didn't, of course, but few people are interested in facts when they argue about economics) to exorbitant levels to carry his ballooning fixed charges. Harriman pointed out that such a scheme, however convenient, was no more open to a railroad than to a manufacturer.

> It would be suicidal for a railroad company to throttle or paralyze the industries along its lines by charging exorbitant rates. Even if there be no direct competition by parallel roads, every industrial plant located along a line of railroad is competing with plants located on other lines, and every railroad is forced to make such low and reasonable rates as will permit the industries in the territory tributary to it to make sales in competitive markets, and thus furnish the traffic from which the railroad company derives its earnings. It is impossible for a railroad company to sever its interests from those of its patrons.

He went on to say that if a railroad's capitalization were too high, it would be too bad for its stockholders, but the notion that a road could extort its customers "in defiance of the laws of trade," as he put it, was just erroneous. The railroad would kill its own territory.

There are two remarkable things about Harriman's little essay on the economics of railroads. First, it is a "long-run" view and has implicit in it the vision of growth and change in the economy. The typical analysis of monopoly pricing is strictly short-run, a changeless world in which the consumer is extorted. In the second place, there is the realization in Harriman's statement that the potential monopoly of a railroad is not the textbook one in which the monopolist must only fear raising profits so high as to attract competition, but rather, that the railroad, which clearly is in little danger of competition, will not see a growth of competition in its market but a disappearance of its market altogether. A monopolist's market can be lost if demand collapses.

Curiously enough, Harriman didn't think of the possibility of government seizure "in the name of the people" which is what is more likely to happen to a huge public utility like a

392 / THE ORGANIZERS

railroad, and which, with all the public pressure upon him
(the Interstate Commerce Commission investigation of his
roads), and the obvious vulnerability of all railroads to the
courts and the law, was a real threat. It seems that Harriman
was almost perfectly insensitive to "public opinion," and his
colleagues afterward maintained that he never gave it a second
thought. He simply refused to try to explain what he was doing
to anyone, even when his friends told him that his silence was
taken to imply that he had no defense. On balance, I doubt
that it would have done his reputation any good to explain
what he was up to. Few people sympathize with millionaires.

Harriman got on the Erie board in 1903. It had to be
arranged with J. P. Morgan and, while Morgan didn't object,
he was not enthusiastic about it. Harriman had given Morgan
lots of trouble. Yet Harriman had a perfect understanding and
appreciation of Morgan's virtues. In 1905 president F. D.
Underwood of the Erie decided that the time had come to
absorb the Cincinnati, Dayton & Hamilton Railroad, a small
Ohio line. Underwood accordingly told Morgan to buy it for
him and then charge the stock, worth $12,000,000, to the
Erie account. What followed must surely be one of history's
largest "money-back" guarantees.

When Harriman, who had been out of the country, came
back and examined the transaction he was appalled. The railroad was virtually bankrupt, and the one thing the Erie didn't
need was more money-losing territory. Harriman knew that
Morgan did no speculative business, and said to Underwood,
according to Underwood's own account (the style is typical
of Harriman):

> You made the trade with Mr. Morgan yourself. No one was
> present. You had better go and see Mr. Morgan, and you had
> better not depend on anyone else but yourself. . . . You had
> better go now.

President Underwood went "now" to Morgan and told the
great man that he had sold the Erie a faulty property. Morgan
could scarcely believe it, called for the balance sheets and,
failing to find them, asked Underwood to give his evidence.
When Underwood explained Harriman's opinion concerning
the Cincinnati, Dayton & Hamilton's condition, Morgan, like
any honest small-town druggist facing the return of a faulty
fountain pen, gave Underwood his money back—$12,000,000.
The Cincinnati, Dayton & Hamilton was soon in receivership;
Morgan was presented by the grateful Erie board with a scroll,

suitably engraved for the ". . . magnificent, unparalleled, and absolutely voluntary offer himself to assume the entire purchase, and to relieve the Erie. . . ." Morgan liked to keep his customers satisfied. In the spring of 1908, Harriman had to save the Erie from receivership out of his own pocket—a matter of lending the railroad $5,500,000 when the management could not borrow the money from anyone else.

Harriman was also on the board of the Equitable Life Assurance Society (assets of $400 million) with some other notables, including Jakob Schiff, James Hill and Henry Frick (now a New Yorker, having left Pittsburgh for the more genteel life of the big city). Harriman knew little about the company's affairs but supported a study by Frick which stated that both factions in an acrimonious management battle were incompetent to run the company. Both factions turned upon the directors and, among other accusations, asserted that Harriman had lent himself money at low rates. Otto Kahn urged Harriman to answer the charges. He replied: "Let them kick. It's all in a day's work. After a while they will tire of it. Nothing tires a man more than to kick against air."

There was nothing to the charges. Some years earlier, and *before* he was on the Equitable's board, Harriman had borrowed some $2.7 million of the Equitable's money, but had paid it back precipitately upon discovering that he could borrow the money cheaper elsewhere. But it was typical of the man to ignore the outcry against him. The Armstrong Committee investigation finally got into the Equitable's affairs, and the subsequent reorganization fell into the willing hands of J. P. Morgan.

One of Harriman's most unhappy experiences came when his old friend and colleague Stuyvesant Fish began to come apart at the financial seams. Fish had been with the Illinois Central for more than thirty years and was its president, but Harriman did not hesitate to throw him overboard once he became a hopeless case financially. In business Harriman was always ruthless. Fish had lent himself $1,500,000 of the Illinois Central's money to deposit in a tottering trust company in which he had a major interest, to keep that company's door open. Fish could not repay the loan. Harriman made Fish a personal loan of $1,200,000—at 5 percent, a rate Harriman said he could get for his money elsewhere—to carry his friend over.

But bad blood developed between them and Harriman led a movement which ousted Fish from the Illinois Central's presidency (in spite of an appeal by Fish that he needed the salary to pay his current living expenses). Fish was also barred from the board. Fish was a prominent and respected man; he charged that Harriman wanted to sell out the Illinois Central to the Union Pacific (a charge which Harriman typically ignored although he did in fact buy some Illinois Central stock for the U. P.), and the fact that Harriman purged Fish did Harriman little good in high places.

Almost to the end Harriman's policies continued to create great public uproars. In 1906 when he sold out his stocks in Hill's lines at such an enormous profit, as we have seen, the Union Pacific had something like $132,000,000 in its cash fund. At this point Harriman blundered. He proceeded to buy more than $130,000,000 worth of stocks in the nation's major railroads. That may have been (and many then and later thought it was) the most serious mistake Harriman made in his management of the Union Pacific.

The wrath of Congress, the press, the competition, the White House and other interested parties descended upon Harriman. He was subjected to a "one-man hunt" by the Interstate Commerce Commission. They failed to find that any crime was committed. But from that interlocking set of interests came the persistent government legal actions, beginning in 1908, which finally, after Harriman's death, resulted in the United States Supreme Court's order, under the Sherman Anti-Trust Law, to break up the Harriman empire, split up the control of the Southern Pacific and the Union Pacific, and divest those lines of Harriman's network of interests across the continent. Like so many empire builders before and after (most recently the DuPonts and General Motors), Harriman had finally gone too far; his interests were considered to be "too big" and a threat to the maintenance of competition.

Moreover, in spite of George Kennan's skillful demolition of Prof. W. Z. Ripley's celebrated inaccurate accounts of Harriman's affairs, there is no doubt that the vast stock acquisitions that followed the dissolution of the Northern Securities Trust and Harriman's uses of the proceeds had armed Harriman's enemies too well. Even if the charges did not stick to Harriman, the innuendos did. He went into the history books as a great monopolist, as well as a malefactor of great wealth, and the Supreme Court's dissolution of Harriman's empire burned the seal of official condemnation into all of it. One wonders how a financier so skilled could make such a wrong estimate of the impact of his actions. But many like him made similar blunders and continue to do so. According to his colleague, Otto Kahn, Harriman obstinately believed that he had made splendid investments with the U. P.'s great cash hoard.

Even in that, aside from the legal and political considerations, Harriman was wrong. What perhaps made his great blunder even more humiliating to himself, to his friends and later to his friendly biographers, was that it wasn't even a smart thing to do financially, as it turned out. The uncanny instinct that told him to sell out in 1906 did not hold up as it had in the period just preceding the Panic of 1893. Instead of staying in cash in 1906, Harriman bought railway stocks at the top of the market and was caught flatfooted a few months later when the Panic of 1907 humbled everyone but Pierpont Morgan. The "Little Giant" was finally the victim of his own hand, and the business cycle.

Perhaps the realization of that fact, among his peers, contributed to the noticeable softening of their attitude toward him in 1907 and the dissolution of the so-called Harriman Extermination League (an informal propaganda organization populated by many prominent financiers). They all had a lot in common now. There was a great deal of humiliation around Wall Street and much contrition among the mighty during the 1907 panic and its aftermath. The crest-fallen tycoons had been forced to file silently in J. P. Morgan's library to get their orders from the old man, who had come back to New York from his Episcopal Church convention to save them all. Wall Street was never quite the same afterward.

The Panic of 1907 disrupted Harriman's last great venture. In 1905 he had taken his family to the Far East. If one could tie a continent together with railroads, why not go the whole route? Harriman wanted to put together ships and railroads under a single management all around the world (and the Supreme Court thought the Union Pacific was big!). The Russo-Japanese War had just ended, with President Roosevelt presiding over the distribution of booty. Now was the time to capitalize on the good feelings. The scheme was not really fantastic, even though it was perhaps a century premature.

Harriman reasoned that the Japanese would be glad to get American capital to develop the South Manchurian Railway, which they had just got from the defeated Russians. The Russians had lost Port Arthur to the Japanese, so they ought to be willing to let Harriman manage their Chinese Eastern line and connect it to the South Manchurian. Since the Czars had traditionally been happy enough to let foreigners develop Russia's railways, the present government would doubtless give Harriman rights to remodel the trans-Siberian, double-track it and hook it up with the others. That much covered Asia and part of Europe. A line to the Baltic ports and a fleet of steamers scheduled from the Baltic to the Atlantic Coast of the United States would finish the job.

It was a railroad venture entirely worthy of the man. He negotiated first with the Japanese. They made a partial commitment, then balked because, under the terms of the Treaty of Portsmouth, the Chinese had to agree to any arrangements made about the South Manchurian Railroad, one of the economic concessions the Heavenly Empire had made to the occidental barbarians. As it turned out, the Chinese refused to allow any but Chinese and Japanese shareholders in the railroad. There was also much opposition among nationalists in Japan to allowing occidentals any of the fruits of the Japanese victory (Harriman and his physician were stoned in Tokyo by a mob). Harriman went to Port Arthur, Tientsin, Peking and to Seoul and the experience whetted his appetite for the venture.

In 1906 Schiff went to Japan and tried to induce the Japanese to reconsider the proposals and possibilities, but with no luck. In 1907 a chance came to build a new railroad in China to the Russian frontier, but in that year Harriman and his colleagues had troubles enough at home. In 1908 another chance to build in China faded with the death of the Emperor and then of the Dowager Empress. There was then too much political upheaval in China for railroad financing. It was too late for the scheme to come to fruition. The next year, Harriman's health began to fail. He went to Europe to take the waters, failed to improve, came home to Arden and death took him Aug. 24, 1909. He was buried at Arden. The world-wide railroad and shipping company died with him.

Many have speculated about what the impact of Harriman's last great vision might have been. The possibilities are of course infinite. But the reality? It is difficult to agree with those who have written that the course of history might have been changed. Efficient transportation systems in Western Europe never brought peace—prosperity yes, but not peace. Efficient transport in Asia would doubtless have brought a greater degree of economic progress than was experienced. The potential effects upon politics, military power and the rest would really be anyone's guess. One wonders what Harriman had in mind beyond profits. Doubtless he had some non-pecuniary motives. After all, he could make plenty of money at home.

VIII

The Little Giant of railroads has been an enigma in our history to a large extent, and will likely so remain. The fact that he was not one of those who explicitly linked his own and the nation's interests together in a flood of speeches and public statements, combined with Roosevelt's attack upon him, left Harriman pretty much in our history books as he was in life, a "loner." The disagreement with Roosevelt began over the financing of political affairs among the Republicans of New York State; but, as usually was the case with T. R., it soon got down to personal vilification. That never helped Harriman's good name.

When the basic railroad lines were completed, and their managements were sinking into bankruptcy and oblivion, the hand of the financier was required. Harriman was a master. He built a great railroad empire on the ruins of a pioneering era. The pieces of his empire remain and serve the needs of American economic growth. Harriman has passed into the nation's folklore as a somewhat shadowy malignancy to the muckrakers and their epigoni, and simply as a great financier to those historians with no doctrinal crosses to bear.

How much else there was to Harriman besides a masterful efficiency and a great intelligence is now, and will be, a question of high controversy. There is no doubt that his public relations program—silence—did nothing to improve the "image" he projected. He seems to have been mainly a man who went about his business in his own way, giving as good as he got where business was concerned and ignoring the rest. When he died, the encomiums poured forth, and even before he died he saw the tide of public opinion turning in his favor. Did it really matter to him one way or another? One can't really know now. Harriman himself observed that he had no time to bother with such matters. He said, "I need all of my time and energy to *do* things."

He did a great many things in a short time; but one thing he did more successfully than all others—he carved his niche in America's history without courting the historians. In spite of the failure of the government's investigation in 1906–07 to find Harriman guilty of any crime, in spite of George

Kennan's exquisite destruction of the specific charges made by Prof. W. Z. Ripley that Harriman's reorganization of the Chicago & Alton Railroad was a classic example of "stock watering," "abuses" and "frauds"—that the Harriman gang had "plundered" the road—(charges still faithfully recited as late as 1965 in history books); in spite of the blunt facts of the financial growth and stability of Harriman's empire; in spite of the Interstate Commerce Commission's admission in 1907:

> It has been no part of the Harriman policy to permit the properties which were brought under Union Pacific control to decline. As railroads, they are better properties today— with lower grades, straighter tracks, and more ample equipment—than they were when they came under that control . . .

—in spite of all that, the historians, for the most part continue to treat Harriman as a near criminal and a robber baron. Leo Durocher's theorem, that "nice guys finish last," is probably not true in the long run, or so it appears in Harriman's case. He wasn't a "nice guy," and he has been finishing last in the history books for a long time now, all evidence to the contrary notwithstanding.

Perhaps it is true that Harriman was simply Adam Smith's *homo economicus,* a man of invincible self-interest who was "led by an invisible hand to promote an end which was not part of his intention." Perhaps he wanted only profits for himself and made his great contribution to America's empire beyond the Missouri by accident. That the Supreme Court finally dissolved the Harriman empire says that the court found it to be too large and a threat to competition (would it be dissolved today, in a new era of giant amalgamations?), not that its construction had been immoral. Harriman made a great contribution to America's growth, but he got a bad press and will, judging from the history books, always have it. Paraphrasing Mary McCarthy on Trotsky, one is tempted to say to Edward Harriman's memory, "Well done, little man"— even though the hall is empty.

CHAPTER 9

J. Pierpont Morgan, the Investment Banker as Statesman

> I don't know what to do myself, but . . . someone
> will come in with a plan that I know will work; and
> then I will tell them what to do.
>
> J. P. Morgan in the Panic of 1907

The point of the quotation is to give a view of a period in American industrial history. Many critical junctures in J. P. Morgan's business career must have contained moments of indecision simply because Morgan, like the new industrial America itself at the turn of the 20th century, was attempting for the first time to find some general order or logic in a bewilderingly changing environment. How many railroad companies should there be? What is competition and what is monopoly? How big is "big" when it comes to the steel industry? Does a private businessman have any public duty? At the end of the 19th century the vestiges of Jefferson's Arcadia were fast disappearing and the nation was trying to learn a most difficult new skill—how to live as an urban, industrialized society. There were no ready-made ground rules. The only precedent was England, a hair-raising example. Amid a chaos of new and old doctrinal panaceas, men and governments simply tried what "worked" in given situations and, if the longer-run consequences appeared to be undesirable, there were always the statute books and the law courts.

John Pierpont Morgan was the one American financier of really titanic stature; the Yankee peer of Cosimo de' Medici, Jakob Fugger, Nathan Rothschild and Sir Francis Baring—a real Jupiter, and that is what men called him.

"Pierpontifex Maximus" Morgan ruled American finance like a Caesar. No one before him had such influence over others, and none since his death has aspired to his diadem. He died in 1913, which seems a long time ago to most Americans, but the consequences of his financial stewardship are still around us. His legacy is clouded to some extent by the remaining dust of the great turbulence of his times and by the memory of his seemingly enigmatic personality.

We still don't fully understand the history of the period in which Morgan's achievements were made, and this makes it very difficult to understand Morgan. Were the years from about 1870 to 1913 a period of progress toward a more efficient competitive economy or were they, as most historians seem to believe, primarily a time when trusts and monopolies threatened to kill the golden American goose? What we think of Pierpont Morgan depends largely upon how we interpret the American economy which developed during his adult years. If we ask whether Morgan was a great force for ultimate progress or simply a greedy, but consummately skilled, money monopolist, we are in a sense asking what American industrial development in the period 1870–1913 was all about. My own view is that the questions we have asked are not correctly framed; I don't believe that the answers could be of the "either/or" variety. Consider the bare economic outlines of the period.

<h1 style="text-align:center">I</h1>

The last quarter of the 19th and the first decade of the 20th century saw tremendous industrial development in the United States. It was in this period that we decisively became an "industry state." In 1873 American steel production had risen to 200,000 tons, still less than English production; by 1913 our steel output was 31 million long tons, more than that of all the European nations combined. We had 52,000 miles of railways in 1870, and 240,000 by 1910. Our coal output of 517 million tons in 1913 was greater than that of all Europe. Whereas our population of 39.9 million in 1870 had been less than Germany's 41 million, by 1910 our 92 million had outstripped Germany's then 65 million by far and was greater than that of Britain and France combined.

Although our population had more than doubled (1910 was 130 percent of the 1870 figure), estimates of national wealth show a fourfold increase over the period. It was the age of our most rapid growth of per capita income; in 1874–83 the rate of growth of per capita income was almost 3 percent per annum, or double the rate of the "roaring" 1920's. The ratio of net investment to national income in 1874–83 may have been as high as 18 to 20 percent. Over the period 1870–1910 as a whole this ratio was higher than in the 1920's. It was a great time for the investor if he didn't suffer from the short-term setbacks of the business cycle.

This great economic change had a profound impact upon the way Americans lived. By 1910 nearly half of the population lived in towns and cities, and more than 20 percent lived in cities larger than 100,000 in population. Such urbanization was a measure of the rise of industry—the old 75 to 80 percent rural economy of ante-bellum America was now just a memory.

The great change brought its own problems. Of the population of 1910, 13.8 million, or more than 1 out of 7, had been born abroad. This was another story. The new industry had been fed an army of foreign-born workers. From 1885 to 1910 more than 14 million came. These increasingly came from Southern and Eastern Europe and less from Northwestern Europe, whose industrial growth was providing for its own growing population. As a result, the workers in the new cities and factories of America were increasingly becoming "foreign" to the native stock which still predominated in the small towns and rural areas. Wages did not increase as did wealth and income per capita; money wages rose only about one-third and "real" wages only about 20 percent from 1873 to 1910. Although labor thus shared in the new abundance to some extent, it might be argued (and it was) that the working-man was not getting his full share.

The farmer too was having his troubles. They were the familiar ones. The nation has not, except in its earliest beginnings, been able to consume its agricultural product at prices which seemed adequate to farmers. From 1873 to 1913 farm acreage more than doubled (25 million to 52 million acres), and prices had fallen throughout the period from 1865 to the 1890's, with only brief cyclical interruptions in the descent. From 1896 on, there had been some improvement, but not enough to wipe out the long slide from the Civil War heights. Long-term farm debts, moreover, year by year became more burdensome as the terms of exchange did not turn in favor of agriculture. The period was mostly one of bitter frustration for farmers, who, time and time again, became involved in politics on an occupational (one might almost say "class") basis.

For those sectors of the population which were not fully sharing the profits of the new industry, the years were made more frustrating by a series of particularly bitter experiences with the business cycle. Downturns in business activity in 1873, 1884, 1893, 1903 and 1907 were associated with financial panics of varying intensity, those of 1873, 1893 and 1907 being especially severe. Periods of mass unemployment in industry, in conjunction with chronic distress in agriculture, were bad enough, but as they were combined also with periodic chaos in the nation's banking system, there was an increasing agitation for "reform."

The net growth of the economy was staggering in spite of the cyclical setbacks and, in an age before income taxes, great fortunes were made (and lost) left and right during the surges of economic activity. Accordingly, the Drews, Fisks, Goulds, Rockefellers, Fricks, Hills, Morgans, Harrimans and Stillmans—those who knew how to turn both booms and panics into profit—became the New American Rich. Their apparent affluence in times of both dearth and plenty gave rise to a belief, still commonly held, that "they" *caused* the bad times. Curiously, the argument was not symmetrical, and few thought to give them credit for the good times too. In the turbulence, not only was industrial America created, but so were the myths and traditions which are still our heritage from that "gilded age."

Perhaps the most important of the new alignments were political. The Republicans, the party of Civil War inflation and the greenbacks, came to associate themselves with the new industrial interests and wedded their traditional policies of protection for manufactures (the legacy of Hamilton, Webster and the old Whigs) to the rising sentiment to abandon the traditional American bimetallism and to put the currency on a more solid basis—gold. Our own GOP is still largely in the tradition of protection and "sound" money as a result.

The Democrats, coming back from the Civil War debacle, increasingly allied themselves with the dissident forces of the "small" businessman, farmer, worker, the men who came to cry for cheap money, greenbacks and "free silver"—for inflation. As a consequence, beginning in 1896, the fantastic and erratic William Jennings Bryan was three times the candidate of the party of the great conservative, Calhoun. The Democrats became, and remained, the party of the small man, the experimenters, the champions of low interest rates and a plentiful money supply. Paradoxically, the Republicans became the party of "business" and the rural North as the farmers became more conservative and alienated from the cities while the Democrats captured the votes of the cities and the rising industrial areas.

The great issues of the period fired the political boilers, and the journalists and historians added their fuel. We know the period today as a Babel of events and conflicting interpretations. Is there any other period so variously and ambiguously defined in our history as 1870–1914? Think of it: the age of the robber barons, the great picnic, the Populist revolt, the age of trusts, the epoch of monopoly capitalism, the railroad era, the time of the farmer's last frontier, the age of American imperialism, the American industrial revolution. The period saw the rise of the American labor movement, the Knights of Labor, the A. F. of L., the I. W. W., the contract labor scandals, the Haymarket massacre and the application of the Sherman Anti-Trust Act to labor-union "monopolies." There was also the great railroad amalgamation movement, the billion-dollar Congress, the anti-trust movement, free silver, the end of traditional American bimetallism and the Gold Standard Act of 1900.

All these events were part of the total fabric of our history in those years. It is fair to say that the most widely accepted interpretation of that period is anti-capitalist and populist in flavor. Such an interpretation may easily be justified, yet it is important to recognize that "history" is what the historians say it is, and in this case, the history of 1870–1914 is very largely what the muckraker historians said it was. That the period which saw such enormous economic growth should become known mainly as one of constricting monopoly is paradoxical to say the least. To say the most, is to say that both cannot have been true. Nevertheless, the muckrakers have been victorious.

It is not my intention to "rehabilitate" anyone. Even if the effort could be justified, I doubt if any pen could undo in a century the brilliant work of the muckrakers. The muckrakers are imperishable, but vulnerable. Vulnerable because of their main source of power, moral outrage. Morals change. The muckrakers left a baffling morass of special pleading and bias which is great fun for the reader but which is largely incoherent except as entertainment.

From our point of view the moral eccentricities of a Rockefeller or a Morgan are of little or no importance, since we are interested in the economic circumstances and impact of their works. Economics will therefore give us a different view of the period than did the moralist's outrage. We don't ask whether a man's acts were "good" or "bad" in a moral sense. It is clear enough, after all, that a lot of camels passed through the eyes of needles before the great American tycoonery of the

19th century ever got into Heaven. But why were they, as opposed to others, the tycoons? That is the interesting economic question.

The free market compensates its participants on the basis of a cold appraisal of their worth, given the state of tastes, incomes and technology. The civil law places bounds upon the actions of individuals vis à vis society. All else is a matter of individual conscience. Some consciences are more restrictive about "money getting" than are others. The interesting economic point about the "masters of capital," the "robber barons" and what have you, is that the burgeoning American economy suddenly began to pay enormous compensation for certain kinds of skills. Since this was so, we ask "which" skills and "why." This tells us a lot about how the economy grew. When Pierpont Morgan died in 1913, *The Economist* of London wrote:

> Mr. Morgan made his money almost entirely in America, and he was a typical American banker—quick, resolute, highly speculative, well versed in all the arts of the stock exchange, in company promotion, in the control of banks and other corporations, and, above all, in trusts, pools, syndicates and agreements. All his competitors regarded him as their superior. He was the Napoleon of Wall Street. . . .

To a muckraker historian this statement might suggest a worthy target for an opprobrious pen. To an economist it describes an obvious master of free-market capitalism in the process of organization and reorganization. Both views might be interesting, but the economist's view suggests a line of thought for understanding the way the man served his times. Morgan could not create his own world—no man has ever been so fortunate—but he could exploit the advantages which came his way and perhaps influence the future course of events. But "to influence" and "to create" are not the same infinitives. Morgan's America was, as we have seen, a land of fabulous industrial growth, and he was a man who was equal to his opportunities. The great market economy might baffle and frustrate a man of the frontier like Brigham Young, but it was a friendly ocean in which the Morgan cetacean flourished.

II

American investment banking grew largely out of international merchant banking, and consisted of the purchase and sale of negotiable bills of exchange drawn against the movement of commodities in international trade. Merchant banking was a highly specialized business in many respects—so highly specialized that until the 1830's there were few Americans in it. English houses handled most of the American trade, the bills drawn against American exports of cotton and grain feeding into the British financial system through the London merchant banks and discount houses. The whole apparatus of trans-Atlantic trade and payments was ultimately buttressed by the Bank of England's support in the discounting of trade bills. Access to the Bank of England's "parlour" (the equivalent of the "discount window" at a Federal Reserve District bank) moved crops from the American interior into international markets. This system was soon to move American securities from the offices of American company promoters into the mainstream of British international investment.

In the days before passports and visas, labor restrictions and the like, men moved as freely as goods throughout the Atlantic economy. As the British industrial economy came to depend increasingly upon the trans-Atlantic exchange of its manufactures for American food and raw materials, and a proliferating American financial system became increasingly involved in the movement of goods, it was natural that Americans should penetrate the trans-Atlantic financial network. It was a matter of specialization and soon enough the famous "Anglo-American" houses appeared in London: Brown-Shipley, Alexanders, Dennistouns, Barings, and George Peabody & Co.

Peabody, a Yankee merchant of Salem, Massachusetts, had pioneered the American entry into the North Atlantic financial hierarchy and was near the end of his long and brilliant career in 1854 when he asked Junius Spencer Morgan to come in as a partner. The new partner and his son were destined to lead the rise of international investment banking out of the nucleus already formed among the merchant bankers of England and the Continent and their far-flung networks of agents. The increasing pervasiveness of the international gold standard established long-term borrowing on a more easily convertible basis, reducing the risk accordingly, and the British appetite for foreign securities, together with the international expansion of railways and corporate industrial ventures, assured a freely flowing supply of securities. The Yankees who had joined in the business of international finance were riding the crest of a wave which was destined to reach great heights.

The Morgans were of old New England stock (the student of American colonial history would need to know little more of J. P. Morgan's genealogical background than that his great-great-grandmother's maiden name was Experience Smith). Miles Morgan, the direct American ancestor of Pierpont Morgan, came to Boston from England in 1636 and settled in Springfield, Massachusetts. Pierpont Morgan's grandfather, Joseph Morgan, a Hartford coffeehouse owner, landowner and founder in 1819 of the Aetna Fire Insurance Co., also discounted commercial paper. He thus was partly a banker. The family remembered his reading habits—he simply read the Bible from front to back, and then over again, and then again and so on through his whole life. The connection between Bible reading and business affluence in the Protestant world has been remarked by Weber, Tawney and others.

Joseph Morgan's son, Junius Spencer Morgan, was born in 1813. He was in every respect "his father's son," going into trade at 16 as a clerk in Boston. He worked in New York and, by 1836, was a partner in the general merchanting business of Howe, Mather & Co. back in Hartford. The firm added the name of Morgan in place of Howe in 1850. A year later Junius Morgan became a partner in the firm known as J. M. Beebe, Morgan & Co. of Boston, which house became heavily involved in merchant banking with George Peabody & Co. as its London correspondent.

Old Peabody liked Morgan and asked him to come over to London as a partner. Peabody had to weather the Panic of 1857 before he could get out of the turbulent world of Anglo-American finance, and he weathered that panic only with a loan of more than a million pounds from the Bank of England against his temporarily frozen assets of nearly £2.5 million sterling. Peabody and Morgan were firm Union supporters during the Civil War and aided the American minister in many ways. In 1865 the firm's name was changed to J. S. Morgan & Co. after Peabody's retirement.

Peabody's money endowed causes ranging from workers' housing in London to Harvard College, and he set up an education fund to assist the growth of learning in the Southern states (the Peabody College in Nashville, Tennessee, was established by his fund). Peabody was offered a baronetcy by Queen Victoria, and when he died in 1869 his body was brought home in a British warship. He was a great man of Anglo-American finance. As the senior partner in the firm which was to be the mainstay of the Morgan dynasty (J. S. Morgan, J. P. Morgan, J. P. Morgan, Jr., and their heirs) old George Peabody, the Yankee merchant banker, should be counted as one of the fathers of investment banking in America.

J. S. Morgan took over a well established and thriving business when Peabody quit. Before Morgan died in 1890 his firm had become legendary; the Morgan name was co-equal with the Barings and the Rothschilds in the galaxy of international financiers. Possibly the greatest single coup organized by Junius Morgan was the syndicate that floated $50 million in French government bonds successfully in 1870 when French fortunes in the war with the Germans were at their nadir. The profit to the syndicate was about 10 percent and the whole operation was a sensation in the financial world. Junius Morgan was a credit to Peabody's trust and built a mighty structure on the foundations of the old Peabody firm. John Pierpont Morgan used that structure to launch the greatest empire of financial power and influence the world has ever seen.

III

It is clear enough that the life of Pierpont Morgan could be no Horatio Alger story. Morgan was the scion of a brilliant, shrewd and powerful line. He was in every sense "to the manor born." It is conceivable that Morgan's aristocratic air was an important element in his power over his fellow tycoons. One thing Morgan had over them all was "style." It was a grandiloquent style, and no one else, no matter how rich, was in his league in that regard. There was also something else. Morgan was not just another shrewd Yankee, cutting a profit from sharp dealings. He had a penetrating and far-seeing mind, and his taste for affairs on the largest scale with long horizons was evidence of his sense of proportion in the roaring new American economy. To again quote *The Economist* when Morgan died, ". . . it should be added that his speculative operations were mainly, if not entirely, on the bull tack. He . . . professed the theory that a bear of American undertakings was bound to be ruined." They added that Morgan was "undoubtedly a man of genius with a strong will power and a commanding personality." He was all that and, for his time and profession, an educated man.

If indeed the child is father to the man, Morgan's personality as a child was an accurate guide to the grown man. His son-in-law, Herbert L. Satterlee, published a largely uncritical but informative biography in 1939 which contained a letter written by the 13-year-old to his teacher at the Hartford Public High School (the punctuation is as given).

> Miss Stevens
>
> I should like to enquire of you the reasons why you as a teacher and of course over me only a scholar should treat me in such an unhumane manner as to send [me] out of the class for laughing a little too loud which I can assure you I am perfectly unable to control and which no punishment will cure me of. . . . If I wanted I could sit still (without saying a word) in a corner and suppose all the class were to do it would not you think that all the class were very stupid indeed and you would have to do all the talking the scholars saying nothing. If I cannot be treated well . . . rather than be treated as I have been I shall next term [transfer to another class] . . . I do not say this hastily in anger but you cannot say but what I have stood it a great while and I think that upon reflection you cannot say but what I have been treated unjustly. . . .
>
> J. Pierpont Morgan.

We do not know how Miss Stevens was affected by young Morgan's carefully measured indignation. The tone of the letter was in many ways prophetic. In later life his forceful character awed and even frightened strong men. He was a careful, confident operator, and in affairs of business was much given to a very heavy hand. He kept his own counsel, chose his subordinates by his own code. The "Morgan men" were, as Frederick Lewis Allen noted, so much like Morgan that they were in many ways virtually incarnations of himself and he could trust them implicitly. His code of business was so rigorous that it astonished those who knew him. His insistence before a Senate Committee that "character" determined credit is still received by students of finance with a smile. Yet there is no doubt that Morgan meant it, but also that by "character" he meant something more than the right actions, the right pose, the right words, the right "image."

Morgan's education was capped by a year at the Institut Sillig, a boys' school at Vevey in Switzerland, in 1854–56 (where the master liked him and noted that he smoked at the age of 17) and at the great old German university of Göttingen from April, 1856, to the summer of 1857. At Göttingen, Morgan's facility with numbers so struck his mathematics professor that he urged the young man to make a career of mathematics, promising him an instructorship after an additional year's work. It was not to be, and before 1857 was out Morgan had entered the business world back in New York.

As a student the young Morgan had gained a reputation for his fine mind and for great physical strength. He was six feet tall, powerfully built and energetic. But he was also bothered by occasional fainting spells, headaches and skin eruptions of unknown origin which later in life settled into his nose and made his face a cartoonist's delight.

Compared to that of most of his peers in late-19th-century finance, Morgan's formal education was extensive. The great breadth of his adult interests together with the record of his schoolboy career indicate that intellectually he was a powerfully gifted man. Yet, somehow Morgan's biographers have failed to re-create a convincing portrait of him. Morgan destroyed the file of the letters he wrote to his father twice every week for years, so that key to his elusive personality is lost. The letters which remain are models of organization and accurate observation. He seems to have been a fun-loving creature, but also much given to admiration of system and order. The latter quality perhaps represented the frustrated mathematician in him.

The great organizer of industry and finance, the collector and patron of the arts, the gay yachtsman and the financial statesman of 1895 and 1907 are parts of a most complex personality. They are all compatible with the conservative New Yorker who would not move his residence to the fashionable part of town, who shunned the "society" of his time, who did not move his summer home from the Hudson cliffs to Long Island as that long strip of quaintness became fashionable.

Morgan always went his own way, following his own interests and instincts. However unfathomable he seemed to become as he grew older, he was always recognizable as the grandson of Joseph Morgan of Hartford, the son and heir of Junius Morgan; the strong-minded schoolboy and the gifted but undeveloped mathematician. If Morgan had not been the equal of the Vanderbilts and Rockefellers, and better than the Goulds and Fisks, it would have been surprising. It is a great advantage to have those qualities which make a "self-made" man in business; it is a much greater advantage, after all, to have all of them together with a brilliant and subtle mind, *and* to be the son of a rich and powerful father. So it was with Pierpont Morgan. He began as a prince of this life, and he carried it off.

But Pierpont Morgan was also true to his Yankee origins, shrewd, bold and religious. Like his Bible-reading grandfather,

Pierpont Morgan maintained his Episcopal faith. In fact he
was a prominent and devoted Episcopal layman, treating the
Bishops to free transcontinental railway tours, endowing holy
building projects and the like. Such activities in Morgan's life
were flamboyant gestures toward respectable, middle-class
America and must have made the cynics happy. Yet Morgan
carried his religious interests further. He was a regular
churchgoer, a church warden and long-time vestryman of St.
George's Episcopal Church in New York (imagine skimping
on the offering with J. P. Morgan passing the plate!). Morgan
sang hymns loudly in church, liking only vigorous and well
known ones. When he died, his will opened with words which
must have unsettled the plungers who emulated the old millionaire.

> I commit my soul into the hands of my Saviour, in full con-
> fidence that having redeemed and washed it in His most pre-
> cious blood he will present it faultless before my Heavenly
> Father. . . .

That, as his biographer Frederick Lewis Allen comments,
was the faith of Hartford, Connecticut, in the 1840's. Morgan
would be an easier subject for his biographers if he had in
fact been the stereotyped ogre of railroads and banks and steel
that the muckrakers wrote about. The difficulty is that the
20-year-old Pierpont Morgan who started out in business in
New York, just in time to witness the Panic of 1857, was flesh
and blood like everyone else. It is only what he accomplished
in his long life that is so difficult to comprehend. J. P. Morgan
was human enough.

IV

Although Morgan's beginnings in the banking business were
entirely conventional, they have been obscured by historians
and biographers who have started him all the way from
cashier down to assistant bookkeeper. The facts are simply
that, upon the young man's leaving Göttingen, his father (who
is quoted as saying at the time, "I don't know what in the
world I'm going to do with Pierpont") arranged a place for
him as a "volunteer" (no pay, or nominal pay) in the well
established house of Duncan, Sherman & Co. in New York.
They did some business with George Peabody & Co. and also
did a correspondent business with other foreign banks. The
system of volunteers is still a tradition in European merchant

banking and was in this country a century ago. It kept banking confined to those with funds—young gentlemen—gave firms a chance to look over their men, and provided a little free labor. It was essentially a very high-class apprenticeship system.

Morgan took up his work late in the summer of 1857, and was on the job in time to witness most of the Panic of 1857 and to hear premature stories of the demise of George Peabody's firm in London where the panic raged more than a month after sixty-two of the sixty-three New York banks suspended gold payments in a body. As an apprentice Morgan was not privy to the important affairs of his employers. This was probably their loss. Morgan was an ambitious and brilliant student. Banking is not unlike mathematics in some respects—there are answers to most of the questions. Jim Goodwin, his cousin, described Pierpont in 1857 as "just crazy to get into business."

Pierpont quickly learned the banking business and Duncan, Sherman & Co. quickly learned about young Morgan. In the summer or fall of 1859 the 22-year-old volunteer, in New Orleans to study the movement of cotton and its attendant financial paper, had purchased on his firm's credit a whole shipload of coffee and sold it at a handsome profit before his astonished employers had time to intercede, which they tried to do. Morgan was always proud of this, his first business coup.

Morgan followed the trade of merchant banking in a fairly conventional manner for a long time. During the Civil War he was involved in some minor affairs over which a great deal of noise was made by the muckrakers. In 1861, when he was doing some banking business of his own he lent $20,000 to one Simon Stevens, against a note of the United States government, to buy some unrifled carbines from the army ordnance, rifle them and ship them to General Frémont. Morgan also lent the money to rifle the carbines. The weapons were bought from the government for $3.50 each and sold back for $22.00 each. Morgan had his money back in thirty-eight days. He had lent money against a U. S. government note. A scandalous proceeding to Gustavus Myers (*History of the Great American Fortunes*), but of no consequence to two official investigations of the "Hall Carbine Affair," and a court ruling after a public trial.

A second "scandal" came in 1863 and involved gold speculation. Since the Federal government's greenbacks were fluctuating in value daily against gold, and hence against foreign exchange, the gold market offered a profit for quick wits. Morgan was in the gold market, at times speculating against the Federal currency. Biographers have considered this to be at best slightly off color or in bad taste, if not downright unpatriotic. Morgan was daily in the business of buying foreign exchange—as a merchant banker that was his everyday affair. Since the prices fluctuated daily, and he was not in business for his health, he bought in the cheapest market and sold in the dearest. I suppose he might have been patriotic and always sold gold at the official greenback price (as much as 40 to 60 percent below the market price) but he wouldn't have been in business long. Biographers should read books about banking.

Morgan also paid $300 for a "substitute" in the draft. As Matthew Josephson noted in *The Robber Barons,* very few of the business leaders of the late 19th century wore the Federal uniform (or the Confederate) in 1861–65. In the North, as in the South, the Civil War was evidently "a rich man's war and a poor man's fight." It is on record, at least, that Morgan "helped out" his substitute, whom he called "the other Pierpont Morgan," for some years after the war. It seems an odd way to raise an army, but the substitute system was general and accepted practice. There were millions of eligible, healthy and brave young American men who did not go to war in 1861–65. Morgan was among them.

Morgan's first, and tragic, marriage occurred in 1861 at about the time he lent Stevens the money for the carbines. On Oct. 7, 1861, Pierpont married his sweetheart, Amelia Sturges, although he knew that she was fatally ill. He took her to Europe, to the South of France, but she was dead within four months. He brought her body home to America. A widower at 24, he was married a second time in May, 1865, to Frances Tracy, daughter of a New York lawyer and the mother of his four children. J. P. Morgan, Jr., the second child and Morgan's heir, was born in September, 1867.

During the years after 1865, when his family was growing and Morgan was establishing himself in New York, Morgan's business interests were slowly expanding. He had taken on as a senior partner, an old acquaintance from Duncan, Sherman, Mr. Charles Dabney, and, accordingly, in 1863 J. P. Morgan & Co. became Dabney, Morgan & Co. They continued as agents for J. S. Morgan in London and followed the usual merchant banking line. Data for foreign-exchange transactions

I have seen indicate a remarkable success of Morgan's firm in international finance in these years.

Morgan had also been importing railway iron and had become sufficiently interested in the railroads to take his wife out to the West Coast and back in 1869, just as soon as the transcontinental line was finished. On this excursion they went down to Salt Lake City for an interview with the old Lion of the Lord. The transcontinental railway, a mortal threat to the old empire builder, was merely a diversion and a source of entertainment to the new empire builder. Every man in his time and element. Soon enough the rails would become a serious concern for the new empire builder. But he would not be threatened by them, he would become their master.

It was in 1869 that J. P. Morgan first showed his strength as an organizer of capital. It was a portent of things to come. When he arrived back in New York in September from his transcontinental tour, the "Susquehanna War" was on. Morgan, the merchant banker, now changed character, and in his first important financial engagement, at the age of 32, the investment banker took over and defeated none other than the Erie barons, Jay Gould and Jim Fisk.

The details of the Susquehanna War make a colorful episode in American railway history, and we will deal with the color. But the Susquehanna War is also a classic example of the process we are studying—the impact of the financial system upon economic growth. It is worth considering in a little detail. In a sense the individuals involved are perfectly irrelevant, especially from the "crude" Marxist view that only processes, and not people, count in the making of history. It is clear, however, that the *techniques* used in a given situation are the consequences of the choices of individuals. Consider the Susquehanna War.

First the process. As the American railway system experienced its booming expansion after the Civil War, much of the construction was done, as in the past, by relatively small companies. However, the technology of railroad operation dictated that in the majority of cases there were great "economies" available in large-scale operating units; larger companies were more efficient than small ones. This was not uniquely an American phenomenon; by the 1860's the English railways were also involved in a mammoth amalgamation process. As in the case of England and, for that matter, in this country today, amalgamation was the handmaiden of the proliferation of railway lines. The older and larger companies found it profitable to absorb branch and connecting lines. In most cases the smaller lines found it profitable to be absorbed. But sometimes they fought back.

Dramatis Personae. Joseph Ramsey, president and director of the Albany & Susquehanna Railway Co., a small line (142 miles long) connecting several main lines including the Erie, and opening a route for the coal of South Central New York and Northern Pennsylvania possibly all the way to the New England markets. *Judge Rufus W. Peckham*, State Supreme Court Judge, friendly to Ramsey. *Jay Gould*, the diminutive Mephistopheles of Wall Street, power in the Erie management, noted company wrecker, student and protégé of Daniel Drew, the wily old cattle drover and stock-market manipulator. Gould was one of the evil geniuses of American finance, favorite target of the muckrakers and probably for good reason. *Jim Fisk*, partner to Gould, big, gaudy, flamboyant and ill-fated (he was murdered). *Judge George G. Barnard*, Gould's judge, "owned" by Gould along with his stable of Governors, Senators and high Federal officials. *Pierpont Morgan*, Napoleon-to-be of Wall Street. *Samuel Hand*, Upstate New York lawyer and counsel to Morgan.

The Albany & Susquehanna Railway was started in 1863 and completed early in 1869. As with most railroads, "government" in one form or other (read Prof. Carter Goodrich's *Government Promotion of American Canals and Railroads 1800–1890*) was critically involved in the financing of construction. In this case, towns along the route traded their bonds to the A. & S. for stock in the road. The municipal bonds were then sold in the capital market to raise cash to finance construction, and the A. & S. stocks were held in municipal treasuries. The directors of the A. & S. represented the municipal stockholders.

Gould decided to add the A. & S. to the Erie network. This was to be done by simply buying the stocks from the municipalities until a controlling interest was acquired and Gould directors and a Gould management ruled the A. & S. There would be no great difficulty for a man with Gould's connections. It was a matter of "influencing" local politicians.

The buying began; Ramsey was alerted and issued enough new stock to keep Gould from control (Gould and Fisk had pulled the same stunt on Commodore Vanderbilt in a fight over the Erie). Accordingly, Judge Barnard issued an injunction restraining Ramsey from interfering with Gould's stock transfers, from acting as president of the A. & S. and from issuing any more stock. The annual election of officers was to be held on Sept. 7, and the stock transfer books were to be closed Aug. 7. With Ramsey under injunction, another director locked up the books and, before the Gould forces could break down the doors (which they did), the books were removed and hidden.

An injunction was now issued restraining Gould's directors, and Judge Peckham appointed a court receiver to run the property until the election. Fisk, in Albany, brandishing Barnard's injunctions, was forcibly ejected, thrown out of the A. & S. offices. All this was done by Aug. 7. With the law thus suitably deadlocked and a receiver "operating" the road, the Susquehanna War began.

Under a further writ from Barnard, the Albany sheriff seized control of the Albany property of the A. & S., and Erie train crews ran the A. & S. trains as far as Harpursville, Gen. Jim Fisk in command. At Harpursville a tunnel was "no man's land" and the Ramsey men ran the A. & S. on the Binghamton end. Private armies of about 6,000 men each camped at both ends of the tunnel; an engine was derailed; violence followed; the tunnel changed hands several times and the Governor ordered out the state militia to impose a truce upon the belligerents. With the state militia under General McQuade involved, private warfare was at a dead end and new strategies were called for. Judge Barnard accordingly issued an order setting aside Judge Peckham's orders. Judge Peckham followed with an order setting aside Judge Barnard's orders.

The air was quickly filled with suits and countersuits. What the law might be in the end, no one knew. Gould was evidently certain that he had sufficient stock and proxies to win the election which was to follow shortly. He turned the final details over to Fisk and concentrated upon the newest operation, bribing high officials in the Grant Administration to stop United States Treasury sales of gold long enough to enable Gould to corner the gold market—the spectacular "Gold Corner" of 1869, another of "Jay's little tricks."

At this point Ramsey was directed to Pierpont Morgan. Why he turned to Morgan is not clear. So far as we know, Morgan, a comparative youngster, had not entered into the industrial battles as any kind of Napoleon; there had not yet even been a "whiff of grapeshot" from Morgan's guns, let alone any major campaigns. Morgan was then a highly successful merchant banker, buying and selling foreign exchange.

He had not been in on the beginning of the Susquehanna War; he had been out West and had only arrived back in New York on Sept. 1, a week before the election. Someone "knew his man" and so Ramsey sought out Morgan. After reading over a memorandum on the situation, Morgan, who disliked Gould intensely, agreed to take on the Erie tycoons if Dabney, Morgan & Co. were given a completely free hand to conduct the campaign (this was to become the model of the later J. P. Morgan, financial Caesar; he did things his own way, the Morgan Way). Ramsey agreed.

Morgan moved quickly: there was little time. Dabney, Morgan & Co. bought 600 shares of A. & S. for their own account (the stock books were open by Barnard's first injunction against Ramsey). Judge Barnard enjoined them. Morgan retained Samuel Hand of Albany as counsel and proceeded. There would be lots of time later for legal proceedings. The A. & S. stock lists were studied carefully and the election was "organized" by Morgan, purging in advance enough Gould votes to ensure a Ramsey victory. The night before the election, Hand discovered dramatically (from the observation platform on the rear of a moving train) that Fisk was coming back to Albany with a train full of Bowery "stockholders" to take over the meeting. On the morning of Sept. 7, Morgan and Ramsey, playing the game according to the developing rules, met Fisk at the top of an outside staircase and the obese Erie tycoon was knocked backward down the stairs (his second violent ejection from A. & S. affairs). Whether Morgan or Ramsey did the physical work is not clear and not important.

Fisk and his "stockholders" had to be kept from controlling the meeting and were. Morgan locked the doors, Ramsey was re-elected president and Morgan himself was made vice president (his first trip as a railroad officer). Judge Barnard enjoined everything, but, before he could be reached, Morgan had leased the A. & S. to the Delaware & Hudson Canal Co. for 99 years. After all the suits and countersuits were duly adjudicated, Morgan won and Gould (recently enriched by successfully cornering the gold market and then breaking it by dumping at the peak just as the Federal government began to sell gold again) had lost. One railroad had passed under Morgan's thumb, going from conflict and chaos into the deep freeze of a Morgan reorganization. Many more would follow. Years later even the Erie was transmogrified by Morgan's reorganizing methods (and E. H. Harriman's ideas). Morgan hated disorganization and corporate chaos. It was later charged that his dislike for chaos was essentially a dislike for competition. We will deal with that in due course.

Thus ended the Susquehanna War. It was a small-scale model, in many respects, of the pattern which American industry followed in the years from the end of the Civil War to the early 20th century. Except for the ordinary criminal code, there were no rules or laws to govern the amalgamation of companies as the size of individual producing units grew in accord with the scale of operations warranted by the growth of the national market. There was groping, by companies, by the courts, groping by government.

Eventually the rules of the corporate amalgamation and reorganization game were agreed upon. But only after the wisdom of experience was gained. The mixing of men and law and money, as in the Susquehanna War, was to be repeated again and again, although not usually with violence, as parts of the raw, new and dynamically growing industrial economy went from adolescence into adulthood. Experience came, industry by industry with growth and aging. We see it all clearly enough now, but because of hindsight. At the time it was a great transformation and Pierpont Morgan became a colossus in that transformation.

Oddly enough, Morgan's victory in the Susquehanna War was no clarion call to him. We like to believe that heroes hear history's beckoning voice and step boldly onto the stage at the appointed hour, just as they do in the Hollywood pictures. History is sometimes too fickle for that sort of thing. In fact, soon after the Susquehanna War, Morgan was contemplating retirement from banking. Following his father's coup with the French bond syndicate in 1870, Pierpont was bothered again with a recurrence of his old headaches and his skin troubles. He had made enough money to provide a comfortable life, and his old partnership with Dabney had run its course. His cousin, Jim Goodwin, a business associate since childhood (they played at business as children), had decided to leave New York and return to Hartford. Morgan faced the prospect of reorganizing his business altogether and, although only 34 years of age, was experiencing enough *Weltschmerz* to consider giving it all up, at least for a few years.

Instead of that he was now to form a partnership with the Drexels of Philadelphia, which brought a great change in his affairs. The Philadelphia banker, Francis M. Drexel, had died in 1863 leaving his firm to his three sons, Francis, Anthony and Joseph. In May, 1871, Anthony Drexel telegraphed Morgan to come to Philadelphia for dinner. Morgan took the train down and came back to New York that night with the terms of a proposed partnership with the Drexels written on the back of an envelope. In response to Pierpont's protestations of ill health, Anthony Drexel had agreed to an immediate one-year leave of absence.

Morgan was to become a full partner in Drexel & Co. of Philadelphia and each Drexel was to be a partner in the New York firm of Drexel, Morgan & Co. By the terms of the partnership each partner shared in the profits on a *pro rata* basis of his contributions to the firm's resources (presumably including "labor"). Morgan agreed to this arrangement; the new partnership began business July 1, 1871, and Morgan sailed within a fortnight with his family for London. It was on this trip that he first visited Egypt, a momentous tour, the consequences of which we will consider in due course.

The new firm was one of great potential power, linking the Drexels of Philadelphia, Pierpont Morgan of New York, J. S. Morgan in London and a Paris affiliate, Drexel Harjes & Co. Within this framework Pierpont Morgan would become one of the most powerful international investment bankers in the history of finance. This international framework provided outlets which enabled a flood of American railway, government and industrial securities to find European buyers discreetly and efficiently. By such placements Morgan was virtually to eclipse his competitors.

The entry of Drexel, Morgan & Co. into the national focus came with the Federal debt refunding in the early 1870's, followed in a few years by the sensational sale of a large share of William Vanderbilt's New York Central stocks. After that there was an increasing number of spectacular financial operations, capped early in the 20th century by the organization of United States Steel, the Northern Securities Trust and an attempt to organize a gigantic international shipping combine. Throughout the period from 1871 to the early 20th century, Morgan's business was closely allied with structural changes in the rapidly growing national economy; the mark of the House of Morgan—tight organization, central control and "community of interest" among former competitors in output and pricing policies—was becoming ubiquitous. At the end of this period street vendors in London were hawking licenses to remain on earth signed by Pierpont Morgan, and Morgan, lavishly courted by king and kaiser, had become the symbol of international financial power. The notoriety both fascinated and repelled him. In his biography of the banker, Frederick Lewis Allen quoted the choicest comments from Finley Peter Dunne's "Mr. Dooley":

> Pierpont Morgan calls in wan iv his office boys, th' prisidint iv a national bank, an' says he, 'James', he says, 'take some change out iv th' damper an' r-run out an' buy Europe f'r me,' he says. 'I intind to reorganize it an' put it on a paying basis,' he says. 'Call up the Czar an' th' Pope an' th' Sultan an' th' Impror Willum, an' tell thim we won't need their savices afther nex' week,' he says. 'Give thim a year's salary in advance. An' James,' he says, 'ye better put that r-red headed bookkeeper near th' dure in charge iv th' continent. He doesn't seem to be doin' much,' he says.

By this time the "rules of the game" of the growing American economy were hardening and a complacent nation had awakened to the realization that "ruinous" and "cutthroat" competition were words which described a world most Americans might prefer to Mr. J. P. Morgan's community of interest when the "community" was limited strictly to management and stockholder. Morgan, the Caesar of Wall Street, organizer of finance, transportation and industry, came to be viewed as "the enemy" by those who fancied that their own views were the views of "the people." A nation which wanted more, not less, competition in industry had a right to change the rules of the game of American capitalism. But it is only justice to observe that, in the process, Morgan became the victim of *ex post facto* proceedings. But so did many others.

An examination of Morgan's main financial operations up to the Northern Securities organization shows a skillful and moralistic player of a part of the game of American economic development. What was involved was the stabilization and reorganization of institutions in certain industries which had to be realistically fitted into an economy which could not, or would not, support their existing structures.

The government refunding operation is illustrative of how economic change produced "technological unemployment" in even so sophisticated a sphere as investment banking, and none other than the fabulous Jay Cooke was to be the victim.

The Federal government's Civil War expenditures had been partly financed by the flotation of bonds at 6 percent. Congress authorized a refunding of 500 million of these bonds at 5 percent to take advantage of lower interest rates and cut

420 / THE ORGANIZERS

the cost of servicing the debt. In 1871, Jay Cooke, the Civil War financier, had formed a syndicate to sell the refunding issue, and the sales, not adequately organized, had not been satisfactory. Cooke needed an international market, but, even with powerful allies, seemed unable to put together a syndicate with sufficient resources.

In 1873 more of the new bonds were to be offered. This time Drexel, Morgan & Co. cut themselves in, allied with J. S. Morgan and Baring Brothers in London, Levi Morton (a partner and business associate with J. S. Morgan years ago in the Boston drygoods trade) and the Rothschilds in New York, London and Paris. For such an operation 1873 was a bad year, but the Morgan syndicate managed to place privately, partly in Europe and partly in the U. S., some 200 million of the refunding issue. Cooke had now been eclipsed and was, in fact, wiped out altogether in the Panic of 1873, leaving Drexel, Morgan & Co. as the leader among the major American financial houses with powerful international connections. The guard had been changed in Wall Street, and Jay Cooke followed Fisk and Drew into the dustbin of history.

Pierpont's international connections paid off again in the spectacular New York Central deal a few years later. The old Commodore, Cornelius Vanderbilt, had gone into railroads in the late 1850's and by the 1870's had put together the enormous New York Central System. When he died in 1877 his great fortune, including some 87 percent of the stock of the New York Central, went to his son William (considered until middle age by the Commodore to be simple-minded and kept on a farm on Staten Island).

William Vanderbilt was distressed at being the target of public abuse as the "owner" of the New York Central. Moreover, the New York Legislature could tax the road with impunity, knowing that the incidence was falling mainly upon a single unhappy, unpopular millionaire. Vanderbilt was advised by his associates to cut the extent of his ownership of the New York Central. The problem was how to market an enormous block of N. Y. C. stock without depressing the prices. Vanderbilt, impressed by Morgan's discreet placement of the government bonds, sought an interview with him. Morgan agreed to form a syndicate to take a total of 250,000 shares, valued at some $25,000,000, and place them quietly abroad. The placement was done successfully and, when news of the deal came out in New York, Morgan's reputation soared even higher. Moreover, his firm held the proxies of the English investors and Morgan, their representative on the Central directorship, was now a power in American railroading.

A year later Drexel, Morgan successfully placed a large issue of Northern Pacific stock. Morgan's firm continued its merchant banking business, and discreetly placed American securities with its European customers too. But Morgan was now a major force in the troubled world of American railroads and in the next two decades his hand was felt with increasing force as the new arteries of commerce were amalgamated and reorganized to move them from a land and construction speculation basis to a Morgan basis—profit making. The railroad economy was settling down to the task of making profits out of day-to-day operations, and Morgan, like Harriman, could see the role that the financier had to play.

Not only were the main trunk lines completed, but branch and connecting lines had been built into every area where a profit might conceivably develop from the rapid growth of towns and cities, the opening of mineral deposits and farm lands. The system had to be reorganized, and efficiency introduced into the ruins of the railway empires. Increasingly, Drexel, Morgan & Co. (J. P. Morgan & Co. after 1895) did the job. But there were others: E. H. Harriman, for example, was playing the same game as Morgan. Railroad reorganization offered a great field for the men of finance.

The first of Morgan's more spectacular settlements came in 1885. William Vanderbilt was in trouble again. In 1883 he had gone in with Carnegie and others to build a line through from Philadelphia to Pittsburgh to drain off traffic from the Pennsylvania Railroad. On the west shore of the Hudson a speculative line had been laid down in earlier years as far as Buffalo by Gould and others, roughly paralleling the Central tracks across the Hudson. This line, the West Shore Railroad, had been built to siphon off enough N. Y. C. traffic to force the Vanderbilt interests to buy it. This did not happen and in June, 1884, the line had slipped into receivership.

It was rumored that George Roberts, hard-bitten head of the Pennsy, would buy control of the West Shore and a rate war would commence between the nation's two largest roads. Morgan had watched this development carefully, and early in 1885 had gone to London to discuss N. Y. C. affairs with his father. Pierpont came back on the same steamer with William Vanderbilt (who had been vacationing) and began developing a plan to bail everyone out. By July, direct negotiations had taken place between Roberts and Chauncey Depew, president of the Central; but Roberts had proved to be "exceedingly obstinate." It was an extraordinarily hot summer and Morgan, who was now living on the princely scale the world remembers, invited the principal figures in the dispute for a cool cruise aboard *Corsair* (the first of three yachts with the same name owned by Morgan). Roberts showed up with his lieutenant, Frank Thompson. The party—Roberts, Thompson, Morgan, Depew and the crew—went aboard at 10 A.M. on the Jersey shore, and Roberts was not on the gangway again until 7 that evening. He had said very little as Depew talked on and on, but, mounting the gangway, he turned to Morgan, shook his hand and said: "I will agree to your plan and do my part."

Morgan now asked Vanderbilt for a Central lawyer and Vanderbilt sent him Judge Ashbel Green. Morgan laid out his plans and asked Green how to do it legally. When Judge Green gave his opinion that it could not be done legally, Morgan's characteristic comment followed: "That is not what I asked you . . . I asked you to tell me how it *could* be done legally. Come back tomorrow or the next day and tell me how it can be done." In the end it was done, and Morgan took the judge back over the scheme step by step and made him admit that it was legal. Morgan always savored his triumphs. It had been legal all right, but only after a great deal of fast court action which, at one point, saw Pierpont Morgan, Chauncey Depew and Judge Green as sole owners of the West Shore Road before they could transfer their newly acquired property to the New York Central. The N. Y. C. ended up with the West Shore Road, and Vanderbilt agreed to abandon the South Pennsylvania Road (Allen points out that part of the Pennsylvania Turnpike today runs over the roadbed of the old South Pennsylvania). Vanderbilt "dropped dead" three days after the West Shore settlement was completed, and the third generation controlled the old Commodore's fortune a scant eight years after he had gone to his reward. The South Shore settlement was especially sweet to Morgan because his Yankee father, upon hearing the details, had finally admitted that the boy (now 48 years old and without a peer in American finance) had talent. Satterlee, Morgan's son-in-law, is worth quoting on this filial point.

> Pierpont's father had never complimented him on anything that he had done but he said to . . . [Pierpont's wife] . . . the next time he saw her, 'Pierpont handled the West Shore affair better than I could have done it myself,' and this pleased Pierpont very much.

Presumably Junius could stop worrying about what in the world he would ever do with Pierpont.

After the South Shore settlement, the railroad reorganizations came thick and fast. By then the world of finance had come to recognize and fear Morgan's tremendous influence. The big laconic man with the blazing eyes and the long cigar not only had earned his father's praise, but Wall Street's deepest felicitations.

In 1886 Morgan decided to end the railroad confusion once and for all. He couldn't buy everyone out. Morgan was, in John D. Rockefeller's immortal words, "not even a wealthy man" (who was by Rockefeller's standards?) and, of course, Morgan had no client with sufficient resources to buy all the railroads in the country. But Morgan could, by the force of his personality and logic, together with the awe in which he generally was held, simply bully the railway tycoons, as he later could bully the bankers. Morgan called a meeting at his home, 219 Madison Avenue, of the heads of the Eastern railways and the relevant bankers. It was a stormy session but the tycoons filed out having, by "gentlemen's agreements," committed themselves to regional associations to regulate their business in an orderly way.

There was as yet no Interstate Commerce Commission to regulate railroad rates. In the absence of government power, Morgan himself filled the vacuum (the Supreme Court later frowned upon these agreements as violations of the Sherman Act). When the Midwestern and Southern railways failed to behave satisfactorily, Morgan rapped their knuckles too. In late 1888 and early 1889, the leaders of most of the Midwestern and Southern roads were summoned to 219 Madison Avenue and treated to Jupiter's views on the railway trade. Drexel, Morgan & Co., Brown Brothers & Co., and Kidder, Peabody & Co. were the relevant bankers represented.

As in the case of the Eastern tycoons, the provincial tycoons became gentlemen by agreement, a temporary one which was renewed periodically until December, 1890, when Morgan summoned them back once more to his parlor for two more days "under his personal guidance." The gentlemen worked out a system, the Railway Advisory Board, to handle their rates in accord with the new Interstate Commerce Act. The newly constituted Interstate Commerce Commission was glad to see such public spirit among the railroad officers, and Morgan viewed his handiwork with pride: "I am thoroughly satisfied with the results accomplished," he said.

In 1886 Drexel, Morgan had reorganized the Philadelphia & Reading; in 1888, the Chesapeake & Ohio. Morgan had been defeated in 1887 in an attempt to reorganize the Baltimore & Ohio, and devised the voting trust (the trust owned the voting stocks and Morgan appointed the trustees) to enable him to control the affairs of the reorganized roads relatively indirectly. Morgan tried to control his reorganized companies because, he felt, he owed their competent management to the stockholders who had become his clients. Morgan was increasingly placed on the boards of railways just for the prestige of his name, but more often to get his services in financial matters.

Morgan always wanted his own way. He would take complete responsibility, but he wanted the power to do the job as he thought it should be done, and he knew what he wanted. Depew said of Morgan some years after his death: "He differed from all other bankers whom I met in my efforts to raise money by his intuitive grasp of the situation and quick decision." Morgan knew his business so well partly because he had built a brilliant organization; his partners, especially Charles Coster, the railway specialist, had become minor gods in Wall Street. No one man could have handled the immense business that Morgan managed. His organizing genius was used on his own affairs as well as upon those of the railroads.

In 1893–94 when Drexel, Morgan reorganized the Richmond Terminal, no fewer than thirty railway companies in the Southern railway system were placed under a single management—Morgan management. In 1895 it was the Erie's turn. Plundered and plundered again by one of the wildest railway managements in American history—Drew, Gould and Fisk, the Erie had never recovered. It finances were now Morganized and Morgan's voting trust took over the management for an initial five-year period. The number of Morgan's railway reorganizations is too great to treat them all individually here. Essentially, the reorganizations had a common pattern: simplification of the corporate structure, reduction of the "water" in the capital structure, linking of small lines into systems wherever possible and control by a Morgan management.

Morgan was slowly bringing order out of chaos all right, but competition is sometimes chaotic indeed, and, as noted earlier, the nation had come to appreciate some of the major benefits of that chaos. Accordingly, with the Northern Securities Trust, a great Morgan railway reorganization became a landmark in Federal government anti-trust policy and a staggering and bitter defeat for Jupiter. The rules had changed and Morgan's methods were outdated, quite suddenly it seemed.

As we noted earlier, E. H. Harriman, financier and reorganizer of the Union Pacific, had attempted to buy control of the Northern Pacific Railway in his struggle with James J. Hill. Morgan was Hill's ally and had engaged in the Northern Pacific battle against Harriman, "that little fellow," and between Hill and Morgan, Northern Pacific stock rose from 112 to over 1,000 in three days—the Northern Pacific Panic—May 6–9, 1901. Morgan and Harriman, the great railway financiers, now had to settle with each other and, as a result, the Northern Securities Co. was formed, uniting the Harriman and Hill forces to be a community of interest among three of the transcontinental roads and all their connections. This had been another spectacular Morgan organization, and there were clearly more to come. But now the tide had begun to run out against Morgan's conception of orderly, organized, cartelized growth. The long-changing political consensus had been given a sudden, sharp focus.

In September, 1901, President McKinley was assassinated and Theodore Roosevelt, "that damned cowboy," as Mark Hanna called him, was in the White House. Both McKinley and Hanna were men of the kind Morgan understood and respected. Roosevelt, although of vintage New York genealogy, had a wild air about him. He railed against the trusts. (A trust was Morgan's notion of the ideal way to organize industries, to spread order and responsibility, but to the courts Morgan's voting trust was deemed simply a monopolistic device "in restraint of trade.") Roosevelt pilloried the old tycoons, the "malefactors of great wealth" as he put it at the Gridiron Club—some of Morgan's best friends were included. The long Victorian boom was ending, and as a counterpart to organization designed to protect the interests of the investors—the Morgan specialty—the pendulum swung back from the business oligarchy and the "Billion-Dollar Congress" era toward political democracy. The "little man," the farmer, the small-town businessman and the worker began once again to be courted by politicians. When McKinley was killed, the nation was, after all, little more than a decade away from the election of Woodrow Wilson. The tide had turned. In fact, the days of Morganized consolidation in corporate growth were already over when the greatest of Morgan's organizational triumphs, the Northern Securities Co., United States Steel and the International Mercantile Marine, were achieved.

In 1902 Morgan was informed that the Attorney General was out to break up the Northern Securities Trust. The banker is reported to have been perfectly outraged at this, mainly because of the implication that something organized by Pierpont Morgan could be deemed either illegal or immoral. He argued plaintively, in an interview with Roosevelt, that it was unfair for the government to attack his creation without prior consultation. Allen quotes Morgan as saying to Roosevelt: "If we have done something wrong, send your man to my man and they can fix it up." The Attorney General's reply told the story of economic and political change: "We don't want to fix it up, we want to stop it."

Morgan had played a vital role in bringing order out of chaos in the national transportation system. But the nation wanted a difficult compromise instead; it wanted both order *and* competition. Morgan and many like him had gone too far on the road to order, and would continue to do so, thus providing work for the Anti-Trust Division of the Justice Department. The new rules said: order but not collusion: competition but not chaos. The nation is still trying to find out how to play those rules (as the electrical company executives recently discovered during their tenures at the Federal prison in Norristown). In 1902 J. Pierpont Morgan was hopelessly out of the new game and he knew it. After the Circuit Court decision went against the Northern Securities Trust, in April, 1903, Morgan said to one of his counsel, Francis Stetson, "You will have a pretty job, unscrambling the eggs and putting them into their shells and getting them back to the original hens." In 1904, the Supreme Court killed the Northern Securities Co., and the hens and the lawyers had to sort it all out. As we saw in the previous chapter, to students of American industrial history the Northern Securities case marks the end of "merger for monopoly" in this country. Monopoly is a bad word. Morgan was not explicitly trying to organize monopolies, he was just trying to limit competition. To him there was a difference. To modern economists the difference is largely imaginary.

In 1902, Morgan attempted to organize another branch of competitive chaos, the ocean traffic, and put together a proposed International Mercantile Marine: 120 ships, owned by many of the larger lines including White Star. The securities didn't sell and by 1906 the scheme had to be abandoned. The oceans remained un-Morganized. An attempt to organize a New England railway network based upon the New Haven also failed, but only after Morgan's death.

Perhaps the failures he was experiencing by the early 1900's were offset in his own mind by the organization of the United States Steel Corp., the greatest merger the world had ever seen, and one which was considered by friend and foe alike to be a portent of the future. Morgan was operating in basic industries; the railroads had brought him into the coal industry, and when in 1901 he combined the greatest financial interests (including Rockefeller money) with the booming steel industry, the Morgan system seemed a blueprint of the future of American heavy industry. Historians have considered U. S. Steel as Morgan's greatest triumph. Possibly Morgan did too; Carl Hovey, who wrote an obsequious "court biography" (Morgan didn't like it) in 1912 "with Mr. Morgan's cognizance," as it says in the publisher's preface, considered U. S. Steel to be simply "his masterpiece." It was indeed a masterpiece of Morgan's organizational genius, and is worth studying from that point of view.

But Morgan's masterpiece was, in fact, the wave of the past. United States Steel did not grow with the industry; its share of output in 1901 was 60 to 70 percent but it could not hold such a share, and it was soon reduced by new growth in the industry (U. S. Steel's share is about 25 percent now). No more steel combines of such (proportional) magnitude were attempted, perhaps because of the law and the changing political climate, perhaps because of economics. More than once the great steel Leviathan's managers have protested that U. S. Steel is too big and unwieldy to be efficient, that it has run into managerial diseconomies because of its great size. It remains the largest single steel company, but in nearly two-thirds of a century no one else has thought that combining two-thirds of the industry's output under a single management would be the road to efficiency—a company which controls two-thirds of steel output could be organized without including U. S. Steel.

The great uproar over the steel corporation was a wasted effort. U. S. Steel was not the future of American industry. Some industries faced markets and technology which made the dominance of a few large firms logical, but other industries had different markets and technology. The subject of "concentration of economic power" is a complex one, but it has been, and is still being, closely studied, and the best students agree that, since 1910, there has probably been an actual decline in industrial concentration in manufacturing output in this country. Nor have the courts been prone to equate bigness with monopoly. The competitive economy was a vital force, and chaotic and wasteful or not, it was retained. Morgan's trusts and cartels, efficient or not, did not receive the public's support.

Doubtless his vast reorganizations were needed where they were successful at the time, and, in those vast reaches of American industrial development, Morgan played a vital role and is deserving of praise rather than censure. After all, half a century later, under partly different and partly similar pressures, the banks and railroads have taken the amalgamation route again. Morgan was neither the first nor the last financier to recognize that mergers are sometimes profitable. Morgan played the organizational game in his time until the limit was reached. The great new industrial economy of 1870–1910 encompassed such growth that many of its basic units had to be reorganized to face an enormous internal market.

The U. S. Steel merger is so well known that we need only trace its basic outlines here to illustrate Morgan's abilities at the peak of his powers. He was in his sixty-fourth year in 1901. For some time he had taken an interest in the possibility of bringing "order" to the steel mills. Morgan was present at a dinner in 1900 when Charles Schwab, of Carnegie Steel, painted a roseate picture of the economies of vertical integration, and Morgan was deeply impressed. He had assisted Judge Elbert Gary in the organization of the Federal Steel Co. in 1898. This company was an amalgamation of several minor companies and their connecting railroads; but if Morganization was to continue further, the most important steel interests must be brought together, and, most difficult, the "old man of steel" himself, Andrew Carnegie, must be bought out. Rockefeller interests controlled the Lake Superior soft-ore mines, most of which Carnegie leased, and the remaining major ore deposits were controlled by Morgan's old ally, James J. Hill, the Great Northern magnate.

Carnegie was a ruthless competitor, the most efficient producer of steel ingots, and had recently started a foray into steel fabrication, and was, at the same time, proceeding with plans to build his own railway from Pittsburgh to the coast to eliminate once and for all his dependence upon the Pennsylvania Railroad. Carnegie threatened the existing industrial and transportation balance in every direction. No one doubted that he could do whatever he pleased if he put his hard-grained mind to it. But it was also known that Carnegie was getting restive about remaining in the steel business at the expense of his plans for universal education and "the world at peace." In fact, he had given Henry Frick, his long-time friend, antagonist, partner, competitor (Frick knew Carnegie well), a $2 million option to buy him out, which Frick had lost. So Morgan faced his most enormous financing task. Would Carnegie sell?

After some conferences with Morgan, Charles Schwab, Carnegie's trusted lieutenant, went up to the St. Andrews Golf Club, played a round with the old man in the dead of winter and then asked him what his price would be. As we know, Carnegie wasn't modest; he wrote down a total in excess of $400 million. Schwab took the figure to Morgan, who accepted it out of hand (and later told Carnegie he would have given him $100 million more if necessary). Arrangements were now made with Rockefeller for the ores, with the companies which had been chosen for amalgamation: Federal Steel, American Bridge, American Tin Plate, National Steel, American Steel Hoop, American Sheet Steel, National Tube, American Steel and Wire. Thus commenced the great steel company, the largest ever created, with facilities for complete fabrication from raw ore to finished product. In March 1901 the world was astonished to find that United States Steel had a capitalization of nearly a billion and a half dollars.

The management was strictly blue-ribbon. Morgan had cut out the more objectionable principals (e.g., John W. "Bet-a-Million" Gates) from the management. Charles Schwab was to be president; Judge Gary, chairman of the executive committee, with Charles Steele as "Morgan's man" on the committee. It was an altogether breathtaking affair, $550 million of preferred stock, $550 million of common and $304 million of bonds.

Initial reaction to the new organization ran to two extremes; naturally enough, after three decades of trusts, mergers, amalgamations, cartels, pools, monopolies and threats of more, followed by rising public sentiment against such arrangements, there was high complaint that the free market was in danger, that the nation's industry was on the road to monopoly, that there would soon be an emperor in the White House and so forth.

On the other side were the men of banking and industry who knew that perhaps half of the Steel Corp.'s capitalization represented nothing more than "blue sky and water," and that the job of placing the securities would be a fantastic task, probably too big even for Morgan. There were also those, evidently including Carnegie, who believed that the steel corporation would fail as a business venture. The wily old Scot knew that more than one previous amalgamation had failed and that the properties had reverted to the bondholders at enormous profits. Carnegie had taken all his personal payment in bonds of the new corporation ($225.6 million), for which Morgan had personally congratulated him on being "the richest man in the world." Carnegie, perhaps in the spirit of sour grapes, had his own characteristic comment, quoted by Satterlee.

> Pierpont is not an ironmaster, he knows nothing about the business of making and selling steel. I managed my trade with him so that I was paid for my properties in bonds, not stocks! He will make a fizzle of the business and default in payment of the interest. I will then foreclose and get my properties back, and Pierpont and his friends will lose all their paper profits. Pierpont feels that he can do anything because he has always got the best of the Jews in Wall Street. It takes a Yankee to beat a Jew, and it takes a Scot to beat a Yankee.

Morgan fooled them all. U. S. Steel was not the road to monopoly control of the American economy; the securities were placed with ease, and Carnegie did not get to foreclose. Schwab did his job, as he had always done under Carnegie, and the corporation's growing assets soon absorbed the water. U. S. Steel was not, in my judgment, Morgan's greatest triumph at all. That was to come in 1907 when Morgan was an old man. United States Steel might have been organized by others. It was, in any case, the capstone of a long development of American industrial growth and was nothing more than a very large company in America's future. Other, less well publicized achievements of Morgan's had, I believe, more of an impact on the future of the country. But in the railway and industrial amalgamation movement, Morgan had been *the* man of his times, and no one can gainsay him that.

By the early 20th century, with the dissolution of Northern Securities by the courts, the failure of the International Mercantile Marine, and the public's option to encourage competitive, rather than Morganized, growth in industry, it was clear enough that Morgan's great organizing ventures, the sensations of the day, would be enveloped by the expanding national economy. The railroad organizations scarcely can be considered the salvation of American railroading (at the time of this writing it is not entirely clear what the future and salvation of the nation's railroads might be), and the great steel company would become simply another giant firm (there is "price leadership" in more industries than steel), and by no means the largest in the country.

V

In his later life Morgan became an art collector on a colossal (such a superlative is justified) scale and it is not inconceivable that he achieved his greatest personal influence in America's destiny by his love of beauty and hence by his patronage of the Metropolitan Museum of Art. There is nothing really paradoxical in this assertion. The overall productive ability of a people (the illusive word "productivity," output per man hour, is used by economists as a pretense toward quantitative knowledge of the phenomenon) is a mysterious and obviously complex combination of traits, not really well understood, but certainly very highly correlated with the general extent of education among all strata of the population. By "education" we include the presence of all those aspirations for the achievement of both material and esthetic objectives which motivate populations and governments toward long-range habits of industry and intelligent organization of resources, habits which make economic and cultural progress possible.

There must be the urge to save and improve. Without such an urge, output is devoted mainly to consumption, and investment with technological change is not possible. The implantation of such aspirations in underdeveloped countries since 1942, the "demonstration effect" (phraseology from the lexicon of recent economics jargon), is judged by many to have been one of the chief revolutionary forces at work in the "new nationalism" which has overthrown the empires of the pre-1914 "new imperialism." In the underdeveloped countries, some of them rich in artistic tradition of their own, the introduction of modern consumer goods produced the desire for economic advance.

In the United States, rich in the gimmickry of modern consumer technology, the introduction of fine art of the highest quality has wrought a desire for quality in the lives of Americans. Without such desires we doubtless would have drowned by now in a sea of household appliances and hillbilly recordings. Morgan's paintings, porcelains, tapestries, sculptures, miniatures and so forth, which he brought to America, have vastly enriched the country; they have provided several generations of students with a free education. Not only must one take into account the more or less direct impact of the Morgan collections upon designers, students, architects and artists, but, perhaps more important, the esthetic impact and the indirect consequences in terms of general "enrichment" of the culture which have been carried away from the Metropolitan by the millions who have filed through the galleries of Morgan's collections for half a century.

Morgan himself seemed to view his great gift to the people in a Victorian way, an attempt to uplift and civilize the savages. Morgan, after all, was no "man of the people"; he was a patrician. But he was perfectly aware that his collections would change the country's life and, for that reason, toward the end of his life he became obsessed with the task of finishing off his collections and making provision for their public use. His collections were nominally valued at $60 million when he died. Morgan wanted the bulk of it to go directly to the Metropolitan Museum, but like many a humbler "do-gooder," Morgan discovered to his dismay that "the people," as represented by their elected officials, were not pressing to be uplifted; the city of New York balked at putting up funds for a museum extension to house the great collection. It was therefore left to his son to dispose of the collections, to "render them permanently available for the instruction and pleasure of the American people," as it was put in Morgan's will. In the event, about 40 percent of Morgan's collections ended up in the Metropolitan Museum, and the rest was scattered. As Aline Saarinen put it in her recent book, *The Proud Possessors:* "The Morgan collections represent the most grandiose gesture of *noblesse oblige* the world has ever known."

Probably a professional analyst could convince himself that he understood Morgan's motives completely. The mere historian will have to settle for less; Morgan was a terribly complex man. Of course it is tempting to just lump Morgan, Carnegie, Rockefeller, Frick, Huntington, Stanford and all the rest together and argue that they somehow had bad consciences about their wealth. While this might seem to make some sense on a priori grounds—they were men of religious belief and knew about their Savior's attitudes regarding idle wealth—it is also clear that this procedure is too simple. It deprives each man of his individuality, and anyhow, where is the *direct* evidence to support such a view? Like the others, Morgan, considering his business career, makes a curious and slightly unbelievable picture of Christian humility. Was it simply a matter of generosity run riot? Certainly Morgan had always been a generous man, but he had other traits.

The objects in the Morgan collections, especially the paintings, represented the streak of New England conservatism in their owner. At the time he seemed to many to be a reckless collector who was buying out the down-at-the-heels European aristocracy at exorbitant prices. Yet it is clear now that he was a shrewd buyer who mainly got what he wanted, proven masterpieces. He had no taste for "modern" work in art or in music. His conservatism was symmetrical. He was a strong supporter of McKinley and practiced his old-fashioned New England Episcopal faith, believing in the efficacy of "good works," of individual Christian charity as the main palliative for the social evils which were so evident in the New York of his time. He supported innumerable personal and public charities, educational institutions (including the Harvard medical school), hospitals, camps for boys and so forth. On these enterprises he lavished several fortunes. But there is no evidence that he recognized any areas in social reform which called for government action.

Morgan was also a strictly old-fashioned family man. So long as Junius Morgan lived (he died in 1890, thrown from a carriage in France at age 77), Pierpont dutifully wrote him his long weekly reports, and every year journeyed to London to visit the old merchant banker. The main holidays were occasions for family reunions and feasts at home. He was senior warden of his church (St. George's) and had the rector regularly for breakfast on Monday morning—a ritual. In 1871 Morgan bought Cragston, near Highland Falls on the Hudson. That remained his summer home till his death. In the fall of 1882 the family moved into their home at 219 Madison Avenue, and that remained Morgan's New York home.

Some biographers have wondered why Morgan never moved his summer residence out to Long Island when the Hudson Valley lost its appeal as a summer retreat, or why he never moved "uptown" with the rest of New York's wealthy families. It would have been strange if he had done so. Morgan was strictly indifferent to changes in styles, tastes and opinions. He was one for family, old friends, established customs, the Episcopal Church and a protected private life.

Even his clothes, frock coat, silk hat, wing collars, were worn without noticeable change in fashion—except for the fancy waistcoats he favored when he was on the yacht.

I don't mean to imply that Morgan was in any sense a "stuffed shirt"; he wasn't. He was just an old-fashioned Victorian gentleman of means with the conservative habits and tastes of a family of Yankee bankers. But there was also something of the prince in Morgan. He enjoyed entertaining, either in his home or wherever he happened to be, on his yachts or, when abroad, in the hotels and on the vessels he favored at sea. He liked good food and good talk, but limited his circle of dinner companions to those he would care to invite into his home. On such occasions, whether they were dinners given in his private capacity, for example, as a prominent Episcopal layman, or in his many official capacities, commodore of the New York Yacht Club, president of the Metropolitan Museum, he entertained lavishly. A fireworks barge drawn up Long Island Sound to amuse the Yacht Club, Louis Sherry and his staff taken to San Francisco to cater for the Episcopal Bishops (on that excursion a lady reported seeing Morgan tip an astonished railway porter with a $100 bill), a selection of solid-gold Egyptian trinkets given to the ladies after dinner as favors, these were domestic gestures typically in the Morgan manner.

He seems to have been interested in sports, but not excessively so. His son-in-law said that Morgan took no exercise of any consequence and ignored most of the "rules" of good health. He did some fishing. He smoked one cigar after another and played endless games of solitaire, the latter doubtlessly representing more of the mathematician than the sportsman. He raised prize collies at Cragston and sponsored racing yachts. His own yachts were used almost as floating homes when he was in the city during the summers and the family was at Cragston.

Morgan continued to be abrupt with people throughout his life. In many ways this represented the simplicity he preferred in all personal dealings. At his office he usually worked in full view of his staff, and he looked after his business affairs meticulously, even to the extent of auditing the accounts (at the New Year in 1913 when he was in his last year and in poor health, the figures from the firm's operations for 1912 were brought to him at his library for his audit). Morgan never "retired" from business. When he was questioned in 1912 by the Pujo committee, his answers were simple and direct and showed that, even in his seventy-fifth year, he was still master of his house. It was on that occasion that he nonplused his inquisitors (and the public and generations of historians) by bluntly asserting that, so far as he was concerned "character" and not collateral was the primary basis of credit: ". . . a man I do not trust could not get money from me on all the bonds in Christendom."

With all the air of mystery around him, Morgan actually was no man of mystery at all—although a complex one—except possibly by way of contrast with the "400" of his day. His habits were perfectly regular, almost like clockwork, including each year a few months abroad, visits to his father in London, regular attendance for the "cure" at Aix-les-Bains, a favorite watering place; visits to galleries and art dealers. In his old age the bulbous nose made him terribly shy and he tried to avoid the inquisitive gaze of the public. He had little use for the popular press anyhow, and the possibilities of photography made him go to some lengths to avoid reporters. This perhaps contributed to the "enigma"; he tried to avoid extensive or close observation by the public. On the other hand, he seemed to enjoy having his *presence* noted wherever he was. On his return from Europe each year the *Corsair* would meet him at Quarantine, streamers and flags aflutter, family aboard, and Morgan, in a boyish gesture, would wave his handkerchief slowly back and forth along the rail to return the salute (the *Corsair* also had a brass cannon which was sometimes fired to salute him).

Morgan had become a fabulous "figure"; he knew it, but did not relish all that went with being a celebrity. It was gratifying to be entertained by the President, the Kaiser and the Prince of Wales, to have Lord Kitchener to dinner, to advise the King of the Belgians on his investments, to have tea with the Archbishop of Canterbury, to be received by the Pope and by the Sultan. It was a pleasure to have one's own yacht come out in the channel to meet the ocean steamer and pilot one safely and directly to one's own mansion overlooking the Hudson. But it was no pleasure to be stared at, to have one's private affairs the subject of speculation in the press. Morgan relished his stature but hated the price he paid for it. "Pierpont the Magnificent" claimed the perquisites of his position, but J. P. Morgan, son of Junius Morgan, scion of old Yankee Bible-reading stock, sometimes could not bear the burdens of his own magnificence. He was plagued, actually to his dying day, by his fame.

It was as an art collector that "Pierpont the Magnificent" seemed farthest in character from J. P. Morgan the investment banker. Morgan went after his collections with gusto. He had been associated with the Metropolitan Museum since its founding in 1870 and was among its first backers. By 1904 he was its president. Morgan wanted to make the Metropolitan the greatest art museum in the world. But he wanted more than that; he wanted it to be an educational institution covering the widest range of fine arts. To achieve these ends it was inevitable that there should be Morganization.

In 1906 he successfully prevailed upon Sir Purdon Clarke, director of London's Kensington Museum, to direct the Metropolitan—Coster in railways, Judge Gary and Schwab at U. S. Steel—Morgan knew the value of intelligent and trustworthy management. The Morgan control, as in industry and finance, was maintained. During Morgan's tenure as president the trustees met at his house—again reminiscent of his business affairs. Moreover, he soon added a glittering bevy of fellow tycoons to the board to assure a solid base.

Morganization was of course extended into the process of acquisition since he was acquiring the majority of the objects initially for his own private collection. He employed agents, placed his confidence in selected dealers and utilized system; wherever possible he relied upon confidential expert valuation of objects in which he had an interest. He built his collection quickly, most of it after the mid-1890's. He bought on an enormous scale and was accused by his detractors of buying in ignorance. As Aline Saarinen pointed out, time has shown that he was shrewd indeed in his purchases; only a small percentage were of questionable value, and an even smaller proportion were fakes. His methods were resented by many and constituted a revolution in the art market. Yet the student of his business career sees nothing really novel in his collecting methods. The typical Morgan patterns are all there. All that is novel is that, after decades of making his fortune, he was now investing it in assets which he proposed to give away.

Since Morgan had always loved quality and cultivated a deep understanding of his own affairs, it is not surprising that, once he turned to collecting, he became a close student of the market in which he was operating. He became especially attached to figurines, miniatures, illuminated manuscripts, early bindings, and manuscripts of noted works. It was not just paintings and statues with Morgan. He was an educated man with sophisticated tastes. After the lovely Morgan Library was completed in 1906, he brought part of his collections together there and spent silent hours with his treasures. As a student at Vevey and Göttingen, Morgan had learned to sift and rake the dirt beneath the stained-glass cathedral windows, finding bits and pieces dropped there centuries earlier by the practitioners of the great medieval art. In the library the glass was fitted into the windows of the West Wing. The old man spent his declining years basking literally in the light of the ages as the sunshine filtered through his youthful collections.

Those who have written that Morgan was merely a rich American mindlessly piling up the treasures of the Old World are lost in ignorance of the man. He was passionately addicted to beauty and symmetry all his life. The touch of the mathematician never left him. Satterlee tells of a basketful of recently unearthed Egyptian baubles brought to Morgan during one of his excursions in Egypt, and Morgan afterward relating that he could feel the beads of nervous sweat running down his back as he watched the small objects being uncovered for his inspection.

Egypt became a special passion. He had first gone there to see the treasures of antiquity in 1871. On later trips he chartered river steamers to carry him up and down the Nile, and finally had a special all-steel steamer built for the same purpose. It was named *Khargeh,* after one of the primary archeological sites of the Metropolitan's expeditions and a favorite spot of Morgan's. In 1909 Morgan had personally inspected the diggings and had all the processes explained to him. After that the Egyptian Department at the Metropolitan was especially generously treated by Morgan in his official capacity, and he financed some excavations himself. In 1911 Morgan personally opened the Metropolitan's magnificent Egyptian exhibition. By that time he was nearly at the end of his tenure as president of the museum and was beginning to gather his vast acquisitions to present them to the Metropolitan, and to the City of New York. He arranged to have customs inspectors go to Europe to examine his collections before shipment so they would need to be crated and uncrated only once.

At this point Morgan tasted the cup of bitterness. In Europe there was public agitation to prevent the movement of his treasures. In New York, the Board of Estimate and Apportionment, under pressure from the Hearst newspapers (strange as *that* seems considering San Simeon) not to assist the old millionaire, balked at appropriating money to build a new wing to house the collections. Morgan, benefactor of the Museum of Natural History, the Metropolitan Opera, Madison Square Garden, the New Theatre, the Cathedral of St. John the Divine, the Lying-In Hospital, a trade school, the Y. M. C. A. and a dozen other of New York City's social investments, and having helped to buy and preserve the New Jersey Palisades from being "developed" as a rock quarry, and who in 1907 had taken over the city's finances as we shall see, was now refused any municipal contribution whatever to house the greatest artistic benefaction in history. The story has been told many times, and need not be told again here.

Morgan's fifteen-year assault on the world's art was, even viewed simply as a way to spend 60-odd million dollars, a fantastic accomplishment. He brought his collection all home anyhow and did not deviate from his scheme to give it all to the City of New York in spite of the willful ingratitude of that city's elected officials. He could have given it to other friendly cities, Boston, London, Hartford, but he stuck with Gotham. Morgan's death in 1913 intervened and, as noted earlier, the City of New York received only about 40 percent of the total. Even so, Morgan had made the Metropolitan Museum indisputably a peer (or better) of the Louvre and the British Museum. For that, if for no other reason, New York, as well as the nation at large, has reason to cherish the old banker's memory.

Why did he face resistance on his scheme for the Metropolitan? This had, after all, developed into his primary interest —the object of his long career. Possibly Morgan the patrician had no idea how the ordinary New York political leader might view a Rembrandt self-portrait. This is not difficult to comprehend—consider the sniggering reception the Kennedy Administration's bill in 1961 to assist the arts was given in the United States Congress. It was Morgan's dream to make the world's great art freely available to the ordinary U. S. citizen—but the ordinary citizen hadn't asked to be thus enlightened. Certainly the political leaders in New York hadn't requested esthetic improvement. If it was not absolute folly in the early 1900's to expect the people's gratitude for such a gesture as Morgan made, it was certainly premature in terms of the nation's cultural advancement, vastly premature. Nevertheless, the nation has used the great collection in due time and has received the benefits of Morgan's largesse, if not in precisely the manner and sequence he might have wanted.

Possibly Morgan's rejection by "the people" in the matter of the museum wing was due to the Panic of 1907 and its aftermath. Morgan, who had played his role in financial reorganization for nearly four decades, had not been allowed to retire quietly to his art collections. In 1907 "history" called him back again to the center of the dynamic and unstable economy, and his actions in stemming the tide of financial panic brought charges that he and a "money trust" controlled the nation. He was investigated in 1912 by the Pujo committee, and his troubles with the officials of New York City may simply have been political; he was too controversial. However, if the events of 1907 contributed later to his temporary undoing at the Metropolitan, Morgan's actions at that time were his greatest personal triumph and, being so singular in our history, will be remembered so long as financial history is written.

VI

Imagine a situation arising in which the presidents of the major financial institutions of New York City would file into the private quarters of a 70-year-old man and agree to use their combined resources in any fashion that the old gentleman might suggest. It sounds like a science-fiction plot. Who could imagine such a thing? Yet that is what happened in 1907. Morgan was the old gentleman, and no other single event in his life so sharply illustrates the personal prestige he had acquired in his lifetime. Morgan's role in the Panic of 1907 also serves to illustrate another aspect of the nation's economic development, the maturing of the commercial banking system which had grown up during the 19th century.

To comprehend Morgan's actions in 1907 one needs to understand three factors: (1) the absence of a central bank, (2) the growth of the commercial banking system and (3) the problems produced by the first two factors during the "business cycle."

There was no central bank in the United States from 1836 to 1914. We had had two institutions which performed essential central-banking functions (mainly government finance and credit control). The First Bank of the United States was chartered by Congress in 1791 for twenty years. In performing its central-banking functions it generated sufficient opposition so that the charter failed to be renewed (by an incredibly close margin: one vote in the House and a Vice Presidential tie-breaking vote in the Senate). After the Federal government's financial disasters in the War of 1812, the virtues of a central bank were appreciated enough so that a new one, the Second Bank of the United States, was chartered for twenty years in 1816. Its charter ran out in 1836, and Andrew Jackson vetoed the recharter bill. He charged that the bank, by constraining the note issues of the commercial banks, was becoming a giant money monopoly (which any self-respecting central bank ought to be, but which the Second Bank of the United States emphatically was not). The charge created a romping ground for historians out of which two Pulitzer prizes have been garnered, for largely opposing viewpoints.

From 1836 to the establishment of the Federal Reserve System in 1914, the United States had no central bank; the Treasury filled in some central-banking functions in times of crisis, but when the Treasury needed a central bank, there was no recourse save private initiative (Morgan's in 1877, 1895, 1903 and 1907) or varying shades of disaster.

During the 19th century the American commercial banking system developed into its present unique form of thousands of banks, mainly without branches across state or even county lines. The system had grown up on the basis of state charters until the National Banking Act of 1863. In that year there were (not including unincorporated commercial or savings banks) more than 1,408 state banks and the 66 national banks. Because the notes of the state banks were taxed and the new national-bank currency was not, the number of state banks had declined to only 277 by 1873 while the number of national banks grew to 1,908, making a total of 2,245 banks in that year.

The number of national banks rose to 6,422 by 1907, but, as the system of demand deposits and checks came into general use, the tax on state banknotes was no longer a hindrance (notes were no longer issued by state banks). The advantages of state charters, which included generally lower reserve requirements and relatively lax auditing methods, brought the state-chartered bank back to popularity with bankers. By 1907 there were 11,469 state banks, making a total of 17,891 commercial banks (compared to 13,462 today *and* a central-banking system) with their correspondent connections, all operating on a fractional-reserve basis, all promising to pay out legal tender and gold coin for deposits.

In addition there had grown up a system of nonbank intermediaries—life insurance companies, savings and loan associations and so forth, which kept deposits with the commercial banks. Finally, the trust business, management of investment portfolios, estates and the like had been wedded to the commercial banking business. In the thousands of small units lay considerable danger.

In a financial system based upon fractional-reserve commercial banking, the system as a whole is illiquid by definition. It cannot pay off all of its deposits at once, or even a very large (larger than its cash reserves) proportion of them. A single bank might borrow from another, and banks in one city might borrow from banks in another city or from abroad; but, unless there exists a central bank empowered to *create money* on its own credit, the financial system must close its doors if the depositors "run" on their deposits. This simple fact is as true today as it was in 1933, 1929, 1907, 1895, 1884, 1873, 1857, 1839, 1837, 1834 or 1819, except that during the crises of those years there was no Federal Deposit Insurance Corporation and before 1914 there was no Federal Reserve System; there were just the "gold standard" (bimetallism before 1900) and fractional-reserve banking—incompatible if there were deposit runs. And there often were.

During downswings in business activity or in periods of deficits in the balance of international payments, the reserves of the banking system tended to be reduced and credit extinguished. With no immediate legal sources for monetary expansion, interest rates rose quickly to high levels. Capital values were reduced and there was credit stringency and, if apprehension mounted sufficiently among depositors in the thousands of tiny independent banking units, wild, blind unreasoning panic broke out like the plague. Runs commenced, sweeping away banks by the score and any temporary economic setback could become a rout, following by deep depression and mass unemployment. The ultimate defense was for the banks to close their doors. There were temporary devices to buoy up "confidence": e.g., the bankers' clearing houses could issue their own "money," scrip used in clearings. The Treasury, if it had the necessary bullion reserves, might make flamboyant gestures, like moving gold into a city in plain sight of the public as it attempted to do in the Panic of 1857 in New York. But time after time the banks were forced to close, dealing a body blow to credit, ruining thousands, and spreading chaos and disorganization in a business community that was already in distress.

Even if there were no central bank, reserves might be pooled to aid individual banks to keep panic from becoming

general and inexorably fatal. But strong leadership of extraordinary quality was needed to organize the terrified bankers
to use their reserves to help each other when their own banks
might be assaulted at any moment by depositors. Such leadership among private bankers in this country did not exist until
Pierpont Morgan came along. He taught the bankers of
Christendom a vital lesson in 1907 and kept an economic
downswing from being intensified by a general banking
collapse.

Morgan had had considerable experience in mobilizing bank
resources on a general scale in the national interest before
1907. In 1877 when Congress adjourned without appropriating money for the army's payroll, Morgan had arranged for
army vouchers to be discounted at cost by commercial banks
to pay the soldiers. Until the Gold Standard Act of 1900, the
country had a bimetallic currency which worked very badly
at times.

In 1893–95, under balance-of-payments pressures plus continuous exchanging of Treasury notes which had been paid
out for newly mined silver by the Treasury (a consequence of
the madcap legislation of the silver interests in Congress) for
gold coin to export, the Treasury's gold reserve was dangerously low. Morgan, in consultation with President Cleveland,
formed a syndicate to market United States government securities in Europe in payment for gold which he *guaranteed*
the President would come into the Treasury, and it did.

The silver interests and professional enemies of Wall Street
were outraged that the American government should be forced
to turn to a private banker. The absence of a central bank to
engage in market operations which would attract gold actually
gave the government little choice beyond refusing to sell gold
—a violation of the currency laws. That the effects of the
transaction wore off and that after six months gold began to
flow out again, further enraged the enemies of Wall Street.
Morgan offered to repeat the transaction but Cleveland decided to try a direct Treasury sale instead.

Morgan, incidentally, was evidently more efficient than a
central bank might have been. If the exchange rates were at
the ordinary gold export points, as they clearly were, the
astonishing aspect of the transaction is that Morgan was
able to assure Cleveland, and come through on his promise,
that the gold would come to this country. Precisely how he
managed this is not known. Even though lasting only six

months, for a private banker to stem the gold outflow of the United States was a breathtaking feat.

What Morgan did in 1907 was in many ways more impressive than his gold operations were in 1895, because in 1907 he was battling the public itself. He played the central banker's role in suppressing the panic, against the clear wishes of the depositing public to run on the banks and get out their money. Although a central-banking tradition had been developed in England, it was by no means so generally accepted as central banking is today. Indeed, as late as 1878 Walter Bagehot, in *Lombard Street*, was still against the tide of opinion when he argued that the Bank of England (which was then privately owned) had public obligations which were stronger than its private interests.

But Morgan's memory was long; in 1907 it was half a century long. He knew from experience that a central bank, even with such limited resources as the Bank of England had, could have powerful effects at the margin during crises if its credit were given liberally at crucial junctures, even if at high rates of interest. In the Panic of 1857, for example, the Bank of England had conducted an inordinately conservative campaign but that campaign had saved the center of the money market, prevented a general bank run and had in the process saved Junius S. Morgan and George Peabody.

Could a similarly conducted campaign at the center of the New York money market suppress the general spread of panic? Morgan had, after all, a business in London and watched from a vantage point the Bank of England's actions during crises in 1857, 1866, 1873, 1884 and 1890 when the tradition of central banking at the Bank of England was maturing. It is conceivable that, on the basis of his own experience alone, by 1900 Pierpont Morgan knew as much about central-bank operations during financial panics as did anyone outside the Bank of England.

During the brief financial upheaval in 1903 Morgan had begun plans for establishing a pool of banking reserves similar to the London pool of 1890 organized by the Bank of England's Governor Lidderdale to save the firm of Baring. The pool was not needed then, but in 1907 the need for centralized reserves was immense, and it took all of Morgan's powers to galvanize the banking fraternity into collective action.

The reasons for the 1907 panic are not clear to this day. Like the other "business cycles" we know about from extensive economic analysis, the 1907 crash was probably highly individualistic and no one but a fool or a charlatan would attribute the crisis to a single cause, like the journalistic "overspeculation." That the 1907 crisis was a financial contraction which followed a "real" downturn in economic activity is clear enough; the few available indicators illustrate that. There were signs of a slackening in the pace of business activity; bank clearings in New York reached a peak in 1906 and declined slowly throughout 1907; building activity throughout 1907 was well below 1906 and even 1905. Interest rates (commercial paper rates) for short-term money had gone up already in 1906 and remained high and went higher in 1907 before the crisis, indicating the "tightness" of money as free bank reserves were reduced to the limits. Business failures had been rising in 1906 and by mid-1907 were up sharply. Finally, stock-market prices had started falling late in 1906 and, by early 1907, the alarm was already out that the market was jittery, dangerously so. Morgan was told that before he left the country on March 13, 1907, for his annual European cruise. Soon afterward, a Morgan syndicate selling railway debentures folded and the securities were absorbed by the syndicate members, because the public had bought only 1 percent of them. Conditions were bad.

The year 1907 was Morgan's seventieth and was begun by his moving into the new library and completing plans for the Wadsworth Athenaeum in Hartford as a memorial to J. S. Morgan. Pierpont also went to Washington and met with President Roosevelt about impending railway legislation and spent some days consulting with Senator Aldrich on proposed banking reforms. The European tour, beginning in March, was of the type which had now become the familiar Morgan summer in Europe—a triumphal tour by the old millionaire and his numerous entourage to the galleries, tourist sights, watering places, official entertainments, all in the glare of an inquiring but largely unwelcome publicity.

In 1907 there was no Egyptian excursion, but the European tour was fairly glorious anyhow—London, Paris, Rome. The *Corsair* had been ordered to meet Morgan on the Adriatic and anchor off Venice. Morgan was back in London on June 22, picked up his wife, who had just come over; off to Paris and back in England on board the *Corsair* by Aug. 1 for the regatta of the Royal Yacht Squadron at Cowes. It was observed that Morgan's yacht was only less impressive than the one belonging to the King of England. By Aug. 21, the banker was back in New York for a while to appraise the

J. PIERPONT MORGAN / 445

business situation and then, as a lay delegate to the Episcopal convention at Richmond, Virginia, rented an appropriate mansion, engaged Louis Sherry to cater for his guests and was off to attend to affairs of the spirit. The ecclesiastical idyll ended abruptly Oct. 19; Morgan's partners wanted him back in New York, and fast.

On Saturday, Oct. 19, Morgan's private railway cars started rolling back to New York and to his most trying and greatest personal triumph. Jersey City Terminal was reached early Sunday morning; Morgan and his party crossed the Hudson and broke up. As Morgan put his daughter Louisa on the train to Highland Falls, he told her that he viewed Monday morning at the Stock Exchange with apprehension. He went directly to his library where a group of his partners and colleagues awaited him. By lunchtime Morgan was hard at his solitaire (he played it intensively in times of crisis). Now the news had spread that he was back. The press was refused admittance to the library and set up a "picket line" (which remained for nearly two weeks) across the street and watched the ashen-faced financiers file in one-by-one to talk to Jupiter. It was time to hang together.

Harriman came, "bold, aggressive, ambitious and over-worked"; the Little Giant of Railroads instinctively came to the one man who could unite the financial world. James Stillman, sardonic and cold, head of the National City Bank and banker to Mr. John D. Rockefeller, came. Stillman knew what Morgan was worth and didn't like to admit it. The great ones filed in and the meetings with the old man lasted until after midnight. There he sat, an enormous old man of few words, implacable, with the bulbous nose and blazing eyes, the wing collar and huge cigar, the steady gaze; each man must make some kind of peace with Morgan. For some it must have been sheer hell. But it was Morgan or isolation. It was late Sunday, Oct. 20, 1907; the Panic of 1907 would begin next day and the "terror-stricken bankers" (the London *Economist*'s words) knew it. Morgan was Wall Street's "greatest practitioner" and no one doubted it. At 70 years of age there was still no one else; his will and presence remained supreme. It was an altogether remarkable thing.

As always, Morgan put together an organization to direct his campaign. His partners, especially George Perkins, were of course privy to the operations—it was their money as well as Morgan's that would be used for grapeshot. In past financial crises the effectiveness of the Bank of England "at the margin" came largely from the bank's command of information regarding the affairs of the main financial firms at the center; no funds must be wasted salvaging firms which could not be saved. The weak must die.

To gain intimate business knowledge quickly, and incredible amounts of knowledge at that, Morgan wanted a staff of bright young men from the main financial houses to do leg work and all-night auditing. He and Perkins chose such a staff at breakfast Monday morning, the 21st. Among the elect was Benjamin Strong, then a young vice president of Bankers Trust and destined, with the blessings of the House of Morgan, to become the first governor (the title for the job is now "president") of the New York Federal Reserve Bank. Governor Strong became, by acclamation, America's greatest central banker, admired even by the enemies of central banking. Morgan chose young men of quality to grapple with the affairs of 1907.

Finally, Morgan kept at his side Messrs. Baker, Stillman and Steele, representing the First National Bank, the National City Bank and J. P. Morgan & Co. Baker and Steele were "Morgan men" from way back, Steele a partner. Stillman was a Rockefeller man and had long since become a confidant of Morgan's, if a highly independent one. Baker and Stillman had joined Morgan in 1903 in the proposed pool of $50 million of central reserves, so all the older men could well imagine what was coming. The young ones soon found out. Strong later reported nights without any sleep spent poring over records and wading through vaults as Morgan's *ad hoc* central bank burrowed its way into Wall Street to find the sources of weakness and strength.

Monday morning was mainly spent in observation. Morgan listened to some financiers; he avoided others. What was it going to be like? No one knew for certain. The first giant financial institution to totter and fall apart was the Knickerbocker Trust. Morgan was a stockholder, knew its affairs were very bad indeed. He made no move. The Knickerbocker Trust was doomed. The Knickerbocker's checks were being refused; lines of depositors were forming, and the panic would soon sweep the bank away. Tragedy or not, resources could not be wasted on such a shell. Meetings among Morgan and his colleagues lasted until late in the night; a more general run, in the wake of the Knickerbocker Trust failure, was expected next day.

On Tuesday, call money on the exchange reached 75 percent. The panic was getting worse. Morgan could now see the outlines of his problem. He summoned the presidents of the major clearing banks, asked for their "figures" and on that basis allocated the amounts of the pool each bank was to prepare for. That day the 70-year-old Morgan had his breakfast at 8 A.M. with Perkins, worked at his office until 6 P.M. and the meetings in the library lasted until 3 A.M. Nineteen hours at the minimum. The old man was suffering from a cold and was clearly exhausting his physical resources.

On the morning of the 23rd, Wednesday, Morgan could be roused from his sleep (his son-in-law describes it as a "stupor") only by the family doctor with an assortment of sprays and gargles. The young men had been up all night examining the books of banks and trust companies likely to be hit by deposit runs.

The feeling of imminent disaster was everywhere that morning. When Morgan reached his office, Henry Frick, Harriman, Thomas Ryan and others were waiting. Was it time to act? Where and how? Ben Strong had been going over the records of the Trust Company of America; it was now undergoing a deposit run and would soon be "over the dam" with the Knickerbocker Trust. Morgan had not met Strong before the crisis but by now was mightily impressed. Did Strong believe that the Trust Company of America could be saved? Strong said, "Yes." Morgan turned to Baker and Stillman and said: "Then this is the place to stop the trouble." Oakleigh Thorne, president of the Trust Company, was instructed to hurry over to Morgan's with his securities as collateral for a loan. Morgan had the names of the securities read to him, jotted them down and quickly estimated their true market values, then had Baker and Stillman loose their cash upon the Trust Company. When the Baker–Stillman money arrived, the Trust Company was down to a mere $180,000 and its frantic depositors at the tellers' windows were pressing in hard; by 3 P.M. closing they had $3 million in the till from Baker and Stillman. Morgan had their securities in his vault.

But that had only been the beginning. The Pittsburgh Stock Exchange had closed its doors, and now a stock-market panic in New York could be expected. That would have to be met head on, but the short interest could be radically reduced simply by a flat threat from Morgan. He had it spread about that, if any member of the exchange sold short during the panic, such a member would be "properly attended to" afterward. That night Morgan called the trust company presidents together again and asked them to pool $10 million. During the bickering discussion he fell asleep in his chair, cigar and all; uopn awakening his patience was at an end. He asked for paper and pencil, called for volunteers and wrote down the subscriptions. He got $8,250,000 and left. He still had to dodge the platoon of newspapermen who haunted his steps at every turn going home (he stayed with the Satterlees during the panic). There was a final conference with Perkins before going to bed. He needed the sleep; next day he would have to save the Stock Exchange.

On Thursday the 24th, the morning papers carried "Morgan" headlines, with front-page pictures. Morgan clearly enjoyed all the fuss. He may have thought that the panic had been beaten the day before, so on Thursday he rode grandiosely down to Wall Street in a brougham drawn by a white horse, like a conquering hero. The crowd, pressed "curb to curb," opened to let him pass with cries (according to Satterlee) of "There goes the Old Man" and "There goes the Big Chief." The Old Man and Big Chief had little time to savor his triumph. He had won a battle but the war was still going on. At his office the bank presidents waited nervously. Morgan's efforts had had some effect; John D. Rockefeller had cracked open a bit and deposited $10 million at the Union Trust Company to be used in the slush fund. But only a beginning had been made.

The stock-market panic was now on; "money" was quoted at 100 percent, which is arithmetic for "try and get it." The president of the New York Stock Exchange was already scared out. He came to Morgan to say that the exchange would have to be closed. Morgan pointed his finger at the unhappy man and, emphasizing each word with a jab, ordered him to keep the Exchange open; Morgan would find money to lend the brokers.

He called an immediate meeting of the clearing-bank presidents. They must supply $25 million within fifteen minutes or the Stock Exchange would go under. Some of the bankers were losing their taste for dramatic actions ". . . and Mr. Morgan had to speak to them pretty plainly." Thus instructed in the ways of righteousness, the bankers formed a pool of $27 million. To get the news instantly to the riot scene on the floor of the exchange, a group, including one Amory Hodges, was chosen to announce that money would be available at 10 percent. Violence roared through the packed humanity as

the chance to survive suddenly appeared. "Everyone surged
to the money post and fought to get his share. Hodges' coat
and waistcoat was torn off. . . ." Even his waistcoat. The
Stock Exchange stayed open until its usual closing time.

That night the library conferences took up again. Hoarding
of currency together with country bank withdrawals made it
necessary to issue Clearing House Certificates in place of legal
tender. Morgan, as a good gold-standard man, didn't like it,
but knew that it had to be done. It would work. Morgan sat
in the West Room of the library alone playing solitaire while
the bankers worked out the strategy in the East Room. All
Morgan had to do was say "yes" or "no"; he knew how to
use a staff.

Next morning it was Baker and Stillman again after breakfast. Money had to be raised for the Trust Company of America again and for the Union Trust Co.; they were still under
siege from long queues of depositors who had waited through
the night. Moreover, panic had broken out again on the floor
of the Stock Exchange where "money" was at 150 percent,
even more nearly impossible to get than it was the day before.
Morgan called the bank presidents together again; he thought
that $15 million would be enough to hold the line at the Stock
Exchange. The bankers gave him $13 million. Morgan left
the Clearing House for his office. His son-in-law described the
old man's progress down Nassau Street in a classic paragraph.

> Anyone who saw Mr. Morgan going from the Clearing House
> back to his office that day will never forget the picture. With
> his coat unbuttoned and flying open, a piece of white paper
> clutched tightly in his right hand, he walked fast down Nassau
> Street. His flat-topped black derby hat was set firmly down on
> his head. Between his teeth he held the paper cigar holder in
> which was one of his long cigars, half smoked. His eyes were
> fixed straight ahead. He swung his arms as he walked and
> took no notice of anyone. He did not seem to see the throngs
> in the street, so intent was his mind on the thing that he was
> doing. Everyone knew him, and people made way for him,
> except some who were equally intent on their own affairs;
> and these he brushed aside. The thing that made his progress
> different from that of all the other people on the street was
> that he did not dodge, or walk in and out, or halt or slacken
> his pace. He simply barged along, as if he had been the only
> man going down Nassau Street hill past the Subtreasury. He
> was the embodiment of power and purpose. Not more than
> two minutes after he disappeared into his office, the cheering

on the floor of the Stock Exchange could be heard out in Broad Street.

The new money was at the money post.

Except for the Knickerbocker Trust, the major trust companies had been kept open and the Stock Exchange had survived a two-day siege. Morgan enjoyed Saturday afternoon and Sunday at Cragston, but Monday, Oct. 28, he was back in the trenches. The City of New York could not meet its current obligations. Morgan called in the Mayor, George B. McClellan, to work out the city's finances; $30 million worth of 6 percent city warrants were to be issued. Stillman and Baker would arrange for the banks to buy them *pro rata* and then exchange them for Clearing House Certificates (money was thus created based upon debt, just as it is today with a managed currency whenever Federal deficits are financed through the banking system). Throughout the week Morgan's men kept at it, a loan here, an admonition there, constant consulting and auditing. It appeared that the defenses would hold. On Saturday, Nov. 2, the last great explosion occurred.

Moore & Schley, a prominent firm of New York brokers, was near the edge. It was decided that they had to be saved. The panic was dying down; it must not be allowed to build up again. At the same time, the trust companies had to form one more pool to save themselves. There was plenty of "battle fatigue" among the financiers now, but Morgan drove them on. Ultimately, the President of the United States (Roosevelt, who had spent most of this time hunting) had to be brought in. Moore & Schley had sold shares of the Tennessee Iron & Coal Co. and had then made loans against the shares as collateral. The brokerage firm was now unable to meet its own current obligations and had nowhere to turn for aid. Its failure would have set up a new train of disasters.

Morgan decided that U. S. Steel would have to acquire the T. I. & C. shares; but Tennessee Iron & Coal was a direct competitor of the steel corporation, and none of the Morgan people was anxious to get into anti-trust trouble again. But if the deal could be made, Moore & Schley would be saved; financing of the stock purchases could be carried, if necessary, with the help of the commercial banks until U. S. Steel could acquire them. Seventeen to nineteen million dollars were involved.

The most famous of the meetings at the library in 1907 was called to get all of this going—the trust company pool and the

Moore & Schley deal. It took Saturday night, Sunday and Sunday night to work it all out. On Saturday night, Morgan put the presidents of the commercial banks in the East Room. The trust company presidents (Morgan figured they would need to pool another $25 million to carry them through) were placed in the West Room. Morgan, waiting for the financial luminaries to work it all out, sat at the desk in the little librarian's office playing solitaire. There could be no turning back. This was to be the last great holding operation of the 1907 crisis. It must work.

The suits slowly sorted themselves out on the table in front of him as Morgan's cigars burned. The Big Chief took no chances. When, in the early morning hours, Ben Strong had made his report to Morgan (evidently regarding the commercial banks) and went to the door to go home, he found that he could not open it. Morgan had locked the bankers in the library and had the key in his pocket. He intended to have his solutions before anyone left. Finally he imposed his own pooling arrangements on the trust companies. Allen describes the scene.

> At last Morgan walked into the West Room and confronted them. He had with him a document which provided that each trust company, according to its resources, would put up its share of the twenty-five million dollars. One of his lawyers read it aloud, then laid it on the table.
>
> "There you are, gentlemen," said Morgan.
>
> No one stepped forward.
>
> Morgan put his hand on the shoulder of Edward King, the dean of the group. "There's the place, King," he said firmly. "And here's the pen." And he put a gold pen in King's hand. King signed. Then they all signed.

It was 4.45 A.M. when Morgan unlocked the doors. The next day the details of the Moore & Schley maneuver were worked out at the library, and Frick and Gary took the midnight train to Washington. Would the President agree not to prosecute under the Sherman Act? After breakfast Roosevelt agreed to Morgan's plan. When the market opened, it rallied. The deposit runs continued for some days, slowly dwindling, but the trust pool was sufficient to keep the doors open. Morgan, Stillman and Baker each took one-third of the T. I. & C. shares, these to be turned over to U. S. Steel as soon as possible. Stillman balked but followed Morgan on his assurance "I know my man" and that the T. I. & C. deal would be enough to save Moore & Schley. The depression of 1908 was relatively mild, not having been detonated by an enormous monetary collapse like the one which came in 1929. After 1908 recovery came fairly rapidly and was strong.

The Panic of 1907 was a profound lesson. If Morgan could avert a catastrophe by mobilizing existing resources (the only new "money" was the increase in Clearing House Certificates), what might a real central bank do? In the next two years Morgan spent a good deal of time with Senator Aldrich on the subject. A National Monetary Commission was appointed to examine the prospects for a new central bank. The Pujo committee of the Senate, looking for bogey men, interviewed Morgan himself to see if there were secret devices, a vast "money trust" which controlled events (naturally they concluded for the "evil men" theory of history).

In the end we got a central bank, the Federal Reserve System in 1914, as a result of the Panic of 1907, the National Monetary Commission, the Pujo committee and a very large dose of partisan politics. The new central bank was to have less than a complete success at playing J. P. Morgan, as the thousands upon thousands (more than 16,000) of bank failures in 1920–34 show. After the 1933 debacle in which all of the nation's banks closed (and more than 4,000 did not re-open), the Federal Reserve System, together with the new Federal Deposit Insurance Corporation, seemed sufficient to cope with the problem; bank failures due to deposit runs have been virtually unknown since.

Morgan was in no sense the "father" of the Federal Reserve System. His actions in 1877, 1895 and 1907 showed that there was indeed a useful function to be played by a central bank, Andrew Jackson's fulminations against the evils of a money monopoly notwithstanding. The "art of central banking" is not generally viewed with approval by economists and bankers to this day. Perhaps central banking is a necessary evil. As the nation's economy became more complex, and industry and finance became inextricably entwined, some degree of Morganization seemed to be cheaper than the wild deposit panics, mass liquidations and bankruptcies followed by mass unemployment and possibly political upheaval which seemed all too real a possibility if there were no central-banking control. The change to extensive central-bank control was not immediate, even after the apparatus for it, the Federal Reserve System, was in operation. But Pierpont Morgan, with his almost irresistible personal power over his peers, showed in 1907 that financial crises of gigantic magnitude could be controlled by intelligent and adroit financial management if that management could overlap all normal institutional frontiers when necessary. The nation's subsequent economic and monetary development owes Morgan a debt of gratitude for the lesson. If ever there was a private individual cast by circumstances into the role of statesman, it was Morgan in 1907. That the lessons of 1907 were not immediately comprehended was not his fault.

VII

Pierpont Morgan died in Rome on the last day of March, 1913, in his seventy-sixth year. When word of his illness was out, the hotel was besieged by art dealers, friends, private art sellers, photographers (they had a room across the street with a telescope trained on his windows) and newspapermen. The old man had been slipping for some months, had been taken ill in Egypt and in the end wanted to go to his home in London. He didn't make it. His affairs were in order. He had arranged to move his massive art collections to New York. He had been disentangling himself from some of his affairs, although not from the banking business itself. Much of his work, as already noted, is still with us today and continues to play a role in the shaping of the American destiny. His son Jack carried on the House of Morgan in the Morgan manner, and in the First World War the arts of international finance developed by Junius and Pierpont Morgan made the Morgan bank the center of finance in the Allied cause.

Such a life as Morgan's could hardly have been blameless and free of controversy. Yet, given the economic environment in which he worked together with the social and political milieu of his own experiences, it is difficult to criticize him with confidence; it was never hard to admire him. The old man, born during the great canal boom of the 1830's, had lived through the railroad era into the age of the airplane. Born when Andrew Jackson was President, Morgan lived to see Woodrow Wilson in the White House; born in the year of the young Victoria's accession, Morgan lived to see her grandson, the German Kaiser, at the brink of war. Born when the United States was in many respects an appendage of British trade and finance, Morgan lived to see and help organize industrial America. His life spanned the great American transformation. He played many roles as circumstances changed but found his greatest success as an organizer. By now few of those works remain as he left them. But his contribution to the Metropolitan Museum of Art remains. In that, and in his other cultural benefactions to the nation, Morgan is still with us. To quote once more the *Economist*'s remarkably prescient obituary:

> . . . Mr. Morgan was undoubtedly a man of genius, with strong will power and a commanding personality. He will stand, as a contemporary remarks, with Carnegie the manufacturer, Rockefeller the commercial organizer, Harriman the railway man, as one of the four most original and typical products of modern America.

And so he has.

PART V

BUREAUCRACY: THE NEED TO MONITOR AND
THE DANGER OF ORGANIZATIONAL GRIDLOCK

The fifth stage of economic life in our survey is bureaucracy —caretaking. Organizations cease to grow; the vital force ebbs. It may die with the founder, and what J. K. Galbraith calls "the entrepreneurial firm" becomes a memory. It is bureaucracy that takes over, and presides and administers in this world in which stability insensibly slips into stasis, stagnation and decline. The entrepreneurial energy is not only lacking; it is not wanted anymore. Routine administration abhors the disruption caused by new ideas. We all know this already, and the media entertain us from time to time with accounts of "whistle blowers" and other kinds of unwanted "idea people" who get forceably ejected from various bureaucracies for disrupting the life of pure administration. As the saying goes (or used to go) in the Chicago political machine, "Go along to get along."

The life of order, routine and structure is the life of bureaucracy. It was reported, in a stellar episode in the annals of bureaucracy, that the American soldiers crashing into Cologne in the spring of 1945 disrupted the annual inventory of office supplies in the *Reichsämter*, to the great consternation of Hitler's hard-working public servants. Lenin was confident that the Tsar's bureaucracy would serve the Revolution as well as it had served the Tsar, and with equal ruthlessness, and Lenin was right. But the ridiculous *can be* sublime. In an ancient Chinese novel there is a God of Promotions and a Temple of Salary Increases serving the administrators of the oldest continuous bureaucracy in the history of the human species. Revolutions, emperors, warlords and heroes triumphed and vanished into the dust, but the imperial examinations were administered each year, through thick and thin. Fiction copies real life. The great irrigation works at Chengdu in Sichuan Province have been in continuous operation for more than 2,200 years—continuously administered, the instructions for dredging channels and maintaining the levies carved in stone by their creator, engineer Li Ping, for the benefit of the succeeding hundreds of generations of administrators. The great dam at Chengdu ought to be the absolute ideal for virtuous bureaucracies everywhere.

Both Henry Ford and Chairman Mao, each in his own way, attempted to recapture dynamism by waging futile campaigns against their own bureaucracies. Ford fired people right and left, and Mao loosed the Red Guards upon his hapless functionaries. Then Ford and Mao died, and the bureaucracies lived on. Many studies, one by a former U.S. president, Herbert Hoover (commissioned for the task by then-President Harry Truman), have been conducted by the federal government in search of ways to cut back, modernize and streamline our enterprise-strangling bureaucracy in Washington. Presidents are elected decade after decade on the promise to cut the bureaucracy. But presidents come and go, and the bureaucracy remains.

The problem is that bureaucracy is both necessary and, in many ways, dangerous. Since bureaucracy is characterized by adherence to rules and forms, it tends toward conservative mindlessness and authoritarianism. Successful and growing social processes become complex. To maintain momentum the complexity must be put into order, and regularity then replaces spontaneity. To achieve regularity someone must devote time to mere monitoring and scheduling. At some point an apparatus of formal organization of the monitors rises up. It consumes part of the net product of the original income- and wealth-creating activity. At first this is a necessary and valuable cost of increasing efficiency through the achievement of orderly production and distribution sequences. Since expertise is needed, formal training for the separate bureaucratic career comes into existence. Those who monitor the work of others need their own space for bookkeeping, and their place of employment moves away from the sites of actual production, away from the fields, the shops, the assembly lines. The special places where the records are kept, where the monitors work, then become complex. They become offices—bureaus. When enough of these special employees are gathered together, they must themselves be organized into formal structures of punctilio, of social relations, to avoid overlapping jurisdictions. The monitors and bookkeepers form organizations that take on lives of their own, increasingly distant from the original real-product producing and nourishing economic activities. Not only do special trainings appear and then become necessity, but titles, perhaps uniforms, even special honors and medals appear; there are limousines for the higher-ups in modern times.

Since, after a point, only the bureaucracy has the means—the records, the time and the necessary expertise to study them—to achieve a global view of the relevant economic and social processes, there is an inevitable tendency for the power to control those processes to slip away from the actual producers and into the hands of the members of the bureaucracy. The accountants replace the production people; "management" takes over from entrepreneurship. The age of J. K. Galbraith's "technostructure" dawns and the future becomes financial, or fiscal—abstract. In private business, people like Carnegie and Ford, with their emphasis on production technologies and the nature of the products themselves, are forgotten. The servants are now in control. The master is gone, but his creation lives on in corporate perpetuity. What such evolution can mean in private industry became graphically obvious in the United States in the early 1980s when it began to appear that the nation of Andrew Carnegie and Henry Ford might only be able to produce basic steel and automobiles in a competitive world under an umbrella of government protection, a sad end to a great tradition. In the impersonal world of corporate finance, even private property—in its "vital form," as Schumpeter put it—vanishes. Control no longer resides in ownership.

In government the tenure of the appointed bureaucrats is longer than that of their elected "bosses"—congressmen, senators, presidents—and the power of the monitors then threatens to exceed that of elected officials merely because knowledge and expertise become lodged, then hidden, in the recesses of the bureaus. Forms and procedures multiply, gain increasing complexity, and the public business becomes arcane—a mystery to elected officials and the general public alike. The federal tax code, for example, which President Jimmy Carter decried as "an insult to western civilization," is after all a Golconda for bureaucrats, lawyers, certified public accountants and neighborhood scribes who prepare the forms each year for their seminumerate fellows. Every law, every regulation, must be monitored to be enforced. The "permanent government" has become the appointed one. Elected officials are merely part of the passing scene. In what the German sociologist Max Weber called "the routinization of charisma" the great men of nonelected "government" like Robert Moses and J. Edgar Hoover become public heroes. If the public business becomes routine enough, it no longer really matters who the elected officials are, or what they believe or say.

Weber, lamenting the utterly conservative nature of bureaucracy, also considered its presence in civilized society to be absolutely necessary.

> Without it [bureaucracy], a society like our own—with a separation of officials, employees, and workers from ownership of the means of administration, dependent on discipline and technical training—could no longer function. The only exception would be those groups, such as the peasantry, who are still in possession of their own means of subsistence.

Large-scale economic and social processes absolutely require bureaucracy to push back the inevitable diseconomies of large-scale activities, to push back the tendency to disintegrate into chaos as more and more people and processes crowd the space-time continuum in which work is done. Quoting Weber again:

> Only by reversion in every field—political, religious, economic . . . to small-scale organization would it be possible to any considerable extent to escape . . . [the bureaucratic] . . . influence.

Weber believed that modern capitalism is the most "rational" form of economic organization ever developed, and since bureaucracy rises initially from the technology of rationalization itself as the scale of operations expands, ". . . capitalism is the most rational basis for bureaucratic administration." He thought, incidentally, that socialism (then only a cloud on the horizon, or a ray of hope, depending on one's preferences) would require much more bureaucracy per unit of productive work because of socialism's centralized decision making. He did not consider that to be rational, but merely necessary for socialism to exist at all. Capitalism, decentralized, would still function, but without scale economies—that is, less efficiently.

Bureaucracy, then, is the essence of all that Henry Ford hated and feared—a world of expertise and titles. The growing bureaucratization of American life has been decried at all levels for decades, even as the universities organized elaborate schools of business administration and public affairs, and then began cranking out graduates equipped only for the life of bureaucracy. We have been, and are, like drunkards decrying the consumption of alcoholic beverages. Louis Galambos, an eminent American historian, paraphrased Franklin D. Roosevelt and wrote that the destiny with which modern Americans really had a rendezvous was bureaucracy. Our massive business organizations and complex economy would be unthinkable without "rational" management. But when bureaucracy ceases to make a net contribution and becomes a strangling parasite, it is at the point of critical mass, the gridlock when the cost of management reduces the net product to zero and beyond. The necessary evil then becomes a luxury and drags the economy down. To stop the apparatus of routine from strangling productive enterprise has become the great problem, in giant enterprises as well as in government. The heart of the problem is how to motivate thought, originality, energy and creative innovation into a social organism—the bureaucracy—whose teleology is routine, perfect routine.

The growth of governmental bureaucracy developed apace with the American population and an increasingly complex national life, just as business bureaucracies grew with the progression of possible economies of scale in business. More and more we asked for, and got, additional government services. To some extent it was the provision of "public goods" we wanted, services used by all, or most, than could not be diminished in total supply by individual consumption. National security is the usual example. To some extent we also wanted services the private sector could not supply, or would not, at prices people wanted to pay. Roads, canals and rural electrification are common examples. It may be true to some extent, as a cynic put it, that "public goods are the epiphenomena of private interests realized," and therefore some demand for more government service was generated by private parties for private profit, the public service in question being an incidental by-product. It may be partly true that demands for government regulation have come in large part from those who can gain positive monopoly rents (profits above competitive rates) from regulation. Premeditated free riding and straightforward corruption no doubt also played roles in this history. It also is true that growth of governmental bureaucracy represented, over time, the outcome of publicly (politically) expressed demands for reforms in national life—for whatever reasons, prohibition, virtue in Wall Street, clean air and water—that could only be imposed from above.

As a result of all such forces our public bureaucracy has grown mightily. Consider some figures for the federal government alone. In 1841 there was just more than one permanent federal employee for every 1,000 of population. By 1871, even after the events of 1861–65, the number per 1,000 was a mere 1.2. By 1900 it had nearly tripled to 3.1. After World War I, in 1921, the number reached 5.2. The New Deal raised it to 10.8 by 1941, and in 1951 the number reached its apparent maximum of 16.1—an increase by a factor of 13.4 over 1871, *a 1,240 percent increase per head of population* in 80 years. Since 1951, with the revolution in modern communications and monitoring—computers—enormously raising the potential output per government employee, the number has stabilized at about 14 per thousand of population.

The total of all government employees has grown apace. In 1981 there were 2,865,000 civilian federal employees, 3,726,000 permanent state and 9,377,000 permanent local government employees, a total of 21,193,000 government employees out of a civilian labor force of 110,800,000—or just more than every fifth person in the labor force. As recently as 1951 that number had not been one in ten.

Not only has the governmental bureaucracy grown in numbers at an astonishing rate, but so has the share of government expenditures out of the total, the gross national product (GNP). In 1950 total government (federal, state and local) expenditures were about $70 billion out of a nominal GNP of $285 billion, just under 25 percent. By 1980 total government expenditures were $959 billion out of a nominal GNP of $2,626 billion, more than 35 percent of the total. Government expenditures had grown nearly half again as fast as GNP. In the first half of the 1980s government expenditures, based on huge deficits at the federal level, continued to outstrip the growth of GNP. The national debt, a consequence of the federal deficits, was doubled in the first five years of the conservative Reagan administration. The supposedly spendthrift New Deal came nowhere near such a proportional increase in the public debt in its first five years. So the proportion of the nation's total allocation of resources under the government's stewardship has grown at an extraordinary pace for five decades, and continues to burn up the track.

Perhaps the most thought-provoking statistic is the change in the ratio of private investment to federal expenditures: 4 to

1 ($16.2 billion to $3.8 billion) in 1929, and just over 1 to 2 ($473.3 billion to $826 billion) in 1983. We are considering here the power to set the nation's agenda. Investment is the private sector's move toward the future, and the rate of expenditure is the federal sector's countermove. At the end of the old regime, in 1929, the private sector disposed of four times the federal power in this regard, and now it has about half. This has been a turnaround in the decision making that shapes this country's destiny of revolutionary proportions.

What does it matter? Some would consider these data to be measures of inexorable progress in the "mixed economy." Others would consider the data to be evidence of an appalling dead weight upon an economy still dependent, nevertheless, on private ownership of productive resources, and private thinking and labor to make those resources yield a desirable social product. With much premeditation (two books written on the topic), I will dodge these metaphysical issues and argue instead that our only realistic choice now is that some public expenditures are more socially desirable than others, that some bureaucratic decisions are "better for the country" than others. This is only common sense. In our national historical development we have already made the basic political decisions that have created the governmental establishment that presides over more than a third of our total national expenditures. The persons in that establishment dispose of a financial power that simply dwarfs any private business or conceivable combination thereof. Neither I nor any other scholar, politician or president, apparently, will change this condition.

So even if there is no way for the bureaucracy and its power to be reduced, we are better off if the bureaucracy is wise than if it is stupid, better off if it is good rather than evil, benevolent rather than malicious. "Bureaucratic entrepreneurship" in the interests of generally acceptable ideals of public virtue (and adherence to the laws of the land) is important to reduce the element of dead-weight loss. Engineer Li Ping's wise instructions, carved in stone, were more valuable for China's long future than were the decisions for us of the private-sector bureaucrats who presided over the competitive decline of many of our great industrial firms, or the waste of resources in such governmental bureaucratic catastrophes as the Teton Dam, or the present embroglios of the government-sponsored and -regulated nuclear power industry. Wisdom matters. Wisdom is a judgment call by a wise person. So we will be better off if our public servants are appointed for intelligence—and common honesty—as well as expertise.

CHAPTER 10

Mary Switzer: Well-Mannered Juggernaut

> I went to bed one night with what I thought was a tre-
> mendous budget of more than 300 million dollars and
> when I awoke the next morning I found it was six billion
> dollars.
>
> Mary Switzer, 1967

I

On August 15, 1967, Mary Elizabeth Switzer was named by
Health, Education and Welfare (HEW) Secretary John Gardner as administrator of HEW's newly organized Social and
Rehabilitation Services. It was the highest any woman had
ever climbed, from within, the bureaucratic ladder in Washington. By 1967 Mary Switzer had a magnificent record of
public service. She was a civil servant and had worked in the
federal government since 1923. She had been the instrumental catalyst in the creation of the 1946 National Mental
Health Act. In the 1950s she had been a driving force in turning around this country's attitudes about disabled people and
their rehabilitation through self-help, therapy, education and
physical medicine. Her philosophy about "investment" in the
disadvantaged had been adopted by President Eisenhower in
1954 as his administration's approach to the problems of social
welfare. It had all been a glorious achievement, involving great
men and women, momentous events.

So Switzer's 1967 promotion could have been seen as a
logical use of a first-class bureaucratic talent, compensation
for rare performance and a personal triumph. Instead it was
her Waterloo. In 1968 the cities were burning, the nation's
poor people were marching and Richard M. Nixon defeated

Hubert Humphrey, ending the New Deal, Fair Deal, New Frontier, Great Society era, which had been broken only by Eisenhower's eight years of relative stability. The era of good feelings toward the poor and the "disadvantaged" that had been sure-fire politics for so long was swamped by the tide of history, and Mary Switzer's 48 years in government service ended on a sour note indeed. She had wanted to resolve the "welfare problem" with her ideas of local initiatives, state and federal cooperation, decentralization of authority, greater reliance on the abilities of her agency's "clients"—she wanted cooperation and good feelings. Do the best you can. These attitudes had served her well for many years.

The future wasn't going to be that way. Mary Switzer was forceably retired at age 70 in 1970. Her time was past. She was dead of cancer not two years later. Now she is still remembered in Washington, and HHS (The Department of Health and Human Services) has a building named after her. Why? The elderly "spinster," as *Time* magazine had ungraciously labeled her when she was appointed in 1967, had in fact realized her moments in this country's history; she was prepared, and when her chances came, she was a champion. That is why she is remembered.

In the life of Mary Switzer three powerful currents came to a confluence in the developing American economy: industrialization, modern medical science and the rise of the welfare state with its concentration of power increasingly in the federal bureaucracy. It was Switzer's fate, as a civil servant, to find herself drawn into the vortex of these merging currents.

II

Mary Switzer was born in Newton Upper Falls, Massachusetts, on February 16, 1900, the daughter of Margaret (Moore) and Julius F. Switzer. He was a manual laborer in a dismal turn-of-the-century New England manufacturing town. Margaret Switzer died when Mary was still a youngster, and her father drifted off. Mary grew up with her mother's Irish family at a time when the life of the working-class Irish of the Boston area was anything but a transcendent economic success story. Mary received her schooling at Classical High School in Newton, and managed in 1917 to gain admittance to Radcliffe College in nearby Cambridge. She could live at home and attend Radcliffe as a day student. She had a scholarship and odd jobs to pay the tuition. Once each day, inside the confines of what was considered to be a school for the daughters of the elite, Mary Switzer acquired a first-class education. She graduated in 1921. Her special interest at Radcliffe was international law, a subject in considerable academic vogue at the time, with the League of Nations being formed and the "war to end all wars" just ended.

In that age of progressivism this educated young woman, like many others, aspired to a career in public service, and away from home. Such a life would achieve security from the grinding poverty of her childhood surroundings, and also the exciting prospects of a wider world. Her first efforts to secure employment in Washington failed, however, and she was forced to return to Boston and a temporary life of odd jobs, even including scrubbing other people's floors, a more "traditional" role in the world for an Irish girl.

The Radcliffe experience, however, saved her from that, producing an opportunity to return to Washington, with a job waiting. One of Mary's friends at Radcliffe had been Elizabeth Brandeis, daughter of the great jurist, and through that important connection Switzer was able to secure a post with the District of Columbia Wage Board. This was to be her first brush with that wider world at its legal heights.

Congress, then governing the District of Columbia and using the mantle of wartime concentration of powers, had written a minimum wage law for the District in 1918. Minimum wage laws were important ambitions of the reformers of the time. Congress had also passed a law in 1916 forbidding the movement in interstate commerce of the products of child labor. These were among several pieces of legislation designed to achieve the aims of progressive and "New Freedom" reformers during a moment of wartime expansion of the federal government's powers in the nation's economy. Also in 1916, the Adamson Act had regulated the hours of railway labor under the commerce power.

Not for the first time or the last, the U.S. Supreme Court proved to be less "forward" in its thinking than the reform-minded Congress of the war years. In that era the Court was still fighting a rear-guard action to preserve the states from the encroaching federal power. Louis Brandeis, after all, was a lifelong champion of such ideas. In 1887 there had been the Interstate Commerce Act setting up the Interstate Commerce Commission, in 1890 the Sherman Antitrust Act, in 1906 the Pure Food Act, in 1913 the Federal Reserve Act, in 1914 the Federal Trade Commission Act and the Clayton Antitrust Act.

There had been more, and then in 1916–19 the war powers had enabled the federal government to establish a sweeping federal bureaucracy which erected the country's first "command economy." Taking off for Europe to fight for the League of Nations, President Woodrow Wilson had ordered the command-economy bureaucracy to fold its tents and go home. The Supreme Court, at the same time, began to dismantle the congressional reforms.

The Adamson Act had stood the court test; the railroads were indubitably part of interstate commerce, and therefore were subject to congressional regulation. But other things were not, such as manufacturing. Already, in 1895 in the "Sugar Trust" case (*E. C. Knight* v. *U.S.*), the Court had ruled that manufacturing was not commerce, and therefore Congress had no power to regulate; the Sherman Act did not apply. In 1918, in *Hammer* v. *Dagenhart*, the Court tossed out the 1916 child labor act on the same ground. Congress responded with a tax, the Child Labor Tax Law, and the Court overturned it in 1922 in *Bailey* v. *Drexel Furniture*, arguing that the tax was a subterfuge to legislate on the subject of child labor. The Court then turned to the District of Columbia's minimum wage law and, in so doing, to young Mary Switzer. Her job was wiped out.

In *Adkins* v. *Children's Hospital* Mr. Justice Sutherland was at his Olympian heights, delivering in ringing words an argument against federal interference with freedom of contract in the wage bargain. He wrote:

> To sustain the individual freedom of action contemplated by the Constitution is not to strike down the common good but to exalt it; for surely the good of society as a whole cannot be better served than by the preservation against arbitrary restraint of the liberties of its constituent members.

The problem was not the judge's rhetoric, but the issue: the Court's majority, by wiping out the District's minimum wage law, was defending, as Edward Berkowitz laconically put it, the freedom of children and women to bargain on equal terms with men. It would take the National Labor Relations Act of 1935 and the Fair Labor Standards Act of 1938 to get past *Adkins*.

Casting about for a future in Washington after the *Adkins* decision, Switzer served briefly as executive secretary of the Women's International League for Peace and Freedom. She also took and passed the civil service examination. She was qualified by that exam, to her surprise, to be a junior-level economist. She started at the bottom rung of the ladder in the U.S. Treasury. It was not difficult work and, as she later wrote, gave her time to explore Washington and its cultural attractions.

At first Switzer lived in the University Women's Club, near Lafayette Square, and as a result met many of the important and unusual women working in and passing through Washington. An interesting new friend of that period was Tracy Copp, also staying at the Club. Copp was to be, like Elizabeth Brandeis, a lifelong friend. By the early 1920s Copp already had lived a varied career in Wisconsin, including jobs in the Wisconsin Anti-Tuberculosis Association and the Wisconsin Industrial Commission. In the latter service she had been a factory inspector and director of the Department of Women and Children. Now in Washington, Copp was a field agent for the new federal excursion into vocational education for the handicapped. She told Switzer about her experiences in the new program.

In 1920 Congress had passed the Vocational Rehabilitation Act—the Smith-Fess Act. The war, with its abundant horrors, had temporarily sensitized the country to the problems of the disabled, and a movement had begun in the states to find ways to rehabilitate them. Before Congress jumped on the bandwagon in 1920 twelve states already had their own rehabilitation laws. In 1918 a rehabilitation act for soldiers had been passed, and even that was antedated by a month by the state of Massachusetts with a law establishing vocational rehabilitation for civilians.

The federal law, when it came, had been backed by both political parties and by both the American Federation of Labor and the National Association of Manufacturers. This kind of broad-based support for social legislation, together with initiatives at the state level, must have impressed the young Switzer, because when her chances came to initiate programs and legislation, she would try to achieve similar backing of all interested parties; it became her hallmark, a special skill she learned. But in the early 1920s, bored at the Treasury, Switzer later said of Tracy Copp's friendship and conversation: "Tracy Copp managed to make her work come alive to a young civil servant in the Treasury." But active association with rehabilitation was still a decade away for Switzer.

Through the 1920s Switzer slowly worked her way up the bureaucratic ladder. But her ascent, rung by rung, continued after 1929 in the gathering murk of an all-enveloping depression that was not understood (it still isn't) and was bad news almost every day at the U.S. Treasury. As the "New Era" slowly sank into the mire of the Great Depression, Switzer's duties came to include cutting and pasting clippings each day from the morning newspapers for the attention of Secretary Mellon and sometimes President Hoover himself. It was a morbid task; the news simply got increasingly dismal and would finally include the defeat of Hoover for reelection. But in those years Switzer was in regular attendance at the Brandeis home, where the justice held sway and where the more liberal element of Washington's young elite regularly assembled to spread and absorb the light. Switzer was a particular favorite of Justice Brandeis. Her job at the Treasury admittedly was, as a "forward-thinking" Harvard friend put it, "in the heart of the present system." But she persevered, making a life for herself as a bachelor career woman in Washington, widening her circle of friends, especially among the "Seven Sisters underground" in the nation's capital.

Switzer had been excited by the brilliant young people surrounding Brandeis, especially the young Dean Acheson, described by Switzer as "one of the glamour boys in Washington." But tragedy also came to her in those early Washington days. She fell in love with Wright McCormick, a World War I veteran and a militant supporter of Irish independence. According to Martha Walker, Switzer's biographer (*Beyond Bureaucracy: Mary Elizabeth Switzer and Rehabilitation*), McCormick was trying to start up a career as a journalist. Also, in Washington he was working for "Friends of Irish Freedom." Switzer knew the lingo of "the movement" from her own family background in the Boston area; her Uncle "Mike" Moore used to take her to rallies in support of Ireland and other causes. So she found an easy rapport with McCormick. He was killed mountain climbing in Mexico, and that door closed for Switzer. Walker writes of no further known romantic interest for the rest of Switzer's life. She had many male friends, some, like Howard Rusk and Nelson Rockefeller in later years, deeply devoted to her. But after McCormick, Mary Switzer turned entirely to her civil service career, a life as an independent single woman in Washington.

The years of the Hoover administration finally ended, and with FDR and Eleanor came Henry and Elinor Morgenthau. Both Eleanor Roosevelt and Elinor Morgenthau were Vassar women, and the Seven Sisters underground began to play a more important role as a support network. Graduates of

Vassar, Barnard, Wellesley, Smith, Mount Holyoke, Radcliffe and Bryn Mawr found their circle of friends and colleagues growing in numbers and influence as the New Deal assembled its version of "the best and the brightest." At the Treasury, Switzer assumed responsibility for Morgenthau's correspondence section, and now gravitated toward the center of New Deal social and professional circles. In 1935, when Switzer was 35 years old, now a middle-aged woman, her first great chance came: the appointment of the dramatic Josephine Roche as Assistant Secretary of the Treasury.

Josephine Roche was a sensation. A Vassar woman, she was just coming off an unsuccessful attempt on the Democratic ticket to become Colorado's first woman governor. A determined woman with a forceful personality, Roche held deeply liberal and reformist political beliefs. She had inherited a coal-mining company from her father, and as president of that enterprise had settled her labor relations problems with the United Mine Workers on mutually agreeable terms. She knew John L. Lewis well, and respected his ambitions for the welfare of his union members. (Lewis would later repay the compliment by appointing Roche to the governing body of the UMW Welfare Fund, of which more later.)

Owing to the peculiarities of the developing American welfare state, the Public Health Service was lodged in the Treasury Department, and Josephine Roche had been tagged by FDR to head that agency. Switzer desperately wanted the job as Roche's assistant, campaigned for it within the Seven Sisters network and in 1935 got the appointment. The patient civil servant would get her chance to mold and influence vital government policies. She made the most of her opportunity.

Switzer now found herself, as she put it, in a "beehive, a merry-go-round, a large gathering of serious thinkers—almost anything . . . a great contrast to the last years of the Hoover administration." Roche and Switzer developed almost immediately an interesting and portentous failure: their effort to have provisions for both national health and disability insurance included in the original social security bill. They came up against problems that have not been solved to this day. Their failure in 1935 was a landmark of sorts. To understand why, we need to make a small diversion into the general history of the "welfare state."

III

A peculiarity of the American welfare state is how utterly disorganized it seems, its apparent lack of any logic. Partly it is federally run, partly by states, counties, cities, even by tiny New England townships. Some needs are adequately met; some are overwhelmed with concerned officials and resources; some are not covered at all. There are overlapping responsibilities. Despite a wealth of examples in other countries of coherent, unified and efficient social insurance and delivery systems, we have gone our own way, gerry-building a rickety structure that is both expensive and deficient. It probably serves better as a reflection of our history than the needs of the present. It is not useful merely to curse our fate, but might be to understand it.

Felt human needs covered by our social agencies and systems today, such as old-age dependency, the long-term consequences of injuries, hunger and permanent disability, were originally matters of charity. In the English tradition that charity had been an affair of the private conscience together with the responsibility of the church—until Henry VIII. After stripping the church of its wealth and pulling down the monasteries, Henry faced a dilemma: what to do about the poor? In 1535 a law was passed, "Charitable Alms," in which Henry charged the parishes of the English church to provide for the poor by local taxes. Private charity outside of gifts at the church poor box was prohibited, and fines were imposed on the parishes for failure to meet their obligations. It became illegal to starve to death in England, although the poor, if they did not "attend to their labours," might be hanged. This was the beginning of the Tudor poor laws, passed to America, as amended, in the colonization, evolved at the town and county levels into almshouses, county poor farms, various forms of home relief, mothers' aid, mixed with private charities, complemented by veterans' pensions, and on into the twentieth century, an incredible jumble that had tumbled to financial disaster by 1933. We were not ready for the collapse of state and local government charitable funds.

The frontier tradition had provided a belief that the poor could always go west or find a farm in the wastelands, buttressed at the higher levels of thought by philosophers like Herbert Spencer, who had contributed such Darwinian gems as ". . . rigorous necessity . . . when allowed to act on them, becomes . . . a spur to the lazy . . . under the natural order of things society is constantly excreting its unhealthy, imbecile, slow, vacillating. . . ." William Graham Sumner, described by Gaston Rimlinger as Spencer's leading American disciple, had put it in a business way:

> In our modern state, and in the United States more than any-
> where else, the social structure is based on contract. . . . It
> follows . . . that one man, in a free state, cannot claim help
> from, and cannot be charged to give help to, another.

One can still hear echoes of such stout sentiments. They no doubt were more commonly held half a century ago than now. The United States had in fact evolved by the turn of this century into an industrial, urban nation, and Sumner's man "in a free state" would have made one lousy neighbor. By 1910 about 46 percent of the population already lived in incorporated towns and cities of more than 2,500 population, and 22 percent already lived in cities with populations exceeding 100,000. By 1930, 56 percent of the population lived and worked in towns and cities, cheek by jowl with each other. For most Americans there was no place left to flee; there was no frontier left. Unless you could somehow barricade yourself away from your fellows, the fittest, the less fit and the helpless now had to live together within settled borders and jurisdictions.

Unlike the major European nations, we had done very close to nothing at the level of central government to cope with the rising problems of health and welfare in an urban industrial world. The federal government had not originally exercised the "police powers"—the protection of health, safety and welfare. Those had been the province of the common law and municipal and state legislative powers. Our old systems in the counties and states, the almshouses and poor farms, were based on a rural world, a world long gone. In 1933 the New Deal faced millions of unemployed, a quarter of the labor force, perhaps more. There was desperation. Despite tradition, people now turned to the federal government. Time was short. There were radical solutions threatening. Emergency relief began immediately with Harry Hopkins and his Civil Works Administration. On May 12, 1933, Congress voted $500 million for immediate relief to be administered by state agencies. In November 1933 the Civil Works Administration was established, and in three months Hopkins spent nearly a billion dollars, putting nearly 4 million to work. FDR hated to be in the relief business and asked for planning of a system of comprehensive social insurance. From this effort grew the modern welfare state.

But that was long-term planning. As history knows, in the short run, the New Deal coped as best it could within its limits, with the famous alphabet soup of emergency employment programs, CCC, PWA, WPA, NYA, subsidies to agriculture, for exports, for reforestation, for conservation, for giant multipurpose dams in the west, TVA in the east, manpower programs, conservation of natural resources, federal highways, bridges—efforts in every direction to try to escape the trap of 1933. By 1941 the WPA alone had employed 8 million people, an estimated 16 percent of the entire labor force.

Meanwhile the president's Committee on Economic Security, headed by Labor Secretary Frances Perkins (Mount Holyoke) began the work that resulted in the 1935 Social Security Act and, it was hoped, a different kind of escape from a return to 1933.

One route to follow could have been found in the example of Imperial Germany. We could have copied the German system, evolved by the early 1930s (before Hitler) into a widely admired comprehensive, centrally administered social security system. Bismarck, contemplating the problems of modern economic life in the early 1880s, had gone directly to the target by the shortest route (translation by Rimlinger): "The State must take the matter in hand." Bending the *Reichstag* to his will, Bismarck got comprehensive health insurance in 1883, accident insurance in 1884 and old age and disability insurance in 1885. That was Bismarck's way of dealing with social problems exploited by the German left: remove them. When he was accused of being socialistic, the Iron Chancellor had said that a bit of socialism was good for the state:

> . . . in our empire the state will have to become used to a little more socialism. . . . If you believe that you can frighten anyone with the word "socialism" you hold a view which I have long overcome.

Socialism still frightened Americans, but the problems could no longer be dodged.

In the English-speaking world mass unemployment produced by business-cycle downswings had been widely discussed since 1909, when William Beveridge published his book, *Unemployment, A Problem of Industry*. In 1931 Gerard Swope's plan for a federally administered system of industrial insurance (against old age, death, disability and cyclical unemployment) had created a sensation; President Hoover labeled it fascism. Also, bills had been introduced in 1909, 1911 and 1927 to create old-age pensions. Indeed, New Zealand had actually introduced publicly supported old-age pensions in 1889. The British had begun a national old-age pension system in 1908, and started unemployment compensation in 1911 after Board of Trade President Winston Churchill had sent Beveridge to Germany to study Bismarck's system.

Laggard as we were in the 1930s, our own history had produced beginnings which could not be, or at least were not, tossed overboard in favor of a comprehensive new plan. The problems were poverty caused by unemployment, by on-the-job accidents, by old age, by short- and long-term disabilities of all sorts, physical, mental, educational. There were also Congress, the states, local governments, labor unions, business associations. All of those interests had to be served somehow. FDR was no Bismarck, and Congress was not the *Reichstag*. But there was political pressure to do *something*. FDR wanted legislation, not only to sidetrack people like Huey Long, but also Doctor Francis Townsend, whose alarmingly simple plan (a $200 monthly pension paid by the federal government to all over 60, the $200 per month to be spent within each 30-day period) was catching on. The Committee on Economic Security was charged with the job of devising passable legislation.

By 1935 agreement had been reached by the Committee on employer-paid unemployment insurance and compensation systems administered by the states, on an old-age insurance pension system run exclusively by the federal government, aid to the blind and to dependent children. That much went through Congress in 1935, and became the first installment of "social security" as a federally sponsored program in this country.

What did not become law in 1935 were national health insurance, insurance against mental illness and disability insurance. Regulation 7 of Harry Hopkins's Federal Emergency Relief Administration stated boldly: "The conservation and maintenance of public health is a function of government." But what was "public health"? Who was healthy and who was not? No one actually knew. As part of the continuing pressure Roche was applying to get national health insurance legislation, Switzer planned and, with the use of WPA labor, conducted a survey of the nation's health. In 1935–36 some 2,500,000 people were interviewed in a sample of 83 cities, and 140,000 more in 23 rural areas. By that sample it seemed that as many as 16,000,000 people, nearly 18 percent of those 15 to 64 years of age, suffered from some form of disability.

The size of the problem amazed those concerned with public health. Not knowing the actual numbers they were dealing with, two specialists working for the Committee, I. S. Falk and Edgar Sydenstriker, had labored since the summer of 1934 on national health and disability insurance, sending in a report recommending legislation in 1935. Their report was held back while Congress debated the rest of the social security bill. Roche and Switzer along with Harry Hopkins pushed for the legislation, but Frances Perkins, monitoring the balking Congress, wrote to FDR: "In view of the controversial character . . . of the subject, I suggest the report not be made public." It was not, according to Berkowitz, until 1962.

FDR signed the new Social Security Act into law on August 14, 1935, and the abandoned problem of federal programs for health and disability began its long evolution. There never would be a comprehensive national health insurance program. The outstanding problems of health and disability would be dealt with in bits and pieces over the years, and there, in a complex evolution in detail, Mary Switzer would play her role.

IV

Utilizing the 1935–36 survey of the nation's health, the Interdepartmental Committee to Coordinate Health and Welfare, headed by Josephine Roche, submitted a report to FDR. Roche then went back to Colorado after working with Switzer to organize a National Health Conference in Washington in 1938 to consider a policy for the federal government to follow. The conference was a very large-scale affair, originally to include an opening address by FDR (he went on a cruise instead). Josephine Roche came back and delivered an address of her own.

Switzer now learned about the American Medical Association and the character of Morris Fishbein. She had said privately that the conference would alert the public to the "death grip of organized medicine on the provision of medical care." The fee-paying public surely knew that already. The conference may well have enlightened Mary Switzer more than it did the general public. She already had slipped some of her Brandeisian moorings. The justice had told her that $8 million would be an excessive federal contribution to public health; that was the business of state and local governments, not the federal government. Switzer observed, after studying the figures gathered in her national health survey: "I cannot look at the figures for Federal aid for services in the last ten years and feel we can ever again leave this load to the localities." So she was, compared to Justice Brandeis, already something of a centrist.

On the other hand, traveling over the country as Roche's assistant, she had become acquainted with the nature of localized delivery systems for public health and the importance of local initiative and responsibility. She also had come to know the leading figures in the Public Health Service (PHS), as well as the leaders in most of the state health services. At the National Health Conference she received her initiation to the AMA. At first she compared them to a well-run labor union, a building trades union. She grossly underestimated Fishbein, the editor of the AMA journal. She thought of him merely as a clever and insincere lobbyist for a well-organized special interest. But listening to the heated debates she gained a deep understanding of the AMA representatives themselves, and the great variability of their opinions within a seemingly narrow ideology. The AMA people were, after all, a very special interest indeed: they gained their livelihoods solely from the delivery of medical care. They held to their beliefs about medicine doggedly. It was *their* profession, *they* owned it, and *they* wanted to run it. They were also not entirely opposed to receiving money from the U.S. Treasury. They would perhaps be influenced, even led a bit. They would not be driven. Also, the country had to have them, they too were part of it, integral to any government policies and programs concerning medicine.

It is easy enough to blame the AMA for the absence of a national health system; we are the only "civilized" country without one. But the AMA did not run Congress, or FDR. After the National Health Conference the AMA in fact had come out in favor of disability insurance and federal medical grants to the needy. The AMA opposed general national health insurance. The 1938 conference produced a legislative effort, the Wagner national health bill, which died in a Senate committee in 1939. The Wagner bill included grants-in-aid to the states for medical care, hospitals and temporary disability payments. National standards were not set for medical services; they were left to the states. In 1939 survivors benefits (hence the title Old Age and Survivors Insurance, OASI) were added to the Social Security Act as amendments, but not disability insurance. Wagner introduced a separate disability bill in 1940. That failed passage. In 1943 the Wagner, Murray, Dingell bill was introduced. It empowered the federal government to create a national health insurance along with both temporary and permanent disability programs as part of a unified social security system. That also failed. One must suppose that somehow the United States, for whatever reasons, was not ready for a unified system of national health in the 1930s, or even in the midst of World War II. It hasn't been ready since, either. The AMA did not want national health insurance, but it took more than the AMA to produce the results just described.

Switzer was a practical and "resourceful" woman, a professional civil servant, not an elected politician. Her job was "to get things done," mostly for other people. She had to see and understand the other fellow's viewpoint if she were to succeed in her job. The results she would achieve would be attained by careful diplomacy, by a delicate weighing of the various interests concerned. From 1938 onward Switzer was careful to cultivate professional medical support for the projects she was pushing. She would rather succeed partly than fail totally, if gloriously. She became known as someone in Washington with influence between the AMA and the government. She described herself in 1951 this way: "I am amazed at myself, at how readily and easily I have fallen into the habit and pattern of an operator." She was a bureaucrat, a uniquely successful one before her career ended. One of her later pamphlets inviting the construction of local rehabilitation clinics was labeled "Here's How To Do It."

The pace of professional life picked up for Switzer in 1939 when the Federal Security Administration (FSA) was organized to put many of the different federal agencies delivering "human" services under a single bureaucratic roof. The Public Health Service, Switzer's special responsibility in the Treasury, was among the agencies being gathered from far afield to join with the new Social Security Board, Tracy Copp's Vocational Rehabilitation unit, the National Youth Administration and others. Politics and the rational growth and permutations of the bureaus were slowly producing a new organism; the next reorganization on this scale would produce HEW in 1953.

The FSA in 1939 was headed by Paul V. McNutt, and Switzer became his assistant, with special responsibility for the agency's health and medical obligations. McNutt, with his great mane of white hair, had presidential ambitions, and some have been unkind enough to suggest that FDR gave him the very visible post of administrator of the new FSA to use him as a "stalking horse" for 1940. When the political battle became more heated, FDR dispatched McNutt to the Philipines. In 1940, of course, FDR, like the walrus with the oysters, decided he would have to take the best for himself and have a third term.

Switzer's comment on leaving the Treasury after so many years was how exciting it now was to be in an agency that was going someplace. After the 1938 recession the Treasury was in the doldrums due to Morgenthau's temporary displacement by Marriner Eccles (next chapter) as FDR's deep thinker on fiscal matters. Since McNutt was a political "big swinger," and not a manager, Switzer, as his assistant, found herself involved in the daily hassles of FSA, mediating between rival agencies, including the Social Security Board, which no longer had access to FDR but only to McNutt. It was then that Switzer developed an aversion to the Social Security Board's ambitions to unify all welfare services. She considered them to be excessively "bureaucratic." That was swinging back a bit toward Mr. Justice Brandeis.

With the outbreak of World War II, Switzer's position (along with Switzer) would become an important link in the defense effort, and she became far more deeply enmeshed in the politics and development of public medicine, now as an advocate with a message. Her life was changed for good. When the war ended she had become a champion of both mental health and "physical medicine," the new medical specialty produced by the existence of thousands of disabled men, and its economic rationale, rehabilitation. It would be her active involvement in the rehabilitation movement that would produce results that finally formed a philosophy underpinning the developing welfare state from Eisenhower to Nixon, via John Kennedy and Lyndon Johnson.

V

With the war McNutt moved to the War Manpower Commission (WMC), and so did Switzer. She was assistant to the chairman of the Procurement and Assignment Service, finding ways to supply both the armed services and the civilian population with physicians, rationing them out. Here she worked regularly with AMA officials and individual medical doctors all across the country. She gained a deep insight into the professional souls of people like Morris Fishbein. She had to understand them now; without the AMA's active help the medical needs of the wartime economy could not be met. This work also involved her in administration of secret research on biological warfare. She saw the frightening possibilities of secret power at the center. This seems to have swung her even farther back toward Justice Brandeis. She wrote to her friend, Elizabeth Brandeis:

> I resist every increase in the centralization of power over the human soul. In the winning of the war, I don't want to lose the ability to break up central power even at the expense of local inefficiency and scandal.

She apparently quietly opposed the Wagner, Murray, Dingall bill in 1943 over the issue of its potential centralization of power.

In her work with organized medicine Switzer served from 1941 to 1946 on the Board of Visitors of St. Elizabeth's Hospital. There and in the WMC she gained an interest in mental health, became a friend of the Menningers and served on the Board of Trustees of the Menninger Foundation. That interest produced an important legislative payoff: the National Mental Health Act of 1946, slipped through Congress quietly, efficiently, effectively. From that act arose, in 1949, the National Institute of Mental Health, one of the seven National Institutes of Health in Switzer's old bailiwick, the PHS. According to Berkowitz, Switzer simply "took over" the mental health legislation. The Surgeon General knew next to nothing about mental health, and Switzer did. When Representative J. Percy Priest of Tennessee called at the PHS for information about mental health, Berkowitz writes, "Mary Switzer presented him with legislation which she had drafted with the help of the National Committee for Mental Hygiene and Menninger brothers. . . ."

The years of patient learning produced a wealth of results of the first magnitude. By 1948 the federal role in medical research had been reorganized and the National Institutes of Health set up and given their name and place within the Public Health Service. Switzer had worked with AMA leaders and the Congress to achieve this vital public involvement in medicine without a full-scale national health service on the European model. Switzer also worked with Vannevar Bush on postwar plans for the federal role in medicine, the Bush Report. Scientists like Bush were alive to the possibility that waiting if only the research funds and facilities were available. With the giant expansion of the government's fiscal power in World War II, the pay-as-you-earn income tax in 1943 and the obvious, that the federal government would never give up that siphon on the GNP, there was one place to go for funding for medicine and science: Washington. Such would be true of the new National Science Foundation, whose legislation in 1950 was decisively influenced by Switzer's desire that even government-funded science be guided by scientists and not by politicians. Such has been true ever since.

The question was how much centralism, and how much reliance on state initiatives? Switzer knew that national health insurance wasn't in the cards (Truman tried the Wagner, Murray, Dingall bill in Congress again after the war, and it failed the congressional test again). Switzer knew from her experience with PHS, vocational education and other funding in FSA that grants-in-aid from the federal government to the states, for services, for medical research, hospitals and clinics, would be well received. It might not be as rational as the Iron Chancellor's methods, or the early hopes of the Social Security Board, but the grant-in-aid method floated. The grant-in-aid was like a happy business deal. People "out in the field," the United States beyond the Potomac, felt involved with their government. No congressman in his right mind would resist it if his district was to receive the Treasury checks.

A great chance came with the Hospital Survey and Construction Act of 1946, the Hill-Burton Act. Here was the possibility for big federal money jointly administered, which would upgrade medicine "for the people" from Maine to California. It would fill the country up with new hospitals. In that program a Federal Hospital Council surveyed hospital construction plans coming in from the states and made awards for federal subsidies. The council advised the Surgeon General on the standards of hospital care built into hospital design. Truman wanted the Council only in an advisory capacity. But the legislation was written so that the Council ruled, independently of the PHS. Half of the Council was made up of people from the medical and hospital fields. Mary Switzer selected the members of the Council.

By the 1940s Switzer's reputation, for a professional civil servant, was extraordinary. She entered the field of public health on the international level when in 1946 she was a U.S. delegate at the UN International Health Conference. In 1948 she was U.S. delegate at the International Congress on Mental Health; she played an important role in creating the World Health Organization. The list of her postwar activities becomes daunting: she was a director of the Georgetown University; she was a member of the Board of Overseers of the Florence Heller Graduate School of Advanced Studies in Social Welfare at Brandeis University; she served on boards, committees for rehabilitation, mental hygiene, workers for the blind. In every direction her expertise was sought whenever there were issues of public health mixed up with the governance of institutions. In all she received some 40 awards in recognition of her work in public health and welfare. It was a most extraordinary achievement for a member of the permanent Washington bureaucracy. Such an effort was not required, after all, for a career in the Civil Service. Mary Switzer "invented" all this for herself, and the rest of humanity. In 1960 she received the prestigious Albert Lasker Award in Medicine for her work in rehabilitation.

The latter was an outcome of the great change in the direction of her interests produced by her wartime service. During the war she had met Howard Rusk and learned of the revolutionary discoveries in rehabilitation medicine, special corrective surgical techniques, therapies, prostheses and psychological support, developed by himself, Henry Kessler and others in military service. Men with terrible crippling wounds could find their way back to productive lives by application of all this. After World War I the average paraplegic would be dead in a year. Medical rehabilitation, physical medicine, had changed all this. Switzer must have thought back to the 1935–36 survey, of the 16,000,000 physically disabled, and the lack of anything in the way of federal programs for most of them. These people, so many of them drains on the nation's resources then, had been pulled into the labor force in 1941–45 to do whatever they *could* do.

With the end of that episode the danger was a lapse back into the status quo ante. Doctors like Rusk and Kessler were following a trail that could lead to better lives for the disabled from advances in medical science. But how to get it to the people in a country with no national health program? It was partly the delivery of this new science to the public that formed the content of Switzer's greatest contribution. She supported rehabilitation medicine wherever she could in its most difficult period, after World War II, when both established medicine and the general public seemed to forget about it. Rusk would later repay Switzer with a dramatic gesture of support. The second chance for Rusk and other practitioners of physical medicine, and a new vocation for Mary Switzer, came from an unlikely source: John L. Lewis and the United Mine Workers.

VI

Disabled people had always been subject to prejudice; in older times they were even feared as "possessed," "witches," and so on. With the coming of manufacturing industry and extensive use of machinery in agriculture, disabled people were produced in assembly-line numbers, like a stream of military casualties. The difference was that this "war" was never going to end. There was still popular prejudice against the disabled, and there was no way the ancient system of charity to the dependent poor could meet the ever-growing needs of this mangled and partly dismembered army.

The remedy at common law, a suit for negligence instituted by an injured worker against his or her employer, was a joke. The rule that liability follows negligence meant the injured worker's lawyer had to prove negligence against the employer and/or the insurance company's lawyers. The "fellow servant" doctrine in law meant that the employer's liability in industrial accidents could be reduced by proof of contributing negligence by a fellow worker in an accident, a common enough situation with people working around machinery. Finally, "contributory negligence" by the injured employee himself or herself would reduce the employer's liability. As Berkowitz points out in his penetrating study of disability and rehabilitation, between 1906 and 1908 Aetna Life Insurance Company, with its skilled lawyers, was able to avoid payment of anything on 88 percent of suits for negligence against its clients by their injured employees. The "remedy at law" obviously was not going to be the worker's salvation.

As we saw, the state of Wisconsin in 1911 passed a workers compensation law to protect its people against the consequences of the industrial casualty rate. In 1920 the federal government, in the afterglow of World War I, had passed its vocational rehabilitation law. Were these a remedy? Hardly.

The federal government's program had always been minimal for two reasons. First, it was a grant-in-aid scheme that had never been energized at the state levels. State officials initiated actions, if any, not the federal government. (In 1941, the last prewar year, the total number rehabilitated in the entire United States under the federal program was about 11,500.) Second, the official attitude toward rehabilitation had been since its inception that only clients with good chances of finding sufficiently paid employment would be acceptable for rehabilitation. It was a kind of mindless cost–benefit analysis. Anyone too seriously injured—high risk—was "infeasible." Paraplegics, for example, were almost never taken, nor were people with multiple sclerosis or heart disease. The idea was that rehabilitation paid the government only if the injured could be put into employments that returned as much (or more) to the tax rolls as their rehabilitation had cost. Needless to say, under these criteria, very few women or blacks or Hispanics were worth rehabilitating, nor were middle-aged men or the uneducated. In the 17 states with the largest black populations, 91.5 percent of the rehabilitated were young white males. Overall, in 1925–41, the median age of a rehabilitation client was under 30. Whatever the intent of the law in 1920, its outcome was a farce, the kind of "government" that produces revolutions if it cannot be changed by peaceful means.

Workers' compensation worked against the idea of rehabilitation altogether, since compensation payments to the injured were reduced if they could manage to earn any money doing anything. The injured worker with compensation would hardly risk losing what little he or she had by trying to get into a rehabilitation program. In any case, if the injuries were permanently disabling, the worker needn't bother the "rehab" people, since he or she was infeasible.

During the World War II labor shortage the disabled were put to work doing whatever they could do, in a sudden burst of reason at high levels. Paul McNutt in 1942 suddenly sounded like the Henry Ford of *My Life and Work* (before he became senile). McNutt called for "appraisal of the physical requirements of a job, an appraisal of a handicapped worker, and a matching of the two." Since Mary Switzer was his assistant, one suspects that McNutt had not himself actually been independently seized of this inspiration. At the same time Vocational Rehabilitation was now raised from a division in an education bureau to its own existence as an office, the Office of Vocational Rehabilitation. However, the VA, state rehabilitation officials, even the organized blind, opposed any significant expansion of its powers. They too wanted to protect what they already had.

But the end of the war threatened a return to the old system, where a paraplegic or a middle-aged man with heart disease would be infeasible. Howard Rusk learned to his dismay that the wartime interest in rehabilitation medicine was dying out once the shooting stopped. In any case, what about the tens of thousands of people who already had been rendered economically useless by industrial injuries and had no place to turn?

By 1945 John L. Lewis had had enough. He had thought little enough of FDR, and less of Harry Truman, but thought a great deal about his miners. They had terrible problems. He would not wait longer for leadership from the political system. It wasn't going to come. From 1906 to 1945, on the average, 1,981 miners were killed at work each year, and many times that number were injured. Their injuries, typically from explosions and falling rocks, with crushed limbs, broken spines and black lung, made them infeasible. As Lewis put it, ". . . there is no industry in the world which pays such a price in blood and bone and human flesh, in the lives of men and the tears of women, as our own bituminous coal industry." The Social Security System, as it existed, was ". . . totally inadequate to meet the problems of the incapacitated man in industry." As for worker compensation in the coal-mining states, no state ". . . provides payments adequate to maintain a widowed family or fairly compensate the injured." The UMW was going to produce its own social security system, but before it came "on line" in 1948, there had been the Centralia, Illinois, coal mine explosion that killed 114 men. The old system was still in existence and the miners' wives were paid $1,000 each for their husbands—what Lewis had been talking about.

Lewis called a strike, shutting down the mines. Truman, using wartime powers, seized the mines on May 21, 1946, in the name of the people. For that reason Interior Secretary

Julius Krug found himself on the hot seat; he now had to bargain with the miners. He found I. S. Falk, still in government service, and they designed the program Lewis wanted, employer-funded (by a 5¢-a-ton royalty) and union-run. The United Mine Workers Welfare and Retirement Fund was set up as a program of old-age and disability benefits for the miners and their families. In setting up the Fund's management, history spoke. Josephine Roche was made the director of the Fund, and she appointed Warren Draper, formerly Assistant Surgeon General (prewar), and a great friend of Switzer's, to be the Fund's medical director. Switzer wrote to Roche of her deep sense of pride in the personnel of the Fund.

When the Fund's medical staff began to examine their problem, they were horrified. They found some 50,000 miners in need of emergency medicine. There were paralyzed men bed-ridden in the hollows who had been without medicine for 30 years. Now, because of wartime developments and the dedication of the physicians who had been involved, physical medicine and rehabilitation were available. The Fund relied on seven rehabilitation institutions, of which three, run by Rusk, Kessler and Herman Kabat, were the most important.

Howard Rusk had been turned down in 1945 as medical director of the Veteran's Administration, and had taken a job at NYU Medical School. He had treated Arthur Hays Sulzberger's crippled hands (the results of surgery), and the grateful publisher responded by giving Rusk his column in the *New York Times* (which was to run for 25 years) as a forum for his ideas about rehabilitation.

The cause of rehabilitation medicine had good luck in an earlier practitioner. Dr. Simon Baruch had been a pioneer of physical medicine, and his son Bernard, in 1944, had given a million dollars to Columbia and other universities, including NYU, for development and research into the subject. Moreover, Baruch organized a blue-ribbon committee on physical medicine which issued a report urging the establishment of community rehabilitation clinics. Rush, who had met Baruch, headed the subcommittee on the establishment of civilian rehabilitation centers. Baruch would later give Rusk direct funding.

Kessler a Navy doctor, and, Rush's wartime colleague in rehabilitation medicine, had gone back to New Jersey to start a civilian rehabilitation clinic, hopefully modeled after the wartime installation. The UMW Fund would make this possible for Kessler.

The third facility came from a different "infeasible" source. This was the Kabat-Kaiser clinic in Vallejo, California. Herman Kabat was a specialist in paralysis and neuromuscular malfunctions. He had successfully treated Henry J. Kaiser, Jr., for multiple sclerosis, and Henry Kaiser backed him in 1946 with a clinic in Washington, D.C., which closed down for lack of patients. Back in California the Kaiser Permanente Foundation backed Kabat with two more clinics.

At first, hope had nearly turned to ashes for these men. Organized medicine was at least indifferent to the appearance of a new specialty. Continued pressure from Rusk, Kessler and Frank Krusen (who had served on Baruch's committee) finally persuaded the AMA board of medical specialties to establish in 1947 a board for physical medicine, which in 1951 was changed to physical medicine and rehabilitation. But that was after success came. Disappointingly, the states did not use the Hill-Burton funds to include rehabilitation clinics with their new hospitals. They tended to build new traditional hospitals. Moreover, the state rehabilitation bureaucrats also stayed away from the new specialty. In 1948 Rusk had been in operation for a year in his NYU-Bellevue rehabilitation center (established by more money from Baruch, the Gimbels and other New York Jewish sources) and had not received a single referral from the people at New York State Vocational Rehabilitation. But he was there and waiting when the first patients came from the Fund.

Kessler had already made a name for himself with the miners for his miraculously successful treatment of Edward McGinnis, a West Virginia miner who had been paralyzed in a rock fall. Both of his legs had been amputated by doctors in West Virginia. Kessler, after eight months of surgery, rehabilitation therapy and two artificial legs, had been able to send McGinnis home on his own power. He worked afterward, as Berkowitz reports, "in a coal town restaurant." Kessler had been working with the Hospital for Crippled Children and Orthopedics in Newark, and the Fund people urged him to go ahead and open his own rehabilitation center. He did, and the Fund sent him his first five patients.

Once the Fund was operative incredible scenes occurred. In June 1948 the first trainload of paraplegic miners, from Tennessee and Kentucky, headed for Vallejo and Kabat-Kaiser. Other trainloads followed. Miners were carried down out of the hollows on stretchers; others lay on railroad platforms waiting for the trains. The Fund sent out 1,284 patients between October 1947 and the end of 1954; nearly half were paraplegics. Most of the Fund's patients were unknown to state vocational rehabilitation agencies, since they rarely took such infeasibles. Three-fourths of Rusk's patients in those years came from the Fund, as did half of those treated by Kabat-Kaiser.

The state rehabilitation agencies at first were unable and unwilling to accept the Fund's patients. Then a slow and steady change occurred. Draper kept pushing from the UMW side, pressure on the Social Security Board, pressure on the PHS, for more help. By 1953 the change was apparent. In that year West Virginia ranked third in per capita rehabilitations. Kentucky's state rehabilitation effort expanded. After a decade, by 1960, the coal-mining states led the nation in rehabilitations. Already in 1953 the Surgeon General had credited the UMW with leading the nation to rehabilitation, and making it possible for the government to follow. The change in "the government" was in fact a change in the Office of Vocational Rehabilitation (OVR), which both controlled the purse strings over grant-in-aid funds and had the power, if used, to energize the state programs.

In 1950 that power came to life: FSA Administrator Oscar Ewing appointed Mary Switzer director of OVR. In a decade the entire landscape of rehabilitation would be transformed. Money for VR was increased year after year as Switzer cajoled Congress, went out to the state agencies, slowly stretched the old and inflexible VR rules.

Switzer was frightened at first by the opportunity. She already had pursued a long and successful career in the federal medical bureaucracy, and had become the master of pulling strings, using influence, making "soup" out of compromises among opposing interests. But a civil servant is largely invisible in Washington. The political appointee who heads each major agency takes both the credit and the heat for successes and failures. Isabella Diamond, with whom Switzer for many years made her home in Alexandria, Virginia, recalled that Switzer told Ewing she was afraid to take the job: "I have always been a second string person." But Ewing insisted.

As an administrator Switzer would stretch the rules whenever she wanted to. She got results, and after it was all over that is all that mattered. She thought nothing, for example, of bringing Howard Rusk along to high-level bureaucratic policy conferences. After all, if one were discussing a subject, why not have competent opinion about it? As OVR director she pursued the uses of personal contact. It was natural to her, but had been inspired too in earlier days. She recalled, in a revealing letter to the daughter of Elizabeth Brandeis, a visit to the Arthurdale (West Virginia) Subsistence Homestead with Eleanor Roosevelt. The New Deal had wanted through its homestead program to put people back in that place from which they already had fled: the farm. It was not the policy that mattered to Switzer, but how it was pursued by Eleanor Roosevelt. Walker quotes Switzer's letter to the younger woman:

> It was accompanying Mrs. Roosevelt around those projects, watching her talk to young people, questioning them, finding out about their families, their dreams . . . seeing what a simple visit could result in. . . . I do believe this is something I did learn from her. . . . For one of the most important things I have been able to do in my present job as I go around the country is stopping . . . in a mentally retarded workshop, a rehabilitation center, a sheltered workshop for the mentally ill. . . . I find an amazing insight comes to one as a result of personal contact. . . .

Writing again of Eleanor Roosevelt, Switzer went on:

> . . . No one knows the number of people she touched, but the tremendous lesson to learn . . . is that the individual does count . . . to win a battle of thousands, the battle of the individual must be won first.

Switzer was to be head of Vocational Rehabilitation for seventeen years during which this country's view of both medical and vocational rehabilitation would be revolutionized; then the concept would be shifted to social rehabilitation with the Great Society. By 1968, 250,000 people would be rehabilitated by VR in a single year. By 1973, two years after Mary Switzer's death, the federal government had 64 federal disability programs going and was spending $40 billion, or 3 percent of the GNP on rehabilitation of the disabled. A time would come when no building built with federal money could be designed without access for the disabled. Millions would have reason to be grateful to the handsome lady from Massachusetts. In 1950, when her chance came, the long years of service paid off. She wasn't really a second stringer after all, but a champion at the arcane art of making things happen in a bureaucratic system designed to achieve and maintain stasis. The 1950s were the years of breakthrough.

The postwar surge of federal expenditures, expansion of the federal role in medicine and hospitals, by 1950 still had done nothing for rehabilitation, vocational or medical. Medical rehabilitation still depended on private donations by individuals like Kaiser, Baruch and the Gimbels, and by interested private organizations. In 1950 the Korean War broke out, and once more the Congress and the administration began to examine the state of the labor force and to cast about for ways to improve its quality and morale. In 1950, in the first significant amendments to the Social Security Act since 1939 (when Survivor's Insurance had been added), Congress opened up OASI to 10 million more participants, this time allowing the self-employed, farm workers and domestic workers the privilege of contributing. The Social Security Board lobbied once more for disability insurance, but the AMA was in opposition, along with others who feared anything that would encourage malingering: "We must always oppose any program which places a brake on the incentives of the sick and disabled to desire recovery," said the AMA. Disability insurance was scrapped again and in its place a new public assistance program was added to the Social Security law, Aid to the Permanent and Totally Disabled (APTD). In addition, Aid to Dependent Children was liberalized to include families with dependent children, and ADC became AFDC. Also, provision was made to permit federal matching funds to be used for medicine for the blind and for the institutionalized aged.

Since there was not going to be an extension of social insurance, including health, to protect the public from the risks of living, as in Britain's "cradle to the grave" social insurance system, emphasis changed to ending "dependency." This was opportunity for Switzer. She wanted to include more medical input into VR, and she also wanted to chip away at the base of disabled people on public aid, still within, of course, the OVR guidelines: that any rehabilitation in question make *economic* sense. OVR should think of ways to reduce the range of infeasibles. Switzer argued that ". . . where disability exists the sufferers will be taken care of one way or another." So why not restore as many as possible to productive life through vocational rehabilitation? In 1951 only one OVR client in eight had come from public aid rolls. By 1952 the number was one in five, a 60 percent increase in a single year—energized.

At that point what was to be almost did not happen. After the long drought from 1932 to 1952, the Republicans, behind their newly acquired leader, General Eisenhower, won the election. The name of the game in changes of administration is patronage—jobs, jobs for supporters, contributors, friends, fellow ideologues, relatives, whatever. Mary Switzer's applecart was almost trashed. The secretary of the new Department of Health, Education and Welfare (HEW), as history will ever remember (owing to the foul-up on polio vaccine production and distribution when Jonas Salk made his discovery), was Oveta Culp Hobby. She was under heavy pressure to open up spots for deserving Republicans in the new HEW. The change-of-administration plans included replacing Switzer with the head of the California Women's Committee for Nixon. This monstrosity was aborted by Dr. Howard Rusk. Through the years since their wartime collaboration Rusk and Switzer had continued a close professional association, and she had supported his plans whenever possible during the lean years. In 1952 he had written a *New York Times* editorial to help OVR get its appropriations from a balking Congress. Now Rusk came to Switzer's aid again, with Oveta Culp Hobby, with Sherman Adams, with Eisenhower's personal physician, with George Merck, head of the big drug company. The pressure was sufficient, and wherever the California Woman for Nixon landed, it would not be in Switzer's chair.

Soon Eisenhower himself was in Switzer's camp. Her philosophy about rehabilitation contained very attractive political meat and potatoes for the Eisenhower Republicans. Their style was a kind of progressive conservatism. They were "modern," and wanted a cost-effective, forward-looking stance, not a return to the ancient regime. After twenty years of New Deal and Fair Deal, it would not be possible for the party in office to face the public with no social policy at all. There now had to be something beyond "bloviation," President Harding's word, in office. Eisenhower had said "no new starts," and there were the perennial issues of the national debt and the budget deficit. But those were not issues Eisenhower wanted. Casting about, the new administration's attention was drawn to Switzer's activities.

Howard Rusk had been chairman of the Health Resources Advisory Board in 1950 and had written to the Office of Defense Mobilization about the role handicapped people could now play in any wartime manpower mobilization. A task force had been formed and in 1952 had published a report in which it was argued that the whole idea of handicap was obsolete. A person need not be "anatomically whole" to perform productively. With community cooperation, utilizing rehabilitation experts including physicians and aided by OVR, the handicapped could play a full part in the labor force.

Such a community-based effort backed by OVR now existed in Knoxville, Tennessee, the location of the Oak Ridge atomic research installation. Employment was up; relief rolls were down. Mary Switzer had proclaimed that "Operation Knoxville" was ". . . setting the pace for the whole country. . . . The same methods that work in Knoxville will work in your city and mine." OVR put out a pamphlet, "Community Organization for Vocational Rehabilitation—Here's How To Do It," outlining in detail the potentials for local service-club action, support by local community organizations. OVR had sent a special task force to Knoxville to use it as a demonstration of what could be done. In an article she wrote for the *International Labour Review*, "Vocational Education in the United States," Switzer outlined her long-argued position on rehabilitation in every community:

> First, rehabilitation restores hope and confidence in the disabled men and women themselves, giving life a new meaning for them. Secondly, it demonstrates to all the people, in a practical way, that every citizen, however difficult his circumstances, has a chance to make his life useful and satisfying. And finally, it brings into the productive strength of a country thousands of workers, many of them with high skills, who might otherwise be a drain upon the national economy.

Eisenhower wanted a new approach to social problems, an approach that would not be seen as a mere extension of the New and Fair Deals. He wanted something positive and dramatic, something more than just throwing money at problems. Hobby was told to come up with something for health that was not "socialistic." Since Mary Switzer's object was the elimination of welfare, or at least its reduction, through rehabilitation, and she could show results, her OVR became the object of intense scrutiny by Hobby, Undersecretary Nelson Rockefeller and Assistant Secretary Roswell Perkins. Before long Hobby herself gave a demonstration of VR's possibilities to an audience of Air Force wives, and Mamie Eisenhower was there. Rockefeller took the show to Eisenhower himself.

Before long rehabilitation became a Washington buzzword.

The Eisenhower government was rehabilitating the states from their dependence on the federal government, the people from their dependence on *any* government, foreign countries to save them from communism. According to Berkowitz, Eisenhower even discussed the idea of rehabilitation as a solution to the growing problems of juvenile delinquency. This thought would become a federal agency when the activists returned to power in the 1960s.

To be in fashion after such a long uphill pull was a welcome change, but money was going to be spent, or not, so the various interests and agencies began the bureaucratic war dance over clashing jurisdictions and budget shares. Switzer was out to get her agency enlarged. She believed that 60 percent of the 200,000 people disabled every year, out of work and thus lost to OASI, could be rehabilitated and brought back into the productive labor force. So she pressed her argument that more money for rehabilitation was really less, since she was causing *total* expenditures on the disabled to fall. She also wanted a National Institute for Rehabilitation inside the NIH system, but was not optimistic about that with a conservative administration in power. She, along with Howard Rusk, also wanted amendments to the Hill-Burton Act to encourage the building of community rehabilitation centers with federal funds. That would be a tall order. Senator Lister Hill would have to be won over, as would the AMA. The program was finally sold on the ground that all interests would find something in it for themselves, and amendments were written so that nursing homes and rehabilitation facilities, as well as hospitals for the chronically ill and impaired, and diagnostic and treatment centers all would qualify under the Hill-Burton Act.

In January 1954 the Eisenhower program was ready, with rehabilitation as its central theme. The disabled should be helped to "return to employment and lives of usefulness, independence and self respect," Eisenhower said in a message to Congress. There were, he said, 2 million Americans who could be rehabilitated, and in the 1950s the rate was still only 50,000 to 60,000 a year. "Conditions of both humanity and national self-interest" justified an increased effort. At the White House ceremony, signing the new vocational rehabilitation act, Eisenhower intoned Switzer's arguments (crudely), with Switzer standing nearby: "It is a humanitarian investment of great importance, yet it saves substantial sums of money." More accurately, he should have said that the program made it possible to spend less money overall than would be spent without it, somehow, by someone, on the disabled who would not be rehabilitated without the new program. In 1956 an amendment to OASI allowed cash benefits from Social Security to disabled persons over 50, the beginning of the federal disability insurance so long sought after in vain.

Although Switzer complained about the "assembly-line" mentality of the Eisenhower bureaucracy, each year she got more money and each year the numbers grew. But vocational and medical rehabilitation took place one person at a time, and to increase the numbers rehabilitated meant increased effort; it was a simple as that. There were no mass-production techniques possible. You had to have counselors in the communities, funding and cooperation at the local and state level. By 1962 there would be another Rose Garden ceremony, now with President Kennedy, celebrating the 100,000th rehabilitation in a single year, something Switzer said ". . . we should make a little splash about." Kennedy then promised that the 200,000-a-year mark would be reached.

Berkowitz argues persuasively that rehabilitation's triumphs in the Eisenhower years were in fact the result of a social compromise between those who wanted to move again into a full expansion of the welfare state ideal and those who wanted minimalism: more, but not too much. For Mary Switzer, who distrusted centralization of power, the 1950s were congenial to her self-help and community-based techniques with the helping hand of the federal power necessary only as extra assistance, the provision of expertise, encouragement and guidelines. For Howard Rusk and the doctors of physical medicine the Eisenhower program brought official recognition, a statement, finally, that their science and healing art had a place for its inherent social value.

What none of these people foresaw was that the rehabilitation idea, taken from strict vocational education and physical medicine, would follow the line inherent in Eisenhower's random thought about juvenile delinquency; rehabilitation could become the rationale and blueprint for community building by the Great Society social engineers to come. In place of the National Rehabilitation Association with its careful lobbying there would be welfare rights groups presenting demands to bureaucrats with no rationale for refusing them. What seemed like big breakthrough in the Eisenhower era would be considered restraints in the 1960s when history caught up with the American Dream, and with Mary Switzer.

Her ideas and methods would suddenly seem out of date.

VIII

Since the American welfare state had been put together piece by piece, with no overall plan, it had no theoretical or real limits. It went nowhere in particular, and therefore it *could* go anywhere. What seemed each time to be final changes, or necessary amendments, were merely higher platforms for the next expansion. The minimalists were in fact defeating their own purposes by refusing to consider carefully where the maxima ought to be relative to some aggregate measure. With no overall targets, categorical assistance schemes could and would be added by every Congress until, by the early 1970s, they occupied 75 percent of the entire federal budget. Discretionary expenditure for the government, freedom to act anew, was to be reduced to a mere quarter of the federal government's resources. Those who had argued against national health insurance in the 1930s on the ground that it would be "too expensive," had they lived to the 1980s, would have seen 10 percent of the GNP spent on medical care and delivery in a crazy quilt of separate insurance and payment schemes, public and private, that were decried both as excessively expensive *and* wholly inadequate to meet the country's needs. The same was true of the rest of the welfare system. Social Security payments to the aged, based on the Social Security Fund and its payroll-tax supports, would now seem to be conservative and under control by comparison. But we anticipate.

On September 1, 1960, Mary Switzer became the first woman to receive the Lasker Award for international achievement. She was cited as ". . . the prime architect of workable rehabilitation services for the nation's physically handicapped." Switzer was doubly pleased because Mary Lasker was a Radcliffe woman. Switzer was also apprehensive about her acceptance speech; it had "no punch," she said. But the audience in New York cheered anyway. Switzer was probably at, or near, the peak of her career. Coming full time to rehabilitation when she was fifty years old, already a bureaucrat seasoned by nearly three decades in Washington, she had charted and followed a clearly defined path for rehabilitation. Now would come the New Frontier and the Great Society, chaos and destruction. By 1967 she would be handed a flaming mess that exploded in her face.

John Kennedy wanted to "get this country moving again." He wanted a national social system that was a "hand of hope." The New Frontier began its social policy planning in an atmosphere of overwhelming optimism. There was talk of "buying out" the poor. About 21 percent of all families in 1959 had been classified as "below low income level," 18 percent of white families, but 56 percent of nonwhite families including fully half of all families headed by females. Why couldn't a renewed effort now solve the problems that produced poverty in a country as rich as this one? The young activists poured into Washington to help chart the course toward this Utopia. Everything seemed possible. Mary Switzer, looking out from the citadel of a long-term program that counted success person by person, year after year, over a long hard road up, commented later on the flood of floundering federal antipoverty programs: "Poor President Kennedy! He probably thought he knew a lot about what he was getting into, but I am convinced he didn't know the half of it."

Mary Switzer was an interesting mixture. For her the best of all possible worlds was certainly "liberal" in the modern sense of that word. She wanted a world in which every disabled person had access to rehabilitation: ". . . an advanced civilization like ours should so order its system that all disabled people will be restored as fully as possible, regardless of any benefits to anyone." But she hadn't written the laws, and her success was always to work *within* them, getting the best for the most from what there was, and suggesting changes that had a chance of passage through Congress. She was "thrilled," as a citizen and as a taxpayer, she wrote, by the Kennedy vision. But she was a conservative about procedures. She attributed this conservative streak to the years of working for Mellon and Morgenthau, together with her New England upbringing. She feared the centralization of power, and was always realistic about the temptation for the opportunity in any subsidy program to attract "free riders," those whose only object was to take advantage of someone else's generosity. So her administration was characterized by personal management, careful delegation of power and a belief that maximum local effort would act as a brake against abuses. Local people knew what was going on. Counselors, if carefully chosen, motivated, trained and supervised with patience, could ensure the right outcomes.

In this philosophy Switzer was, had she known it, in agreement with the great English economist David Ricardo, who argued in his *Principles of Political Economy and Taxation* (1819) that the "poor rates" (taxes collected for relief payments) must always be gathered and dispersed locally, *never* put by law into a central fund. Ricardo had written:

> If by law every human being wanting support could be sure to obtain it . . . in such a degree as to make life tolerably comfortable, theory would lead us to expect that all other taxes . . . would be light compared to . . . the poor rates. The principle of gravitation is not more certain than the tendency of such laws to change wealth into misery and weakness. . . .

For Switzer the participation of the states by grants-in-aid was the hands-on guarantee against the Ricardian nightmare in which well-intentioned public welfare expenditures would ". . . call away the exertions of labour from every object . . . until at last all classes would be infected with the plague of universal poverty."

Martha Walker gives examples of Switzer's resistance to centralization in an exchange with Elliot Richardson late in the Eisenhower administration. Social Security, after 1956, began making cash payments to the disabled over 50 years of age. So why not centralize things? Why not put Vocational Rehabilitation together with the Social Security Board? Switzer, defending her turf ("market share" in Niskanen's analysis), pointed out that such an arrangement would end her carefully constructed system of state and federal cooperation: "Does the administration wish to reverse itself on the oft-reiterated principle that the states are a responsible part of this man's government?" In the present system OVR had to go to Congress for its money just like all other agencies, and make a case—sell its product—in competition with the others. You had to beat the competition to increase your share. The process set limits that Richardson would eliminate: "The temptation to dip into the Trust Fund for support of the rehabilitation programs rather than support from the general revenues would become irresistible."

Such conservative financial ideas were not destined to thrive in the 1960s. As the "federal gold rush" of 1964–65 mounted, competition was attracted and Switzer began to lose ground to more aggressive, and younger, bureaucratic entrepreneurs in the competition for the now-generous money flows.

John Kennedy's assassination in November 1963 brought Lyndon Johnson to the White House and transformed the ambitious social-welfare plans of the New Frontier into a martyr's cause. The New Frontier passed into the Great Society. The 89th Congress, the "Congress of Fulfillment," assembling in 1965, began passing an avalanche of social legislation. Johnson wanted all this even while he was mounting his Vietnam War. In the first session alone the 89th Congress passed 25 new programs for HEW to administer, including the Social Security amendments establishing Medicaid and Medicare, also the Higher Education Act, and assorted bills for health, Mental Retardation and Community Health Centers Construction, and special programs to fund attacks on heart disease, cancer and stroke. Already in 1964 Switzer complained that her VR forces were being spread too thinly. She still fought for her independence: ". . . so long as I am responsible for this program [it] must be a self-contained, independent operation with freedom to move about and accomplish its mission." Her reputation was immense by now in Washington. Congresswoman Edith Green of Oregon said in hearings before the Subcommittee on Education: "I think that the vocational rehabilitation program is, without question, the best antipoverty program we ever had in this country."

Other programs were now growing faster, in part because of Switzer's success. The 1962 amendments to Public Welfare had set up a category of grants under Social Services to the states to purchase services, in a vain attempt to change welfare into rehabilitation. Where free riding can occur, it will. There were no statutory limits on these purchases, and welfare expenditures soared, but not from a sudden appearance of hoards of unwed "welfare mothers." The free riding came from sharp hustlers in the state governments taking advantage of HEW's largesse, shifting their bureaucracies into areas where the new unlimited grants-in-aid could be found— "where the money was," as bankrobber Willie Sutton once explained his career. The people Switzer had always trusted to hold the line now went instead "for the gold." The early champion at this game was California, followed quickly enough by Illinois and then New York before Congress put on a lid. Other states had their moments too. Martha Derthick, in her study *Uncontrollable Spending for Social Services Grants*, quoted a California assembly study, "California Welfare: A Legislative Program for Reform," showing where this would go. As for rehabilitation money, citing the 1962 act: "We propose to deploy these existing expenditures in a way which will produce an optimum return of federal dollars for a minimum amount of state and local dollars." Since Social Services expenditures had no ceiling: "The first task would be to shift existing rehabilitation services that would qualify . . . from rehabilitation to the Social Service Amendments, thus freeing federal rehabilitation dollars." So much for the deserving poor and the disabled. California's new gold rush would be in Washington, D.C.

The booming Welfare Administration of HEW temporarily acquired Ellin Winston from North Carolina to ride herd on this runaway. Her new agency included the Children's Bureau, the Office of Juvenile Delinquency, the Bureau of Aging, the Cuban Refugee Program and Medicaid. There were no statutory spending limits in these and free riding was irresistible. A lot of money was made "servicing" these agencies of HEW by persons not poor or disabled in any way.

Some programs in HEW became targets of ridicule. In the Community Work and Training Program and the Work Experience and Training Program, 90 percent of the expenditures had gone to subsidize the employment of AFDC fathers. That was somehow considered to be an outrageous waste, proving that the new welfare programs could not work. But what was the purpose of those programs? The critics didn't care.

Switzer had hoped to expand VR techniques and criteria into the expanding welfare areas, but Winston went her own route (and soon, back to North Carolina).

In 1958 Switzer had been instrumental in writing legislation to fund captioned films for the deaf. A new entreprenur, Patricia Winalski, had seen these films, was inspired by the possibilities and came to HEW's Office of Education to play a role. She went after the handicapped children (left behind in 1943 when OVR left the Office of Education), and in 1963 the Bureau of Education for Handicapped Children came into existence run by Winalski. That had been a bitter loss to Switzer, destroying for good her hopes to have her agency (now renamed the Vocational Rehabilitation Administration, VRA, with Switzer now styled the Commissioner) acquire a monopoly on vocational rehabilitation for the entire population. Still, Switzer's agency thrived in the Great Society in 1965–66 despite the competition. She did not complain of lack of work for rehabilitation.

Total Federal welfare expenditures, $25 billion in 1960, more than doubled to $53 billion by 1967. The problem became how to expand fast enough to keep up with the money. In 1965–66 HEW's budget rose 41 percent in a single year.

Employment at HEW went from 87,316 to 99,810 in response, an increase of more than 12,000 new employees in a single year. Mary Switzer's state rehabilitation agencies had their budgets doubled in a single year. She worried aloud that such abundant funding would wipe away any believable excuses for failure.

But the accompanying euphoria was soon gone. By 1967 the Vietnam horror show had seeped from the evening TV news into the Treasury and was sapping the Great Society. The hopes, now suddenly dashed, were going to produce a violent reaction. Martin Luther King had warned of it: "The bombs we drop in Vietnam will explode in America's cities." Mary Switzer wrote in 1967:

> The legislation passed a year ago is suffering, as all the new programs are suffering, from under-financing, and this has a subtle, deflationary effect not only on the projects that have to be postponed but also on the general morale of the groups.

In August 1967, Senator Lister Hill heaped Emersonian praise on Mary Switzer: "An institution is the lengthened shadow of a man . . . you are that individual in rehabilitation." But in that same month John Gardner, the sixth HEW secretary in 14 years, passed a smoldering explosive to Mary Switzer. With rising criticism of HEW's wasted opportunities and funds, he saw in Commissioner Switzer and her VRA staff what he wanted to see: a piece of unvarnished success. It was a valuable HEW asset, and he decided to cash in on it. He called Switzer a "dynamo," called VRA his "Marine Corps," and promised that "she will make history for all of us." What he did was make Switzer the head, the "Administrator," of a single new agency, Social and Rehabilitation Services (SRS), which contained nearly all of HEW's current troubles, including unresolved problems of the aging and welfare. The concept of rehabilitation was now, in Gardner's words, to "embrace millions, not thousands."

Mary Switzer was 67 years old by then. She was a veteran, a wise and powerful Washington figure. So why did she take the job? Was it arrogance, foolishness, senility? She failed in it, of course. So has everyone else since, if by success you mean ending "poverty" and all that it implies for the nation's "underclass"—a new buzzword, a euphemism for "hopeless."

Three points might be mentioned. First, it was not yet 1968. So the flaming cities and rioting poor had not yet been seen, and were not anticipated, except by King. Second, there was still the hope in 1967 that the United States could extract itself from Vietnam and return to managing its own affairs. In those days the war would be over "in six months" (every six months) and light was shining "at the end of the tunnel." The Tet offensive had not yet come. Third, Mary Switzer really did believe in the philosophy of rehabilitation, and despite her aversion to the "mass production" of it, she may have thought that, given a few years, she could bring order and purpose to the federal welfare programs. Finally, one is here considering the life of a career civil servant, a professional bureaucrat who had been in Washington since Harding was in the White House, had lived through the entire vast growth of the federal government since World War I. She may very well have believed that growth of the federal government was inevitable (it is now *much* larger than it was in 1967), and the record showed that she could do the job as well as or better than anyone else. Her own success, after all, had made rehabilitation the only game in town by 1967. Everyone and everything needy, from crippled babies to giant urban slums and their populations, now had rehabilitation as their only hope for improvement. Her career was a monumental success, so they made Mary Switzer the "captain of the Titanic."

IX

Before disaster came Mary Switzer savored one more sweet triumph. Her years of work to get architectural help to the disabled paid off. The National Commission on Architectural Barriers to Rehabilitation of the Handicapped gave its report to Johnson. On June 3, 1968, he sent the report to Congress. After that no construction utilizing federal funds could be approved without making access provisions for the handicapped. Walker quotes Switzer upbraiding a conference of architects: "It's your fault [that] there are barriers in hospitals, schools, libraries and court houses." The physical world in this country opened up for the handicapped after 1968, wherever federal money was being spent, which was almost everywhere outside the home.

Switzer began her new task at SRS with a restatement of her belief in rehabilitation. It was now to be inserted into ". . . all programs that serve those who cannot achieve their rightful place in our society without some assistance." She now had to reorganize some 1,900 of the HEW labor force to service (Walker's numbers) 7,600,000 people receiving welfare payments (4 percent of the entire 1967 population), 6,000,000 people in receipt of Medicaid, 600,000 childlren needing "foster parenting," 450,000 handicapped children receiving special medical care, and, in the world of sexual freedom, already 250,000 receiving free birth-control technology. In addition there were millions of old and aging people whose fates had to be contemplated.

With the best of luck Switzer's prospects were dismal to achieve measurable, accountable success of the kind known to her old rehabilitation programs. Moreover, not everyone loved Mary Switzer, and that made a difference now. She had played plenty of Washington "hardball." She had been the victor over the years in a thousand and one bureaucratic struggles. Many of those who had lost programs and funds (and therefore promotions and salary increases) to Mary Switzer's well-mannered juggernaut were now her direct subordinates. Their cooperation with their old bureaucratic rival was now essential, and problematical. She knew that and made speeches and sent memos to them saying that they would all now have to stand or fall together. She was not entirely successful in this. Martha Derthick is extremely critical of Switzer's administrative methods, her informality, her hatred of red tape—exemplified by the oft-cited sign in her office taken from Shakespeare's *Henry VI*: "The first thing we do, let's kill all the lawyers." Switzer was no longer working with her old "rehabilitation family." She now had to rely on people who were not her friends, who had not been chosen by her, and many of whom did not want to go her way.

SRS began as a crisis reorganization. Welfare costs were soaring and no one knew how to get it all under control. Derthick, to be fair, does not blame all the chaos on Switzer's informal administrative methods. The job was unbounded, had never been thought out or coordinated. Not only were the newly radicalized "recipient groups" (those receiving the Treasury checks) demanding a role in policy formation, but so were politicians, and even the president. Switzer had been brought to the top of this in a relief pitcher's role, to "put out the fire." Derthick writes: "Leaders of the Department of Health, Education and Welfare . . . thought that if anyone could help the welfare poor get to work and show Congress that HEW was trying, Mary Switzer could."

She might have too, but Switzer would not be in charge of SRS long enough to find out if her ideas would have worked.

No one was going to make order out of decades of chaotic growth in a few months. One point is clear: if anyone expected *less* welfare expenditure once she took the throttle, they were probably wrong. True, she had always been a careful player of the Washington game. But since her days with Roche in the Treasury, Switzer had wanted true national health insurance. She considered Medicare an imperfect substitute, merely better than nothing. Switzer wanted disability care in reach of *all* the disabled for humanitarian as well as economic reasons. She knew, after all, how little was spent on welfare compared to war and preparation for it, and it was clear where her interests lay. She was no starry-eyed idealist. She knew "how things are." Consider her comments on acquiring medical care for welfare clients:

> . . . The most disadvantaged are not attractive patients. They do not think as a physician thinks. They don't take responsibilities that he thinks they should. They stink. They are not a good advertisement in the waiting room. They don't follow up. They don't have the money to buy their medicine. . . . How do we get physicians to give comprehensive and goal oriented care to the bottom of the barrel persons widely regarded as . . . undesirables?

In December 1967, John Gardner resigned, going the way of the other HEW secretaries, and was replaced by Wilbur Cohen, HEW's seventh secretary in 14 years. Cohen's tenure was destined to be very short. He had come to Washington long ago from Wisconsin, accompanying Professor E. E. Witte to plan the original Social Security Act. Cohen knew where everything had come from and why. Cohen and Switzer might have made a first-class team at HEW. But time was now running out for people who thought like they did. In April 1968, following the assassination of Martin Luther King, the black poor rose up and torched and looted downtown Washington. Standing now where revolutionaries the world over had dreamed of being, instead of overthrowing the government, they spent their energies carrying off TV sets, furniture, air conditioners and refrigerators. It was a strange spectacle.

The marching began. The poor descended on Washington and built Resurrection City out of rubbish. Mary Switzer went there to meet them and talk. She stood shoulder to shoulder with Cohen when the poor surged into HEW headquarters and were invited by their leader, Hosea Williams, to run their "bare feet through some of these thick carpets." In the dying months of the Johnson administration the poorest made their statement. They had to do it then because Richard Nixon was coming. Although a world-class welfare spender (federal welfare spending, $60.3 billion in 1968, skyrocketed to $106 billion by 1972), he would hardly be interested in their ideas. They only wanted more, so he gave them more.

What the poor people really wanted was a realization of all the promises of the Great Society. Instead there was the war in Vietnam consuming their sons and the substance that might have made the Great Society work for them, might have opened the gates to prosperity, might have ended poverty and blight. Their hopes had been raised and dashed. It was the prospect that had turned bad, not the reality. Real income had risen substantially in the 1960s. Lyndon Johnson was right when he told the union leaders that they had never had it so good. There was no discernible slack in the rate of growth of the economy. Unemployment, 5.5 percent for the labor force in 1960, had fallen sharply to a mere 3.6 percent by 1968. Black unemployment had fallen even more, declining from 12.4 percent to 6.7 percent in the same period. The proportion living in poverty had been reduced drastically, from 22 percent in 1960 to 13 percent in 1968. Unless none of this improvement had reached the marching poor, either it was felt to be insufficient or their complaints were aimed at something else. Looking back, one could argue that the chaos of 1968 marked the end of a period of hope for the black poor. King was assassinated; then Robert Kennedy was killed. The champions of the poor were being killed off and fading into history as the era of "benign neglect" dawned.

Switzer's reaction was to reach out. She now advocated more decentralization, more local involvement, the keys, after all, to the success of years of rehabilitation, she believed. This seething, cursing, violent clientele did not frighten her. They were her job, and she meant to do that job.

> I am concerned with our responsibility and our commitment for helping the poor, the deprived, the disabled, the hopeless, to move from the road down, onto the road back. . . . We have not been wise enough to establish the right training programs at the right times . . . to open up avenues of work . . . to see the effects of rejection and failure . . . to enforce Civil Rights . . . to have equal justice before the law . . . to recognize what has been happening in our cities. . . .

That was a speech given in June 1969, and it could have been her valedictory. The same month Switzer hosted the National Citizens' Conference on Rehabilitation of the Disabled and the Disadvantaged at the Mayflower Hotel in Washington. There were 700 in attendance and the federal bureaucracy got an earful. Martha Walker puts the scene in nice understatement:

> What became obvious during the Conference was that minority participants knew little about rehabilitation and that many rehabilitation professionals were being exposed for the first time to the language and bitterness of minority groups.

The professionals in Switzer's shop were in fact appalled by the militancy, the loud demands, the cursing. Walker quotes a comment from one of the professionals in attendance:

> I believe we can find people who will tell it like it is, people who will call us to task and make us reconsider our objectives, without the obscenity and vulgarity and without the belligerency that alienates rather than illuminates.

Switzer criticized her own welfare personnel, calling them hardened. Where was the "shared caring" of her rehabilitation people? She told a church group:

> How pleased we all are to be so comfortable within our own private shells of material comforts. . . . However remote the Poor People's Campaign may seem, it is as close to your doorstep as it is to mine. They are *our* neighbors. . . . I hope you can sense their plight as I feel their presence—in our camp, in my office, in our Department's cafeteria or auditorium.

Some of Switzer's criticisms of the federal welfare establishment and policies made headlines in the newspapers. That hardly soothed her colleagues. Most important, though, after November 1968, her time was nearly up. It wasn't California Women for Nixon this time; it was Nixon himself, and her job would be gone. In 1970 Switzer would be 70 years old. By Civil Service standards, that was enough. She did not want to quit, and tried to get her old allies Howard Rusk and Claude Pepper to fight for her once more. But on December 19, 1969, Robert Finch, HEW secretary number 8, announced that "with regret" he was accepting Mary Switzer's resignation. She was replaced as SRS administrator by a political appointee, and he by another, and another.

There is no happy ending. Welfare expenditures now dwarf the levels of Switzer's time. There are thousands of homeless poor in the great cities in winter; there is starving while government warehouses are filled to overflowing with surplus food. Perhaps someday Americans will discover a successful formula for their welfare state. By the mid-1980s, with the year 2000 on the horizon, the time is not yet. In the very long run there has been improvement, of course. In Shakespeare's time the poor were hanged for the third offense of vagrancy. Two hundred years later Jefferson could write with pride in his *Notes on the State of Virginia*: "Vagabonds, without visible property or vocation, are placed in workhouses, where they are well clothed, fed, lodged and made to labor." It beat hanging, and forced labor is "full employment" of a sort, but that was not the right formula either. Mary Switzer thought the right formula might be a massive dose of vocational rehabilitation. She said we would succeed if we emphasized it as much as we do "automatic transmissions, lunar exploration, or irrigation." Maybe so.

X

Switzer said her farewell after 48 years in public service quoting Carl Sandberg: "I see great days ahead, great days possible to men and women of will and wisdom." She died on October 16, 1971, at age 71. After leaving office she served her remaining days as vice-president of the World Rehabilitation Fund. Elliot Richardson said of her:

> She made a difference. Countless of the handicapped the world over led fuller and more rewarding lives because of her unflagging inspiration, caring deeply—here is an unforgettable spirit.

Mary Switzer lit a candle—rehabilitation—in the darkened world of the disabled and outcast. No one else has lighted another. The young woman from Newton and Radcliffe College achieved a career in the ordinary federal civil service that is astounding to recall. But, really, it is easy to remember her: whenever you see a ramp by a stairway in a public building or a parking space reserved for the disabled, think of Mary Switzer.

CHAPTER 11

Marriner Eccles: Logician in Wonderland

We were never able to take up the large amount of slack
that existed throughout the economy. We did not take it
up because we did not spend enough. . . . We were told
that the doctrine of compensatory economy was a failure
—despite the fact that it had never been tried, except to
a mild degree.

Marriner Eccles, 1951

I

Marriner Eccles was the perfect man for his time. He knew
what was right, wise and logical, and he had a missionary zeal
to enlighten his fellow citizens about it. Therefore, in the
perverse way of our historical era, he was destined in the
arena of public life to be frustrated and to fail, in part or
entirely, again and again. The great issues for Eccles were to
be the structure of the banking system, fiscal policy, the
financing of war, the avoidance of inflation, monopoly power,
recognition of Red China, the Korean War, the Vietnam War,
the arms race and world population control. A man like
Marriner Eccles finally would be excluded from public life
after a brilliant personal effort, and men like Lyndon Johnson
and Richard Nixon would be presidents of the United States.
It was our destiny that fools, knaves, and the prophets of folly
would win out, and that the appalling history we have experienced would happen.

Marriner Eccles would continue to lose on the great issues
of the time, right up to the day he died. He lived out the
prime of his life in government service, for years alone, in a
Washington, D.C., hotel, in a self-created emotional drought
that withered the lives of those he loved the most. He knew
it, regretted it, couldn't stop himself, but suffered no self-
delusions about it. Why he chose that road is a mystery, not
explained by himself or by those who studied his life after he
was gone.

In the passage quoted above from his memoirs, *Beckoning Frontiers*, Eccles was summing up the years of his service in Washington before World War II. War came again to the world in 1939, and American factories, mines, farms and lumber mills began finally to arouse themselves from the terrible malaise of the depression of the 1930s. After two Roosevelt administrations and the New Deal, celebrated in song and story by American historians for "saving the country," the nominal GNP still lay below 1929 and a whopping 17.2 percent of the labor force was still unemployed. (If you counted those on various forms of government work-relief as employed, the percentage was still 11.2.) The depression was ended by World War II, not by the New Deal. War, as it had for thousands of years, absorbed, swallowed up, "excess" men and materials.

Eccles knew the truth about the New Deal and the depression from bitter experience. Five years after his memoirs were published science verified the conclusions he had written. Professor Cary Brown of MIT published a famous econometric study in 1956 which contained some of the most-quoted words of any paper ever published in *The American Economic Review*. Brown found the New Deal expenditures to have been so conservative that the federal budget was actually a drag on the economy. He wrote:

> For recovery to have been achieved in this period, private demand would have had to be higher out of a given private disposable income than it was in 1929. Fiscal policy, then, seems to have been an unsuccessful recovery device in the thirties—not because it did not work, but because it was not tried.

Professor Brown's study, indeed, has been found by subsequent research to have been too kind to the New Deal's reputation as a gang of wild-eyed spenders. Larry Peppers, reworking Brown's numbers nearly two decades later in 1973, found that at (assumed) full-employment levels of growth in the 1930's the New Deal would have been running surpluses in every year—actually slowing down the economy's growth. There had been much hairy-chested talk among the New Dealers similar to Rexford Tugwell's famous boast about rolling up his sleeves and remaking the American economy. In fact, it was different. In Henry Morgenthau's diaries (as reported by John Morton Blum) one finds plenty of "advanced" social thinking, but there, in the U.S. Treasury, at the heart of the "federal spending machine," what one finds is trembling fiscal timidity, and a creationist-like devotion to the ideal of balanced budgets—the divine order. In those pages Marriner Eccles lurks like a demon, the threat of fiscal heresy, spreading the red-ink stain of his subversive doctrines inexorably through the New Deal bureaucracy.

Marriner Eccles, the western business tycoon, temporarily abandoned his private empire in 1934 to join the New Deal effort to remake the world. By 1951, despite his reputation in "thinking circles" in the nation's capital, Eccles knew that he had failed in his one great mission: to stabilize the American economy's erratic growth patterns—boom and bust, and boom again—by adroit management of monetary and fiscal policies. Eccles achieved only parts of his plan and is honored today for his partial successes.

Intellectually, though, his greatest achievement was the one in whose interests he labored most valiantly and unsuccessfully. Eccles, on his own, pondering the economic problems of the Intermountain West, had discovered by 1932 the basic elements of macroeconomics—the economic logic of the creation of national income. This was an impressive feat, but not a unique one. In later years some people, mainly professors, doubted that a banker "out west" could have made such a discovery untutored by emissaries of higher learning (Eccles never went to college). But it had been done before, for example, by English banker Henry Thornton in *The Paper Pound* (1818), and in a later generation by London banker and financial writer William Newmarch in Vol. VI of *Tooke's History of Prices* (1857), among others. Farther back, and in a foreign tongue, Antonio Serra, the sixteenth-century Italian mercantilist, understood it, multipliers and all. Macroeconomics is a "real world" topic; one can discover it by studying reality, and many did, before Keynes. For that matter, John Law (1671–1729), the father of modern public finance—print money, spend it—surely understood the basics of macroeconomics. The memory of those discoveries had died out. Thornton's advocacy of countercyclical monetary policy and Newmarch's analysis of domestic and international income multipliers (used to explain the income effects of the then-recent Californian and Australian gold discoveries) vanished without trace in mainstream economic doctrine. In 1932, John Maynard Keynes was just coming away from the triumphal publication of his *Treatise on Money* (1930), in which national income advanced or fell because of the inequalities of saving and investment. In 1936, Keynes would get it right in *The General Theory of Employment Interest and Money* and start a revolution in economic thought.

But already in 1932, Marriner Eccles fully comprehended the policy implications of macroeconomics, and began to lectrue to captive (and baffled) audiences of bankers and businessmen about the promise of compensatory economic policy. In February 1933, during the hiatus between the Hoover and the Roosevelt administrations, Eccles would upend a senate committee, and the attending corps of newspaper reporters, with his ideas. There was too much saving. The federal budget should expand by deficit spending. You had to *spend*, not save, your way out of the depression. The drive to cut expenditures and balance the federal budget was all wrong. Hoover couldn't do it, and FDR had promised to do it, if elected. That was all wrong, in the circumstances.

Eccles joined the New Deal in 1934, and in 1951, after 17 weary years (as "Pharaoh's Steward," as he put it), went home to Utah after a final victory: he beat Harry Truman in a bitter battle over the inflationary consequences of increased federal expenditures in a full-employment economy. The victory trophy was the Treasury–Federal Reserve "Accord" which freed the Fed from its "Babylonian captivity," the obligation to monetize the outstanding national debt by supporting with Federal Reserve buying the market for federal debt obligations. Eccles went home, accompanied by the fading strains of Truman's curses, and resumed his career as financial capitalist extraordinaire. He died in 1977, a week before Christmas, at age 87 in Salt Lake City, a man of great personal wealth, "more feared than loved." In 1982 they renamed the Federal Reserve Building in Washington after him. Who was Marriner Eccles?

II

Marriner Stoddard Eccles, the eldest child of David and Ellen Stoddard Eccles, was born September 9, 1890, in Logan, Utah. The Eccles family story begins where we left Brigham Young and his saints, high in the mountain deserts of the Great Basin, polygamy and all. The Mormons had tried to fill their empty empire with converts to the doctrines of Joseph Smith. A large part of their missionary work was in Europe. Among those snared abroad were William Eccles, a nearly blind wood turner in Paisley, Scotland, along with his wife Sarah and their seven children. The Perpetual Emigration (or Emigrating) Fund had been established in 1849 to aid poor immigrants, and as we have already seen, within a year some 2,500 were able to use its resources to make the journey across the ocean, plains and mountains to Zion, the gathering place.

In 1863 the time came for the Eccles family. The PEF advanced the family £75 (roughly $375). They came on a sailing vessel, the *Cynosure*. The ocean voyage took four weeks and three days, and they arrived in New York harbor July 1, after an experience they all remembered in later years with distaste. From there the journey went by train to St. Joseph, Missouri, and thence by wagon to Florence, Nebraska ("Winter Quarters" in 1846–47). There the family joined a wagon company for the trek west across the plains and mountains. Mormon teamsters from Utah by the 1860s had the trek organized carefully. It had become routine—hard routine. It was mostly walking, with the wagons carrying the provisions. Old William, although very nearly blind, walked most of the way. By October 5, 1863, a mere four months after leaving Scotland, the Eccles family stood where Brigham Young had stood in July 1847, on the "east bench" of the valley with the view of the Great Salt Lake stretching westward. By 1863 there was a city down below on the valley floor. The great American future for the Eccles clan now began.

In Scotland young David Eccles had sold his father's wooden handicrafts door to door in Paisley and Glasgow. The Eccles family had been among the poorest. Marriner Eccles later wrote of them that whatever qualms they may have had about the Prophet Joseph and the golden plates were academic. To believe meant a chance for America; to disbelieve meant continued existence in the slums of Paisley and Glasgow. They had nothing to lose, as Eccles wrote of his grandfather's family, ". . . they couldn't fall any further." Now, in Utah, the early mercantile experience of young David Eccles would mix with many elements into a sensational lifetime payoff.

Pioneering in Utah was still hard. There were few resources easily accessible. It was cold in winter and hot in summer, there was very little rainfall and the landscape was rugged. The Eccles family lived at first in miserable conditions, lean-tos, shacks, cabins, mainly in small outlying Utah settlements. One winter they sheltered their only remaining ox in the house, only to see it bloat and die from consumption of springtime grasses. The mainstay of Mormon life then was farming, and

William Eccles was no farmer. In various settlements he made wooden objects for David to peddle, as in Scotland, but now walking down the rough mountain pathways. Once, nearly freezing in a blizzard between Huntsville and Ogden, he swore to himself he would someday build a railroad there. He did, too. It lost money, but he kept his promise.

After more than three years in Utah, mainly getting nowhere, the family migrated again, temporarily, to the Willamette Valley in Oregon to find work in a new woolen mill being constructed. That was another thousand-mile trek, this time across the lava rocks of southern Idaho past newly made graves from an Indian massacre. In Oregon City they built a log cabin and started again. They cut wood by contract for the mill and for private customers. They tried other ventures, including a distillery, and young David Eccles saw in the vast stands of virgin timber of the Northwest and the new lumber mills being built a vision of enterprises to come. After two years most of the family went back to Utah with the "stake" they had earned in Oregon. Year after year young David worked, cutting wood, hauling logs, freighting for railroads, loading coal cars in Wyoming, always working, always watching, always learning. When he failed in a job involving elementary bookkeeping he took some time out to pay for a few months of formal schooling (at about age 21) in two successive winters at an academy in Ogden operated by Professor Louis Moench. That and the bit of schooling in Scotland constituted all the formal education David Eccles ever had.

He had something else, though, like his fellow Scot, Andrew Carnegie. David Eccles possessed a sure instinct for business. The West was growing, and Eccles was the right man in the right place. First a sawmill, then another, then a lumber yard, then milling, manufacturing, railroads, sugar refining (he founded Amalgamated Sugar), construction, cattle, horses, canneries, banks, condensed milk factories, even a candy company. David Eccles became an entrepreneur of fabulous magnitude by the hard-scrabble standards of the Mountain West. He made millions in the barren wastes of Utah and Idaho. Leonard Arrington, in a biography of David Eccles, lists 54 separate enterprises founded by the man. He lived to become a legend in his own lifetime, and died in 1912 "the richest man in Utah." He owned real property in seven states and in Canada. He was president of 7 banks and 16 industrial corporations. In all he was an officer of 47 corporate enterprises and owned stock in 76 companies. He also kept few written records of his tangled interests.

By all accounts David Eccles was a generous, witty and charming man. But he believed in the doctrine of hard work and thrift. Like his fellow Scot, Carnegie (and later on, Henry Ford), he believed his enterprises should generate their own capital. He did not borrow. He took partners, sometimes loaning gifted but poor men the money to buy their shares, the money to be paid back from the earnings of the enterprises. He was also, by two measures, a devout Mormon; he not only tithed himself every year of his working life (toward the end more than $10,000 a year), but he also obeyed the precepts of his religious leaders and married more than one wife. He maintained two stately homes, one in Ogden for his first wife, Bertha, and their twelve children, and another in Logan for his second wife, Ellen, and their nine children. The energy, thought and devotion consumed by such marital obligations boggle the modern mind. To raise 21 children to upper-class opulence, having started from scratch, is by itself a singular achievement. When he was not traveling to oversee his business affairs he spent weeknights with the Ogden family and weekends in Logan. He tried to be a real father to them all. His physician in Logan had warned him against his exertions, advised him to get his affairs in order, said that he had hardening of the arteries. The man dropped dead at age 63 in Salt Lake City, rushing to catch the 9:00 P.M. train to Ogden. He had spent the day and early evening in business conferences. A completely "self-made man," he had lived a rich life, with abundant reward. But it was cut tragically short.

III

The night his father died, Marriner Eccles was in a work camp in Blacksmith Fork Canyon, near Logan, where he was employed by his father to oversee the latest Eccles enterprise, a hydroelectric power plant under construction. Marriner, a mere 22, was just home from serving two years as a Mormon missionary in Scotland. His father had put him right to work. Marriner was used to that. His father had started Marriner in one of his lumber mills, carrying boxes for 50¢ a day, when the lad was only 8 years old, telling him he could buy a stock in the company for $100 if he could save that much from his wages. It took Marriner three summers to accumulate the money, and according to bargain David sold Marriner the stock, much underpriced. Marriner remembered it fondly:

"The feat won a treasured compliment from my father. . . .
I've never ceased being a capitalist since then."

Eccles was devastated by his father's death, but the event
forced the youngster into the full stream of his father's enterprises. Marriner now had to assume the responsibility for the
Logan family. He knew how to work, how to think about his
work and how to start new enterprises. Unlike David Eccles,
Marriner was not starting from scratch. Adding in the widow's
dower (one-third of the net estate), which went only to the
mother of the Ogden family by common law, the twelve shares
of the Ogden family and the nine children of the Logan family,
perhaps best thought of as the junior or "cadet" Eccles family,
the estate was divided into five-sevenths for the senior and
two-sevenths for the cadet branch.

Another putative family—one wife, one child—was awarded
$250,000 by a jury. It was next to impossible for the two
known families to defend against other marital claimants of
the estate of a known polygamist. By 1912 polygamy was out
of fashion among the Mormons. The cadet family had begun
in 1885, and in 1890 the Mormon church disavowed polygamy. Law now filled in the void left by the change in religious
doctrine. The law recognized only one wife and family at a
time. But the law, since the Northwest Ordinance of 1787,
recognized no discrimination against the "half-blood." All the
children of David Eccles, from whatever family, owned equal
shares in his estate. When we consider the problems of the
estate of the late Howard Hughes, the Eccles families were
perhaps lucky to have lived in earlier, simpler times. Nevertheless, there were many attempts at extortion made against
the Eccles families and fortunes after David's death.

In the next two decades Marriner Eccles exceeded his brilliant father as a business tycoon, and also suffered two emotion-
ally wrenching experiences. At first there was an intrafamily
struggle over control of the intermingled assets. Marriner
described that in a chapter, "Joseph and His Brothers," of
Beckoning Frontiers. In 1950 he found it still a sorrowful
memory: "What happened between us is not an uplifting story,
but neither is the story of the tensions between the sons of
Leah and the sons of Rachel in Biblical times."

The second experience came at the end of Marriner's
triumphal early business career when he realized that many of
his father's ultra-orthodox business beliefs, while right for the
individual enterprise, could be profoundly damaging to the
community at large. He worked out for himself "the fallacy

of composition" on his way to discovering the elements of macroeconomics. It was an ideological parting of the ways with the precepts of his beloved father that made an "economic radical"—as he was soon to be called—out of Marriner Eccles. At first, though, economic orthodoxy paid off for Marriner, as it had for David.

The net estate of David Eccles was valued in 1912 at about $7 million. In his book Marriner estimated that at 1950 prices the estate would have been worth about $25 million. Using the consumer price index (1967 = 100), 72.5 in 1950 and about 322 in mid-1985, the Eccles estate of 1912 would be worth about $115 million in 1985 dollars—even with modern inflation, no small beginning. The cadet family's two-sevenths share would have been roughly $33 million by modern standards. That is where, financially, Marriner Eccles began.

Two family holding companies were formed to control this fortune: the David Eccles Company for management of the senior family's holdings and the Eccles Investment Company for the cadet branch. Marriner wrote that many of his father's business associates urged him to try to maintain unity of interests with his half-siblings, but that an uncle, Robert Anderson, urged Marriner to separate the cadet family's shares. It took nerve for the young man to separate from his older half-brothers, but he did. Marriner was only 22, and his eight brothers and sisters were all minors. But the uncle believed in Marriner's superior abilities, and ". . . I incorporated the Eccles Investment Company." The uncle knew who was "his father's son" in the universe of business acumen. The uncle was a wise man.

Banking was to be the most innovative element in Marriner's expansion of his father's legacy. David Eccles had acquired or founded banks in connection with his productive enterprises. He thought little of his banks, "a bundle of notes." His attitude about business was almost identical to that of Carnegie—"the perfect mill is the way to wealth"—or, later, to Henry Ford's ethereal disdain for the very idea of moneymaking. Arrington quotes David Eccles on moneymaking:

> Never work for money . . . this is the wrong attitude . . . always work for the success of the business . . . if you will keep your mind and attention on the business, you'll never go wrong and the money will come.

It had certainly come for David Eccles, but from building

where nothing had existed before, from production, from job-creating enterprises. Marriner wrote with pride that none of his father's wealth came from windfalls, gold, silver or copper mines, or from unearned increments in urban growth. It all had been done the hard way. Writing like a PR man for a work-ethic festival, Marriner boasted of his father's "courage, hard work, self-denial, thrift," but also of a "clear view of the kind of economic development that could succeed in a new area." *There* was the innovation, the great entrepreneurial ability. David Eccles had left behind lumber operations, sugar factories, coal mines, heavy construction, banking and utilities. To "prove himself" to his father's memory and not be just another rich boy, Marriner Eccles was going to have to beat the legend, the pioneer, David Eccles. He would continue in his father's footsteps, but the bundles of notes were going to lead to the country's first multibank holding company.

Of the cadet family's two-sevenths share of the David Eccles estate Marriner Eccles could say, sixteen years later, "I made the most of it." Of his own holdings by 1928, now very large, the presidencies and directorships were still mainly where his father had been before him. But there was one big change, the First Security Corporation, an invention of Marriner Eccles and his associates and an innovation that was destined to change the financial structure of the country in ways we still cannot imagine. The evolution of the multibank holding company continues, and the pressure for true interstate banking builds as a result.

First Security was an outgrowth of David Eccles's long-time close association with Utah's Browning clan. Jonathan Browning, a Mormon convert in the 1840s, was the fabled gunsmith of Nauvoo. He went west on the trek and by 1852 was in business in Ogden. John Moses Browning, a son by Browning's second wife, also was a maker of firearms, including the lethal Browning Automatic Rifle of World War II fame. His brother, Matthew, was the family businessman. Both men, the sons of Jonathan Browning, had shared in business ventures with David Eccles, including stock participations in several banks. Young Marriner Eccles, almost immediately after his father's death, became president of one of the banks by virtue of his inherited stock. It was the small Hyrum State Bank in Cache Valley, Utah. The Eccles-Browning joint banking interests also included a bank in Richmond, Utah. Marriner Eccles had become president of the Ogden First National Bank and the Ogden Savings Bank as a result of bitter settlements splitting up the intermingled stock interests of the two Eccles families. The Brownings also owned an Ogden bank separately, the Utah National Bank, just across the street from Ogden First National Bank. The year was now 1922, "Matt" Browning was 65 and Marriner was a mere 32, still living in Logan, despite his growing interests elsewhere in the region.

Matt Browning called on Eccles and pointed out that "since we were associates in other ventures, there was no point in being competitors in the banking business." One of Browning's conditions for a merger was that Marriner move his family (he had married in 1913) from Logan down to Ogden and become president of the newly merged bank. That was done. Shortly thereafter Eccles Investment Company made a $1.5 million profit selling its shares in a condensed milk firm to Pet, a milk products company. That had resulted from a daring follow-through and stock-acquisition coup by Marriner involving a pioneering David Eccles venture, the construction of the first condensed milk factories west of Denver. The result of the Pet sale was that Eccles Investment Company could now join forces with the Brownings in more bank acquisitions.

They looked around for likely buys. The isolated settlement of Montpelier, Idaho, had become bankless. Its two banks had succumbed in 1924 and 1925, partly because of the depression in agriculture and partly because their managements, more fearful of bank robbery than of deficient liquidity, had persisted in policies of absolutely minimal cash balances. The Bank of Montpelier, chartered in 1891, had actually recorded among its robbers the ragtag duo, last of the western badmen, Butch Cassidy and the Sundance Kid—a kind of fame.

The other Montpelier bank, the First National, had failed in April 1925. The Brownings owned a small bank in nearby Paris, Idaho, and thus knew the ground. Young Marriner Browning (son of Matt Browning, who died in 1925, and, like Marriner Eccles, named after the Mormon apostle, Marriner Merrill) drove up through the mountains from Ogden and bought both Montpelier banks. They were the first Eccles-Browning banks. Then came one in Rock Springs, Wyoming, where the Eccles-Browning group had coal interests. At the same time another bank in a nearby Wyoming settlement was purchased. The group then moved into Blackfoot, Idaho, to repurchase control of a bank once owned and subsequently disposed of by Eccles. By early 1926 the group had purchased eight banks. The next move was again in Idaho, the Anderson Bank in Idaho Falls, this time snaring significant new executive talent, E. G. Bennett, a virtuoso banker (in 1933 to be the first head of the Federal Deposit Insurance Corporation), who agreed to come in as a stockholder, vice-president, and manager of the Eccles-Browning banks located outside Ogden.

Because the National Bank Act of 1864 read that ". . . usual business shall be transacted at an office or banking house in the place specified in its organizational certificate," the national banks could not be branched. No bank could buy stock in another bank, but a single person could own stocks in several banks. Each bank in the Eccles-Browning group was therefore operated as a single firm. At this point the officers of the Eccles-Browning group made the decision to organize the banks like the Eccles Investment Corporation, which was, after all, a holding company for the business interests and stocks of the cadet Eccles family. There would be a new company, a single organization, not itself a bank, owning significant or controlling interest in all the banks. Such an organization could create scale and external economies for separate small banks, could deal in national markets for securities and other bank investments, could keep abreast of nationwide developments and could offer consulting and other valuable (and expensive) services for the member banks. No single country bank could afford such a hierarchy—bureaucracy—to operate in the financial "big time." Eccles wrote that they made a study to estimate how many banks they would need to generate sufficient profits to support the kind of overarching central organization they had in mind. They needed between 15 and 20 of the sizes they had been acquiring. They went ahead and by early 1928 had bought the banks they needed.

On June 15, 1928, the men from Utah and Idaho were in Dover, Delaware, for the formal charade in which First Security Corporation was chartered as a Delaware corporation. There was no inheritance tax in Delaware and the filing fees were half the levels of Utah and Idaho. Marriner Eccles was president of the new corporation, Marriner Browning was vice-president, E. G. Bennett was managing vice-president and young George Eccles (another innovative banker-to-be), Marriner's brother, was secretary–treasurer. The authorized capital was $6.5 million, of which $3 million was paid up.

There were then 17 banks plus one savings and loan company in the new system. First Security Corporation exchanged its stocks with those of the Eccles-Browning group, and the other bank stockholders were invited to make the switch on the same basis. The great advance over other chain banks was that First Security Corporation was managed by a large central organization which was not a bank, not subject to bank regulation; only its member banks were. They could continue their businesses as country banks, but with superior expertise and organization at their disposal. By 1928 the corporation's 21 subsidiary firms had net earnings of $427,000, of which First Security's share was $375,000 (88 percent). The system continued its expansion, adding more banks, including the National Copper Bank in Salt Lake City. In 1930, First Security Corporation's earnings topped $713,000 (in the fullness of time, by 1984 First Security had assets of about $5 billion). In nearby California, A. P. Giannini must have been fascinated. A major innovation had appeared in the financial world.

Eccles quoted Polonius: "By indirection I found direction out." He wrote that he had originally no intention to enter banking on any "sizable scale." But events had taken their course. Eccles would say with pride: "These business successes reaffirmed me in my father's faith. . . . In the banking field I had outdistanced him and was still young in years."

Eccles was a multidimensional entrepreneur—he had to be, given the pace his father had set. There were many businesses to master, including the family's major interest in Amalgamated Sugar. One of the businesses with a major Eccles interest was Utah Construction, a property originally acquired by David Eccles to build railroads. It already had an impressive record in David's lifetime, including dams and urban water-supply projects. In 1930, Marriner negotiated a loan with the Crocker Bank in San Francisco for a million dollars and took Utah Construction into a syndicate to build Boulder Dam. The special corporation, called the Six Companies, included as other participants Henry Kaiser, the Bechtels and Morrison-Knudsen. The giant dam was built successfully and profitably. But by 1930 the great American gasbag was leaking badly, the effects of the 1929 Wall Street crash were now eating into the vitals of the American economy and the triumphant Marriner Eccles was to know the series of crises that changed the course of his life.

IV

In his memoirs Eccles points out that in October 1929, when Wall Street's roof fell in, the crops in the Intermountain West had already been sold. But the next year the full impact of the crash was felt in the West as well. Farm prices fell 16 percent that year; the number of bank failures nearly doubled, hitting 1,350 nationwide; unemployment lept from 3.2 to 8.7 percent. The economy was "imploding," and worse, much worse, was coming. The country's leaders were still preaching confidence and urging cuts in government expenditures and, fervent hope, a balanced budget. But Eccles, with his widespread interests, knew what was happening at many levels in the economy, his economy, and he was adding it up. There were no quarterly GNP estimates flashing from the Department of Commerce in those days (Simon Kuznets had not yet done his Nobel Prize-winning work), so an informed general viewpoint was not common. Each business leader knew his own firm or industry. Eccles knew dozens of different industries and what was going wrong, from his own financial statements. He could not explain it. Accordingly: "During 1930 I awoke to find myself at the bottom of a pit without any known means of scaling its sheer sides." He wrote that he knew the "techniques" of the worlds of finance and industry; he was the proven master of that, after all. In the platitudes of the business world, he had "met a payroll." He had met many payrolls. But meeting payrolls was just business, and business was bad.

A rare bird, Eccles also had a social conscience, ". . . having been reared by my father to accept the responsibilities of wealth and having been placed by circumstances at the helm of many enterprises." As guardian of the estates of his family and friends, as well as the deposits in First Security banks, he was in, as he put it, a "sensitive" position. He was, in fact, in misery, and was desperate to find a way out. He had been elected president of the Utah Bankers Association in 1925, and had given dozens of the usual booster speeches (excerpts of which, for the touch of irony, he printed in his own book) to assembled business leaders. Coming from Eccles, they naturally contain interesting thoughts, but they are also puffed out with the usual gaseous rhetoric so familiar to bored luncheon-club boosters everywhere. Eccles just had not thought "beyond the counting house." As he said of those years: "When asked for an opinion, I bowed to the East and paraphrased the latest statements of someone like Ogden Mills and Andrew Mellon . . . or of Alfred Wiggin, Charles Mitchell, and J. P. Morgan. . . ." By 1930, ". . . all I could find within myself was despair." Eccles felt his inadequacy keenly. People expected him, the leader of leaders, to know the way out. He did not, and he knew it. Unlike the modern State Department,

Eccles did not believe his own propaganda: "I felt the whole depression was a personal affront. . . . Night after night I would return home exhausted by the pretensions of knowledge I was forced to wear in a daytime masquerade."

What one sees here is an extraordinary and rare specimen of humanity, someone with a critical mind. To get at an explanation of his world he had first to unlearn—not an easy thing. A self-taught musician has the most difficult time if he gets lessons from a skilled professional. The autodidact already knows how to play the instrument—wrong. Every step, every finger movement, every instinct, every tropism has to be disconnected, and all of it "rewired." There was a conventional view about economic life, which Eccles had learned, thoroughly intertwined with morals, politics, personal values and ethics: "thrift, initiative, competition and free enterprise" were the watchwords. It was all supported by the accepted (selected) teaching of writers on economics from Adam Smith down. David Eccles had been the self-taught devotee of that scheme of thought and his son had always agreed: "I nodded my head approvingly."

Marriner now subjected those ideas to logic, based on his own store of facts, to discover why he could not explain what was happening to the world around him. He began to chart unknown seas of the mind. For example, why would his lumber mills still lose money even if the workers came to work for free? Eccles had to learn to theorize—facts and logic, and conclusions. His father's maxim, derived from experience, was that "a business, like an individual, could only remain free if it kept out of debt." Unlike David Eccles, who disdained those "bundles of notes," Marriner, the founder of First Security Corporation, had paid close attention to what those notes were.

He reasoned in this regard a little like Cotton Mather had, long before, examining the church's doctrine prohibiting usury. Mather had found the gospel wanting. In *Magnalia Christi Americana*, Mather had probed deeply into the logic of interest rates and sin. If he had a surplus, and his neighbor wanted to borrow it to put it to use, would it not be a sin to refuse his neighbor? But if his neighbor made a profit from the loan, would it not be a sin for his neighbor to refuse to share the profit with Mather? A simple interest payment for sharing the surplus and the risk would relieve both men of the deadly threat to their eternal salvation.

Eccles realized that if no one was in debt, the surplus of one could never be used by another; ". . . there would be no capitalist system." He understood the first principle of macroeconomics: actual saving always equals actual investment, expressed in money terms. He wrote:

> The very essence of capitalism implies a debtor–creditor relationship . . . to save successfully, someone has to borrow what is saved . . . bankers, the arch symbols of capitalism, are the greatest borrowers. . . .

You save; the bank borrows it from you and lends it to someone who invests. David Eccles would have owned no banks if no one saved and no one borrowed. David Eccles, in fact, borrowed when his banks accepted deposits. There could be too much saving. The unsold inventories of commodities and goods were also "investment," unwanted investment, and they could only be reduced if consumption were increased, if spending rose. The sum of spending, consumption plus investment, was equal to the total amount available to be spent, consumption plus that which was not consumed, saving.

Also, the cost of output is the income of the factors used to produce it. There was a real as well as a money way to view economic life. When inventories rose there appeared to have been too much production, but that was "in reality underconsumption when judged in terms of the real world instead of the money world." There is the second principle of macroeconomics: output equals income. There was also productive and unproductive investment. High savings would not always lead to productive investment; it might lead to idle cash balanced by unsold goods. Consumption was the key. If consumption were too low the condition "brought about a fall in prices and employment."

Eccles also realized that investment in plant and equipment created productive capacity and that unsold goods made that capacity "excess"—a brake on further investment.

> What passed as a "lack of confidence" was really nothing more than an investor's recognition of the fact that new plant facilities were not needed . . . that the existing plant was overbuilt when judged in terms of the effective demand consumers could make on the output of that plant.

No amount of inspired advocacy of "business confidence" by the nation's leaders could overcome that kind of hard assessment of the facts. Talking would not reduce excess capacity and make new investment pay.

Moreover, the only way economic growth could continue was if the changing balance of consumption and savings over time could "provide men with buying power equal to the amount of goods and services offered by the nation's economic machinery." With this Eccles not only had grasped the bookkeeping essentials of elementary macroeconomics, but he realized the dynamic properties as well. The wrong ratios of consumption to savings could cause the growing system to plow itself into the ground. It was Roy Harrod's 1948 book on economic dynamics that first explained in formal terms the paradox of self-destructive macroeconomic growth.

Eccles even knew, intuitively, about income and investment multipliers. He saw it in a practical way, based on induced spending, not just a stream of spending caused by a single increase in expenditure, and in the early 1930s was agitating for government expenditures in various areas of the economy to entice private capital out of hoards so that the total spent because of the government's "seed money" would greatly exceed the amount of the original government outlay. Vernon Mund, a fairly slow-track professor of economics at the University of Washington, had published an essay in 1930 on that question. Mund went down in history as one of the inventors of the multiplier. Since he didn't know about geometric progressions (the increments ultimately heading by infinitesimally small amounts toward zero), Mund's multiplier tended to get out of hand. A year later, in 1931, Richard Kahn at Cambridge University published an essay, "The Relation of Home Investment to Unemployment," in which he got it right. Keynes borrowed Kahn's multiplier to underpin the message in *The General Theory* in 1936. Eccles already knew it.

All intuition? The search for the origins of these deductions by Eccles had gone far and wide, usually landing on William Foster and Wadill Catchings. Eccles had read their book on underconsumption, *The Road to Plenty*. But he also could have received the message earlier from the English economist, John Hobson, or from reading Karl Marx, for that matter. The doctrine of underconsumption was not new. In any case, in his understanding of both sides of economic life, real exchanges and money exchanges—output equals income—the necessary equality of savings and investment, the danger of too much savings as the economy expanded, Eccles had gone beyond the simple underconsumptionist doctrine, and Keynes was not yet in the picture. Eccles said later that he had learned it all by "naked eye" experience out west. He also perfectly understood the circular flow of income, both loops, real and money. And why not? His own enterprises were located all the way around the circle. In those little western communities he knew what happened when bank loans expanded or contracted in the world of output, sales and the resulting bank deposits.

Eccles also figured out "the fallacy of composition." What was good for the bankers in a depression was bad for everyone else:

> By forcing the liquidation of loans and securities to meet the demands of depositors, were we not helping to drive prices down and thereby making it increasingly difficult for our debtors to pay back what they had borrowed from us?

Is "what's bad for Ford good for the country"? Not even if you work for General Motors, in the world of macroeconomics. The liquidation of loans by the bankers would consume the banks themselves. And that is what happened.

How could the situation be turned around? In earlier times, in the nineteenth century, one might have heard arguments for printing greenbacks and for free coinage of silver. And given the cultural lag, one did, all over Washington, and in the Thomas Amendment to the Agricultural Adjustment Act of 1933. Eccles, however, turned in a different direction.

In June 1932, Eccles stiffened the assembled Utah Bankers Association with:

> The theory of hard work and thrift as a means of pulling us out of the depression is unsound economically. True hard work means more production, but thrift and economy mean less consumption. Now reconcile those two forces, will you? . . . There is only one agency . . . that can turn the cycle upward and that is the government. The government . . . must so regulate . . . the economic structure as to give men who are able, worthy, and willing to work, the opportunity to work, and to guarantee to them sustenance for their families and protection against want and destitution.

The depression "will not correct itself." Marriner Eccles had discovered "compensatory" fiscal policy. He had concluded that government should raise its expenditures in a depression by deficit spending and put men to work. Then, when prosperity returned, reverse directions, easing the budget into balance.

Later, facing the post–World War II inflation, he would advocate surpluses and debt retirement. It was all a matter of "timing and method." Moreover, it should be done so as to encourage "a maximum amount of private expenditures with a minimum amount of public expenditures"—pump priming. Eccles, the capitalist par excellence, was no advocate of "seizing the means of production in the name of the people." He wanted to use the power, deftly, that only the federal government had, to create money and spend it, to raise income to full employment levels.

He said he had heard "grass roots" demands that "the government" should "do something" about the depression, and he had wondered what and how. He thought it out, and Eccles, the returned Mormon missionary, now had a new gospel which he drummed into the ears (many of them nearly deaf) of all who would listen, for years to come.

Where did Eccles get his ideas about such a compassionate and responsible government? From Foster and Catchings? Not likely; the federal government had never done such things. Surely not from observing the panic-stricken statesmen in Washington in 1932. Eccles had been well aware that in World War I the government had exerted its fiscal powers to achieve its ends by deficit finance without "ruining the country." He didn't need Foster and Catchings to know that public debt counted as an asset to those who owned it. But he also knew, growing up in the afterglow of Brigham Young's Utah, that such efforts by the central power were effective and did not necessarily threaten private property—the bugaboo of the budget balancers and expenditure cutters in the eastern financial establishment. Eccles knew of the Mormons' great collective efforts to colonize, which had hardly made socialists of them, after all. We recall Brigham Young upbraiding those who challenged his own miniature "compensatory fiscal policy":

> I build walls, dig ditches, make bridges . . . I annually expend hundreds and thousands of dollars almost solely to furnish employment to those in want of labor. Why? I have potatoes, flour, beef, and other articles of food, which I wish my brethren to have; and it is better for them to labor for those articles . . . than to have them given to them.

Brigham "paid the laborers their wages" and put public expenditure where private expenditure was lacking—and Zion flourished.

Dean May is surely correct in his essay, "Sources of Marriner S. Eccles's Economic Thought," about its origins. It lay not in books, but all around Eccles in Utah, still. Eccles reinforced his theorizing with his own knowledge of the facts, and as many an infuriated senator and congressman would soon learn, Eccles was a "mean" man with the facts. Eccles did pay tribute to the Mormon church's efforts to care for its own in the early 1930s, but as chairman of the Utah Committee on Relief, Eccles knew the problem of destitution by 1932 was beyond the grasp of private charity sources, or indeed of the states themselves.

His new gospel had some amusing consequences. His colleague, E. G. Bennett, feared for the First Security banks; the depositors might "run" for their money, knowing the new turn of mind of their chief steward. The president of a western railroad thought "poor Marriner" had lost his mind under the strain of the bank runs his organization had endured.

This is a well-known part of the Eccles legend, now routinely reprinted in textbooks for college students of courses in "Money and Banking"—pay off slowly with small bills the first day, and stay open late. Open early on the second day, pay off in big bills immediately, let no queues form for any reason. Bring in notes in a flashy way—armored cars, police guards—and assure the depositors there is plenty for all. After many a harrowing hour, no First Security bank closed its doors; no First Security depositor lost a penny. The corporation's reputation soared, and that of Marriner Eccles with it. He had worked out a set of tactics, used throughout the First Security system, to hold off the panics ignited by the failures of nearby banks. The corporation in fact expanded, absorbing banks by emergency means to save the rest of the regional banking system from collapse. There had been wild scenes, midnight dramas. When the dust cleared Marriner could say, "I thanked God for the nerves I had inherited from my father and mother."

By then Eccles was ready to spread his new gospel to a wider audience, and by fits and starts he left Utah to join the New Deal. In Utah, as in the rest of the country, 1933 dawned with bank holidays; state by state and then finally by presidential order, all the banks in the nation closed their doors. "Scrip" issued by local bank clearinghouses was going to be money, as had been done by Morgan in the 1907 panic, and then as allowed under the Aldrich-Vreeland Act of 1908. Will Rogers caught some of the flavor of the times when he said we were the only country that ever rode to the poorhouse in automobiles. Leonard Arrington reported a memoir that catches some of the madcap mood of the day. Lionel Olson, a Utah banker, was printing scrip with Marriner's brother, George:

> . . . all the bankers gathered at the Rocky Mountain Bank Note Company for the purpose of printing and signing their own scrip money, which was to be used in lieu of the old sawbucks if necessary. George and I got on a machine in a dark corner and started running off the real McCoy, twenty-dollar greenbacks. The machine went haywire and started printing eighteen-dollar bills. . . . I thought I'd better try one on a small grocery store before dumping them on the banks. I asked the hillbilly in the grocery store if he would break an eighteen-dollar bill for me. . . . He replied, "Do you want two nines or three sixes?"

The time for funny money schemes had arrived in Washington, too, and Marriner Eccles would soon go there to join the exotic circus of characters who formed the personnel of the New Deal.

V

As part of his extracurricular intellectual activities, Eccles had joined an informal discussion group in Ogden. In that connection he met and talked with Paul Douglas, then still one of the lights of the University of Chicago's economics department, and he met a leading national journalist, Stuart Chase. They were impressed. One member of the group, Robert Hinckley, was a cousin of Utah Senator William King, and he invited Marriner to testify before the lame-duck Senate Finance Committee holding hearings on the depression and what to do about it in Washington in February 1933. It was a chance to be heard, and Eccles accepted. He described those meetings as "the last, dim, weird battle of the West." Eccles had been interested in the "brains trust" around Roosevelt, and made an appointment to meet Rexford Tugwell, then still filling his role as professor of economics at Columbia University. Also, Eccles had been appalled by FDR's speeches, promising if elected to balance the budget. Eccles had already been pointing out that the unbalanced federal budget was not a cause of the depression, but a consequence of an unbalanced, sagging economy.

That issue is worth a momentary digression just to set the

record straight. Before Andrew Jackson paid it off, the national debt had been a sure-fire issue for politicians. Inconvertibility of the greenbacks provided stump material until 1879. Later on attention shifted to silver and gold as ballast for electioneering. There had been big deficits in the federal budget in fiscal years 1918 and 1919, followed by a string of surpluses (with debt retirement) through fiscal 1930. In 1931 a small federal deficit appeared; there was a larger one in 1932. Here was a grand new issue for political rhetoric, and has been ever since. What it means is interesting. A balanced federal cash budget, revenues equal to expenditures—any sort, annual, cyclical, moving-five-year-averages—would be some sort of a fiscal target, *a policy*, and as such is no doubt superior to no fiscal policy at all. But the latter, really, is what we have actually experienced. After 1930, Truman managed two small budget surpluses, in 1947 and 1948; Eisenhower achieved minuscule surpluses in 1956, 1957 and 1960 (each associated with recessions); and Nixon accidentally found himself with a small surplus in fiscal 1968–69, before he could do anything about it. *That is all*. In the past 55 years there has never been a balanced budget, and only six small surpluses. All the rest of the time, 49 out of 55 years, 89 percent of those years, we have had deficits. And the republic survives. Balancing the budget, like free silver, is in fact political hooey, used to attract votes. Its importance as economics is trivial. As a guide to policy it is a dream, now pursued with a proposed constitutional amendment and legislation. The idea, however, quickly came to grip the minds of people like Henry Morgenthau, possibly in lieu of anything else to hand.

Writing of his 1933 testimony in *Beckoning Frontiers*, Eccles recalled with amusement some of the depthy advice of those who preceded him before the panel. From Bernard Baruch, the windy and self-infatuated "adviser to presidents": "Reject all plans which oppose or postpone the working of natural processes. . . . Cut government spending. . . . Delay in balancing the budget is trifling with disaster. . . ."

Eccles quoted from several examples of such energetic new thinking in his memoirs. He also outlined his own advice, decried later by the *New York Times* as "bombastic" and "inflamed"—before there was a New Deal:

1. Make an immediate gift of $500 million to the states for the balance of 1933 "to take care of the destitute and unemployed."
2. Lend at low rates of interest $2.5 billion, more if neces-

sary, to the states for self-liquidating public works.

3. Adopt a domestic allotment plan for agriculture to regulate output and raise farm prices.
4. Refinance the country's outstanding farm mortgages, long term, and at low interest rates.
5. Settle the question of World War I inter-ally debts, preferably by cancelling them (this was Keynes of *The Economic Consequences of the Peace*, not, however, read by Eccles).
6. Unify the national and state-chartered banking system under a single, effective regulation by the Federal Reserve System.
7. Raise both income and inheritance taxes.
8. Legislate federal child labor and minimum wage laws.
9. Introduce a system of national unemployment insurance with old-age pensions.
10. Create federal regulation of new capital issues.
11. Recreate a national planning board similar to that of World War I.
12. Introduce federal insurance of bank deposits.

There was more, and one can sympathize with Eccles when, for months afterward, he languished, unbidden, back in Utah while the New Deal began to arise as if out of his own testimony, and even his conservative associate, E. G. Bennett, was invited to Washington to be the first director of the new Federal Deposit Insurance Corporation. For the record, Eccles never claimed credit for the transmutation of his blueprint into reality. But two years later, Archibald MacLeish wrote a long article in *Fortune* about the (finally) rising new star over the Potomac, saying that "M. S. Eccles of Ogden, Utah, was not only a Mormon but a prophet."

At first nothing much fell Marriner's way from the nation's capital. In New York City he had an ambiguous meeting with Tugwell in a booth of a Broadway drugstore off the Columbia campus, and then went back to Utah for months of mounting frustration, firing off letters of advice to those in the seats of power. Finally, in October 1933, Tugwell wrote from Washington asking if Eccles might be coming east again, and if so to drop by—still the touch of the academic marketplace in Tugwell's head; no one is really interested in what is on everyone's mind. Eccles replied that in fact he would be going east again on private business, the appropriate response. In the capital Tugwell introduced Eccles to the Agriculture Department's great statistician, Mordecai Ezekial, and to Henry Wallace. There was no time to talk, so Eccles suggested a

dinner at the Shoreham. Tugwell phoned Eccles to ask if he
might bring along a couple more guests. He brought along
Harry Hopkins and Jerome Frank. Eccles invited two of his
Utah banking associates, George Dern (FDR's nominee to be
secretary of the War Department) and Bennett now struggling
manfully to organize the FDIC. Eccles thought the others had
never heard of either Bennett or the FDIC. They talked long
and hard about economic issues and the beliefs of various
members of FDR's inner circle. The next night Tugwell
brought Dean Acheson, then undersecretary of the Treasury
(soon to resign). Tugwell introduced Eccles to Harold Ickes,
and then offered to arrange a meeting with FDR. Eccles got
cold feet at that point and modestly demurred, not wanting to
take any of the great man's time. Tugwell then said that they
wanted to bring Eccles into the government. What if an offer
were made? Eccles said he would consider it.

Again, nothing happened. Eccles went back to Utah, in part
convinced that he had been put on exhibit mainly because of
his "bizarre" reputation as the millionaire radical. But he was
no sooner home than a telegram came from the office of Henry
Morgenthau, now the new secretary of the Treasury. Would
Eccles come to Washington? He called Bennett, and although
Bennett knew of nothing afoot, he advised Marriner to trek
east again. On New Year's night, 1934, Eccles made the fateful journey back to Washington.

When they met, cautious Henry Morgenthau stalled Eccles.
Would Eccles like to write a report on money and banking?
Eccles met some more Treasury people and cooled his heels
for several days. Finally he said he was fed up and was leaving. This produced an immediate invitation to Morgenthau's
home. Morgenthau now questioned Eccles closely about his
personal affairs, about his businesses. Had any of them ever
been bankrupt? He may have wondered if Eccles had too
many wives. It didn't come up. Finally he came out with it:
Would Eccles consider an appointment as an assistant secretary
of the Treasury?

Now the ball was in Marriner's court. Here was his chance.
He could now "put up or shut up." He had always been his
own boss; he "didn't know a damned thing about government
or law making." Here was this strange bird, Morgenthau, the
carefully polished graduate of Phillips Exeter Academy, bosom
friend of the president, wearing a pince nez, asking Marriner
Eccles, the western tycoon, to put his shoulder to the New
Deal's wheel. Eccles went to New York on business, then back

to Washington, and told Morgenthau he would have to put his private affairs in order and could come back February 1, for one year. The United States thus hired Marriner Stoddard Eccles for $10,000 a year—no mean feat.

In the years the followed Morgenthau must often have cursed his fate. Eccles could be intolerable, but he was indispensable in the government. It is imperative to have *someone* who knows independently what he is doing, regardless of the shifts and flows of opinions. That was Eccles. And it no doubt was the source of his power in Washington in years to come and his undoing when Harry Truman came to the presidency. The Morgenthau-Eccles relationship is endlessly amusing to the student of the New Deal. They infuriated each other. Morgenthau, sensitive, haughty, cautious, socially correct, was bound in harness with Eccles, direct, forceful, insensitive and usually correct in the other way. Blum published the following exchange in the fall of 1937, when Eccles, as Chairman of the Board of Governors of the Federal Reserve System, had playfully but honestly offered to expand the Fed's notes against a deposit of gold certificates. The hard-pressed Morgenthau, facing a collapsing economy, along with his cherished policy, the balanced budget, blew up in his way:

> There's never any use talking to you Marriner. I try to be nice and then . . . you've got the audacity to put it up to me that you want . . . to know whether I want to be relieved of some gold. I say it's an insult for you to ask me a question like that. It's an insult.

Eccles, who came from a part of the country where one was not lightly, if ever, accused of "audacity," replied in his way:

> You get irritated every time I come over here and present anything, and I'm getting tired of it. . . . Maybe the thing for me to do is get up and walk out, because I'm getting goddam sick and tired of it.

It was one of the famous pieces of FDR's political genius, placing men against each other in such a way as to generate maximum energy (for example, Ickes and Hopkins). Eccles and Morgenthau would make a fantastic "odd couple" in the years ahead.

In that instance the great economist, Jacob Viner, was present and suggested that both men grow up and attend to the country's problems.

VI

FDR seemed to find Eccles likable, or amusing; in any case, he seemed genuinely fond of the man. Eccles, notoriously, had no "small talk." He realized that his blunt manner and tenacious methods of argument tired the president, and in later years would sometimes purposely stay away from the White House for that reason. He never had, or tried to have, an informal entrée with FDR. Eccles was not in the president's intimate group. He usually met with the president on strictly business issues, or tried to. It wasn't easy to bind FDR to economic issues if he was interested in something else. FDR was a great politician—elected four times to the White House —whether you like it or not. But many things, including his dog Fala, could be more interesting at times to Roosevelt than Marriner Eccles with his firehose presentation of "the facts."

A classic example of Eccles in action came in April 1938, when he was called before the House Committee on Banking and Currency. Wright Patman, the all-purpose Populist from Texas, was introducing a bill (backed by 160 other congressional statesmen) to take over the actual ownership of the Federal Reserve System. Eccles didn't like that idea, and buried the congressman with facts and argument. But before that testimony, Eccles dealt with another part of the bill. Patman had decided to solve all the country's problems at once by ordering the Fed to engage in open-market purchases of government securities until prices regained their 1926 levels. A few lines give the flavor of Eccles at full force:

> The proposal is that the Board of Governors bring the commodity price index up to at least the 1926 level. The average for that year is about 25 percent above the present level and an advance of that magnitude, except over an extended period, would cause speculative buying and would lead to boom conditions which would culminate in a break and a depression. Furthermore, in periods of rapid advance disparities between prices of different groups of commodities generally become more pronounced and yet, both from the point of view of justice and of economic stability, the most important thing in regard to prices is the maintenance of proper relations between prices of different commodities that are exchanged for each other. Activity of producers depends on the relationship between their costs, including principally prices of materials, labor, taxes, and debt service, and the prices at which they can sell their products. . . . In directing the Board to achieve price stability and full employment through open-market operations,

the proposed mandate disregards the limitations on the effectiveness of this instrument of credit policy. It assumes that open-market operations can always create or destroy deposits and that changes in the volume of deposits in turn are immediately reflected in the price level. The fact is that open-market operations do not always create deposits, since purchases of securities from the banks do not increase deposits. Whether open-market purchases result directly in an increase in deposits or not, they do result in the creation of a corresponding amount of reserves. These reserves may or may not result in the creation of deposits, depending on whether conditions are favorable for the expansion of loans and investment by banks. The great bulk of deposits in the banks of the United States are created through such an expansion. A given volume of reserves created by Board action, therefore, might result in no increase in deposits at all; or on the other hand, might result in a growth of deposits several times as large as the reserves. Which of these developments would actually occur would depend on forces that are largely, if not wholly, outside the control of the Board of Governors.

It is not true, furthermore, that the creation of deposits necessarily results in an equivalent rise in prices.

Eccles then went on to explain *that* in the same deadpan block verbiage in which he had enlightened the congressman about what may or may not happen to bank deposits as an outcome of an open-market purchase. Many pages later he turned to the proposal to "nationalize" the Federal Reserve System and poured it on Patman. He was remorseless. Sidney Hyman, in his biography of Eccles, quotes Herbert Corey in the *Financial Observer* about Eccles and his fantastic knowledge. Corey was watching a luncheon meeting; the bankers were attempting to bait Eccles. The time dragged on:

> Eccles was so much interested in the ideas he wished to put over, and in the questions he wanted to ask that he did not even notice they were trying to take him for a ride. At first, he aroused my protective instinct. He made me think of a nice, gentle little boy surrounded by high school bullies, and I was sorry for him. Before he got through, I was sorry for the bankers. He knew everything about banking—by periods, details, totals. panics, causes and effects.

Hyman also quotes Raymond Clapper in *The Review of Reviews*. Clapper wrote that Eccles was "the strangest character in that strange wonderland of Washington," a "brilliant master of capital, sitting at the head of the country's national banking structure and advocating 'revolutionary ideas' about fiscal policy, money and credit that bring shudders to most of his fellow capitalists." George Creel had said that Eccles looked at first glance like an undertaker, small, spare, "with his pallor, jet black hair and eyes." But then when you listened, "the whole of him glowed with a certain incandescence." His talk was "electric"; his presentation gave "every idea the drive of a bullet." If you tangled with Eccles, you lost, at least the argument.

But you didn't have to believe. Many years later a retired great man of New York banking recalled being taken as a youngster by a senior New York banker to meet Eccles in his office. "Now I'm going to introduce you to the 'boogyman.' Just listen to what he says. Don't talk. If you believe what he says, I won't think much of you."

FDR had come to Washington to be president, and had invited his Dutchess County neighbor, Henry Morgenthau, along to "have fun." Eccles, on the other hand, had gone to Washington to "save the country." So one difference in style was simply motivation. Morgenthau, judging from his diaries, had little enough "fun." Eccles was not amused much either. FDR was, and as history knows, tilted this way and that over the years, usually depending on immediate circumstances. In November 1937, Morgenthau gave a budget-balancing speech before the Academy of Political Science, which Roosevelt actually had helped draft. Eccles was outraged, beside himself at the duplicity and stupidity of it. The economy was diving, and Eccles thought he had been bringing FDR around to some compensating deficit spending. Even in his 1951 book Eccles was still angry. On November 10, 1937, in the afternoon, FDR had seemingly approved of a shift of fiscal policy toward the deficit. That night Morgenthau dropped his bomb (to the accompaniment of some drunken laughter in the audience). Eccles wrote:

> The contradictions between the afternoon and evening . . . made me wonder at this time whether the New Deal was merely a political slogan or if Roosevelt really knew what the New Deal was. This is an ungenerous comment, yet it faithfully reports what I felt at the time.

The road of the true believer is a hard one. Eccles traveled it, but FDR didn't bother. He made his own roads. Shortly thereafter, once "Henry" had experienced his big moment,

FDR turned and supported an increased deficit. As Lily Tomlin said about the phone company, he didn't care, because he didn't have to.

In his first two years in the Roosevelt administration Eccles was responsible for the new Federal Housing Administration act, and then for the 1935 bank act; at the same time Senator Carter Glass was trying to bomb Eccles and his legislation clean out of Washington, by opposing both the "Eccles Bank Bill" and the Senate's confirmation of Eccles to the Federal Reserve Board.

The FHA bill was Marriner's first real introduction to the ways of Washington politics. He had been brought in as the Treasury representative on the president's Emergency Committee on Housing. The housing industry, so important in every community as an employer of labor and consumer of materials, had started stalling in 1925 and by 1934 was a shambles. The Committee included New Deal luminaries Harry Hopkins, Frances Perkins, Henry Wallace, Tugwell, Edward Harriman's son Averill (the "tame millionaire") and John Fahey, chairman of the Federal Home Loan Bank Board. Eccles listened in at several meetings, and was unimpressed by what he heard; it mostly sounded to him like "social-service-worker" thinking.

Eccles had something else in mind. He planned a scheme that was a financial revolution in home finance. The traditional system of home mortgages was a big (commonly 50 percent) down payment, together with high interest rates and short payoffs. Most people in fact could not manage such terms. So second and third mortgages, at even higher interest rates, were common. The whole system had crashed, the first mortgage holders ending up with unsalable properties, the second and third mortgage holders with nothing and the mortgagors in the street. Eccles wanted to create a system to employ long-term mortgages, with low downpayments, low interest rates and a regular schedule of affordable payments backed up by a federal guarantee.

He proposed that a subcommittee be established to draft actual legislation for the full committee to consider. The others jumped at the chance to shift the responsibility, naturally, to the man brash enough to make the proposal. So Eccles was to chair the subcommittee. He put together an able staff and they went to work. The ultimate result was the Federal Housing Authority, and the now-familiar system of FHA-backed mortgages.

But before that happened Eccles found himself liberally dipped in the venality and self-serving that motivates so much of the nation's legislation. The commercial banking community lined up en bloc against him. The Home Loan Bank Board would have to be served by adding Title IV to establish the Federal Savings and Loan Insurance Corporation to underwrite the building and loan associations. A Mr. Bodfish, lobbyist for the building and loan associations, had to be ejected from the discussion by Marriner's direct order to his patron, John Fahey. There were long and rocky sessions before committees of the Congress and the Senate, at which every oar was dipped, and the bill was twisted this way and that, much to the unhappiness of Eccles. On the Senate Banking and Currency Committee sat Senator Thomas Gore of Oklahoma, who had been at the 1933 lame-duck Senate Finance Committee hearings and, Eccles wrote, had "evidently not yet recovered from the shock of my testimony." Parts were added, parts were dropped, parts were emasculated as every interest was served, or tried to be.

The bill was finally passed because of the clock. Congress was due to adjourn on June 30, 1934, and that was an election year—time to campaign, not swelter in Washington. The clock was stopped until the bill was finally reported out of a conference committee. Then the statesmen went home. At first the FHA was not a great success, for complex reasons, including appointments of important personnel Eccles considered to be incompetent. The Reconstruction Finance Corporation finally had to organize the Federal National Mortgage Association (FNMA, "Fanny May"), the secondary market for the mortgages. The private banks could have done that themselves, for themselves, but would not. Even in 1951, Eccles was still baffled by such obstinacy. As the saying goes, "you can lead a horse to water . . ."

Eccles was bitter about the outcome. But by another standard, Washington's, this young millionaire Utah banker had deeply impressed. In August, Morgenthau whispered to Eccles at a White House conference that he had recommended him to FDR to replace Eugene Black as Governor of the Federal Reserve Board. Eccles was taken aback: "For once in my life I was mum." He had not considered staying on in Washington beyond June of 1935, when schools for his children would let out. He had intended to return to Utah to resume his private life. The Federal Reserve appointment would be a long-term thing.

This was the beginning of the Marriner Eccles of Federal Reserve legend. Eccles knew all about the Federal Reserve System (FRS), and most of what he knew he didn't like.

As we know from the career of Pierpont Morgan, the Federal Reserve Act of 1913 was an outcome of the 1907 panic. Morgan's son-in-law wrote that, in the years 1908–11, "Mr. Morgan" had been consulting with Senator Nelson Aldrich about reforming the nation's banking system. Aldrich published his proposal in 1911, *Suggested Plan for Monetary Legislation*, and in 1912 the National Monetary Commission published its report, a facsimile of the Aldrich proposal except for some preliminary scathing of the nation's banking nonsystem. In 1912 the Democrats won and, with Woodrow Wilson in the White House, took over the legislation. Other strands of thought, including the doctrine of "real bills" (below), were introduced, as described by Robert Craig West in his definitive study, *Banking Reform and the Federal Reserve 1863–1923*. What came out were 12 separate district reserve banks (Aldrich had called for 15), privately owned, held together by the Federal Reserve Board, presidentially appointed, in Washington. The system began operations in 1914, and so did World War I. The system thus began in a flood of deficit finance. There had been no blueprint—anywhere—on how to run a 13-part central bank. In the 1920s Ben Strong (Morgan's right-hand man in 1907) was head of the New York Federal Reserve Bank, and he figured out how: by buying and selling government securities for the system as a whole, open-market operations. The system had thus operated in the 1920s and the disasters of 1929–33.

Who controlled it? The chairman of each bank was designated by the Federal Reserve Board, but the bankers themselves, in each district, decided who the chief executive officer would be. He was called the "Governor," unofficially. Hence, Governor Strong, the host in New York City in the 1920s to famous visits by *Reichsbankpräsident* Hjalmar Horace Greeley Schacht and Lord Norman, governor of the Bank of England. Strong died in 1928, before things got really hot, and was replaced by George Harrison as governor of the New York Bank. The committee, the Governor's Committee, conducting open-market operations, had gone through several permutations by 1933, but had remained in the control of the New York financial community, via the governor of the NYFRB. Strong, with his great prestige, had the ear of the Treasury and the president when he (rarely) needed higher authority for his actions. Harrison, Eccles charged, went instead to Senator Carter Glass of Virginia, an original sponsor of the 1913 legislation, and author of other financial legislation afterward. In any case, the individual district reserve banks had remained free to withhold their cooperation and funds from the Open Market Committee if they so pleased.

Eccles thought the entire business had become a sour joke: "A more effective way of diffusing responsibility and encouraging inertia and indecision could not very well have been devised."

Indeed, the Fed's record had been amazing. In 1914 there were but 152 bank failures out of some 28,000 banks. By 1926 out of 28,350 banks there were 976 failures; by 1930, 1350; by 1931, 2293. Between 1929 and 1933 the number of banks had fallen by half to 14,771, of which 9,755 were outright failures. Was the Fed responsible? Who said the Fed was supposed to save banks from failing? How? The nominal money supply in 1929–33 had fallen by 25 percent. Was the Fed responsible? Under the 1913 act it was supposed to issue its own notes against rediscounts of certain grades of commercial paper, "real bills" (alluding to nonfinancial bills of exchange, already nearly a vanished species in 1913). The total supply of such paper in the whole country (not all of it eligible) in 1933 was about $2 billion—not much of a basis for monetary expansion. The Fed had bought securities, increased its holdings of federal debt by a factor of five, from $500 million to $2.5 billion between 1929 and 1933. But, see Eccles above, the banks had not made the appropriate increases in loans and investments and, instead, their excess reserves had soared. Moreover, of the 14,771 surviving banks in 1933, some were national banks, some were state banks and some had no charters at all. Some were members of the FRS, and some were not. In addition there was no uniformity in accepted banking practice; the banks were subject to three different sets of federal auditors: the FRS, the (new) FDIC and the Comptroller of the Currency. The Federal Reserve Board included as members, ex officio, the Secretary of the Treasury and the Comptroller of the Currency.

These and other imperfections were in banker Eccles's mind when FDR asked him how he would like to be governor of the Federal Reserve Board? Eccles answered that he wouldn't touch it unless he could rewrite the law governing the Federal Reserve System. Roosevelt, who *admired* audacity, asked Eccles for a memo about that. The result was the Banking Act of 1935 and a sensational Washington dust-up.

Marriner Eccles had nothing against New York bankers, as people. But he believed the New York domination of the FRS had been bad for the country. Since the system was established by the federal power, he believed the control of it should be primarily in the hands of those who were part of the federal government, and that meant the Federal Reserve Board. He got that, mostly. He believed the FRS should be able to deal directly with the Treasury on a large scale when necessary, without paying commissions to private dealers of federal securities. He did not get that. He wanted the banking system unified, with a single bank examination authority and set of standards. He did not get any of that. But he got much of what he wanted.

After making an appeal at the beginning of his memo about the need for real control and for a compensatory monetary policy, the memo contained an outline of simple but fundamental changes:

1. The power over open-market operations should reside in the Federal Reserve Board.
2. The office of the chairman of the board of directors of each district bank should be abolished, and its powers merged with that of the governor of each bank, who would be appointed annually subject to approval or rejection by the Federal Reserve Board.
3. The embodiment of the "real bills doctrine," eligible paper, should be changed to "sound assets," the definition of which would be up to the Board in Washington.

These simple proposals would switch the control to Washington, centralize the lines of power and make a broad range of assets eligible as collateral for Federal Reserve credit.

FDR talked with Eccles for two hours, then said:

Marriner, that's quite an action program you want. It will be a knock-down and drag-out fight to get it through. But we might as well undertake it now as at any other time. It seems to be necessary.

Roosevelt added that Eccles should know that there was significant opposition building up against his rumored appointment as governor. FDR added, however, that he didn't "give a damn." To which Eccles replied boldly, "Mr. President, if you don't give a damn, I don't see why I should." Eccles later thought he might have been of a different mind had he known what was coming. On November 10, 1934, FDR announced the appointment of Marriner Eccles to be governor of the Federal Reserve Board, and his office handed out a statement of the man's financial and general business achievements—a long statement. That amused Eccles, who thought such an extraordinary move was to counter the view current in Washington "that every official in the New Deal was a crackpot and a visionary unqualified to hold public office because he had never met a payroll. . . ."

When it was all over Eccles was Chairman of the Board of Governors of the Federal Reserve System. The Governors had 14-year staggered terms, and the Chairman had a four-year term as Chairman, but served in that capacity at the President's discretion. The district banks now had presidents and vice-presidents who could be removed by the Board. The Board had an automatic majority (seven Governors) of the new 12-member Open Market Committee, which met in Washington. The Board could initiate changes in the rediscount rate. The Board at its own discretion had the power to raise and lower the reserve requirements of the member banks, and would get the power to set the margin requirements for bank loans made to security dealers. The Comptroller of the Currency and the Secretary of the Treasury lost their spots as ex officio members of the Board. In a late draft the Comptroller kept his membership, while his superior, the Secretary of the Treasury, was left out. Morgenthau was deeply offended, but then the Comptroller was dropped too. Eccles wrote that "this is one case where the public result of Morgenthau's fragile feelings was highly beneficial."

The Board of Governors could now be an economic policy powerhouse, in the right conditions, with the right members and the right Chairman. Eccles had succeeded with much of his program, and may in some cases have gotten more than he hoped for. In the years ahead, having freed the Federal Reserve System from New York domination, Eccles would have to fight a mortal battle to free it from the control of the Treasury. The system was still privately owned. The Board was charged with the conduct of monetary policy, and was in theory responsible to Congress. "Our creature," said Senator Paul Douglas. "Independent," said President Dwight David Eisenhower. To this day there are ambiguities. But what Eccles now had was a far cry from what he found—to the deep consternation of many, then and forevermore.

Senator Glass, whose opinion of his own role in 1913 had become much inflated by 1934, was offended by Eccles and by his manner. Glass was a courtly elder statesman, childishly egotistical but powerful. The senator had not been consulted about changing the bank law in advance. Eccles said he regretted that, and tried to make amends. He failed. The war began. Eccles had two fundamental allies: FDR's seemingly shifting and vacillating (but in the end sufficient) support and the arrangement of the bill. Title I rechartered the FDIC, which the bankers desperately wanted; Title II contained the changes in the FRS that Eccles wanted; Title III amended the banking laws in various ways, but included changing an anti-"money changer" bit passed in 1933 whereby if by July 1, 1935, bank officers had not paid back the loans they had made to themselves from their own banks they had to resign their positions. Eccles knew that the act would get through by August 1935, and he was right. So long as the three parts of the bill were held together, and Eccles's opponents would make every effort to separate them, the bill was bound to pass.

Morgenthau entered as Eccles's ally, as did other talented men in government and the Congress. Glass quickly established at his committee hearings that no present member of the Federal Reserve Board, and none of the past luminaries in its history, such as Paul Warburg, had been consulted by Eccles. At first Glass had high hopes of "wrecking" the Eccles Bank Bill. "I have some hope also of wrecking Eccles," he wrote in a letter to Professor Parker Willis (who, in his own book, rather considered himself to have been the primary architect of the 1913 act). Glass snooped around for some dirt on Eccles, charging that he was a dangerous man, radical, ambitious, that he still had banking interests (Eccles had to divest himself of his bank stocks to avoid conflict of interest).

The battle over the bill was a dirty business, described by Eccles himself and his biographer, Sidney Hyman. It was at the height of the battle that *Time* in a cover story wrote: "Many people in Washington are convinced that Marriner Eccles is all that stands between this country and disaster." The *New York Times*, which had called Eccles "bombastic," after viewing him in action day after weary day, defending, explaining, enlarging upon, before hostile committees, surrendered. It editorialized that "Mr. Eccles established himself in this trial by fire as a man of the first capacity." Senator Glass got to have input on the bill and it passed.

Glass was still after Marriner personally, and that dragged

over into 1936 before FDR finessed the whole business; the new governors were appointed and took office. Eccles settled some old scores very abruptly with opponents inside the system, with Harrison and with the members of the Federal Advisory Council—an odd bit left over from the 1913 Act, which passed through into further life in the 1935 bill. Then Eccles insensibly became the captive of his own creation; he was to become the premier pillar of the Federal Reserve System itself. He would be called Governor Eccles for the rest of his life. The honor went with him after he finally left Washington.

VII

Creating the new system was one thing; making it more than it had been before turned out to be something else. The organization was now in place, but to what end? By 1936 the economy was improving; in fact, there were some rather odd phenomena to consider. Industrial production was making a roaring comeback. It had fallen by nearly 50 percent, from 58 (1947–49 = 100) to 30 in 1929–33, but was back to 55 in 1936, and would actually hit 60 in 1937, exceeding the 1929 level. Yet in 1936 unemployment was still nearly 17 percent of the labor force. This disturbed Eccles, especially in the light of a 38 percent increase in the hourly wages of those who had jobs in manufacturing. How was this possible? (It is not understood to this day). Consumer prices had advanced in 1933–36 by a mere 11 percent, but wholesale prices were up by a full third, and this alarmed Eccles. Consumer prices could be next. Gold was pouring into the country and bank reserves in excess of required reserves, 1.8 percent in 1932, 74.4 percent in 1935 and still 65.7 percent in 1936 after an abrupt rise in the currency outstanding and bank deposits of 15 percent in just three years. By the standards of the time such an increase was alarming. The increase of excess reserves by a factor of 41 contained the possibility of an inflationary explosion in bank lending. Morgenthau and Eccles faced the puzzling prospect of high unemployment and inflation simultaneously. It was the fear of inflation gripping both Eccles and Morgenthau that gave rise to one of Keynes's choicest quips: "They profess to fear that for which they dare not hope."

What they did is merely amusing now, since it had no measurable economic consequences. The Treasury borrowed money to buy gold, and did not issue gold certificates to the

Federal Reserve System, thus "sterilizing" gold—the imports sold to the Treasury did not increase bank reserves because the Treasury had borrowed an equal amount of reserves from the banks through its security sales. The Board of Governors, for its part, by two steps raised the reserve requirements to their legal maxima, sharply reducing excess reserves, but in the circumstances still leaving them vastly in excess of normal levels. Eccles, now a "central banker," wanted to get within closer reach of "control" of bank lending, and had no hope of it at all with the excess reserves existing in 1936. Since neither set of moves created so much as a blip in the economic data, they are not worth discussing except as historical curiosities, but it was all accompanied by extensive internecine sniping between Eccles and Morgenthau.

There was a far larger game afoot that did have consequences: budget balancing. Morgenthau still hankered after a balanced budget, and in 1936, with an election on, FDR was with him. Hapless Alf Landon would campaign against FDR with "I believe a man can be a liberal without being a spendthrift." Meaty stuff. The deficit in 1936, augmented by a one-time veterans' bonus of $1.7 billion, would hit $4.4 billion, the largest of any New Deal year to date. That had fueled the recovery. But Marriner Eccles could both add *and* subtract. In 1937 there would be no bonus and the new Social Security taxes would heist an additional $2 billion out of the spending stream. Even without any other budget-balancing nonsense the government's contribution to the economy in 1937 would fall by nearly $4 billion. If expenditures were cut in addition, it would be worse. Eccles had no faith in Morgenthau's gods, "business confidence" and whatever. Eccles was a man of facts.

To balance the budget in fiscal 1938, or, rather, to promise to balance it in the 1936 election, there would need to be a great reduction in expenditures. Eccles, looking at his numbers and the huge unemployment level, was opposed. He lost out. To Morgenthau and his staff it even seemed that the strength of the recovery might eliminate the need for relief payments altogether. Roosevelt won the election, but the budget-balancing idea was taking hold around him. Already at the end of 1936, Harry Hopkins was making plans to cut back federal relief and WPA. In December 1936, Eccles sent FDR a memorandum stoutly opposing any attempt to cut back or to balance the budget; the idea of a balanced budget in fiscal 1938 would be "dangerously premature." Despite all other problems, millions were still unemployed and the recovery had a long way to go to absorb them.

Blum wrote that the Eccles memorandum was a "tremendous challenge to Morgenthau." The secretary wrote in his diary that if he failed to "dynamite" the Eccles memo, ". . . he would find that Eccles will become the President's fiscal adviser." Morgenthau talked FDR around, the recovery kept going, but federal revenues were falling. The only way to achieve a balance was to cut back, and FDR demanded retrenchment by Executive Order on April 7, 1937. Morgenthau "rejoiced." He crowed to his daily assembly of Treasury subordinates, his "morning group," "I wish you'd hear the President talk about balancing the budget to Eccles. . . . God if he'd only say publicly what he told him, it would be marvelous."

Eccles caved in to FDR. By fall of 1937 the economy caved in too, and panic struck the New Deal. The depression of 1937–38 was on, giving rise among other things to a reversal of both Treasury and Federal Reserve policies, again with no known effects. In addition there were Marriner's anguish about FDR's sincerity regarding the New Deal and the colloquy between Eccles and Morgenthau about gold desterilization quoted above, and there would be a recrudescence of Eccles as the prophet of compensatory fiscal policy. Now FDR would listen. But in late 1937, when the New Deal's house of cards was falling apart, Eccles remarked sarcastically that at least for the first half of 1937 the Treasury had indeed achieved an actual cash balance.

Eccles got going vigorously, and FDR went with him, but changing policies and producing an impact takes many months; 1938 would therefore be gloomy year. Unemployment, about 14 percent on average in 1937, jumped to 19 percent. The deficit in 1938, a mere $1.2 billion, was only 18 percent of federal expenditures, the lowest since 1931 (it had been 52 percent in 1936). People were pointing fingers. Eccles was blamed for wrecking business confidence with his advocacy of increased business taxes, including one on undistributed profits. New Dealers were now blaming monopolists and economic royalists. Thurmon Arnold was authorized to raise the antitrust laws from the dead, and the Department of Justice began to pursue monopolists. There was to be a new bank holding-company bill. A. P. Giannini had been deeply impressed by young Marriner and his First Security Corporation, and now Giannini's Transamerica Corporation was going to town out west and, some thought, was going too far.

On one tack Eccles went back to his FHA ideas. He wanted a drastic reduction in down payments and interest rates to shore up the sagging home construction industry. FDR didn't mind doing that. Why not call the relevant agency heads together and suggest it? "If you do that," Eccles replied, "you can count me out." "Why?" asked FDR. Eccles pointed out that, with each one defending his own bailiwick, they would never agree on anything. A committee of people from outside the bureaucracy should be called in. FDR agreed and appointed a blue-ribbon group including Gerard Swope of G.E. and Robert Wood of Sears Roebuck. The committee was doing its work with Eccles in November 1937 and had met with FDR when Morgenthau had made his budget-balancing speech. Following that shock, the work proceeded and liberalized FHA terms were authorized by Congress. Hopkins produced proposals for new spending projects. Morgenthau, who had not been seriously consulted on all this, was appalled, felt utterly defeated and contemplated his resignation until FDR jollied him out of it. There would be big increases in spending on all fronts. On April 14, 1938, Roosevelt sent his new spending message to Congress.

Eccles and those who thought like him were now in the driver's seat as Roosevelt's economic advisers. The conservatives did not take it lying down and counterattacked vigorously. On December 10, 1938, Senator Harry Byrd (Democrat of Virginia) made a nationwide radio broadcast denouncing FDR, Eccles, the New Deal and "nine years of fiscal insanity," followed by the usual homilies about free enterprise, initiative, thrift and so on. Eccles told FDR that he would write a rebuttal to Byrd in the form of a letter of the sort that would be "in the front pages." Roosevelt was delighted. Then nothing happened. Roosevelt phoned Eccles and asked, "Marriner, what's happened to the letter? You're not backing down, are you?" Eccles explained that he had a Virginia problem. He had forgotten that on December 23 they would be unveiling a plaque at the Federal Reserve Board to commemorate Senator Carter Glass and his many contributions to its welfare: ". . . I felt it would cause some embarrassment to assail the junior United States Senator from Virginia while immortalizing the senior one." Eccles wrote that "Roosevelt roared with laughter. . . . Two days after the plaque to Senator Glass was unveiled I unveiled my letter to Senator Byrd." It was Byrd's turn in front of the firehose. Eccles began: "I think I may be forgiven for feeling some impatience when a responsible public official like yourself so misconstrues my viewpoint . . . ," and then blasted the senator's arguments in small detail, root and branch, page after page, in the Eccles manner, explaining to him about compensatory fiscal policy, the economics of the public debt, the "burden" of taxation relative to ability to pay, the salvation of private enterprise by government expenditure, the paradox of thrift, the responsibilities of government in a democratic society, the dignity of man, the right to work, social security, the inability of empty stomachs to build character, ending up with: "I am convinced that your program is . . . a defeatist one, a program of retrogression . . . that it would jeopardize the salvation of our democracy, which I know you are sincerely desirous of preserving as I am." Eccles was mighty pleased with himself: "The uproar in the press following this letter was highly gratifying, though hardly any editorial writers agreed with me." Byrd replied on January 16, 1939, with, according to Eccles, *"Poor Richard's Almanac, Bartlett's Quotations*, Will Rogers . . . condensed versions of the lives of Thomas Jefferson and Andrew Jackson, and the history of the Federalist party, and of the English people in modern times." Byrd and Eccles were invited by NBC to go at each other on national radio. Both accepted. Byrd spoke first, on January 16. Marriner's reply came a week later. Roosevelt phoned the next morning: "Well, I just called to *condemn* you and to *commend* you. I usually go to bed at ten. But you kept me up until ten thirty listening to your speech. But now I want to commend you. I think your address was excellent. You made the problem so simple that even I was able to understand it." Now at least FDR knew what Eccles thought the New Deal was, or was supposed to be.

But note the date. The depression was still on, but history was now closing down the New Deal road show. The Japanese were on the march; the Germans had divided up Czechoslovakia, were going to devour it and would soon launch World War II in Europe. The great issues and arguments of the 1930s would suddenly become part of history's dust.

VIII

The sum of the deficits from 1933 to 1940 was $25.2 billion. In 1942 alone the deficit was $20.8 billion, and in 1943 it was $54.9 billion. In 1940 the national debt was $42.8 billion; in 1945 it was $235.2 billion. The nominal GNP in

1945 was $100.5 billion; in 1945, $213.6 billion. The money supply, currency plus demand deposits, $38.7 billion in 1940, was $94.1 billion in 1945. The civilian labor force had expanded by 50 percent even while some 13 million men and women served in the armed forces. Unemployment vanished.

In 1942 the Board of Governors announced that they would buy and sell Treasury bills in unlimited quantities at 0.38 percent discount. This "pegged" the prices of government securities at incredibly high levels, in a fixed pattern. The commercial banks were allowed to buy bonds with "war loan" accounts that required neither reserve requirements nor deposit insurance. This was simply interest-bearing cash. Coming out of the rock-bottom interest rates of the 1930s (prime rates mainly at less than 1 percent), World War II was financed at incredibly low interest rates. For Morgenthau it was a great triumph, and justifiably so from the Treasury viewpoint. But for Eccles the war finance was a source of (necessary) anguish. Morgenthau stuffed federal securities into the banking system like an Alsatian farmer stuffs a Strasbourg goose. The banking system was filled with federal securities by Morgenthau. Total bank holdings of public debt (including the Reserve banks), $21.9 billion in 1940, were an astounding $118 billion in 1945.

Eccles ruefully admitted that "each of us who served in Washington in 1940–45 fought a civil war within an international war." How could the vast monetary expansion be kept from igniting an equally vast inflation? The goods of war did not enter the market; the money paid for them did. Eccles was full of plans for the contribution to be made by the Fed. In fact, by pegging the market, the Fed's role became mainly that of the goose. Prices were held down and kept in line mainly by that apparatus of direct regulation, the Office of Price Administration, described by J. K. Galbraith in *A Theory of Price Control* and by Hugh Rockoff in *Drastic Measures*. Eccles agreed that only direct controls had prevented a disastrous inflation. The first problem after all was goods and arms. In fact, there were no purely monetary measures possible. The problem of wartime finance is always to extract men and resources from the economy. Men were drafted, resources were paid for with 60 percent borrowed money at prices held down by direct controls. Civilians got rationing and black markets. Compared to the war, the legendary fiscal problems of the New Deal were peanuts.

From June 30, 1940, to December 31, 1945, federal expenditures were (Eccles's own figures) $380 billion; $153 billion (about 40 percent) paid for by taxes and $228 billion by borrowing; $133 billion were borrowed outside the banking system, and $95 billion by stuffing the goose.

Eccles was endlessly frustrated during the war by his fears of what would happen when the war ended and controls were lifted. He wanted more savings bonds sold to the public, fewer marketable bonds to the banks. He wanted higher taxes. He attempted to change the war strategy, to starve Japan out, slowing down the buildup and starting to convert to civilian production to get goods produced and on the market that could sop up the money. What would happen when the war ended and the huge volume of marketable debt hung over the financial system? This threat dwarfed the excess reserves of the 1930s (they disappeared forever in 1942).

No one knew what would happen, of course. Some feared a renewed depression when the war ended. Others, including Eccles, feared an inflation. Roosevelt died, Morgenthau went home, the war ended, times changed, and Eccles was still in Washington, himself now a relic. He didn't quit. The controls were lifted, too fast for Eccles's tastes. He contrived some ingenious substitutes, controls over consumer credit manipulated by the Fed, a system of secondary reserves for the commercial banks. Prices rose, but the Fed, cooperating with the Treasury, maintained the peg on the bond market. This policy "monetized" the debt as banks and others cashed in their holdings to get Federal Reserve notes to make loans and investments. The great postwar boom came, and prices rose by 50 percent in the three years from 1945 to 1948. Still the peg remained. The Fed remained immobile. It had become, in Eccles's immortal words, "the engine of inflation."

Eccles had not wanted to stay on in Washington in 1940, but Roosevelt had reappointed him to a full 14-year term in 1940, pleading that he had to have him. Then, with the war, Eccles like others "stayed at their posts." Eccles offered to resign as chairman in 1945, pointing out to Truman that the President had a right to his own Chairman. Truman and the Treasury preferred to stick with the veteran Chairman in the face of the giant postwar debt refinancing problems coming up. Eccles by then was preaching the other side of his compensatory message. Had he been endowed with the powers of Li Ping, he would have carved it in stone: "Low interest rates, higher expenditures, deficits, lower taxes in depressions: higher interest rates, lower expenditures, surpluses and higher taxes in expansions." In those days even economists believed in the real possibility of "full employment and price stability," as the saying used to go. Eccles wasn't mad—or at least, not mad alone. In the Employment Act of 1946, Congress had committed the federal government to something resembling price stability and full employment, a weird overestimate of the government's abilities, as it turned out, in the next four decades.

Eccles had been involved in the Bretton Woods negotiations which set up the postwar international financial institutions; so had his younger brother, George, now a rising star in his own right in the world of finance. In 1945, Eccles wrote out the terms of the British loan. He presented them in person to Keynes, who came to call at the Federal Reserve Building. When Keynes complained that they were too stiff, Eccles, the banker, said that they were meant to get through Congress. If Eccles had his own way it would all be a gift, out of gratitude for what the British had done for the Allied cause.

Then the new politics of Washington got Eccles. In 1948, Truman "dropped the pilot." Without warning Eccles was informed that he would not be reappointed as chairman. Eccles was staggered, wounded. When he asked why, Truman said merely that he wanted someone else, that he was in no way dissatisfied with Eccles. It was a mystery. Moreover, Truman pleaded with Eccles to stay on as vice-chairman. He repeated, according to Eccles, "Please stay and help me. I need your help." The bewildered Eccles agreed. Truman then reneged on the vice-chairmanship, so Eccles stayed on as ordinary governor.

By then Eccles's personal life was at a very low ebb. His wife of many years, May Campbell Young, the girl he had met in Scotland and married in 1913, had come to Washington in 1934 with their three children. The children had grown up hardly knowing their father, with his day-and-night work schedules. Mrs. Eccles had had enough of Washington by 1941 (it is not to everyone's taste), went home to Utah, and stayed. Eccles lived on alone at the Shoreham, year after year, an eccentric figure. He had gone back to Utah at Christmas in 1948 (on part of his annual leave; he never took a vacation) to make the final agreements for a divorce. When he came back Truman's bombshell awaited him. Eccles believed Giannini had gotten him by power politics in payment for the government's harassment of Transamerica. Sidney Hyman, writing in 1976, still could not explain it. Perhaps it will never be known why Truman sacked Eccles. One point we do know unambiguously: the little man from Missouri did not like to be disagreed with.

Eccles, living alone in Washington in 1951, wrote of his marital failure with great sadness. His intense work habits had kept him away from his family. The intensity had "touched innocent lives" and never should have. He had been deficient both as a husband and as a father, and he knew it. He found no comfort in the fact that Washington was full of similar stories. Now it was too late to make amends.

Beckoning Frontiers ends in the gloom of mid-1951, before, as it turned out, Eccles had one of his finest Washington hours. He roused himself from his torpor, and started the battle with Truman and Treasury Secretary John Snyder, that was to liberate the Federal Reserve System. Eccles then walked away from Washington at age 61, remarried, remembered who he had been back in 1933 and started a rich new life. The pessimistic ending of his memoirs was revised by life itself, by renewed enterprises to come.

IX

The U.S.S.R. had entered the war against Japan at the last moment, and grabbed all of the Japanese-held territory it could. Stalin, with his eye on the long term, held onto North Korea, organizing a communist government there, arming it, training its soldiers. South Korea was organized by the Americans, along American lines (in theory), and its soldiers were armed and trained by the United States. After a period of intense military confrontation, in June 1950, a North Korean tank army burst into South Korea. President Truman committed U.S. forces and appealed to the UN for approval. The Korean War was on.

For Eccles this meant more inflation on the way. World War II had only been over for five years and its financial hangover still ached. The Truman government began erecting a smallish facsimilie of World War II direct controls. Eccles yearned for the power to use standard central banking techniques to combat rising prices, but the peg remained. The FRS, meant to be an agency independent of direct political control since its inception in the 1913 legislation, had been the Treasury's instrument since 1941, and the Truman administration intended to continue that relationship.

On January 9, 1951, Secretary John Snyder made a speech

in New York announcing an agreement between the Treasury and the FRS to continue the peg. Thomas McCabe, Truman's new chairman, said nothing. Since Snyder's statement was not true, Allan Sproul, the outspoken president of the New York Federal Reserve Bank, responded with a speech before the New York State Banking Association that implied disagreement with Snyder. Ironically, Eccles himself, by defanging the power of the district reserve bank presidents, was responsible for Sproul's inability to speak more authoritatively. Sproul, a great central banker in his own right, was but one member of 12 of the Open Market Committee. So was Eccles now, but he didn't care. He did more than imply; he went before the Joint Committee on the Economic Report (a product of the 1946 Employment Act), and argued straight out against Snyder. That was *big news*. Truman then invited the entire Open Market Committee to the White House for a chat. A very general discussion occurred in which Truman laid out his problems, and Chairman McCabe discussed the Committee's problems. Someone on the Committee apparently "got that feeling," as John Dean would in a later White House meeting, that someone was being "set up." So one of the Committee members, Governor R. M. Evans, immediately wrote up a memorandum containing the substance of the White House meeting. The memo was circulated and each member penciled in his corrections. The memo, in that pre-tape-recorder age, contained the combined memory of the 12 Committee members of what had transpired.

The administration then put out a statement that the Board of Governors had agreed to maintain the peg. Eccles, on his own, leaked to the press that the administration's statement was not in accord with the facts. There followed an exchange at the Board between Governor J. K. Vardaman (a Truman appointee and crony from Missouri) and Eccles. Who gave that information to the press? Eccles said he did. McCabe that morning showed the Board members a private letter from Truman thanking them for their agreement to maintain the peg. The governors were astounded. It was Friday. That evening the others had gone home. Eccles, with no home to go to, was still in his office. Felix Belair of the *New York Times* phoned and read Eccles the text of Truman's private letter to McCabe. The administration had released it. What did Eccles have to say about that? Now Eccles acted, alone. He believed it was an attempt "by the Treasury to impose its will on the Federal Reserve. If swift action was not taken . . . the Federal

Reserve would no longer have a voice in deciding monetary and credit policies."

He put Belair off. He phoned the Board's secretary, Sam Carpenter, at his home. Carpenter had a copy, the only copy, of the Evans memo in his safe. Eccles had Carpenter come back into town, and give him the memo. Eccles then had his own secretary make copies of it. By then it was 11:00 P.M. Eccles phoned Belair to say that he might have a statement to make, but "wanted to sleep on it." The next morning Belair appeared at the Shoreham. Eccles gave him a statement, together with a copy of the Evans memorandum. Belair gave copies to the *Washington Post* and the *Washington Star*. The whole business was headlines in the Sunday papers, and had been timed that way. Eccles wrote, "By Monday morning the fat was in the fire."

McCabe called a meeting of the Open Market Committee for Tuesday, February 6. Allan Sproul made a statement defending Eccles. Eccles then made a little speech, telling the Committee that they now had to stand up to the administration. They should have done it earlier. It was their duty to defend their own independence: "If Congress objects to our actions it can change the law; but until it does that, we have a clear responsibility to check inflation. . . ."

More negotiations now followed and the Fed agreed only to maintain the peg up to an additional $500 million. The Treasury accepted the plan, "the Accord," and in March 1951, in three days, the $500 million evaporated into an ocean of new debt expansion. The Fed was liberated from the Babylonian captivity, as wits inside the system had called it, and cautiously, ever so cautiously, edged back into the world of central banking control—but without Eccles.

In 1950, Eccles had written an article in *Fortune* critical of the foundations of American foreign policy, and in particular of the continued support of Chiang Kai-shek. Eccles knew who had made the money. *Fortune*'s editors, failing to get Eccles to delete the offensive parts, and considering publisher Henry Luce's views, published the article with a footnote disassociating themselves on the China issue. Eccles advocated recognizing Red China as soon as the Korean War ended. He was already far ahead of Washington in his thinking. This would continue. On June 4, 1951, Eccles was back in his hometown, Logan, Utah addressing the graduates of the Utah State Agricultural College. He blasted away at the follies of the era, of the Truman government, of war; economic underdevelopment in Asia, Africa and Latin America; overpopulation in the poorest nations and our own inability to cope realistically with the causes of social upheavals and revolutions abroad. Moreover, he said darkly, we had found no way at home to maintain our economy except "war or preparation for war." Still the radical, still audacious. Nine years later Eisenhower would utter the same dark thoughts.

The Washington years, 17 of them, were now clearly at a dead end. Eccles had seen it coming and was planning to go in any case. After the fight with Truman and Snyder, the sooner the better. On June 20 he submitted his resignation to Truman. The president said goodbye and good luck, but not thank you for the years of public service. Others did, though. There was an outpouring of good will and praise from those who knew Eccles and had watched the final drama. As the *New York Times* put it: "The grip of the Treasury on Federal Reserve policy was finally broken. . . ." The *Washington Post* wrote of a man who had stuck to his own ideals and beliefs in that town, those years, saying that Eccles was "pretty well unique." In Dallas, the *Morning News* wrote: "No political crony of Mr. Truman can fill his shoes." *Life* called Eccles the "real hero" of the current fight against inflation and said he deserved a medal. He would not be getting it from Harry Truman.

He liked flattery as well as the next man, but Marriner Eccles was the ultimate realist and could see the world that was coming—our world. He did not like the vision. But he was still the son of David Eccles, the capitalist, and was going to swim with the tide of endless inflation, endless deficits, endless expansion of "big government," and not drown in it. Shortly before returning to private life he wrote in the annual report of the Utah Construction Company that "Your management" had recognized the inevitability of inflation, and therefore would be devoting more resources to acquisition of basic raw materials, "ownership of which would serve as a source of profit as well as a hedge. . . ." The policy and the company were going to become, in due course, Utah International, a vast worldwide mineral, mining, metals, construction and shipping enterprise with Eccles as its chairman. The next 25 years, longer than his years of public service, would bring out the old Eccles blood and talents. Build, his father had said.

Before that he regained a normal emotional equilibrium. The life of the hermit of the Shoreham Hotel ended. By good luck he had met a lady in Washington in November 1950. Sallie Madison Glassie found "the Governor" both interesting and amusing. After (according to Sidney Hyman's account) one of the lower-key courtships of the modern era, Eccles was married again in New York City on December 29, 1951. He had pushed up the nuptials to 48 hours before January 1 for "tax reasons." In his 62nd year, when some men are thinking about and hoping for retirement, he was thinking about what he had missed.

But he did try to convert his great, good Washington fame into a seat in the U.S. Senate. It was the country's bad fortune, no doubt, that the currency of the nation's capital is not really fungible out in Utah politics. The country did learn to its amusement that Marriner Eccles was in fact a Republican, always had been. He lost his bid in the Utah Republican primary to unseat incumbent, colorless and conservative Arthur Watkins. After that Eccles spent plenty of time on political issues, but on his own terms. He never bothered with the pursuit of public office again.

X

In its 1951 annual report First Security announced, with no small pride, the return of Marriner Eccles as chairman of the board. Eccles was barred by law for two years from direct participation in the affairs of the First Security banks themselves. But he had other things in mind, mainly his interests in Amalgamated Sugar and Utah Construction. Eccles was chairman of both, and presided over major changes in both. Amalgamated was in a fairly stagnant industry, encased in government allotments and controls (until 1974). But you could still make money with greater efficiency in your own corner. Eccles often boasted of Amalgamated's management, the men he had brought in himself. The management was of high quality and Eccles now played his role in the financing of major technological innovations, relocations of plants and changes that gave Amalgamated the reputation as the best-managed firm in the sugarbeet industry. In 1966 the company paid tribute to Marriner's half-century on its board. That membership had been one legacy of David Eccles, well tended.

Utah Construction was another, and its development after Eccles "came home" was to be world class. Eccles knew the company needed to shift emphasis in an inflationary world, and knew he needed an infusion of younger management.

Eccles had taken the opportunity in 1946 to sell off the great "Seven U" ranch, holdings of some 600,000 acres of grazing land around the slopes of northern Nevada's spectacular Jarbidge range and the uplands at the T junction of Utah, Idaho and Nevada. His father had used this land long ago to raise livestock, cattle, horses and mules for his construction enterprises. When the lands were sold it was proposed that Utah Construction be wound up. Eccles had prevailed upon the other directors to continue, but to begin acquiring raw materials. This they did, adding to properties such as the Wyoming coal already owned, going back to David Eccles.

Marriner Eccles always had possessed a nice judgment about men, particularly those with executive talents, and had in fact been surrounded by men of brilliance; for example, Winfield Riefler drafting the FHA bill or Lauchlin Currie on the 1935 bank act and later at the Board. Eccles also had deep respect for bureaucrats who did their work well, and *Beckoning Frontiers* is studded with praise for such people. Consider what he wrote of Herman Oliphant, a Treasury Department official with whom Eccles had many conflicts: "He was one of those men, little known to the public, who work outside the glare of a spotlight, but without whose tedious labors the men in the spotlight would flounder helplessly."

Solid and innovative management had always been characteristic of Eccles enterprises; they were both dynamic and "sound," and difficult competitors. When Eccles thought of Utah Construction's future he went after the men for his company who could deliver. A brilliant example was George Ishiyama, a *Nisei*, an American whose parents, *Issei*, had been born in Japan. Ishiyama's specialty was to study and learn the ways of his parents' homeland. Utah International was to do hundreds of millions of dollars worth of business with Japanese firms, and long before it was fashionable elsewhere in this country, Utah knew that "the Japanese way" was not like ours—and learned about it. In 1949, Ishiyama negotiated a sale from the mines in Cedar City, Utah, of iron ore to Japanese steel mills struggling out of the ashes of war. After that, as Hyman put it, "all subsequent" contracts in Japan were negotiated by Ishiyama. Utah Construction and then Utah International were to make a fortune in business with the Japanese as their post–World War II economic miracle blossomed.

Utah Construction had been founded by early Utah pioneers, four Corey brothers who came to Zion in the 1850s, and by J. E. Spaulding, who came in 1847 with Brigham Young. The Coreys also ran a grocery business, and it was all called Corey Brothers & Co. The Wattis brothers, Ed and William, had joined the firm on the construction end as partners in the 1890s. Their banker had been First National of Ogden—David Eccles. The floundering company was reorganized in 1900 with David Eccles coming in for a third. Under Marriner's later direction, as we have seen, the company was a major contractor on the Boulder Dam. Now, with Marriner's belief that the country's fiscal policies would generate endless inflation, the company was moving into raw materials and their devlopment. Eccles was looking for talent.

His eye had been on Edmund W. Littlefield, a grandson of old Ed Wattis, the construction man. Littlefield had worked for Standard Oil, and had served during the war in the Petroleum Administration. Eccles had kept in touch with the young man. After the Rose Bowl game in 1951, while Marriner was still in public service but thinking of leaving, he approached young Littlefield to help with the ancestral firm. At first Littlefield wasn't interested. Eccles persisted. He wanted Littlefield as financial vice-president and treasurer, pointing out that one day, via his mother's shares, Littlefield was destined to be an owner of Utah Construction, so why not come and help out? Finally, Littlefield agreed, but he wanted conditions peculiar to the circumstances. First Marriner had to promise that Littlefield's decisions would not be overturned by other members with inherited spots in the company. Eccles said not to worry; he knew that more firms were ruined by nepotism than by business conditions. Second, Littlefield said, knowing Eccles, that he wanted a pledge that he could leave the office at night and go home to his wife and children. Eccles said OK.

The rest is history. By the time Eccles gave up his chairmanship in 1971, 20 years after the Washington years had ended and after 50 years on Utah's board, Littlefield was its president, and the stockholders had seen their shares increase in value by a factor of 70—a $1,000 share had grown to $70,000. Utah International was a worldwide conglomerate with interests all over the West, in Canada, in Latin America, in Australia, New Zealand and Asia. There were fleets of ships, ocean-going dredges, coal, iron ore, uranium; the company had built a fleet of double-duty (ore out, crude oil back) cargo tankers. Its merger with G.E. in 1976, the year before Marriner's death, was the largest corporate merger in American history. In 1984, Utah International, with Littlefield still on its board, had 6,500 employees and revenues of $1.6 billion. (It was purchased by the giant Australian firm, Broken Hill Proprietary Company, in 1985 for $2.6 billion.)

Marriner had moved its headquarters to San Francisco, where "the Governor" could better oversee his worldwide interests and where his wife could enjoy the more expansive cultural life of "everyone's favorite city in the world." Eccles also kept his suite in Salt Lake City in the grand old Hotel Utah, right across the street from Brigham's Temple and the old Tabernacle. A large statue of Brigham stands in the intersection, as the saying goes in Utah (here bowdlerized), "with his back to the Temple and his hand outstretched to the bank."

By the 1970s, now with a second career in a single lifetime as the great western tycoon behind him, one would suppose that Washington and all that might have been forgotten. It was not so. Eccles never had lost his taste for great issues, nor his understanding of why they usually were dealt with so badly. Remember, Eccles had once proposed to "save the country" by the product of pure thinking. At age 82, in his last public speech, he laid it on again: ". . . the wrong road was taken every time we had a chance to alter course. . . ." We had ignored the needs of our own country, we had misunderstood the world around us, we had tried to force people by military violence to bend to our will and we had so mismanaged our domestic economy that our economic structure now "made the control of inflation impossible." Despite his own fabulous achievements in a long life, Eccles was an angry old man. We could have been so much better than we were. No one could call Marriner Eccles a "visionary," a "crackpot," someone who didn't really know how things worked. He really did know how things worked, and he didn't like it.

X

If you were a mature person in 1950 and hated folly, war, corruption, crime in high places, foreign aggression, militarism, waste, inflation—you were going to be unhappy about much of American public life in the coming decades. That was Eccles. Already, in 1954, he was on Washington's case. In a speech in Salt Lake City before the National Association of University Presidents, he turned the firehose on again. "We should know by now," he said, that isolated military cam-

paigns around the world would not stop communism. Such
efforts would be "endless and futile." We should instead try
to correct the political corruption and economic mismanage-
ment upon which communism thrived. We should stop backing "reactionary governments that lack the confidence and
support of their people." In that regard, he named Chiang
Kai-shek, Syngman Rhee and "the French colonial government of Indochina." We should recognize Red China, as
Britain and most of our allies already had done. He noted
the infernal stupidity and bad manners of John Foster Dulles,
who in Geneva had refused even to look at Premier Chou
En-lai. He included, for good measure, Senator Joe McCarthy
on his list of the world's imperfections.

He kept it up. He participated in the CED's Commission
on Money and Credit. He went back to Washington in 1961
to argue before the Joint Committee on the Economic Report
the unfinished reforms in the banking system. He wanted the
district bank presidents off the Open Market Committee; he
wanted the Board reduced from seven to five members, with
no restrictions on their occupations or origins. He still wanted
unification in the commercial banking system. He wanted the
wording of the 1946 Employment Act amended to include
stability, and he wanted the Federal Reserve's written warrant
amended in the same manner. He warned that the economy
was becoming uncompetitive in the world markets because of
monopoly practices by both management and labor, that we
were becoming, as a result, technologically backward and
would be unable to compete with world-market prices. We
could not in these conditions continue long to be the world's
banker. The balance of payments would soon turn against us.
All this in 1961.

Eccles brought down the wrath of both the Catholic and
Mormon hierarchies by his support of planned parenthood.
He was outraged that we would provide third-world nations
with the means to lower their death rates and then sabotage
that achievement by refusing them the means to reduce their
birth rates. This was folly which would produce unmanage-
able disasters of swarming populations where they could not
find even subsistence.

But history, a century from now, may well record Marriner's finest hour as an after-dinner blast in the face of the
president of the United States. Eccles had been appalled by
Senator Barry Goldwater's bellicosity, and had supported
Lyndon Baines Johnson, the self-proclaimed peace candidate

in the 1964 presidential campaign. Eccles had even introduced Johnson to an audience in Salt Lake City. (He would do the same for Bobby Kennedy four years later.) In July 1965, Johnson, having won the election, was at war in Vietnam. Eccles was invited to dinner at the White House. Johnson had invited the members of the committe of independent business-men who had backed him. Once the speaking began it was clear they had been brought there to generate support for Johnson's war in Vietnam. Johnson spoke. Dean Rusk spoke. Defense Secretary Robert McNamara spoke, aided by his usual array of data, charts, diagrams and printouts. It was entirely by chance that Eccles was designated to make a little speech in response to the heavy thoughts that had been laid out. Eccles had known Johnson for many years. Appar-ently Johnson didn't know Eccles very well. The 75-year-old former New Dealer opened up on Lyndon Johnson:

> . . . I regret that I cannot follow or subscribe in any sense to what the seven preceding speakers have said concerning Viet-nam, or what I heard a while ago from members of the cabinet. I believe the administration's policy toward Vietnam to be based on fatal errors, and that our national interest would be best served if the administration disentangled itself from a course of action that is bound to be ruinous.

Eccles then produced from his pocket a draft resolution writ-ten by a New York business friend, Palmer Weber, advocating an immediate ceasefire and negotiations to end the war. There was stunned silence. Johnson turned to his slow-witted secre-tary of state for a reply. Rusk failed him. There was no reply.

Eccles went on to help organize Business Executives Move for Vietnam Peace; he spoke against the war wherever and whenever he could, calling it a "tragedy of errors." He wrote long letters to the newspapers. He was passionately against the "senseless, bloody debacle," the blind mass killings by bombing raids of the helpless peasants below, the destruction of their homes and fields. He warned his fellow adults that the radicalized long-haired youths in the streets were going to be this country's leaders in due course whether they liked it or not, that the country must change course and make its peace with the chanting marchers.

It seemed all in vain. By 1972 the killing and bombing were still going on. Richard Nixon was now in the place where Washington and Jefferson had once headed a nation of youth and hope. Eccles, then 82, was making his final public speech, at an occasion in his honor in San Francisco: "There . . . is a bloodbath . . . it is our doing. We are guilty . . . no amount of rhetoric about a 'generation of peace' will make it go away. It will not be forgotten—or forgiven. Nor should it be." He continued: ". . . killing and carnage do not bring us honor . . . we are appalled at the savagery we have unleashed on a small Asian country which has in no way offended us."

Eccles lived long enough to see on television the final disastrous American exit by helicopter from the roof of the U.S. embassy in Saigon. "Ruinous," he had warned Lyndon Johnson in vain.

XI

Marriner Eccles died just a few months over a century after the death of Brigham Young. They are both buried in Salt Lake City. Marriner's will provided bequests to foundations, universities, the arts, science. His name will live on, mainly in the West, through those bequests.

So who was Marriner Eccles? He was an example of the very best this country could ever produce. We never got the benefits of his life and abilities that were possible. But that's the way we are. We soldier on in our bumbling way, a democracy, good and bad, wise and foolish. As the saying goes, "Every dog has his day," and since we are a lucky country, once in a while a Marriner Eccles comes along.

For the memory of Eccles one has a warm feeling, knowing what his standards were, and that he lived and died facing them:

> The World has need of willing men,
> Who wear the worker's seal;
> Come, help the good work move along;
> Put your shoulder to the wheel.

The music of a Utah childhood, long ago.

PART VI

THE AMERICAN LEGACY AND ITS FUTURE

It scarcely seems reasonable, two-thirds of the way through the 20th century, to prate about the pioneer virtues. And I don't intend to do that. But we can, I think, gain a certain perspective from our history, a perspective on the universal problem of economic life—the battle against scarcity. Here is where the history of American economic development is critically important to us. To be sure, many things have changed, but the fundamental problem, scarcity, has not, and neither has the formal organization of the American economy —it is still capitalism. Marx might be dazzled by our economy's prodigious output, but that restless inquirer would soon discover that most of the productive resources in the American economy are privately owned, as they were in his day. The modern economy is the child of the past, and the family inheritance is an important determinant of the present and, therefore, the future. The past is thus important; we are its product and need to understand our history to understand ourselves.

Probably the strongest lesson of American economic history is that continuous *change* is a legacy from our past. Americans adopted radical political and social institutions at the beginning, occupied the land and created a system of economic development based upon ceaseless technological change. Thus far our political and social institutions have adapted, with varying degrees of success, to continuous change. Failure to adapt successfully to change produces stagnation or inflation, vast unemployment and wasted production capacity, or a creeping shoddiness in economic life which comes from long periods of exhilarated demand as money income rises at a more rapid rate than physical output.

Americans have mastered a changing technology by all practicable methods—sometimes accepting market decisions, sometimes using our collectivity or "government" by deciding to act through government subsidies, outright government construction of dams, roads, schools and whatever else we vote for if the social benefits seem to justify a refusal to accept the market decisions made by individual firms. American history shows a flexible approach to the economics of change. Eli Whitney was primarily a government contractor; the government intervened in the affairs of Harriman, Morgan and Edison when the public good seemed to call for intervention. On the other hand, vast empires, like Carnegie's and Ford's, were built with a minimum of government influence. We have been plainly pragmatic. As changes came, our population moved about the country and redirected the uses of the nation's resources under the dictates of a changing technology.

Like no other people, Americans have conditioned their society and their plans for the future in terms of economic change. It is a greatly rewarding life in material terms. It is also a life of uncertainty and continuous social and economic upheaval. It is not a simple way to live.

In spite of this, as Sir Denis Brogan emphasized in his *American Politics,* we have also maintained a studied conservatism about certain things. Ours is, then, a land of the "old" in many ways, with a continuous set of social institutions based upon the Federal Constitution, a document written and ascribed to eons ago if measured in terms of technological change. That is a paradox, but it is a tribute to the good sense of Americans to accept change (and once to enforce it by a bloody Civil War) and yet carry forward the best of the old traditions and culture. Sometimes these were superficially transformed, but they were still based upon the old American radicalism, the *dream* of a perfect egalitarian democracy, and the *experience* that, however difficult to maintain, the competitive society, in both public and private affairs, yields the highest returns in the development of economic resources for the use of all the people. Carnegie and Ford, as we saw, were alive to the knowledge that they were creating more than they were destroying. The competitive economy imposed a life of vigor, but also the chance for great abundance.

There are, of course, those who would stop the clock now —or turn it back—those who have deluded themselves into believing that the past was better than the present, and that, moreover, we could actually go back to it. A neat trick in a nation steadily approaching a population of 200 million. There are also those who hate capitalism, the system of private incentives and rewards, who would throw most of the competitive society over for the dream of some more perfect system, planned, presumably, by perfect planners. Either could be attempted, and peacefully, if that were the decision of the voters. But neither extreme could produce the promised state of social and economic euphoria (the one based upon some kind of income aristocracy, the other upon values "higher" than mere self-interest), without stopping or controlling the far-reaching technological and social change that has been our way of life.

It is argued by some that the traditional American system of change is meaningless, that the continuing drive to raise the standard of living is an endless will-o'-the-wisp. Material-ism, so the argument goes, is pointless. The argument is a caricature. Great material wealth provides human beings with the means to achieve any amount of "psychic income" they wish to have. A millionaire is not bound to try to eat all of his income or spend it on luxuries. A Pierpont Morgan could spend a fortune on miniatures, but, and this is all the critics ask, he could study and be mentally enriched by his acquisi-tions. Being wealthy, he could even share his culture with the rest of his country.

But the whole argument is pointless anyway. I fail to see how American notions of "general welfare" are any less meaningful than either the "stationary state" envisaged by the extreme right or the completely "planned" economy of the far left. I see no particular value in either stagnation or planning as such. Stagnation or planning for what? In any case, unless the American public should voluntarily relinquish its taste for change, the "stability" of either the extreme right or the ex-treme left is probably incompatible with political democracy in America. Both social and economic stagnation and planning require more coercion than Americans are likely to tolerate from any set of political leaders. We are too disorderly.

There remains the problem of utilization of our human resources effectively in the future. The reader of this book must be aware that in our past Americans have utilized a vast range of talents, possessed by men from all parts of society. It was an "open" society, not perfectly so of course, but a vastly more open society than most others have had. The indi-viduals who have been treated in our scheme of thought in this book could be replaced by others, millions of others, in our history, and indeed by millions living and at work today in all sorts of fields, whether labor, agriculture, education or serv-ices.

To gain the maximum benefits of American capitalism both

the competitive market and the mobile, open society are required. The opposite, the adoption of a rigid social and economic structure, is the road to stagnation. The notion that there is a "correct" approach to all kinds of human activity is sheer folly in a world of continuous technical change, and any society that chooses its leadership, in science, the arts, government or business, on the basis of formalized credentials alone, rather than by performance, is asking for the ultimate rule of organized stupidity.

Writing about the men in this book I have often been amused by the fantasy playing in my mind of these people applying for admission to one of the better schools of business administration (Brigham Young at Harvard?). The fantasy becomes less amusing when one considers the extent to which we have already taken the route toward becoming a nation of credentials inspectors. Some large businesses, governmental and educational institutions within my ken resemble nothing so much as the pre-1914 Austro-Hungarian civil service.

To structure the economy mainly on the basis of credentials and "proper" attitudes toward problems is to choose the worst of all worlds. Talent is largely distributed at random. This talent is easily overlooked. To provide the best educational opportunities (best because, even if made universally accessible, the schools and universities will doubtless never all be equal in quality) on the basis of parental income, as we still do in the majority of cases, is systematically to throw away the majority of our best talents. The distribution of income, where it is not due to inheritance from the distant past, is based upon the talents of the parents, not the children. The systematic discrimination on the basis of race, color, sex and religion is too monstrously wasteful to bear comment and is rightfully condemned officially, even if practiced privately.

The paths to economic progress could easily be choked with a multitude of way stations manned by credentials examiners. Credentials are useful as guide posts, but not at the expense of informed judgment. The national tradition of idealism modified by radical pragmatism is a powerful legacy and should remain a source of strength. "What works the best" and "who works the best" were the questions the old-time builders of the American economy asked. Asking those questions, America avoided the mindless "Manchuism" based upon credentials that blocked economic progress for so long among so much of humanity.

Innovation in all parts of the national life, in government, in business, in the arts and education is required for efficiency so long as Americans prefer relentless technological change as a way of life. Problems change and require fresh analysis. The best people ought to think about such problems no matter what their formal credentials may look like. Carnegie said Americans used to believe, "The tools to those who can use them!" What a completely revolutionary slogan that is. But how incompatible such thinking is with any hierarchical social structure in a world of technological change!

When social attitudes get mixed up with economic decisions, a systematic bias toward the waste of human resources is introduced. If there is some general consensus in favor of the kind of discrimination in force, it can be maintained almost indefinitely and human resources thrown away generation after generation. In this regard the loss to the country of talented Negroes and other minority members has obviously been great, but happily the barriers of racial bigotry in America seem at last to be crumbling.

So long as competition is maintained, those who do so discriminate are punished quickly and impartially by the market mechanism. But where the "credentials society" becomes dominant, competition is destroyed and economic progress increasingly comes to depend upon the talents of specialized income groups and occupational groups and their children. The labor force could be reduced to the level of noncompeting groups. That is a thing to be abhorred and avoided.

The point of this little harangue is very simple: the lessons of our history are useful stimulants to thought but are not directly applicable to all of our problems. Our world is not like the one grandfather lived in. There is, it seems to me, one cloud on the horizon especially worth watching carefully in this regard. That cloud is the power of higher education. A hundred years hence the Penns, Edisons, Fords and Morgans are likely to be men of extensive formal education. One of America's great gifts was the absence of a landed aristocracy —a line of economic bluebloods with economic power passed through the generations solely on the basis of the accident of birth. It would be a pity if the nation's progress were to be crippled by the rise of a hereditary intellectual aristocracy. But that is a possibility now, for the economic power of our scientifically determined future, the world of computery, automated manufacturing, space communications and the like, clearly will be largely controlled by formally trained intellects,

564 / THE AMERICAN LEGACY

just as land in the age of agricultural feudalism was the basis of economic power in the medieval age.

Unless the national pool of talent has access to the required education, the future will largely be in the hands of those whose parents are already on the right track. It is interesting to me that those concerned with "hard core" unemployment have realized this. To be in the "labor force" at all, ten years hence, may well require high school graduation, and in the future the route to effective leadership for the virtuoso is likely to be the university much more than was the case in the past.

Education, however, is only one problem. The United States has vast and complex economic issues to face; some, like those related to the business cycle and economic growth, inflation and depression, are old stories, even if they have never been dealt with very effectively by government. Other problems, like automation, the accelerated displacement of skills by technological change, the festering slums engulfing the cities, are relatively new in the national focus. It is well enough to discuss these as "national problems" and to plan to deal with them through the instruments of monetary and fiscal control available to the Federal government, perhaps to the extent of more "planning" than Americans have experienced in their past.

Yet none of these problems will be solved by any governmental policies if the population itself is not able to absorb the necessary doses of economic and social change. This means that either we preserve and improve the mobility and adaptability of our working at *all* levels, or we must somehow "freeze" the technology. Otherwise there is the distinct danger that the economy will be unable to cope with the problems which continuous technological change produces. It seems to me that the future can, in fact, learn from the past; that leadership can be found, the kind of leadership that arises readily enough in an open society, but a kind which is desperately short in supply in highly structured societies where the genius of the people lies hidden behind an iron mask of precedence and privilege. Failure, in the latter circumstances, tends to perpetuate itself.

Can the same degree of social and economic mobility be maintained in the future as was achieved in the past by the old open society? One hopes so. Technological progress can only be as effective as the people allow. However trite that may sound, it is a mystery that has long escaped millions, their governments and their economic advisers. Tedious as it is to be reminded of it again, "government" is no panacea for economic ailments. Capable leadership and an adaptable population come as close as anything is ever likely to come to being a cure-all for economic troubles. Capable leadership and adaptable populations are typical products of open societies in the long run; both are rare phenomena in societies of caste and procedure.

This brings us to the fifth and final "stage" in our scheme of organization: the role of bureaucracy, and the very difficult problem of maintaining maximum efficiency within a nearly stable organization. Although this is not necessarily a problem on a *national scale*, it certainly is, and is bound to be, in many parts of the economy, at any time. After a period of growth in any economic process is completed, there will be decline, but there may also be a period of near stability. The "committee man," or what have you, comes into his own in the great industrial, educational and governmental bureaucracies. Now bureaucracies can be useful things. They do a job that is necessary sometimes—the management of successful economic operations that may require no great changes, or changers, in the daily routine.

The competitive market will tell any business bureaucracy quite bluntly when the time for major change has come. But in education and government things are not so simple. As W. W. Rostow phrased it in his thought-provoking book, *The United States in the World Arena:* "How shall change be instituted to meet new circumstances in large-scale units which, because they are committed to comparatively static standards of efficiency, limit the capacity of those relatively few creative men capable of innovation and leadership?" In general, I would argue that the answer to that question must depend quite simply upon the quality of the people who govern such large units. In general, except for good fortune, it is difficult to conceive of first-rate solutions coming systematically from second-rate people.

The problem of keeping bureaucracy as intelligent as possible is important to Americans, not only because the governmental and educational systems tend to have fairly rigid power hierarchies, but because so does "big business," and a great deal of American business is very big indeed. In a recent year, of more than 2,800,000 firms employing nearly 40,000,000 people covered by Social Security, 14,000,000 of the people, or 35 percent, were employed by a mere 3,100 firms, a minute part (.0011+ percent) of the total number. Wherever economies of large-scale output have been possible, we have developed (within the confines of the anti-trust laws, and their current interpretations by the Supreme Court) large firms. Many of the great innovators and organizers specialized in this particular kind of economic development, the achievement of the economies of large size. The 20 largest firms by the late 1950's made the following proportions of total shipments in their respective industries: petroleum refining (153 firms in all), 20 firms produced 84 percent; motor vehicles and parts (991 firms in all), 87 percent; steel works and mills (102 firms in all), 85 percent; aircraft (46 firms in all), 96 percent. In smaller industries there is also a great deal of "concentration"; for example, in 1954 the 4 largest producers of tires and inner tubes produced 79 percent of total output in an industry with 27 producers. Of 202 manufacturers of organic chemicals, the 4 largest companies produced 59 percent of total output.

Large companies tend to have enormous managements. We therefore have a great deal of bureaucracy in American industry, and it obviously is of prime importance that the bureaucracies be competent at their jobs. The inexorability of "Parkinson's law" of bureaucratic growth (roughly put: bureaucracy tends to increase in size at a constant rate regardless of the work done) in our economy can be counteracted to some extent by thought, but only by thinking people.

The need for the maintenance and promotion of an open society in America is nowhere made more evident than in the historical record of the country's growth. Technological change in the economy destroys in order to build. New firms grow to a large extent at the expense of older ones in a changing technology. As we saw, Carnegie built partly on the economically dead bodies of Pittsburgh's "Fathers in Israel." Simon Kuznets, in his great paper (published first in 1929) "The Retardation of Industrial Growth," pointed out the unevenness of such growth, arguing that available data for industrial countries showed a common pattern:

> . . . we can observe a succession of different branches of activity in the vanguard of the country's economic development, and within each industry we can notice a conspicuous slackening in the rate of increase.

Arthur F. Burns continued the argument a few years later, pointing out in 1934 that, in the 104 selected sectors of the American economy which he studied, industrial retardation was very marked and, further, that only growth itself seemed to assure life in industry. Once a firm or an industry ceased to grow it began to die, sometimes moving quickly toward oblivion. The growth of the economy over time comes primarily from new processes, new firms, new industries, and that growth "feeds" to a large extent upon older processes, firms and industries. Thus we saw Carnegie and Ford devour their rivals, Harriman and Morgan absorb firms too small or conservative successfully to resist merger.

Burns was so bold in 1934 as to argue from his work that, even at the depths of the Great Depression, there was no tendency for the slowing down of growth and actual decline in individual industries due to this aging process, to retard the long-run growth of the overall national economy. He argued that the young more than replaced the old. That took a lot of nerve to say in 1934, and it turned out that Burns was right.

Such a world of change is one in which there seems to be no comfortable resting place. Growth is not inevitable but it must be actively created. Carnegie's history alone is sufficient proof of the economic payoff that comes from thinking, and his array of brilliant young men who planned and managed Carnegie Steel is evidence enough of the wisdom of searching for talent wherever it is and using it when you find it. When Ford refused to do that, his great company fell into stagnation.

What are the main motives required to keep American society pushing on efficiently? Our subjects in this book were, except for Penn, essentially men of the 19th century. A question arises concerning their motivation, whether there is any reason to suppose that the economic achievements of our forefathers, as individuals, were in any important respect based upon what are commonly thought of as the Victorian mores. The question arises because of the fairly thoroughgoing destruction of the 19th century's ethical value system (or the one we believe existed then) which has taken place since the First World War. There are four central areas in which this destruction occurred.

First there was the destruction of effective social prestige based solely upon independent wealth. Egalitarian democracy, following the 1929–33 debacle, eliminated the pretension that people of wealth were to have any special place in the country's future except as education makes them useful in the world of economics or the arts, or wealth makes a political career possible where it might be barred to the more humble. This loss of prestige attaching to "Society" was of course accelerated by the vast prestige acquired by the newly rich of Hollywood, the communications industry and the world of popular entertainments, people who flamboyantly pursued personal lives which were repugnant to the traditional codes of morality and destructive of either the continuation of the family as we have known it or even of society as a whole. With the aid of a partly clothed pornography, our gutter press and certain magazines, the lives of these moral troglodytes became NEWS. Such people were wealthy, and appalling.

Second, the income and inheritance taxes made the tax-free foundation, presided over by depersonalized boards of managers, trustees, expert consultants and the like, the primary way in which great wealth could be safely perpetuated. Hence, just as the corporation tended to separate ownership from control, so the foundations largely separated benefactions from the intentions of the benefactors. Indeed many of the processes of "project formation" among the great foundations make the benefactee responsible for the nature and the amount of the benefaction. This is of no small importance in economic life as the foundations preside over hundreds of millions of expenditures and utilize our best scholarly and scientific talent. I do not mean to say that is bad. But if the post-mortem uses of large personal fortunes were in any way motivations for accumulating those fortunes, the income and inheritance taxes must have had some dampening effect upon the incentive to accumulate great wealth and to build giant firms, efficient in a *competitive* economy, which made such accumulation possible.

Third, the catastrophic wars of the 20th century, together with the rise of the "peace of mutual terror" of the Cold War, made the building of personal "stewardship" (remember, we are discussing the Victorians)—the attempt to influence public affairs by the moral greatness of one's own actions—mainly futile if not, indeed, a sour joke. No single life, no matter how great and blameless, seems to be sufficient to affect the terrible logic of the nuclear age. The moral stature of nations no longer seems to be the business of individual citizens.

Fourth, the terrors of the 20th century among the Western nations—millions upon millions slaughtered on the battlefields, together with such atrocities as mass bombings of civilian populations, the distinctly German "contribution" perfected at Auschwitz, the colonial revolt after 1945 and the abandoned brutality of the unsuccessful attempts to repress it—withholding political freedom from masses of humanity—all these things have made the very idea of old Pierpont Morgan's "Christendom" a farce. The notion that Christian civilization per se had a special mission in the world was evidently a powerful force in the affairs of Europeans and Americans before 1914 (demonstrated nowhere more convincingly regarding the British than in Lytton Strachey's *Eminent Victorians*). Now that is gone. Gone from us, and no one would take us seriously if we believed it anyway. Indeed, "moral leadership" in the world community had pretty plainly gravitated (until the Indian invasion of Goa and the other Portuguese dependencies) to the "uncommitted" nations. Commitment to anything beyond raw self-interest becomes ipso facto proof of moral debasement among a large segment of humanity, or so it appeared at the United Nations.

Such considerations as these breed a grim pessimism. But perhaps they are not important; perhaps the 19th-century Americans didn't really believe any of that anyway, or perhaps we still believe it all in spite of modern history. However, even if the demolition of the old value system is important, we are still stuck with ourselves and must face the consequences of past actions with more actions. We cannot escape the effects of our history. One sees no sure and clear way out of this predicament, but since the tragedies and errors of the past cannot be undone, Americans must continue to build as best they know how. It seems obvious to me, in the light of the evidence explored in this book, that the maintenance and improvement of our open society is the best hope for the future, as it was in the past. Since Americans will not accept the dictates of foreign lawgivers, we will need to do the job ourselves. How? As always, by democratic procedures, relying upon the old American Adam, the "common man." Even if a new Messiah appeared with the answers to *all* of our problems, under our Constitution, Americans would still need to be convinced or at least reduced to a silent neutrality.

The United States has been profoundly blessed in its economic history. The population included the Penns, Youngs, Whitneys, Edisons, Fords, Carnegies, Harrimans, Morgans and the millions of men and women represented by those names in our scheme of thought. Their achievements were enormous. But, paradoxically, the job continues, and the requirements for future achievement are just as great as ever, because the country is constantly changing. Hence at the end of Brigham Young's great life, a new generation had to undertake a different kind of pioneering all over again. A hundred years after the old frontier had nearly vanished, the "New Frontier" focused upon problems no less arduous and dangerous than those faced by the pioneers. Unless someone can "stop the world," the new frontier will be ever recurring—technological, social and economic changes assure us of that much.

We have our idealists, inventors, innovators and organizers all around us, and in a vast mechanism of economic and social change there is work for all kinds to do, if only the men and women and the jobs can find each other. The competitive, open society, judging from our unique economic prowess compared to the works of closed and structured societies, is the most efficient way for Americans to bring together the supply of talent and the demand for it. In the American government, people and institutions resides the power to accomplish virtually anything in the realm of economic achievement. Moreover, we can more readily build an acceptably ethical society upon rising material wealth than upon economic stagnation, simply because more resources can be made available for moral and cultural development. It may not be done, but it could be; the opportunity is there. If one believes that the United States has a responsibility to less fortunate peoples, surely that responsibility can be best met by building the American economy soundly. If Americans fail to realize their national potential, they will have only themselves to blame. A great legacy exists to build upon.

Bibliographical Notes

GENERAL

This bibliographical essay is meant to provide the interested reader with a skeletal bibliography on the wide range of subjects treated in this book. I have included only secondary sources. But first it is only fair that I provide some background reading references. I would recommend two works. Every reader should have a working knowledge of general American history before undertaking the more specialized study of American economic history. There exists a simply enormous literature in American history; my own favorite general treatment is at the college textbook level: Samuel Eliot Morison and Henry Steele Commager, *The Growth of the American Republic,* New York, Oxford Press, various editions, two volumes.

American economic history is a specialized and fragmented discipline and what one needs to begin its study is a descriptive synthesis. To my mind the best remains Chester W. Wright, *Economic History of the United States,* New York, McGraw-Hill, 1941.

Beyond these two works lies an enormous and sometimes excellent literature, general and specific, descriptive and analytical, at the textbook level, the popular monograph level and the technical monograph level, articles in learned journals and special publications—all of which I shall forbear to discuss here except as references to such works occur directly in the present volume. It would be folly even to attempt to guide the reader into the whole range of American historical writings in a bibliography to a book such as this one; it would also be inappropriate and presumptuous.

For economic data generally the reader is directed to *Historical Statistics of the United States,* Washington: Department of Commerce, 1960.

Short accounts of the lives and careers of many individuals mentioned in this book will be found in Thomas Cochran and William Miller, *The Age of Enterprise,* New York, Macmillan, 1951. In this well known monograph an attempt is made to place the great industrial transformation of the United States in a broad context of social and institutional change.

It might be useful to deal here briefly with the general literature on the classic American tycoonery. The American business tycoons of the late 19th century have been the subjects of many studies and the objects of crude as well as brilliant vituperation. These men have also been subjected to some almost unbelievably saccharine biographical writing. There is a classic trilogy of debunking: Gustavus Myers, *History of the Great American Fortunes*, Chicago: Charles Kerr, 1910; John Moody's small but entertaining *The Masters of Capital*, Yale University Press, 1919; and Matthew Josephson, *The Robber Barons*, New York: Harcourt, Brace & Co., 1934. Of these Josephson is, in my opinion, the most important. He utilized, and followed closely in many respects, the main materials on the tycoons that were available up to the 1930's. His book had a great impact upon the thinking of American historians. Its major defect, in my opinion, is a simple one: he viewed capitalism and capitalists as being, ipso facto, immoral. That is perfectly all right as one man's opinion except that, as an intellectual framework for the study of a capitalist economy, *The Robber Barons* viewpoint leads to a cataclysm when, in fact, depressions and all, and with all its faults, American capitalism led to vast economic growth, social reform, the maintenance of political liberty, and helped to create a fluid and adaptable society. Americans have scarcely been impoverished by their system of economic change based upon self-interest—however hard that fact is to swallow for those who hanker after more perfect economic systems.

Recent writing on the subject is vast and I will forbear to discuss it. But some additional influential views on the great age of the tycoonery are worth listing as a matter of historical interest. The main books are: C. W. Baron, *They Told Baron*, New York, Harper & Bros., 1930; C. A. and M. R. Beard, *The Rise of American Civilization*, New York: Macmillan, 1930; Henry Clews, *Fifty Years in Wall Street*, New York, Irving, 1908; L. M. Hacker, *The Triumph of American Capitalism*, New York, Columbia Press, 1947; L. M. Hacker and B. B. Kendrick, *The U. S. Since 1865*, New York: F. S. Crofts, 1932; T. W. Lawson, *Frenzied Finance*, New York, Ridgway-Thayer, 1905; A. D. Noyes, *Forty Years of American Finance*, New York, Putnam's Sons, 1925; R. E. Riegel, *The Story of the Western Railroads*, New York: Macmillan, 1926; W. Z. Ripley, *Trusts, Pools and Corporations*, New York, Ginn & Co., 1916; Ida M. Tarbell, *History of The Standard Oil Company*, New York, Macmillan, 1925. An outstanding recent treatment of research concerning American business leadership, together with a bibliography is: Arthur F. Cole, *Business Enterprise in Its Social Setting*, Harvard, 1959. Finally, J. H. Chamberlain's *Enterprising Americans*, New York, Harper & Row, 1961, is a useful textbook level treatment of some of the matters treated above.

CHAPTER 2, WILLIAM PENN

George Bancroft, *History of the United States of America*, Vol. II, Boston, Little, Brown & Co., 1879 ed. Chapters XX, XXIV on Quakers and Pennsylvania; Mabel Richmond Brailsford, *The Mak-*

ing of William Penn, New York, 1930; William Charles Braith-
waite, *Beginnings of Quakerism*, London, 1912; Augustus C. Buell,
William Penn, New York: Appleton Co., 1904. Anti-Quaker
biography. A serious effort; definitely calls Penn's mother English;
Edward Channing, "William Penn," *Annual Report*, American
Historical Association, 1906, Vol. I. This is a general "apprecia-
tion" of Penn's role in American history; G. N. Clark, *The Later
Stuarts*, Oxford, 1934. Definitive general treatment; H. S. Commager, *Documents of American History*, early charters, the *Con-
cession* of 1681, and "The Earliest Protest Against Slavery,"
Germantown Mennonites, Feb. 18, 1698, and Penn's Plan of Union
1697, finally the *Charter of Privileges* of 1701; Godfrey Davies,
The Early Stuarts, Oxford, 1937. Definitive general treatment;
W. I. T. Dixon, *A History of William Penn Founder of Pennsylvania*, New York, 1902; Maurice Dobb, *Studies in the Development of Capitalism*, New York: International Publishers, 1947.
This work is especially suggestive concerning the economic mean-
ing of the Puritan revolution. The bias is a strict economic deter-
minism; C. R. Fay, *The Corn Laws and Social England*, Cambridge
Press, 1932, Chapters I and II discuss origins and early operation
of the "corn bounty"; Sir Charles Firth (Regius Prof., Oxon.),
Oliver Cromwell and the Rule of the Puritans in England, New
York: Oxford Press, World's Classics ed., 1953; *Journal of George
Fox*, George Fox, revised, Cambridge, 1952; J. L. Hammond and
Barbara Hammond, *The Rise of Modern Industry*, London, 1951
(eighth ed.), Chapters I and II discuss conditions in late 17th,
early 18th century and Europe's new position in Atlantic and shift
from Mediterranean; Marcus Lee Hansen, *The Atlantic Migration
1607–1860*, Harvard, 1940; Christopher Hill, *Puritanism and
Revolution*, London, Martin Secker & Warburg, Ltd., 1958. A bril-
liant and controversial set of essays on the forces underlying the
Civil War; George Hodges, *William Penn*, Boston, Houghton
Mifflin, 1901. A good little study. Definitely identifies Penn's
mother as Dutch, Peare claims she was English; Rupert S. Holland,
William Penn, Macmillan, 1925. A popular biography that follows
Buell rather too closely; J. K. Horsefield, *British Monetary Experi-
ments 1650–1710*, Harvard, 1960. Contains discussion at points on
Stuart financial troubles; William I. Hull, *William Penn, a Topical
Biography*, New York, 1937; E. Lipson, *A Planned Economy or
Free Enterprise, The Lessons of History*, London, 1946. See Chapter II on Tudor economic legislation and its results; E. Lipson,
The Economic History of England, Vol. II, Age of Mercantilism,
London, Black, sixth ed., 1956, five general, especially Chapter II
on the Royal Trading; Wallace Notestein, *The English People on
the Eve of Colonization 1603–1630*, New York, Harper, 1954. A
general survey of population structure and institutions from which
the original settlements in the New World were launched. Catherine Owens Peare, *William Penn*, Philadelphia, Lippincott, 1957.
An exhaustive account, with a complete bibliography; A. M.

Schlesinger (Sr.), *The Colonial Merchants and the American Revolution*, N. Y., 1939. The first chapter touches the tail end of 17th-century affairs; Francis Newton Thorpe, ed., *The Federal and State Constitutions, Colonial Charters and other Organic Laws*, Washington, D. C., Government Printing Office, 1909; G. M. Trevelyan, *History of England*, Vol. II, Tudors and William and Mary Stuart, third ed., 1952. Doubleday Anchor ed. This old work is still a standard treatment; A. P. Usher, *The Industrial History of England*, Boston, 1920 (Houghton Mifflin). Selected chapters cover the whole ground both in general and in detail.

CHAPTER 3, BRIGHAM YOUNG

A Mormon Chronicle, The Diaries of John D. Lee 1848–1876, edited by Robert Glass Cleland and Juanita Brooks, Huntington Library, San Marino, Calif., 1955. A rare and controversial witness to trials of early Mormons; Leonard J. Arrington, *Great Basin Kingdom*, Harvard, 1958. The definitive economic history of the Mormons from 1830 to 1900; Harry M. Beardsley, *Joseph Smith and His Mormon Empire*, Boston, Houghton Mifflin, 1931. An unfriendly account; Fawn M. Brodie, *No Man Knows My History*, New York, Knopf, 1946. Critical and thorough biography of Joseph Smith. Probably best non-Mormon account of Smith's life; Bernard De Voto *The Year of Decision 1846*, Boston, Little, Brown, 1943. A beautifully written and critically friendly account of the trek within the framework of the larger national issues of the period and of 1846–48. With exceptions De Voto states, p. 512, "There are practically no trustworthy authorities about the Mormons"; *Doctrine and Covenants, Pearl of Great Price*. In one volume, L. D. S. Church, Salt Lake City, 1952. Revelations of Joseph Smith, one to Brigham Young and the polygamy "Manifesto of 1890." Also some further writings of Smith; Susan Young Gates and Leah D. Widtsoe, *The Life Story of Brigham Young*, New York, Macmillan, 1930. One of his daughters. Contains interesting material but is suffocating cant for most part; Dale L. Morgan, *The Great Salt Lake*, Bobbs-Merrill, New York and Indianapolis, 1942. Most extensive monograph on the Great Salt Lake and its history beginning with the physical geology of the area, the first explorers, the mountain men on down through Mormon history to the immediate post-World War II period. The most *extensive* book on the valley and its history, both authoritative and written with great imagination. The treatment of the Mormons is objective and not without both sympathy and humor; *The Book of Mormon*, Salt Lake City, 1952. "The Golden Bible." This is the scripture claimed by Joseph Smith to have been copied from the Golden Plates under divine guidance; William Mulder and A. Russell Mortensen, *Among the Mormons*, Knopf, 1958. Selections from contemporary accounts, eyewitnesses, etc.; B. H. Roberts, *A Comprehensive History of the Church of Jesus Christ of Latter-day Saints,* Salt Lake City, 1930, an official history; Clarissa Young Spencer and Mabel Harmer, *One Who Was Valiant,* Caxton Printers, Caldwell, Idaho, 1940. Another daughter. Not so serious a study as Gates and Widtsoe but some charming detail; Wallace Stegner, *Mormon Country,* 1942, Duell, Sloan & Pearce, New York. Immensely readable essays covering broad areas of Mormon life and history. The author's materials are extensive, accurate. A well informed and informative book on the Mormons, their history, myths and the land they settled; T. B. H. Stenhouse, *The Rocky Mountain Saints,* D. Appleton & Co., New York, 1873. A violent denunciation by a former Mormon official, yet contains interesting information. West rates it as one of the most damaging books ever written about the Mormons; Mark Twain, *Roughing It.* Harpers, first edition in 1874. Chapters XII–XX, on Mormons and life in Great Basin after the Civil War. Appendix to Vol. II on Mormons; M. R. Werner, *Brigham Young,* Harcourt, Brace, 1925. Critical and scholarly biography. Best non-Mormon account of Young's life; Ray B. West, Jr., *Kingdom of the Saints,* Viking Press, 1957. A serious pro-Mormon study of Brigham Young and Mormons. A reasonable treatment; Kimball Young, *Isn't One Wife Enough?,* New York, Henry Holt, 1954. A grandson of Brigham Young and well known American sociologist. Friendly, scholarly, critical. Traces polygamy and its many domestic problems from origins to modern times. An interesting store of information about history, organization and operations of Latter-day Saints.

Chapter 4, Eli Whitney

Alfred H. Conrad and John R. Meyer, "The Economics of Slavery in the Ante Bellum South," *The Journal of Political Economy,* April, 1958. A celebrated and disputed piece of historical and statistical detective work which, mixed with economic analysis, has partly destroyed the view that slavery would necessarily have withered away of its own accord and that the Civil War would not have been needed to demolish that system in the United States; M. V. Clark, *History of Manufactures,* Washington, D. C., Carnegie Institution, 1929, Vol. I contains materials on Whitney's contributions; E. J. Donnell, *Chronological and Statistical History of Cotton,* New York, 1872. Covers rise of the industry in America; Thomas Ellison, *The Cotton Trade of Great Britain,* 1886. Statistical materials relating to early British cotton industry; Lewis C. Gray, *History of Agriculture in the Southern United States to 1860,* Washington, the Carnegie Institution, 1932, 2 vols. This is the classic study of Southern agriculture before the Civil War. Clearheaded, scholarly, objective, a landmark in scholarship on the South; Constance Green, *Eli Whitney and the Birth of American Technology,* Boston, Little, Brown, 1956. Based upon Yale papers. Slightly sharper on some of the details of Whitney's contributions in machinery than Mirsky and Nevins. Curiously, no mention in this serious work is made of Mirsky and Nevins; H. J. Habakkuk, *British and American Technology in the Nineteenth Century*, Cambridge University Press, 1962. The latest examination, and an excellent one, of the divergence of technique in industry between the two Anglo-Saxon industrial nations. He pursues the questions: Why was U. S. A. so much more efficient by the end of the century than Britain? and, Was Britain penalized for her early lead?; Frederick L. Lewton, "Historical Notes on the Cotton Gin," Smithsonian Institution, *Annual Report*, Washington, 1937; Jeanette Mirsky and Allan Nevins, *The World of Eli Whitney*, New York, Macmillan, 1952. A thorough job. An attempt to relate Whitney's life to the developing nation. Research utilized Whitney papers at Yale and other previously unused materials. Contains essay on the state of science, practical and theoretical, in Whitney's time; Joseph Wickham Roe, *English and American Tool Builders*, Yale University Press, 1916, New Haven. Contains excellent material on Whitney; The following have sections on Eli Whitney: Dwight Goddard, *Eminent Engineers*, 1906, New York, Derry-Collard; Philip G. Hubert, *Inventors*, Scribner's Sons, New York, 1896; Grace Humphry, *Stories of Our Great Inventions*, 1927, Bobbs Merrill, Indianapolis; Classics on the Industrial Revolution are: Paul Mantoux, *The Industrial Revolution in the Eighteenth Century*, London, Jonathan Cape, 1928; T. S. Ashton, *The Industrial Revolution*, London, Oxford University Press, 1948; Arnold Toynbee, *Lectures on the Industrial Revolution*, London, Longmans, Green, 1908.

CHAPTER 5, THOMAS EDISON

George S. Bryan, *Edison, the Man and His Work*, New York, Knopf, 1926. A thoughtful, full-scale biography, well written, containing interesting contemporary information; James G. Crowther, *Famous American Men of Science*, New York, Norton, 1937, also, *Six Great Inventors*, London, Hamish Hamilton, 1954, each contains a biographical essay of Edison with discussion of his main work; F. L. Dyer, T. C. Martin, and W. H. Meadowcroft, *Edison, His Life and Inventions*, New York, 1929. This is considered to be the "official" biography; Henry Ford, in collaboration with Samuel Crowther, *My Friend Mr. Edison*, London, Ernest Benn, 1930. A collection of Ford's reminiscences concerning Edison, together with a description of the Edison Institute at Dearborn; Gordon Hendricks, *The Edison Motion Picture Myth*, Berkeley, University of California Press, 1961. An effort to correctly apportion credit for the motion picture inventions; Francis Jehl, *Menlo Park Reminiscences*, Dearborn, Edison Institute, 1936–41. Jehl was one of the long-time Edison associates and his volumes provide a rich source of materials about Edison's career; Francis A. Jones, *Thomas Alva Edison, An Intimate Portrait*, London, Hodder & Stoughton, 1924. A worshipful study by an English journalist, good on descriptions of Edison as an old man, his personality and habits; Matthew Josephson, *Edison, A Biography,* New York, McGraw-Hill, 1959. The latest and in many ways the most interesting biography. Written in great detail, based upon extensive research. A thoughtful study by a writer well known for his critical expertise on the major economic and political issues of Edison's lifetime; D. T. Marshall, *Recollections of Edison,* Boston, Christopher, 1931; Forrest McDonald, *Insull,* Chicago, University of Chicago Press, 1962. Parts relating to Insull's early career contain useful information on Edison and formation of General Electric; F. T. Miller, *Thomas A. Edison,* London, Stanley Paul, 1932. This curious and interesting biography is extensive and yet written on a level appropriate for teen-age readers; Harold C. Passer, *The Electrical Manufacturers, 1875–1900,* Cambridge, Harvard Press, 1953. A fine economic study of the early days of the industry, very good on Edison and his competitors. This is a major effort to write industrial history in the Schumpeterian mould; National Electric Light Association, "In Memoriam, Thomas A. Edison," *N.E.L.A. Bulletin,* November, 1931, Sec. 2; David Sarnoff, *Edison, 1847–1931,* New York, Newcomen Society, 1948. There are a number of older biographies; among the better ones are: W. K. L. and Antonia Dickson, *The Life and Inventions of Thomas Alva Edison,* London, Chatto & Windus, 1894; F. L. Dyer, *Edison, His Life and Inventions,* New York, Harper & Bros., 1910; F. W. Rolt-Wheeler, *Thomas A. Edison,* New York, Macmillan, 1915. There is an extensive literature at the juvenile level, including a number of biographies. There are also serious studies in the scholarly journals, and even a curious German study of the Edison high-school tests, A. Horschitz and Paul Oestreich, *Edison and His Competition,* with an introduction by J. A. Fleming, London, Foyle, 1932, which tars Edison as a crypto-fascist. J. A. Fleming's *Fifty Years of Electricity,* London, 1924, contains a careful, lucid account of the origins of the incandescent as well as the arc lights with copious drawings and diagrams.

CHAPTER 6, ANDREW CARNEGIE

David Brody, *Steelworkers in America,* Harvard Press, 1960. A remarkable opening chapter on "The Psychology and Method of Steelmaking" is by itself justification for this sound, original, scholarly and objective piece of work. The book is a history of unionism and labor in steel down to the end of the 1920's. Three chapters on "The Skilled Workers," "The Immigrants" and "The Mill Towns" are also very fine; D. L. Burn, *The Economic History of Steelmaking 1867–1939,* Cambridge University Press, 1961. The general study most useful in detailed comparison between American, British and European practices in growth of steel; Andrew Carnegie, *Autobiography,* Boston, Houghton Mifflin, 1924.

Of all Carnegie's books and articles this one is the most valuable. It was largely dictated to a secretary and was published only after Carnegie's death. It is a remarkable "apologia and explanation" kind of book, entirely frank and personal. In this book the reader can quickly acquire experience in the views of Victorian America; *Andrew Carnegie Century,* New York, 1935, Carnegie Corporation of New York, contains memorials and addresses by men who knew him; V. S. Clark, *History of Manufacturers,* 1929, McGraw-Hill, for the Carnegie Institution. A classic in American industrial history. Vol. II contains relevant information on American steel industry during Carnegie's lifetime; Burton J. Hendrick, *The Life of Andrew Carnegie,* New York, Doubleday, 1932. The definitive study. Objective and thorough. Good on both personal and business affairs; *A Manual of the Public Benefactions of Andrew Carnegie,* Washington, 1919, by the Carnegie Endowment for International Peace, contains a summary up to the time of Carnegie's death, with relevant letters from Carnegie to trustees, charters, and so forth in addition to a quantitative summary of the expenditures.

Chapter 7, Henry Ford

For more complete bibliographies on Ford, see Burlingame, Nevins and Hill, and Sward. H. H. Bennett, *We Never Called Him Henry,* New York, Fawcett, 1951. These are Bennett's apologies for his stewardship as Ford's policeman. Bennett's account gives Ford's vindictiveness a fuller illumination in many respects than does Sward's full-scale assault (below); Roger Burlingame, *Henry Ford,* New York, Knopf, 1957. A readable impressionistic study, balanced, objective and short; Among the works written by Ford with the help of Samuel Crowther, *My Life and Work,* New York, Doubleday, Page, 1922, is the most useful statement of Ford's views on industry, economics and life in general. The factual material in it, however, is untrustworthy. It was evidently thrown together to some extent by Crowther on the basis of conversations with Ford, so that when the master said he had an automobile running in 1893 that is how it was printed; Garet Garrett, *The Wild Wheel,* New York, Pantheon Books, 1952. A delightfully readable account of Ford's life by one who knew him; Allan Nevins and F. E. Hill, Vol. I, *Ford: The Times, The Man, The Company,* New York, Scribner's, 1954; Vol. II, *Ford: Expansion and Challenge 1915–1933,* Scribner's, 1957; Vol. III, *Ford: Decline and Rebirth, 1933–1962,* Scribner's, 1963. The Nevins and Hill study is the most exhaustive account of Ford's career to date. Use is made of the Ford archives at Dearborn. This is doubtless destined to be one of the most influential biographies of Ford. The attempt to stay on middle ground regarding Ford's less admirable characteristics is strained. The book is academic in tone. There is a full bibliography; W. A. Simonds, *Henry Ford,* Los Angeles, F. Clymer, 1946. A most uncritical account of Ford's career written by an admirer; known as the "court biography" of Ford, it is nevertheless a mine of information and has been thoroughly used by other biographers; Charles E. Sorensen, *Forty Years With Ford,* London, Jonathan Cape, 1957. One of the most important pieces of reminiscence concerning the growth of Ford Motors. Sorensen's candid views on Henry Ford and his career form a unique contribution to American industrial history; Keith Sward, *The Legend of Henry Ford,* New York, Rinehart, 1948. The first serious, and most damaging to Ford, scholarly effort. An attack on the benevolent picture of Ford which had been built up during Ford's lifetime. It is a bitter and thoroughgoing demolition job, with little effort made to find anything favorable to say about Ford. Contains a bibliography. Well written and extremely readable; Richard Lee Strout and E. B. White, "Farewell My Lovely," *A Subtreasury of American Humor,* New York, Modern Library, 1941, an appealing little essay on the great car; other books of interest on Ford include: S. S. Marquis, *Henry Ford,* Boston, Little, Brown, 1923, the confessions of Ford's onetime spiritual adviser; William Greenleaf, *Monopoly on Wheels: Henry Ford and the Selden Automobile Patent,* Detroit, Wayne State University Press, 1961; C. C. Caldwell, *Henry Ford,* New York, Messner, 1949; Charles Merz, *And Then Came Ford,* New York, Doubleday, Doran, 1929; J. N. Leonard, *The Tragedy of Henry Ford,* New York, Putnam's Sons, 1932; Upton Sinclair, *The Flivver King,* Pasadena, the Author, 1937; William C. Richards, *The Last Billionaire,* New York, Scribner's Sons, 1950; Louise Albright Neyhart, *Henry Ford, Engineer,* Boston, Houghton Mifflin, 1950. There are, in addition, any number of less-serious studies, including several fairly noxious panegyrics:

CHAPTER 8, E. H. HARRIMAN

C. J. Corliss, *Main Line in Mid-America,* New York, Creative Age Press, 1950. A history of the Illinois Central Railroad; Stuart Daggart, *Chapters on the History of the Southern Pacific,* New York, Ronald Press, 1922. The standard history; Robert W. Fogel, *The Union Pacific Railroad; a Case of Premature Enterprise,* Baltimore, The Johns Hopkins University Press, 1960. A brilliant economic analysis of the Union Pacific's early financial difficulties and the problem of "building ahead of demand"; George Kennan, *The Chicago and Alton Case,* Garden City, New York, Country Life Press, 1916. Kennan's original defense of Harriman against charges that his actions had "milked" the Chicago & Alton. Not substantially different from the account given in *E. H. Harriman* (below); George Kennan, *E. H. Harriman,* Boston, Houghton Mifflin, 1922. This is the definitive biography. It is extremely sympathetic, although not altogether uncritical. It has the virtue that it goes far into the details of Harriman's business ventures. Like most biographies of business tycoons, the tone is extraordinarily obsequious, which can become tiresome; Robert A. Lovett, *Forty Years After,* New York, Newcomen Society, 1949. A survey on the fortieth anniversary of Harriman's death of his contribution; C. H. Merriam, *The Harriman Alaska Expedition,* Doubleday, Page & Co., New York, 1901. A survey of the expedition and its results with photographs and maps; F. H. Newell, "The Salton Sea," Smithsonian Institution, *Annual Report,* January, 1907. An account is given of the operations in 1906 and early 1907 to put the Colorado River back into its channel and to save the Imperial Valley; John Muir, *Edward Henry Harriman,* New York, Doubleday, Page & Co., 1911. An "appreciation" by Muir of Harriman the man and of the Alaska expedition; *Reports* of the Interstate Commerce Commission, "The Consolidation and Combination of Carriers, etc.," Government Printing Office, Washington, D. C., 1908. This is the report of the official investigation into Harriman's railroads; Carl Snyder, "Harriman, Colossus of Roads," *Review of Reviews,* January, 1907. An account is given of Harriman's railroad empire and of his coup in the sale of the Great Northern and Northern Pacific Stocks; John F. Stover, *American Railroads,* Chicago, University of Chicago Press, 1961. A scholarly study of the whole field of American railway history. On the subject of Harriman and the Chicago & Alton, Stover follows the W. Z. Ripley account in spite of Kennan's refutation of the charges; Nelson Trottman, *History of the Union Pacific,* New York, Ronald Press, 1923. The standard history; N. C. Wilson, *Southern Pacific,* New York, McGraw-Hill, 1952. A popular and readable study of the Southern Pacific's colorful history.

Chapter 9, J. P. Morgan

Frederick Lewis Allen, *The Great Pierpont Morgan,* Harper, 1949. The most recent biography, also available in paperback from Bantam Books. A generally sound work in which the author had access to private Morgan papers; Lewis Corey, *The House of Morgan,* G. H. Watt, New York, 1930. An assault on high finance; Carl Hovey, *The Life Story of J. Pierpont Morgan,* London, Heinemann, 1912. Mainly a superficial work, originally appeared as a series of magazine articles, but it does contain some interesting materials since it was written by a contemporary of Morgan's; Aline Saarinen, *The Proud Possessors,* Random House, New York, 1958, contains a perceptive essay on Morgan; Herbert L. Satterlee, *J. Pierpont Morgan,* New York, Macmillan, 1939. A personal biography by Morgan's son-in-law. Rich in personal detail, altogether uncritical and selective regarding the more controversial aspects of Morgan's career. The book is organized entirely chronologically; Francis Henry Taylor, *Pierpont Morgan as Collector and Patron,* New York, Morgan Library, 1957; J. K. Winkler, *Morgan the Magnificent,* New York, Vanguard, 1930; Materials generally related to banking and monetary matters treated here may be found in Davis R. Dewey, *Financial History of the United States*, New York, 1934, Longmans, Green; Hepburn A. Barton, *History of Coinage and Currency*, New York, Macmillan, 1924; Margaret Myers, *The New York Money Market*, New York, Columbia Press, 1931–32; Paul Studenski and Herman E. Kroos, *Financial History of the United States*. On the role of merchant banking in the evolution of investment banking see Lance E. Davis, Jonathan R. T. Hughes and Duncan McDougall, *American Economic History*, Homewood, Illinois, Irwin, 1961, Chapter 14.

CHAPTER 10, MARY SWITZER

There is not a great volume of published work on the life of Mary Switzer. Martha Lentz Walker's book, *Beyond Bureaucracy: Mary Elizabeth Switzer and Rehabilitation*, Lanham, Maryland, University Press of America, 1985, is a new full-scale biography with exhaustive bibliography. Since Walker is herself a trained rehabilitation specialist, her study is comprehensive and accurate on technical matters. It is an original monograph utilizing the Switzer papers now on deposit at Radcliffe College. Edward Berkowitz's unpublished Ph.D. dissertation, *Rehabilitation: The Federal Government's Response to Disability, 1935–1954*, Northwestern University, 1976, contains a separate chapter on Mary Switzer and her achievements. Berkowitz has also published short summary items, including "Mary Switzer: The Entrepreneur Within the Welfare State," *American Journal of Economics and Sociology*, vol. 39, January 1979. Jean Christie wrote a short biographical note in *Notable Women*, Cambridge, Belknap Press of Harvard University Press, 1980. I also used Mary Switzer's own essay, "Vocational Rehabilitation in the United States," *International Labour Review*, vol. LXVII, no. 3, March 1958. The most interesting and original recent work on the American welfare state is Edward Berkowitz and Kim McQuaid, *Creating the Welfare State: The Political Economy of Twentieth-Century Reform*, New York, Praeger, 1980. For a rare international comparison of the development of modern welfare states by a scholar who both understands the issues and can read the necessary languages, see Gaston V. Rimlinger's *Welfare Policy and Industrialization in Europe, America and Russia*, New York, John Wiley and Sons, 1971. The remote origins of the American welfare state in England and the American colonies may be found in my own book, *Social Control in the Colonial Economy*, Charlottesville, University Press of Virginia, 1976.

CHAPTER 11, MARRINER ECCLES

John Morton Blum, *From the Morgenthau Diaries: Years of Crisis, 1928–1938*, Boston, Houghton Mifflin, 1959, is a reliable source for the politics and major issues of the New Deal from inside the U.S. Treasury. Sidney Hyman, *Marriner S. Eccles: Private Entrepreneur and Public Servant*, Stanford, Stanford University Graduate School of Business, 1976 is the major source of collected information about Eccles after 1951. Before 1951, Hyman's text follows *Beckoning Frontiers* (below) closely. Leonard J. Arrington, *David Eccles: Pioneer Western Industrialist*, Logan, Utah State University Press, 1975, is a thorough and readable investigation of the life and enterprises of David Eccles. Also by Arrington is *Bankers Extraordinary: A History of the First Security Corporation 1928–1973*, an unpublished manuscript. The details of all the acquisitions by First Security are given, including the historic roles of Butch Cassidy and the Sundance Kid in Montpelier, together with the $18 bills of 1933. The major book to read on Eccles is his own, Marriner S. Eccles, *Beckoning Frontiers: Public and Personal Recollections*, edited by Sidney Hyman, New York, Alfred Knopf, 1951. Eccles is very candid about his own background and his feelings, and is not bashful to note his achievements in public office. It is a revealing and surprisingly compelling memoir, the ultimate sourcebook for all subsequent students of his life up to 1951, ending, however, before the final showdown with Snyder and Truman. *Economic Balance and a Balanced Budget: Public Papers of Marriner S. Eccles*, edited by Rudolph Weissman, New York, Harper & Brothers, 1940, is a fairly stiff dose of the Eccles firehose, but contains several of his encounters with congressional committees and assorted speeches, including his 1939 radio address together with the letter to Senator Byrd. Some of the confrontation with congressional committees makes fairly delicious reading for those with a good background in economics and politics. Especially recommended in this regard is the chapter entitled "The Fallacies of the Silver Program," in which Eccles tries to explain why silver does not contain the magical qualities so beloved by silver enthusiasts of old. The introduction by Weissman is a good, general, critical survey of the book's contents. There is a "Credo" by Eccles containing a statement of his beliefs about monetary and fiscal policies as they existed in 1940. Weissman also provides a useful introduction to the issues presented in each chapter. Professor Dean L. May kindly provided me with several of his searching studies of the life and contributions of Marriner Eccles. May's book, *From New Deal to New Economics: The American Liberal Response to the Recession of 1937*, New York, Garland Publishing Company, 1981, has as its emphasis the victory of Eccles and those who thought like him within the Roosevelt administration after the 1937–38 recession. Throughout, the emphasis is on Eccles and his program for compensatory finance. May kindly provided me with a copy of his unpublished manuscript, "The Banking Act of 1935." In addition, May explores the influence of Eccles's Mormon heritage on his thinking about the proper role of government in "Sources of Marriner S. Eccles's Economic Thought," from *The Journal of*

Mormon History, vol. 3, 1976. The argument concerning the Mormon influence is mainly inference. Eccles himself said little in *Beckoning Frontiers* to directly credit Utah's history with any inspiration. Indeed, Eccles quotes a passage from Adam Smith's *The Wealth of Nations* as his inspiration about the role of government. The contents of Leonard Arrington's masterpiece about pioneer Morman economic history, *Great Basin Kingdom*, Cambridge, Harvard University Press, 1958, would not have been known to Eccles. The physical remains, all over Utah, of Mormon communitarian enterprises would have been known to anyone with eyes to see and ears to hear the reminiscences of David Eccles and his generation. Dams, irrigation works, railroads, the telegraph, the Utah-Idaho Sugar Company, Zion's Cooperative Mercentile Industries—the Mormon Welfare System—it was all pretty obvious when Eccles was growing up. Also by May is a brief survey with bibliography, "Eccles, Marriner Stoddard," in *Roosevelt, His Life and Times: An Encyclopedic View*, edited by Otis L. Graham, Jr., and Moglau Robinson Wunder, Boston, G. K. Hall & Co., 1985. The best book now available on the early history and intellectual origins of the Federal Reserve System and the peculiar role of the real bills doctrine, which gave rise to the Fed's obsolete "rules of eligibility," is Robert Craig West, *Banking Reform and the Federal Reserve, 1863–1923*, Ithaca, Cornell University Press, 1977. For a straightforward and readable account of the monetary and fiscal problems of the 1930s, see the relevant parts of Herbert Stein's *The Fiscal Revolution in America*, Chicago, University of Chicago Press, 1969. A conservative himself, Stein provided an objective statement and evaluation of the "Keynesian" concepts of fiscal and monetary policies in the 1930s. On the failure of the New Deal fiscal policy, see Cary Brown, "Fiscal Policy in the Thirties: a Reappraisal," *American Economic Review*, vol. XLVI, no. 5, December 1956; and L. C. Peppers, "Full Employment Surplus Analysis and Structural Changes: The 1930s," *Explorations in Economic History*, vol. 10, no. 2, Winter 1973.

Index

DATE DUE

BRODART, INC.

Cat. No. 23-221